C H A R T

Apico-alveolar	Fronto-palatal	Dorso-velar	Uvular	Glottal
t d	(c ɟ)	k g		ʔ
(ʈ̥ ɽ)		(x ɣ)		h ɦ
s z	š ž			
č ǰ				
ṛ (r̈)			(ʀ̈)	
(n̥) n	(ɲ)	ŋ		
ḷ̥ l ɬ	(ʎ)	ɫ L		
ṛ̥ r	j	w̥ w		
		(ẇ)		

Unrounded [̣]; Fortis [ͺ]; Lenis [ͺ]; Fronted [ͺ]; Retracted [.].

Trager – Smith (handwritten)

P H O N E M E S

Stops: /p t k b d g/

Affricates: /č ǰ/

Fricatives: /f θ v ð/

Sibilants: /s š z ž/

Nasals: /m n ŋ/

Lateral: /l/

Semivowels: /r w y h/

Vowels:

i	ɨ	u
e	ə	o
æ	a	ɔ

Stresses: /ˊ ˆ ˋ ˇ/

Pitches: /1 2 3 4/

Junctures: /+ | ‖ #/

Nena Wolfson

W. Nelson Francis is Professor of Linguistics
and English at Brown University. He received his
B.A. from Harvard University and his M.A. and
Ph.D. from the University of Pennsylvania, and
was a Fulbright Research Scholar at the University of Leeds, England.

Raven I. McDavid, Jr., Ph.D., Duke University, is Professor of English at the University of Chicago. The *Workbook*
that accompanies *The Structure of American English* was
prepared by Dr. McDavid and Donald C. Green of the University of Chicago.

THE
STRUCTURE
OF
AMERICAN ENGLISH

by

W. Nelson Francis
Brown University

WITH A CHAPTER ON
AMERICAN ENGLISH DIALECTS
BY
RAVEN I. McDAVID, JR.
UNIVERSITY OF CHICAGO

THE RONALD PRESS COMPANY · NEW YORK

Preface

This book was written to fill my own need for a suitable text to be used in an introductory course in the structure of English. It is intended for upper-division undergraduates and graduate students making their first acquaintance with the study of the English language as an end in itself. No previous training in linguistics is needed in order to use it. It does, however, make two important assumptions about the reader. The first is that he is what linguists call a *native speaker* of English, preferably American English—that is, one who learned it in infancy as his first language. As such he has a tremendous store of knowledge about it, much of which he is unaware of. One purpose of this book is to bring this fund of knowledge into awareness. The second assumption is that the student is prepared to approach the analytical study of his language with the same interest and open-mindedness he would bring to any other new subject. This means that he is asked to refrain from hasty judgments even when some of his most cherished notions about his native language seem to be called into question. Only so can the dispassionate inquiry which is essential to a scientific study be carried on.

The book is intended to provide the material for a rather full one-semester course, comprising half of the year's course in the English language which all English majors and candidates for the master's degree should have. It can advantageously be followed by a second semester devoted to the history of the language and the nature and sources of the vocabulary. Such a survey will give the nonlinguist an adequate idea of the nature of linguistic study

iii

and what it can contribute to the myriad human activities in which language plays a part. A survey of that sort is essential for those who are going to teach English at any level; the final chapter is especially directed to them. It also is the best introduction to the subject for those who intend to go on to further linguistic study. In any case, an extra laboratory hour each week devoted to drill in phonetic and phonemic transcription is strongly recommended.

A word should be said about technical terms: No attempt has been made to suppress them in this book. Indeed, to have done so would have been a disservice to the reader, since a mastery of the terminology is an important part of the introduction to any new science. Where possible, new terms have been introduced in a context making their meaning clear, and have been printed in boldface type at their first appearance. In addition, the most important ones have been brought together and defined in the Glossary at the end of the text.

This book does not presume to present completely original material, although some new notions are put forward in the chapters on grammar and graphics. It is, instead, an attempt to bring together in one place a synthesis of current linguistic knowledge, especially as applied to present-day American English. This being so, my first and greatest debt is to the teachers who have made that knowledge available to me. Among these I should particularly mention Albert C. Baugh, Bernard Bloch, Hans Kurath, Robert Lado, Floyd Lounsbury, Albert Marckwardt, and the late P. V. D. Shelly. Not all of these will agree with all that is written here, any more than they would agree wholly with one another except on the one point on which all linguists are agreed—the fascination of the subject itself.

A second great debt is owed to colleagues, friends, and students who in question and discussion have helped me to formulate and clarify my material and my ideas. I want especially to thank those who have read all or part of the book in preliminary form and whose comments—often extensive, usually perceptive, and always honestly and straightforwardly expressed—have saved me from error. One or two of these are to me anonymous; the others are Harold B. Allen, Richard Beal, Dan Desberg, Robert J. Geist, Sumner Ives, Donald Lloyd, Albert Marckwardt, James Sledd,

Henry Lee Smith, Jr., and William J. Stevens. Needless to say, they cannot be held responsible for what I have written, and only they know what I had written before they set me right. My collaborator, Raven I. McDavid, Jr., has contributed much more than the chapter which bears his name; his responsibility, of course, ends with that chapter, though his influence has been felt in all the rest. His partner in scholarship, as well as in marriage, Mrs. Virginia Glenn McDavid, prepared the maps, and both of them read proofs on the entire book.

Finally I should like to thank those at Franklin and Marshall College who have made my task of writing easier. A. G. Breidenstine, former dean of the college, arranged that my teaching load should be reduced during the year when most of the writing was done. Both he and his successor, Dean J. M. Darlington, as well as Professor M. Ray Adams, chairman of the English Department, have been sympathetic and encouraging throughout the time the book was in plan and process. Valuable help has been given by the librarian of the Fackenthal Library, Herbert Anstaett, and his staff, and by the staff of the Recorder's office, especially Mrs. Marion M. Harper, who helped solve the problem of duplicating a preliminary version for classroom trial.

W. Nelson Francis

Lancaster, Pennsylvania

April, 1958

Contents

THE
STRUCTURE
OF
AMERICAN
ENGLISH

Chapter 1

Language, Languages and Linguistic Science

HUMAN SPEECH

Man is a talking animal. More precisely, man is *the* talking animal. Among all the creatures of the earth there is no other that uses articulate speech for communication. It is true that some animals use sounds to communicate, but their cries can hardly be called articulate. And while certain birds can produce an uncanny imitation of human speech, they communicate nothing by their parrotings. If man is to talk—and he seems unable to refrain from doing so—he is obliged to talk to his fellow man. Furthermore, he always will be. Astronomers assure us with virtual unanimity that none of the other planets of our system can be inhabited by any creatures higher in the scale of evolution than vegetation. And though the laws of probability make it virtually certain that somewhere in the unimaginably vast reaches of the universe there are other highly developed forms of life, the distances between the stars are so great that, notwithstanding the imaginative flights of the science-fiction writers, we shall never meet the inhabitants of other systems face to face. The human race is destined to spend the rest of its allotted span talking to itself.

In order to carry on this characteristically and uniquely human activity, man has developed an intricate apparatus made up of bits

3

and pieces of anatomy whose primary functions are quite different from those they perform in speech. It will be our business in the next chapter to look at this apparatus in some detail; for the present we need only recognize that from the diaphragm to the lips, the various organs that take part in producing talk all have other work to do that is biologically more fundamental. So obvious are the primary functions of lips, teeth, and tongue, nose, throat, and lungs that there is no need to describe them here. "What about the vocal cords?" one may ask. Let him try to lift a heavy weight while singing or speaking, and he will soon find that the vocal cords—or **vocal bands,** as we shall henceforth call them—have as their primary function to shut off the windpipe so that the chest muscles may brace themselves against the compressed air of the lungs. Without them we should be even more feeble creatures than we are.

This kind of improvisation is, of course, not confined to man's speech organs. The whale's tail, the seal's flippers, and the bat's wing all remind us that it is Nature's way to patch up an astonishingly efficient mechanism out of organs whose original purpose was quite different, even as a boy makes a scooter out of soapboxes, old expresswagon wheels, and odds and ends of all sorts from behind the garage. Evolution cannot go to the hardware store and pick the parts it needs to produce the organs it has in mind because evolution doesn't know what it has in mind. It just seems to keep tinkering with what is there until something happens. In the case of the speech machinery, it tinkered with a miscellaneous group of organs dedicated largely to the basic tasks of eating and breathing. Out of them and the very breath of life itself it made speech.

There is another and even more mysterious side to it. This complexly modulated stream of sound is not mere random or instinctive behavior. It is under the direction of the most remarkable of all Nature's patchworks, the brain. All but a minute fraction of speech— the cry or groan of pain, the grunt of extreme physical exertion—is purposive. It is produced to evoke a response, to assist man in his lifelong task of controlling his environment. In order to do this, it somehow gets formed into patterns, which are themselves purely arbitrary, but which are associated in the brain with notions about the world around us and how it works. It is the business of the philosopher, not the linguist, to go into the question of the nature of these notions and the extent to which they are an accurate report of the environment. Here we shall simply remark that these notions exist, and that they are in some way related to infinitely complicated connections among the cells of that myriad-circuited switchboard, the cortex of the brain.

The switchboard itself is the province of the neurologist, who is coming to know quite a bit about it. He tells us, for instance, that some of its billions of circuits are already hooked up at birth. A new-born infant is a helpless thing indeed, but it is capable of doing a good many things that require considerable coordination, such as breathing, sucking, wiggling its hands and feet, and crying. It comes equipped with the ability to perform the fundamental acts which with practice and coordination will make up speech: it can make a sustained sound, and it can move various parts of its breathing and sucking apparatus in such a way as to modulate that sound. But not for a year or more does it turn these accomplishments to the task of speaking. The reason is a simple one: the circuits of the brain which will ultimately store a vocabulary of thousands of words, along with a complicated set of patterns of arranging them, are at birth completely nonexistent. The cells are there, but they are of no more use than disconnected wires on the floor of the telephone exchange. They must be hitched up into a network of interconnecting circuits whose complexity is beyond our power to visualize—which is only another way of saying that while voice and the capacity to articulate are inborn, *speech must be learned.*

Of course, it needs no neurologist come from the laboratory to tell us that. Most of us have watched a baby develop from crying to babbling, and from babbling to the momentous utterance of its "first word" (which sounds like "mama" to Mama and like "dada" to Daddy). But because this process is going on at the same time that the baby is learning other things—to stand up, to grasp and hold, to fit together, and so on—we may not realize that it is really a different kind of learning. A baby kept alive by amiable apes or the traditional wolves would eventually learn to stand, to grasp, and to hold, but it would never learn to speak. The three areas of the left hemisphere of the cerebral cortex which are reserved for speaking would remain forever as blank as they were at birth, just like the corresponding areas on the right side, which none of us use unless a brain injury in infancy leads us to use them as substitutes.

Here, then, is a paradox. Speech, the universal human activity, the very mark and defining criterion of humanity and its unique possession, is not an innate part of man's nature at all. Each individual member of the race must experience in himself the task of learning it from other humans, with or without their conscious assistance. It is a tremendous task, and a magnificent accomplishment—nonetheless magnificent though all attain it. It occupies the center of our attention for several years in early childhood, and though it continues in greater or less degree through life, most of the work has been done by the age of six. Admittedly some few seem so exhausted by the task that they don't learn much else for the rest of their lives; but by learning to speak they have certified their humanity and claimed their place in society. Most of us take it for granted and go on to other things. But no matter what else we study and learn, all our life long we are aware—sometimes only dimly, sometimes with painful vividness—of our dependence on speech to get done the things we feel must be done. And yet, for all this unrivaled importance of speech in human life, most people really know very little about it, and a good deal of what they do "know" is wrong. It is the purpose of this book to correct some of that error and remove some of the fallacies upon which it is based by bringing together some of the facts about language in general and the twentieth-century American brand of English in particular. We cannot hope to be complete in our investigations of the various facets of language study; in fact, so new is the scientific study of language that many interesting areas are as yet unexplored. But we can, perhaps, draw a sort of map of the territory, which will help each individual student to direct his own natural interest in language intelligently and efficiently.

LANGUAGE AS SOCIAL BEHAVIOR

The first point we must make about language, then, is that it is a *social*, rather than a *biological*, aspect of human life. The point is so important that it must be labored here, even at the expense of overstating the obvious. Let us define as biological those parts of our behavior which are concerned with preserving and prolonging our life, both as individual organisms and as a species. We need not go beyond the immediately obvious categories of breathing, eating, eliminating, reproducing, and nurturing the young. On the other hand, those parts of our behavior which are concerned with preserving and prolonging patterns of relationship among individuals can be called social. Here again the obvious list includes property arrangements, marriage, kinship relations, laws, and customs of all sorts. There is, of course, yet another group of actions which is concerned with what, for lack of a better term, we can call the psychic aspects of our life, both as individuals and as organized groups. Here belong religion, art, and part, at least, of philosophy and learning. It is true that language is a fundamental part of our actions in this field, which we like to think of as embracing the "highest" qualities of our nature. But because the use of language in this field does not submit itself to the kind of analysis which the linguist uses, we must mark it as the province of the rhetorician, the philosopher, the theologian, and the literary critic. These experts can profit by the linguist's findings, but they must go further by means of their own methods, which are not his.

Having neatly separated biological and social behavior, we must immediately set about to blur this oversimplified division. It is in the nature of man to mingle the biological and social aspects of his behavior in complicated combinations which are infinitely varied in different times and places. Thus we complicate the essentially biological act of eating by overlaying it with a more or less elaborate set of table manners, which are social in nature and origin. It is biologically more efficient to eat with the fingers; it is socially more acceptable to use a fork. Not even the most primitive of peoples treat sexual intercourse as a purely biological device for insuring the continuity of the species; all human societies make it part of an elaborate pattern of social customs and relationships which are intricately bound up with other forms of social structure and behavior. Most of them also add a third dimension of psychic events and concepts which are embodied in artistic and religious attitudes toward sexual love.

But in spite of these complications, it is always possible to separate the biological and the social aspects of any given kind of behavior, by taking thought and especially by making comparisons. We know that all people eat, so we must mark this down as a biological necessity. But if we have even the least bit of experience outside our own narrow circle, we know that different people eat different things in different ways, so we must attribute both the menu and the table manners to social custom. It seems to be natural for people to attribute to a biological basis many aspects of behavior which are really social. This may be one device by which we preserve and bolster up our social customs. Thus the average American is revolted by the idea of eating grasshoppers or other humans and feels that there is something essentially wholesome about drinking milk. In other words he feels that these preferences are biologically determined. It is only when he learns that there are people who consider grasshoppers or human flesh great delicacies and others who are physically revolted by the idea of drinking milk that he comes to realize that these preferences and aversions are not part of inherent biological behavior at all, but of acquired social behavior. The revulsion may be none the less physical in nature for being social in origin. And not all people accept with docility all the dietary preferences of their society—which is a rather pompous way of saying that some Europeans and Americans never get up courage enough to eat their first oyster.

Simply stated, our point is this: Speech is a form of behavior which is social in origin and in application; it must be newly learned by each individual as part of his conditioning within the society to which he belongs; it varies arbitrarily from place to place and from time to time; in any group it is intricately bound up with other aspects of social behavior which make up the total repertory or *culture* of that society.

Some corollaries of these facts are important and will engage our attention at various stages of our survey of American English. Since some of them at least are contrary to many widely accepted ideas about language, they may at first appear questionable if not downright wrong. But they flow inevitably from the incontrovertible facts stated above, and upon them the whole substance of linguistic science, and hence of this book, is based. For that reason the more important ones will be brought together here, though the exploration of their implications may come much later.

1. There is no such thing as a "natural" language in the sense of one which is dictated by the nature of things. If there were, all men would speak the same language, instead of several thousand different ones. Each language is, thus, the artificial, arbitrary invention of a social group. This does not, of course, mean that the members of a given group all sat down one day and made up a language. The process is a gradual one, and largely unconscious. But it is nonetheless a process of creation, not of discovery. This is true in spite of the

fact that most peoples firmly believe that they have the secret of the *real* way to talk, while foreigners have more or less perverse and ridiculous caricatures thereof.

2. The nature and form of every language is adapted to the social requirements of the society that uses it. The Eskimos have no single word for what we call *snow*; instead, they have a series of words describing many different kinds of things which we lump together under this single term. These things obviously are central in their society but peripheral in ours. But when an American takes up skiing, he finds that he needs an elaborate vocabulary of snow terms because snow now has become central to him. He further finds that the subgroup of our culture that is interested in skiing has already made up the language of snow-as-it-pertains-to-the-sport-of-skiing. This language he will learn as an essential part of learning how to ski and to hold his own in the society of skiers.

3. It follows from the preceding that we must be very cautious about calling any language intrinsically better or worse than any other. Each language is "good" for the culture that uses it; in fact, it is the language best adapted to that culture. It may not, of course, be the best possible language for that culture, because no man-made things are perfect. To evaluate languages comparatively is, thus, impossible; they are on the whole incommensurable. Classical Greek was the "best" language for ancient Greece, Latin was the "best" language for Rome, American English is the "best" language for Americans, Hottentot is the "best" language for Hottentots. When we compare languages this way, we are really comparing cultures. To say that French is a better language than English is only to say that French culture is better than English culture. This in turn is probably only another way of saying that we like French ways of doing things better than English ways. It would be more accurate to say, for instance, that French is a better language than English for gourmets because French culture pays more attention to the preparation of food than does English culture. Or to put it another

way, the menus of stylish restaurants are full of French words for the same reason that their kitchens are full of French cooks.

4. Similarly, no one language is any more *beautiful* than any other. The question of whether there are any universal standards in aesthetics is one which I gladly leave to philosophers. But as a working principle I think it is safe to say that a large proportion of our aesthetic preferences and judgments, which we consider to be universally valid, are simply expressions of our mastery of the aesthetic standards of our own culture. Again comparisons bring this out very clearly. Certainly there is a vast difference between the Chinese, the American, and the Zulu view of what constitutes a beautiful girl, a beautiful song, or a beautiful view. Our judgments in these areas are dictated almost wholly by what we are used to and what we have been taught, and hardly if at all by any appeal to absolute standards. It is, of course, true that a member of one culture can liberate himself from slavish adherence to its standards. He can, in other words, become a cosmopolitan, who can appreciate the beauty of Zulu drumbeating and Scottish bagpipe music in the same way, though perhaps not to the same degree, that he does a string quartet or a hot trumpet. Similarly, the speaker of English may come to have an aesthetic feeling for Italian, or Chinese, or Hottentot poetry. But he is unlikely to get completely over the feeling that no speech is capable of matching his mother tongue in beauty. Yet the source of this pleasure is almost entirely the associated meanings rather than the sounds themselves. "*Spit* is an ugly word," the advertisements used to say. What this means really is that the act of spitting is frowned upon by our culture for a complex of reasons. But the sounds of the word itself are not ugly when we find them embedded in a word like *hospitable*, which refers to a trait that our culture approves of.

5. Finally, as the last corollary of our acceptance of the social nature of language, we are obliged to assume that there is no standard by which we can judge language other than an estimate of its success in accomplishing the social functions that are demanded of it. This

means, for instance, that any Zulu who is accepted by Zulu society as an efficient adult capable of meeting the linguistic needs of that society is by definition a speaker of "good Zulu." Any differences between his Zulu and that of his next-door neighbor are significant only if they have social consequences. Furthermore, if he moves to another village where his brand of Zulu produces different and less happy social consequences than it did at home, his "good Zulu" has by definition become "bad Zulu," although it has not changed its intrinsic nature in the least. If being an accepted and efficient member of society is essential to his happiness, it behooves him either to learn what his new village considers "good Zulu" or go back home.

This corollary does not mean that there are not great differences of skill among the native speakers of a given language. We are all individuals, not automata, and some of us can do some things better than others. So it is, of course, with any of the activities that a culture considers important. I am sure that to a Scot there is good and bad bagpipe-playing, though not being a Scot myself, I am equally sure I could not tell them apart. Similarly, a person who knew no English could not possibly judge between the English used by Harold Macmillan addressing the Commons and that of a Cockney agitator addressing a London crowd. In fact, if the outcome of Mr. Macmillan's speech was a lost vote, and the outcome of the Cockney's harangue was a successful strike, the outsider might conclude that the Cockney spoke "better English" than the Prime Minister. And how could we prove him wrong? We could do it, I suspect, only by showing him that our culture vests such prestige in the figure of a Prime Minister that it values *all* his utterances, successful and unsuccessful, at a higher rate than those of a minor agitator. This may well be the case; if so, it is, you will note, a statement of the value judgments of our particular culture and says nothing about the intrinsic "goodness" or "badness" of Mr. Macmillan's or the Cockney's English. It is, of course, our privilege to build such standards into our culture, which is ours to do with as we will. But we should also realize that our judgment is valid only within the framework of our own society. A parallel event in another society which set a tremendous value on success and none at all on political rank might well result in the agitator's successful language being valued as "good" and to be imitated, and the unsuccessful cabinet minister's language being counted "bad" and to be shunned. In short, most of our judgments ostensibly about language are really judgments about the people who use language. In our own society we are inclined to label as "good English" that characteristically used by people of education and assured position.

So far, then, we have been concerned with locating language in the scheme of things, so to speak. We have found that from a biological point of view it is a secondary activity, which makes use of special adaptations of organs whose primary functions are quite different. Psychologically we have seen that language is an acquired rather than an innate skill and that each individual must learn it from the beginning. These two facts led us to the conclusion that language is in origin and largely in use a social phenomenon, a part of the complex of modes of behavior that anthropologists call culture. This in turn led us to a series of corollaries: that all languages are equally arbitrary and artificial; that each language is the best existing language for the society that uses it; that attempts to demonstrate that one language is better than another only result in value judgments about their respective cultures; that aesthetic judgments about languages are inevitably strongly influenced by cultural bias; and that the only valid standard by which we can judge any given specimen of a language is social effectiveness within the society that uses that language.

Definition: A language is an arbitrary system of articulated sounds made use of by a group of humans as a means of carrying on the affairs of their society.

LINGUISTICS, THE SCIENCE OF LANGUAGE

The alert reader will perhaps have observed that in the course of the preceding section a rather important transition was made. We began by talking about *language* as a generalized form of human behavior; before long we were discussing *languages* as the creations and possessions of human societies; we closed with a definition of *a language* as a form of behavior limited to a specific human society. The reader may justly feel that since our subject is professedly twentieth-century American English, this progressive narrowing of the field is movement in the right direction. But there is another reason for the rather hasty abandonment of the discussion of language in the abstract. This is that, from the linguistic point of view there is not much to be said about language in the abstract. People don't speak language; they speak languages. Some people—a relatively small number—are capable of speaking more than one language, but nobody can speak more than one at a time. To the neurologist investigating the cerebral circuits used in speech, or to the oto-laryngologist observing the mechanism of the vocal bands in producing voice, it is of no moment what language is being spoken. But for the linguist, whose subject of observation is the articulate sounds themselves, it is essential to begin, at least, with a single language. Time enough when he knows a great deal about a large number of languages to make statements about language in general.

Before we go on to describe how the linguist operates, it would be well to make clear just what we mean by **linguistics** and **linguist.** To begin with, linguistics is a science. It is, in fact, often called **linguistic science** in order to emphasize this point. This will occasionally happen in this book, most likely at those places where the scientific nature of linguistics must be emphasized. But in general the shorter term, analogous as it is to *mathematics* and *physics*, is sufficient. Now a form of study or a body of knowledge if it is to call itself a science must conform to certain generally recognized requirements. They are these:

1. A science directs its attention to a coherent body of facts, entities, or events which can be separated from the rest of the universe by consistent and clearly statable definitions. This is its *subject matter*. The subject matter of geology, for instance, is the earth, especially its crust, and all nonliving things found within it. It is bounded on the one side by the subject matter of astronomy, and on the other by that of biology.

2. A science directs upon its subject matter a close and unprejudiced scrutiny and attempts to record the results of this scrutiny in such a manner that they can be verified by any competent observer. It produces, in short, *careful objective descriptions*.

3. A science further attempts to put together the results of its descriptions in such a way that they form orderly and systematic patterns which display the relationships that exist within its subject matter. In brief, it *makes generalizations*.

4. A science tests its generalizations by applying them to parts of its subject matter not used in forming the generalizations. In other words, it *makes predictions*.

5. Finally, a science examines the outcome of its predictions and, in the light of their success or failure, corroborates or revises its generalizations. If the corroboration is satisfactory, it may call its generalizations *laws*, which are simply statements of predictable behavior.

In any active science, all five of these processes are going on at the same time. Science is constantly redefining its subject matter, refining its observations, restating and revising its generalizations. It may also occupy itself in working out practical applications of its discoveries, but this is by no means a necessary or even typical part of science. Science as such has fulfilled its function when it has produced laws upon which accurate predictions may be based.

Let us now apply these criteria to linguistic science.

1. The *subject matter* of linguistics is all the systems of articulated sounds used today by humans in the carrying on of their affairs, that is, all living languages. It further includes records, in writing and in such media as phonograph records and magnetic tapes, of languages that have been used at some time in the past.

2. The methods of observation used by linguistics are various, including simple listening, phonetic transcription, and the use of various instruments, such as oscillographs, sound-spectrographs, and kymographs. Records made in these ways constitute various kinds of *objective description*.

3. The kinds of *generalization* made by linguistics are primarily statements about the systematic selection and arrangement of significant sounds and groups of sounds which are actually used by native speakers. Other kinds of generalization include statements about the changes which have taken place in specific languages in the past and about the genetic and other relationships between languages both at present and in the past.

4. The *predictions* made by linguistics are principally of the nature of grammars and dictionaries, which say, in effect, "If you use these sounds and groups of sounds in the patterns of arrangement here described, native speakers of this language will understand you and will respond in the predicted way."

5. Since linguistics is a very active science just now, it is constantly engaged in revising and overhauling all parts of its methods, findings, and generalizations. In fact, so rapidly is it moving that parts of this book may well be out of date by the time it is printed. This would also be true of a textbook in physics, chemistry, or, indeed, any other active science.

A person who engages in the methodical exercise of some or all of these five pursuits is a **linguist.** Not all such people are wholly content with this term, because it has another well-established meaning: "a person who knows several languages and uses them with facility; a person who learns languages easily." Linguists in the scientific sense are usually, but not necessarily, linguists in this sense as well. But linguists in the popular sense are seldom linguists in the scientific sense; they may be travelers, cosmopolitan playboys, waiters, diplomats, international business men, students of literature, or just plain citizens with a fondness for languages. In this book, *linguist* invariably means "linguistic scientist"; if it is necessary to refer to the person who knows many languages, some such term as *polyglot* will be used.

LINGUISTICS IN RELATION TO OTHER STUDIES

Just as we felt it necessary to find the place of language in the total scheme of things, so it seems wise at this point to place linguistics among the other branches of study. We must certainly do this before we can decide what it can and cannot do, before, that is, we can answer the question, "What use is it?" From another point of view, we want to know in at least general terms what its boundaries are so that we can avoid straying out of its territory into the domain of some neighboring discipline. As anyone knows, it is not always easy to draw precise boundaries between two branches of learning. Sometimes the subject matter becomes ambiguous at the borderline, as, for example, in the case of certain single-celled organisms that can be assigned equally well to the provinces of botany and zoology. But border areas of this sort do not disturb us; either we draw an arbitrary line somewhere, as we do in making political boundaries, or else we create separate, overlapping fields whose very names often indicate their nature, such as biochemistry, physical chemistry, and economic geography.

Language, which we have stated to be the subject matter of linguistics, is such an ever-present and multipurposed form of human behavior that it turns up as part, at least, of the subject matter of many other disciplines beside linguistics. Some sort of linguistic factor is involved in most of the things we humans do. It may be only an unimportant and chiefly irrelevant accompaniment, as in golf, where the only essential use made of language is to yell "Fore!" Or it may be one of the most important and central parts of the activity, as in praying or political campaigning. This means, in turn, that people who study and teach the many hundreds of human activities must devote a part, at least, and sometimes a pretty large part, of their attention to the related uses of language. This seems very obvious, and indeed it is, as a general rule. But a good many mistakes have been made and continue to be made by people who do not take it sufficiently into account. For this reason, and because some important points about linguistics depend upon it, we must here labor the obvious a bit more.

First, we might look at the large field of activity that we can call by some such general term as "special skills." Here belong games, like golf, bridge, and baseball; occupational techniques, like carpentry, automobile mechanics, and gardening; useful acquirements of varied application, like driving a car, dressmaking, and first aid; social graces, like dancing, ballroom etiquette, and formal entertaining. The list could be greatly extended, but enough examples have been cited to make it obvious that each of these skills has its own linguistic accompaniment, which the beginner must learn as he masters the activity itself. Usually the language element is a vocabulary of terms designating objects and the manner of manipulating them, as in "clutch," "throttle," "steering wheel," "put on the brake." Less often it may consist of a collection of utterances that must be repeated in certain circumstances, such as "I pass," "Come on, seven!" and "I've had a delightful evening." In any case, the person who simply learns and teaches these special areas of language is not thereby engaging in linguistics. But a person who collects these special vocabularies and subjects them to observation, objective description, and generalization is acting in accordance with scientific method and is, therefore, to some degree at least a linguist.

Next, we might consider a group of human activities which use language not as an accompaniment to more important nonlinguistic actions, but as the actual medium in which actions are conducted. This is a vast field indeed. It includes almost all of what we call "thinking," which I shall not attempt to define. It therefore includes all the branches of study that have thinking as their subject matter: a good part of philosophy and psychology. It also includes a large part of all the branches of learning which study (that is, think about) all the other subject matters, simply because one of the most important ways they have of carrying on their thinking and expressing its results is by using language. There are, of course, other ways— mathematics, diagrams, and manipulative experiments—but language is always there too. No matter what a branch of study may be, in addition to its laboratories it always has its textbooks and lecture-rooms. Furthermore this large field includes those activities which use language as a medium of artistic creation and performance. Here belong rhetoric, literature, oratory, storytelling, and part, at least, of acting and singing. A fourth area in which language is central is religion, since language is the medium of prayer and for much of ritual. Still another great area of human activity uses language as a medium of social, political, and economic manipulation and control. Here fall advertising, propaganda, pedagogy, political caucusing and campaigning, and a large part of what we loosely call "human relations." Finally, though not exhaustively, we might mention a few miscellaneous activities which use language as their main medium in varied and interesting ways, such as psychoanalysis, games like "Twenty Questions" and "Scrabble," polite conversation, journalism, criticism of all sorts, hypnotism, magic and incantation generally, and the desultory interchange of personal reminiscences, prejudices, and bits of information which serves to fill an idle silence and is variously known as "chat," "gossip," or "shooting the breeze."

All these multifarious activities are deeply concerned with language, and their practitioners spend a good deal of their time studying, thinking about, and discussing various qualities, phases, uses, and kinds of language. But they must all be excluded from the field of linguistics proper, for one or both of two reasons. Either they fail to make language itself, as we have defined it, their total subject matter, or they fail to use the methods of science as we have previously described them, or both. A few examples will make this clear. Logic, for instance, might seem to qualify because it deals in a scientific manner with language as a tool of thought. But those last five words rule it out; its subject matter is not language but thought, which does not consist of "a system of articulated sounds," though it may depend on one for its existence. Similarly rhetoric, which studies the use of language as a means of effective communication and persuasion, is disqualified because its subject matter is not language pure and simple, but language as a means to some ultralinguistic end.

It would be an instructive exercise to go over the list we have just given and see the detailed reasons why each of these language-employing activities must be ruled out of our definition of linguistic science. The reader is urged to do so. He may sometimes have trouble putting his finger on the disqualifying element. In fact, many linguists occasionally or habitually venture into one or more of these fields, and they are not always aware that in so doing they cease to be linguists in the precise sense of the word. We shall undoubtedly do so ourselves many times in this book, because many of these fields are closely related to linguistics, and many of them are areas where linguistics can either learn something of help to itself, or be of service to some other discipline. This last point will be explored in some detail in Chapter 10, "Linguistics and the Teacher of English," where we shall see some of the ways in which a knowledge of linguistics can be of value to teachers of reading, writing, spelling, composition, and literature. But for the present we shall have to postpone the consideration of practical application, which can only be intelligently discussed against a background of fact and theory.

FIELDS AND ASPECTS OF LINGUISTICS

As with all the other sciences in our day, it is not possible for any one man to take all linguistics for his province. Therefore linguistics has many subdivisions, representing various ways in which the subject matter can be cut up. We may recognize three groups of these divisions, which can be called *fields*, *aspects*, and *branches*.[1]

The various **fields** of linguistics are arrived at by dividing the total subject matter (which, you will remember, is all language, present and past) into various language groups, language families, and individual languages. Thus we can speak of Indo-European, Semitic, or Algonkian linguistics, all of which deal with large language families. Or the field may be progressively narrowed. Our field, American English, belongs in the largest sense to Indo-European linguistics. This includes many lesser fields, among them Germanic, which in turn includes English. By restricting ourselves to American English, we limit our field to only part of a single language. At that we shall have more than we can do.

The **aspects** of linguistics are divisions of the subject matter on the basis of time or point of view. Here the fundamental distinction is between *synchronic* and *diachronic* linguistics. **Synchronic,** a term also used in other fields such as anthropology, means "dealing with the state of affairs at a given point of time." It takes no account of history, in other words. On the other hand, **diachronic,** also used in other sciences, means "dealing with changes that occur in time." History is its material. This distinction between synchronic and diachronic linguistics is very important because many mistakes and fallacies result from overlooking it. Let us then pause briefly in our subdividing of linguistics in order to take a closer look at this distinction and the way it influences the kinds of description and generalization that a linguistic scientist can make.

[1] These are not standard terms, but are introduced by the author in the meanings used here. Linguists, like other scientists, sometimes disagree over both the subdivision and the nomenclature of their science.

In the first place, since everything in this time-bound world of ours changes from year to year, even from moment to moment, this distinction recognizes two fundamental ways of looking at and describing almost anything. We usually mix them together in our descriptions of things. Thus *Webster's New International Dictionary*, under the entry "Unitarian," makes the following statements (somewhat abbreviated here):

> The churches of the Unitarian denomination are congregational in polity, except in Hungary where they are organized under a bishop. They have never issued any authoritative confession of faith, one of their most distinctive principles being the right of private judgment in theological matters. They formerly differed widely among themselves . . . . Later there came to be virtual unity on the broad basis of [certain] doctrines . . . but the denomination now includes in its ministry as well as its membership a number of nontheistic humanists.

It is obvious that this paragraph contains both synchronic and diachronic statements. What is more, the synchronic statements do not all deal with the same point in time. Thus the first sentence makes a synchronic statement about the Unitarian denomination "now," that is at the time of writing (presumably shortly before 1934, when the dictionary was published). The first part of the next sentence, as far as the comma, makes a diachronic statement covering the whole history of the denomination. The second half of that sentence is ambiguous; from one point of view it is synchronic ("one of their most distinctive principles *is* . . ."); from another it is diachronic ("one of their most distinctive principles *has always been*..."). Probably the latter was intended. The next sentence is also ambiguous, depending on how we interpret *formerly*. If we take it to mean "at an unnamed point of time in the past," the statement is a synchronic one; if we take it to mean "during a good part of their past history," it is diachronic. The first part of the next sentence is clearly diachronic because of the verb *came*, which describes a process going on in time. Finally, the last sentence returns to a synchronic statement of the time of writing, as is clearly indicated by the words *now includes.*

It is, of course, quite proper for the two kinds of statement to be mingled in this paragraph since people who look for information about the Unitarian denomination in the dictionary undoubtedly are interested not only in what it is now but also in how it got that way. But when we are dealing with statements about language, particularly if they are precise enough statements to warrant being called scientific, it is of considerable importance to keep our synchronic and our diachronic statements separate. This usually is not difficult; it simply involves being aware of the distinction and being careful about making it. Let us look at a few examples from familiar linguistic material.

Coming across "this was the most unkindest cut of all" in Shakespeare's *Julius Caesar,* I can make several statements about it. I can say, for instance, "About the year 1600 an exceedingly popular playwright at a critical point in a serious play put into the mouth of an important and dignified character an expression involving a double superlative." This is an objective description and it is a purely synchronic statement. It is not evidence enough to permit a generalization, but if I searched about I would find some more examples, such as "the calmest and most stillest night" (*2 Hen. IV*, III.i.28); "this most bravest vessel of the world" (*Cym.*, IV.ii.319); "the basest and most poorest shape" (*Lear*, II.iii.7). I might eventually feel justified in saying, "The double superlative was a rather rare but perfectly acceptable construction in the standard English of the late sixteenth century." This is a generalization, still synchronic. After observing the usage of some of my educated friends, and relying somewhat on my own knowledge as a native speaker of English, I might make another generalization: "The double superlative is not used by cultivated speakers of present-day English." This is also a synchronic statement, but about a different point of time than the preceding one. But if I say, "The double superlative has disappeared from cultivated use since Shakespeare's time," I have made a dia-chronic generalization because I have described a change taking place in the course of time.

There are, of course, other statements that I might make. I might say, for instance, "It is all right to use a double superlative because Shakespeare did," or, "Even Shakespeare made mistakes, witness his use of the double superlative, which is not permissible in English." It may be seen at once that both these statements are utterly unsci-entific, and hence from the point of view of linguistics they are worthless, whatever may be their value as indications of the speaker's prejudices. One reason they are unscientific is that they are neither synchronic nor diachronic. One bases a generalization about present-day English on observation of late sixteenth-century English; the other reverses the process and bases a conclusion about Shakespeare's English upon a generalization about present-day English.

Sometimes the distinction between synchronic and diachronic is not so easy to observe. Take, for instance, two ways of describing the relationship between the English words *agree* and *agreement:* (1) "*agreement* was formed from *agree* by adding the noun-forming suffix -*ment*"; (2) "*agree* and *agreement* differ in that *agreement* has the noun-suffix -*ment*, otherwise they are alike." At first glance these seem to be merely two slightly different ways of saying the same thing. But closer scrutiny reveals that the first is a diachronic state-ment because it assumes that *agree* existed first and that -*ment* was added to it. This is a statement about a change taking place in time; hence, by definition it is diachronic. The second statement, on the other hand, simply describes a state of affairs that exists at the present time; hence, it is synchronic.

The study of language in its diachronic aspect is often called **historical linguistics.** This is a perfectly acceptable term, of course, since history is indeed the description of changes taking place in time. Likewise, the study of language in its synchronic aspect is often called **descriptive linguistics.** This, however, is much less acceptable, because by definition all linguistics is basically descriptive. Hence, this term is misleading. It once enjoyed quite a vogue, however, and is still used, so the student should know about it. But he should avoid using it and stick to *synchronic* as the more accurate term.

One minor point might be mentioned here because it might create occasional difficulties. This is that a truly synchronic description as we have defined it is an impossibility because there is no such thing as "a point of time." Actually, a synchronic statement may cover a duration of time of months or even years. Lorenzo Dow Turner's study of the Gullah dialect spoken in the Sea Islands of Georgia and South Carolina occupied him for fifteen years. Yet it contains a description of this dialect which can quite properly be called synchronic. The reader is frankly told about the time involved in collecting and studying the material and can make adjustments accordingly. On the other hand a statement covering a much shorter span, or even appearing to be confined to a point of time, may be diachronic if it describes a process rather than a state of affairs. For instance, the statement "the verb *contact* is well on the way to being accepted in cultivated English" is really a diachronic statement, because it says, in effect, "the verb *contact* was once not accepted at all in cultivated English, but it is accepted by a good number of cultivated speakers now, and I predict that it will be accepted by the large majority of them in the future."

In this book our major interest is in a synchronic description of present-day American English. But diachronic statements will appear from time to time. The reader must be constantly alert to keep them separate and to recognize the differing kinds of validity they have. In one chapter we shall use a relatively large amount of historical or diachronic material—Chapter 9, "The Dialects of American English."

There is another kind of statement we can make about language, which, in effect, means there is another aspect under which we can study it. If we return to Shakespeare's "most unkindest cut of all," it is apparent that we can make a statement of this sort: "The double superlative was used in Shakespeare's English, but it is not used in the English of the twentieth century." What has been done here is to *compare* two synchronic statements about two points of time. The comparison may suggest a diachronic conclusion, but it does not state it. There are many other kinds of comparative statements that can be made, such as "the Germanic dative survives in German but has disappeared in English" (comparison of two diachronic statements about different but related languages), or, "the German definite article is inflected, but the English one is not" (comparative synchronic statements about two languages at the same point of time) and so on. The study of language from this point of view is **comparative linguistics.** It is always based on a foundation of synchronic or historical linguistics, or both, simply because comparisons are impossible without something to compare.

Finally, before we take leave of this rather lengthy discussion of the subdivision of linguistics according to aspect, we should take note of the term **structural linguistics.** This is used to denominate the kind of linguistics which is primarily interested in discovering and describing as concisely and accurately as possible the interrelationships and patterns which make up the intricate structures of languages. In a way, structural linguistics can be called the mathematics of language study because it is likely to be rather abstract and preoccupied with methods. It is the most rigorously scientific form of linguistics, and its practitioners sometimes claim to be the only true linguists, just as mathematicians sometimes claim to be the only pure scientists. The structural linguists may be indulged in this claim because they have developed methods and standards of procedure that have contributed more than anything else to making linguistics the most scientific of the social sciences. It is largely owing to their work during the last three decades that the study of language has taken on new vitality and interest in our day.

BRANCHES OF STRUCTURAL LINGUISTICS

The third method by which the subject matter of linguistics can be subdivided is on the basis of the various parts, or layers of structure, which go to make up speech. This gives us the various **branches** of linguistics, which are listed on page 30. But first we must look more closely at the principle of division, because it is not so immediately obvious as the division by fields and aspects.

Language, as we shall see in detail later on, is a highly organized affair. Now most highly organized things exhibit various degrees, levels, or layers of organization, whereby the original smallest units are built into larger units, which in turn are built into larger ones, until the largest desired unit is reached. In our political organization, for instance, the unit is the individual citizen. If the citizen is a city dweller, he is grouped with his neighbors into a precinct, a group of precincts are organized into a ward, a group of wards make a city, a group of cities and townships make a county, counties are organized into states, and states into the largest unit we recognize, the nation. The world is at present trying to find a satisfactory way to organize nations into even larger political units. Perhaps the very survival of the human race depends on the success of this effort. Other examples of organization by layers will come to mind readily, such as the military, which builds individual soldiers into squads, squads into platoons, and so on through company, battalion, regiment, division, and army. Here, too, our country has added one more degree of organization by creating a Department of Defense to bring together all the branches of the military into one unit.

This method of organizing things is not man made; it is Nature's way. "What a piece of work is a man!" Hamlet said. A knowledge of modern science would certainly have confirmed him in his opinion, though today he might say instead, "What a miracle of organization is a man!" A relatively small variety of unit particles—charges of electricity, bundles of energy, or what you will—are organized into a somewhat larger number of types of atoms, which in turn are organized into a very large variety of molecules. Selections of these are organized into cells, the cells into organs, and the organs into the total man, who walks about like a single thing (our very word *individual* comes from Latin elements meaning "not to be divided up"), totally unconcerned by the fact that he is a complex of at least five layers of organization.

Before we go on to see how all this applies to language, we should note two facts about this kind of organization:

1. The old axiom from Euclid, "the whole is equal to the sum of all its parts," does not apply to *organized* wholes. An organized whole is always *greater* than the sum of all its parts, because it is equal to the sum of its parts *plus the way they are organized*. Everybody knows that water, H_2O, is made up of hydrogen and oxygen. But one could not put two tanks of hydrogen and one of oxygen into a sealed room, open the valves, and expect to come back an hour later to find a room full of water. The hydrogen and oxygen would be there in the right proportions, but they would be simply *mixed*, not *organized*. In the same way both an army and a rabble are wholes made up of the sum of many individual persons, but because it is organized, the army has many properties which the rabble has not.

2. As a result of this principle, the person who studies or uses material which is organized in this way may move up and down from one level to another, and as he does so, he may treat what is a collection of parts on one level as a unit on the next higher level. A general may manipulate regiments in much the same way a squad leader manipulates individual men. Similarly, as we move up the scale of the organization of the universe, we find the nuclear physicist preoccupied with the smallest units, the subatomic particles; then the chemist, studying atoms and molecules; the structural geologist, studying various kinds of rocks and their organization; and finally, the astronomer, whose units are stars, galaxies, and supergalaxies.

Another chain would take us from the chemist to the cytologist, who studies cells, to the histologist, who studies tissues, to the anatomist, who studies organs. All these scientists are to a large degree concerned with studying patterns of organization, or structures, and how they affect the behavior of all the many things to be found in this fascinating universe. In fact, if one were asked to name the most characteristic feature of science at the middle of the twentieth century, he would be bound to reply, "its preoccupation with *structure*." Here, as we have already seen, linguistics is no exception; whatever may be the other interests of modern linguistic science, its heart and center is an interest in the *structure of language*.

We shall have a good deal to say about the details of linguistic structure later on. For the present we need only take a quick look at it in order to see how its various levels become the subject matter of the various branches of linguistics. When we hear a person say something in a language we understand, such as, for instance, "It's going to rain this afternoon," spoken with a rather heavy stress on *rain* and a descending intonation from there to the end, we are subconsciously aware of a good many things at once. We recognize, for instance, that the speaker is expressing an *opinion*. This we gather from the over-all structure of what is said. A change in this structure, such as giving the intonation an upward turn at the end, or changing the beginning to "Is it," would change our interpretation of the whole utterance from an opinion to a question. We further are aware that the over-all structure is made up of smaller structures we call *words*. We may also be aware that these in turn are made up of *sounds* (or, if we are highly literate, we may think of *letters*). This is about as far as the ordinary person goes in his thinking about language structure; it corresponds to about the H_2O level of thinking about chemical structure. But a bit of closer scrutiny will reveal that some of the sounds are important—of structural significance— and some are not. We can pronounce *rain* in a good many different ways before somebody thinks we are saying "run," or "ran," or "ruin." Finally, even closer scrutiny will reveal that the various sounds are themselves structures made up of various features, such as whether we are talking through our nose, as in the last part of *rain*, or through our mouth, as in the first part of *afternoon*, and so forth. These **features** or **qualities** of sounds are, in the present state of linguistics at least, the atoms of speech.

To reverse the process and start from the small end, we may say that in an act of speech, features are organized into sounds, these are selected and organized into significant groups, these in turn are organized in various combinations into words and parts of words, which in turn are organized into an utterance. Each level of organization in this process, which we all perform at incredible speed every time we speak, is the subject matter of a branch of structural linguistics. For our purposes in this book, four branches may be recognized. They are:

Phonetics, whose subject matter is sound-features or qualities and their organization into speech-sounds, or **phones.**

Phonemics, whose subject matter is the organization of phones into groups or families, called **phonemes,** whose members are the *significant* sounds of speech.

Morphemics, whose subject matter is the organization of phonemes into meaningful groups called **morphs.** It is also concerned with the organization of these morphs into family groups, called **morphemes,** and the combination of morphemes into *words*.

Grammar, whose subject matter is the organization of words into various combinations, often representing many layers of structure, such as phrases, sentences, and complete utterances.

Beyond this, linguistics does not at present go. Further levels of organization, such as the paragraphs, sections, and chapters of this book, are the province of rhetoric, which, as we have seen, is not a part of linguistics.

Three more terms which are often used in structural linguistics should be mentioned here. **Phonology** is a cover term embracing phonetics and phonemics. It is sometimes convenient, for example, to speak of "the phonology of English," meaning all matters relating to the sound-system of English. **Morphology** and **Syntax** are subdivisions of grammar; the former deals with the structure of words, the latter with the structure of word groups. Thus, a discussion of how English plurals are formed would belong to morphology, while a discussion of prepositional phrases would belong to syntax.

FOUR MORE BRANCHES OF LINGUISTICS

In addition to the four branches of structural linguistics which we have just described, there are four more branches of linguistics that will concern us to a greater or less degree in this book. They are *semantics*, *graphics*, *linguistic geography*, and *lexicography*. They have in common two qualities: (1) they represent attempts to apply the findings and methods of linguistics to the solution of problems and the attainment of ends that are not strictly within the field of linguistics proper, and (2) they draw upon materials, ideas, and methods from other fields of study outside the strictly defined limits of linguistics. They thus are of the nature both of the applied sciences (such as surgery, engineering, and forestry) and of what may be called the "liaison" sciences, which occupy the border territory between two fields (like biochemistry, social psychology, and geopolitics).

1. **Semantics** is a term much heard these days, and it is used to describe many different fields of study, not all of them scientific.[2] In its broad sense it means "the study of meaning." One would think that this would put it well within the field of linguistics, since meaning is certainly an important part of language. The catch is in deciding just what meaning is. If we think of meaning as "the ideas,

[2] Those who are interested in the origin, history, and multiple meanings of the term *semantics* will find an admirably clear and compendious treatment of the subject in an article by Allen Walker Read, "An Account of the Word 'Semantics,'" *Word*, IV (1948), 78–97.

concepts, images, and feelings which are associated in the mind with words," anyone who has followed the discussion in this chapter to this point will immediately see that meaning in this sense is outside both the subject matter and the methods of linguistics. We have defined the subject matter of linguistics as language, which we in turn have defined as "an arbitrary system of articulated sounds." An idea or image or feeling may be either the stimulus for or the response to an articulated sound, but it is not the sound itself. Furthermore, ideas, notions, feelings, and the like may be observed and studied only by the person in whose mind they occur. This means that they cannot be "verified by any competent observer," a requirement that we set up as essential to scientific method (p. 15). It is conceivable that in the future the human race may develop powers of telepathy and "mind-reading" far beyond the exceedingly rudimentary ones some individuals now possess. If so, "ideas, concepts, images, and feelings" will come under the observation of science. But not till then. For the present, this kind of meaning, which we can call **notional meaning,** belongs to philosophy, not to science, and, hence, not to linguistics.

But this is not the only definition of meaning. It can also be defined as "an object, relationship, or class of objects or relationships in the outside world that is referred to by a word." This can be called **referential meaning,** and the object, relationship, etc., in the outside world to which a word refers is often called its **referent.** We make extensive use of referential meaning in the early stages of learning to talk, as anyone knows who has observed a child pointing to things and asking "What's this?" Now, since objects and relationships in the outside world can be subjected to scrutiny, objective description, and generalization, a semantics based on referential meaning can be scientific. But it is not truly a branch of linguistics, because its subject matter is not *language* but *referents.* This kind of semantics, to which the well-known "General Semantics" of Count Korzybski and his followers belongs, is a "liaison science," which investigates the relationship of words and things and thus partly invades the field of linguistics. It has shown great results already, and has even greater potentialities. But it is beyond our range, and we cannot go into it in this book.[3]

There is yet a third definition of meaning which can properly be called linguistic and thus can open the way to a kind of semantics within the field of linguistics as we have defined it. Going back once more to our definition of a language, let us recollect that we defined it as "a *system* of articulated sounds . . ." The existence of a *system* implies the existence of patterns of arrangement and order other than those that would result from mere chance. If I spilled a boxful of the little lettered squares used in playing "Anagrams" or "Scrabble" onto a table, the chances that they would fall into a pattern of arrangement similar to this page or any page in any book are exceedingly remote. Yet, anyone who turns the pages of this book or any other, even if he does not know how to read, will perceive patterns that recur again and again, and will be aware that there is some sort of system behind these patterns. Try it yourself with a book in some language, preferably also some alphabet, that you don't know, such as Greek, Hebrew, Russian, or Sanskrit. Now we can define the meaning of a word as "all the positions it fills in the system of the language of which it is a part." This is as much as to say that a word means the sum total of what it contributes to all the utterances in which it appears. It can be seen at once that this is a definition of meaning that brings it completely within the scope of linguistics as we have defined it. It does not bring in any subject matter (such as ideas or referents) from outside the language, and it allows the kinds of objective description and generalization which we have called scientific to be carried on. Some kind of linguistic semantics is, thus, a theoretical possibility. Since in its pure form it is a virtually

[3] Those interested in looking farther into General Semantics will find a convenient summary in an article by S. I. Hayakawa, "Linguistics and the Future: Some Implications of General Semantics," *ETC*, I (1944), 148–53.

unexplored field, we shall do very little with it in this book. But when we use the term *meaning*, we shall try to restrict it to this kind of contextual, systematic, or **distributional meaning,** rather than either notional or referential meaning.

The idea of distributional meaning put forward in the last paragraph may at first seem both strange and difficult. But a little thought on the subject of how we learn the meanings of words should make it clear. We have already seen that in the early stages of the language-learning process a child makes extensive use of referential meaning. He points to something, or touches it, or holds it up in order to get some adult to repeat the word which is associated with that thing—which "means" that thing in the referential sense. Some children do this quite systematically. One linguist reports that when his two-year-old daughter first learned the word *clock* from him, she took him by the hand and led him through the whole house, stopping before every clock and getting him to repeat the word.[4] In this way she extended the referent of *clock* from a single object (the clock she first pointed to) to a class of objects (all the clocks in the house).

An adult finding himself among people to whom he could not talk would be forced back upon the child's method of learning by referential meaning. But in our own native speech, or the later stages of learning a foreign language, we largely abandon the use of referential meaning and come to rely more and more upon context to guide us to the meaning of new words. We see or hear a strange word and guess at its meaning from our idea of the total meaning of the sentence in which it occurs. Then, as we observe it in other, different contexts, we begin to build up a collection of associations with it. Finally, we may become so sure of what it can contribute to a context that we use it ourselves. If we are mistaken (if our generalization about what it can contribute to a context is based on insufficient evidence), we may be laughed at, politely corrected, or asked to

[4] H. V. Velten, "The Growth of Phonemic and Lexical Patterns in Infant Language," *Language*, XIX (1943), 283.

explain. This whole procedure is one of finding out what positions the new word fills in the system of the language (in what contexts it can be used and what it contributes to those contexts). And this is precisely our definition of distributional meaning.

One more illustration, this time from outside the immediate field of language, may help to clarify this important concept. From one point of view it may be said that the "meaning" of one person to another is the total of what he contributes to the environments in which he appears. For instance, we may buy our meat from a Mr. Smith at the corner market. So long as our experience of Mr. Smith is confined to this, his "meaning" for us may be something like "cheerful, honest, skilful butcher." Then one day we may see him at the county fair, conducting a small child among the wonders of the midway with apparent enjoyment. At first, the context is so different from that of the butcher shop that we may not even identify him, but simply have a vague feeling of having seen him before. But if we do recognize him, we will add to his "meaning" something like "patient, good-tempered, sympathetic father." Then, as we encounter him in other places—at church, at PTA meetings, at the baseball game, or perhaps drunk and disorderly at the corner tavern —we find each new context adding to his meaning for us. If he should die, we might remark to a friend, "I miss Mr. Smith; he meant a lot to me."

To sum up, then, semantics is the study of meaning. If it deals with notional meaning, it is philosophical semantics. If it deals with referential meaning, it is referential or, in a special sense, general semantics. Only if it deals strictly with distributional meaning can it be called linguistic semantics. It would be well if we were always careful to label the word with the appropriate adjective whenever we use it.

2. **Graphics** is a convenient term to use for the branch of linguistics whose subject matter is all the conventions used in representing speech in writing. We shall treat this branch, as it relates to American English, in Chapter 8, "Writing It Down." At this point our concern

is to place it in its relationship to the other branches of our science. To do this we must make three points.

a) Writing is not language and language is not writing. We have defined language as "an arbitrary system of articulated sounds," a definition which certainly does not include marks on paper, stone, and metal, or patterns of neon tubes, smoke in the sky, tracks in the snow, or any of the other fanciful or practical media we use for writing. If we should substitute "an arbitrary system of visual shapes" in our definition, we should be on the way to defining writing. But we should still have to find some way of excluding other visual shapes which we use in carrying on the affairs of our society.

b) There are basically two kinds of writing, one of which is linguistic and the other outside the linguistic field. By this we mean that a written record or message may use a system of visual shapes that represent the *sounds of speech* which the writer would use if he were in the presence of the person for whom it is intended, or it may use a system of visual shapes that represent the *referents* which the writer would point to if he were in the presence of the receiver of the message. The first method is **alphabetic** (or sometimes **syllabic**) writing; the second is **pictographic** or **ideographic**. A familiar illustration will make this clear.

Driving along an American highway, a motorist might encounter a sign like this:

This sign has a simple message to deliver, and it does so twice. The upper part is a **pictogram,** giving a conventionalized picture of the referent, a curve to the right. It could be used on any highway in the world because it is nonlinguistic. It does not mean the *word* we pronounce "curve," but the *thing itself.* It is part of a system of similar pictograms, used to describe the different kinds of hazard to be found on the highway. The lower part of the sign uses five *alphabetic characters* to represent a series of sounds which a person who reads English will recognize as a word. It is, thus, a linguistic message. But unless a speaker of English has learned the arbitrary relationship between the alphabetic characters and the sounds of English, he will be unable to make anything out of the lower part of the sign, and will be forced to depend on the upper part, just as he would if he were a speaker of some foreign tongue.

c) It follows from the preceding point that pictographic writing is completely outside the field of linguistics because it deals only with visual shapes and referents, by-passing language entirely.[5] Linguistics does take account of alphabetic and syllabic writing, for two principal reasons: first, because until the invention of the phonograph there was no other way of preserving specimens of language for study; and secondly (really a corollary of this), because older forms of "living" (i.e., still spoken) languages and all survivals of "dead" (i.e., no longer spoken) languages are in written form, and therefore historical (diachronic) linguistics would be impossible without recourse to written materials. But the linguist never forgets that in dealing with written material he is not dealing with language itself but with an arbitrary system of written symbols which more or less accurately represents the arbitrary system of articulated sounds which is the language. In short, he is constantly aware of three

---

[5] This statement is actually an oversimplification. It is probable that pictographic signs often involve a linguistic intermediary in fact, however they may exclude it in theory. But in any case this belongs to the field of psychology, not linguistics.

points that must be always in the mind of the reader of this
book:

> Writing is not language, though it usually represents language.
> Letters are not sounds, though they may represent sounds.
> Combinations of letters are not words, though they may represent
> words.

Half of the world's population—the half that cannot read—does not
need to be told these things. But literate people, particularly those
who read a great deal, frequently forget them and are betrayed into
many wrong and fallacious notions about language as a result.

3. **Linguistic geography,** or **area linguistics** as it is sometimes
called, is the branch of linguistics which is interested in the geographic distribution of dialects within the general system of a language. These dialects may differ from one another in many ways: in
their phonology, their grammar, their vocabulary, and their semantics. The nature of dialects will be taken up later in this chapter, and
the whole question of the linguistic geography of the United States
will occupy us at some length in Chapter 9, "The Dialects of American English." For the present, we need only make two observations
about linguistic geography:

a) It uses the methods of all three of the principal aspects of linguistics, as we have defined them above. It usually begins with a
synchronic description, based upon collections of samples of the
actual speech of the region under investigation. It then uses *comparative* methods to study the differences between parallel samples
drawn from different speakers. Finally, it draws *historical* conclusions
concerning parallel, divergent, and convergent changes in the systems
of speech used by different areas or social classes. Because its conclusions are usually stated in diachronic terms, it is often classed as a
branch of historical linguistics, but it should not be forgotten that it
uses synchronic and comparative methods as well.

b) Linguistic geography is a "liaison science," because it uses material drawn from other subject-matter fields than that of linguistics proper. The most important of these fields are history, economics, sociology, and demography. In fact, not only does it draw upon these disciplines, it contributes to them as well. As we shall see in the chapter on American dialects, such a project as the *Linguistic Atlas of the United States and Canada* is a mine of information about the settlement history of our country, and about such other subjects as social stratification and mobility, regional and class folkways, and many other matters of interest to the social scientist.

A term sometimes heard is **dialectology,** often used as a synonym of linguistic geography. If it is a separate branch of linguistics, it certainly overlaps linguistic geography to a large degree, differing more in emphasis and interpretation than in subject matter and method, though as a broader term it includes also the study of social, as well as regional, dialects.

It should also be observed that linguistic geography does not always limit itself to differences between the dialects of a single language. In its broadest aspect it is interested in the distribution of all the languages of man and in their influences upon each other where their speakers come in contact. From the historical point of view it describes the spread, radiation, and migration of languages and their shrinkage and disappearance; one might borrow a term from biological science and call this *linguistic ecology.* A special branch of it deals with the interesting question of **bilingualism** and **multilingualism** in those parts of the world where people habitually speak more than one language.

4. The last branch of linguistics to be discussed here is **lexicography,** the preparing of dictionaries. This is pretty certainly the most important branch of applied linguistics, and the one most familiar to the general public. Indeed, the dictionary is often the only point of contact between the ordinary citizen and the whole field of linguistic science. For this reason, many notions, not all of them

accurate, prevail about the nature and use of dictionaries. For our purposes, three facts about lexicography are important:

a) Although lexicography is an applied science, one that is concerned with the practical needs of users of a language, it is still a science. This means that good dictionaries use the methods of objective description, generalization, and constant revision which we have said are essential to the scientific method. Insofar as a dictionary uses guesswork or prejudice as a basis for its generalizations, it is unscientific and, hence, unreliable.

b) Lexicography, like linguistic geography, uses the methods of all three aspects of linguistics, and makes statements of relevance to most of the main branches. Thus, a usual dictionary entry may contain the following information about a word: (1) spelling (graphics); (2) pronunciation (phonology); (3) part of speech (syntax); (4) inflections (morphology); (5) etymology (comparative historical morphemics); (6) present meaning or meanings (comparative synchronic semantics); (7) older meanings (historical semantics); (8) usage labels (dialectology); (9) derivative words (morphology); (10) synonyms (comparative semantics again). In addition, the modern dictionary frequently feels called upon to give information not only about words themselves, but about their referents, as in the passage about the Unitarian church quoted on page 22. Here the dictionary departs from linguistics entirely and invades the field of the encyclopedia.

c) Dictionaries are likely to use all three kinds of meaning, as we have defined them above. They may define a word by synonyms or longer expressions which attempt to suggest the idea or concept or feeling associated with a word; that is, its *notional meaning*. They may use other words, descriptions, or even pictures and diagrams, that point out the referent; that is, its *referential meaning*. The larger dictionaries, notably such magnificent works as the *Oxford English Dictionary*, give many illustrative quotations, which is a way of at least sketching the *distributional meaning*.

THE SUBDIVISIONS OF LINGUISTICS (SUMMARY)

The various subdivisions of linguistics may be summarized in outline form, as follows:

I. Fields of Linguistics

    A. Language families: Indo-European, Semitic, etc.

    B. Individual languages: French, English, etc.

    C. Subdivisions of languages: Canadian French, American English, etc.

II. Aspects of Linguistics

    A. Synchronic (or Descriptive)

    B. Diachronic (or Historical)

    C. Comparative

    D. Structural

III. Branches of Linguistics

    A. Four main branches of Structural Linguistics

        1. Phonetics

        2. Phonemics

        3. Morphemics

        4. Grammar

            a) Morphology

            b) Syntax

    B. Four kinds of Applied Linguistics

        1. Semantics

        2. Graphics

        3. Linguistic Geography (Area Linguistics, Dialectology)

        4. Lexicography

SPEECH-COMMUNITIES AND DIALECTS

So far we have been working with a rather broad and simple definition of a language. It is accurate enough to serve the purpose for which we have used it—to help us separate linguistics from other studies dealing with language and to subdivide linguistics itself into its fields, aspects, and branches. But when we come to look more closely at a single language, such as English, we find that our definition leaves many questions unanswered. Perhaps the one most often asked is, "When do two different ways of speaking a language become so different that they are really two languages?" A version of this question often heard is, "Is there a separate American language, or is it part of English?" We have implied the latter by using "American English" in our title. On the other hand, H. L. Mencken called his classic book *The American Language*. On the whole we are inclined to feel that Mr. Mencken overstated the case in his title, and that our language is only a variant version of the mother tongue. After all, most Americans can converse freely with most Englishmen without making more than minor alterations in their ways. But if an Alabama farmer, a Scottish shepherd, a London Cockney, and a Maine lobsterman were to be suddenly thrown together, they might have considerable trouble before they were able to converse with any mutual understanding. Yet each one would stoutly maintain that he was speaking English.

This is a real and vexing question, and it must be answered before we can begin our detailed examination of American English. The answer is to be sought by giving attention to the second part of our definition of a language. The first part, you will remember, defined a language as "an arbitrary system of articulated sounds." The second part went on to state that this system is "made use of by a group of humans as a means of carrying on the affairs of their society." The key phrases here are *a group of humans* and *their society*. These phrases had to be left vague, so that they would cover both a language spoken only by a few hundred people in a small village and a language spoken by many millions in many areas of the earth. But we need now to look at some of the differences there would inevitably be between two such languages.

In order to simplify the problem, let us imagine a village of a hundred people, completely cut off from the rest of the world. Let us further imagine that this village has a very simple and democratic kind of social life. All political problems and other matters affecting the whole village are settled in a weekly town meeting, which is attended by the entire adult population and presided over by a citizen chosen by lot. Everybody belongs to the same church, and all the children attend the same school. All business is carried on in the market place, where craftsmen bring their handiwork and farmers their produce. Nobody is very rich or very poor. It is, in short, a simple community, which you might consider Utopian or intolerably boring, depending on your tastes.

In such a village as we have described, the chances are that every individual would speak with every other individual many times in the course of his life. If we represented each citizen by a dot on the map of the village and drew a line between him and every other citizen he conversed with in any one year, our map would be covered by so many lines that it would be virtually obliterated. Now it is clear that in order to keep this intricate network operating, no individual could allow his own speech to get very far out of line. In fact, we could call this village a single **speech-community.** Its speech would not only be a single language, but a single dialect, since **dialect** may be defined as "The variety of language spoken by the members of a single homogeneous speech-community."

Now, let us assume that the population of our imaginary village doubles in the course of time. To avoid crowding, half of the people move to a new site about a day's journey away and set up a new village on the model of the old one. In general, each village goes its own way, but there is considerable visiting back and forth in the course of trade and on holidays. Since only a few of the people of the second village converse with a few of the people of the first village, and that on rare occasions, there is a relatively thin network of lines of communication between the two. We still have a single speech-community, but it has two centers, rather weakly bound together. Some new fashion in language in one village—perhaps some expression adopted from the vocabulary of those fertile inventors of slang, the teen-agers—may or may not be copied in the other village. We have the beginning of a split into two speech-communities, each with its own dialect.

To carry our hypothetical case a bit farther, let us imagine that some event—earthquake or flood, or perhaps simple estrangement —cuts off all communication between the two villages. Each one has now become as separate and self-contained as the first one was in the beginning. We now have two distinct speech-communities. At first, they will both still speak the same dialect. But if the breach continues long enough—two or three generations, let us say—the innovations made independently in each village's speech-habits will add up into clearly recognizable dialect differences. If communications are re-established, visitors from one village will find that although they can make themselves understood well enough, the citizens of the foreign village sound a bit queer and use some unfamiliar words and expressions now and then. In short, they will be speaking different **regional dialects** of the same language.

Now, let us return to our original village at the time when it was feeling the pressure of a doubled population. Let us suppose that the citizens solve the problem not by emigration but by expanding their village and changing their political structure. Instead of everybody belonging to town meeting, only those who have a certain amount of property are considered full citizens. The rest of the population is barred from political participation and restricted in other ways. The town-meeting crowd take over the profitable occupations and get rich. They no longer work with their hands but become a white-collar class. Their children receive a special education, while the working people's children are required to stop their education at an early age. Finally, the aristocratic town-meeting class set up their own church, which they can attend without rubbing elbows with the miserable workers.

The result of all this is clear. There will be two speech-communities within the same village, each one closely knit within itself. A member of the working class may converse a hundred times with other members of his class for every single conversation he has with a member of the ruling class. And since the occupations, education, and religion of each group differ sharply from those of the other, it is clear that before long they will develop marked differences in vocabulary, at least, and probably in pronunciation and grammar as well. They will, in fact, be speaking different **social** or **class dialects,** even though they live in the same village.

It is clear that if regional and class dialects can exist under the theoretically simplified conditions we have just imagined, the situation in any language spoken over a wide area by large numbers of people of widely varying social classes and customs must be very complicated. And indeed it is. Every language is a collection of many dialects, all more or less mutually intelligible and sharing a common core of structure, but differing from one another in many ways. Each dialect is adapted to the needs and interests of the speech-community that uses it, while at the same time making use of the main features of structure that constitute the common language.

The number of different dialects and the extent of their diversity differ very much from one language area to another. In parts of the world that have been settled for a long time by a stable population, there may be a separate dialect for virtually every village. This is true of many European countries. On the other hand, areas recently settled by a relatively homogeneous population, given to moving about a good deal, may have relatively few dialects. In the United States, for instance, one can travel from the Pennsylvania-Ohio line to the Pacific Coast without being aware of any but the slightest dialect differences—one of the largest dialect areas and speech-communities in the world. This is an important fact about America, to which we shall return in Chapter 9.

STANDARD AND LITERARY DIALECTS

We must take account of one more phenomenon before we can conclude this introductory discussion of dialect. Let us return to the village that developed a marked class structure, with upper- and lower-class social dialects. In such a community the aristocratic class will inevitably regard its members as superior to the members of the working class. This attitude will extend to all the possessions and attributes of the aristocratic class—its politics, its customs, its manners, its clothing, and its dialect. Meanwhile, the members of the working class, unwilling perhaps to grant the superior worth of the aristocracy, will certainly admit their superior comfort and fortune. They may well envy them, or at least hope that their children may join them. And since the way a person talks is usually the most obvious clue to his position in the social order, a prerequisite to entry into the ruling class will be learning its dialect. Linguists call such a dialect a **prestige dialect.** If it is widely accepted by the majority of speakers of a language as the "best" dialect of that language, it is a **standard dialect.** Thus, the language spoken by educated Englishmen in the south of England is called Received Standard English. It is, of course, not standard to Americans, who call it "an English accent," and sometimes make fun of it.

The preceding paragraph described in simplified form the way in which a standard dialect may develop from a class dialect which acquires prestige and ultimately becomes the key to superior social status, or one of the symbols thereof. In the same way, a regional dialect may become the standard dialect of its language. Again, however, the reasons will be social rather than linguistic. If a given locality becomes dominant in its language area to the extent that its inhabitants become the class to whom the other regions look for leadership, the dialect of that locality may very well acquire such prestige as to become standard. This happened in both English and French in the later Middle Ages. In the earlier medieval period, no single one of the many dialects of either English or French was considered standard. But as London and Paris grew into prominence as centers of government and trade, their dialects acquired prestige. By the fifteenth century, London English and Parisian French were accepted as standard by nearly everybody, including those who did not speak them.

Actually, it is usually a combination of these causes that produces a standard dialect. In most languages where a standard dialect is recognized, it will be found to be the dialect of the educated and socially, economically, politically, and artistically prominent citizens of the dominant region, usually including the capital city.

If a language is spread over a wide area, it may well have several standard dialects, each one recognized over part of its territory. This is the case with such widely disseminated languages as English, French, and Spanish. Whatever may be the opinion of Englishmen, it is a plain fact that Received Standard English is not the standard dialect of Australia, Canada, or the United States. We must also recognize a standard Canadian French, Mexican Spanish, Brazilian Portuguese, and so on. It is true that many speakers of these dialects may feel that their speech is in some way inferior to that of London, Paris, Madrid, or Lisbon. On the other hand, others may take an exaggerated attitude, often strongly influenced by political nationalism, regarding the right of their dialect to be considered standard. This is not the place to go into the complicated attitudes people may have about their dialects, which are matter for the psychologist and sociologist rather than for the linguist. We will, however, go into them in somewhat more detail in the Chapter 10, "Linguistics and the Teacher of English."

One more type of standard dialect should be recognized at this point. That is the **literary dialect.** Any dialect may be a medium for literature, of course, as anyone knows who has read *Huckleberry Finn, Uncle Remus*, or the poems of Robert Burns. But it often happens that a single dialect is considered the appropriate one for artistic and scholarly composition. It may, of course, be the same as the standard spoken dialect, as is the case with most modern European languages. This is likely to be true when literacy is widespread and many people engage in literature, whether it be reciting and listening to epic poems or writing and reading novels. On the other hand, when literacy is restricted to a rather small and sometimes exclusive group—a scholar class—this group may use a special dialect for its writing. Often this is an older form of the language, as it appears in literary classics which the scholar class is intimately familiar with. Sanskrit is such an archaic literary dialect. The extreme is reached when a literary dialect is actually another language, as was the case with classical Latin in Western Europe during the Renaissance.

We may sum up the material of the last two sections in six points; as follows:

1. A language is usually a collection of dialects, spoken by the members of different speech-communities, sharing the main structural features of the language, but differing to a greater or less degree in details of phonology, grammar, and vocabulary.

2. Dialects spoken in speech-communities occupying different parts of the general territory of a language are *regional dialects.*

3. Dialects spoken by different social groups within the same region are *social* or *class dialects.*

4. A dialect admired and emulated by the speakers of other dialects is a *prestige dialect.*

5. A dialect generally admitted by the majority of speakers to be

superior to all the other dialects in its language is the *standard dialect* of that language, or simply the *standard language*. It is usually that used by the educated and ruling classes.

6. A dialect used primarily by writers and scholars is a *literary dialect*.

It should hardly be necessary to say that the word *dialect* as used by linguists is a technical term, free from any emotional connotations or value judgments. It will be so used constantly throughout this book, and the reader must train himself to use it in a purely objective, scientific way.

NOTE ON COLLATERAL READING

In general, items are listed in the order in which they should be read by the beginning student. The arrangement is governed by three considerations, which sometimes conflict: application to the central, fundamental matter of the chapter; amplification of points and lines of study not fully treated in the chapter; and degree of difficulty.

On the whole, the readings have been chosen from recognized classics of linguistic literature and scholarship, many of them pioneer works or memorable syntheses. Works of secondary importance, however, have been freely drawn upon if they serve any of the three functions listed above.

There is considerable overlapping among the readings suggested in any single group, a fact which permits them to be selectively assigned. The first two or three items in each list should be sufficient for undergraduates; graduate students should read all items.

The assignment of these readings is, of course, a matter for the discretion of the instructor, who may choose to omit them entirely, or to supplement or replace them with other material from the General Bibliography or of his own choosing.

COLLATERAL READING, CHAPTER 1

Bloch, Bernard, and Trager, George L. *Outline of Linguistic Analysis*. Baltimore, Linguistic Society of America, 1942. Chap. i, "Language and Linguistics," pp. 5–9.

Sapir, Edward. *Language: An Introduction to the Study of Speech*. New York: Harcourt, Brace & Co., Inc., 1921. Chap. i, "Introductory: Language Defined," pp. 1–23.

Gleason, H. A. *An Introduction to Descriptive Linguistics*. New York: Henry Holt & Co., Inc., 1955. Chap. i, "Language," pp. 1–13.

Bloomfield, Leonard. *Language*. New York: Henry Holt & Co., Inc., 1933. Chap. ii, "The Use of Language," pp. 21–41; chap. iii, "Speech-Communities," pp. 42–56.

Sturtevant, Edgar H. *An Introduction to Linguistic Science*. New Haven: Yale University Press, 1947. Chap. i, "Introductory," pp. 1–8; chap. vi, "Descriptive Linguistics," pp. 51–64.

Carroll, John B. *The Study of Language: A Survey of Linguistics and Related Disciplines in America*. Cambridge: Harvard University Press, 1953. Chap. ii, "The Science of Linguistics," pp. 7–29.

Trager, George L. *The Field of Linguistics*. Studies in Linguistics, Occasional Papers, No. 1. Norman, Okla.: Battenburg Press, 1949. Pp. 1–8.

Chapter 2

The Sounds of Speech: Phonetics

THE COMPLEXITY OF SPEECH

Talking is such an incessant and habitual mode of human behavior that most of us take it for granted. We greet each other, pass the time of day, discuss our daily affairs, ask and answer, chat and argue from the moment we get up in the morning, or before, until the moment we retire, or after. Yet a large part of this flow of talk is of very little practical consequence. In the course of an average day the normal city-dweller may take part in several hundred conversations, yet when he looks back over the day, he will remember only two or three of them. This seems like a tremendous waste of time and energy, and from one point of view it is. Moralists of the more utilitarian sort are fond of coining proverbs like "Talkers are no great doers," and all of us know people who fit the description. No one is more annoying than the person who insists on talking when we want to do something else, such as read, sleep, think, or talk ourselves.

But from another point of view this seemingly wasteful and unnecessary use of talk seems to be of great importance to us. We discover this fact when for some reason we are prevented from talking, by severe laryngitis, let us say, or by finding ourselves among people whose language we cannot speak. In fact, prolonged depriva-

51

tion of the opportunity for conversation is a very trying experience indeed. Solitary confinement is traditionally considered a very severe form of punishment, largely because it cuts its victim off from talk. General William F. Dean preserved his sanity when a prisoner in Korea by talking to himself, and Robinson Crusoe on his island carried on long conversations with his dog and parrot. Talking thus seems to be more than just a practical means of communication. We saw in the last chapter that speech is a unique human attribute; apparently there is a compulsion to exercise it. Perhaps it is one way of reassuring ourselves that we are still members in good standing of the human race.

Most of the activities involved in a conversation are habitual; they are directed by channels and circuits in our nervous system so well-worn that we are totally unaware of them. These habits we acquired with considerable trouble during our childhood, and most of them are so deeply ingrained that they will not leave us until we die. A person suffering from amnesia may forget his name and all his past life, but he will talk as naturally as he breathes. As a result of this, it requires quite an effort of mind and imagination to see a simple conversation as the vastly complicated thing it is. Yet this is the first step we must take in becoming linguists. We can take nothing for granted; we must examine every minutest detail with care and patience lest we overlook some essential part of the intricate patterns of speech.

Suppose, having trained ourselves to observe in this way, we turn our attention to a conversation between two friends meeting on the street. Let us assume that they speak a language we do not know; in that case we will miss some of the substance of their conversation, but we will be the better able to observe things about its nature.

First, we might observe some matters that did not involve speech at all, such as which one saw the other first, whether the street was crowded or deserted, what the weather was like, how the two friends were dressed, what they were carrying, whether they stopped to talk or walked along together, and so on. All these things we can call parts of the **nonlinguistic context.** In general, they are outside the scope of linguistic study, though sometimes we have to know about them to explain certain linguistic facts.

Next, we might note some other things which seemed to accompany the stream of speech without exactly being a part of it. Among these might be bowing, shaking hands, removing hats, various motions of hands, arms, and shoulders, nodding and shaking of heads, smiles, frowns, and pursing of lips. All these things can be grouped together as **gestures.** Some of them are so closely bound up with speech that we might have quite a bit of difficulty deciding where to draw the line. That they are a habitual part of the act of talking is illustrated by the fact that a person talking on the telephone will use the same kind of facial expressions and even hand gestures that he customarily uses when face to face with the other party to the conversation. Yet, in the present state of linguistics, gesture is left largely out of consideration, so we shall have nothing much to say about it in this book. In passing, however, we should observe that a large part of gesture is not individual but social. Gestures, like table manners and languages, are parts of culture which we must learn like all the rest. Within the repertory of gesture, as within that of language, there is room both for regional and social "dialects" and for individual styles.

The first thing we would note about the vocal part of our hypothetical conversation would be that the two speakers talked in turn, rather than in chorus, with occasional brief periods of overlapping and occasional periods of silence. Then we would observe certain large and obvious qualities of voice. Our two speakers might shout at each other, or they might murmur or even whisper. If one was a child and the other his parent we might hear a whining, wheedling tone on the one hand and either a clipped, overemphatic, scolding tone or an ingratiating, songlike tone on the other. These **vocal qualifiers,** as they are called, would certainly contribute a good deal to the interchange, and as accurate reporters we should have to include them in any description of the conversation.

If the conversation endured long enough, we might find that during a large part of it, each speaker made use of a tone of voice which we could call "normal" for him. We would further note that the normal voices of the two speakers were distinctive, so that we could tell without watching them which one was talking. Further observation of other conversations would lead us to the conclusion that "normal tone of voice" covers a wide range of variation, including some differences purely individual and others attributable to nationality, sex, age, and social class. We should discover that most adults are able to recognize and distinguish several hundred different individual voices so well that they never mistake them over the telephone. On the whole, we should learn that **individual voice quality** is almost entirely disregarded in speech. We actually train ourselves to recognize two utterances or speech-sounds as being "the same" linguistically, though they may vary greatly in pitch and in vocal quality. This in itself is not as simple as it seems; it is a matter of interest to psychologists, like the ability to recognize a melody as "the same" even though it is played on different instruments in different keys. Since individual vocal quality is a nondistinctive feature in language, linguistics takes no account of it.

Having, so to speak, peeled off and set aside several layers of structure or modulation in our imagined conversation—the non-linguistic context, gesture, vocal qualifiers, and individual vocal quality—we would find ourselves with a residue that we could call speech in the narrow sense of the word. What is this like? It is hard to describe it in a few words, because it is like nothing else on earth. We could note that it is on the whole a continuous noise, occasionally interrupted by longer or shorter pauses, varying from second to second in musical pitch and in degree of loudness, and composed of sounds of many different sorts, following one upon another with incredible speed. We do not notice the speed so much if it is our own language, but speakers of strange tongues always seem to speak very fast. So bewilderingly complicated, so intangible, and so relentlessly rapid is this stream of speech that it seems a miracle that we can learn to catch it on the wing, as it were, assign meaning to it, respond to it, and even duplicate it ourselves. Yet every child sets about this seemingly impossible task and carries it through to a more or less successful conclusion. He is able to do so because this apparently chaotic stream of sound is a highly organized system of structures, which can be learned, remembered, and reproduced.

In order to begin the study of these structures as they are found in present-day American English, we must have a means of describing, classifying, and recording as many as possible of the minimum discernible features of the stream of speech. The science which concerns itself with such matters is *phonetics*.

THE THREE BRANCHES OF PHONETICS

The simplest act of speech, such as saying "Hello!" to a friend, has seven distinct phases. These are:

1. An idea, notion, desire, or similar event in one person's consciousness, which has
2. A neurological counterpart in the brain cells and other parts of the nervous system, which sets off
3. A complex series of maneuvers of the organs of speech, which produces
4. A series of pressure-patterns in the air, called sound waves, which in turn produce
5. A complex series of vibrations of the hearing organs of another person, which are converted into
6. A congruent series of nerve impulses to the cells of the brain, which are in some way related to
7. An event in the second person's consciousness.

This chain of events can be schematically represented by a diagram:

SPEAKER		OUTSIDE WORLD	HEARER	
1–2	3	4	5	6–7

| Mind 1 |
| "Idea" |

| Nervous System 1 | → | Vocal Tract | → | Air | → | Ear | → | Nervous System 2 |
| Stimulus | | Speech Act | | Sound Waves | | Hearing Act | | Response |

| Mind 2 |
| "Under-standing" |

Time

Parts 1, 2, and 3 of this series take place inside one individual, the speaker, parts 5, 6, and 7 inside another, the hearer,[1] and part 4 in the outside world. Parts 1 and 2 have been lumped together because the connection between them is outside the field of linguistics, and because we know little or nothing about it anyhow. The same is true of parts 6 and 7; the little double-headed arrows in the diagram are a confession of ignorance, not a claim of knowledge. What we are concerned with here is parts 3, 4, and 5, which make up the speech act as a physical event that can be subjected to the kind of study we defined in our last chapter as scientific.

[1] The speaker, unless he is deaf, is also a hearer, and the fact that he listens to his own speech is of some importance. But for simplicity's sake this "feedback" has been omitted from the diagram.

The fact that there are three parts to this physical act of speech suggests that there might be three ways of attacking the problem of describing it. We could concentrate on the production of speech sounds by the various organs of the vocal tract (3). Or we could study the vibrations of the delicate hearing mechanism of the ear (5). Finally, we could study the sound waves in the air (4). As might be suspected, all three approaches have been investigated, so that there are three branches of phonetics: **articulatory phonetics,** which deals with speech *production,* **auditory phonetics,** which deals with speech *reception,* and **acoustic phonetics,** which deals with speech *transmission.*

Throughout this book we shall deal almost exclusively with articulatory phonetics. There are three reasons for this apparently arbitrary limitation:

1. Articulatory phonetics is the oldest and most completely developed of the three branches. Acoustic phonetics has made tremendous advances since World War II, but it is still in the developmental stages. Auditory phonetics is much less advanced.

2. Investigation in articulatory phonetics can be carried on with a minimum of elaborate equipment. Refined observations, it is true, make use of X-ray photographs and motion pictures, palatograms, and other paraphernalia of the laboratory. But many of the most important phenomena can be observed with a mirror and flashlight or by kinesthetic sense, or "feel." Acoustic phonetics, on the other hand, requires elaborate electronic equipment and knowledge of higher mathematics.

3. Most of the phonetic literature that a practicing teacher of English, or any other language, needs to read is expressed in articulatory terms. Likewise, most methods of visual recording (phonetic alphabets), including the one used in this book, are based on articulatory classifications.

In addition to limiting our discussion to articulatory phonetics, we shall further restrict ourselves to those aspects which are of importance for the study of English. No language uses more than a small part of the extensive repertory of speech-sounds. It is the business of the general phonetician and of the linguist working with unfamiliar languages to know the whole gamut; but for our purposes here, it is enough to study the sounds actually used in the various dialects of American English. Those interested in going farther may do so by reading some of the books on phonetics in the General Bibliography, or, better yet, by taking a course under an experienced phonetician.

SEGMENTING THE STREAM OF SPEECH

We said (p. 54) that speech is "on the whole a *continuous* noise." This fact must be emphasized. As literate persons, we are so accustomed to seeing the divisions of written language into words and letters that we think we hear them when we listen to someone talking. Printed words and letters are separate and distinct entities; each one ends before the next one begins. They are marshalled on the page like soldiers on dress parade, in orderly rows, each individual alongside his neighbor but not touching him.

Literate people, accustomed to think in terms of the written language, are not the only ones to think of the continuum of speech as broken up into neat units. Because of matters which we shall discuss in the next chapter, when we listen to someone speaking a language we know well, we pick out certain **distinctive features** as they go by in the flowing stream of speech. These we use to divide up what we hear into separate units; the rest we disregard. This is not done consciously, of course. It is simply a habit acquired in the process of learning to speak a language. An exceedingly valuable habit, to be sure; it is what makes possible the rapidity of speech. But it makes it all the harder for us to be objective observers of our own language.

A simple experiment will demonstrate more clearly than any amount of explanation that speech is really a continuous flow, and that its division into clearly distinct words and sounds is an illusion. Listen to someone speaking normally in a language totally unknown to you, and try to detect the divisions between words and between separate sounds. You will find that it is impossible, although to the native speaker of that language it will seem obvious. His habits are different from yours.

Nevertheless, if we are to make a beginning in the study of the stream of speech, we must divide it up in some way into units that can be described and classified. In so doing we may misrepresent the facts a bit, but this will do no harm provided we always remember how we obtained our units in the first place. Science must frequently resort to rather arbitrary methods of this sort. In order to find out how living bodies work, we dissect dead bodies. The anatomist separates and names the various bones, nerves, and muscles; but he does not forget that in the living body they are all working together in an intricate relationship of cooperative and overlapping interaction. In the same way the phonetician dissects the stream of speech into separate sounds or **phones,** which he names and describes. But he does not forget that in the living speech they flow into and overlap each other in a modulated stream. Speech is like a river flowing along a variegated channel, not like a file of soldiers marching across a plain.

It is not necessary here to go into the details of the careful process by which the phonetician cuts up or **segments** the speech-stream. We can begin instead from our own rather crude and unscientific awareness of what we call speech sounds. As has been pointed out, in literate people this awareness is all tangled up with their awareness of letters as shapes. This situation is essential to the practice of reading, however regrettable it may be from the point of view of phonetics. It makes it necessary for us to insist with all the emphasis at our command that the student must make every possible effort from this point on to free his mind of notions about language and ways of discussing it that confuse the living speech with the written record. This is not easy to do. It is particularly hard for people who read a great deal. But it is not impossible; if it were, there would be no phoneticians except illiterate ones. The biggest step toward clarifying our thinking on this point is to be exceedingly careful about our expression. And the beginning of accurate expression is always to speak of a unit of speech—a set of three-dimensional wrinkles in the atmosphere—as a *sound* or *phone*, and always to speak of a unit of writing as a *letter* or *character*. One cannot see a sound; one cannot hear a letter.

Let us pick out of the stream of speech a few samples to listen to, such as the words we write *bib*, *bin*, and *nib*. Listening to them repeated several times over, we become aware of certain similarities. The first two, *bib* and *bin*, are the same over most of their duration. If we start to say one of them and stop just before the end, a hearer cannot tell which one we were in the act of saying. (If there is a potential hearer present as you read this, try it out on him.) In the same way, *bib* and *nib* are the same over most of their length. Further observation would reveal several more facts, such as that all three have something in common in the middle, that the first and last parts of *bib* are alike in certain ways, and that *nib* has the first and last parts of *bin* reversed. We would ultimately come to the conclusion that each of these units could be cut up into three smaller units, or **segments,** and that the nine segments or phones resulting could be collected into three groups or **phone-types**: (1) the one that appears in the middle of all three; (2) the one that appears at the beginning of *bib* and *bin* and at the end of *bib* and *nib*; (3) the one that appears at the beginning of *nib* and at the end of *bin*. Further observation would show us that each of these three not only sounds different to the ear but is produced by different maneuvers of the vocal tract. In other words, there are both *auditory* and *articulatory* differences between them. And if we had one of the various machines that make visual patterns corresponding to the pressure patterns in the air, we would see that there are *acoustic* differences as well.

The preceding paragraph may seem like going to a great deal of trouble to discover the obvious. But we must begin somewhere, and there are advantages to beginning with the obvious. If this procedure of examination and comparison were to be carried out with a large number of short samples of English speech, we would very soon have a rather large collection of phone-types similar to the three in *bib*, *bin*, and *nib*. What is more, the more closely we listened to our samples, the more different kinds of phones we would discover. Nor would everything we found be obvious to all speakers of English. We would find, for instance, that the last sound in *pill* is different from the first sound in *lip*, and that the second sound in *spill* is different from both the first sound in *pill* and the last sound in *lip*. Many of the things we discovered would depend on the part of the country we come from. Those from Tidewater Virginia, for instance, would notice that the central sound of *loud* is different from the central sound of *louse*. People from western Pennsylvania and eastern Ohio would observe that the central sounds in *cot* and *caught* are the same, while people from Philadelphia would find that the central sound of *can* differs according to whether it means "is able to" or "put in a can."

Whatever we discovered, it would soon be obvious that we need a system for describing and recording these observations that is accurate without being cumbersome. We could not get very far if we had to write "the sound in the middle of *can* when it means 'is able to'" every time we wanted to refer to this particular sound. We should soon find that building any kind of system of descriptions and generalizations out of such statements is about as difficult as doing differential calculus with Roman numerals. Fortunately, articulatory phonetics provides two consistent and relatively uncomplicated systems, one for describing and the other for recording phonetic observations. The former requires some knowledge of the speech organs and how they work; the latter requires that we learn a **phonetic alphabet** in which a separate character is provided for every sound-type. Most of the rest of this chapter will be concerned with the details of these two systems.

THE ORGANS OF SPEECH

Early in Chapter 1 we noted that none of the organs which are used in speech was originally evolved for that purpose. Instead, they all have something else to do, mostly concerning breathing and eating. Yet the rapidity and complexity of speech is evidence of how thoroughly these organs have become adapted to their secondary functions. In the course of evolution, many of them have developed properties and mechanisms going far beyond those needed for their primary functions. In this respect the **larynx**, or voice-box, is undoubtedly the most remarkable. From a relatively simple open-and-shut valve, it has developed an elaborate set of delicate muscles and cartilages, balanced against one another in complicated ways that make it potentially the most versatile musical instrument known.

The diagram on page 63 displays most of the organs of speech. We shall now take them up in order, and describe briefly the part each one plays in speaking. As he reads what follows, the student should locate as many of them as he can in two ways: by actual observation with a small mirror and pocket flashlight; and by kinesthetic sense, by moving them and getting the "feel" of where they are in relation to one another.

We can begin by dividing the speech organs into three groups, depending on the part they play. Since the whole business of speaking depends on some kind of air movement, we can call the process of getting the air moving **initiation.** Secondly, during parts at least of the stream of speech, voice is used; the production of voice is **phonation.** Finally, most of the differences between sounds are produced by changes in the shape and size of various resonance cavities or passages for the air stream; changes of this sort are called **articulation.**

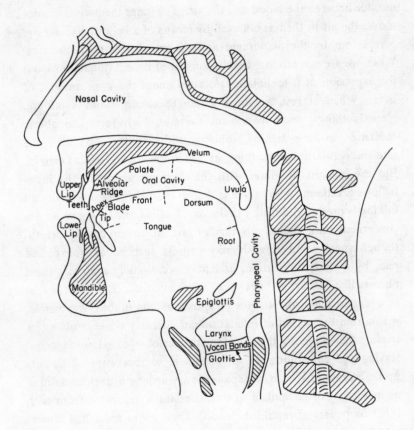

Cross Section of Head, Showing Principal Speech Organs.

INITIATION. The principal initiator of the air stream that is modulated into speech does not show on the diagram; it is, of course, the **lungs.** The lungs are air sacs, divided into many small chambers, whose purpose is to permit an interchange of oxygen and carbon dioxide between the blood and the air. The lungs themselves cannot move; the air in them is changed by means of a bellows-like action, carried out by the diaphragm and the muscles between the ribs. When we are not talking, the drawing in of breath (inhalation) and the expulsion of it (exhalation) occupy about the same amount of time. When at rest, we breathe ten to twenty times a minute. Various things, such as violent exercise, high fever, coughing, sneezing, yawning, sighing, sobbing, and laughing, may alter the rate and regularity of breathing, as well as the volume of air taken in. But the greatest interferer with the rhythmic action of the lung-bellows is talking. The reason is that in most languages virtually all talking is produced during exhalation. English, the language we are concerned with, makes no regular use of the in-drawn breath, though speakers of English may express surprise or unexpected pain by a sharp inhalation, and may occasionally even say short phrases like "O.K." or "Let's see" while inhaling. The result is that in order to make the stream of speech as continuous as possible, we shorten the period of inhalation considerably while doubling or tripling the volume, and we prolong the period of exhalation by conserving and controlling the air stream in various ways. This cuts up the stream of speech into spans of varying length, each containing as much as can be spoken in one exhalation, separated from each other by pauses of rapid inhalation. These spans are called **breath-groups.**

The part played by breath-control in speech is better known to trained public speakers, actors, and singers than it is to the rest of us. It was vividly brought home to the writer when he conversed with a person in the kind of respirator known as an "iron lung." The respirator, by alternating pressure and vacuum on the whole body, reproduces the regular rhythm of normal breathing. Since the person in the respirator has no control over the rate of exhalation, the breath-groups of his speech may end in the middle of a phrase or even a word, and he must wait for the next exhalation before he can continue.

English, unlike some other languages, uses only the lungs to initiate speech-sounds.

PHONATION. The loudest of the sounds of speech are produced by **voice,** which is in turn produced by various kinds of complicated vibrations taking place in the larynx. The larynx is situated at the top of the trachea, or windpipe. It is composed of a complex system of muscles, membranes, and cartilages, enclosed in a heavy outer sheath, the thyroid cartilage, or "Adam's apple." The whole of the larynx can be moved a considerable distance upward and downward from its normal position. Its various parts are capable of a wide variety of adjustments and movements, far too complicated to go into here. What concerns us primarily is the role of the vocal bands in producing voice.

The **vocal bands** are a pair of bundles of muscle and cartilage, about three-fifths of an inch long, attached to the walls of the larynx. They can be adjusted to various positions, from wide open to tight shut, partly by means of their own muscles and partly by means of muscles and cartilages to which they are attached. They may also be subjected to various degrees of tension, both by the contraction of their own muscles and by the stretching of their length resulting from movements of the larynx. The combination of various degrees of tension, various degrees of opening, and various modifications of shape of the vocal bands makes possible many different types and pitches of voice, which are of interest to specialists in speech and singing. We shall concern ourselves with only three of the many possibilities.

1. *Completely open position.* During normal breathing and during many of the sounds of speech, the vocal bands are relaxed, making

larynx

the opening between them, called the **glottis,** wide enough to permit the unobstructed passage of air. Speech sounds produced with open glottis are said to be **voiceless.** An example is the "Shh!" we use to request silence.

2. *Completely closed position.* The vocal bands may be pressed together so tightly as to resist considerable air pressure from the lungs. As has been previously mentioned, this is their primary function. It permits the muscles of the ribs, diaphragm, and abdomen to brace themselves against the compressed air of the lungs. This bracing is essential, not only in the lifting of heavy objects, but in such natural functions as defecation and childbirth. The closed position of the glottis occurs frequently in speech, and is of great importance in some languages. It is called the **glottal stop.** A clear glottal stop may be heard between the two parts of the negative expression often written "hnh-hnh." In the phonetic alphabet we shall use, it is symbolized by [ʔ].

3. *Position for voice.* In describing the closed position of the vocal bands, we were really discussing articulation rather than phonation. True **voice** occurs when the vocal bands are brought so close together that the air passing through the glottis causes them to vibrate, producing a sound with the regular vibratory character we recognize as **tone.** Speech-sounds produced while the vocal bands are vibrating are said to be **voiced.** You can feel the vibration of the vocal bands in producing voice if you put your fingers on your Adam's apple while saying "Ah."

The **glottal tone** produced by the vocal bands varies considerably in pitch and quality, even in the speech of one person. But for our purposes we can consider it as relatively constant, varying in pitch less than an octave. It has one property that is of considerable importance. Unlike the tone produced by a musical instrument, the glottal tone is made up of a series of harmonics of almost equal intensity from the fundamental pitch of 100–300 cycles per second up to 2200 or more cycles. This means that the various resonance cavities of the mouth and nose, which act as filters, may allow different sets of vibrations to pass while suppressing others, all without appreciably affecting the loudness or pitch of the sound. This sounds rather technical. What it amounts to is that the central sound of *cat* is recognizably different from the central sound of *kit*, no matter who says them or what pitch or "tone of voice" he uses.

Without this remarkable property of the glottal tone, speech as we know it would be impossible. It is due to a complicated kind of vibration of the vocal bands duplicated by no man-made musical instrument. Only with the development of electronics has man been able to imitate the glottal tone and thus produce artificial speech.

In addition to normal voice, various other kinds of phonation can be produced by special adjustments of the vocal bands and other parts of the larynx. Among these may be mentioned various kinds of whispering, rasp, murmur, falsetto, and the so-called "whistle voice" of coloratura sopranos. We have no room to say anything more about these in this brief and elementary discussion.

ARTICULATION. We have already seen that the vocal bands themselves can act as articulators when they close completely to make the glottal stop. In addition, virtually all parts of the throat and lower head above the glottis which are accessible to the stream of air from the lungs can take part in articulation. We may conveniently divide them into three groups: resonating cavities, articulators, and points of articulation.

Resonating Cavities. It is evident from the diagram on page 63 that air passing through the glottis and out of the larynx goes past the epiglottis into the **pharynx** or **pharyngeal cavity.** This is a space formed by the root of the tongue and the walls of the throat. Though it obviously affects the quality of the sound by its shape, no further use of it is made in English. Some languages, notably Arabic, have sounds articulated in the pharynx.

When the organs are in the position represented in the diagram, air moving outward through the pharynx has a choice of routes.

It may pass above the **velum,** or "soft palate," through the **nasal cavity,** and out the nostrils. Or it may pass below the velum into the **oral cavity** or mouth, and ultimately out through the lips. Various adjustments of the velum and root or back of the tongue may alter this situation. On the one hand, the velum may be drawn up and back against the pharyngeal wall, forcing all the air to pass through the oral cavity. On the other hand, the velum may be dropped and the extreme back of the tongue raised until they meet, thereby blocking off the mouth and forcing all the air to pass through the nasal cavity. These two positions should be observed with flashlight and mirror. The first may be produced by saying "Ah" as the doctor requests when he wants to examine your throat; the second by prolonging the final sound of *song.*

These three cavities—pharyngeal, oral, and nasal—are quite complicated in shape, with various side chambers and cavities connecting to them. Furthermore, all of them, but especially the oral cavity, can be altered in shape and size by the action of various articulators. Their function is to act as **filters** and to a lesser degree as **resonators.** The explanation of how these processes operate is a matter of acoustic phonetics and, hence, beyond our scope here. We can, however, describe their results in nontechnical terms. A sound-filter is a chamber or passage which has the effect of allowing some frequencies of vibration to pass through with virtually un-diminished strength, while suppressing others. A resonator is a similar chamber or passage (or other vibrating object) so placed in relation to the source of vibration that it strengthens some frequencies and suppresses others. Most musical instruments depend on some sort of resonator to increase the intensity of their original sound.

Articulators and **Points of Articulation.** These are best considered together, since they work together. The articulators are various movable organs that can modulate the glottal tone or produce secondary noises by their motion in relation to fixed points of articulation. The principal articulators are the **lower lip,** the **tongue,** the **velum** and the **uvula** (the small appendage at the end of the velum). The principal points of articulation are the **upper lip,** the **upper teeth** (and to some extent the lower front teeth), the gum behind the upper teeth, called the **alveolar ridge,** the bony roof of the mouth, or **palate,** and the **velum** again. Before reading any farther, the student should locate all of these, first on the diagram on page 63, and then in his own mouth by means of flashlight and mirror.

It is no accident that in many languages the word for *speech* is derived from the word for *tongue.* The tongue is the most versatile of all the articulators, since it is capable not only of many positions, but also of radical changes in its own shape. It can curve its surface in many different ways, or flatten it out. It can protrude some distance out of the mouth, or be pulled far back in. It can be spread wide or bunched together. Its tip can be held level, tipped down, or curled back almost to the uvula. Many of these motions, as well as combinations of them, are used in producing articulate speech. As may be seen from the diagram, names have been given to various parts of the tongue. Since it is actually all of a piece, with no natural division into parts, the terms used are arbitrary in their application; their sole purpose is to make it easier to describe various articulations. Thus, from the extreme point back about a quarter of an inch above and below is called the **tip,** and the next half inch or so of the upper surface is called the **blade.** Tip and blade together make up the **apex.** The rest of the upper surface all the way back to the epiglottis is divided into three roughly equal parts, the **front,** the **dorsum** or **back,** and the **root.** As the diagram shows, when the tongue is in the position of rest in the bottom of the mouth, with the tip near or against the lower teeth, the apex is opposite the alveolar ridge, the front is opposite the palate, the dorsum is opposite the velum and uvula, and the root is opposite the pharyngeal wall.

One more articulator should be mentioned: the whole **lower jaw** or **mandible.** Its only significant form of motion is up and down, primarily to diminish or increase the volume of the oral cavity. This can also be done in other ways, since it is possible to speak understandably, if not elegantly, with the teeth clenched or with a pencil gripped between them. Yet the up-and-down movement of the jaw is such a characteristic part of speech that it has given rise to slang expressions for talking like "chewing the rag" and "beating the gums."

THREE MAIN TYPES OF SOUNDS

The articulators, combining with the points of articulation in a large number of different positions or rapid motions, with or without voice from the larynx, produce the almost infinite variety of speech sounds. Different languages use different selections of these. Those which are used in English, and hence of concern to us, can be classed in three major groups, according to the degree to which the air stream from the lungs is impeded.

1. If an articulator is brought so firmly against a point of articulation that the air stream is completely interrupted, the resulting sound is a **stop** (sometimes called a **plosive**). It is rather a misnomer to call this effect a sound, since its most characteristic feature is complete or almost complete absence of sound. A special class of stops are the **affricates.** When the momentary closure of a stop is released gradually rather than abruptly, a slight friction noise can be heard; such a stop is an affricated stop, or simply an **affricate.**

2. If an articulator is brought so close to a point of articulation that the air passing between them is made turbulent and produces frictional noise, the resulting sound is called a **fricative** or **spirant.** A special class of fricatives are the s-like sounds made by channeling the blade (and sometimes the tip) of the tongue so as to project a jet of air against some point of articulation. These are sometimes called **sibilants** or **blade spirants.**

3. If an articulator is moved in such a way that it neither stops the air stream nor constricts it in such a way as to produce noise, the

resulting sound is a **sonorant.** Sonorants differ from one another primarily in the shape of the oral cavity, and hence in the particular combinations of harmonics which make them up. Special classes of sonorants which will be defined and described below are **vowels, semivowels, nasals,** and **laterals.**

All three types of sounds—stops, fricatives, and sonorants—may be voiced or voiceless, depending on whether or not the vocal bands vibrate during their production.

It is sometimes useful to have a cover term for all types of sounds except vowels; for this the traditional name **consonant** will serve. The term **continuant** is sometimes used for those sounds which may be produced for the whole duration of an exhalation. This group includes vowels, fricatives, nasals, laterals, and trills; it excludes stops, affricates, semivowels, and **flaps,** a special group which is defined on page 88.

The system of nomenclature we have just reviewed, based upon the positions and movements of the various speech organs, makes it possible to describe the sounds of speech with a fair degree of accuracy, so that they may be referred to unambiguously. The description involves as a minimum four parts: (1) the distinction between voiced and voiceless; (2) the name of the articulator; (3) the name of the point of articulation; (4) the sound type. The names of the articulator and point of articulation are usually hyphenated together. Thus, the central consonant of *locker* may be described as a *voiceless dorso-velar stop.* It will be noticed that nothing is said about the initiator or the direction of the air-stream. That is because, as we have seen (p. 64), all sounds in English are made with exhaled air from the lungs. In describing sounds in other languages, it is sometimes necessary to add to the description a statement concerning the initiator and the direction of the air-stream.

It should be realized that descriptions like "voiceless dorso-velar stop" are only approximations. Many different sounds can be distinguished which fall within such a general description, though they will all be very much alike, particularly to the untrained ear. Increasing refinement of discrimination requires greater precision of statement. In the discussion of individual sounds which follows we shall introduce such refinements as are usually needed by the student and teacher of American English. But we shall leave unexplored many distinctions among sounds which are of great importance in other languages. And since a phonetic alphabet is only a sort of shorthand for phonetic description, the same principle will guide us in presenting the technique of phonetic transcription. The alphabet we shall use, a modification of the 1951 revision of the International Phonetic Alphabet (IPA), will include only those symbols and diacritics which are needed for transcribing the various dialects of American English.[2]

In the earlier descriptions it will be necessary to use some characters which have not yet been identified, in order to cite representative words in complete phonetic transcription. Since the standard spelling is also given, the student should have no trouble with these, but can take them for granted and concentrate his attention on the specific sounds being illustrated. One point which should be noted carefully, however, is the position of the symbols for **strongest, strong, and medium stress**: [ˈˈ], [ˈ], and [ˌ]. These are placed immediately *before* the syllable bearing the stress, not after it, as in most dictionaries. In citing individual words, stress marks will be given only with words consisting of two or more syllables, since the stress can fall in only one place in a one-syllable word which is spoken in isolation.

STOPS

As we have seen, the characteristic feature of stops is a complete stoppage of the outgoing air-stream. Actually the complete articulation of a stop, such as the central sound in *locker*, has three phases: (1) a preliminary closing, during which the articulator is brought

[2] The complete IPA is reproduced on pp. 586–87.

into close contact with the point of articulation; (2) an intermediate **closure,** or period of silence, or, in the case of voiced stops, of subdued voice, during which the close contact is maintained; and (3) a final **release,** during which the articulator is separated from the point of articulation. If a stop comes at the beginning of an utterance, after another stop, or after a sound articulated in the same position (**homorganic** sound), the closing may be absent, since the articulators may already be in position for the stop: examples might be the first sound in "Put it down!" or the last sound in *ant.* Likewise, if a stop comes at the end of a phrase, breath-group, or utterance, it may be **unreleased,** the speech organs simply being retained in the position of closure. Unreleased stops are marked with the diacritic [⌐] following the appropriate character.

When the release is present, it may be of three main types. (1) If the articulator is brought away sharply, without friction and without an audible release of the air compressed behind it, the stop is **unaspirated,** and it is symbolized by the simple phonetic character; thus [p] stands for the *unaspirated voiceless bilabial stop.* (2) If the articulator is brought away sharply, but the compressed air is released in a puff clearly audible before the next sound begins (as at the beginning of *puff*), the stop is **aspirated** and the aspiration is indicated by ['] following the phonetic symbol; thus [pʿ] stands for the *aspirated voiceless bilabial stop.* (3) If the articulator is brought away slowly, so that the compressed air escapes with a fricative sound, the result is an **affricated** stop, or simply an **affricate.** Affricates are usually represented by separate characters. We will discuss the important affricates of English in a separate section, following the discussion of fricatives.

English makes use of seven types of stops: two bilabial, two apico-alveolar, two dorso-velar, and the glottal stop. We shall begin our numbered series of English phone-types with these seven.

1. The *voiceless bilabial stop,* [p]. This is formed by closing the lips tightly. In initial position it is usually aspirated; in final position

it may be aspirated, unaspirated, or unreleased. Thus, *pep* may be variously pronounced [pʰɛp], [pʰɛpˀ], and [pʰɛp̚]. After initial [s] it is usually unaspirated, as in *sped* [spɛd]. Before another stop it may be unreleased, as in *pepped* [pʰɛp̚t]. Nasal and lateral release of this and other stops will be discussed later on, after we have considered the nasal and lateral sounds.

2. The *voiced bilabial stop*, [b], is formed like [p] but with the addition of voice. A stop may be voiced even during the middle period when the air-stream is stopped, because even though the air-stream is completely blocked at the point of articulation, air can continue to pass through the glottis and actuate the vocal bands until the pressure in the oral cavity equals that in the lungs. If the stop is not released by the time this happens, the remainder of it must be voiceless, since the vocal bands cannot vibrate unless there is air passing between them. [b] is unaspirated in all positions in English. It may be unreleased when final or when followed by another stop, as in *web* [wɛb̚] and *abduct* [æb̚ˈdʌk̚tˀ].

3. The *voiceless apico-alveolar stop*, [t]. This is usually formed by bringing the tongue tip against the alveolar ridge, while the sides of the tongue are held firmly against the upper teeth. Like [p] it is usually aspirated initially and may be aspirated, unaspirated, or unreleased when final; thus *tat* may be pronounced [tʰæt], [tʰætˀ] or [tʰæt̚]. After initial [s] it is unaspirated, as in *step* [stɛp]. In various preconsonantal positions it may be unreleased, as in *outdo* [ˌaʊt̚ˈduu]. Certain varieties of [t] and substitutions for it often appearing between vowels will be discussed later on.

4. The *voiced apico-alveolar stop*, [d], is formed like [t] with the addition of voice. Like [b] it is unaspirated and may be unreleased in certain positions. Thus *dead* may be [dɛd] or [dɛd̚]; *bedbug* [ˈbɛd̚ˌbʌg].

5. The *voiceless dorso-velar stop*, [k], is formed by placing the back of the tongue firmly against the velum. The exact point of contact may vary considerably under the influence of neighboring sounds,

but these variations are unimportant in English, and need not concern us here. Like the other voiceless stops, [k] is usually aspirated when initial, unaspirated after initial [s], and in final position may be aspirated, unaspirated, or unreleased. Thus *coke* may be pronounced [kʻoᵤk], [kʻoᵤkʻ], or [kʻoᵤk⁻]. [k] may also be unreleased in various preconsonantal positions, as in *tactic* [ˈtʻækˉtʻɪk].

6. The *voiced dorso-velar stop*, [g], is formed like [k] with the addition of voice. Like [k] its position varies considerably under the influence of neighboring sounds. Like the other voiced stops in English, [g] is always unaspirated and may be unreleased in certain positions. Thus *gag* may be [gæg] or [gæg⁻]; *pigpen* [ˈpʻɪgˉ ˌpʻɛn].

7. The *glottal stop*, [ʔ], has already been described (p. 66). It is quite frequent in American English, but usually goes unnoticed by all except those with phonetic training, because its presence or absence does not distinguish one word from another. It may often appear at the beginning of words which at other times begin with a vowel. This is especially true when such words are given strong or contrastive stress; thus in "I said *ám*, not *ís*!" the two italicized words would be [ˈllʔæm] and [ˈllʔɪz]. The glottal stop may also appear between a stressed vowel and a final unreleased stop, as in *cat* when pronounced [kʻæʔt⁻]. In this last case it may come at the same time as the final stop, in which case the two may be joined by a **link** to show that thay are simultaneous, as in [kʻæ͡ʔt⁻]. In some dialects the glottal stop is substituted for [t] before a syllabic lateral or nasal, as in *bottle* and *button* when pronounced [ˈbɑʔɬ] and [ˈbʌʔn̩].

It is easy to miss the glottal stop when it comes in initial or final position. The student should practice pronouncing it in various positions; this will make it easier for him to hear it in the speech of others.

At least one dialect of English (Gullah, which is discussed in Chapter 9) has a voiced and voiceless pair of *fronto-palatal stops*, formed by closing the front of the tongue against the palate. These will not be included in the series of numbered sounds here, since they are so unusual in English. The IPA characters are [c] for the voiceless variety and [ɟ] for the voiced.

FRICATIVES

The characteristic quality of the fricatives is noise produced by the stream of breath passing through the constricted opening between an articulator and a point of articulation. When fricatives are voiced, two kinds of sound are present at the same time: the voice, or glottal tone, and the local friction-noise. A large variety of fricatives can be made, including many not heard in present-day standard American English. As we did with the stops, we shall take up first the ones that are important in the principal dialects of American English; then we will mention a few others that turn up in a few dialects or were important at some time in the past. The main group includes ten sound-types: two labio-dental and two apico-dental fricatives, two apico-alveolar and two fronto-palatal sibilants or blade spirants, and two glottal fricatives.

8. The *voiceless labio-dental fricative*, [f], is produced by bringing the lower lip close to or against the edge of the upper teeth, so that the breath passing through may be heard. There are no significant varieties of [f]. It is heard in all positions in the word, as in *fat* [fæt], *sofa* ['soᵾfə], *lift* [lɪft], *off* [ɔf].

9. The *voiced labio-dental fricative*, [v], is made like [f] with the addition of voice. It is the same in all positions, as in *vat* [væt], *oven* ['ʌvən], and *have* [hæv].

10. The *voiceless apico-dental fricative*, [θ], is made by air friction between the tip of the tongue and the upper front teeth. It is common initially, as in *thin* [θɪn], and finally, as in *wrath* [ræθ]; rather rare medially, as in *ether* ['iθɚ] and *deathly* ['dɛθli]. One variety, common in New York City, uses the blade rather than the tip, the tip being placed against the lower front teeth. To many this sounds more like [t], and it is often so written in attempts at indicating "Brooklyn" dialect.

11. The *voiced apico-dental fricative*, [ð], is made in the same way as [θ] with the addition of voice. It appears in all positions, as in *then* [ðɛn], *either* [ˈiðɚ], and *bathe* [beɪ̯ð]. Students who have difficulty distinguishing between [ð] and [θ] should practice alternately pronouncing *this* and *thin* with finger and thumb on the larynx or with both hands over the ears.

12. The *voiceless apico-alveolar sibilant*, [s], is usually made by producing a rather deep groove in the center of the apex of the tongue, forming a narrow channel through which a jet of air is directed at the lower edge of the upper front teeth. The tip may be variously placed; some speakers even put it against the lower front teeth. This pulls the whole tongue forward, involving the blade and front, rather than the tip and blade, in making the air channel. Whatever version of [s] a speaker of English may use, he will probably use the same one in all positions in the word. [s] is a very common sound in English, occurring in all parts of words, as in *sit* [sɪt], *assist* [əˈsɪst], *hiss* [hɪs], and *hats* [hæts].

13. The *voiced apico-alveolar sibilant*, [z], is formed like [s] with the addition of voice. It has variations corresponding to those of [s], but it is likely to remain constant in the dialect of a given speaker. Like other voiced sounds, however, it may be partly unvoiced, a point which will be taken up below. It is not very common in initial position, but occurs frequently between vowels and finally. The student should not be misled by spelling, since [z] is often spelled with an *s*. Some examples of its occurrence are *zoo* [ˈzʊu̯], *lazy* [ˈleɪ̯zi], *raisin* [ˈreɪ̯zɪn], *daze* [dɛɪ̯z], *days* [dɛɪ̯z].

14. The *voiceless fronto-palatal sibilant*, [š], is formed in somewhat the same manner as [s], but instead of the apex, the blade and front of the tongue are used to direct a somewhat wider stream of air against the alveolar ridge, rather than the teeth. Its exact articulation may vary considerably from speaker to speaker. Within a single person's speech it does not have positional variants. It is widely distributed in all word positions. Some examples of its occurrence

are *shed* [šɛd], *ocean* [ˈoʊ̯šən], *issue* [ˈɪšʊ̯], *machine* [məˈšin], *fiction* [ˈfɪkšən], *hash* [hæš]. The standard IPA character is [ʃ], which is widely used and should be learned, though [š], which seems to be finding increasing favor with American linguists, will be used in this book.

15. The *voiced fronto-palatal sibilant*, [ž], is made like [š] with the addition of voice, and has a similar range of variant articulations. It is of limited distribution, appearing in final position only in a small group of words recently borrowed from French, and initially being totally missing except in the quasi-French pronunciation of some French loan-words and proper names. Some speakers use [ž] only in medial position, where it is of fairly frequent occurrence. Thus it is standard in *pleasure* [ˈpˤlɛžɚ], usual in *rouge* [rʊ̯už], often heard in *prestige* [ɪpˤrɛsˈtiž] and *garage* [gəˈraž], occasional in *Jean* [žã] and *Jacques* [žak]. The standard IPA character is [ʒ], which should be learned, though this book will use [ž] throughout.

16. The *voiceless glottal fricative*, [h], is formed with the oral cavity totally unobstructed, and with a very slight fricative sound produced either by the relaxed vocal bands or the walls of the pharynx. Very often there is no fricative sound at all, in which case this sound is no longer a fricative but a voiceless vowel (see p. 105). [h] appears only at the beginning of syllables, usually stressed syllables. In intervocalic position it varies with voiced [ɦ], the next sound to be discussed. Some examples of its occurrence are *hymn* [hɪm], *uphold* [ʌpˈhoʊ̯ld], emphatic pronunciation of *ahead* [əˈhɛd]. In the personal pronouns *he*, *him*, etc., [h] is usually present only when the pronoun is stressed; compare *téll him* [ˈtˤ ɛlɪm] and *tell hím* [ɪtɛɫ ˈˈhɪm].

17. The *voiced glottal fricative*, [ɦ], is produced like [h] with the addition of the subdued kind of voice called **murmur.** Full voice turns it into a vowel. It is heard only between voiced sounds in relatively unemphatic context, as in *ahead* [əˈɦɛd], or in *roadhog*

[ˈroᶷd‾ɦɑg] as compared with more emphatic [ˈroᶷdₗhɑg], in which the [d] is released and voiceless [h] is heard.

In addition to these ten fricatives of standard English, three more should be mentioned here, since they occur in dialectal or variant pronunciations. The *voiceless bilabial fricative*, [ɸ], formed by air friction between the lips, may occur in bilabial environment, as in *camphor* [ˈkˤæmɸɚ], *Humphrey* [ˈhʌmɸri]. Similarly, the *voiced bilabial fricative*, [β], may occur in words like *triumvirate* [tˤṛaɪ̯-ˈʌmβərɪt]. It is also common in the English of Pennsylvania Dutch speakers. These two fricatives regularly take the places of [f] and [v] in Gullah. A third sound, the *voiceless dorso-velar fricative*, [x], produced by air rushing through a narrow constriction between the back of the tongue and the velum, is of historical importance in English, though it does not occur in any present-day American dialect known to the author.[3] It is common in Scottish English and a few dialects of the north of England. It is always either final or preconsonantal, and its point of articulation may vary with the surrounding sounds, as in Scottish *loch* [lɔx] and *bright* [brɪx̣t].

AFFRICATES

As defined above, an affricate is a stop with a release sufficiently slow to produce a momentary fricative effect before the next sound begins. For this reason, some phoneticians treat affricates as merely stop + fricative in close conjunction. There seems to be a difference, however, principally in length. The closure, or period of silence between closing and release, is much shorter in an affricate than in the corresponding stop, and the period of friction is shorter than the corresponding fricative, though longer than the usual release of a stop. Furthermore, the syllable break cannot fall between the closure and the affrication. All these tend to produce an impression that the affricate is a single sound, rather than a combination of two.

[3] I am informed that it is commonly used as the first sound of words like *here* and *huge* in the dialect of Atlanta, Georgia.

The difference is exemplified in the contrast between *hatchet* [ˈhæčɪt] and *hat-shop* [ˈhætˌšɒp].

Affricates are possible in every articulatory position where stops occur, and virtually all the possibilities can be heard in English speech. Only two, however, are important enough in English to warrant distinct phonetic symbols and inclusion in our numbered list of phone-types. They are the voiced and voiceless apico-alveolar affricates.

18. The *voiceless apico-alveolar affricate*, [č], is formed by bringing the apex of the tongue to the alveolar ridge somewhat back of the usual position for [t] and immediately bringing it away somewhat more slowly than in the release of [t], so that a distinct but brief fricative sound is heard. The release may also be somewhat aspirated, especially in initial position. [č] may occur in all principal positions, as in *church* [čɚč], *pitcher* [ˈpˤɪčɚ], *picture* [ˈpˤɪkčɚ], *benches* [ˈbɛnčɪz], *patched* [ˈpˤæčt], *nature* [ˈnɛɪčɚ].

19. The *voiced apico-alveolar affricate*, [j], is made like [č] with the addition of voice. It is unaspirated in all positions. When it is initial, the closure may be voiceless; when final, the release may be voiceless. Examples of its occurrence are *judge* [jʌj], *badges* [ˈbæˤjɪz], *pledged* [ˈpˤl̩ɛjd], *range* [rɛɪnj]; it is heard commonly in *garage* [gəˈrɑj] or [gəˈræj].

As we said above, many other affricates occur as nondistinctive variants of stops or stop + fricative combinations. Rather than learn the elaborate set of IPA symbols for these, the student who wishes to record them can use the appropriate stop and fricative characters joined together with a link. Thus slowly released bilabial stops will produce the affricates [p͡ɸ] and [b͡β]. Voiced and voiceless apico-dental affricates are heard in many dialects, notably in New York City, in place of [θ] and [ð]; they may be written [t͡θ] and [d͡ð]. The combination [t⌐] + [s] is often heard as the affricate [t͡s], especially when final, as in *rats* [ræt͡s]. One may even occasionally hear the dorso-velar affricate [k͡x] in place of initial [kˤ].

The voiced versions of these last two are more rare; if they are heard, they should be written [d͡ʒ] and [ɟ͡ɣ] ([ɣ] is the IPA symbol for the voiced dorso-velar spirant).

NASALS

In the production of nasals the oral cavity is completely stopped at one of the points of articulation, but since the velum is slightly lowered, there is free passage for air and sound through the nasal cavity and out the nostrils. The closure of the oral cavity may take place at any of the positions where stops occur. The varying shapes and volumes of the part of the oral cavity which is joined to the nasal cavity account for the different sounds of the several nasals. Congestion of the nasal cavity alters the resonance of nasal sounds, and when the nose is completely blocked the nasals cannot be produced at all. The attempt to make them produces instead the homorganic stops.

Virtually all types of English make use of three distinct nasals: the bilabial, the apico-alveolar, and the dorso-velar. All of them are customarily voiced but have voiceless variants; all of them may be **syllabic,** that is, constitute the center or **nucleus** of a syllable. A syllabic consonant is indicated by the mark [ˌ] directly below the appropriate character.

20. The *voiced bilabial nasal*, [m], is formed by closing the lips tightly while the velum is lowered and the vocal bands are producing voice. It has no variants and may occur in all word positions, as in *met* [mɛt], *tame* [tˤeɪm], *comet* [ˈkˤɑmɪt], *dimmed* [dɪmd]. It may be syllabic in certain pronunciations of *Clapham* [ˈkl̥æp⁻m̩], *grab 'em* [ˈgræb⁻m̩], and the like.

21. The *voiced apico-alveolar nasal*, [n], is made with the tongue in position for [d] but the velum lowered. It is a common sound in all word positions, as in *net* [nɛt], *ten* [tˤɛn], *tenant* [ˈtˤɛnənt], *tend* [tˤɛnd], and so forth. It is frequently syllabic, especially in rapid speech, as in *certain* [ˈsɝt⁻n̩], *mountain* [ˈmaʊ̃nt⁻n̩] or [ˈmaʊ̃nʔn̩],

hot and cold [ˈhɑt⁻n̩ˈˈkˤoʊ̯ld], *isn't* [ˈɪzn̩t], and so on. A voiceless variety, written [n̥], is occasionally heard; it sounds like a mild sniff, as in the affirmative expression [ˈʔn̥n̥n̥] (with rising intonation).

22. The *voiced dorso-velar nasal*, [ŋ], is formed with the back of the tongue against the velum, which is slightly dropped so as to open a passage from the pharynx to the nasal cavity. As in the case of the dorso-velar stops, [k] and [g], the exact point of articulation varies under the influence of neighboring sounds. [ŋ] never appears initially in any variety of English. It is common in final position, and medially between vowels and before [k] and [g]. It may be syllabic as a variant of syllabic [n̩] after [k] or [g] in rapid speech. Some examples of its positions are *singer* [ˈsɪŋɚ], *finger* [ˈfɪŋgɚ], *sinking* [ˈsɪŋkɪŋ], *bacon* [ˈbeɪk⁻ŋ̩] (or [ˈbeɪkn̩] or [ˈbeɪkˤən]), *dog and cat* spoken rapidly [ˈdɔg⁻ŋ̩ˈˈkˤæt]. Note that the pronunciation often called "dropping the *g*" is really a replacement of [ŋ] by [n], as in *singin'* [ˈsɪŋɪn]. A similar replacement is heard in *strength* pronounced [strɛnθ] instead of [strɛŋθ] or [strɛŋkθ].

These are the only nasals that appear regularly in English. Two others of occasional occurrence may be mentioned. The *voiced fronto-palatal nasal*, [ɲ], formed, as the description indicates, by closing the oral cavity at the palate with the front of the tongue, is a regular sound in the Gullah dialect. It also may appear in careful pronunciation of Spanish loan-words like *señor* [sɛˈɲoɾ] and *piñon* [piˈɲon]. Most English speakers use [nj] instead, as in [sɛnˈjɔɚ] and [pˤinˈjoʊ̯n]. The *voiced labio-dental nasal*, [ɱ], sometimes occurs before [f] or [v], as in *comfort* [ˈkˤʌɱfɚt] varying with [ˈkˤʌmfɚt] and [ˈkˤʌmɸɚt]. It may occasionally replace [n] also, as in *convenience* [kˤəɱˈvinjəns].

LATERALS

In the formation of laterals, most of the air passage of the mouth is closed off by placing part of the tongue against the roof of the mouth while leaving an opening on one or both sides. The result is a characteristic continuant sound, which may be voiced or voiceless, may have some frictional component, and varies in quality depending on the part of the mouth where the partial occlusion takes place. Many varieties are found in various languages; for most dialects of American English it is sufficient to recognize four. These are the voiced and voiceless apico-alveolar laterals, the voiced apico-alveolar lateral with dorso-velar coarticulation, and the voiced dorso-velar lateral.

23. The *voiced apico-alveolar lateral*, [l], the so-called "clear *l*," is regular in most American English dialects in initial position and between a voiced consonant and following vowel. As the name implies, it is formed with the tongue tip in approximately the position for [t], [d], or [n], but with an opening between one or both sides of the tongue and the side and back teeth. The front of the tongue is relatively flat and the back somewhat lowered. Examples of its occurrence are *link* [lɪŋk], *loot* [lut], *glance* [glæ˔ns], *black* [blæk]. It often appears after vowels in some Southern dialects.

24. The *voiceless apico-alveolar lateral*, [l̥], is made like the preceding sound without voice. When heard at all in American English, it is usually after voiceless consonants, as in *flip* [fl̥ɪp], *slam* [sl̥æ˔m], *clean* [kʿl̥in], *please* [pʿl̥iz], *atlas* [ˈætˡl̥əs] (the lateral release of the stop will be taken up later on). This sound is never heard initially in English, so that Welsh proper names which begin with [l̥] sound to English speakers as though they begin with a voiceless fricative or even a voiceless aspirated stop. Hence, beside the name *Lloyd* we find *Floyd* and *Cloyd.* Presumably the [fl] and [kʿl] combinations were selected as substitutes rather than the phonetically closer [tʿl] because the initial combination [tʿl] is less common in English.

25. The *voiced apico-alveolar lateral with dorso-velar coarticulation*, [ɫ], is the usual variety of so-called "dark *l*," found after vowels and as a syllabic nucleus in English. The tongue tip is again against the alveolar ridge, but the blade and front slope sharply downward.

The dorsum is raised fairly close to the velum, so that there is a pronounced hollow in the center of the tongue, between the high tip and high back. Examples of usual positions of this sound are *full* [fʊɬ], *gulf* [gʌɬf], *spelling* [ˈspɛɬɪŋ], *bottle* [ˈbɑtˤɬ] (sometimes [ˈbɑˀɬ]), *muscle* [ˈmʌsɬ]. As noted above, some Southern dialects have [l] in some or all of these positions.

26. The *voiced dorso-velar lateral*, [L], is formed like the preceding, except that the tongue tip is against the lower front teeth, so that the apico-alveolar articulation is missing. It is an occasional dialectal or individual variant of [ɬ], replacing it in some or all positions. If the tongue back does not touch the velum to produce the characteristic lateral effect, this sound becomes a high back unround vowel, [ɯ]. Thus *milk* may be variously pronounced as [mɪɬk], [mɪLk], and [mɪɯ̯k].

In the pronunciation of Spanish loan-words, some careful speakers may use a fronto-palatal lateral [ʎ]; but this is usually replaced by [j], as in *olla* [ˈoʎa], or [ˈojə]. *Llama* is almost always [ˈlɑmɑ].

SEMIVOWELS

We classed as sonorants (see pp. 70–71) all those sounds which are produced without any stoppage or friction-producing occlusion above the larynx. They derive their individual qualities from the filtering and resonating functions of the variously shaped chambers formed by differing action of articulators. The nasals and laterals already discussed are sounds of this type, easy to describe because of their characteristic articulations. The remaining two groups, **vowels** and **semivowels,** are distinguished from each other not so much by articulatory differences as by word position and duration. Thus, vowels are found in the center or nucleus of syllables, always the most prominent elements in the syllables to which they belong. Furthermore, although vowels vary greatly in length, a vowel always lasts long enough for its characteristic **color** or distinguishing auditory effect to be perceived.

Semivowels, on the other hand, are found in consonantal positions; that is, they are always in the same syllable with a true vowel, which is the nucleus. They also are of very brief duration; or rather they have no single position of articulation which gives them a certain color. Instead, they consist of a rapid movement of the articulators from a characteristic initial position to the position for the vowel that follows, or the reverse, a rapid movement from the position of the preceding vowel to a characteristic final position. Because of this rapid motion, these sounds are sometimes called **glides,** though we shall use that term in a somewhat broader sense to mean any transitional sound. If the student will examine his own mouth —especially the tongue—with mirror and flashlight while producing the sounds described below, he will clearly perceive the rapid motion of the tongue that takes place in the production of semivowels.

There are five semivowels of sufficiently frequent occurrence in American English to occupy us here. They are the voiced and voiceless labiovelar semivowels, the voiced and voiceless apico-alveolar retroflex semivowels, and the voiced fronto-palatal semivowel. One or two others of occasional occurrence will be noted later.

27. The *voiced labiovelar semivowel,* [w], is formed by rounding the lips slightly while raising the dorsum of the tongue toward the velum and then moving it rapidly into position for the next vowel. The amount of rounding of the lips depends on the following vowel; it is greatest in the neighborhood of rounded vowels like [u], least in the neighborhood of unrounded vowels like [æ]. The height of the dorsum is also conditioned by the nature of the following vowel. It is very high before high vowels, somewhat lower before low vowels. This difference can be clearly seen by observing with flashlight and mirror while alternately pronouncing *wood* and *wad.* [w] occurs initially, between vowels, and between consonant and vowel either at the beginning or in the middle of words, as in *wish* [wɪš], *away* [əˈwɛɪ], *quick* [kʿwɪk], and *acquire* [əˈkʿwaɪ̯ɚ]. Phoneticians differ in

their practices of transcribing the final sound of *cow* or the next to last sound of *loud*. Since these are glides which reverse the formation of [w] in [wɑd], these are sometimes written [w]. However, the practice of writing these as nonsyllabic vowels, [u̯] or [ʊ̯], is more common and will be used in this book.

28. The *voiceless labiovelar semivowel*, [w̥], is formed like [w], but without voice. It is sometimes accompanied by considerable aspiration; if so, it may be written [w̥] or [hw͡]. The IPA symbol is [ʍ], but since in handwritten script this may be confused with [m], it is better to use the [w] symbol with the diacritic for voicelessness. This sound may be heard initially in those dialects in which a distinction is made between *witch* [wɪč] and *which* [w̥ɪč]. It may also sometimes be heard medially in *somewhat* [ˈsʌmˌw̥ɑt], *anywhere* [ˈɛniˌw̥ɛɚ], and similar words, and after voiceless stops, as in *twist* [tˤw̥ɪst], *quick* [kˤw̥ɪk].

29. The *voiced apico-alveolar retroflex semivowel*, [r], the characteristic "American *r*," is formed in various ways in different dialects and by different individual speakers. The following description applies to the variety common in the author's own eastern Midland speech; something quite similar is general throughout the Midland area, the upper Middle West and Far West. The sides of the tongue are against the back teeth, as for [n]; the front is lowered considerably; the blade and tip are turned upward and withdrawn a bit toward the back of the mouth (hence the term *retroflex*, or "bent back"); the tip points to the extreme back of the alveolar ridge where it joins the palate, considerably back of the position of contact for the alveolar consonants [t], [d], and [n]. The separation between the tongue tip and the alveolar ridge is about one-eighth to one-quarter inch. From this position the apex flicks rapidly forward and down into the position for the following vowel.

This sound appears in initial and intervocalic positions, and between an initial voiced consonant and following vowel, as in *red* [rɛd], *arrow* [ˈæˌroʊ̯], *dread* [drɛd]. In some dialects it may occasionally appear between a word normally ending with a vowel and another word beginning with a vowel, as in *china and glass* [ˈčˈaɪnər-ənd⁻ˈˈglæs]. This is the so-called "linking *r*." The problem of final or preconsonantal position, as in the Midland pronunciation of *bare* and *bared*, is similar to that of [w], and will be handled in the same way; that is, this sound will be represented as the nonsyllabic retroflex vowel [ɚ], as in [bɛɚ], [bɛɚd]. It should be noted that the IPA symbol [r] denotes an alveolar trill, the symbol for the retroflex semivowel being [ɹ]. But since no trill occurs in American English, and since it is easier to write *r* right-side-up than upside-down, we shall use [r] for the retroflex. The trill may be indicated by placing two dots over the character thus [r̈].

30. The *voiceless apico-alveolar retroflex semivowel*, [r̥], is formed like [r] without voice. It may sometimes be heard between a voiceless stop and a vowel, particularly a high front vowel, as in *prim* [pˈr̥ɪm] and *creep* [kˈr̥iip]. In most cases probably only the first part is voiceless. If the voice begins at any time during the retroflex sound, it is best to write it [r].

31. The *voiced fronto-palatal semivowel*, [j], is formed by bringing the front of the tongue close to the palate and back part of the alveolar ridge, with the tip either pointing toward the upper teeth or held against the lower front teeth. The tongue is then moved rapidly down into position for the following vowel. The degree of separation between tongue and palate is influenced by the next vowel; the higher the vowel, the closer and tenser the position of the tongue at the beginning of [j]. All versions of this semivowel may, however, be represented by the same symbol, as in *yield* [jiɫd], *yawl* [jɔɫ], *pure* [pˈjʊɚ], *lawyer* [ˈlɔjɚ], *inure* [ɪnˈjʊɚ]. Consistent with our treatment of the other semivowels, when something resembling this sound occurs after vowels it will be treated as a nonsyllabic vowel [i̯] or [ɪ̯], as in *say* [sɛi̯], *saying* [ˈsɛi̯ɪŋ]. It should be observed that medially the position of the syllable-break will determine the character of the transcription; compare [ˈsɛi̯-ɪŋ] and [ˈsɛ-ˌjɪŋ].

Some American phoneticians prefer to use [y] instead of [j] to transcribe the fronto-palatal semivowel. But since most phonetic transcriptions the student is likely to encounter use [j], and since [y] is the IPA symbol for a high front rounded vowel, common in French and German and not unknown in English, we shall use [j]. The student is cautioned to distinguish it carefully from the voiced apico-alveolar affricate [j].

Two more semivowels of occasional occurrence—both of them variants of [r] or substitutes for it—may be mentioned here. After [t], particularly at the beginning of words, many speakers use a slightly retroflex voiceless alveolar sound, often with considerable fricative quality. If it is desired to distinguish this from [r], the symbol [ɹ̥] may be used. If it is felt to be so closely allied to the stop as to form an affricate, the two may be bound with a link. Thus, *trick* may be [t̄ɹ̥ɪk], [t͡ɹ̥ɪk], or even [čɹ̥ɪk].

In place of the retroflex [r], many speakers substitute a dorso-velar semivowel with pronounced action of the lips. The back of the tongue is brought close to the velum, the apex is tipped slightly upward, and the lips, especially the lower one, are somewhat pro-truded. The articulation of this sound is very similar to that of [w], the principal difference being the slight retroflexion of the apex of the tongue. It is sometimes represented by *w* in pseudophonetic spelling, as in *wabbit* for *rabbit*. This substitution is an individual rather than a dialectal trait, but it is more common in some regions (New York City, for instance) than in others. If it is desired to distinguish it from [r], the symbol [ɰ̈] may be used, indicating a *voiced frictionless labiovelar semivowel*.

FLAPS AND TRILLS

A **flap** is a sound made by touching some part of the tongue very briefly to some point of articulation and bringing it away sharply before the characteristic quality of a stop or affricate can be heard; that is, before any pressure can build up behind the point of closure. In a **trill** an articulator (usually the tongue tip or uvula) is set momentarily into vibration. The vibration is well below the rate at which it would be heard as a continuous low-pitched sound (16–18 cycles per second), so that it is heard as a rapid-fire series of sounds, about six to ten per second. Both these types of sound, which are very common in many languages, are rare in American English. In fact, the author has never heard a true trill as a normal feature of any dialect of American English. In the speech of foreigners who have learned English, in the careful pronunciation of loan-words, and in some dialects of British English, the apical trill [r̈] and the uvular trill [ʀ̈] may be heard.

32. One **flap** is of common occurrence in many dialects of American English as a substitute for [t] between vowels and in some other medial positions. In all cases it is apico-alveolar and at least partially voiced, though the exact point at which the tongue tip touches the alveolar ridge, the duration of the contact, and the amount of voice used all vary from region to region and from speaker to speaker. The problem for the phonetician is whether to represent the sound as a true flap [ṙ], as in British English *very* [ˈvɛṙɪ]; as a somewhat more lax (lenis) variety of [t], which can be written [t̤]; as a slightly voiced [t], which can be written [t̬], or as a true [d]. In the author's own east Midland speech, it is best treated as [ṙ], since the point of brief contact of the tongue tip is behind that for [d], and the front of the tongue is lowered considerably more than for [t] and [d], producing some retroflex quality. Accordingly, words like *latter* and *wanted*, when pronounced with this flap, will be represented in this book as [ˈlæṙɚ] and [ˈwɔ̃ṙɪd]. Others may prefer to write [ˈlæt̤ɚ] or [ˈlæt̬ɚ]. There are dialects in which a true [d] appears in this position, though most Americans distinguish between *latter* and *ladder*. A good test sentence is, "I have a ladder and a pole; the latter is leaning against the house." Pronounce the sentence and then ask the listener what is leaning against the house. If you can persuade him that you are quite sane and not involving him in riddles, the answer will indicate whether or not you distinguish these words.

CONSONANT SUMMARY

In the preceding sections we have identified and described thirty-two consonant sounds of common occurrence in American English, and fourteen more that may appear in the speech of some regions or individuals. A system of phonetic characters to be used in transcribing these sounds has also been presented. These characters could be brought together in an arbitrary series like an alphabet. It is easier to learn and remember them, however, if they are presented in a chart like the one on page 92, which is also printed on the endpapers of this book. Here the symbols are arranged in *rows* according to the *type* of articulation and in *columns* according to the *articulator* and *point of articulation*. In many of the spaces thus marked off, two characters will be found; the one on the left represents the voiceless sound. The fourteen supplementary symbols are enclosed in parentheses.

It may be noted that of the thirty-two main characters used, eighteen are from the regular Roman alphabet, nine more are Roman characters with additional diacritics, and only five are new. Of these five, one (θ) is from the Greek alphabet, one (ð) from the Old English and Old Norse alphabet, and three (ʔ, ɦ, ŋ) are more or less arbitrary innovations. It is because of this extensive use of standard Roman characters that phonetic transcriptions are always enclosed in square brackets, to avoid any possible confusion with standard spelling. Among the supplementary characters, the number of familiar letters is lower: of the total fourteen, two (c, x) are regular Roman letters, three (n̥, ɨ, ɨ̈) are Roman letters with diacritics, six (ɟ, ɲ, ɱ, ʎ, ɹ, ɣ̆) are modifications or distortions of Roman letters, and three (ɸ, β, γ) are from the Greek alphabet.

These characters should always be written in the same way, since what may seem to the writer an innocent variation may indicate an important difference to the trained phonetician. Use printed forms rather than cursive script. Especially avoid using capitals to distinguish the beginning of sentences and proper names. Each character has only one form, and capitals are always separate characters indicating distinct sounds, as we have seen in the case of [L] and [ʀ].

In oral discussion of *sounds*, the sounds themselves should be used if they are separately pronounceable. In oral discussion of *characters*, at least of those for consonants, names may be used drawn from or analogous to the ordinary names of the alphabet, or in some cases abbreviated descriptions of the sounds signified. The following is an acceptable nomenclature for the forty-six characters here introduced:

1. p [pʿi]
2. b [bi]
3. t [tʿi]
4. d [di]
5. k [kʿɛɪ̯]
6. g [ǰi] or [gɑ]
7. ʔ *glottal stop*
8. f [ɛf]
9. v [vi]
10. θ [ˈθɛɪ̯tə]
11. ð [ɛð]
12. s [ɛs]
13. z [zi] or [zɛd]
14. š [ɛš]
15. ž [ži]
16. h [ɛɪ̯č] or [hɑ]
17. ɦ *voiced* [ɛɪ̯č]
18. č [čɑ]
19. ǰ [ǰɑ]
20. m [ɛm]
21. n [ɛn]
22. ŋ [ɛŋ]
23. l [ɛł] or *clear* [ɛł]
24. l̥ *voiceless* [ɛł]
25. ł *apicovelar* [ɛł] or *dark* [ɛł]
26. L *velar* [ɛł]
27. w [ˈdʌbłˌju]
28. w̥ *voiceless* [ˈdʌbłˌju]
29. r [ɑɚ̯]
30. r̥ *voiceless* [ɑɚ̯]
31. j [ǰɛɪ̯] or [jot]
32. ṙ *alveolar flap*
33. c [si]
34. ɟ *voiced palatal stop*
35. ɸ [fi] or [ɸi]
36. β [ˈbɛɪ̯tə] or [ˈβetɑ]
35. x [ɛks] or [xi]
38. γ [ˈgæmə]
39. n̥ *voiceless* [ɛn]
40. ɲ [ɛɲə]
41. ɱ *labio-dental* [ɛm]
42. ʎ [ˈɛʎə]
43. ɹ̥ *fricative* [ɑɚ̯]
44. ɹ̇ *labiovelar* [ɑɚ̯]
45. r̈ *trilled* [ɑɚ̯]
46. ʀ̈ *uvular trill*

CONSONANT CHART

	Bila-bial	Labio-dental	Apico-dental	Apico-alve-olar	Fron-topa-latal	Dor-sove-lar	Uvu-lar	Glot-tal
Stops	p b			t d	(c ɟ)	k g		ʔ
Fricatives	(ɸ β)	f v	θ ð	(ɹ̥)		(x γ)		h ɦ
Sibilants				s z	š ž			
Affricates				č ǰ				
Flaps and Trills				ṙ (r̈)			(r̈)	
Nasals	m	(ɱ)		(n̥)n	(ɲ)	ŋ		
Laterals				l̥ l ɫ	(ʎ)	L ł		
Semivowels	w̥ w (ɡ̇)			ɹ̥ r	j	w̥ w (ɡ̇)		

Diacritics: Syllabic [ˌ]; Voiceless [̥]; Aspirated [ʰ]; Rounded [̮];
    Fortis[4] [ˌ]; Lenis[4] [̮].
Shift Signs: Forward [̭]; Backward [̍].

[4] These terms will be explained later in this chapter (p. 111).

On the principle that the name of a character should contain the sound it represents, the names [gɑ], [jot], [ɸi], ['βetɑ], and [xi] are preferable to their more familiar alternates. This is especially important with [gɑ] and [jot] because of possible confusion arising from English spelling.

The **shift signs** [ˌ] and [.] may be used beneath consonant characters to indicate articulation respectively farther front or farther back than the normal one. Thus, an *apico-dental stop* may be indicated by [ṭ] or [ḍ], a *prevelar stop* (that is, one farther front than [k] but not so far front as [c]) by [ḵ], an *apico-palatal sibilant* by [ṣ̌] or [ṣ], and so forth.

VOWELS AND DIPHTHONGS

We have already found that two qualities distinguish **vowels** from other sounds. In the first place they are formed without any stoppage of the oral cavity or any constriction so narrow as to create local sound. In the second place they are **syllabic** or **nuclear;** that is, a vowel is always the most prominent sound in the syllable to which it belongs. Therefore, the presence of a vowel indicates the presence of a syllable (the special case of nonsyllabic vowels will be discussed shortly). The reverse is not always true; some English syllables have no vowel. We have already noted the cases of syllabic [ḷ], [m̩], and [n̩] in *muscle* ['mʌsḷ], *drop 'em* ['drɑp⁻m̩], and *button* ['bʌt⁻n̩]. One or two unusual cases can be cited in addition, such as [pʻṣt] and [š], used respectively to attract attention and to request quiet. In rapid speech, other consonants may become syllabic.

The distinguishing auditory quality of a vowel is its **color,** which is due to the particular combination of harmonics which the articulators permit to pass while they suppress or *damp* the others. We should note two important things about vowels: (1) vowel color is independent of other qualities, such as pitch and loudness; and (2) there are no clear-cut distinctions between vowels; instead, there are gradual transitions from one to another, permitting an almost indefinite number of minute gradations. This last point emphasizes the aptness of the term *color* for describing vowels, since they "shade into" one another as gradually as do the colors of the rainbow. Therefore, in naming them we do as we do with colors. We locate a certain number of points in the continuous spectrum of the vowels and refer the intermediate sounds to these as a surveyor refers points on his map to his bench marks and triangulation points. The result is a system which is capable of indicating any distinction that can be heard. The more precisely the phonetician has trained his "ear" to discriminate among closely similar sounds, the more refined will be his system of transcription. Since we are concerned here with only the grosser distinctions in a single language, we shall be able to get along with eighteen vowel-types and hence with eighteen characters to represent them.

Before we come to these, however, we should discuss the matter of **diphthongs.** To understand about them, we must re-emphasize the continuous nature of speech, which was discussed at some length early in this chapter (p. 58). Speech-sounds, we saw, are not separate, individual units, moving along like soldiers in single file. They are joined together in a continuous flow, so that at the places where they join, the **junctures,** they often blur gradually one into another. Why this must be so is apparent from considering the nature of movements made by the various articulators. In a word like *zoo*, for instance, the first part is formed by the apex and front of the tongue in close proximity to the alveolar ridge, and the last part by the dorsum raised toward the velum. The two articulations are so different that there is bound to be a transitional sound of some sort between them.

Most of these transitional sounds go by so rapidly that we cannot detect them, although they may show up in visual records of speech such as those produced by the sound-spectrograph. Sometimes, however, they are distinct enough and last long enough to be heard. In that case they are called **glides.** Theoretically, almost all glides come between two sounds, but usually it is more convenient to speak of them in relation to one of the neighboring sounds, rather than to both. Thus, a glide coming *before* another sound is called an **on-glide,** and a glide coming *after* another sound is called an **off-glide.** Some of these glides are consonantal, such as the fricative release that characterizes affricates (pp. 73, 79). But a large number of them are *vocalic* (vowel-like) sounds, coming between the syllabic vowel and a preceding or following consonant. We have already described the semivowels, a group of on-glides which are so prominent as to deserve recognition as separate segments. We may also have prominent off-glides, which follow the syllabic vowel and are long enough in duration to take over some of the syllabic nucleus from the syllabic vowel. The nucleus then consists of a longer and more strongly stressed first part, with a short and swift transition to another vowel position at the end. A nucleus of this sort is called a **diphthong,** and its second part or off-glide is a **nonsyllabic vowel.**

Diphthongs are very frequent and important sounds in English. In fact, there are dialects of both British and American English in which all the stressed syllabics and some of the unstressed ones are diphthongs; in these dialects, so-called "pure" vowels do not appear at all, except a few in unstressed positions. This is not a matter of "slurred" or "sloppy" speech; it is simply a characteristic of English which distinguishes it from many other languages. This is why it is necessary to take up diphthongs before going on to the pure vowels. Many of the pure vowels appear only or primarily as parts of diphthongal syllabics. This makes it rather difficult to illustrate them in sample words—a difficulty which is increased by the fact that the readers of this book speak many different dialects, which differ from each other principally in the vowels they use. For that reason, the sample words used here are not to be given too much weight. The student must learn the anchor points of the vowel system from his instructor, or from specially prepared phonograph records.

The **color** of a vowel, as we have said, is the distinctive *auditory* effect it has in the ear of a hearer. An instrumental analysis of the components of the complicated sound wave that produces the auditory effect gives us an *acoustic* description of the vowel. This, in turn, is correlated more or less precisely with certain positions of the jaw, tongue, and lips. The description of these positions gives us *articulatory* descriptions of the vowels, parallel to those we have already given for the consonants. The following descriptions, then, are primarily articulatory, but their validity is substantiated by the findings of acoustic phonetics.

A satisfactory description of a vowel sound must account for five dimensions in which contrasts may occur. These are: (1) *jaw height*, or the degree of closeness of the lower jaw to the upper; (2) *tongue position*, or the location in the mouth of the highest part of the tongue; (3) *lip position*, or the amount of rounding or spreading of the lips; (4) *tension*, the degree of general tension of the whole vocal tract; and (5) *length*, or the actual duration of the sound in time. Let us look at these separately.

1. As one runs down the scale of *beet, bit, bait, bet, bat, bot*, he will observe that his lower jaw drops wider and wider open. We may thus describe the vowels of the first two of these words as **high,** those of the next two as **mid,** and those of the last two as **low.**

2. Pronouncing the series *beet, Bert, boot*, one may feel (or watch in a mirror) the tongue moving progressively backward in the mouth. The first of these vowels may then be classed as **front,** the second as **central,** and the third as **back.** (Remember that *mid* refers to *height* and *central* to *tongue position*.)

3. Pronouncing the pairs *beet:bit* and *pool:pull*, one may feel a certain degree of relaxation of the tongue and perhaps of the other parts of the mouth in saying the second member of each pair. This distinction is not as noticeable in English as it is in other languages, such as French. But it still permits us to call the vowels of *beet* and *pool* **tense** and the vowels of *bit* and *pull* **lax.**

4. If one watches his lips in a mirror while alternately pronouncing *see:sue*, he will observe that for *see* they are either relaxed or some-

what spread, and for *sue* they are somewhat pursed and protruded, or **rounded.** Thus, we may call the vowel of *see* **unround** and the vowel of *sue* **round.**

5. The matter of **length,** or **quantity,** does not involve the position or condition of the articulators, but the length of time they are held in a certain position. Thus, any vowel may be made **long** by prolonging it and **short** by clipping it off. Since length by itself is seldom a distinguishing feature of vowels in English, native speakers have difficulty observing differences of length. Careful listening to alternate pronunciations of *bit*:*bid* and *bet*:*bed* will reveal that the vowel of the first word in each pair is considerably shorter than that of the second.

By describing its nature in each of these five dimensions, we may identify a vowel. Thus, the [ε] of *bet* in most dialects of English is a *mid front lax short unround* vowel, and the vowel of *caught* (again allowing for dialect differences) is a *mid back lax long round* vowel.

In practice we do not always need to account for all five of these qualities when dealing with most American English vowels. That is because of certain almost universal correlations. In the first place, as we have already seen, *length* is seldom a distinctive feature; it varies with the environment of the sound and often with the general rhythm or tone of the sentence. Secondly, in most standard American English dialects, all back vowels are *round* and all front and central vowels are *unround.* We therefore need to specify "round" only in the case of atypically round front and central vowels; conversely, we have to specify "unround" only in the case of unround back vowels. Thirdly, no vowels differ only in degree of tension; they differ in position as well. It is, thus, often not necessary to specify "tense" or "lax," since the position automatically determines this distinction. Nonetheless, we should remember that a *full* description of a vowel necessitates all five distinctions.

We are now ready to look at our eighteen vowel types. Instead of taking them up individually right away, it is more feasible to display them all at once, arranged on a chart that roughly indicates their position in regard to the first two of the distinguishing features discussed above; that is, *height* and *tongue position*. The third criterion is taken care of by the fact that the five back vowels are round in varying degrees, and the other thirteen unround. The other two criteria will be discussed in connection with the individual sounds later on.

The chart we use is called the **vowel quadrangle.**

THE VOWEL QUADRANGLE

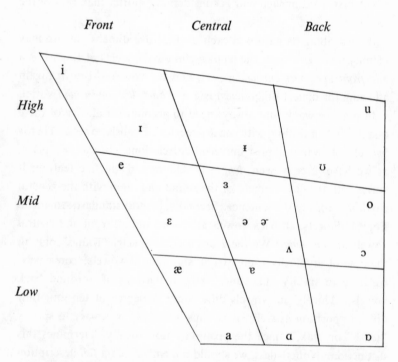

This quadrangle is always made with the front vowels to the left, just as the cross section of the vocal organs (p. 63) always faces left. This convention makes it possible to use a standard set of

shift signs to indicate vowels whose positions are somewhat different from those charted. We shall use four shift signs, [˗] for *fronted*, [˗] for *retracted*, [˕] for *raised*, and [˕] for *lowered*. Thus [ɪ˗] means a retracted version of [ɪ]; that is, one which is nearer to [ɨ] than is the [ɪ] in the diagram. Similarly, [i˕] means a lowered version of [i], nearer the position of [ɪ].

Another set of diacritics is used with vowel characters to indicate varying degrees of length. Thus [·] following a vowel character represents a vowel somewhat longer than the shortest version; similarly [:] signifies an even longer vowel, and [::] an extra-long one. If an abnormally short vowel occurs, it may be marked with [˘]. As has been pointed out before, length is seldom an important feature of English vowels. For this reason the length diacritics will not always be used in our transcriptions. Since consonants may also be long or short, the same diacritics may be used with them. Thus, a common pronunciation of *penknife* has a long [n] in the middle [ˈpˤɛn:aɪf].

FRONT VOWELS

A look at the vowel quadrangle shows that we recognize six **front vowels,** from the highest [i], to the lowest [a]. These arrange themselves into two series. The first contains [i], [e], and [æ], which are relatively long and tense; the second series, [ɪ], [ɛ], and [a], are relatively lax and short. They can thus be treated in pairs, [i, ɪ], [e, ɛ], and [æ, a], each pair containing one longer tense vowel and one shorter lax vowel. In each pair the tense member tends to be diphthongal; in fact, [i] and [e] especially are very seldom found in pure form in American or British English. The lax member of each pair is lower and more central than its tense companion. All six vowels are unround.

1. *High front tense* [i] is the vowel of *seat* [sit] when it is spoken without a diphthong. It may occur in all stressed positions: initially in *east* [ist], medially in *seat*, finally in *see* [si·], *guarantee* [ˌgærənˈtˤi].

In some dialects it may also appear in unstressed position, particularly finally, as in *pretty*, *city*, when the final vowel is clearly higher than the stressed vowel: [ˈpˤɹɪtˤi], [ˈsɪtˤi] or [ˈpˤɹɪɾi], [ˈsɪɾi]. A useful pair of test words here is *candid* and *candied*. If the final syllables of these are different, the second one probably has [i], perhaps a slightly lower, shorter, and laxer version of it than is found in stressed syllables; the word may be transcribed [ˈkˤæ⁺ndiˑd].

2. *Lower high front lax* [ɪ] is the vowel of *sit* [sɪt] in most dialects. It is usually quite short, though before voiced consonants, as in *bid* and *fin*, it is somewhat longer. It occurs initially and medially in stressed syllables, as in *itch* [ɪč] and *witch* [wɪč], but almost never in final stressed position, though I have heard *here* pronounced [ˈhɪˑ] by an educated New Yorker. It is common in unstressed syllables, where it may vary with [i], [ɨ], and [ə] in different positions and dialects: thus, *believe* and *deceive* may have any one of these four vowels in the first syllable. The final syllable of words like *catches* and *batted* may have [ɪ], [ɨ], or [ə].

3. *Mid front tense* [e] very seldom occurs in undiphthongal form in English. It is the vowel of French *été* [ete], though this is somewhat tenser and higher than the usual English version. Some American pronunciations of the first syllable of *chaotic*, or the last syllable of *real estate* have a pure [e]. Usually the nucleus of words like *same*, *fade*, *waste*, *day*, *able* is some sort of diphthong, such as [ei̯, eɪ, ɛi̯, ɛɪ]. In this book, these words are usually written with [ɛɪ], simply because it is the author's pronunciation, thus [sɛɪm, fɛɪd, wɛɪst, dɛɪ, ˈɛɪbl̩].

4. *Lower mid front lax* [ɛ] is the vowel of *bet* [bɛt] in most dialects. Stressed, it occurs initially and medially, as in *etch*, *protect*, but not finally. It may occur in all positions in unstressed syllables, though it is rare in final position and often replaced by [ɪ], [ɨ], or [ə] elsewhere. Thus, *exact* may be [ˌɛgˈzækt] when spoken alone in careful pronunciation, but in the stream of speech it usually begins with [ɪg-], [ɨg-], or [əg-].

5. *Higher low front tense* [æ] is the vowel of *sat* [sæt] in most dialects. It occurs initially stressed, and medially both stressed and semistressed, as in *atlas* [ˈætˈləs], *contract* (vb.) [kˈənˈtˈɹækˉt], and *contract* (n.) [ˈkˈanˌtɹækˉt]. It may appear in unstressed position in words pronounced in isolation, but in normal pronunciation these words will have [ə]: thus, *attempt* is [ʔæˈtɛmt] only in overprecise pronunciation. Similarly, *effect* and *affect* (vb.) are both pronounced [əˈfɛkˉt], except when the latter is artificially pronounced [ˌʔæˈfɛkˉt] to distinguish it. In the dialect of the eastern Midland (Philadelphia area) spoken by the writer, two versions of [æ] are heard, one longer and somewhat higher than the other: thus, *can* meaning "put into a can" is [kˈæˑ:n], but *can* meaning "is able" is [kˈæn].

6. *Low front lax* [a] is the so-called "broad *a*" heard naturally in Boston and some other parts of New England in words like *ask*, *half, path, can't* (but not *cant*), *aunt*. It is a "prestige pronunciation" in some social dialects of American English, but speakers who attempt to adopt it in their dialects often use it in words where Bostonian English does not have it naturally (overcorrections of this sort are called **hyper-forms**). It is not present in most American dialects except as the first element of diphthongs. Many American speakers use it, however, perhaps as a prestige form, in the one word *aunt* [ant] which is thus distinguished from *ant* [æˑnt], [æɪnt], [æˑənt], or [ɛənt].

BACK VOWELS

The five back vowels on our vowel quadrangle are all rounded. The rounding is most pronounced in the highest, [u], and decreases with decreasing height. The tense-lax distinction is much less pronounced in the back vowels, being significant only in the high pair, [u,ʊ]. As with the front vowels, the lax member of the pair, [ʊ], is lower and more central.

7. *High back tense round* [u] is the vowel of *loot* [lut], when pronounced without a diphthong. It may appear initially, as in

ooze [uˑz], and in some unstressed positions, as in *lieutenant* [lu-
ˈtˤɛnənt], though frequently replaced by [ʊ] when unstressed, as in
dubiety [dʊˈbaɪəˌtiˀ] as compared with *dubious* [ˈdubiəs], [dɹʊ̈biəs],
or [ˈdjubiəs]. When final, [u] is usually diphthongized to something
like [ʊ̯u̯] or [uu̯ˀ], as in *do* [dʊu̯], *kangaroo* [ˌkˤæŋɡəˈrʊu̯].

8. *Lower high back lax round* [ʊ] is the vowel of *put* [pˤʊt]. Its
usual position is medial; it is very rarely heard initially and never
finally. It varies with [u] as the stressed vowel of a number of words
deriving their syllabic vowel from ō in Middle English, spelled *oo*,
such as *room, coop, hoof, root,* etc.

9. *Mid back round* [o], sometimes called "close *o*," appears in
English chiefly as the first element of the diphthong [oʊ̯] or [oʊ̯].
It sometimes appears undiphthongized in semistressed or unstressed
position, as in the first syllable of *obey* or the last syllable of *lifeboat*.
A lax, centralized version, [oˀ], appears in some New England
pronunciations of *won't, home, only, boat, road,* etc.

10. *Lower mid back round* [ɔ], sometimes called "open *o*," is the
vowel of *caught* [kˤɔˑt] and *clawed* [kˤlɔˑd] in most varieties of
American English. It varies considerably in length, degree of
rounding, and degree of tenseness. It may appear initially, as in
auger [ˈɔɡɚ], or finally, as in *law* [lɔː]. When final, it tends to become
diphthongized to [ɔə̯] or [ɔʊ̯]. A short, unstressed version may
sometimes be heard in the first syllable of words like *autumnal*
[ɔˈtˤʌmnəɫ].

11. *Low back round* [ɒ], considerably lower, less round, and shorter
than the preceding, is the vowel of the "short-*o* words" in British
English and some eastern dialects of American English, as in *not,
top, dock.* Most Americans have unround central [ɑ] or low back
unround [ɑ] in these words. A good test pair for this sound is
balm:bomb. If the two are unlike, the second probably has [ɒ] or [ɑ].

Unround back vowels are so unusual in American English that they
can be disregarded here. If the student hears them and wishes to
indicate them, he may use either the IPA characters (see pp. 586–87)

or the characters for the round vowels with the diacritic for un-rounding [ˌ]. Thus, the high back unround vowel sometimes heard instead of the [ɨ] in *milk* may be written either [ɯ] or [ɰ].

CENTRAL VOWELS; DIACRITICS

The seven central vowels of our vowel quadrangle are all unround. Two of them, [ə] and [ɨ], occur most commonly in unstressed syllables (including, of course, unstressed versions of words like *and* which also may have stressed forms). One, [ɐ], occurs chiefly as the first element of diphthongs. Thus only four, [ɜ, ə, ʌ, ɑ], customarily appear as syllabic vowels of stressed syllables. All the central vowels except perhaps [ɜ] can be classed as lax.

12. *Lower high central unround* [ɨ] is a common sound in unstressed syllables, as in the adverb *just* as it is usually pronounced in speech. As previously noted (p. 100), it is common in the unstressed syllables of *believe, parted, candid, houses,* where it varies with [ɪ] and [ə]. It may appear as the stressed vowel in some pronunciations of words like *sister* [ˈsɪstɚ], *dinner* [ˈdɪnɚ], and *jury* [ˈjɨrɪ]. It occurs as the first element of the diphthong [ɨu̯] in some pronunciations of *Tuesday, due,* and similar words.

13. *Higher mid central unround* [ɜ] is the vowel of *bird, word, turn, herd, heard* in Received Standard English and those dialects of American English—predominantly in eastern New England, New York City, and parts of the South—which do not have a retroflex vowel or a diphthong here. It is also the first element of the diphthong [ɜɪ̯] which appears in these words in some dialects of New York City and the deep South, especially Louisiana and Mississippi.

14. *Mid central unround* [ə], variously called the "obscure vowel," "neutral vowel," or **schwa,** is an exceedingly common vowel in unstressed position in all dialects of American English. It appears initially, medially, and finally, as in *about* [əˈbaʊ̯t], *enemy* [ˈɛnəmiˑ], and *sofa* [ˈsoʊ̯fə]. In some dialects it is virtually the only vowel in unstressed position except its retroflex counterpart [ɚ], so that

believe, exact, houses, and *sifted* have [bə-], [əg-], [-zəz], and [-təd] as their initial or final syllables. Other dialects have [ɪ], [ɨ], and sometimes [iˑ] in any or all of these positions. [ə] is very common as the nonsyllabic element of diphthongs.

15. *Mid central retroflex* [ɚ] is like [ə], except that the tongue tip is curved up toward the alveolar ridge, as in the formation of [r]. It is, in fact, quite similar to [r], differing in only two respects: it is a true vowel rather than a glide, and the front of the tongue is lower than in the usual position for [r]. It is commonly the syllabic vowel of *bird, word, turn, herd, heard* in those dialects which do not have [ɜ] or [ɜɹ]; in such words it is rather long, thus [bɚˑd, wɚˑd, tʼɚˑn, hɚˑd, hɚˑd].[5] It is frequent in unstressed syllables, especially final, as in *father* [ˈfaðɚ], and medially before consonants, as *super-vene* [ˌsupʻɚˈviˑn]. Medially before vowels it varies with [ə] + [r] or simple [r] in words like *history* [ˈhɪstɚiˑ], [ˈhɪstəriˑ], or dissyllabic [ˈhɪstriˑ]. It is common as the nonsyllabic element of diphthongs, as in *fear* [fɪɚ], *bear* [bɛɚ], or triphthongs, as in *fire* [faɪɚ]. Many dialects in England, New England, New York City, and the South do not have this sound at all; they are the so-called "*r*-less" dialects.

16. *Retracted lower mid central unround* [ʌ] is the vowel of *cut* in most American dialects. It may also be considered a fronted version of the unround back vowel for which this symbol is used in the IPA. It is common initially and medially in stressed syllables, as in *utter, mutter, hurry* (often with [ɚ], however): [ˈʌtɚ, ˈmʌtɚ, ˈhʌriˑ]. It does not occur finally, and in unstressed position is usually replaced by [ə] or [ɪ]; compare *suspect* (n.) [ˈsʌspʻɛk̄t] and *suspect* (vb.) [səˈspɛk̄t] or [sɪˈspɛk̄t]. The sound usually written [ʌ] in transcriptions of British English is lower and more central; in our system of transcription it would appear as [ɑˑ] or [ɐˑ].

17. *Higher low central unround* [ɐ] is not a common sound in

---

[5] The character [ɝ] is sometimes used for this vowel in stressed position. But since there is no difference between the two vowels of *Herbert* except stress and perhaps length, it is only confusing to use separate characters.

American English. It is included here because it appears as the first element of diphthongs.

18. *Low central unround* [ɑ], the vowel of *father* in most American dialects, is also common in *calm* [kʻɑ·m] and similar words, and in shorter form as the vowel of *not*, *top*, *dock*, and so forth. In some dialects it varies with [ɒ] and [ɔ] in words like *loss*, *soft*, *caught*, *forest*, *sorry*, *on*, *off*, *frog*, and many others. In the "*r*-less" dialects it is the vowel of *cart*, *barn*, etc., except in parts of New England that have [a·] or even [æ·] in these words. Some Southwest dialects, especially in Texas, have it before [ɚ] in *short*, *cord* [šɑɚ̯t, kʻɑɚ̯d]. Thus, in one dialect or another of American English, the following pairs may be **homophones** (words of identical sound): *cord–card*; *cot–caught*; *cot–cart*; *balm–bomb*.

These eighteen vowel-types are sufficient to serve as focal points for all American vowels—in fact, for the vowels of most English dialects. They may be adapted to the requirements of refined transcription by the use of various **diacritics,** some of which have already been introduced. We will bring them all together here.

1. *Length* is indicated by [·] for half-long, [:] for long, [::] for overlong, in all cases following the vowel character.
2. *Shift Signs* [˔ ˕ ˖ ˗] are used following the vowel character to indicate raised, lowered, fronted, and retracted variants.
3. *Rounding* is indicated by [̹], *unrounding* by [̜], beneath the vowel character.
4. *Nasalization* is indicated by [˜] above the vowel character. A nasalized vowel is formed in the usual way except that the velum is slightly dropped, allowing part of the sound to go out the nose, and giving the vowel a different color.
5. *Voicelessness* is indicated by [̥] beneath the vowel character, as with consonants. The various varieties of [h] heard in *heel*, *hit*, *hat*, *hot*, *hoot*, *home*, *haul*, *hurt*, *hut* become voiceless vowels [i̥, ɪ̥, e̥, æ̥, ɑ̥, u̥, o̥, ɔ̥, ə̥, ʌ̥] if the glottal friction is absent.
6. *Nonsyllabic* position is indicated by [̯] beneath the vowel charac-

ter. This is the same diacritic as the one used with consonants to indicate fronting, but since the two never conflict, no confusion arises.

7. *Stress* is indicated by [ˈˈ] for strongest stress, [ˈ] for strong stress, [ˌ] for medium stress, placed just before the character which begins the stressed syllable. Unstressed syllables are left unmarked.

DIPHTHONGS

So many and so various are the diphthongs to be found in the various dialects of American English that it is neither feasible nor desirable to list them all here. What we can do, however, is to recognize certain main types. The student can then readily observe and describe the numerous varieties as he hears them in the speech about him. And since in every case they may be considered combinations of vowels, in which one vowel is the syllabic center and the other a nonsyllabic glide, no new characters are needed to transcribe them. A good many have, in fact, already been illustrated in the course of the discussion of consonants and vowels earlier in this chapter.

The first distinction we should take account of is that between so-called **rising** and **falling diphthongs.** The terms refer to the position in time of the stressed, syllabic part of the diphthong in relation to that of the glide. Thus, a diphthong consisting of a preliminary on-glide followed by a syllabic vowel is called *rising* because the intensity of stress increases as the syllable goes on. On the other hand, a diphthong consisting of the syllabic vowel followed by an off-glide is called *falling*, because the intensity of the syllable decreases.

In our treatment of the semivowels, we implied a special treatment of rising diphthongs, which is consistently followed in this book and in most discussions of American English phonetics. They can for most practical purposes be considered combinations of *semivowel plus vowel.* Thus, the nuclei of *mule*, *trick*, and *twit* are here treated as [ju], [rɪ], and [wɪ], rather than as [i̯u], [ʒ̍ɪ], and [u̯ɪ]. This is to some degree a simplification of the phonetic facts, especially in the case of diphthongs with a high front on-glide, but it does no serious harm to our discussion here and greatly simplifies transcription.

We cannot, however, introduce a similar simplification of the falling diphthongs, because of the great variety of vowels that may appear as off-glides. We shall find later on, however, when we come to *phonemics*, that simplification of this sort is possible at a later stage of linguistic analysis. But we must postpone it until then.

It is possible, however, to classify the falling diphthongs in three main groups, according to the nature of the off-glide. These groups are: diphthongs with a mid or high front off-glide; diphthongs with a mid or high back off-glide; diphthongs with a mid central off-glide.

1. The diphthongs with a mid or high front off-glide have as their syllabic element any one of the vowels except [i] and [u]; any of the vowels, that is, included in the shaded area of the following chart:

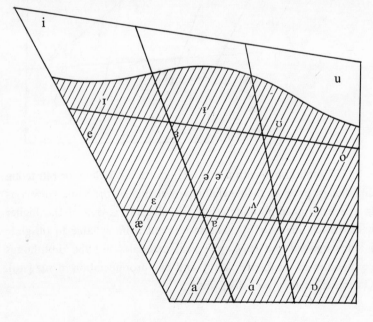

They have as their off-glide one of the high or mid front vowels [i, ɪ, ɪ˙, e, ɛ]. The off-glide is always higher than the syllabic vowel. Thus, the movement from syllabic to off-glide is *upward and forward*, so that these diphthongs may be conveniently called **fronting diphthongs.** Typical examples are the diphthongs commonly heard in *ray* [reι̯], *rye* [raι̯], and Roy [rɔι̯]. These can be represented by arrows on the vowel chart:

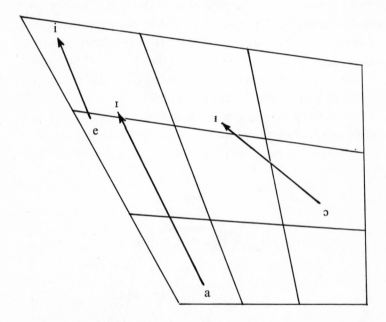

2. The diphthongs with a mid or high back off-glide, or **retracting diphthongs,** have as their syllabic vowel one of the same vowels as in the fronting diphthongs, but the off-glide is one of the higher back vowels [u, ʊ, o, ɔ]. The movement from syllabic to off-glide is thus *upward and back*. Typical examples are the diphthongs common in *so* [soṷ], *cow* [kʻaṷ], and one pronunciation of *sue* [sɪṷ]. On the chart they look like this:

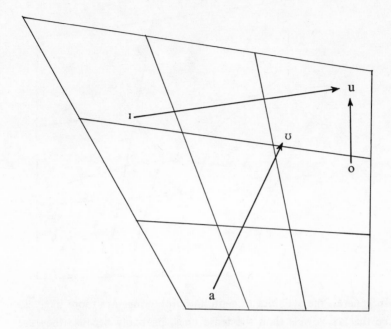

3. The diphthongs with a mid central off-glide, the **centering diphthongs,** may have as syllabic any of the vowels around the whole outside of the vowel quadrangle, including [ʌ]; that is, any of the eighteen except [ɜ, ə, ɚ]. As off-glide they may have [ə] or [ɚ]. There is a large group of dialects which do not have the retroflex off-glide [ɚ], the "*r*-less" dialects to which we have already referred (p. 104). Where the other dialects have diphthongs in [ɚ], these dialects usually have either the corresponding diphthong in [ə], or simply a long vowel with no off-glide at all. Thus, where the other dialects have [ɑɚ], as in *barn,* the "*r*-less" dialects may have either [ɑə] or [ɑ·], as in [bɑə̯n] and [bɑ·n]. Typical centering diphthongs are those of *barn* [bɑɚ̯n], *idea* [ˌaɪˈdɪə̯], *horse* [hɔɚ̯s], *bear* (or *bare*) [bɛɚ̯], and *poor* (one pronunciation) [pʻʊɚ̯]. They may be charted as in the following:

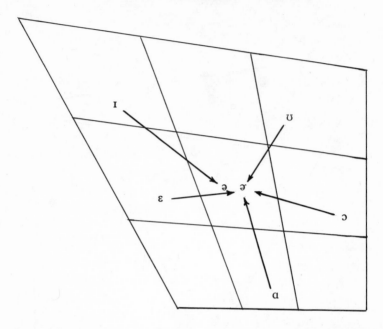

In general, the syllabics of centering diphthongs are more likely to be the lax vowels than the tense ones, probably because they are already nearer the central position of the off-glide. But the tense vowels may also appear.

A FEW FINE POINTS

Before we can conclude our discussion of phonetics, a few fine points should be mentioned. Three of them relate to consonants and the rest to the transcription of connected speech.

PARTIALLY VOICED CONSONANTS. The beginning and ending of phonation by the vocal bands does not always exactly coincide with the movement of articulators into position for a new sound. In other words, voicing may begin or end in the middle of a consonant, especially a fricative or affricate. The result is a sound that is partly voiced and partly voiceless. This is particularly likely to happen at the beginnings and endings of words, breath-groups, and utterances.

Thus, when words that ordinarily begin with [v, ð, z] or [j] come at the beginning of an utterance or phrase, there may be a brief occurrence of [f, θ, s] or [č] before voicing sets in. In the same way, words which normally end in [v, ð, z] or [j] may end with a brief voiceless [f, θ, s] or [č] when they come at the end of an utterance or phrase. This may be indicated by treating the voiceless sound as an on- or off-glide, and writing [f͡v, θ͡ð, s͡z, č͡j] or [v͡f, ð͡θ, z͡s, j͡č]. If the voiceless part of the sound seems longer than a mere glide, the diacritic for voicelessness may be used. Thus [v̥ɪm] indicates that the first half or more of the initial [v] is voiceless, and [hæv̥] means that the last half or more of the final [v] is voiceless. Many speakers of American English unvoice a good part of the [z] which forms the plurals of nouns whose singulars end in a vowel or voiced consonant. Thus in reporting their speech, *days* and *bags* may be written [dɛɪz͡s] and [bægz͡s] or [dɛɪz̥] and [bægz̥]. If in the hearer's judgment the voice does not continue into the final sibilant at all, these words should be transcribed with a lenis [s̬]: [dɛɪs̬] and [bægs̬]. But this complete unvoicing seldom occurs in the speech of native speakers.

FORTIS AND LENIS STOPS AND FRICATIVES. Stops and fricatives are often characterized as **fortis** (tense) or **lenis** (slack), according to the degree of tension which accompanies the articulation. The diacritics [ˌ] for fortis and [ˌ] for lenis are used beneath the consonant character to mark this distinction. In English, the voiceless consonants are usually fortis and the voiced consonants are usually lenis. This may be considered the normal state of affairs and need not be marked. Occasionally, however, a lenis voiceless consonant or a fortis voiced consonant is heard, in which case the proper diacritic should be used. Thus, in many American dialects the medial consonant in *water* is a *lenis voiceless alveolar stop*, which may be written [t̬].

NASAL AND LATERAL RELEASE. When a stop is followed by a nasal, its release may take place through the nose, instead of through the mouth. This **nasal release** can be indicated by using the diacritic [ᴺ] following the consonant character. Thus, *acknowledge* may be pronounced [əkᴺ'nɑɫɪj], or it may begin [əkn-] or [ək⁻n-] or sometimes even [ək'n-]. Similarly, we may hear *utmost* ['ʌtᴺˌmoʊ̯st], *dragnet* ['drægᴺˌnɛt], and so on. In the same fashion, when a stop is followed by [l] or [ɫ] it may have a **lateral release**; that is, the release may be withheld until the tongue is in position for [l]. The diacritic for this is [ˈ], as in *atlas* ['æt˞l̥əs], *acclaim* [ə'k˞l̥ɛɪm].

CONNECTED TRANSCRIPTION

WORD DIVISION. So far our examples of phonetic transcription have almost all been of isolated words. When we transcribe connected speech, we are faced with the problem of what word boundaries to indicate. The point was made early in this chapter (p. 58) that speech is a continuous flow, not a series of distinct sounds grouped into clearly distinguishable words. In listening to our native language we mentally divide up the continuous stream into individual words, partly on the basis of our intimate knowledge of the spoken language, and partly because of our familiarity with conventional writing and printing, in which words are set neatly apart. But if we listen to an unknown language, or with a truly objective ear to our own, we can hear very few clear indications of word division. In fact, we may not be able to distinguish with certainty any discrete units shorter than the breath-group. Thus, a phonetician who knows no English, upon hearing "Isn't he coming today?" might feel that he had no other way to transcribe this than [ˌɪzn̩tiˈk˂ʌmɪntəˈˈdeɪ].

No great harm is ordinarily done, however, if in transcribing English we take advantage of our knowledge as native speakers of the language and introduce some word divisions. But we should not set off everything that is customarily printed as a separate word. Our knowledge of the language will simply sharpen our ears to the minute signals of pause and retarded tempo that mark the divisions between words. Thus, a speaker of English might hear "Isn't he coming today?" as [ˌɪzn̩ti ˈk˂ʌmɪŋ t˂əˈˈdeɪ]. Similarly, groups like *instead of* and *in spite of* will often be written [ɪn'stedəv] and [ɪnˈspaɪ̯təv] to show that no indication of division is audible in them. Thus, a space in our phonetic transcription will primarily indicate a point at which we hear the kind of slight pause or retarding of tempo, or **open juncture,** which often coincides with the point where we divide words in standard writing.

Occasionally in listening to connected speech we will observe pauses of greater length than the very short ones which separate words. These may be marked with a strong vertical line or bar [|]. Longer pauses may be marked with two or three bars; individual transcribers are likely to develop their own practices in this regard. It is convenient to mark the end of an utterance—the point at which the speaker lapses into silence—with a **double cross** [#]. We thus have various indications of word division and pause, the three basic ones being the *space*, the *bar*, and the *double cross*.

STRESS IN CONNECTED TRANSCRIPTION. We have already presented a set of diacritics for indicating stress in individual words, the three marks [ˈ] for strongest stress, [ˈ] for strong stress, and [ˌ] for medium stress. In connected speech these are distributed differently from the way they appear in isolated words (called **citation forms** by linguists). Usually there are fewer of them, and strong stresses are often reduced to medium. Thus, we write *Monday* [ˈmʌndiʳ] with strong stress as a citation form, but in "I saw him Monday night," it may have medium stress: [ˌaɪ̯ ˈsɔɪm ˌmʌndiʳ ˈˈnaɪ̯t]. This sentence also illustrates how one syllable within a phrase or breath-group may have its strong stress increased to strongest; thus [naɪ̯t] is marked with [ˈˈ] to show that it receives more stress than anything else in the phrase.

PITCH. When we hear people talking at a distance or through some muffling obstacle, we may not be able to distinguish individual words at all; instead, we may hear only a more or less continuous rumble. Under such circumstances it is especially apparent that the stream of speech is not all at the same pitch, and that there are ups and downs ranging over as much as an octave. These variations in pitch are not accidental or random; they are a part of the structure of speech. It is the duty of the phonetician who wishes to present a complete record to take account of them.

Musical notation, it is true, supplies a very accurate and refined system for recording changes in pitch. Theoretically the phonetician could simply run a five-line staff parallel to his phonetic transcription and indicate the "tune" of an utterance in the usual musical symbols. But this has some obvious disadvantages. In the first place, it would require that the phonetician have perfect pitch, unless he wanted to carry a set of tuning forks about with him. Secondly, it would be too precise a method of notation. Very seldom do we need to know the exact pitch of various parts of an utterance. What is important in most languages is *relative* pitch and *changes* in pitch. We recognize an utterance as the same, even though it may be spoken once by a bass and again by a soprano two octaves higher, if both of them follow the same ups and downs. Therefore, all that is needed is some way of indicating the major differences of pitch between the different parts of an utterance.

In many languages, called tone languages, a designated level or change of pitch is an important part of every word, so that the only difference between two words may be a matter of pitch. In languages of that sort, it is essential that the pitch of every syllable be recorded as accurately as the distinctions of the particular language require. English, however, is not a tone language. When we say [hæt], the lexical meaning does not differ if we say it on a high, low, level, rising, or falling pitch. Certain other aspects of meaning do change, however, if we alter the succession and type of pitches in pronouncing a whole sentence. "He is coming," for instance, is a statement if the voice drops at the end, but it is a question if the pitch goes up. It is these significant levels and changes of pitch that make up the **intonation** of an utterance. They are what the phonetician must record.

For our purposes it is sufficient to recognize four levels of pitch in recording English. They can be most simply represented if we imagine our transcription to be written in the middle space of a four-line staff, whose lines are numbered 1 to 4 from the bottom up:

4 _____

3 _____

2 ___(Transcription goes here.)___

1 _____

Actually, we do not draw in all four lines. We simply draw opposite each part of an utterance the line corresponding to the pitch on which it is spoken. Thus "not today" spoken on a level tone at pitch 2, which is the most common one for unemotional utterances, is written:

[ˌnɑt tˤə ˈˈdɛɪ#]

Actually, of course, we very seldom say a complete utterance without any change of pitch. We shift back and forth, principally among the three lower levels. Level 4, the highest, is reserved for especially emphatic and emotional utterances. These shifts are of two sorts: sudden jumps and gradual glides. A sudden change of pitch can be indicated by simply stopping one line and starting another on the level of the new pitch. A gradual change can be indicated by a slanting line right through the syllable in which it occurs. Thus, a common way of saying "Come right in" would be with pitch 2 on the first two words, a break to pitch 3 at the beginning of "in", and a gradual drop to pitch 1 at the end. This would be written:

[ˌkˤʌm ˈraɪt ˈˈin#]

When one is transcribing rapidly, it is convenient to omit all but the important changes of pitch. Since pitch 2 is by far the most common, we can adopt the convention that all syllables not otherwise marked are spoken on pitch 2. This will have the effect not only of simplifying transcription, but of bringing out the important changes of pitch more emphatically. Thus, the sentence "Now that you're here, let's get it done" would normally begin on pitch 2, jump to 3 at the beginning of *here*, slide back to 2 during the speaking of *here*, continue on 2 through *it*, jump to 3 and slide down to 1 at the end. This would be indicated as follows:

[ˈnaʊ̯ðətˌjʊɚ̯ ˈˈhɪɚ̯ | ˌlɛts ˈgɛṙɪt¯ ˈˈdʌn#]

This is now as complete a transcription of speech as we are usually called upon to make. It indicates not only the individual sounds, but the way they are joined, the stresses they bear, and the intonation of the utterance. It should be possible for anyone who has learned the system to repeat the sentence in substantially the way it was uttered. It should be observed, however, that this transcription does not indicate three things which might sometimes be important. It says nothing about absolute pitch; the sentence might be spoken in a deep bass or in a childish treble three octaves higher. It likewise says nothing about vocal qualifiers (p. 53); the sentence might be shouted, murmured, or rasped (it could not, however, be whispered, because whisper cannot change pitch). Finally, it does not indicate the individual vocal quality (p. 54) of the speaker. If it is necessary to include something about these, the phonetician must simply make a note to go with his transcription.

READING PASSAGE

For practice in reading, there follows a transcription of a well-known test passage, as spoken by the author. The student should first work out the individual sounds and words carefully, then put them together with attention to juncture, stress, and intonation.

ˈˈgrɪp¯ | ðə ˈˈræt

ˈwʌns ðɚwəzə ˌjʌŋ ˈˈræt | hu ˈkˤʊdn̩t ˌmɛɪ̯k ˈʌpɪz ˈˈmɑ·e̯nd || wɛnˌɛvɚ ðɪˌʌðɚ ˌræts ˈˈæ˔·stɪm | ɪfiwəd ˈlɐɪ̯k tɪ kəm ˈˈaʊ̯t ˌwɪðəm | ˌhɪi̯ wəd ˈˈæ˔·nsɚ | ˀˌɑ·ɪ̯ ˌdoʊ̯̃ntᴺˈnoʊ̯ || ˀən ˈwɛn ˌðɛɪ̯ ˈˈsɛ·d | ˌwʊdžə ˈlɐɪ̯k¯tˤə

ˈstapˤət ‖hoṵm‖|ˌhi̧ ˌwʊdnat |sɛı̯ ‖jɛṣ|ɚ ˈnoṵ ‖iðɚ‖|ˌhi̧wəd
|ɔɫwɪž |šɚk |meı̯kıŋə ‖čɔı̯s‖|ˈwʌn |deı̯ hız|ant ‖sɛd⁻tʊım|ˌnaṵ ‖lʊk ⁵
‖hıɟ‖|ˌnoṵwʌn wɪɫ ˌɛvɚ ‖kˤɛ·ɚ fɚjʊṵ|f·jʊṵ ˈkˤæriˑ ˌɔn|leı̯k ‖ðıs‖|jʊ
hæv ˌnoṵ ˌmɔ·ɚ‖ˈma·ɛ̧nd|ðənəˈbleı̧d əv‖græˑs‖|ðə ˌjʌŋ ˌræt ˈkˤɔ·ft
ən ‖lʊk⁻t ‖waɛ̧z|əz ‖jʊṵžəliˑ‖|bət⁻ ˌsɛd ‖nʌθıŋ‖|ˌdončʊ ‖θıŋk ˈsoʊ
|sɛdız ˈant|ˈstæˑmpˤıŋ ˌwıðɚ ‖fʊt|ˌfɚši ˈkˤʊdn̩t ‖bɛ·ɚ tˤəˌsiı̧ ðə ˌjʌŋ
ˈrætˤ|soˑ ˌko·ɫd‖blʌdɪd‖|ʔaˑı̧ ˌdo ‖noṵ|wəzɪɔ·ɫ ðə ˌjʌŋ ˌræt ‖ɛvɚ ¹⁰
ˈæˑnsɚd‖|ən ˈðɛn hiwəd ˈwɔ·k ‖ɔ·f|tˤə ‖θıŋk fɚ ən|aṵɚ|ˌwɛðɚišəd
ˈsteı̧ınız ˈho·ɫ ˌıŋ·ə ‖graṵnd|ʔɔɚ ˌgoṵ ˈaṵt ˌınðə ‖lɒft‖|ˈwʌn ˈneı̯t
|ðə ˌræts ˌhɚdə ˈgreı̯t ‖nɔı̯z ıŋ·ə ˌlɒft‖|ıʔwəzə ˌveriˑ ‖drıɟiˑ
ˌoṵɫdˤˌlɒft‖|ðə ˈru·f ˌleı̯ın ðə ‖reı̯n|ðə ˈbrı̧mzn̩ ˈræftɚz wɚ ˌʔɔ·ɫ
‖rɒtᴺn̩|ˌsoðəɚ̧⁻ðə ˌpˤļeı̯s wəz ˌrædɚ ˌʔʌn‖seı̯f‖|ʔætˤ ˌlæˑ·st⁻ ˌwʌnəðə ¹⁵
ˈjɔı̯s ˌgeı̯v ‖weı̧|ʔənðə ‖brı̧mz ˈfɛɫ|wıð ˈwʌn ˌend ˌɒnðə ‖fļoˑɚ‖|ðə
ˈwɔ·ɫz ‖šʊkˤ|ən ˈɔ·ɫ ðə ˌræts ‖hɛ·ɚ|ˌstʊdɒn ‖end|wıð ˈfıɚ ən
‖hɒrɚ‖|ˌðıs ˌwoṵn̩t⁻‖dʊṵ|ˌsɛd⁻ðə ˈčıɟf‖|ˌwımṣt ‖lı̧ı̧v ˌðıs ˈpˤļeı̯s‖
soðɛı̧ ˈsɛnt ˌaṵt ‖skaṵʔts|tˤə ˈsɚč fɚə ˈnı̧ṵ ‖hoṵm‖|ıŋ·ə‖neı̯t|ðə
ˌskaṵts ˈkˤeı̯m ‖bæk|ənd ˌsɛd⁻ ðɛı̧ həd ˈfaṵnd ən ˌoṵɫd⁻ ˈkˤʊṵpˤəvə ²⁰
‖baɚn|ˌw̧ɛˈðɚˌwʊd|biˑ ˈrʊmn̩ ‖bɔ·ɚd|fɚðəm ‖ɔ·ɫ|ɛt ˈwʌns ðəˈčıɟf
ˌgeı̯v ðıˤ ‖ɔɚdɚ‖|ˈfɔɚm ˌın ‖la·ɛn‖|ðəˌræʔts ˈkˤɔ·ɫd aṵtə ðɛɚ
‖hoṵɫz|ın ˈstʊd ɒnðə ‖fļoˑɚ|ınə ‖ɔ·ŋ ‖la·ɛn‖|ˈjıs ˌðɛn ði ‖oṵɫd⁻ˈræt
|ˈkˤɔ·t ˈseı̯ţəvˌjʌŋ ‖grıpˤ‖|ˈðæʔ wəz ðə ˈneı̯məðə ‖šɚkɚ‖|ˌhiı̧ wəzˌnɒt
‖ınnə ‖la̧ɛn|ən ˌhiı̧wəz ˌnɒt ıgˈzækliˑ aṵʔ ‖tsaɛ̧dıt|rı̧ ˈstʊd jıst⁻‖ba·ɛ̧ ²⁵
ıt‖|ˌwaɛ̧ ˈdoṵnčʊ ‖sprı̧k|ˌsɛd⁻ði ˌoṵɫd⁻ˈræt ‖kˤɔ·ɚsliˑ‖|əv ˈkˤɔɚs
ˌjʊɚ ‖kˤʌmıŋ‖|ˌaɛ̧ˌdoṵnt ‖no·ṵ|ˌsɛd ˈgrıp⁻ ‖ka·mliˑ‖|ði ˌa·ɛ̧‖dıɚ
ˌɒvıt‖|waɛ̧ ˌjʊ ˈdoṵnt⁻ˌθıŋkıts ‖seı̯f|‖dʊṵ ˌjʊṵ|ˌıʔaɛ̧m ˈnɒt ‖sɚt⁻n̩‖
ˌsɛd ˈgrıp ˌʌn‖dɔ·ntɪd|ˌðə ˈrʊṵf ˌmeı̧ ˈnɒt ˌkˤʌm ˈdaṵn ‖jɛt⁻‖|‖wɛɫ
ˌsɛd⁻ ði ˌoṵɫd ˌræt|wıı̧ ˈkˤæˑ·nt ‖weı̯t|fɚ ‖jʊṵ tˤə ˈjɔı̯nəs‖|ˈreı̯t ³⁰
əˌba·ṵt ‖fɛs‖|ˈmaɚč‖|ənd⁻ðə ‖ɔ·ŋ ‖la·ɛn|ˌmaɚčt ‖aṵţəðə ˌlɒft|
ˌwaɛ̧ɫ ðə ˈjʌŋ ˈræt ‖wɒčtəm‖|əˈθıŋk ˌaɫ ˈgoṵ tˤʊ‖mɒ·roˑ|ˌhi ˈsɛd⁻tʊ
ım‖sɛɫf|bət⁻ðən əˈgen|ˈaɛ̧ ˌdont ‖noṵ|ˌıt·so ˈneı̯sn̩ ‖snʌg ˈhıɚ‖|
əˈθıŋk aɫˈgo ˈbæk⁻ tˤʊˌmaɛ̧ ‖hoṵɫ|ˌʌndɚðə ‖lɒg fɚə ˌbıt|ˈjəstə
ˈmeı̯k ˌʌp⁻mɛ ‖ma·ɛ̧nd⁻‖|ˈðæt⁻ ‖neı̯t|ðɚwəzə ˈbıg ‖kˤræš‖|ˈdaṵn ³⁵
ˌkˤeı̯m ‖brı̧mẓ‖|ˈræˑ·ftɚẓ‖|ˈjɔı̯s·|ðə ˈhoɫ ‖rʊṵf‖|ˌnɛks ‖mɔɚnıŋ|

ˌɪʔwəzə ‖ˈfɒɡiˑ ˈdeɪ│səm ‖ˈmɛn ˈkˤɛɪm│tˤə ‖ˈlʊkət⁻ðə ‖ˈlɒft‖ˌðɛɪ ˈθɔɹ̇ɪt ‖ˈɒd⁻│ðəţ ˌɪʔwəz ˌnɒtˤ ˈhɔˑnţɪd ˌbɑɡ ‖ˈræts‖bəɹ̇əţ⁻ ‖ˈæˑˑst│ˈwʌnəðəm ˈhæpəntˤə ˌmʊu̯v ə ‖ˈboɡ̇d│ɛni ˈkˤɔt ‖ˈseɪ̇t│əvə ˈjʌŋ ‖ˈræt│ˈkˤweɪt⁻ ˈdɛd│ˈhæf ‖ˈɪn│ˈhæf ˈau̯təv ˌhɪz ‖ˈhoʊ̇ł‖ˈðʌs ðə ‖ˈšə̇kə̇│ˈhædˌhɪz   40 ‖ˈdɪʊ̯u̯#

COLLATERAL READING, CHAPTER 2

Books previously listed are cited by author only.

Bloch and Trager. Chap. ii, "Phonetics," pp. 10–37.

Gleason. Chap. xiv, "Articulatory Phonetics," pp. 187–204.

Kenyon, John S. *American Pronunciation*, 10th ed. Ann Arbor: George Wahr, 1951. Sections 28–78, pp. 33–65.

Thomas, Charles K. *An Introduction to the Phonetics of American English*, New York: The Ronald Press Co.,1958,2d ed. Chap. ii, "The Mechanism of Speech," pp. 13–31; chap. iii, "The Classification of Speech Sounds," pp. 32–41.

Jones, Daniel. *The Pronunciation of English*, 3d ed. Cambridge, Eng.: Cambridge University Press, 1950. Pp. 3–30. (For Received Standard British.)

Heffner, R-M. S. *General Phonetics*. Madison: University of Wisconsin Press, 1949. Chap. ii, "The Physiology of Speech," pp. 9–41.

Pike, Kenneth L. *Phonetics: A Critical Analysis of Phonetic Theory and a Technic for the Practical Description of Sounds*. Ann Arbor: University of Michigan Press, 1943. Chap. vi, "Productive Mechanisms," pp. 85–106; chap. vii, "Controlling Mechanisms," pp. 107–48; chap. viii, "Conclusions," pp. 149–56.

Curry, Robert O. L. *The Mechanism of the Human Voice*. New York: Longmans, Green & Co., Inc., 1940. Chap. ii, "The Anatomy of the Vocal Organs," pp. 9–38; chap. iv, "The Physiology of Phonation," pp. 61–84.

Phonograph Records.

Greet, W. Cabell. *The Sounds of English: American Speech*. Linguaphone Institute.

Jones, Daniel. *Cardinal Vowels*. Linguaphone Institute.

Chapter 3

The Significant Sounds of Speech: Phonemics

THE PHONEME DEFINED

The full phonetic transcription with which the last chapter ended is a complicated thing indeed. It was complicated to prepare and complicated to print; no doubt the reader found it complicated to read. But we must remember that, complicated though it is, it is not as complicated as speech itself. In other words, the transcription seemed more difficult to read than the sad story of "Grip the Rat" would be to listen to; but this difficulty is the result of unfamiliarity, not of unreasonable complication by the phonetician. After all, we have been learning to read phonetic transcription for only a short time, whereas we have been working at the job of learning to listen since before we were a year old. It is no wonder the phonetic writing still seems strange and difficult.

One of the things we learn to do in the course of learning to listen is to pick out the *significant features* from the stream of speech and let the rest go. We have already seen the beginning of this process in our disregard of individual voice quality, absolute pitch, and vocal qualifiers. These things may influence us to some degree —we may enjoy being quietly addressed in a musical feminine voice more than being yelled at in a loud, harsh baritone. But they do not influence the linguistic content of what is said, and we can

119

disregard them in getting at the message. Actually, we carry the process much farther. Many of the differences which we observe as phoneticians we will find are not important *phonemically*; that is, they do not influence the message. The task of finding out just what elements in the stream of speech *do* carry the message is the task of **phonemics.**

Another way of looking at it is to say phonemics begins the job of analysis and generalization which we found to be one of the major operations of science. Phonetics supplies the raw material, described as objectively as possible, so that if another phonetician using the same phonetic alphabet were to write down the story of Grip as it was spoken by the writer, he would produce a transcription almost identical with ours. Any differences would be due to one or another form of human fallibility. This objective description of speech is what phonemics takes and studies in order to see what generalizations can be made about its structure. What these generalizations are will be the subject of this chapter.

Let us take a few samples from the transcription to serve as an illustration of how phonemics operates. Specifically, let us consider the following words (we should really call them "sound-groups," since we haven't yet defined words, but no great harm is done by using the familiar term):

lɐɪk (line 2)	ˈɔɫwɪž (5)	pˈɭɛɪs (15, 18)
lʊk (5)	wɪɫ (6)	fḷoˈɚ (16)
ˈˈblɛɪd (7)	kˈoˑɫd⁻ (10)	
ˈblʌdɪd (10)	ɔˑɫ (10)	
lɒft (12)	fɛɫ (16)	
lɹiv (18)	ɪmˈˈsɛɫf (33)	
ɪgˈzækliˀ (25)		
ˈˈkˈɔɹ̝sliˀ (26)		

All these words have some kind of *lateral consonant* in them. The ones in the first column have the voiced apico-alveolar lateral [l];

the ones in the second column have the voiced apico-alveolar lateral with dorso-velar coarticulation [ɫ]; and the ones in the third column have the voiceless apico-alveolar lateral [l̥]. In short, the three columns exemplify some of the occurrences of three different phone-types in our transcription.

Taking a closer look at these words, especially at the positions where the lateral phones occur, we can make some interesting observations. For instance: (1) four out of eight words in column 1 have [l] at the beginning, but [ɫ] and [l̥] do not come at the beginning of any of the words in columns 2 and 3; (2) two more words in column 1 (the last two) have [l] at the beginning of a syllable, in both cases [liˀ]; on the other hand, [ɫ] and [l̥] do not come at the beginning of any syllable; (3) the remaining two words in column 1 have [l] between [b] and a vowel; (4) the two words in column 3 have [l̥] between the voiceless consonants [pˤ] and [f] and a vowel; (5) all the words in column 2 have [ɫ] either at the end of a syllable, as in [ˈɔɫwɪž], at the end of the word, as in [wɪɫ, ɔ·ɫ, fɛɫ], or between a vowel and a consonant, as in [kˤo·ɫd⁻] and [ˈˈsɛɫf].

When we study these generalizations a bit further, we can draw the interesting conclusion that there is no type of environment in which one of these phone-types appears in which either of the others also appears. We do not find [ɫ] at the beginning of a word or syllable; we do not find [l] between a vowel and a consonant; we do not find [l̥] between a voiced consonant and a vowel, and so on. In short, they act like members of a well-organized team, in which each knows his place and does not try to trespass on somebody else's territory. Furthermore, if we study the various territories occupied by each, we find that they add up to a complete covering of the field.

The territory covered by a phone-type—that is, all the kinds of environment in which it can occur—is called its **range** or its **distribution**. When, as in this case, a group of phone-types of similar phonetic nature (in this case all laterals) occupy various territories that do not overlap, their distribution is called **complementary.** Such a well-organized team of phone-types is called a **phoneme.** This is such an important term that we will restate our description of it:

Definition: A phoneme is a group of one or more phone-types that are phonetically similar and in complementary distribution.

The different phone-types that make up a phoneme are called its **members** or **allophones.** An **allophone,** then, is a phone-type which belongs to a phoneme. In the examples we have been looking at, we can call [l], [ɫ], and [l̥] the allophones of the l-phoneme of American English. It is customary to write symbols for phonemes between slanted lines, just as we write characters for phones between square brackets; we can then write /l/ instead of "the l-phoneme."

With this new terminology to help us, we can now restate some of our generalizations in more precise terms:

1. In the dialect of American English represented by the transcript on pages 116–18, the phoneme /l/ has three allophones: [l], [ɫ], and [l̥].

2. The allophone [l] appears in word-initial and syllable-initial position, and between a voiced consonant and following vowel.

3. The allophone [ɫ] appears in word- and syllable-final position, and between a vowel and following consonant.

4. The allophone [l̥] appears between a voiceless consonant and following vowel.

If these generalizations are of any value, they should be a basis for accurate predictions. The body of material, or **corpus,** available to us (the transcription of "Grip the Rat") is rather scanty, but it does corroborate some, at least, of these generalizations. That is, we can go back to the transcription and pick out some more words that we did not use in making the generalizations, such as [ˌlɛ́rɪn] (14); [ˌoʊld˕ ˌlɒft] (14), [waɛ̣ɫ] (32), and so on. We find that they do indeed follow the rules of distribution we formulated above. When we know the environment, we can accurately predict which allophone will occur. Our generalizations hold water. And since the nature of the environment decides or **determines** which allophone will appear, in a **phonemic transcription** we can use the same character for all the allophones belonging to a given phoneme. In our case, we can use /l/ for all three of its allophones, remembering that in *phonetic* terms this character may sometimes stand for [l], and sometimes for [ɫ] or [l̩]. A phonemic transcription is therefore simpler to look at than a phonetic one, but it requires that the reader have more knowledge of the language. It requires him to know what allophones appear in what environments. The native speaker knows this by long habit, but the foreigner who wishes to use the "right pronunciation" must use a phonetic transcription if he is to get the allophones in the right places and thus avoid being accused of having a "foreign accent." To see how strange a simple transposition of allophones can make a word sound, try pronouncing *lilt* as [ɫɪlt]. Here [l] and [ɫ] have changed places; they are "off-side" as it were.

We have established two requirements that must be fulfilled if two or more phone-types are to be considered allophones of a single phoneme: phonetic similarity and complementary distribution. It would be well to take a closer look at each of these requirements before we go ahead to call the roll of American English phonemes. And while we are at it, we might make explicitly a point that has already been implied: that is, a phoneme always belongs to a specific dialect or language. Thus, the allophones of American English /l/ in the dialect here being considered are, as we have seen, [l], [ɫ], and [l̩]. There are other dialects, however, in which /l/ might lack one or more of these allophones, or might have additional ones, like [L]. There are languages (Japanese, for instance) which have no laterals at all, hence no /l/ phoneme. Therefore, while [l] as a phone-type may occur in many languages and does not need to be labeled "American English [l]" or "French [l]" (unless, of course, we are arbitrarily using the same phonetic character to represent different sounds, in which case we must explain our action), as soon as we speak of a *phoneme* /l/ we are speaking of a group of phone-types whose membership and distribution are unique to the language or dialect we are talking about. For this reason, when we speak of a phoneme, we must identify the dialect or language to which it belongs, unless this is clearly implied in the context.

PHONETIC SIMILARITY. The classification and discussion of speech sounds in the last chapter gives us a good basis for understanding phonetic similarity. Sounds may be phonetically similar according to any of the various dimensions in which they resemble or differ from one another. Thus [m], [p], [b], and [β] are all phonetically similar because they are bilabials. Likewise [m], [n], and [ɲ] are phonetically similar because they are all voiced nasals. Since [f], [θ], and [s] are all voiceless fricatives, they too are phonetically similar. Many other groups could be made up which fit the general pattern of phonetic similarity. In phonemics, however, a somewhat more rigorous concept is employed. We require that to be considered phonetically similar for the purpose of being classed as allophones of the same phoneme, a group of phone-types must share some feature or group of features not shared by any other phone-type in the language. To be on the team, as it were, all the players must wear a uniform not worn by any outsiders. We met this requirement with our sample case, because our group of allophones of /l/ included all the lateral phone-types there are in the passage studied. In fact, *laterality* and *apico-alveolar articulation* were the pair of features that the three allophones had in common. We could not have included [n] in the group because while it is apico-alveolar, it is not a lateral. Or if we wanted to base phonetic similarity on apico-alveolar articulation alone, we could have included [n], but we would also have had to include all the other apico-alveolar phone-types, such as [t, t⁻, tʻ, d, d⁻, ḍ], and so on. But as soon as we looked at the distribution of all these, we would find that it was no longer complementary; there would be sets like *light – tight – night* in which three of these phone-types appear in the same position. They would meet the requirement of phonetic similarity, but not that of complementary distribution.

Phonetic similarity must be broad enough, then, to include all the sounds sharing a given group of phonetic features; it must be narrow enough to make sure of complementary distribution. In any case, a group of sounds defined as phonetically similar must be exclusive; there must be some way of defining it that includes all the sounds we need to include and excludes all others. In our case, the allophones of /l/ can be sufficiently described as *laterals*, since this includes [l], [ɫ], and [l̩] and excludes everything else in the dialect. But if distribution required us to set up two lateral phonemes, we should have to find some way to define each of them that would exclude all the allophones of the other.

COMPLEMENTARY DISTRIBUTION. The idea of complementary distribution can perhaps be clarified by a few simple illustrations from fields outside linguistics. One year I had a pair of identical twins as students. I had no difficulty identifying them in class, however, because Ed was in section A and Dave was in section B. Therefore, they were in complementary distribution as far as my classes went. For all I know, Dave may have occasionally come to section A and Ed to section B; if so I never knew the difference. But the next year they both were enrolled in the same section. Now I had to study the differences between them and learn to tell them apart. They were no longer in complementary distribution; instead, the linguist would say that they were **in contrast.** That is, they both appeared in the same environment and, therefore, had to be distinguished from one another. In the same way [l] and [r] are in contrast in English because both may come at the beginnings of words, and we must know the difference between *right* and *light*. But [l] and [ɫ] are not in contrast; if we accidentally say [ɫaɪt] instead of [laɪt] it may sound a bit odd, but no confusion or error will arise. One more illustration: at the beginning of any inning of a baseball game, the members of the two teams are in complementary distribution because one team is in the field and the other is in the dugout, except for the one player who is batting, and he stands in a position or "box" where no defensive player is allowed to stand. But as soon as a runner gets to first base, he and the first baseman are now in the same environment; they are in contrast. That is why the players of the home team wear white suits and the visiting team gray ones. Players, umpires, and spectators must have some visible contrast to distinguish baseman from base-runner.

The definition of a phoneme given on page 122 is incomplete in one regard. It needs to be slightly amended before it can be permanently adopted. The nature of the amendment will become clear if we select some more sample words from our transcription, this time words containing *voiceless bilabial stops*.

ˈʌpɪz (1)	stɑpˤ (4)	grɪp¯ (title)
spɹik (26)	pˤḷɛɪs (15, 18)	grɪp¯ (27)
grɪp (29)	grɪpˤ (24)	ʌp¯ (35)
ˈhæpəntˤə (39)	kˤʊup ˤ (20)	

Here we again have three phone-types: the unaspirated bilabial stop, [p]; the aspirated bilabial stop [pˤ]; and the unreleased bilabial stop, [p¯]. All three are voiceless, and they are the only three voiceless bilabial stops that occur in the passage, so there is no doubt about their phonetic similarity. But when we come to examine their distribution, we find that things do not work out quite so neatly as they did with the allophones of /l/. For instance, the name of Grip, the hero of the story, appears four times, once with [p], once with [pˤ], and twice with [p¯]. This is certainly not complementary distribution.

Neither is it contrast, however. The reason it is not is that *it makes no difference which one of the three we use*. No matter whether we say [grɪp] or [grɪpˤ] or [grɪp¯], it always refers to the same unfortunate rat. The only conclusion we can come to is that any of the three phone-types can appear at the end of a word. Phonemicists call this state of affairs **free variation**. To go back to one of our nonlinguistic illustrations, it is as though nobody cared which twin was enrolled in my class. Sometimes Ed would come and sometimes Dave; I would simply call them both "Mr. Smith" and not try to tell them apart. They would then be in free variation. Two allophones which are in free variation can belong to the same phoneme with no difficulty. We can then revise our temporary definition slightly, and this time produce a final:

Definition: A phoneme is a group of phone-types which are phonetically similar and either in complementary distribution or in free variation.

CONSONANT PHONEMES

The process of finding out and formulating the phonemic structure of a language consists of applying the tests of phonetic similarity, complementary distribution, and free variation to all the phone-types of the language, combining them wherever the circumstances permit into phonemes. Sometimes a single phone-type has to be set apart as a phoneme by itself; in that case the phoneme has only one allophone. Sometimes a phoneme may have eight or ten or more allophones. There is no rule governing the number; it is entirely a matter of the organization of the language itself. The phonemicist does not create or arbitrarily set up the phonemes; he merely tries to discover what sets of phone-types native speakers unconsciously recognize as being members of the same phoneme. Thus, if you ask a native speaker of English, untrained in phonetics, if the first and last sounds of *lull* are "the same," he will probably say that they are, though as phoneticians we know that one is [l] and the other [ɬ] or even [L].

Since phonemes usually are families of two or more phone-types, we would expect that in any language there are fewer phonemes than there are phone-types. This is indeed the case. In American English, virtually all dialects fit into a phonemic system of twenty-four consonants, nine vowels, four stresses, four pitches, and four junctures —a total of forty-five phonemes, of which thirty-three (vowels and consonants) are **segmental,** and twelve (stresses, pitches, and junctures) **suprasegmental.** We shall now take these up in order, with a brief look at their various allophones primarily in the dialects of the Midland, the Middle West, and the Far West. Apologies are offered to New Englanders, New Yorkers, and Southerners for apparently slighting their dialects. Our choice is not meant to imply that the dialects discussed are standard or in any way superior to those neglected. The dialects selected, which are sometimes lumped together under the inaccurate title "General American," are chosen for three reasons: they are spoken by a majority of Americans; they are fairly homogeneous; as a native Pennsylvanian, the author is more familiar with them. Amends will be made to the other dialects, it is hoped, in Chapter 9, "The Dialects of American English."

The twenty-four consonant phonemes comprise six stops, two affricates, four fricatives, four sibilants, three nasals, one lateral, and four semivowels. Let us look at them one by one; again, as with the phone-types in Chapter 2, we will number them in series.

STOPS. There are three pairs of stop phonemes, each pair consisting of one fortis voiceless phoneme and one lenis voiced. The three pairs are the bilabial, the apico-alveolar, and the dorso-velar. We will take up the voiceless ones first, then the voiced.[1]

---

[1] The order followed in the discussion of consonant-phonemes is that of the list in G. L. Trager and H. L. Smith, *An Outline of English Structure* (Norman, Oklahoma: Battenburg Press, 1951), p. 35. Since this is the most up-to-date and compendious treatment of English phonemics, and since it seems well on the way to general acceptance as the standard treatment, it has been followed quite closely in this chapter, though there are numerous departures from it in matters of detail.

1. *The voiceless bilabial stop*, /p/, we have already looked at, sufficiently to observe that it has three principal allophones, unaspirated [p], aspirated [pʻ], and unreleased [p⁻], which are in free variation in final position. We may further observe that in word-initial position we find [pʻ], while after initial [s] we have [p], as in *speak* [spɹik]. In syllable-initial position before stressed vowels we have [pʻ], as in *apart* [əˈpʻaɚt]; before unstressed vowels [p], as in *happen* [ˈhæpən]. Two more allophones of /p/ that sometimes occur are nasally released [pᴺ] before nasals and laterally released [pˡ] before laterals, as in *help 'em* [ˈhɛɫpᴺm̩] and *apple* [ˈæpˡ].

2. *The voiceless apico-alveolar stop*, /t/, has three allophones, [t], [tʻ], and [t⁻], whose distribution corresponds to that of the principal allophones of /p/. Thus [t] occurs after [s], in word-final position, and in syllable-final position when the next syllable begins with a consonant; in these last two positions [t] is in free variation with [t⁻]. Examples are *stop* [stɑp], *hat* [hæt] or [hæt⁻], and *outgo* [ˈaʊtˌgoʊ] or [ˈaʊt⁻ˌgoʊ]. Some speakers may also have the combination [ʔt⁻] or even just [ʔ] in syllable-final or word-final position, as in *cat* [kʻæʔt⁻] and *button* [bʌʔn̩]. [tʻ] occurs in initial position before stressed vowels, and in free variation with [t] before unstressed. As in the case of /p/, we may have nasally and laterally released allophones of /t/.

A phonemic problem is presented by a group of phone-types, [t̪], [t̬], and [ɾ], which occur between vowels, in the position called **ambisyllabic** because it belongs partly to each of the syllables on either side. Actually, a sound-change is probably occurring at this point in most American dialects, which may result in these becoming allophones of /d/. Some phonemicists put them there now,[2] or class them as belonging to both /t/ and /d/. We may count them as allophones of /t/ for a large number, perhaps a majority, of American

---

[2] See Victor A. Oswald, Jr., "Voiced 't'—a Misnomer," *American Speech*, XVIII (1943), 18–25, and W. P. Lehmann, "A Note on the Change of American English /t/," *American Speech*, XXVIII (1953), 271–75.

English speakers, but with the reservation that both variation and change can be expected at this critical point. Note that in British English [ɨ] is an allophone not of /t/ or /d/ but of /r/.

Thus, the /t/ phoneme comprises a rather large group of allophones: [t, tˤ, t̄, ˀt̄, ˀ, ʈ, t̬, ɨ, tᴺ, tˡ][3].

3. *The voiceless dorsovelar stop*, /k/, has allophones [k, kˤ, k̄, kᴺ, kˡ] in much the same distributional pattern as the similar allophones of /p/, as in *kick* [kˤɪk] or [kˤɪk̄]; *acknowledge* [əkᴺˈnɑɫɪj] and *acclaim* [əˈkˡlɛɪm]. A lenis version, [k̬], is often heard between unstressed vowels, as in *significant* [sɪgˈnɪfɪk̬ənt]; for many speakers this is indistinguishable from the [g] of *elegant*, and should thus be assigned to /g/. In the company of front vowels, all the allophones of /k/ are considerably fronted, and in back-vowel environment they are retracted. These can be phonetically written [k̟], [k̠], etc., if desired; phonemically they are all allophones of /k/.

4. The *voiced bilabial stop*, /b/, has the allophones [b, b̄, b̥, bᴺ, bˡ]. Of these, [b] may appear anywhere, so the others are in free variation with it in one position or another. Thus [b̥], more accurately written [p͡b] or [b͡p], may be initial or final; [b̄] may be word- or syllable-final; [bᴺ] and [bˡ] are syllable-final before nasals and laterals respectively.

5. The *voiced apico-alveolar stop*, /d/, has the allophones [d, d̄, d̥, dᴺ, dˡ], distributed like the allophones of /b/. As has already been suggested, in those dialects where no distinction is made between *latter* and *ladder*, [t̬], [t̬], and [ɨ] must be classed as allophones of /d/ rather than of /t/.

6. The *voiced dorso-velar stop*, /g/, has a set of allophones parallel to those of /b/ and /d/: [g, ḡ, g̥, gᴺ, gˡ], in similar distribution. All of them may occur in fronted or retracted versions, depending on the neighboring vowels.

---

[3] [ˀ] is an allophone of /t/ only in final or preconsonantal position. When it comes before a vowel, it is best considered a special type of vowel onset. Thus [ˀæ] is in free variation with [æ] in word-initial position.

AFFRICATES. Concerning the treatment of the phone-types [č, čʻ] and [ǰ, ǰ] phonemicists differ. One theory is that these affricates may be phonemically treated as compound sounds, composed in the one case of allophones of /t/ + allophones of /š/, and in the other of /d/ + /ž/. The other theory is that they must be set up as independent phonemes because the central sound of *why choose* [ˌwaɪˈčʊuz] is in contrast with the central pair of sounds in *white shoes* [ˌwaɪtˈšʊuz]. A good case may be put up for either side; we will throw in our lot with the adherents of the second theory, who include the proponents of what is, at present at least, the most widely accepted treatment of English phonemics.[4] We thus recognize two affricate phonemes, one fortis voiceless and one lenis voiced.

7. The *voiceless apico-alveolar affricate*, /č/, has two principal allophones, unaspirated [č] and aspirated [čʻ]. These are in free variation in initial position; elsewhere [č] appears.

8. The *voiced apico-alveolar affricate*, /ǰ/, has three allophones, [ǰ], [ǰ̥], and [ǰ̥]. The last two can both be written [ǰ], with the understanding that either the first or last part of the sound is unvoiced, depending on whether it is initial or final. Of these three, [ǰ] may appear in all positions; initially, it is in free variation with [ǰ̥] and finally, with [ǰ̥]. Thus, *judge* can variously be [ǰʌǰ], [ǰ̥ʌǰ], [ǰʌǰ̥], or [ǰ̥ʌǰ̥]. Phonemically these are all written /ǰəǰ/. In at least one dialect—that of many bilingual speakers of Pennsylvania Dutch and English—this phoneme is missing, being regularly replaced by /č/.

FRICATIVES AND SIBILANTS. The four fricative phonemes of English are two labio-dentals and two apico-dentals; there are also two apico-alveolar and two fronto-palatal sibilants. In all cases, one of each pair is fortis and voiceless and the other is lenis and voiced.

9. The *voiceless labio-dental fricative*, /f/, has two allophones, [f] and [ɸ]. Of these two, [f] may appear in all positions; it is in free variation with [ɸ] following bilabial consonants, as in *comfort*

[4] Trager and Smith, *op. cit.*

[ˈkˈʌmɸət] and *cupful* [ˈkˈʌp⁻ɸʊɫ], alternating with [ˈkˈʌmfət] and [ˈkˈʌp⁻fʊɫ].

10. The *voiceless apico-dental fricative*, /θ/, has only the single allophone [θ] in most dialects. This allophone may appear in all positions.

11. The *voiceless apico-alveolar sibilant*, /s/, also has a single allophone [s], which may appear in all positions. Different speakers may have varying versions of this sound, but these must be counted as individual or dialectal variations, not allophonic ones.

12. The *voiceless fronto-palatal sibilant*, /š/, also has the single allophone [š], appearing in all word positions.

13. The *voiced labiodental fricative*, /v/, has four allophones, [v], [β], [f͡v], and [v͡f]. Of these, [v] may appear in all positions. It is in free variation with [f͡v] (also written [v̯]) initially; with [v͡f] (also [v̯]) finally; and with [β] after bilabials.

14. The *voiced apicodental fricative*, /ð/, has three principal allophones, [ð], [θ͡ð], and [ð͡θ], whose distribution parallels that of the main allophones of /v/. That is, [ð] and [θ͡ð] are in free variation initially, and [ð] and [ð͡θ] finally; elsewhere only [ð] appears.

A bit of a problem for the phonemicist is posed by a set of sound-groups in our transcription which, as native speakers, we recognize as representing what we write as *in the* or *on the*. They are

ɪnðə (12)	ɪnn̪ə (25)	ɪŋ̪:ə (12)
ɒnðə (16)		ɪŋ̪:ə (13)
		ɪŋ̪:ə (19)

There is no question about those in the first column; they clearly have /n/ + /ð/ between the vowels. But what about [ɪnn̪ə], with apico-alveolar [n] followed by apico-dental [n̪]? On grounds of phonetic similarity, [n̪] can be allied with either [n] or [ð], since it shares nasal quality with [n] and apicodental articulation with [ð]. Distribution leads us to class it with [ð], however, since the whole group [ɪnn̯ə] is clearly in free variation with [ɪnðə]. We therefore establish [n̯] as another allophone of /ð/.

This solution guides us to the answer to the problem of [n̯:], which appears in the words in the third column. These also are in free variation with [ɪnðə] and [ɪnn̯ə]. Therefore, we analyze the long [n̯:] as being composed of [n] + [n̯], hence as representing /nð/ phonemically.

Observe that both [ɪnn̯ə] and [ɪn̯:ə] are plainly in contrast with [ɪnə] (23), which has simple [n], an allophone of /n/, between the vowels. Since it has only the single short sound in this position, it must be interpreted phonemically as /inə/, which we write *in a* in conventional orthography.

We thus add [n̯] to the list of allophones of /ð/. Its distribution is quite limited, since in the transcription it appears only between [n] and unstressed [ə]. Further observation would also reveal that it sometimes occurs between [n] and other unstressed or medium stressed vowels, as in *in this* [ɪnn̯ɪs] and *in that* [ɪnn̯æt].

15. The *voiced apico-alveolar sibilant*, /z/, has three principal allophones, [z], [ŝẑ], and [ẑš], whose distribution is parallel to that of the three main allophones of /v/ and /ð/. There is some question as to what to do with the lenis [s̬] which some speakers have in final position after vowels and voiced consonants. If this is in contrast with [s], as in such a pair as *lees: lease*, it is to be considered another allophone of /z/, in free variation with [z] and [ẑš].

16. The *voiced fronto-palatal sibilant*, /ž/, has two allophones, [ž] and [ẑš] (or [ž̧]). This phoneme has incomplete distribution. It never occurs in word- or syllable-initial position.[5] [ž] appears between vowels, as in *measure* [ˈmɛžɚ], and is in free variation with [ẑš] in final position in a few words like *rouge* [ruʊž] or [ruʊẑš].

NASALS. The three nasal phonemes of English are the bilabial, the apico-alveolar, and the dorso-velar.

---

[5] Except in learned pronunciation of French words; see page 78.

17. The *bilabial nasal*, /m/, has one principal allophone, [m]. As we noted in Chapter 2 (p. 82), a labiodental nasal, [ɱ], is sometimes heard before [f] and [v]; this may be classed as another allophone of /m/ in free variation with [m] before labio-dentals. We should also note that a longer version, [m·], may appear in final position. The extra-long [m:] heard in such compounds as *home-made* is phonemically /m/+/m/. Syllabic [m̩] is phonemically treated as /əm/ or /im/, for reasons which will be discussed later on.

18. The *apico-alveolar nasal*, /n/, has one principal allophone, [n]. As with /m/, a longer version, [n·], may appear finally. The extra-long [n:] of *penknife* is phonemically /n/+/n/. Voiceless [n̥] is sometimes heard between initial [s] and following vowel, as in [sn̥ɪp], and in some other environments; it is always in free variation with [n]. Syllabic [n̩], like [m̩], is phonemically treated as /ən/ or /in/. We have already seen that the apico-dental nasal [n̪] may be considered an allophone of /ð/.

19. The *dorsovelar nasal*, /ŋ/, has one main allophone, [ŋ], which is of limited distribution. It never appears in word- or syllable-initial position; it is always either word- or syllable-final or intervocalic, as in *singer* [ˈsɪŋɚ], or preconsonantal, as in *link* [lɪŋk]. As with the other nasals, it has a longer version, [ŋ·], which may appear in word-final position, as in *song* [sɔŋ·]. Like the other dorso-velar consonants /k/ and /g/, it has a fronted version, which can be phonetically written [ŋ̟], and a retracted version, [ŋ̠]; their distribution is determined by the neighboring vowel. Syllabic [ŋ̩] is phonemically /əŋ/ or /iŋ/; this will be discussed later on.

20. The *lateral* phoneme /l/ has already been discussed. Its allophone [l] appears in word- and syllable-initial position and after voiced consonants. [ɫ] appears in syllable- and word-final position, intervocalically, as in *spelling* [ˈspɛɫɪŋ], and between a vowel and following consonant. Some dialects or speakers have [L] in these positions, either always or in free variation with [ɫ]. [l̥] appears only between a voiceless consonant and following vowel.

SEMIVOWELS. The four semivowel phonemes are the retroflex /r/, the labiovelar /w/, the frontal /y/, and the central /h/.

21. The *retroflex semivowel*, /r/, varies considerably in the nature and distribution of its allophones from dialect to dialect, and to a lesser degree between individual speakers of the same dialect. Therefore, it is not possible to make a general statement that will be valid for the majority of speakers of American English. The best that can be done at this point is to describe the state of affairs in the author's own eastern Midland dialect and note a few variations. The phonemics of the so-called "*r*-less" dialects will be touched on in our treatment of vowel phonemes later on in this chapter, and will occupy us more fully in Chapter 9.

In the first place, we may take note of the allophone [r], which we described in Chapter 2 (p. 86) as a *voiced apico-alveolar retroflex semivowel*. It occurs commonly in initial position and between an initial /b/ or /g/ and following vowel, as in *red, brown, green* [rɛd, braṵn, grɪ̣in]. Between /p, f, θ, š, k/ and a following vowel, [r] may be in free variation with its voiceless counterpart, [r̥]. After /t/, many speakers use a voiceless alveolar retroflex fricative [ɹ̥], and after /d/ its voiced counterpart [ɹ]. Examples are *trick* [t͡ɹ̥ɪk] and *drunk* [d̄ɹʌŋk].

Nonsyllabic [ɚ], which occurs as the off-glide of some of the centering diphthongs, is phonetically similar to the other allophones of /r/ and in complementary distribution with them. That is, [r, r̥, ɹ̥, ɹ] always occur before vowels, and [ɚ] always occurs after them. Therefore, it meets the requirements for an allophone of /r/ and will be so treated.

Syllabic [ɚ] is exactly parallel in its distribution to syllabic [m̩, n̩, l̩] and, like them, can be phonemically analyzed as /ə/ or /ɨ/ + semivowel, i.e., /ər/ or /ɨr/. Thus, there are five allophones of /r/ in the author's dialect: [r, r̥, ɹ, ɹ̥, ɚ]. All of them are phonemically written /r/.

The case of labiovelar [w̥] (p. 88) presents no problems. It is an individual or dialectal variant, appearing instead of any or all of the other allophones in the speech of some regions or speakers. In a few cases its labiovelar quality may be so prominent as to make it indistinguishable from [w]; for such speakers, it must be classed as an allophone of /w/.

22. The *labiovelar semivowel*, /w/, has a group of allophones which can be described as very short nonsyllabic high or higher mid back round vowels, acting either as on-glides before vowels or as off-glides following them. Thus, *dwindle* and *woo* can be phonetically written [ˈdu̯ɪndɫ̩], [u̯ou̯]; *wade*, *wed*, and *woad* are [o̯eɪd], [o̯ɛd], [o̯oo̯d]; *wad* is [ɔ̯ad] or [ɔ̯ɒd]. In each of these words, the first sound is a nonsyllabic round back vowel, somewhat higher than the syllabic vowel. Thus [u̯] is higher than [ɪ] and [ʊ]; [o̯] is higher than [e], [ɛ], and [o], and [ɔ̯] is higher than [a] and [ɒ]. These three nonsyllabic vowels, [u̯, o̯, ɔ̯], are thus in complementary distribution in prevocalic position. As high round back vowels they are phonetically similar. They may thus be grouped together as allophones of a single phoneme, which we can call /w/.

When we examine the nonsyllabic vowels which act as off-glides in the retracting diphthongs (p. 108) we find the same three, [u̯, o̯, ɔ̯], also either in complementary distribution or in free variation. They thus fulfil all the requirements of allophones, and we can now write the retracting diphthongs phonemically as /uw, ow, aw/, and so forth, remembering that the /w/ stands for one of the higher back round vowels as an off-glide.

The case of [ʍ] in those dialects that distinguish *Wales* from *whales* presents somewhat of a phonemic problem. It can be set up as a separate phoneme, appearing only in syllable-initial position or after an initial voiceless consonant. This is a simple solution, but not wholly satisfactory. On the other hand, we cannot call [ʍ] simply an allophone of /w/, because it is in contrast with various other allophones of /w/ in pairs like *wheel–weal*, *when–wen*, etc. But a re-examination, or a relistening, suggests a solution. In the speech of those who distinguish *wheel* and *weal*, the former of these not only has initial [w̥]; it also has considerable aspiration, producing some glottal, pharyngeal, or oral friction, along with it. Thus, it should properly be written [ẘ], as distinct from the unaspirated [w̥] sometimes heard in *quick* [kʿwɪk]. We can thus treat [w̥] as an allophone of /w/, and the aspiration that accompanies it in initial position as a simultaneous occurrence of [h]. Thus [ẘ] can be phonemically written /hw/.

The allophones of /w/, then, are [u̯, ʊ̯, o̯, w̥].

23. The *frontal semivowel*, /y/, presents a parallel case to that of /w/. This time the allophones are the nonsyllabic higher front vowels [i̯, ɪ̯, e̯, ɛ̯], which may appear as on-glides in *yip* [i̯ɪp], *Yale* [ɪe̯ɪl], *yoke* [e̯oʊk], and so on. These are the same sounds that appear as the off-glides of the fronting diphthongs (p. 108). We may thus treat them all as allophones of one phoneme, /y/.[6] A very high fronto-palatal glide is sometimes heard in those dialects which have an undiphthongal [i] in words like *yield, yeast*. Phonetically, this may be written either [i̯ᵀ] or [j]. In any case, it is clearly an allophone of /y/.

The principal allophones of /y/, then, are [j, i̯, ɪ̯, e̯, ɛ̯].

24. The *central semivowel*, /h/, presents a set of allophones on the whole parallel to those of /w/ and /y/. In words like *heat, hate, hoot, hole, haunt*, the initial sound is actually a voiceless nonsyllabic vowel with accompanying friction-noise, constituting an on-glide which is in all cases more central than the syllabic vowel. In phonetics it was convenient to emphasize the fricative nature of these sounds and to classify them as a single glottal fricative (p. 78). But for purposes of phonemic analysis, the vowel-like aspect of these sounds allows us to handle them in much the same way we did /w/ and /y/. Thus we could write the words listed above [i̥it, e̥ɪt, u̥ʊt,

---

[6] The objection to using y as a *phonetic* character for IPA [j], made on page 88, does not apply to *phonemics*, where we are free to choose the characters most commonly used in the standard orthography.

ɜ̣⁺oʊ̣ɫ] and [ᵇ̣ɔ·nt], in which the initial sounds have the diacritics for aspiration, voicelessness, and nonsyllabicity. The nonsyllabic vowels are thus *aspirated central on-glides*, and can all be treated as allophones of one phoneme /h/. Similarly, the off-glides of the centering diphthongs of *idea, yeah, boa*, and many words in the "*r*-less" dialects, since they are also nonsyllabic central vowels, may also be treated as allophones of /h/. The fact that they lack the friction characteristic of the on-glide allophones need not disturb us, since they are still phonetically similar to them and in complementary distribution with them.

In our treatment of phonetics, we recognized a sound [ɦ] which was like [h] except for the addition of murmur-voice (p. 78). This too can be considered as a group of murmured nonsyllabic central vowels accompanied by friction noise and, hence, as a further group of allophones of /h/.

/h/, thus, has a large group of allophones, all nonsyllabic central vowels, either voiceless or murmured, and either with or without glottal, pharyngeal, or oral friction-noise.

CONSONANT SUMMARY. The twenty-four consonant phonemes of American English may now be brought together in the following summary list:

Six stops: /p, t, k, b, d, g/
Two affricates: /č, ǰ/
Four fricatives: /f, θ, v, ð/
Four sibilants: /s, š, z, ž/
Three nasals: /m, n, ŋ/
One lateral: /l/
Four semivowels: /r, w, y, h/.

VOWEL PHONEMES

The system of twenty-four consonant phonemes which we have presented in the preceding section is shared by virtually all dialects.

The differences between dialects in the use of consonants are principally of two sorts: (1) variation in the nature and distribution of
the allophones of the different phonemes, and (2) some variation
in the distribution of the phonemes themselves. But virtually all of
them use the same set of twenty-four phonemes.

When it comes to vowels, the situation at first seems more complex.
Our vowel quadrangle on page 98 presented eighteen vowel-types;
allowing eight possible shift signs or pairs of shift signs for each
raises the number to 162; four degrees of length increase the possibilities to 648; rounding of the front and central vowels and un-
rounding of the back vowels doubles this number to 1296; nasalization again doubles the number to 2592. With all these possibilities,
how are we ever to find a phonemic system that will accommodate
the main dialects without being hopelessly complicated?

Yet, so efficient is the organization of language that such a system
has been discovered. In the form worked out by the linguists G. L.
Trager and H. L. Smith,[7] it is an exceedingly simple one, containing
nine vowel phonemes. These can best be examined together first,
arranged in a symmetrical pattern which is simply a more formalized
version of the vowel quadrangle.

	Front	Central	Back
High	i	ɨ	u
Mid	e	ə	o
Low	æ	a	ɔ

The allophones of these nine phonemes, either by themselves or
in combination with the semivowel phonemes /r, w, y, h/, make up

[7] In *An Outline of English Structure.*

the syllabic nuclei of most of the dialects of American English. We shall first take up the simple vowels, then go on to the various combinations. Again, the first examples will be drawn from the "General American" dialects. Later we will see how other dialectal forms fit the pattern.

1. The *high front vowel, /i/,* has as its allophones the various versions of [ɪ]—raised, lowered, fronted, retracted, nasalized, lengthened —that may be heard in such words as *bit, bid, window, will, sister.* Note that while these are phonetically represented by the IPA character [ɪ] with various diacritics, we can represent them *phonemically* by the more readily available /i/. Thus, our five sample words will be phonemically written /bit, bid, window, wil, sistər/. It is of interest to note that this phonemic spelling departs only twice from the standard spelling, which really means that the standard spelling of these five words is nearly phonemic. We shall not always be so lucky.

2. The *mid front vowel, /e/,* has as its allophones the various raised, lowered, fronted, retracted, nasalized, and partially lengthened versions of [ɛ], as in *bet, bed, bend, bell, best.* These words may thus be phonemically written /bet, bed, bend, bel, best/. Again we choose the more available e rather than ɛ, and again we find the standard spellings almost exactly phonemic.

3. The *low front vowel, /æ/,* has the various versions of [æ] as its allophones, though in those dialects which distinguish *can* [kʻæᶥ·n] from [kʻæn], the raised and lengthened [æᶥ·] is in contrast with [æ] and must therefore be separately considered. As we shall see, it works out to be /æh/. In some dialects [a] may also be an allophone of /æ/. Words illustrating the various allophones of /æ/ are *bat, bass* (fish), *back, lad,* and so forth. These are phonemically written /bæt, bæs, bæk, læd/. This time we cannot use the *a* of the standard spelling, since it is needed for the low central vowel phoneme.

4. The *high central vowel, /i/,* has as its allophones various unround high and high mid central vowels, variants of [ɨ], [ɨ], [ɜ], and [ɚ].

It is rare as a stressed vowel, but quite common as an unstressed vowel and as the syllabic of diphthongs in many dialects. In some Southern speech it is the regular syllabic of words like *wish*, *sister*, *Christmas*, *milk*, *children*, *dinner*, that have /i/ in other dialects.

5. The *mid central vowel*, /ə/, has as its allophones various versions of [ʌ], [ə], and [ɐ]. The [ʌ] allophone with its raised, fronted, and lengthened variants is the usual syllabic vowel of *cut*, *bud*, *rung*, and often of *hurry*; these words can be phonemically written /kət, bəd, rəŋ, həriy/. The various versions of [ə] appear in unstressed positions very frequently, varying from one dialect to another and from one set of words to another with allophones of /i/, /ɨ/, and even /iy/. The distribution of these unstressed vowels is very complex, and no general rule can be laid down for them. Some linguists have even suggested a separate phonemic system for the unstressed vowels.[8] But as far as basic phonemic analysis goes, this is unnecessary; they fit perfectly well into the nine-vowel system. The question of how they are distributed in various words by various speakers is a matter of morphophonemics or dialectology and hence not our present concern.

The [ɐ]-type allophones of /ə/ are heard principally as syllabic nuclei of diphthongs, especially in certain districts of the coastal South.

6. The *low central vowel*, /a/, has as its allophones the various versions of [ɑ], raised, fronted, and retracted. [a] may also be an allophone of /a/, or may belong to /æ/, depending on the over-all phonemic pattern of the dialect. /a/ is the syllabic phoneme of the "short-o words" for the great majority of speakers of American English who do not have a low back rounded vowel in these words; examples are *not*, *box*, *rod*, *lost*, *soft*, *cloth*, and so on. For such

[8] See Nathaniel M. Caffee, "The Phonemic Structure of Unstressed Vowels in English," *American Speech*, XXVI (1951), 103–9; also Allan F. Hubbell, "The Phonemic Analysis of Unstressed Vowels," *American Speech*, XXV (1950), 105–11.

speakers these words are phonemically /nat, baks, rad, last, saft, klaθ/. Others have /ɔ/ in some or all of these words.

7. The *high back vowel*, /u/, has for its allophones the various versions of [ʊ]. It is the syllabic vowel of *push, pull, put*, and similar words. It often appears in unstressed or semistressed position in words like *today* /tudéy/. It is also the syllabic of a group of words spelled with *oo*, such as *good* and *hood*. Many other words of this group, such as *food*, have /uw/, and still others vary between the two in very complicated patterns. Some of the test words here are *roof, hoof, coop, hoop, Cooper, room, broom, soot, root, soon*.

8. The *mid back vowel*, /o/, has as its allophones various versions of [o], lax, fronted, raised, and lowered. In most American dialects it is rare or missing as a stressed syllabic, appearing only in semi-stressed or unstressed position or as the syllabic element in diphthongs. Some speakers, including the author, have it in *whole* /hol/, as distinct from *hole* /howl/. It is relatively common in eastern New England as the syllabic vowel of *won't, coat, boat, home*, and similar words.

9. The *low back vowel*, /ɔ/, has as its allophones various versions of [ɒ] and [ɔ]. It is the vowel of *water* for many speakers who do not have /a/ in that word. It is also the syllabic of the "short-o words," especially before /f, s, θ/, for many American English speakers, and of *on* in the south Midland and Southeast. It is also important as the syllabic element of diphthongs.

Not all speakers have all nine of these vowels as regular syllabic nuclei. In fact, most people have only six or seven of them in large numbers of words; the other two or three may be missing entirely, or present in just a few words, sometimes under special conditions of stress. But virtually all the simple syllabic vowels that do occur in the speech of any region or individual will be found to fit into this nine-vowel system.[9] The remaining syllabics are various forms

---

[9] Certain dialects, especially in the Southeast, make use of a tenth vowel, a retracted low front between /æ/ and /a/.

of diphthongs, consisting of one or another of these nine vowels plus one or more semivowels. We can now have a look at some of these.

FRONTING DIPHTHONGS

We have seen that the fronting diphthongs are formed by one of a large choice of syllabic vowels followed by a high front off-glide. (p. 107). We have also seen that the various off-glides can all be treated as allophones of /y/ (p. 137). The syllabics may also be assigned to phonemes. We find that those which fall in the shaded area of the diagram shown on page 107 include allophones of all nine vowels. Therefore, all nine theoretically possible fronting diphthongs may occur; they are /iy, ey, æy, ay, uy, ɔy, oy, ɨy, əy/. Of these, the most common in "General American" speech are /iy/ as in *beat* /biyt/; /ey/ as in *bait* /beyt/; /ay/ as in *bite* /bayt/; /oy/ as in *boy* /boy/. The others occur in various dialects. The author has [ɐɪ] in *right* and [ɑ·ɛ̣] in *ride*, a pattern not uncommon in eastern and southern parts of the country. These can be phonemically treated as /əy/ and /ay/, so that the sample words are /rəyt/ and /rayd/. Southern dialects often have something like [æ·ɪ̣] in words like *pants*, *Daddy*; this is phonemically /æy/. In the author's speech, *buoy* has /uy/, while for others this word is homophonous with *boy*. The diphthong /uy/ is also used in words like *push* by some Middle Western speakers, who will also use /ɔy/ in *wash*. The diphthong [ɨɪ] commonly heard in *me*, *see* in the Philadelphia area is phonemically /ɨy/. Diphthongs of the type [ɨɪˑ], [ɜɪ] heard in such words as *bird* in New York City and parts of the South, can be classed as /əy/ or /ɨy/, depending on the other types of diphthongs present in the dialect. Thus for a dialect which has the [ɐɪ] type of diphthong in words like *right* and the [ɜɪ] type in *bird*, the first is phonemically /əy/ and the second /ɨy/. For a dialect which does not have the [ɐɪ] type of diphthong, the [ɜɪ] of *bird* will be phonemically /əy/. This does not mean that the phonemicist manipulates his symbols at will; it simply means that he is observing the essential principle of phonemics, that phone-types which are in contrast must belong to different phonemes. The assignment of phone-types to various phonemes can be done only on the basis of the whole phonemic structure of the dialect. That is why we can give only very general statements here.

No single dialect, then, has all nine of the phonemically possible fronting diphthongs. But by selecting from various dialects, we can give examples of the whole repertory:

/iy/ "General American" *beat.*

/ey/ "General American" *bait.*

/æy/ Southern *pants*; southern Middle Western *ash.*

/ɨy/ New York City, Louisiana *bird*; Philadelphia *me.*

/əy/ various dialects, including Ontario, *like.*

/ay/ "General American" *ride.*

/uy/ *buoy*; southern Middle West *push.*

/oy/ *boy* for many speakers.

/ɔy/ *boy* for others; southern Middle West *wash.*

RETRACTING DIPHTHONGS

We saw in our discussion of phonetics that the retracting diphthongs are characterized by a syllabic nucleus followed by a high back round off-glide. The off-glide, we have seen (p. 136), can be phonemically classified as /w/. Therefore, there are nine possible retracting diphthongs: /iw, ew, æw, ɨw, əw, aw, uw, ow, ɔw/. Again not all of these are present in any one dialect. The most common ones are /uw/ as in *boot* /buwt/; /æw/ or /aw/ in *bout* /bæwt, bawt/; and /ow/ in *boat* /bowt/. The others are to be found in one or another dialect. Thus, the author has /ɨw/ in *duke, Tuesday*; this diphthong also occurs in some Midland versions of words like *food, moon*, which have /uw/ for most other speakers. Some New Englanders and some from the South have /iw/ in *duke, Tuesday, lute,* and the like (most Southerners have the triphthong /yuw/ in these words). /ew/ is rare in American English, but some eastern speakers have it in *go, so,* etc., perhaps in conscious imitation of British English. /əw/ is regular before voiceless consonants, as in *out, house,* in eastern Virginia, contrasting with /æw/ in final position or before voiced consonants, as in *cow, houses, crowd.* Many Middle Western and Canadian speakers have /aw/ in the pronunciation of both *out* and *crowd.* /ɔw/ appears in words like *law* in the southeastern part of the country.

Thus, we can make up the complete repertory of retracting diphthongs by again drawing on various dialects:

/iw/ New England *duke.*

/ew/ British and some eastern U.S. *go.*

/æw/ New England, Midland, Southern *cow, crowd.*

/ɨw/ South Midland and northern South *duke.*

/əw/ Eastern Virginia *out.*

/aw/ Midland *out, crowd.*

/uw/ *boot.*

/ow/ *boat.*

/ɔw/ Southeastern *law.*

CENTERING DIPHTHONGS AND TRIPHTHONGS

The centering diphthongs fall into two groups, depending on the nature of the off-glide: (1) those with a nonretroflex off-glide, which we have seen is phonemically /h/; and (2) those with a retroflex off-glide, phonemically /r/. The nature and distribution of these diphthongs varies widely from one dialect to another, the major differences being due to the absence of the retroflex off-glide in the "r-less" dialects of New England, New York City, and the South. We will first deal with the situation in the "General American" dialects that have /r/, and then attempt a general statement covering the situation in the "*r*-less" dialects.

(1) *Centering diphthongs with off-glide* /h/. Not many of the eight theoretically possible diphthongs in this group are found in the "General American" dialects. We may note that [ɪə] in *idea* and [iᵊɪᵊ] in *theater* both are phonemically /ih/. The widespread American affirmative "yeah" is phonemically /yeh/. Many speakers have this diphthong also in *man, hand, bad,* and so on. Others, including the author, have /æh/ in these words. Those who distinguish *can* "is able" from *can* "put into a can" have /æh/ or /eh/ in the latter and simple /æ/ in the former. /oh/ is rare; the only word at all common in which it appears is *boa,* though some New York City speakers have it in *law.*

Quite a few speakers of American English have long and short versions of the low central and low back vowels which are in contrast and must thus be phonemically distinguished. Examples are *cot–caught, balm–bomb, clod–clawed,* and so on. For many, of course, the syllabic vowels of these words may be different, *cot, balm, clod* having /a/ and *caught, bomb, clawed* having /ɔ/. But others distinguish primarily by length; this is thus an exception to our statement earlier that length is seldom significant in American English. Where this distinction exists, the long forms may be treated as centering diphthongs in /h/, even though they may have no perceptible off-glide. This is phonemically justifiable, though we cannot here go into the arguments behind it. In any case this gives us /ah/ in *balm, palm, calm,* and so on, and in some dialects in *caught, taught, clawed,* contrasting with *bomb* /bam/ and *cot, tot, clod* /kat, tat, klad/. In other dialects we have /ɔh/ in *caught,* contrasting with /ɔ/ in *cot,* and in still others there is no contrast at all.

These various possibilities may be brought together in a tabular form such as that which follows. This form shows the differing contrasts:

	/a/	/ah/	/ɔ/	/ɔh/
Dialect A	cot	caught		
	bomb	balm		
Dialect B	cot		caught	
	balm		bomb	
Dialect C			cot	caught
		balm	bomb	
Dialect D			cot	
			caught	
			balm	
			bomb	

The author's own speech, as reported in the transcription of "Grip the Rat," is of the "Dialect C" type. Still other contrasts exist.

(2) *Centering Diphthongs with off-glide* /r/. In the various "r-pronouncing dialects" of American English, all nine of the possible diphthongs in this group may be heard. In fact, all nine of them can be illustrated from the author's own predominantly eastern Pennsylvania dialect. Others may lack as many as four or five of the nine possiblities. The following list, then, is representative of eastern Midland speech:

/ir/ *mirror.*
/er/ *merry, ferry, Kerry, bury, berry.*
/ær/ *marry, carry.*
/ɨr/ *hurt, bird.*
/ər/ *hurry, flurry.*
/ar/ *cart, bard.*
/ur/ *jury.*
/or/ *story, fort, morbid.*
/ɔr/ *sorry.*

This still does not exhaust the list of syllabic nuclei in the "*r*-pro-nouncing" dialects of American English. We must still take account of a group of triphthongs, which have one of the three types of diphthongs followed by a further off-glide /r/. Six of the eight possibilities with vowel + /hr/ occur in the author's dialect, and the other two may be illustrated from other dialects. The complete list is as follows:

/ihr/   *dear, dearer.*
/ehr/   *bear, Mary, fairy, vary.*
/æhr/   *hairy,* when it contrasts with *marry* and *Mary.*
/ihr/   *furred,* contrasting with *Ferd.*
/əhr/   *worry,* contrasting with *hurry.*
/ahr/   *barred,* contrasting with *bard.*
/uhr/   *poor; Jewry* contrasting with *jury.*
/ohr/   *mourning, course,* contrasting with *morning, coarse.*
/ɔhr/   *morning, coarse.*

Of the theoretically possible triphthongs in vowel + /yr/ and vowel + /wr/, not many are often heard. The tendency is for these either to break into two syllables by developing the vowel /ə/ or /i/ between the /y, w/ and the /r/, or to simplify the nucleus by dropping the /y/ or /w/. Thus, in many persons' speech *fire* and similar words have /ayr/ in careful pronunciation, but in the stream of speech, especially when not under primary stress, they have /ar/. Similarly, *our* varies between /awr/ and /ar/. On the other hand, *flour* and *flower* tend to become /flawər/; in other persons' speech within the same dialect area, /flar/ or /flahr/ may also be heard. In the same way, *rower* is more often /rowər/ than /rowr/, in either case contrasting with *roar* /rohr/. The combination /ɔyr/ appears in the unusual word *coir*, which is hardly an active element in the vocabulary of many people.

The centering diphthongs in the "*r*-less" dialects are considerably simpler; in fact, there is only one series, with off-glide /h/. The following pattern is characteristic of speakers in the Boston area; it is quite similar to that of Received Standard British. New York City and parts of the South have similar patterns, though differing in details of distribution and in the nature of the allophones used.

/ih/   dear, idea, beard.
/eh/   dare, yeah, dared.
/æh/   (eastern New England far, barn).
/ɨh/   fur, bird.
/ah/   far, barn.
/uh/   poor.
/oh/   pour, boa, board; (Southern poor).
/ɔh/   pore, bored.

Speakers of "r-less" dialects have dissyllabic /ayə/ or /æyə/ in fire when they distinguish between fire and far, and either /awə/, /æwə/, or /ah/ in our, flour.

SYLLABIC CONSONANTS

We have seen in our discussion of phonetics that the nasals [m], [n], and [ŋ] and the lateral [ɬ] can all stand by themselves as syllabic nuclei, as in drop 'em [ˈdrɑpᴺm̩], button [ˈbʌtᴺn̩], bacon [ˈbɛɪkᴺŋ̩], bottle [ˈbɑtˤɬ]. These are all in free variation with forms having vowels: [ˈdrɑpəm, ˈbʌtɨn, ˈbɛɪkən, ˈbɑtəɬ]. Since this is the case, we can say that the syllabic quality of these consonants is an allophone of the unstressed vowels /ɨ/ and /ə/. The question of which vowel phoneme a given syllabic belongs to is a matter of dialect; thus, for some the alternative form of button may have [ə] rather than [ɨ] as above, and so on. In any case, this analysis guides us in interpreting the syllabic consonants as /ɨm, əm; ɨn, ən; ɨŋ, əŋ; ɨl, əl/, as the case may be.

A similar treatment of syllabic [ɚ] is also logical. We may consider this mid central retroflex vowel to be a composite of two allophones: the mid central vowel quality is an allophone of /ə/, and the retroflex quality is an allophone of /r/. All occurrences of [ɚ] as a syllabic nucleus can thus be treated as /ər/. The version with somewhat raised vowel [ɚ˔], common in *bird, word, turn*, etc., we have already analyzed as /ɨr/ (p. 147). When long, as in *furred*, it is /ɨhr/ (p. 148).

Other syllabic consonants that occasionally turn up in the stream of speech may be phonemically treated in the same way. Thus, in line 18 of our transcription of "Grip the Rat" (p. 117) we find [ˌwimṣt], which we can write phonemically /wiymɨst/. This treatment, quite justified by the structure of English, permits us to make the important generalization that, phonemically speaking, *every syllable has a single vowel, and every vowel is the nucleus of a syllable.*

VOWEL AND DIPHTHONG PHONEMES SUMMARIZED

The accompanying table supplies a phonemic framework into which the stressed syllabic nuclei of American English dialects may be fitted. Examples of all possibilities in the author's dialect have been filled in, the standard spelling appearing in the upper table and the phonemic spelling in the lower table. Every student should now make a similar table for his own dialect, and make lists of sample words for each position in the table which is illustrated in his speech. In that way he will familiarize himself with the vowel phonemes of his own speech.

SUPRASEGMENTAL PHONEMES

Before we can proceed to retranscribe the story of Grip in a phonemic transcription, we must take account of the suprasegmental phonemes of stress and pitch. This will be relatively simple, because we actually have used a phonemic rather than a phonetic approach to them from the beginning.

	V	V + y	V + w	V + h	V + r	V + h + r	V + y + r	V + w + r
i	bit	beat		idea	mirror	dearer		
e	bet	bait		yeah	merry	Mary		
æ	bat, lad		bout	bad, man	marry			flour
ɨ	just (unstressed)	(me)	duke		bird	burred		
ə	but	bite	(bout)		hurry	worry		
a	father	bide		calm	cart	starry	fire	
u	put	buoy	boot		jury	poor		
o	whole	boy	boat	boa	story	wore	coir	
ɔ	pot, log			caught, dog	sorry			
i	bit	biyt		aydíh	mírər	dihrər		
e	bet	beyt		yeh	mériy	méhriy		
æ	bæt, læd	(miy)	bæwt	bæhd, mæhn	mǽriy.			flæwr
ɨ	jɨst	bɨyt	diwk		bird	bihrd		
ə	bət	bəyt			hóriy	wóhriy		
a	fáðər	bayd	(bawt)	kahm	kart	stáhriy	fayr	
u	put	buy	buwt		júriy	puhr		
o	hol	boy	bowt	boh	stóriy	wohr	koyr	
ɔ	pɔt, lɔg			kɔht, dɔhg	sóriy			

These phonemes are called **suprasegmental** because they seem like an extra layer of structure, superposed on the basic **segmental** phonemes—the twenty-four consonants and nine vowels that we have been considering. Actually this is an illusion; it is no more possible to speak a sound (or phone) without stress of some sort than it is to breathe without expanding the lungs. The stress may be minimum, but it is there, since there is always more energy exerted in speaking than in remaining quiet. The stress is therefore an integral part of the segment.

The same may be said of pitch, at least in regard to voiced sounds. Pitch is an inevitable quality of sounds that have tone, as distinct from noise. Therefore, the voiced segments of speech, which are accompanied by glottal tone, are always spoken on one or another pitch, while the voiceless sounds never have any pitch at all. Yet, for purposes of analysis it is convenient to separate pitch and stress from the segmental phonemes as features that can be treated by themselves. In the same way we can talk about the *line* and the *color* in a painting, or the *rhythm* and the *melody* in a piece of music, though these qualities may actually be inextricably bound up together. If we keep this in mind, we may use the term *suprasegmental phonemes* for pitch and stress without unduly misrepresenting the facts.

STRESS. In phonetics we recognized four degrees of stress: a strongest, which we marked [ˈ]; a strong, which we marked [ˈ]; a medium, which we marked [ˌ]; and zero or unstressed, which we left unmarked. These four degrees of stress are actually phonemes, whose allophones are the various minute gradations of stress perceptible in actual speech. Stress phonemes are established in much the same way segmental phonemes are: by studying distribution and contrast. Several independent studies have come to the same conclusion: that there are four distinct phonemes of stress in English. Some phonemicists, however, distinguish only three, or treat the completely unstressed condition as the absence of any stress phoneme.

But for reasons given above, it seems best to consider totally unstressed syllables as representing a phoneme of minimum stress,
rather than none at all.

For purposes of transcription and description, we could perfectly
well use in phonemics the same sets of symbols and terms for the
four stresses that we use in phonetics. Unfortunately for consistency,
however, the prevailing systems now in use employ a slightly different
set of names and a new set of symbols. No doubt this duplication
will eventually be eliminated, but for the present we must simply
learn a new set of habits for phonemic transcription.

In phonemics, then, the strongest stress is called *primary*, and is
marked by the acute accent, /´/, above the character representing
the nucleus of the stressed syllable. The next strongest stress,
secondary, is marked by the circumflex accent, /ˆ/; then the *tertiary*
stress, marked by the grave accent, /`/. Weakest or *zero* stress is
left unmarked, as in phonetics, or may be indicated by /˘/. An
advantage of this system is that it puts the stress mark at the point
of strongest stress in the syllable, the nucleus. The four stress
phonemes may all be observed in a normal pronunciation of the
four-syllable sentence "Tell me the truth": /têl mìy ðə trúwθ/.

An important fact about English is that there is only one primary
stress in every word group or phrase. A **phrase** is as much of an
utterance as is spoken between two clearly distinguishable pauses,
or **terminal junctures,** which will shortly be defined. For the present,
it is enough to know that these terminal junctures come at the pauses
in our phonetic transcription, which we marked by bars or double
crosses. We will thus find that there will be one and only one
primary stress between two such pauses. Other stressed syllables
will have secondary or tertiary stress, as indicated by contrast. Thus
in the sentence, "Tell me the truth," we can plainly observe the
primary stress on *truth*. Then, since *me* receives considerably more
stress than *the* and less than *Tell*, we mark *me* tertiary and *Tell*
secondary. If the sentence were simply "Tell the truth," we might

have considerable trouble deciding whether to label *Tell* with secondary or tertiary stress. Actually, it would not matter since no contrast is involved. But it does matter if we reverse the stresses in "Tell me the truth." Pronounce the following aloud and note the change of meaning as the stresses change:

/tèl miy ðə trúwθ/
/têl mìy ðə trúwθ/
/tèl mîy ðə trúwθ/
/tèl míy ðə trûwθ/

PITCH. As in the case of stresses, the four levels of pitch we recognized in our discussion of phonetics are **pitch phonemes.** That is, there are actually many slight variations in pitch from one syllable to another which do not affect the meaning. Many of these variations we disregard; they may be considered allophones of the same pitch phoneme. But when we hear a change of pitch that influences the meaning, or in some other way is noticeable even to the untrained ear, this change is probably a shift from one of the four pitch phonemes to another. Thus, if we listen closely to the sentence "Now that you're here, let's get it done," which we used as an illustration on page 116, we will note that there is a slight progressive lowering of pitch from *Now* to *you're*, and again from *let's* to *it*. Yet this slight change is nonsignificant. It could, in fact, be reversed, so that there was a slight rise in pitch over each of these two spans. Therefore, we are justified in saying that the whole of each of these spans is in pitch phoneme 2; in other words, the slight lowering of pitch involves only a series of allophones of this phoneme. But when the pitch changes at the beginning of *here* and *done*, and when it drops in the course of each of these syllables, we are aware of significant, or phonemic, changes of pitch—up to pitch 3 in both cases, then rapidly down, to 2 in the first case and to 1 in the second. Each half of the sentence thus has three pitch phonemes: 2-3-2 in the first half and 2-3-1 in the second.

In phonemic notation, instead of using the staff arrangement we used in phonetics, we simply use small raised numbers, 1, 2, 3, and 4, indicating as simply and unambiguously as possible the span covered by each phoneme. The rules for using the numbers are relatively simple. They are three:

1. Before the first segmental phoneme of each phrase, place the number of the pitch on which the first voiced segmental phone is spoken. Thus our sample sentence begins /²nǽw.../.

2. Use no more numbers until there is either a new phrase or a change of pitch phoneme. If the change of pitch is a sudden one, without a gradual glide from one pitch to another, simply place the number of the new pitch at the beginning of the syllable with which the new pitch begins. Thus the jump to pitch 3 at *here* appears as /...yùhr ³híhr.../.

3. If a change of pitch is a glide from one pitch to another, place the numbers of the beginning and ending pitches of the glide at the beginning and ending of the span in which the change takes place. This is usually one or two syllables long, very seldom longer. Thus the glide from 3 to 2 in the course of *here* is indicated by /...³híhr²|.../. Note that when the glide covers an interval of more than one pitch, as from 3 to 1, it must pass through the intermediate level, 2. But the actual position of 2 is nonsignificant and almost impossible to identify. For phonemic (and later for grammatical) purposes, the important thing is to identify the beginning and the end of the glide. The rest can be disregarded.

JUNCTURE. In our discussion of the phonetic transcription of connected speech (pp. 112-13), we indicated the pauses or slight delays in the continuous flow of speech, of the kind that we customarily think of as marking word divisions, by leaving a space. Longer pauses we marked by single and multiple bars, and the end of an utterance by the double cross [#]. At the phonetic level, this is about as much as can be recognized. But phonemicists have come to the conclusion that there are three significant types of joints or transitions between phonemes, one of which has three subtypes. These three are called respectively **close juncture** (or **normal transition**), **open** (or **plus**) **juncture**, and **terminal juncture**. These combine with pitch and stress patterns to make the complex prosodic patterns which are one of the most important features of the grammar of spoken English. Whether or not we consider these junctures phonemes (there is some debate about it), they should be marked in any complete phonemic transcription. Accordingly we shall define them here, and mark them in future transcriptions.

1. **Close Juncture** is the normal rapid transition from one phoneme to another within the syllable, as between the /p/ and /l/ or the /l/ and /e/ of /pley/. It is indicated simply by putting the phonemic symbols together, without intervening space.

2. **Open Juncture** often called **plus juncture** because it is commonly indicated by the symbol /+/ between phonemes, is easy to recognize but hard to describe. It is marked by a slight retardation of the first phoneme and a sort of "fresh start" with the second. Normal pronunciation of *a name* contrasted with *an aim* will reveal it. Thus *a name* is /ə+néym/, while *an aim* is /ən+éym/, sometimes with a glottal closure at the beginning of the /e/. Another illustration may be heard in three pronunciations of the proper name *Plato*. It may be pronounced with open juncture before the /t/, something like *play-tow*, in which case it should be written /pléy+tòw/; or the open juncture may come after the /t/ (*plate-oh*), phonemically written /pléyt+òw/; or there may be normal transition throughout: /pléytòw/ or /pléytow/. In this last case, many American speakers will have [t̪], [t̠], or [ɾ] as the allophone of /t/, while in /pléy+tòw/ they will have [tˤ], and in /pléyt+òw/ most likely [t].

In detailed phonemic transcription, all open transitions are marked by the /+/ symbol. We shall commonly omit this symbol and leave a space instead, for the sake of producing a less cluttered transcription. But we shall use the /+/ frequently and the reader should become familiar with it, since he will encounter it constantly in his reading in present-day linguistic materials.

3. **Terminal Junctures** are characterized by pauses of varying length, some very short, following various distinctive ways of cutting off speech. If the voice is cut off rather sharply, on a level pitch, the result is a **sustained terminal juncture**, commonly called **single-bar juncture** from the symbol /|/ used to represent it. It is often heard on both sides of an appositive, as in "Miss Smith, the teacher, came in," which is phonemically written

$$/{}^2\text{mìs} + {}^3\text{smíθ}^2 \,|\, {}^2\text{ðə} + {}^3\text{tíyčər}^2 \,|\, {}^2\text{kêym} + {}^3\text{ín}^1 \,\#/$$

If the pitch rises a bit just before the pause, with somewhat less abrupt cessation of voice, the result is a **rising terminal juncture**, called **double-bar juncture** from its symbol /‖/. It is frequently used in counting, after all but the last number in a series, as in

$$/{}^2\text{wɔ́n} \,\|\, {}^2\text{túw} \,\|\, {}^2\text{θríy} \,\|\, {}^3\text{fóhr}^1 \,\#/$$

Finally, if the pause is preceded by a drop in pitch and the voice fades off into silence, the result is a **falling terminal juncture**, called **double-cross juncture** from its symbol /#/. It can be heard at the end of most American English utterances, including single words cited in isolation.

We can now write the model sentence (p. 116) in full phonemic transcription. For comparative purposes, phonetic transcription and standard or *graphic* transcriptions are placed above and below it:

Phonetic: [ˈnaʊ̯ðət ˌjʊ·ɹ̩ ‖hɹ̩ʒ | ˌlɛts ˈgɛrɪt ‖dʌ\n #]
Phonemic: /²nǽwðət + yùhr + ³híhr² |²lèts + gêtit + ³dɔ́n¹ #/
Graphic: ⟨Now that you're here, let's get it done.⟩

READING PASSAGE

We are now ready for a phonemic transcription of the story of Grip, the shirker. It is of vital importance that the student be able to read and write accurate phonemic transcriptions, since the next five chapters, dealing with morphemics, grammar, and graphics, will make extensive use of them. In fact, once the linguist has worked ɔut the phonemics of a language, he uses phonemic transcriptions almost exclusively in subsequent analysis. He can do this because, if the phonemic transcription is accurately made, it retains all the significant features of the passage transcribed, but discards the non-significant details. It therefore permits him to concentrate on what is important, without being distracted by the accidental or irrelevant accompaniments.

At this point, the question may be asked, "Why learn all the minute details that clutter up our phonetic transcription with strange characters and diacritics if we are going to disregard them again in a phonemic transcription?" In short, "What use is phonetics?"

The answer is that phonetics is important for at least three reasons:

1. Until we have made an objective phonetic description in as much detail as we can, we have no way of knowing what details are important and what are not. We cannot arrive at a knowledge of what the phonemes are until we have listed all the different phone-types and studied their phonetic nature and their distribution. The phonemicist is like a doctor making a diagnosis; he does not know what symptoms are indicative and what are merely accidental. Only after he has made his diagnosis can he afford to disregard the accidental symptoms, because only then will he know which symptoms are significant. What this means for us is that *phonetics is a necessary preliminary to phonemics.*

2. A phonemic transcription is not of much use to someone attempting to learn to pronounce a language as a native speaker does. The fine points which phonetics includes and phonemics discards do not influence the message, it is true, but they mark the native speaker. The learner who wishes to have not only an intelligible but a graceful command of a language must approach it through phonetics.

3. Phonetics is essential to the study of dialectology, one of the most fascinating branches of linguistics. When linguists get together socially, often their idea of amusement is to compare their dialects, as stamp-collectors compare their acquisitions and golfers their scores. And since many of the distinctions between dialects are subphonemic (that is, phonetic), a knowledge of phonetics is essential to dialectology. To the person trained in phonetics, such a work as the *Linguistic Atlas of New England* is a mine of fascinating material.

For these reasons, then, and there are others, the knowledge of phonetics is indispensable to the linguist. But when he moves ahead into his analysis of language structure, the tool he uses is phonemics. So the sad story of Grip must now undergo a transformation and a simplification, from a phonetic to a phonemic transcription.

$$^3\text{gríp}^2 \mid {}^2\text{ðə} + {}^3\text{ræt}^1 \#$$

^{2}wə̂ns+ðərwəzə+yə̀ŋ+^{3}ræt^2 | ^{2}hu+kûdənt+mèyk+ə̂piz+^{3}máynd^1#
^{2}wenèvər+ðìə̀ðər+ræts+^{3}ǽhstim^2 | ^{2}ifìywəd+lə̂yk+tɨkə̀m+^{3}ǽwt+
wɨ̀ðəm^2 | ^{2}hìy + wəd + ^{1}ǽhnsər^2 || ^{2}ày + dòwnt + ^{3}nów^1#^{2}ənwên+ðèy+
séd || ^{2}wùjə+lə̂yktə+ stâp+ət+^{3}hówm^2 || ^{2}hìy+wûd+nàt+sèy+^{2}yés^3 ||
^{2}ər+nôw+^{3}íyðər^2#^{2}hìywəd+^{3}ɔ̀lwɨž+šɨrk^2+mèykiŋə+^{3}čóys^1#^{2}wə̂n+ 5
dèy+hiz+^{3}ǽnt^2+séd+tuim^2 || ^{3}nǽw+lûk+^{3}híhr^1#^{2}nòw+wən+wil+
èvər+^{3}kéhr+fəryùw^2 | ^{2}f+yuw+kǽriy+ɔ̀n+lə̀yk+^{3}ðís^1#^{2}yùw+hǽv+
nôw+mɔ̂hr+^{2}máynd^3 || ^{2}ðənə+blêyd+əv+^{3}grǽhs^1#^{2}ðə+yə̀ŋ+ræt+
^{3}kɔ̂hft^2+ən+lûkt+^{3}wáyz^2 | ^{2}əz+^{3}yúwžəliy^2 | ^{2}bət+sèd+^{3}nə́θiŋ^1#
^{2}dònču+^{3}θíŋk+sôw+sèdiz+ænt^3 | ^{3}stǽhmpiŋ+wìðər+fút^3 || ^{2}fə̀ršiy+ 10
kûdənt+^{3}béhr^2+təsìy+ðə+yə̀ŋ+^{3}ræt^2 | ^{2}so+^{3}kòwld+blə́dɨd^1#^{2}ay+
dò^{3}nów^2 || ^{2}wəzɔ̀hl+ðə+yə̀ŋ+ræt+^{3}évər+ǽhnsərd^1#^{2}ən+^{3}ðên^2+
hìywəd+^{3}wɔ̂hk+ɔ́hf^2 | ^{2}tə+^{3}θíŋk^2+fər+ən+^{2}ǽwər^2 || ^{2}wèðəriyšəd+

³stêyiniz+hôwl²+inðə+³gráwnd²|²ɔr+gòw+ǽwt+inðə+³lɔ́ft¹#³wə́n+

nə̂yt²|²ðə + rǽts + hɨ̀rdə + ³grêyt + nɔ́yz² + inðə+²lɔ́ft¹#²itwəzə+ 15

³vèriy+dríhriy+òwld+lɔ̀ft¹#²ðə+³rûwf+lètîn+ðə+³réyn²||²ðə+bîym-

zən+rǽftərz+wər+³ɔ̀hl+rɔ́tən²|²sòðətðə+plèys+wəz+rǽðər+ə̀n+

³séyf¹#²æt+lǽhst+wə̀nəðə+jôys+gèyv+³wéy²||²ənðə+³bíymz+fêl²|

²wið+wə̂n+ènd+ɔ̀nðə+³flóhr¹#²ðə+³wɔ̂hlz+šúk²||ən+³ɔ̀hl + ðə+

rǽts+héhr²|²stùdɔn+³énd²|²wið+fîhr+ən+³hɔ́rər¹#³ðìs+wòwnt²+ 20

³dúw¹#²sèdðə+³číyf¹#²wìymɨst+³líyv+ðìs+plêys¹#soðey+³sênt+

ǽwt+skǽwts²||²tə+sîrč+fərə+³nîw+hówm¹#²inðə+³nɔ́yt²|²ðə+

skǽwts+kêym+³bǽk²|²ənd+sèd+ðey+həd+fâwnd+ən+òwld+

³kûwpəvə+bárn²||hwèhðər+wùd+bìy+³rûmən+bɔ́hrd²|²fərðəm+

²ɔ́hl¹#²et+wə̂ns+ðəčîyf+gèyv+ðiy+³ɔ́rdər¹#²fɔ́rm+in+³láyn¹#²ðə+ 25

rǽts+krɔ̀hld+æwtə+ðehr+³hówlz²||ɨn+stûd+ɔnðə+³flóhr²|²inə+

³lɔ̀hŋ+láyn¹#³jîs+ðèn²+ðiy+³ówld+rǽt²|²kɔ̀ht+sɔ̂ytəv+yə̀ŋ+

³gríp¹#²ðǽtwəz+ðə+³nêyməðə+³šɨ̀rkər¹#²hìy+wəz+nɔ̀t+⁴ínðə+

lâyn²||²ən+hìywəz+nɔ̀t+ɨgzǽkliy+æw³tsáydit²||²iy+stûd+jist+³báy+

it¹#²hwày+dôwnču+³spíyk²|²sèdðiy+òwld+rǽt+kɔ́hrsliy²||²əv+ 30

³kɔ̀rs²+yùhr+³kə́miŋ²||²ày+dòwnt+³nów²||²sèd+grîp+²káhmliy¹#

ðiy+ày+³díh+ɔvit²#²way+yù+dôwnt+θìŋkits+⁴séyf²|²dúw+yùw²||

àym+nɔ̂t+³sírtən¹#¹sèd+grîp+ə̀n+dóhntid#²ðə+rûwf+mèy+nɔ̂t+

kə̀m+dǽwn+³yét¹#³wél²+sèd+ðiy+òwld+rǽt|²wìy+kǽhnt+³wéyt²|

²fər+³yúw+tə+jɔ̀ynəs²||³rə̂yt+əbàwt+féys³||³márč¹#²əndðə+³lɔ̀hŋ+ 35

láyn²|²màrčt+³ǽwtəðə+lɔ́ft²||²wàyl+ðə+yə̂ŋ+rǽt+²wóčtəm¹#²ə

³θîŋk+àl+gôw+tumɔ́ro²|²hìy+sèd+tu+imsélf||²bət+³ðên+əgén²|

³ây+dònt+nów²||ìt+so+³nə̂ysən²+³snə́g+hîhr²||²ə+θînk+al+gôw+

bǽk+tumày+³hówl²|²ə̀ndərðə+³lɔ́g+fərə+bìt²||²jə̂stə+mêyk+ə̀p+

mə+³máynd¹#³ðǽt+²nɔ́yt|²ðərwəzə+bîg+³krǽš¹#²dǽwn+kèym+ 40

³bíymz|³rǽhftərz|³jɔ́ys|²ðə+³hôl+rúwf¹#²nèks+³mórniŋ²||²ìtwəzə+

³fɔ́giy+dêy²||²səm+³mén+kêym²|²tə+³lûkətðə+lɔ́ft¹#²ðèy+θɔ̀tit+

³ɔ́d²|²ðət+itwəz+nɔ̀t+³hɔ̀hntid²+bày+³rǽts¹#²bətət+³lǽhst²|

²wə̂nəðəm+³hǽpəntə²+mùwv+ə+³bóhrd²||²eniy+kɔ̂t+³sɔ́yt²|²əvə+

³yə̂ŋ+rǽt²|³kwɔ́yt+²dêd||²hǽf+ín²||hǽf+³ǽwtəv+hìz+hówl¹#³ðɔ̂s+ 45

ðə+³šɨ̀rkər²||³hǽd+hìz+³díw¹#

COLLATERAL READING CHAPTER 3

Books previously listed are cited by author only.

Bloch and Trager. Chap. iii, "Phonemics," pp. 38–52.

Sapir. Chap. iii, "The Sounds of Language," pp. 43–58.

Bloomfield. Chap. v, "The Phoneme," pp. 74–92; chap. vi, "Types of Phonemes," pp. 93–108.

Gleason. Chap. ii, "English Consonants," pp. 14–26; chap. iii, "The English Vowel System," pp. 27–39.

Pike, Kenneth L. *Phonemics: A Technique for Reducing Languages to Writing.* Ann Arbor: University of Michigan Press, 1947. Chap. iv, "The Premises of Practical Phonemics," pp. 57–66.

Trager, G. L., and Smith, H. L. *An Outline of English Structure.* Norman, Okla.: Battenburg Press, 1951. Part I, "Phonology," pp. 11–52.

Chapter 4

Building Blocks of Speech: Morphemics

MORPHS AND ALLOMORPHS

The linguist who has completed a phonemic analysis of a language, similar to the one we made for English in the last chapter, is in about the position a chemist would be in when he had succeeded in isolating the elements. We have somewhat of an advantage over the chemist, for while he must keep track of a hundred and two elements, we have only forty-five phonemes to worry about. But this doesn't help us a great deal. The number of possible combinations of our forty-five phonemes is for all practical purposes as great as the number of possible compounds of a hundred and two elements. There are so many, in fact, that only a small percentage of them are used in actual speech. Our next duty in studying the structure of English, therefore, is to see what combinations are used, and what they are like. The study of these matters is the province of **morphemics.**

Let us make a beginning by taking a look at our phonemic transcription of "Grip the Rat" from the point of view of a stranger who knows all about English phonemes but nothing about what English means. Fairly early in the course of such an objective study we would observe that certain groups of phonemes occur more often than they would by mere chance. This is only what we might expect, because we are assured that the passage *means* something,

yet we know that phonemes by themselves have no meaning. Therefore, we conclude that the meaning must somehow be associated
with the way the phonemes are combined. So we proceed to extract
from our text some more or less similar combinations of phonemes.
One list we might make is as follows (the numbers in parentheses
refer to the line numbers on pp. 159–60:

^{3}rǽt^1 (title)	^{2}ræts (2, 15, 28)
^{3}rǽt^2 (1, 45)	^{2}ræts (20)
^{2}ræt (8, 12, 34)	^{3}ræts^1 (43)
^{3}rǽt^2 (11)	
^{2}ræt (30, 36)	

Pretty obviously in making this collection of forms we were guided
by similarity in the segmental phonemes they contain. In the first
column, for instance, all five of the combinations listed have the same
three segmental phonemes, /r/, /æ/, and /t/, in the same order. In
fact, the unwary reader, used to ordinary systems of writing, might
be inclined to say that these five are all the same. But the linguist,
who has gone to some pains to train himself to take account of
suprasegmental phonemes, is not so hasty. For him, /^{2}ræt/ and
/^{3}ræt/, for instance, differ in one respect, that of *pitch*. Both have the
segmental phonemes /r/, /æ/, and /t/, and the tertiary stress phoneme
/`/, but the first has pitch phoneme /^{2}/ and the second has pitch
phoneme /^{3}/. Similarly, /^{2}ræt/ and /^{2}rǽt/ have the same segmental
phonemes and the same pitch phoneme, but they differ in stress, the
first having the tertiary stress phoneme /`/ and the second having the
secondary stress phoneme /^/. Other differences of pitch and stress
distinguish the other combinations in this first column. We cannot
call all six of these "the same" unless we can prove that these differences in pitch and stress, like the differences between allophones
of the same phoneme, are *nonsignificant* on the level of structure we are examining. How is this to be determined?
   First we must get clear just what level of structure we *are*

examining. Let us define it as the level on which the sound-units or
phones, recognized as belonging to various families, or *phonemes*, are
combined into the smallest meaningful units of speech. Because
these units have recognizable shape, we call them **morphs,** a name
derived from the Greek word for shape or form. A **morph,** then,
is a combination of phones that has a meaning. Note that each
morph, like each phone, or each person or each day, happens only
once and then it is gone. Another very similar combination of very
similar phones may come along right after it; if so, we will call this
second combination another morph similar to the first one. If we
are sure enough of the similarity, which must include similarity of
both the phones and the meaning, we can say that the two morphs
belong to the same morph-type or **allomorph.** An **allomorph** can
thus be defined as a family of morphs which are alike in two ways:
(1) in the allophones of which they are composed, and (2) in the
meaning which they have. Or if we wish to be a bit more precise,
we can define an allomorph as *a class of phonemically and semantically identical morphs.*

So far, so good.. But just how far are we? If we have built ourselves a firm enough foundation in the last two chapters, we should
have no difficulty with the first part of this definition. Provided our
phonemic transcription at the end of the previous chapter is correct,
we can see plainly that /²ræt/ in line 30 and /²ræt/ in line 36 are
phonemically identical. But what about the second part of the
definition? How are we to tell whether they have the same *meaning?*
Since we have devised a system of transcription that makes phonemes
visible, we can put the two combinations side by side and compare
them point by point. But our transcription doesn't seem to tell us
anything about meaning. Up to now we have been disregarding
it—perhaps even consciously trying to forget about it—while we
focused our attention on such matters as phonetic similarity,
complementary distribution, free variation, and contrast. But now
we have brought in meaning as part of a definition, and we can

disregard it no longer. Our hypothetical linguist who knows all about the phonemes of English but nothing about its meaning seems to have come to the end of the trail. He must either find a way to deal with meaning or abandon his study just when it begins to look promising. If he is gifted with the stubborn persistence that characterizes scientists in other fields, to give up at this stage would be unthinkable. What, then, can he do?

Let us first look back to our definition of meaning in Chapter 1 (pp. 31–35). We saw there that there are three kinds of meaning that language can have. The first kind is *notional* meaning, or the ideas, concepts, or feelings in someone's mind associated with linguistic forms. Then there is *referential* meaning, or the objects, qualities, and relationships in the outside world which are pointed out by linguistic forms. Finally, there is *distributional* meaning, or the total contribution which linguistic forms make to the environments in which they occur. This would seem to suggest that there are three avenues open to the linguist when he wants to test two similar combinations of phonemes to see if they have the same meaning, and thus can be classed as members of the same allomorph. He can find some way to discover if they are associated with the same *notion* in the mind of a speaker of the language. Or he can get a native speaker to point out the object in the outside world, the *referent*, to which each refers, and himself then judge whether these referents are identical. Finally, he can study the *environments* in which the two phoneme-groups occur, and compare them with a large number of other environments where similar groups occur, and thus come to some conclusion on the basis of distribution, without having recourse to the native speaker at all.

Each of these methods has its advantages and its disadvantages. The great advantage of the use of notional meaning is that it is quick and easy. Faced with the question whether /²ræt/ in line 30 has the same meaning as /²ræt/ in line 36, the linguist simply reads the sentences in which they occur, to a native speaker—or if he is himself a native speaker, he consults his own knowledge of the language. The responses will vary somewhat, depending on the mind, personality, and education of the informant. One might respond rather curtly, "Of course they're the same. As far as I'm concerned, a rat's a rat, young or old." Another might answer more deliberately, "Yes, I'd call them the same. Of course, in line 30 he's talking about an *old* rat and in line 36 about a *young* one. But then that comes from the context. I'd say that the *rat* part in both cases refers to a member of the same species—*Rattus rattus*, I believe the biologists call it. Or perhaps *Rattus norvegicus*. Amounts to the same thing as far as I'm concerned."

The disadvantage of the notional meaning approach, on the other hand, is that it is inexact and unscientific. As we said in Chapter 1, an idea or concept in the mind of a speaker is at present beyond the reach of scientific observation. It can only be got at through language, a fact which suggests that we are in danger of using circular reasoning when it is language itself that is under observation. A scientist likes to do his own observing if he possibly can. Failing that, he prefers to have it done by impersonal instruments, or at the least by other scientists. Yet it is a well-founded axiom of linguistics that linguists themselves and literate people generally are not very good informants, because they have too many preconceived ideas about their speech. Of course if the linguist is a native speaker of the language he is observing, he can examine his own notions about meaning at first hand. But there are drawbacks to this introspective method as well, the chief of which is that the self-examiner may unconsciously tend to find what he would like to find, rather than what is actually there.

A simple illustration will point out the kind of error that might result from the use of notional meaning. Suppose the linguist is investigating the following phrases:

/²ən âyl inðə ³síy¹#/
/²ən âyl inðə ³čə́rč¹#/

He will note that the morph /²âyl/ in the first phrase is identical in phonemic content with the morph /²âyl/ in the second phrase. But before he can class them as members of the same allomorph, the linguist must determine whether or not they have the same meaning. Suppose he goes to a native speaker who answers, "Well, they've got a good deal in common. The first one means a bare, dry area surrounded by water, and the second means a bare space between the pews. Of course there's a big difference, too." Unsatisfied, the linguist goes to another informant, whose reaction is "How could they be the same? The first one's spelled *isle* and the second *aisle*. Anybody can *see* that they're different!" Having thus totally confused the written forms with the sounds themselves, this second informant is sure he has the answer. And the linguist is not much the wiser.

The advantage of using referential meaning is that it gives the linguist some opportunity to judge for himself. He is not wholly dependent on ideas and notions about words, expressed in other words. In many cases, at least, the informant can point out two objects and let the linguist make up his own mind about them. It might be a bit inconvenient to find an actual isle and an actual aisle in most neighborhoods. But the informant could at least draw pictures, from which the sensible conclusion could be reached that these morphs, though identical in phoneme structure, are different in meaning and hence not members of the same allomorph. On the other hand, the use of referential meaning has the disadvantage of being awkward, cumbersome, and sometimes impossible. One is reminded of the learned scholars of the Grand Academy of Lagado in *Gulliver's Travels*, who carried large bundles of referents around on their backs so that they could carry on a conversation without the use of words. And how would you point out the referent of *love* or *life*?

The advantage of using distributional meaning is that it sets the linguist free of dependence on anything except adequate samples of

<u>language</u>. He is in the position a scientist most likes to be in—alone with his materials and his own powers of observation and generalization. On the other hand, ideal though this method is, it has some <u>serious drawbacks</u>. In the first place, it requires long, painful, exacting work to collect enough material to supply the basis for a decision on even the smallest point. Few people have the time, patience, or leisure to do it. Secondly, the methods themselves have not been worked out to a point where they are standardized or even generally agreed upon by linguists. The whole question of the rigorously scientific study of linguistic meaning is a fascinating one, but one which is only just being opened up by pioneering scholars. It is not for us in an elementary treatment such as this to attempt to follow them.

We will depend, then, on a rather rough-and-ready combination of notional and referential meaning to make our decisions about the classifying of morphs. After all, we have assumed from the beginning that we are all native speakers of American English, and therefore, by definition, authorities on a good many things about it. And though we cannot see a notional meaning, we can console ourselves with the thought that scientists in other fields often deal with things they cannot see. After all, no one has seen a proton or an alpha-particle, only the trail of water-drops they leave behind in a Wilson cloud-chamber. But the physicists know enough about such things to build a hydrogen bomb! Furthermore, when we use notional meaning, we shall not usually have to be concerned with fine distinctions. Our interest will mostly be in finding out whether the meanings of two morphs can be called "the same" or "different." The nature and extent of the difference will not often concern us at this stage.

We are now almost ready to decide whether the nine different occurrences of the sequence of segmental phonemes /ræt/ which we listed in the lefthand column on page 163 are to be considered as representing five different allomorphs or only one. Our answer to this problem depends on what we decide to do about the suprasegmental phonemes of stress and pitch. If we find that we must consider these as integral parts of the morphs, on the same basis as the segmental phonemes, then we must conclude that /³ræt¹/ and /³ræt²/, for instance, cannot belong to the same allomorph. On the other hand, if we decide that the suprasegmental phonemes belong to a different level of structure from the segmental ones, so that they can be temporarily set aside, then we can say that since all six of the forms on the list are similar in their segmental phonemes, they all belong to the same allomorph /ræt/.

A good many arguments pro and con can be presented for both these solutions. But the general consensus of linguists is that in English the suprasegmental phonemes of stress and pitch can be separated from the segmental phonemes of vowels and consonants for purposes of analysis. The principal reason for this is that in English stress and pitch seem to be related not to the individual morphs but to the way they are arranged in larger units of structure. Unlike Chinese, for instance, where the pitch or *tone* with which a morph is pronounced is essential to the lexical meaning of the morph itself, in English the pitch is part of the grammatical meaning of a whole phrase or sentence. We shall have more to say about this later on. For the present we shall simply establish the point that two or more morphs which have the same selection and arrangement of segmental phonemes and the same meaning are members of the same allomorph. In English, a /ræt/ is a /ræt/, whether we speak it with primary, secondary, or tertiary stress, or with high, low, level, rising, or falling pitch.

We must also establish one more point about morphs. That is, a morph is not just any group of phonemes having meaning; it is a *minimal* such group. It cannot be subdivided into smaller groups which have their own meanings. If we came across the form /spíndəl/, for instance, we might be tempted to call it all one morph, since the phonemes are all closely bound in normal transition, and the whole seems to have a unit meaning. But if we searched through adequate samples of the language, we would find not only forms like /spíniŋ/ and /spínər/, but the separate allomorph /spin/. We would thus be brought to the conclusion that /spíndəl/ must be divided into two morphs, one belonging to the allomorph /spin/ and the other to an allomorph /-dəl/, which we recognize as being present in a few other words such as *treadle*, *handle*, and *paddle*. We shall have a good deal more to say about this kind of division later on in this chapter.

We may sum up the material of this section, then, as follows:

A **morph** is a meaningful group of phones which cannot be sub-divided into smaller meaningful units.

An **allomorph** is a class of morphs which are phonemically and semantically identical; that is, they have the same phonemes in the same order and the same meaning. (For the present, "the same phonemes" means for us "the same segmental phonemes.")

MORPHEMES

With the recognition of the uniquely occurring morphs and their association in sets of identical allomorphs, we have made a good start toward moving up the ladder of linguistic structure to the next level. One thing seems certain even this early: we shall find a much greater number and variety of units on this level than we did on the phonemic level. The number of different combinations that can be made from thirty-three segmental phonemes is very large indeed. In fact, we can be sure that no matter how many allomorphs we may discover, they will be only a small percentage of the total mathematical possibility. It is here, in fact, that the great diversity and adaptability of language begins to show itself. And it is here that we must give up the hope of being as exhaustive in our treatment as we were in our discussions of phonetics and phonemics. That is, we cannot hope to list all the allomorphs in English. Instead, we can deal only with representative types and illustrations of morphemic structure.

Returning once more to our small sample of American English, the story of Grip, we can now go through it looking for more examples of recurring allomorphs. One that turns up quite frequently is /ðə/, which appears both by itself and in various combinations. Furthermore, it seems to have a couple of close relatives, /ði/ and /ðiy/. Let us list some of the occurrences of these three allomorphs:

ðə	(title, 8, 11, 12, etc.)	ðiəðər (2)	ðiy	(25, 27, 32)
inðə	(14, 15, 22, 28)		sèdðiy (30)	
ɔnðə	(19, 26)			
ðəčîyf	(25)			

Looking at the first column, we can see first that /ðə/ appears most frequently by itself, that is, not in close juncture with other elements. Study of the combinations like /inðə/ and /ðəčîyf/ makes it clear that these are not single morphs, but combinations of two. We find /in/ separately at line 25, and /čiyf/ at line 21, which supports our feeling that /inðə/ is composed of the two allomorphs /in/ and /ðə/ and /ðəčîyf/ of /ðə/ and /čiyf/. In the same way we can separate /ði/ from /əðər/ in the middle column and /ðiy/ from /sed/ in the right-hand column. We are thus left with three allomorphs, /ðə/, /ði/, and /ðiy/.

Our first and natural impulse is to feel that these three allomorphs somehow go together. But we cannot act wholly on impulse if we are to be at all scientific in our attitude toward language. Instead, let us take a look at some of the environments where these three allomorphs occur:

(a) /ðə/ occurs several times in the combination /ðə+yəŋ+ræt/
(b) /ði/ occurs only in the combination /ðiəðər+ræts/
(c) /ðiy/ occurs several times in the combination /ðiy+owld+ræt/.

Any native speaker would probably tell us that all the difference in meaning there is between /ðə + yəŋ + ræt/ and /ðiy + owld + ræt/ lies in the contrast between /yəŋ/ and /owld/. That is, he would confirm our suspicion that /ðə ... ræt/ and /ðiy ... ræt/ are exactly the same in meaning. He would also tell us that the difference in meaning between /ðə + yəŋ + ræt/ and /ðiəðər + ræts/ lies in the contrast between /yəŋ/ and /əðər/ and in the /s/ attached to /ræt/ in the second expression. Thus, we find that /ðə ... ræt/, /ðiy ... ræt/, and /ði ... ræt/ all mean the same thing. And since we have already established the fact that /ræt/ has the same meaning in all of them, we are led almost mathematically to the conclusion that the three allomorphs /ðə/, /ði/, and /ðiy/ also have the same meaning; that is, they are **semantically similar.**

Next, let us take a closer look at the environments where we find these different allomorphs, especially with regard to the phonemes immediately following them. Here are a few:

ðə + yəŋ + ræt	(8, 11, 12, etc.)
ðə + grawnd	(14)
ðə + ræts	(15)
ðə + biymz	(16,18)
ðə + pleys	(17)
ðə + čiyf	(21)
ðəčiyf	(25)
ðiəðər	(2)
ðiy + ɔrdər	(25)
ðiy + owld + ræt	(27, 30)
ðiy + ay + dih	(32)

If we study this list for a moment, we will observe some interesting things about the distribution of these three allomorphs. Specifically:

1. /ðə/ appears only before a morph beginning with a consonant

phoneme, or before open juncture followed by a consonant phoneme.

2. /ði/ appears only once, in close juncture with a morph beginning with a vowel phoneme.

3. /ðiy/ appears only before open juncture followed by a morph beginning with a vowel phoneme.

This pattern looks like something we have seen before. And indeed we have—in the last chapter. There we gave it the name of **complementary distribution** (pp. 122, 125–26). Furthermore, we established the rule that a group of allophones that are phonetically similar and in complementary distribution make up a phoneme. We may apply exactly this same principle at this point in our discussion of allomorphs. Specifically, we can call a group of *allomorphs* that are *semantically* similar and in complementary distribution a **morpheme.**

Definition: A **morpheme** is a group of allomorphs that are semantically similar and in complementary distribution.

As we have suggested in the title of this chapter, morphemes are the building blocks out of which the meaningful utterances of speech are put together. A morpheme is a group of allomorphs, each of which is a combination of phonemes; but, as we pointed out in the first chapter, in structure of the kind that language shares with many other natural and man-made phenomena, the whole is more than the sum of all its parts. When phonemes are organized into an allomorph, meaning is added to make a new thing, just as when hydrogen and oxygen are organized into water, a substance emerges that has new and different qualities which could not have been guessed from a knowledge of the qualities of its components. From here on up the ladder of increasingly complex linguistic structure, we shall observe increasingly complex and precise indications of meaning. For after all it is to communicate meanings that language has been created. Therefore, morphemes, the smallest structural units possessing meaning, occupy a key position in linguistic structure. They are the fundamental building blocks out of which everything we say is built.

BASES AND AFFIXES

The reader may recall that we have left some unfinished business in our lists on page 163. We have seen that by disregarding the suprasegmental phonemes, we can class all the occurrences of the phoneme combination /ræt/ in the left-hand column as members of the same allomorph. But what about the three combinations—representing five individual morphs—in the right-hand column? If we set aside pitch and stress, we find that they all share the phoneme combination /ræts/. This certainly looks as though it has something to do with /ræt/, as indeed we all know it has. Just how are we to describe the relationship?

In the first place, it is obvious that the first three phonemes of /ræts/ are identical with the three phonemes of /ræt/ and in the same order. We may thus tentatively divide /ræts/ into two allomorphs, /ræt/ and /s/, just as we divided /spíndəl/ into /spín/ and /dəl/. We cannot be sure our division is correct, however, until we have established *semantic* as well as phonemic similarity. This is not hard to do. Any native speaker will assure us that the difference in meaning between /ræts/ and /ræt/ lies in the /s/ part of the former. We thus are justified in drawing two conclusions: /ræts/ is a combination of two allomorphs, /ræt/ and /s/; and the allomorph /ræt/ which appears in this combination is the same one we have already recognized as occurring by itself. It is, in fact, the only allomorph of the morpheme to which it belongs.

The last sentence suggests that we need some handy way of writing morphemes if we are to handle them with any dexterity and success. The convention has grown up of placing them within braces, { }, just as we put phones between square brackets and phonemes between slanting lines. What is to be put within the braces depends on the type of morpheme we are dealing with. The distinguishing qualities of the members of a morpheme, it will be remembered, are *semantic similarity* and *complementary distribution*. Nothing at all is said about phonetic or phonemic similarity. Therefore in naming some morphemes we may entirely abandon transcription based on sound in favor of one based on meaning. It actually happens, however, that there is usually a fairly high degree of phonemic similarity among the allomorphs of a given morpheme. We have seen, for instance, that the morpheme which in conventional grammar we call "the definite article" has the three allomorphs /ðə/, /ði/, and /ðiy/. All of these begin with the phoneme /ð/, which is followed by one of three different syllabic nuclei. Probably the simplest way to describe this morpheme is by using the standard spelling, which remains the same regardless of the particular allomorph that it represents. Thus we can write {*the*}, which means "the morpheme comprising the allomorphs /ðə, ði, ðiy/."

When a morpheme has a single allomorph, like /ræt/, we could use either the traditional spelling {*rat*} or the phonemic spelling {ræt}. But since random variation between these would lead to confusion, we will consistently use italicized traditional spellings to describe all morphemes that can be so described. This gives us {*the*} and {*rat*} for the two morphemes so far distinguished.

On the preceding page we split /ræts/ into two parts, /ræt/ and /s/. The first of these we found to be the allomorph /ræt/, belonging to the morpheme {*rat*}. Now we must decide what is to be done with the second part, /s/. There are two possible solutions we can come to: either it is itself an allomorph and, hence, a member of a morpheme, or it is a left-over fragment, a sort of phonemic chip on the floor of the morphemic workshop. If we have the abhorrence of untidiness that usually characterizes scientific thought, this last solution will be a last resort, to be adopted only if every other attempt fails. Our sense of the symmetry of language leads us to feel that every bit and piece of our phonemic analysis of speech should fit into an appropriate place in the morphemic structure. We don't want to find ourselves in the position of the man who had some wheels left over when he reassembled his watch.[1] Let us then see what can be done about fitting /s/ into a morphemic pattern.

In the first place, we may observe that this /s/ appears five times in our materials, always attached in close juncture to the end of the allomorph /ræt/. Furthermore, we saw earlier that it accounts for the difference in meaning between /ræt/ and /ræts/. Just what that difference in meaning is we can get at in several ways. From the notional point of view, the native speaker would tell us that the /s/ part of /ræts/ means "more than one." From the distributional point of view, we could draw the algebraic sort of conclusion that the meaning of /s/ equals the meaning of /ræts/ minus the meaning of /ræt/. And since all the occurrences of /ræts/ have "the same meaning," and all the occurrences of /ræt/ have "the same meaning," then logic tells us that all five occurrences of this particular /s/ also have "the same meaning." They are thus both phonemically and semantically the same. Since these are the criteria for belonging to the same allomorph, we can conclude that these five occurrences of /s/ are five morphs that belong to the same allomorph. So far, so good. We have no "phonemic chip."

We ought not to stop here, however. We should push our study far enough ahead to answer two more questions:

Are there any other morphs in our materials that are also members of this allomorph?

Does this allomorph /s/, meaning "more than one," constitute a morpheme all by itself, or are there other allomorphs associated with it? If there are, what are they?

---

[1] Of course, if the watch went just as well without the wheels, the fault was with the original structure of the watch, not with the way it was put back together. Similarly, if we have "phonemic chips" left over after a morphemic analysis, the fault is ours only if the "reassembled" passage does not have the same meaning as the original. If it does, the "fault" is in the structure of the language itself.

1. In order to answer the first question affirmatively, we must find some other phoneme groups that fulfil three conditions. They must

    a) end in /s/;

    b) be matched by other groups identical except for the final /s/;

    c) in some way involve the meaning "more than one."

Actually, to find such groups we must go beyond our limited corpus, the story of Grip. In that material we can find plenty of groups that satisfy requirement (a) alone, such as /græs/, /pleys/, and /kɔhrs/. We can find a few pairs that satisfy requirements (a) and (b) but not (c), such as /wən – wəns/, /ðə – ðəs/. Finally there are two that satisfy requirements (a) and (c) but not (b): /joys/ and /skæwts/.

If we draw upon our own knowledge or that of some other native speaker, however, we can find many phoneme groups that satisfy all three conditions. Some that are suggested by our materials are the following pairs of forms:

ænt – ænts	nəyt – nəyts
lɔft – lɔfts	kuwp – kuwps
skæwt – skæwts	čiyf – čiyfs

In every one of these pairs it is clear that the right-hand form is made up of two morphs, the left-hand one plus /s/. Therefore, we can conclude that /s/ with the meaning "more than one" is an allomorph of fairly wide distribution.

2. In order to answer our second question—whether there are other allomorphs grouped in a morpheme with /s/—we must search our materials for phoneme groups that comprise two morphs, one of which has the meaning "more than one." Then, we must compare its distribution with that of /s/ to make sure that it is complementary.

Once again our corpus proves too short to supply us with all the materials we need for definite conclusions. There is, however, one very helpful pair of forms: /howl/ and /howlz/. The relationship between these two so far as meaning goes seems to be just the same as that between /ræt/ and /ræts/. Therefore, we must recognize /z/ as an allomorph having the meaning "more than one."

Once more seeking out our native speaker and trying the "same or different" test on him, we can make up quite a list of forms which consist of a separate morph followed by /z/ meaning "more than one." Some of these are the following pairs:

bleyd – bleydz	flohr – flohrz
lɔg – lɔgz	æwər – æwərz
biym – biymz	dey – deyz
layn – laynz	dɨw – dɨwz
wɔhl – wɔhlz	ay+díh – ay+díhz

We shall come back to this list when we come to study the distribution of the various allomorphs meaning "more than one." First, however, we must take account of one more allomorph which appears in the right-hand member of each of the following pairs:

čoys – čɔysɨz
pleys – pleysɨz
nɔyz – nɔyzɨz
kræš – kræšɨz

Here it is clear that the extra morph appearing in the right-hand forms is not /z/ but /ɨz/.[2] This then constitutes another allomorph with the meaning "more than one." We now have three such allomorphs, /s/, /z/, and /ɨz/. It would be very satisfactory if we could group these together as members of a single morpheme, as we did with /ðə/, /ði/, and /ðiy/. But before we can do so, we must establish that their distribution is complementary.

Since these three types of morphs are always found attached to the *end* of other morphs, the first place to look for factors influencing their distribution is the ends of the morphs to which they are

---

[2] This is the form this allomorph takes in the author's dialect. Other speakers may have /iz/ or /əz/ in some or all places where /ɨz/ appears in this discussion.

attached. For convenience of examination, let us bring together our three lists of samples in parallel columns:

Forms taking /s/	Forms taking /z/	Forms taking /ɨz/
ænt	bleyd	čoys
lɔft	lɔg	pleys
skæwt	biym	nɔyz
nəyt	layn	kræš
kuwp	wɔhl	
čiyf	flohr	
	ǽwər	
	dey	
	dɨw	
	ày+díh	

Comparison of these lists reveals the fact that *the final phonemes are in complementary distribution*. That is, in column 1 we have the final phonemes /t, p, f/, none of which appears in final position in either of the other columns. In column 2, the final phonemes are /d, g, m, n, l, r, y, w, h/, none of which appears in final position in columns 1 and 3; and in column 3 the final phonemes are /s, z, š/, none of which appears in final position in columns 1 and 2. And since each column represents the distribution of one of our three allomorphs /s, z, ɨz/, it is clear that these allomorphs are also in complementary distribution. We thus recognize them as members of the same morpheme, which we can write {-es}, having the meaning "more than one."

Actually, to be sure that the distribution of the three allomorphs /s/, /z/, and /ɨz/ is truly complementary, we should test all possible environments in which they may occur. We have seen that the factor in the environment that determines which of these three is to appear is the final phoneme of the preceding morph. We should thus supplement the lists we have already made with examples of morphs ending in all the other phonemes that may come in final position.

So far we have established that /s/ follows /t, p, f/, /z/ follows /d, g, m, n, l, r, y, w, h/, and /ɨz/ follows /s, z, š/. If we consult the list of segmental phonemes on the endpapers, we will note that we still have to find examples in which the final phonemes are /k, č, b, ǰ, θ, v, ð, ž, ŋ/, and whatever vowels may be final. In the author's dialect this means only /ə/.

Arranging our sample morphs in columns similar to those on page 179, we get:

Forms taking /s/	Forms taking /z/	Forms taking /ɨz/
bæk	rib	piyč
leŋkθ	hayv	riǰ
	tayð	gəráž
	sɔŋ	
	sówfə	

Bringing together all the facts we have discovered about the distribution of these allomorphs, we may make three generalizations:

1. /s/ appears with morphs ending in /p, t, k, f, θ/;

2. /z/ appears with morphs ending in /b, d, g, v, ð, m, n, ŋ, l, r, y, w, h, ə/;

3. /ɨz/ appears with morphs ending in /s, z, š, ž, č, ǰ/.

If we study these statements in an attempt to find a principle governing this distribution, we will discover that these generalizations can be restated in even more general terms, as follows:

1. /s/ appears after morphs ending in *voiceless consonants*, except the sibilants and affricate /s, š, č/.

2. /z/ appears after morphs ending in *vowels* or *voiced consonants*, except the sibilants and affricate /z, ž, ǰ/.

3. /ɨz/ appears after morphs ending in *sibilants* or *affricates*.

These three statements comprise a concise and accurate statement of the distribution of the principal allomorphs of the morpheme

{-es}, whose meaning is "more than one," or, to use a grammatical term everybody is familiar with, "noun plural."

By now it should be clear that we are dealing with two kinds of morphemes. One kind includes those that carry the principal meaning in structures like /ræts/, /spíndəl/, and the like. These are called **bases.** Usually, but not always, a base has at least one allomorph that may appear by itself, either as a complete utterance or between terminal junctures, that is, a **free** allomorph. Phonemically a base consists of segmental phonemes in normal transition; it never contains plus junctures nor, of course, terminal junctures. The other kind of morphemes are called **affixes.** Affixes have no free allomorphs; they always appear with a base, to which they are **bound,** either directly or with one or more intervening affixes, by normal transition or plus juncture. The position of affixes in relation to the base is determined: those that precede the base are **prefixes** and those that follow are **suffixes.** In order to distinguish these types of morphemes, we shall write prefixes with a following hyphen, suffixes with a preceding hyphen, and bases with no hyphen. Thus /pleys/ is the base {place}; /rìypléys/ consists of the prefix {re-} and this base; /rìypléysmənt/ consists of this prefix and base and the suffix {-ment}.

BOUND AND FREE ALLOMORPHS; HOMOPHONES

The reader may have noticed that in our discussion of the allomorphs of {-es} we avoided some forms that would have complicated the discussion. Now, however, we must face up to them. If our generalizations are to be of any real value, they must be watertight; if there are exceptions that do not fit, we must do one of three things: (1) recast the generalizations so that they take care of the exceptions; (2) make up a complete list of the exceptions and append it to the generalizations; or (3) scrap the generalizations entirely. The old (and misunderstood) adage "It is the exception that proves the rule" certainly does not apply to any field of science.   Any scientist will say that the exception *disproves* the rule.   Let us see, then, what we can do about the exceptions to our distribution rules for /-s, -z, -ɨz/, the allomorphs of {*-es*}, meaning "more than one."

The first kind of exceptions we should look at are illustrated in the following list, which contains pairs of forms of three types.   The first two are quite common in English, and the third type, while unique, is of similar pattern to the other two:

pæθ – pæðz	layf – layvz	haws – hawzɨz
riyθ – riyðz	liyf – liyvz	
buwθ – buwðz	lowf – lowvz	

If we look only at the right-hand form in each pair, nothing seems exceptional.   We find /-z/ following /ð, v/, and /-ɨz/ following /z/, quite according to the rules we drew up on page 180.   But when we look at the left-hand members of these pairs, we note that the free forms there end not in /ð, v, z/ but in /θ, f, s/.

When we remember that a morpheme may have more than one allomorph, the solution to this problem becomes apparent.   In the case of /pæθ – pæðz/, for instance, we can say that the morpheme {*path*} has two allomorphs, /pæθ/ and /pæð/, whose distribution is complementary.   The allomorph /pæð/ appears only in combination with the "noun plural" morpheme {*-es*}, and is thus not a free but a bound allomorph.   The allomorph /pæθ/ appears in all other positions.   It may thus be free or combined with other morphemes in forms like /pǽθ+wèy/ and /pǽθ+fàyndər/.   All the forms on the list above and all that fall into the same pattern are of the same type.   Thus we may say that {*wreath*} has the two allomorphs /riyθ/ and /riyð/, {*leaf*} has the two allomorphs /liyf/ and /liyv/, {*house*} has the two allomorphs /haws/ and /hawz/, and so forth.   In each case the allomorph ending in the *voiced* consonant is bound and appears with the appropriate allomorph of {*-es*}, while the allomorph ending in the *voiceless* consonant appears in all other positions.   Note that in those dialects where the nature of the syllabic diphthong depends on whether the following consonant is voiced or voiceless, the two allomorphs may differ not only in the final consonant but in the syllabic as well. In the writer's dialect, for instance, the two allomorphs of {*life*} are /ləyf/ and /layv/, and in the dialect of eastern Virginia the two allomorphs of {*house*} are /həws/ and /hæwz/. But since, as we have seen, the allomorphs of a given morpheme do not have to be phonemically similar, this creates no problem.

A problem does seem to be created, however, by the reverse situation; that is, there are morphs that are phonemically similar but do not meet the requirement of similarity of meaning. We have seen, for instance, that /pæθ/ is an allomorph of {*path*} which appears in such forms as /pǽθ+wèy/ and /pǽθ+fàyndər/. What about the /pæθ/ that appears in forms like /pæθáləjiy/ and /sáykopæ̀θ/? However we describe the meaning of {*path*}, we cannot possibly recognize it in these combinations. Yet they clearly contain morphs which are phonemically identical with the /pæθ/ of /pǽθ+wèy/.[3]

The answer is that there is nothing to prevent the existence of allomorphs which are phonemically identical, but which belong to different morphemes. They are called **homophones,** which is Greek for "sound-alikes." They very seldom produce confusion or ambiguity, principally because the environments in which they appear are so different that the hearer automatically recognizes which one is intended; that is, they are not *in contrast.* Thus, we never confuse /pæθ/, the allomorph of {*path*} meaning "track," with /pæθ/, the allomorph of {*path*} meaning "feel, suffer," because there is no conceivable environment in which either one may appear. We are probably guided by other things as well. For instance, the allomorph of {*path*} ("track"), which we can call /pæθ$_1$/, is usually a free form, and when it appears in combination it usually has primary or secondary stress. On the other hand, /pæθ$_2$/, the allomorph of

[3] This is not true of all dialects. Some have {*path*} "track" as /paθ/, /pæhθ/, or /pehθ/ and {*path*} of *psychopath* as /pæθ/.

{*path*} ("suffer"), is always a bound form, and usually has tertiary stress. It may also frequently be replaced by the other allomorph of {*path*}, /pəθ/, as, for instance, in *sympathetic* /sìmpəθétik/.

It is true that homophones may sometimes cause confusion or even complete breakdown of communication. But this doesn't happen very often. We usually have to go pretty far to find an instance of complete ambiguity. On the other hand, homophones are the basis for a good deal of linguistic humor, such as punning and other word-play. Thus, a man whose business is making paths might jokingly call himself a *pathologist*. The linguist would say that he has made humorous capital out of the fact that the free allomorph of {*path*} "track" and the bound allomorph of {*path*} "suffer" which appears in the complex form *pathologist* are homophones. Which is a pretty cumbersome explanation of a joke that wasn't very good to start with—but then, technical explanations of humor have a way of being cumbersome.

PARADIGMS AND ZERO ALLOMORPHS

In the last two sections we have had a good deal to do with pairs of forms which differ by the fact that one means "more than one" of whatever the other one means. We found that this difference in meaning is accompanied by a difference in form; specifically, the form meaning "more than one" has a suffix which we were able to describe as one of the allomorphs of the morpheme {*-es*}. The remainder of this "more than one" form, we found, is in most cases identical with the singular form, as in /ræt – ræts/, /howl – howlz/, and /čoys – čoysɨz/. In some cases, however, we found it to be another allomorph, differing in some respects from the singular form, as in /pæθ – pæðz/, /layf – layvz/, and /haws – hawzɨz/. But we found that both these groups show orderly complementary distribution of the various allomorphs of {*-es*}.

This is not the end of the matter, however. Any native speaker can tell us that there are some other pairs which show exactly the

same kind of difference of meaning, but in which the "more than one"
member of the pair does not contain any of the three allomorphs of
{-es} that we have described.   If he has had a bit of conventional
grammar training, our native American English informant will call
these "irregular noun plurals."   But whether he can give a name to
them or not, he will feel that we cannot stop without somehow
accounting for them.   If asked for examples, he might give us some
such list as the following:

aks – áksən	šiyp – šiyp	mæhn – men
čayld – číldrən	fiš – fiš *or* fíšiz	tuwθ – tiyθ

Any native speaker could supply us with these.   One who had
received some education and had read a bit might add some more,
such as:

> stréytəm – stréytə
> jíynəs – jénərə
> kràytíhriyən – kràytíhriyə
> ələ́mnəs – ələ́mnày

The first question we must settle is whether these pairs actually do
represent the same situation as /ræt – ræts/ and the others we have
already discussed.   The method we use to settle this question is one
frequently used in linguistics as well as in other sciences: the method
of *controlled substitution with minimum variation*.   What this means
is that we find an environment or set of environments where certain
forms or sets of forms fit, and then try substituting other forms while
preserving the environment unchanged.   In this way we get groups
or classes of forms which fit into the same structure without forcing
us to alter it.   There is nothing mysterious or farfetched about this
method; we use it every day.   For example, a mechanic who wants
to find out whether two machine screws have the same thread has
two ways of going about it.   He may use various gauges and calipers

to measure them and see if the measurements correspond.   More likely, however, he will find a nut into which one of them fits and see if the other will go into it also.   In this case the nut is the "structural environment" which is kept unchanged, and the screws are the various forms which are substituted.   If the mechanic tests a large number, he can set aside in one place all those screws which fit the given thread.   Note that they don't have to be of the same material or the same length and their heads may be variously shaped.   It is the same way with our linguistic forms.   They do not have to be *semantically* the same so long as they are *structurally* the same.   Because of their meanings, some of them may be so incongruous in the environment as to turn it into nonsense.   But if they comply with the structural pattern, we can say they belong to the same structural group or **form-class.**

Let us, then, find a pair of environments into which the pairs of words we have already analyzed will fit, and see whether the new pairs will fit equally well.   For purposes of contrast, we need write phonemically only the forms under examination; the environment can be in standard spelling:

> This /ræt/ is good.
> These /ræts/ are good.

If we try the sample forms from the list on page 185 in these environments, we find that they do indeed fit quite satisfactorily:

$$
\text{This} \begin{Bmatrix} \text{/aks/} \\ \text{/čayld/} \\ \text{/šiyp/} \\ \text{/fiš/} \\ \\ \text{/mæhn/} \\ \text{/tuwθ/} \end{Bmatrix} \text{is good} \qquad \text{These} \begin{Bmatrix} \text{/áksən/} \\ \text{/číldrən/} \\ \text{/šiyp/} \\ \text{/fiš/} \\ \text{/fišiz/} \\ \text{/men/} \\ \text{/tiyθ/} \end{Bmatrix} \text{are good}
$$

We may thus take it as established that our instinct as native speakers to class these with our earlier pairs was well founded.

What we have actually established is what linguists call a **paradigm,** a name derived from the Greek word for "pattern." A paradigm is thus a system of morphemic variations which is correlated with a parallel system of variations in environment. What it boils down to is a series of changes in the shape of linguistic forms which matches a series of changes in position. To go back to our illustration from mechanics, a set of machine screws of the same material and shape, differing only in the thread which enabled them to fit into a graduated series of nuts, we could call a "paradigmatic set," though I am sure no machinist would know what we were talking about if we did.

In order to describe a paradigm morphemically, we designate the element that remains morphemically constant as the **stem.** The items that make up a paradigmatic set then have a common stem and differ from one another by the presence or absence of additional morphemes of the type we have called *affixes*. Note that a stem always contains a *base*. It may also contain affixes. Thus, in the paradigmatic set *rat*: *rats*, the stem is the base {*rat*}; while in the paradigmatic set *reader*: *readers* the stem is *reader*, which is itself made up of the base {*read*} and the suffix {*-er*}. This terminology leads us to an efficient and brief description of a paradigm. Thus, the paradigm we have been considering has two sets of forms, or **form-classes:** one that fits into the structure "This ——— is good" and one that fits into the structure "These ——— are good." We may now designate the first form of this paradigm as "stem alone" and the second as "stem + {*-es*}." This last expression is to be understood as meaning "stem plus the allomorph of {*-es*} which is determined by the phonemic structure of the stem, according to the complementary distribution which we described on page 180." We should further note that *stem* is a morphemic term, which may cover various allomorphs of its morphemic constituents. In some cases like *rat* the stem may be a single morpheme having only one allomorph, which appears in both forms of the paradigmatic set, while in other cases, such as *path*, the allomorph of the stem which appears with {*-es*} differs from the one which appears by itself. This makes no difference to our general description of the paradigm, but requires us to include a statement of the distribution of the allomorphs in any description of a morpheme. We must say, for instance, that "the morpheme {*path*} has two allomorphs: /pæð/, which appears in combination with {*-es*}, and /pæθ/, which appears in all other positions."

The next problem we must settle is how to reconcile our "irregular" group—/áksən, cíldrən/, and the rest—with our description of this paradigm as "stem alone and stem + {*-es*}." Since we have established that these irregulars do belong to the paradigm, we must either find a way to describe them in terms of "stem + {*-es*}" or we must broaden our description of the paradigm to take them in. There is no other alternative in logic.

The first pair, /aks – áksən/, presents no problem. The second form here clearly consists of two morphs, /aks/ and /-ən/. The first of these is the same allomorph as the one that appears in the singular form /aks/. This is the stem {*ox*}. Furthermore, since /-ən/ never appears with any of the forms we have already described (we cannot say /*rǽtən/ or /*hówlən/ or /*čóysən/, etc.[4]), and since /ɨz/ never appears with /aks/ (we do not say /*áksɨz/[5]), it is clear that /-ən/ is in complementary distribution with the allomorphs of {*-es*}. Since it occupies the same position in the paradigm as these allomorphs, it must have the same meaning as they do. Thus we find that /-ən/ fulfils the two requirements for membership in the morpheme {*-es*}, complementary distribution and semantic similarity. We now have four allomorphs of this morpheme: /-s, -z, ɨz, -ən/.

We must now re-examine our statements about the distribution

---

[4] The asterisk (*) is regularly used to mark hypothetical forms not actually found in speech or record.

[5] We are of course not concerned here with the genitive form *ox's* /áksɨz/, which belongs to another paradigm.

of the allomorphs of {-es} (p. 180). Those statements were so phrased as to cover all possibilities in terms of the three allomorphs /-s, -z, iz/. Now that a fourth has appeared on the scene, we must revise our statements to make room for it. Its needs in the over-all pattern of distribution are modest, as we shall see, but they cannot be overlooked. It is something like the situation that would arise if a Socialist or a Prohibitionist were to be elected to the U.S. Senate. As we know, the usual custom is for Republican Senators to sit on one side of the main aisle and Democrats on the other. This is complementary distribution of a simple and clear-cut sort. But if even a single member of a third party shows up, he cannot, theoretically at least, sit on either side. The distribution must be corrected to accommodate him.

I have no idea as to how the sergeant-at-arms or parliamentarian or whoever is responsible would settle the problem in the Senate. But the linguist has two ways open to him. He may either refine his statements of distribution by taking account of some hitherto overlooked formal features, or simply make a complete list of all the exceptions to his statements and include the list with the statements. Let us see which of these we must adopt to fit /-ən/ into the distribution pattern of the allomorphs of {-es}.

A bit of trial will convince us that the first method will not work in this case. The forms that are nearest to /aks/ are /baks/ and /faks/, both of which follow the regular course to /báksiz/ and /fáksiz/. It is true that we can find a pair /kaks – káksən/, but it falls down on grounds of semantic similarity, since the first form is the personal name *Cox* and the other is a singular form (that is, it fits the environment "This ——— is good") meaning "helmsman, steersman" (spelled *coxswain*). Other forms, like /laks, daks, raks, čaks, saks, haks/, are already "plurals," fitting into the position in the paradigm occupied by /áksən/. Our only alternative, then, is to list /áksən/ as an exception to the statement that /-iz/ regularly appears with morphs ending in sibilants or affricates (statement 3 on page 180).

The disposition of the second pair on our list of irregulars, /čayld – číldrən/, is now apparent. We simply state that the morpheme {*child*} has two allomorphs, /čayld/ and /čildr/, the latter being a bound allomorph which appears only in combination with /-ən/, one of the allomorphs of {*-es*}. One other form, /bréðrən/ (and in some dialects /sístrən/), completes the distribution of the /-ən/ allomorph in present-day English. It was, of course, much more frequent in older English.

The next pair on our list of irregulars seems to pose a difficult problem. In fact, it can hardly be called a "pair" at all, since the same form, /šiyp/, appears in both positions in our paradigm. At first we might think that the simplest solution is just to make this statement, list /šiyp/ among our exceptions, and let it go at that. This would indeed solve the problem, but it would involve us in a worse one, because it would invalidate our description of the second form in the paradigm as "stem + {*-es*}." Yet this is such a neat and efficient way to describe this paradigm that we would like to save it if we can. Certainly we hate to have to throw it out just because of *sheep* and a few other forms (*deer, moose, swine*, etc.).

The solution is to treat the form /šiyp/ that fits the environment "These ——— are good" as consisting of the stem /šiyp/ + *zero*. This is, of course, a fiction. But it is a fiction of a kind that science often makes use of in order to simplify an operation. No harm is done so long as everybody is aware of the fictitiousness of the fiction. In this case, it permits us to set up zero, which we can write /∅/, as another allomorph of {*-es*}, whose distribution is limited to a short list of forms which must be appended to our statements on page 180. We now have five allomorphs of {*-es*}, namely /-s, -z, iz, -ən, -∅/, and we can continue to describe the second form of our paradigm as "stem + {*-es*}."

The remaining items on our first list of irregulars can now be readily disposed of. In the case of the alternative forms /fiš, fíšiz/, we can see that the second one is "regular" in that it adds the allomorph /-ɨz/ to a stem ending in the sibilant phoneme /š/; while the first is like /šiyp/ in having the zero allomorph of {-es}. We may either treat this as a case of *free variation* or discover complementary distribution for the two plural forms /fiš/ and /fíšɨz/. The latter is probably the better solution, though morphemicists differ on this point. If the two forms are in complementary distribution, there is wide dialectal and individual variation in the details of the environments in which the two forms appear. The writer, for instance, uses /fiš/ almost always; he uses /fíšɨz/ in playful or humorous context only.

Our next "irregular" is /mæhn – men/. We can now see that this fits the "stem + {-es}" pattern if we recognize that the morpheme {man} has two allomorphs, /mæhn/ and /men/, the latter appearing with the zero allomorph of {-es} in the "plural" position of the paradigm.[6] A similar solution accounts for /guws – giys, tuwθ – tiyθ, fut – fiyt, maws – mays, laws – lays, wúmən – wímɨn/. All of these "irregular" forms must, of course, be listed as exceptions to the distribution rules for /-s, -z, -ɨz/.

The second list of exceptions on page 185 (a list which could be considerably extended) suggests that the paradigm we have been discussing has further complexities. We do not have the space to go into these here; their full morphemic treatment is one for a more advanced study than this. We may, however, observe two things about this group. One is that almost all the forms it contains are what are sometimes called "learned words." What this means is that these forms appear only in the dialect of people of considerable education. Often they are restricted to occupational dialects, such as those of botanists or physicians. Secondly, these forms are "loanwords," adopted into English from other languages, especially Latin and Greek. They are none the less English for that, of course. In most cases they conform to the phonemic patterns of English. But

---

[6] Actually {man} has another allomorph, /mən/, which appears in compounds like *postman, freshman,* etc.

their morphemic structure reflects the paradigms of the languages from which they are borrowed. Many of them have alternative plural forms conforming with the regular morphemic structure of English, e.g. /jíyniyəs/, which has either /jíyniyày/ or /jíyniyəsɨz/ as its plural form. This suggests one solution to this problem, which is to set up a second "plural" morpheme for learned words, which is in complementary distribution with {-es} in the case of many of these forms. But this takes us beyond our present bounds.

SUMMARY. Let us summarize the material of this section in a series of definitions.

1. A system of morphemic variations which corresponds to a parallel system of variations in environment (and hence of structural meaning) is a **paradigm.**

2. A set of linguistic forms which fits into a given position in a paradigm is a **form-class.**

3. English paradigms can be described in terms of a **stem,** consisting of or containing a **base,** and various **affixes.**

4. Forms which belong to a paradigm but do not follow a pattern of distribution that can be described in general terms are exceptions or **irregular forms,** which must be exhaustively listed in any description of the paradigm.

5. The concept of a **zero allomorph** of an affix is used in order to fit a form lacking the affix into the description of a given paradigm.

A word of caution needs to be entered here concerning this last point—the zero allomorph of an affix that forms a paradigm. Morphemicists are exceedingly cautious about using this "fiction." The rule is that it can legitimately be used only when it helps to fit a relatively small number of irregular forms into a paradigm established by an overwhelmingly large majority of the forms involved. This is certainly true of the zero allomorph of {-es}. We need to use it for only a handful of forms—less than fifty in most dialects— compared with the thousands of forms that have one of the regular allomorphs of {-es}. On the other hand, it is not good practice to introduce the zero allomorph in order to adapt a large number of forms to a pattern set by a few. For instance, let us consider the forms that fit into the following environments:

This ——— is a man.

This ——— is a woman.

We can find several pairs, such as /ǽktər – ǽktris, hə́ntər – hə́ntris, pówit – pówitis/, in which the form that fits the second environment can be described as "stem + {-ess}." But there is a far larger group of forms that can occupy either environment without morphemic alteration, such as *teacher, student, doctor, driver, friend, relative, person,* and so on. It is obviously being unrealistic to describe the members of this last group when they appear in the environment "This ——— is a woman" as consisting of "stem + zero allomorph of {-ess}." That would be to make the fiction the rule and the fact the exception.

SUPERFIXES

Some time back (p. 169) we decided that we could temporarily set aside the suprasegmental phonemes of stress and pitch in making our classification of phoneme groups into allomorphs and morphemes. In general these suprasegmental features become effective on a higher level of structure than the morphemic one. They serve as elements in the larger structures of phrase and sentence which are the subject matter of grammar. But there are some groups of stress phonemes which operate as morphemes. We shall take a brief look at some representative examples here.

Let us first examine some forms that will fit into the following two environments:

a) He will ——— (it).

b) He has a(n) ———.

We may make up two lists, one fitting environment (a) and the other fitting environment (b), as follows:

(a)	(b)
səspékt	sóspèkt
riyléy	ríylèy
imprínt	ímprìnt
pərmít	pórmìt
kəntrǽkt	kántrǽkt
kəmbǽt	kámbǽt

These lists are mutually exclusive. That is, we cannot put any form from the (b) list into environment (a),[7] nor can we put any form from the (a) list into environment (b).[8] We therefore have what looks like a paradigmatic relationship between the two lists. If they do indeed make up a paradigm, we must look for some formal morphemic contrast which corresponds to the complementary distribution of the two lists. Examining just the first four pairs on the two lists, we find that as far as their *segmental phonemes* go, the (a) form is identical with the (b) form. The only difference is in stress. The (a) forms have weak stress on the first syllable and primary stress on the second; the (b) forms have primary stress on the first syllable and tertiary stress on the second. This contrast also appears in the last two pairs on the list, where we also observe that the (a) forms have the vowel /ə/ in the first syllable while the (b) forms have /a/. We shall discuss this kind of difference in a later section; for the present, we can be sure that the important difference between /kəntrǽkt/ and /kántrǽkt/ is in their stress patterns, not the vowel of their first syllables.

If we remember that stresses are phonemes, and that sequences of phonemes associated with a meaning are allomorphs, it seems plain

---

[7] Some dialects might have "He will /ríylèy/ it." The author's does not, however.

[8] Again we must allow in some dialects for "He has a /pərmít/."

that the stress sequence weak + primary, or /˘ ´/, is an allomorph
with the meaning "verb" and the stress sequence primary + tertiary,
or /´ `/, is an allomorph with the meaning "noun."[9] Since these
allomorphs are composed of stress phonemes, which seem to be
superposed on the segmental phonemes, they are called **superfixes.**

If we change our environments slightly, we will find that we get a
corresponding change in the stress patterns:

> c) Hè will /səspêkt/ it tomórrow.
> d) Hè has a /sᶯspèkt/ hìmsélf.

The difference is that when we add a primary stressed form at the end
of the sentence without introducing a terminal juncture before the
end, the previous primary stress becomes secondary. We thus get
two more stress allomorphs, /˘ ^/ and /^ `/. But we find that this
shift from primary to secondary has made no difference in the
meaning of the item under the superfix. Therefore, we can group
/˘ ´/ and /˘ ^/ together as allomorphs of a superfix which we can
write {˘ ´}. Similarly we can group the allomorphs /´ `/ and /^ `/
together in a superfix {´ `}.

Going back to our lists on page 194, we may further note that
many of these words—for some speakers, perhaps all of them—may
also be pronounced with an internal open juncture, as /im+prínt,
ím+prìnt/, etc. This leads us to recognize two more allomorphs,
which we can write /˘ + ´/ and /´ + `/. The former is an allomorph
of the superfix {˘ ´} and the latter of {´ `}. A superfix, then, is a
morpheme consisting of stress phonemes with or without plus junctures.

We can now see that in order to describe a form like /sᶯspèkt/ in
morphemic terms, we must say that it is made up of three mor-

---

[9] We have not yet defined *noun* and *verb*, which are, of course, terms of
grammar, not of morphemics. They are used here simply as short cuts; the
reader who wishes to be more rigorous may substitute "Fitting the environment
'He will —— (it)'" for *verb* and "Fitting the environment 'He has a(n) ——'"
for *noun*.

phemes, the prefix {*sub-*}, the base {*spect*}, and the superfix {´ `}. Likewise, we describe /kəntrǽkt/ as having the three morphemes {*con-*}, {*tract*}, and {˘ ´}. Finally, we can describe this paradigm as comprising two form-classes: (1) a "noun" class with a stem consisting of prefix plus stem and the superfix {´ `}; and (2) a "verb" class consisting of the same prefix and stem and the superfix {˘ ´}.

INFLECTION AND DERIVATION

So far we have distinguished two principal types of morphemes: *bases*, like {*rat*}, and *affixes*, which are either *prefixes*, like {*re-*}, or *suffixes*, like {*-es*}. Before we can proceed to the identification of *words*, which is the ultimate goal of morphemics, we must look a bit more closely at the various types of affixes and the ways in which they occur.

Let us take, for example, a collection of forms in all of which we find the base *agree*, which has only one allomorph, /əgríy/:

A	B	C	D
əgríyz	əgríymənt		əgríymənts
əgríyd	əgríyəbəl	əgríyəbəlnìs	əgríyəbəlnìsiz

The first thing that we note is that the forms in the first two columns all consist of the stem {*agree*} plus a suffix. We can identify the suffixes in column A as {*-s*} and {*-ed*}, and those in column B as {*-ment*} and {*-able*}. All of them are true suffixes—single bound morphemes following a stem. But there is one important difference between the suffixes in column A and those in column B. If we study the forms in columns C and D, we can see that other suffixes have been added after those in column B but not after those in column A. Thus, the combination {*agree*} + {*-able*} becomes a stem, to which the suffix {*-ness*} is added to make the form /əgríyəbəlnìs/. Still another suffix, our old friend {*-es*}, can be added to this to make /əgríyəbəlnìsiz/. On the other hand, once the suffixes in column A have been added to a stem, further additions are no longer possible. We may have other *free* morphemes after /əgríyd/, for instance, as in /əgrîyd wið míy/, but we cannot have any more suffixes.

This difference allows us to make a distinction between these two types of suffixes, a distinction that will be of considerable importance in our discussion of words, as well as when we come to discuss grammar in the next chapter. Those suffixes which must always come at the end of the morpheme groups to which they belong we will call **inflectional suffixes.**[10] Those which may be followed by other suffixes we will call **derivational suffixes.** We can make a similar distinction between the types of paradigms in which these suffixes take part. Thus a paradigm like /əgríy – əgríyd/, the second form of which consists of the stem plus the inflectional suffix {*-ed*}, can be called an **inflectional paradigm,** and the form /əgríyd/ can be called an **inflected form** of {*agree*}. On the other hand, the pair /əgríy – əgríymənt/ illustrate a **derivational paradigm,** and the form /əgríymənt/ is a **derivative form** or simply a **derivative** of {*agree*}.[11]

[10] Speaking precisely, we should note an exception to this in the case of the possessive plural of nouns, which must be morphologically analyzed as having both plural and possessive inflectional suffixes. But it should be noted that in all cases except one, one or the other of these suffixes appears in its zero allomorph, which, as we have seen above, is an analytical fiction. Thus /menz/ (*men's*) consists of the stem {*man*}, the zero allomorph of the plural suffix {*-es*}, and the /-z/ allomorph of the possessive suffix {*-'s*}. /léydiyz/ (*ladies'*), on the other hand, consists of stem {*lady*}, the /-z/ allomorph of {*-es*}, and the zero allomorph of {*-'s*}. The only exception to this is the small group of words in /-ən/ + /-z/: *children's, oxen's, brethren's.*

[11] It should be emphasized that in this context *derivative* is a purely descriptive term, denoting a type of formal contrast between linguistic forms. It is not to be construed as indicating the historical order of formation. Thus *editor* is in this sense a derivative of *edit*, though historical linguistics tells us that *editor* is the older form and that *edit* is a so-called "back-formation" which came into the language by cutting the apparent suffix {*-er*} from *editor* to make a new free form. Ideally, new terms should be found to replace *derive, derivative*, etc., to avoid the connotation of history or process which they have, but none have as yet been proposed.

One further difference distinguishes inflectional from derivational suffixes in English. The inflectional suffixes have a very wide distribution; that is, the form-classes which they mark have a great many members. We have seen that one or another of the various allomorphs of {-es}, for instance, is part of virtually every form that can fit the environment "These ——— are good." In fact, when we come to grammar, we shall discover that this "plural inflection" is one of the distinguishing marks of the very large class of words called *nouns*.

Derivational suffixes, on the other hand, have a more limited distribution. For example, the number of bases to which {-ment} may be attached is relatively small. Furthermore, there is no single pair of environments which will determine the paradigm "stem + {-ment}." We can say, for instance, "He and I *agree*; we are in *agreement*." But many of the other bases that can fill the first position, such as *fight, love, cooperate, work*, etc., do not have derivatives such as **fightment* to fit the second position. We may also be faced with a choice between various derivational suffixes that are more or less arbitrary in their application; consider such pairs as *agree – agreement, disturb – disturbance, accrue – accrual, accuse – accusation*. We must learn, as part of the task of learning our language, which derivational suffixes may combine with which bases. We must also learn this about inflections, of course, but the rules are much simpler and more general. For instance, a native speaker of English learning the word /əgríymənt/ for the first time would not hesitate to form its plural by adding /-s/, the appropriate allomorph of the inflectional suffix {-es}, thus forming /əgríymənts/. But faced with the problem of making a derivative of /əgríyəbəl/ to fit into the environment "His ——— was pleasant," he would have no way to choose between /*əgrîyəbílitiy/ and /əgríyəbəlnìs/. He would have to do what we all usually do under such circumstances: consult either a dictionary or another native speaker. He might also guess, of course, which is what we all usually do in unrehearsed speech. It was a pair of wrong guesses of this kind that led a student being examined on *Hamlet* to speak of Hamlet's "unableness to overcome his undecidedness."

The suffixes of present-day English can thus be divided into two groups, inflectional suffixes and derivational suffixes. No such distinction exists in the case of prefixes, however; they are all derivational. By means of a prefix like /dis-/, for instance, a whole new set of derivatives of {*agree*} can be made, corresponding to the derivatives already formed by adding suffixes. In turn, these new derivatives may add inflectional suffixes, so that we may get such forms as *disagreed*, *disagreements*, and *disagreeablenesses*. Since in adding suffixes all derivational ones must be added to the base before the final inflectional one, we assume the same of prefixes. That is, inflection takes place on a level of structure higher than that of derivation. What this comes to is that, in terms of our examples, we treat a form like *disagreements* as consisting of /dìsəgríymənt/ + {*-es*}, rather than {*dis-*} + /əgríymənts/. Or, looking at it from the other direction, we may say that in analyzing linguistic forms into their constituent morphemes, we separate inflectional suffixes first, before we separate derivational prefixes or suffixes. This is a phase of the general question of **immediate constituents,** which will be taken up in full in Chapter 6.

BOUND BASES. If we study such combinations as *conclude*, *conceive*, and *consist*, we can observe that the stem of a derivative is not always a free form; it may be bound. Thus, by comparing *conclude* with *occlude*, *preclude*, *include*, and *exclude*, we come to the conclusion that there is a morpheme {*-clude*}, which serves as a stem for these various derivational forms. Yet we never find it as a free form; that is, we can find no environment into which {*-clude*} fits in which it is immediately preceded by silence or a terminal juncture. Our other examples work out the same way. We find a bound morpheme {*-ceive*}, present in *receive*, *perceive*, *deceive*, etc., and a bound morpheme {*-sist*}, present in *desist*, *resist*, *subsist*, and so on. (Note that {*-sist*} has two allomorphs: /-zist/, appearing with prefixes ending in a vowel, and /-sist/, with prefixes ending in a consonant.) Stems of this sort can be called **bound bases.**

SUMMARY. The material of this section may now be summarized in a series of concise statements about bound morphemes in English:

1. Bound morphemes are of three types, suffixes, prefixes, and bound bases.

2. Suffixes are either inflectional or derivational.

    a) Inflectional suffixes are always final in the morpheme groups to which they belong. They are of wide occurrence, marking large form-classes. Their distribution tends to be regular.

    b) Derivational suffixes may be final in the morpheme groups to which they belong, or they may be followed by other derivational suffixes or by inflectional suffixes. They are of relatively limited occurrence, and their distribution tends to be arbitrary.

3. Prefixes are always derivational.[12]

4. Bound bases are morphemes which serve as stems for derivational forms but which never appear as free forms.

WORDS

We are now in a position to attempt a description of one of the most elusive of the linguistic units of English—the word. Certainly to have proceeded this far in a book on the English language without saying what a word is seems at first glance very dilatory. In extenuation, it may be said that there are many books on the English language that never do get around to defining the word at all; they simply assume that everybody knows and go ahead from there. To some degree we have been guilty of such a cavalier attitude in this book, though the reader will perhaps have observed a determined

---

[12] It should be remembered that this statement, like all the rest in this section applies only to present-day English. In other languages and in the older stages of English there are inflectional prefixes, such as the *ge-* of German and Old English past participles.

attempt to talk about "linguistic forms" and "morpheme groups" when it might have been easier to say "words" and be done with it. Indeed, it would have been easier; but it would also have been unfair to the reader, who has a right to know what a term means before it is used in any important statements. Therefore, if we are to talk about words, we cannot in all honesty dodge at least an attempt at a definition.

That linguists are aware of the difficulties involved in isolating and identifying words is clear from the following statement by one of them:

> The problems associated with the proper determination of the word unit are some of the most complex in the analysis of linguistic structure. The units of the syllable, the morpheme, and the utterance are more easily definable. Determining the word unit involves many difficulties, for the criteria employed in establishing it are of different types, and each language constitutes a separate system, with its own patterns of formations and its own types of structural units.[13]

What this comes to is that all languages seem to have some kind of structural units between the morpheme and the complete utterance, but each language has its own way of distinguishing them. Fortunately, since we are concerned in this book only with present-day American English, our problem is not so difficult as that of the general linguist, who must accommodate not only English words but those of Bantu, Turkish, Chinese, and Oneida in his definitions. At that, we shall find our definition of the word a good deal more complex than at first thought seems necessary. If the reader is inclined to feel that we are overcomplicating a simple matter, let him seek out a chemist's definition of *air*, or try to explain to a Frenchman what a *strike* is in baseball. Many things which we all know about and talk about glibly every day turn out to be very complex when we scrutinize them with an objective eye.

Let us, however, start our examination from the "common sense"

[13] Eugene A. Nida, *Morphology: The Descriptive Analysis of Words* (Ann Arbor: University of Michigan Press, 1946), p. 149.

position that "everybody knows what a word is." Such a statement, of course, has very little scientific validity. From one point of view, the history of science looks rather like a tornado track littered with the shattered fragments of what everybody once knew. Everybody once knew, for instance, that malaria is caused by poisonous air; the very etymology of the word itself (Italian *mala*, "bad," and *aria*, "air") reveals it. Meanwhile, the real villain of the piece, the mosquito, continued, unsuspected, to transmit the disease from person to person.

In our case, however, there is something to be said for "common knowledge." Words, after all, unlike the malaria parasite, are manmade, and man may be expected to know something (though by no means all) about his own creations. Or, as the linguist quoted above puts it, "The naïve reactions of the native speaker of a language are very valuable and frequently quite reliable in determining word units."[14] What this really means is that the occurrence of linguistic forms in environments like the following is valuable evidence that these forms are significant structural units having independent existence:

What does *exonerate* mean?
Spit is an ugly word.
Assistance and *help* are two words for the same thing.

Native speakers recognize that certain free bases, like *spit* and *help*, and certain morpheme groups, like *assistance* and *exonerate*, all belong in a common class of units called **words,** and that other single morphemes and morpheme groups, like *-ceive* and *longer than*, do not belong in this class. It is the linguist's task to find out what criteria are used to distinguish the words from the nonwords.

Literate people are likely to be rather strongly influenced by writing practice in their decisions about words. It seems to them obvious that *seashore*, for example, is one word, while *sea breeze* is two. Anyone can tell by looking at them. When in doubt, there is always

[14] Ibid., p. 149.

the dictionary, which will tell us with complete assurance that *backwash* is "one word" and *back talk* is two, though the two desk-size dictionaries available to me as I write are both silent on *back yard* and *back fence*.

The principal trouble with using the written language to answer the question "What is a word?" is that to do so is to put the cart before the horse. As has been pointed out earlier in this book (pp. 37–38), the written language is derived from the spoken; it is merely an arbitrary set of symbols used in recording an approximation of what is said. If our only criterion for judging whether a certain combination of morphemes is or is not a word is to ask how it is written, we are using the arbitrary symbol to judge of the actuality, rather than the other way around. We do not appeal to a man's picture to decide the color of his hair when the man himself is available. Or to put it another way, if our only method of identifying words is to appeal to written language, we are in effect denying that there are such things as words in the spoken language. Which would bring us to the curious conclusion that there was no such thing as a word until writing was invented. Yet this goes counter to the point already made; that is, that in their speech people show an awareness of the word as a structural unit having its place between the morpheme and the phrase.

Furthermore, in English the written language is notoriously inconsistent about words. On a stroll about town, one may pass a *book-store* and a *drug store*, walk on a *sidewalk* or a *side street*, eat at a *tearoom* or a *lunch room*, and buy some *chinaware* at a *china shop*. There are some orderly rules behind some of this apparent irregularity, but they are not sufficient to serve as criteria for defining words. The fact of the matter is, of course, that words are units of speech. The written language, while in most cases accurately representing them, has conventions of its own, some of which are arbitrary, and some of which are simply different from those of speech. They must be learned as part of the process of learning to read and write. We thus come to the perfectly reasonable conclusion that *word* means one thing when we are talking about the written language, and another when we are talking about speech. There is considerable overlapping between the two, but they are not identical. In writing, a word is simply "that part of a given passage which is customarily written with space on either side." Can we find a similar definition for the word of speech?

The corresponding definition would be, I suppose, "that part of a given utterance which is customarily spoken between open junctures." At first view this might seem to fill the bill. But closer examination uncovers some difficulties. Consider, for instance, two different occasions on which the same speaker might speak the sentence "He is a friend of mine." If he were speaking slowly, precisely, and formally, he might say:

$$/^2\text{hîy} + \text{ìz} + \text{ə} + {}^3\text{frénd} + \text{əv} + \text{màyn}^1 \#/$$

In this case we would recognize six "words" in his utterance. On the other hand, speaking rapidly and informally he might say:

$$/^2\text{hìyzə} + {}^3\text{fréndəmàyn}^1 \#/$$

Judging by junctures alone, we would be able to distinguish only two "words" in this utterance. This definition would thus force us to one of two conclusions, either of which would be unsatisfactory: either spoken words are very unstable units, in which morphemes come together and break up like raindrops on a windowpane, or everyone speaks a great variety of dialects differing in speed and precision of utterance, each having its own kind of words.

We can, however, arrive at a linguistically sound concept of the word if we bring together some of the ideas about morphemic structure which we have presented earlier in this chapter. We may define a **morphemic word** as a linguistic form consisting of a base and a superfix, with or without one or more affixes. This permits us to make a clear distinction between a combination like /fréndə-màyn/ and one like /kǽlsəmàyn/. The former has three segmental morphemes, all three of which can appear before or after a terminal juncture; hence it consists of three morphemic words. The superfix {ˊ ˇ ˋ} must thus be considered a **phrase-superfix**, i.e., one that joins words together in a grammatical structure. /kǽlsəmàyn/, on the other hand, has two segmental morphemes, the bound base {*kalso-*} and the suffix {*-mine*}, with the word-superfix {ˊ ˇ ˋ}.

It is apparent from this definition that spoken English has several types of words, considered from the point of view of their morphemic constituents. Specifically we can recognize three principal types: (1) **simple words;** (2) **complex words with a bound stem;** and (3) **complex words with a free stem.** To these we may add a useful, though inexact, category of **compound words.** Let us take a brief look at each of these types. For the sake of brevity, the mathematical symbol ± will be used to mean "with or without."

1. **Simple words** are those that consist of a single free base and a superfix ± an inflectional suffix. Since English permits only one inflectional suffix (p. 197), simple words can consist of no more than two segmental morphemes. Some examples of simple words are *take, takes, took, taken, taking, stronger, earliest, geniuses, apparatus.*

2. **Complex words with a bound stem,** sometimes called **primary derivatives,** are composed of two bound morphemes, one of which is a base, and a superfix ± an inflectional suffix. The second bound morpheme may be a prefix, as in *conceive, disturb, prepare,* or a suffix, as in *missile, version, amity.* These words may in turn have inflectional suffixes, as in *disturbed, preparing, missiles.*

3. **Complex words with a free stem,** sometimes called **secondary derivatives,** consist of a stem which is itself a word + a prefix or derivational suffix + a superfix ± an inflectional suffix. Note that the stem may be either 1 or 2 above; that is, it may be either a single free form, as in *lover, undo, hopeless,* or a complex word with bound base, as in *receiver, misconceive, fissionable.* Either type may in turn have an inflectional suffix, as in *undoes* and *misconceived.* Note that whenever possible in analyzing a word, each time we divide it

into two parts (called *immediate constituents*), we make one of them
a free form if possible. Thus, in analyzing *receivers*, we first remove
the inflectional suffix {-es}, giving us *receiver* + {-es}. Then we cut
off the derivational suffix, giving us *receive* + {-er}. Finally, we
separate *receive* into {re-} + {-ceive}, or prefix + bound base. This
is the logical way to analyze words, since it is the reverse of the way
in which they are built up. It would make less sense to divide
receivers into {re-} + *ceivers*, or *receive* + *ers*; such analysis would
obscure rather than reveal the structure of the language.

COMPOUND WORDS. There is one further group of morpheme
sequences which are commonly called words but which do not fit
our definition of morphemic words because they contain more than
one base. The following are a few examples:

blǽk+bə̀rd
réd+kæ̀p
háws+flày

These combinations, consisting of two bases and the superfix /ˊ + ˋ/,
are different in meaning from combinations like /blǽk+bə́rd/, with
the same segmental morphemes but a different superfix, as may be
seen by comparing the two utterances:

a) /²ày+sɔ̂h+ə+³blǽk+bə̀rd¹#/
b) /²ày+sɔ̂h+ə+blæ̀k+³bə́rd¹#/

What was reported as seen in (a) is a specific kind of bird, whereas in
(b) it might be a crow, a raven, or any other bird colored black.

From the point of view of morphemics, we must say that both
/blǽk+bə̀rd/ and /blæ̀k+bə́rd/ are *phrases* whose difference of
meaning is syntactic. Speaking rather unscientifically, however, we
can use the term **compound word** to describe certain phrases of common occurrence, whose distribution is similar to that of words. We
should note that we have no inflexible criteria for deciding which
phrases can be called compound words and which cannot. It is this

uncertainty, indeed, that accounts for the varying practice in the written language to which we have already referred. Thus *bedroom* is no different in its morphemic constituency from *throne room*; both consist of two bases and the superfix /' + `/. The fact that *bedroom* is written as one word and *throne room* as two is purely a convention of the written language.

It is possible to add derivational suffixes to compounds, producing words that may be called *compound-complex* if we wish to set up a separate category for them. Some examples are *outfielder*, *New Dealer*, *oldmaidish*. On the other hand, there are compounds like *life-preserver* and *oil-burner* in which one of the words going to make up the compound already has a derivational suffix; thus the immediate constituents of *oil-burner* are *oil* and *burner*, not *oil-burn* and *-er*.

SUMMARY. The best way to summarize this discussion of words is to present a systematic classification with some further examples of each type. For simplicity's sake, no illustrations of inflectional suffixes will be given with the various kinds of complex and compound words; but it should be remembered that many of them can take one inflectional suffix in addition to the stems and derivational affixes of which they are made up.

I. Simple Words
   A. Base only
       house, copper, aspirin, macaroni.
   B. Base + inflectional suffix
       swims, simplest, covering,[15] *impresarios.*
II. Complex Words
   A. With bound stem + derivational suffix
       placate, rupture, legible.
   B. With prefix + bound stem.
       circumvent, corrupt, inert, uncouth.

[15] This consists of base + inflectional suffix in such environments as "He is *covering* the pot." In "The *covering* of the bed was green," we have instead a complex word, with a derivational suffix {-ing_2}. This is shown by the fact that the inflectional suffix {-es} can be added, as in "The *coverings* of the bed were green." Since a word can have only one inflectional suffix, -*ing* in this case must be derivational.

C. With free stem + derivational suffix
  1. Stem a simple word
     singer, pliable, manly, easy.
  2. Stem a complex word
     conductor, pliability, manliness, easily.
D. With prefix + free stem
  1. Stem a simple word
     untie, gainsay, imply, disprove, retool.
  2. Stem a complex word
     reconvert, uneasy, subatomic, intramural.
III. Compound Words
  A. Two elements, both simple words
     blackboard, hothouse, house-coat, drug store, by-pass, lookout.
  B. Three elements, all simple words
     son-in-law,[16] *longshoreman, nevertheless, instead of, in spite of.*
  C. Two elements, one complex
     adhesive tape, homing pigeon, Christmas tree, postage-stamp, easy chair, tax-collector.
  D. Two elements, both complex
     elevator-operator, cigarette lighter, movie actor, sínging stùdent (i.e. "student of singing" not "student who is singing.")
  E. Two elements, one or both compound
     lookout tower, football player, tightrope-walker, hardware-salesman.
IV. Compound-Complex Words
  A. Compound word + derivational suffix
     dry-cleaner, forthrightness, folklorist, moonshiner.
  B. Prefix + compound word
     ex-housewife, supersalesman, rebroadcast.

A BIT OF MORPHOPHONEMICS

In our study of morphemes and their combination into words we have frequently noted that a morpheme may have several allomorphs which occur in complementary distribution. We found, for instance, that {*path*} has two allomorphs: /pæθ/, which occurs both as a free form (simple word) and as a combining form in compound words like *pathway* and *pathfinder*, and /pæð/, which occurs only as a bound

---

[16] This presents a problem. If it is accepted as a single word, we must recognize an **inflectional infix** in the plural *sons-in-law*, with an additional inflectional suffix in *sons-in-law's*.

form with /-z/, the allomorph of the inflectional suffix {-es} that regularly occurs after voiced consonants. Many similar examples can be found on the preceding pages.

Early in our discussion of morphemes we made the point that two allomorphs do not have to show phonemic similarity in order to be assigned to the same morpheme. Thus we were able to assign the /-ən/ suffix of *oxen* to the "noun-plural" morpheme {-es}, even though it has no phonemes in common with /-s, -z, -ɨz/, the other allomorphs of {-es}. We did this because of *semantic similarity* and *complementary distribution*, the distinguishing qualities of the members of a morpheme. Our decision receives powerful corroboration from the fact that the pair *ox – oxen* fits perfectly into the paradigm that includes *rat – rats* and countless other pairs.

It is true, then, that phonemic similarity is not an essential requirement for morpheme membership. It is nevertheless obvious that we are strongly influenced by phonemic considerations in setting up morphemes. The two allomorphs /pæθ/ and /pæð/ are, after all, phonemically identical except for the final phoneme, which is voiceless in one case and voiced in the other. We do not hesitate very long before being sure that they belong together. We would probably hesitate a bit longer before deciding that the /fɪf/ of *fifty* and *fifteen* belongs in the same morpheme as /fayv/, since only the first phoneme is common to both. The same may be said for pairs like /bay – bɔht/ and /siyk – sɔht/. But the force of the paradigm, together with the common first phoneme, still reassures us that they belong to the same morpheme. But when we are faced with total phonemic dissimilarity, as in the case of such a pair as /gow – went/, we feel that we must be very sure of our ground before we assign such forms to the same morpheme.

The reason for this is that in English, as in all languages, there is normally a fairly high degree of phonemic similarity among the allomorphs of a given morpheme. Furthermore, historical and comparative linguistics can often supply explanations of the phonemic differences that do exist. Frequently they are the result of phonemic changes that have taken place during the history of the language. We know, for instance, that in Old English the phone-types [θ] and [ð] belonged to the same phoneme, and that they have become separate phonemes since. Here, then, is the historical explanation of the distinction between /pæθ/ and /pæð/. Similar historical information serves to explain irregular pairs like /briŋ – brɔht/ and /fut – fiyt/. But from the point of view of synchronic linguistics, it is desirable to describe the phonemic relationships between allomorphs without resorting to historical (or diachronic) considerations. The branch of structural linguistics which deals with this subject matter is called **morphophonemics.** Specifically, morphophonemics deals with the variations in the phonemic structure of allomorphs which accompany their grouping into words.

The morphophonemics of English is a rather complicated subject, and one which linguists have by no means fully worked out. We shall, therefore, not attempt a complete treatment of the subject. Instead, we shall simply glance at some of the most noticeable phenomena, with an example or two of each. The student is encouraged to find more examples, and to observe the importance of morphophonemic events in the total structure of present-day English.

In comparing the allomorphs of a given morpheme, it is convenient to call one of them the **normal** form, and describe the others as *variations* or *changes* from the normal. Thus we may say that the normal allomorph of {*path*} is /pæθ/, and that the final phoneme becomes voiced to /ð/ before the inflectional suffix {*-es*}. In this case we choose as normal the allomorph which has the wider distribution. In general, we are guided primarily by simplicity of statement; we choose as normal the allomorph which allows us to describe the variations with the least complexity. This means that the form described as normal will not always be the one which is the oldest, or the original from which the others developed, as revealed by historical linguistics. Thus, we might select the free form /fayv/ as the normal allomorph of {*five*}, though actually the bound form /fíf-/ is closer phonemically to the historical ancestor of them both. This practice is not an inconsistent one; it simply results from a difference of point of view between synchronic and historical linguistics. Synchronic linguistics is concerned with formulating the simplest possible description of the existing structure of a language. Historical linguistics, on the other hand, is concerned with the most accurate description of the changes that have taken place during the history of a language.

The types of morphophonemic change which we shall briefly notice are ten: (1) loss of phonemes; (2) addition of phonemes; (3) simple consonant change; (4) assimilation; (5) dissimilation; (6) synthesis; (7) change of syllabic vowel or diphthong; (8) stress shift; (9) gradation; (10) suppletion.

LOSS OF PHONEMES. One or more phonemes that are present in the normal allomorph of a morpheme may simply be missing in another allomorph. Thus we may properly call /in-/ the normal allomorph of the negative prefix {*in-*}; it appears in combination with allomorphs beginning with vowels or with the consonants /t, d, k, g, f, v, s, ǰ, h/. Some examples are *inert, intemperate, indirect, incorrect, ingratitude, infelicity, invisible, insecure, injudicious, inhospitable.* But before morphemes beginning with /m, r, l/ and usually /n/, another allomorph, simple /i-/ appears, as in *immodest, irreligious, illegal, innoxious.*[17] We can then say that the /n/ of the normal form is dropped before /m, r, l/ and usually /n/. Another example of a lost consonant phoneme is the /t/ of the stem {*-crat*} before the derivational {*-cy*}, as in *democracy, aristocracy,* etc. The loss of a consonant phoneme is a common morphophonemic change. Study of the following pairs will reveal other cases, which the student should analyze for himself.

---

[17] We should not be misled by the standard spelling here into considering the prefix to be /im-/, /ir-/, or /il-/. Phonemically these words are /imádist/, /irəlíǰəs/, /ilíygəl/, and /ináksəs/, though variants with C + C are also possible, e.g. /il + líygəl/.

íyziy	íyziliy
táyrənt	tírəniy
salv	səlúwšən
nest	nésəl
sɔhft	sɔ́hfən

Vowel phonemes may also be lost, though less commonly than consonants. For example, the normal allomorph of {veget-} is /vejət-/, as in *vegetate* and its derivatives, but the allomorph /vejt-/ occurs in *vegetable*. Likewise the best description of the regular allomorphs of {-es} is to consider /-iz/ the normal form and /-z/ as having lost the vowel phoneme; /-s/ exhibits the same loss of vowel together with the further change of *unvoicing*, which will be discussed below. Some other pairs showing loss of vowel or diphthong are the following:

énəmiy	énmitiy	ə *lost*
rimémbər	rimémbrəns	ə *lost*
míytər	métrik	ə *lost*
čélow	čélist	ow *lost*
kriyéyt	kríyčər	ey *lost*

ADDITION OF PHONEMES. Usually when one of two allomorphs of a morpheme lacks one or more phonemes which are present in the other, it is more convenient to consider that the longer one is normal and the other has lost one or more phonemes. Occasionally, however, the simpler description results from treating the shorter form as the normal one, to which a phoneme or phonemes are *added* to form the other allomorph. In the case of {idle}, for instance, the bound form /aydl-/, as in *idler, idling*, can be called normal, and /ə/ is added to it to make the free form /áydəl/. Likewise the normal form of {solemn} is /sáləm/, to which /n/ is added before the derivational suffix /ayz/ to make /sáləmnàyz/. Another example of an added consonant appears in the set /lɔhŋ – lɔ́hŋgər – lɔ́hŋgist/, where

/g/ appears before the inflectional suffixes {*-er*} and {*-est*}, but not before other morphemes beginning with a vowel, as in /lɔ́hŋiŋ/.[18]

SIMPLE CONSONANT CHANGE. Sometimes an alternative allomorph of a morpheme differs from the normal in showing a change of one or more consonants. Usually it is the final consonant that is changed. Thus, the normal form of the stem {*mit*} is /mit/, as in *permit, committee*, etc. But before certain suffixes, the final /t/ changes to /s/, as in *permissive, permissible*, etc. A further change, to /š/ as in *commission*, is an example of **synthesis**, which will be discussed below. Other examples of simple consonant change appear in the following pairs:

diráyd	diráysiv
θɔ́hræks	θɔ̀hrǽsik
ekstíŋkt	ekstíŋgwiš

A common type of consonant change is *voicing*. Thus, when a voiceless consonant in the normal allomorph is replaced by its voiced counterpart, the process is called **voicing.** We have already seen an example in the pair /pǽθ – pǽðz/, where the allomorph /pǽð/ of the plural form shows voicing of the final consonant. Voicing of the first consonant of a morpheme appears in /riyzíst/ as compared with /kənsíst/, etc.

Occasionally, the reverse process of **unvoicing** occurs. Thus, as we have seen, the normal form of the plural suffix {*-es*} is /-iz/, which loses its vowel after morphemes ending in voiced consonants except /z, ž, ǰ/. After voiceless consonants except /s, š, č/ this is unvoiced to /-s/, as in /ræts, kæps/, etc.

ASSIMILATION. Often a phonemic change which takes place when two morphemes are combined results in neighboring phonemes becoming more like each other. Such a change is called **assimilation.**

---

[18] However, in those dialects which regularly have /g/ in this word before a vowel, as in *Long Island* /lɔ̀hŋgáylənd/, we would call the form /lɔhŋg/ normal, with loss of final consonant before following consonant, open juncture, or terminal juncture.

By "more like" is meant "sharing more articulatory features." For example, /p/ and /m/ are alike in one feature only, their bilabialness. Otherwise /p/ is *voiceless* and a *stop*, while /m/ is *voiced* and a *nasal*. On the other hand, /b/ is more like /m/ than /p/ is, because it shares with it two features, bilabialness and voice, rather than just one.

Assimilation is a common explanation of consonant change in English. It frequently produces voicing or unvoicing, as in the already noted change of /-z/ to /-s/ after voiceless consonants. Another common change due to assimilation is that of /n/ to /m/ before bilabial consonants. Thus the negative prefix {in-} has an allomorph /im-/ which occurs before /p, b/, as in *impossible, imbalance*. Similarly, the prefix {en-} has an allomorph /em-/, occurring before /p, b/ in *empower, embitter*, and the like.

DISSIMILATION. The opposite of assimilation is **dissimilation,** which sometimes takes place when the combining of two morphemes brings together two identical phonemes; it results in the change of one of them to a phoneme less like its neighbor. It is rare in English. One example, taken over from Latin, is the allomorph /ig-/, which replaces /in-/ before some morphemes beginning with /n/, as in *ignoble, ignominious*.

SYNTHESIS. A rather special kind of consonant change, quite common in modern English, is **synthesis.** This is the fusion of two consonants, brought together by morpheme combination, into a single new phoneme, different from both of its constituents. The new phoneme must be considered to belong to both the allomorphs whose junction-point it represents. For example, when the morphemes {*moist*} and {*-ure*} are combined, the result is not /*mɔystyər/ but /mɔysc̆ər/. The /c̆/ here, phonetically the affricate [c̆], represents the synthesis into a single phoneme of /t/ and /y/. We thus analyze the word into the stem /mɔysc̆-/, an allomorph of {*moist*}, and the suffix /-c̆ər/, an allomorph of {*-ure*}. The phoneme /c̆/ belongs to them both. This kind of change, sometimes called palatalization, occurs quite commonly in present-day English when the combining of morphemes brings together an alveolar (or sometimes velar) consonant and /y/. The following are further examples (the symbol > means "becomes, changes to"):

t + y > č	neyt- + -yər > néyčər
t + y > š	ækt + -yən > ǽkšən
s + y > š	pres + -yər > préšər
k + y > š	myúwzik + yən₂ > myùwzíšən
z + y > ž	viz- + -yən > vížən
d + y > ž	sweyd + -yən > sweyžən
s + y > ž	pǽris + -yən₂ > pærížən
d + y > ǰ	pròwsíyd + -yər > pròwsíyǰər

The combining into one of two identical phonemes brought together by morpheme combination is best treated as a form of synthesis. Thus, the combination of {*eight*} with the suffix {*-ty*} brings two /t/'s together. The result is not /*eyttiy/, however, but /éytiy/. Here the single /t/ is best considered a synthesis of the final /t/ of /eyt/ and the initial /t/ of /-tiy/. This could, of course, be considered an example of loss of consonant; after all, one /t/ does disappear. But such an analysis would raise the difficult question "Which allomorph lost the /t/?" In other words, is /éytiy/ a combination of /ey/ and /tiy/, or of /eyt/ and /iy/? In either case we would have to set up a rather embarrassing allomorph—either /ey/ or /iy/. It is a simpler, and hence more desirable, solution to consider the /t/ a synthesis and, hence, a part of both allomorphs. This also is the solution of the /t/ of *eighteen*, and the single /l/ that results when the suffix {*-ly*} is added to morphemes already ending in /l/, as in *really*, *ideally*, *wholly*, which are phonemically /ríhliy, aydíhliy, hówliy/, and morphemically {*real + -ly, ideal + -ly, whole + -ly*}.

Of course, if we can find in other environments an allomorph from which the consonant in question has been dropped, we do not need to resort to synthesis as an explanation of cases like these. For instance, the negative prefix {in-} has an allomorph /i-/, which appears before /r/, /l/, and /m/, as in *irreligious, illegal,* and *immodest,* so that we can explain such a form as *innocuous* as /i-/ + /nákyuwəs/, without bringing in synthesis of the two /n/'s.

CHANGE OF SYLLABIC VOWEL OR DIPHTHONG. A type of morphophonemic change which is very prevalent in English is the substitution of another syllabic vowel or diphthong for the one which appears in the normal allomorph. I suppose the most obvious example of this, the one that everybody is quite conscious of, is the change of syllabic in the past tense of the so-called strong verbs. Pairs like /teyk – tuk/, /rayd – rowd/, and /siy – sɔh/ are familiar to everybody; in fact, learning the correct vowel substitutions to make in these words is one of the troublesome points in learning English, for foreigners and native speakers alike. There is also considerable dialectal variation, both regional and social, in many of them, which frequently leads to uncertainty as to what the preferred form is. For our present purposes, we need only note that this is one important type of morphophonemic variation.

Change of syllabic is not limited, however, to the strong verbs. We have already noted a small group of irregular noun plurals which show it, among them /guws – giys/ and /maws – mays/. These we also are quite aware of; in fact, children take pleasure in making spurious analogies like "If *goose – geese* is correct, why not *moose – meese?*" But there are many other changes of syllabic nucleus that we are less conscious of, partly because the words in which they occur are less common, and partly because standard orthography often conceals changes that take place in the spoken language. Thus, the regular spelling of the pair *nation – national* conceals the change of syllabic from /ey/ to /æ/, which is clearly revealed in the phonemic spelling /néyšən – nǽšənəl/. The following list contains some more examples of this very common kind of change, sometimes accompanied by other changes of the types we have already discussed.

e > ow	swel	swówlən
ay > i	priysáys	priysížən
iy > e	pliyz	plézənt
ih > ə	hihr	hərd
ih > æ	klihr	klǽrɨtiy
ow > a	glowb	glábyulər
ɔh > e	lɔhŋ	leŋkθ

Many other examples will readily occur to the student.

STRESS SHIFT. All native speakers of English are familiar with many cases where the addition of an affix to a word is accompanied by a shift in stress. For instance, when the suffix {-ic} is added to {despot}, the primary stress moves from the first to the second syllable, giving us the pair /déspat – despátik/. Examples of stress shift of this sort, without an accompanying vowel change, are rather rare in English. The following, however, seem to be clear cases, at least in the dialect of the author:

ímpəls	impə́lsiv
síntæks	sintǽktik
líŋgwìst	liŋgwístik
ímpɔ̀rt	impɔ́rtənt

GRADATION. In English, when the process of derivation involves stress shift, it usually also involves certain types of vowel change. The other vowels and diphthongs tend to be replaced by /i/, /ɨ/, or /ə/ when the stress shifts to another syllable, and *vice versa*. This kind of vowel change resulting from shift of stress is called **gradation.** The conditions determining which of the three vowels /i, ɨ, ə/ appears in syllables that lose their stress are complex and not completely worked out; furthermore, they vary greatly from one dialect to another. For these reasons, nothing approaching a complete statement of these gradational vowel changes will be attempted here. Instead, we shall simply list examples of the more usual kinds of gradational vowel change in the dialect of the author. It should be noted that there are two kinds of such change: (1) the change of "full" vowels and diphthongs to /i, ɨ, ə/ when the stress shifts *away from* the syllable, and (2) the change of /i, ɨ, ə/ to "full" vowels or diphthongs when the stress shifts *onto* the syllable. These changes are listed in the third and fourth columns of the following table.

		Vowel Change	
Stem	Derivative	In syllable losing stress	In syllable acquiring stress
ínstrumənt	ìnstruméntəl		ə > e
místəriy	mistíriyəs		ə > i
símbəl	simbálik		ə > a
sénsər	sensóriyəs		ə > ɔ
lɔ́kšəriy	ləgžúriyəs		ə > u
rifɔ́r	réfərəns		i > e
sigár	sígərèt	a > ə	
inspáyr	ìnspɨréyšən	ay > ɨ	
məríyn	mǽrinər	iy > ɨ	ə > æ
éybəl	əbílɨtiy	ey > ə	ə > i
kəmbáyn	kàmbɨnéyšən	ay > ɨ	ə > a
dípləmæ̀t	diplówməsiy	æ > ə	ə > ow
kəndówl	kándələns	ow > ə	ə > a
dispéhr	déspərit	eh > ə	i > e
ədvǽntij	æ̀dvəntéyjəs	æ > ə	ə > æ; i > ey
démɔkræ̀t	dəmákrəsiy	e > ə; æ > ə	ə > a

Many more examples, of course, could be cited. But these should be enough to reveal how common gradation is, and how varied are the vowel changes it involves.

SUPPLETION. The final type of morphophonemic change (or, speaking synchronically, phonemic contrast) is the occurrence of an allomorph completely different in its phonemic structure from the normal form. It will be remembered that we observed early in this chapter (p. 175) that phonemic similarity, while the usual condition among the members of a morpheme, is not essential. What is essential is semantic similarity and complementary distribution. Another way of putting it is to say that when an allomorph fits into a paradigm with another allomorph, the two belong to the same morpheme even though they may be phonemically completely different. When this occurs, the morphophonemic change involved is called **suppletion.**

We have already observed a case of suppletion in our discussion of the plural morpheme {-es}. Consider the following group of words, illustrating part of the form-class of "plural nouns":

$$/méyziz/ = \{maze\} + /\text{-}iz/$$
$$/dɔgz/ = \{dog\} + /\text{-}z/$$
$$/ræts/ = \{rat\} + /\text{-}s/$$
$$/áksən/ = \{ox\} + /\text{-}ən/$$

Here it is plain that the four suffixes /-iz, -z, -s, -ən/ all occupy the same position in the paradigm. In other words, they are semantically similar and in complementary distribution. The first three, furthermore, exhibit some phonemic similarity. Thus if we establish /-iz/ as the normal form, we can describe /-z/ as /-iz/ with loss of the vowel phoneme, and we can describe /-s/ as /-iz/ with loss of the vowel phoneme and unvoicing of the final consonant. But when we come to /-ən/, all we can say is that it *replaces* the normal form /-iz/, to which it is in no way phonemically similar. This is suppletion.

Another place where suppletion occurs is in the past tense forms of verbs. Consider the following list:

Base	Inflected Form
fret	frétid
reyd	réydid
rab	rabd
pley	pleyd

wɔhk	wɔhkt
teyk	tuk
gow	went

If we describe this inflection as "stem + {-ed_1}," we can see that all the forms in the right-hand column involve one or another of the allomorphs of {-ed_1}, that is /-ɨd, -d, -t, Ø/. Furthermore, in all but the last pair, the allomorph of the base to which the suffix is joined is phonemically similar to the free form in the left-hand column. In fact, in the first five examples, the base and the free form are identical. In the pair /teyk – tuk/ we have change of syllabic nucleus with addition of the zero allomorph of {-ed_1}. But in the pair /gow – went/, the form /wen-/, which is the base of the inflected form, is phonemically completely different from the free form /gow/. Yet the paradigm requires that we assign it to the same morpheme, and describe the morphophonemic change that takes place as suppletion.

Suppletion is relatively rare in English, compared with other languages. But, as the two illustrations we have cited show, when it does occur, it is often in an important word or paradigm. Historical linguistics often can explain it as due to the coming together in a single paradigmatic set of elements originally belonging to different words. This is the case with *go – went*, and with the multiplicity of phonemically unlike forms of the verb *be*, not only in English, but in Latin, French, German, and other languages.

COLLATERAL READING, CHAPTER 4

Books previously listed are cited by author only.

Bloch and Trager. Chap. iv, "Morphology," pp. 53–70.

Gleason. Chap. v, "The Morpheme," pp. 51–64; chap. vii, "Classing Allomorphs into Morphemes," pp. 78–91.

Trager and Smith. From Part II, "Morphemics," pp. 53–67.

Bloomfield. From chap. x, "Grammatical Forms," pp. 158–69; chap. xiii, "Morphology," pp. 207–26.

Nida, Eugene A. *Morphology: The Descriptive Analysis of Words*. 2d ed., Ann Arbor: University of Michigan Press, 1949. Chap. ii, "The Identification of Morphemes," pp. 6–61.

Note: The most complete treatment of morphemics and morphophonemics at present available is contained in Zellig S. Harris, *Methods in Structural Linguistics* (Chicago: The University of Chicago Press, 1951), chaps. xii–xix, pp. 156–360. But this is exceedingly difficult reading and is not recommended for the beginning student.

Chapter 5

Grammar–Part I:
The Parts of Speech

STRUCTURAL GRAMMAR

The words *phonetics, phonemics, morphemics,* and *morphophonemics,* which we have used to name the branches of structural linguistics so far discussed, are technical terms. This means that they are used almost exclusively by students of these subjects, who either know a great deal about them or are prepared to learn from those who do. The term *grammar,* on the other hand, is a word in the general vocabulary, which means that it is used not only by linguistic specialists and students but also by many people whose knowledge of the subject is relatively sketchy, inaccurate, or even erroneous. This, in turn, means that the reference of the term is by no means so precise, so accurate, or so generally agreed upon by all those who use it as is the reference of a technical term like *phonemics.* When two linguists discuss phonemics, they may disagree about details, but at least there is no doubt in either's mind as to what they are talking about. But when two people talk about grammar, they may actually be discussing two different areas of subject matter entirely; they may be as much at cross-purposes as a Russian and an American discussing democracy, or a fashion-designer and a literary critic discussing style. For this reason it is very important to get clear at the outset just what will be meant by *grammar* in the following chapters.

In the first place we should note that the term is commonly used to refer to both a branch of study and the subject matter of that study. When we say, for instance, that teachers of English should "know some grammar," we mean that they should have devoted time and attention to a certain branch of linguistic study. On the other hand, when we compare "English grammar" with "Latin grammar," we are usually talking about certain parts of the actual structure of these languages. The ambiguity here is similar to that of the term *anatomy*. In such a context as "Anatomy is an essential part of medical education," the term refers to the study of physical structure; whereas in "The anatomy of vertebrates differs from that of insects," the term refers to the physical structure itself.

Although we usually know which meaning of *grammar* is intended in a given context, there are potential ambiguities that make it desirable to avoid using the word in both senses when we are trying to be clear and exact. Accordingly, we shall restrict our use of it to contexts where we intend to talk about a branch of study. When we are talking about the subject matter with which the study deals, we shall use the term **structure.** Or if more precision is needed to distinguish the subject matter of grammar from the kinds of structure dealt with by phonemics and morphemics, we shall speak of **grammatical structure.** By grammatical structure is meant the organizing of morphemes and words into larger meaningful utterances. Grammar, then, can be defined as the branch of linguistics which deals with the organization of morphemic units into meaningful combinations larger than words.

It should be noted that this definition eliminates yet another common meaning of the word *grammar* as it is used in ordinary speech. We often hear it said that a certain person "uses good grammar," or that a given expression is "bad grammar." Remarks of this sort are not usually intended as comments either about grammatical structure or about the study thereof. Instead, they are judgments as to the appropriateness and social acceptability of individual expressions in a given dialect. Linguists do not use the term *grammar* in this sense; they treat such matters as, for instance, the acceptability of "It's me" in standard spoken American English as **points of usage.** We shall have a little to say about usage in Chapter 10, "Linguistics and the Teacher of English." This present chapter on grammar neither can nor should attempt to decide about detailed points of usage. Its concern is with grammatical structure: the elaborate interlocking system of mechanisms which speakers of English use when they build words into larger and more meaningful units. This is the proper business of the science of grammar, as the term is used and understood by linguists.

So elaborate is the structural system of English—or indeed of any language—that a full and detailed treatment of it would fill many volumes. Even a relatively superficial treatment would fill a book the size of this. Therefore, what is offered in this and the two following chapters does not pretend to be in any way a complete grammar of English. All we have room to do here is to survey the broad features of English structure, in order to lay a foundation for the reader's future study. When the main principles upon which English grammatical structure is based have been recognized, described, and understood, the student can go ahead confidently with his own analysis of individual patterns and problems. It may stimulate him to know that in so doing he may well be venturing into unexplored territory. For although English grammar has been studied for centuries, the recent findings of linguists have rendered out of date most grammatical writings over twenty years old. No one has yet written a complete structural grammar of English.

The principles upon which such a structural grammar must be based and the methods which will be used in preparing it are the same as those that have guided us in our treatment of phonetics, phonemics, and morphemics, the earlier stages of structural analysis. Since most people are not accustomed to thinking about grammar as a science, it is of great importance that we understand from the beginning what the principles and methods of scientific grammar are. Only if we do so understand will we be able to use and appreciate the work of the structural grammarians and to recognize and escape from the inconsistencies and fallacies of prescientific grammar. Four main principles, then, will guide us in our study of grammar in this chapter. They are these.

1. The subject matter of grammar includes, first, the mechanisms and devices by which words are combined into larger units of discourse; and second, the total linguistic structure of such units.

2. Grammar studies primarily the spoken language, listening to sounds in the air rather than examining shapes upon paper. Practically, of course, grammarians work mostly with written records, since it is the nature of our minds to be more efficient when dealing with the visible than with the audible, and since some way is needed of fixing the fleeting sounds of speech so that they may be studied. But the scientific grammarian always tries to hear the actual sound in "the mind's ear," and he has frequent recourse to native speakers —either in the flesh or as recorded on discs or tape—to make sure that he is not overlooking structural elements that are available only to the ear.

There are two implications of this principle: (a) In their study of structure, grammarians disregard those elements of the traditional method of writing that do not represent anything in the spoken language—that is, a large part of spelling, punctuation, sentence division, and capitalization. In Chapter 8 we shall examine these important devices and see the part they play in the written record of speech. But in so far as they do not reflect actualities in speech, they must for the present be disregarded. No one can hear the difference between *rite* and *wright*, between *cats* and *cat's*, or between a period and a semicolon. These distinctions belong to the written record only; they are not part of the basic structure of English.

(b) Instead of the standard writing, the grammarian must use for his analysis the methods of transcription worked out by the phonemicist and morphemicist. He is, after all, only carrying their work into a higher level of structure, and therefore he builds upon the foundation they have laid. In practice, we shall frequently use the standard written record (without punctuation or capitals) rather than a phonemic or morphemic one. But whenever we are in danger of error because the standard record either omits an important element of structure that is present in speech or includes a distinction that is not present in speech, we shall resort to phonemic or morphemic representation. The student who has mastered the last two chapters should be able to follow such transcriptions without difficulty.

3. The grammarian, like the linguist in other fields, uses the methods of scientific procedure which we described in Chapter 1 (pp. 14–16). That is, he begins his study by collecting adequate samples of actual speech. These he submits to objective examination and analysis, leading to generalizations concerning the devices and patterns of their structure. When he is content that his generalizations are valid, he states them in the form of rules, lists, charts, diagrams, or other convenient ways of representing the patterns of structure he has discovered. A more or less complete collection of generalizations covering the structural patterns of a given language or dialect can properly be called a grammar of that language or dialect.

4. It is to be noted that the method described above implies that the structural grammarian regularly begins with an objective description of the *forms* of language and moves from form toward meaning. Here his approach is directly opposite to that of the traditional pre-scientific grammarian, who often used meaning as a basis for his classifications and formulas. The structural grammarian is concerned with meaning, of course. But his concern is with how the forms of language are used to express meaning. Meaning is, as it were, the end-product; therefore, it cannot also be part of the process. For this reason, the structural grammarian uses meaning as the morphemicist does (p. 168); that is, in making his generalizations he is

interested in finding out only whether the structural meaning (defined below) of two utterances is "the same" or "different."[1]

These principles, then—attention to structure, study of the spoken language, use of the inductive method of scientific analysis, and working from form to meaning—characterize the work of the structural grammarian. They will be our guides in the brief sketch of English grammar to be presented in this and the two following chapters.

LEXICAL AND STRUCTURAL MEANING

Let us begin by observing once again a fact emphasized earlier in this book: that an organized whole is greater than the mere sum of its parts. What this means in linguistics is that at each major step up the ladder of increasingly complex linguistic organization, something new emerges which was not either present or predictable at the level before the step was taken. Thus we have seen that when phonemes are organized into allomorphs, they take on *meaning*, which is not a quality associated with the individual phonemes at all, but is solely a function of the way they are combined. In the same way, when morphemes (or the groups of morphemes we call words) are organized into utterances, a new kind of meaning emerges which is not associated with the individual morphemes at all, but is solely a function of the way they are combined. This we shall call **structural meaning.** In order to avoid possible confusion, we shall henceforth call the kind of meaning associated with the separate morphemes or words **lexical meaning,** because it is the kind of meaning that is described in a *lexicon* or dictionary.

An illustration will make clear the difference between these two kinds of meaning. Suppose we take a group of eleven words whose lexical (or dictionary) meanings are familiar to all native speakers of English.

---

[1] This is sometimes called using meaning as a *diacritic*, as a distinguishing mark.

busy	go	people	watch
come	idly	stand	window
curious	man	street	

This list is simply an accumulation; it is not an organization. The meaning of the list is no more than the sum total of the lexical meanings of its eleven members. The words are presented in "alphabetical order," but this is a purely mechanical matter; they could have been listed according to the number of letters in their spelling or the position of their stressed vowels in the vowel quadrangle. None of these arrangements would have imparted any further meaning to the list as a whole. The eleven words would continue to be like loose parts in a box; if you shake the box they will take new positions in relation to each other, but they will still be just loose parts.

If we try putting our loose words together in pairs, wholly at random, with the phrase-superfix {^ + ´} and the intonation pattern {231#}, we will get many combinations like "busy idly," "stand window," "people man." Any native speaker will tell us that each of these pairs is "meaningless," by which he would really mean that the total meaning of the pair is no more than the sum of the individual meanings of the words which make it up. Every now and then, however, our random matching would produce pairs like "curious window," "busy man," "people go," "stand idly." The reaction of the native speaker to these pairs would be quite different. He would assure us that they "make sense," by which he would be revealing that these pairs are not just accidental conjunctions of words, but little linguistic *structures*. They have a *structural meaning* over and above the lexical meanings of the words of which they are composed.

If we pressed our native speaker to tell us why some pairs of words "make sense" and others are "meaningless," he would probably be at a loss. But this would be bad linguistic method; we must never try to make our informant become introspective about language. The properly trained linguist uses an informant as a chemist uses litmus paper or a physicist a photoelectric cell—as an unself-conscious indicator. But we could ask our informant (who in this case could well be ourselves) whether any two of these structures are "the same" or "different." If he understood our question, he might tell us that "busy man," "people go," and "stand idly" are all different, but that "busy man" and "curious window" are in some sort the same, not in their lexical meaning, of course, but in their structural meaning. Furthermore, if we asked him to make other combinations of words from our list which fit the same structural pattern, he would readily produce such pairs as "busy street," "curious man," "busy window," and "curious watch." If we listened carefully to the way these were spoken, we would observe that they would all have the intonation pattern $\{231\#\}$ and the superfix $\{^\wedge + ´\}$. Putting all these findings together, we would realize we had uncovered one of the ways in which two separate words may be organized into a larger structure—a structure to which each word contributes without losing its own identity, and which has a structural meaning beyond the sum of the lexical meanings of the two words that make it up. We would, in short, have made our first step in grammar.

FIVE SIGNALS OF SYNTACTIC STRUCTURE

In the two-word syntactic structures we observed in the last section, the words were bound into a structure—and recognized as such—primarily by simple proximity in fixed order, though pitch and stress also played a part. By the mere act of placing one word after another in the stream of speech, a little nucleus of structural meaning was formed. Since the native speaker would allow that only certain ones of the possible pairs take on this extra meaning, there must be something about the words themselves that influenced him in his decision. What that is we shall discuss later on. For the present, we note that two things—proximity in a certain order, and a combination of pitch and stress sequences and a terminal juncture—are sometimes enough to bind two words into a meaningful unit. The certain order is important; if we reverse our pairs to "window curious," "man busy," and so on, we no longer have meaningful structures, but are back to random pairs. Here, then, are two of the devices that create syntactic structures. Proximity of words in a certain order we shall call **word order;** combinations of pitch, stress, and juncture sequences we shall call **prosodic patterns.** More about them later. But first we must single out three more such devices.

To do so, let us jump several intervening stages and attempt to incorporate all eleven of the "loose" words on our list into one over-all structure. We shall have to use some other words too, and make some morphemic alterations in some of the original eleven. Granted this much leeway, here are four different utterances involving our eleven words:

1. the *curious man stood* by the *window idly watching* the *busy people coming* and *going* in the *street*
2. *come stand* by the *window busy man* and *watch* the *curious people* who are *going idly* up the *street*
3. why are the *curious people standing* in the *street idly watching* that *busy man come* and *go* through a *window*
4. this *curious street goes* by some *windows* where *people* can *stand* and *idly watch busy men coming*

These structures are much more complicated than the two-word ones like "busy man;" in fact, each of them contains two such minimum structures, which themselves form units in larger patterns. The two structural devices we have so far identified are clearly at work. Thus in no two of these utterances is the order of the eleven basic words (which have been italicized) the same. We have to say them aloud to perceive the part played by prosody. If we do, we shall probably be most struck by the pitch /3/ at the beginning of (3), contrasting with the pitch /2/ at the beginnings of the others. We may also note in (2) a single-bar juncture before *busy man* and a double-bar after it, the whole phrase *busy man* being on pitch /1/, all of which gives these two words a distinctive structural meaning, different from anything else in the four examples.

But we also observe some other devices at work, helping to build these eleven words into well-knit organizations with over-all meanings. Most obvious, I suppose, is the fact that we have used seven to nine additional words in each utterance. They are the words not italicized. Even though they stand out plainly, let us repeat them here:

1. the, by, the, the, and, in, the
2. by, the, and, the, who, are, up, the
3. why, are, the, in, the, a, and, through, a
4. this, by, some, where, a, can, and

These words, all of them quite short, which help greatly to build the eleven basic words into complex structures, are **function words.** They are so called because, while they have little or no lexical meaning of their own, they serve to vary the functions of the lexical words with which they appear, according to the needs of the over-all structure. They are, as it were, humble servants of the more impressive lexical words. Like many humble servants in other walks of life, they are virtually indispensable. It is possible to build short structures without them, but longer and more complicated ones are impossible without their aid. For example, I cannot get more than eight of the eleven basic words into a single meaningful utterance without function words: "Curious people stand idly, watching busy men go." Perhaps the reader's ingenuity can go farther. No matter if it can; the point is that such structures are relatively rare. Seldom will we find structures of more than three or four lexical words without a function word. Something like the usual proportion is indicated by our four sample utterances, which have forty-four lexical words and thirty-one occurrences of thirteen different function words.

When we compare our four organized utterances with one another and with the unorganized list of eleven words with which we
started, another thing should strike us. That is that we have made
morphemic changes in one to four of the eleven lexical words
in each utterance. Thus *stand* appears as *stood* in (1) and as
standing in (3); *go* appears as *going* in (1) and (2) and as *goes* in (4);
man appears as *men* in (4), and so on. In all there are ten such
changes, involving six different words. If we study them, we will see
that they are all of the kind we called **inflections** in the last chapter
(pp. 196–99). We shall identify them all later on; for the present,
it is enough to recognize that one of them is our old friend {*-es*},
appearing in its /-z/ allomorph in *windows* (4) and in its /Ø/ (zero)
allomorph in *men* (4).

Inflections are not as frequent as function words: the proportion
of ten inflections to thirty-one function words, roughly 1:3, in our
materials is typical. Time was when they were much more frequent
in English than they are today. But they are still of vital importance.
After all, about two out of every nine (10/44) of the lexical words in
our sample utterances have them; this is about the usual proportion
in normal present-day speech. If we try to get along without them,
we realize how cramped we are. The following, for instance, is an
utterance using all eleven of our basic words in their uninflected
forms:

> busy man come to the window to stand and watch
> the curious people go idly along the street

How many more such utterances could we make that would sound
natural to a native speaker of present-day English?

For the fifth and last of our structural devices, we have to go
beyond the evidence of our four sample utterances. Not far beyond,
however; in fact, we can illustrate it by a few minor alterations in one
of them. Consider (1):

the curious man stood by the window idly watching the busy people coming and going in the street

Suppose we wish to make two relatively simple changes in word
order: (1) interchanging *idly* and *curious*, and (2) moving *busy* to a
position between *going* and *in*. If we do this without making any
other changes, we get

the idly man stood by the window curious watching the people coming and going busy in the street

Virtually any native speaker would reject this immediately, with
more or less indignation, depending on his temper and the strength
of his attachment to "good grammar." He would require us to
change it to

the idle man stood by the window curiously
watching the people coming and going busily in
the street

Just what have we done here? In terms of morphemics, we have
removed the derivational suffix {-*ly*} from *idly*, leaving the base
form {*idle*}, and we have added the same suffix to *curious* and *busy*.
To a certain degree these changes alter the lexical meaning of the
words. But they are actually necessitated not by lexical but by
structural considerations; that is, a change in one structural device,
word order, necessitated these derivational changes in certain lexical
words. Thus, we must recognize that derivational change, or, to
speak more accurately, **derivational contrast,** plays a part in structural as well as in lexical meaning.

These five, then, are the devices which English speakers make use
of to build words into larger organized combinations or structures.
Or, from the listener's point of view, these five are the kinds of
signals which reveal the patterns of structural meaning in which
words are arranged. As a summary of this section, let us list them

and briefly describe them. We shall have more to say about them
later.

1. **Word Order** is the linear or time sequence in which words
appear in an utterance.

2. **Prosody** is the over-all musical pattern of stress, pitch, and
juncture in which the words of an utterance are spoken.

3. **Function Words** are words largely devoid of lexical meaning
which are used to indicate various functional relationships among
the lexical words of an utterance.

4. **Inflections** are morphemic changes—the addition of suffixes and
concomitant morphophonemic adjustments—which adapt words to
perform certain structural functions without changing their lexical
meaning.

5. **Derivational Contrast** is the contrast between words which have
the same base but differ in the number and nature of their derivational affixes.

PARTS OF SPEECH

Earlier in this chapter we saw that when words from a list such as
that on page 228 are paired with one another in random fashion they
sometimes produce meaningful structures and sometimes do not.
We further found that once a meaningful structure has been established some of the other words in the list can be substituted in it
without destroying or changing its structural meaning, while others
cannot. Thus, once we have hit upon ^2péople $^3stánd^1$ # as a meaningful structure, we can substitute *watch*, *go*, or *come* for *stand* without
changing the structural meaning. (Needless to say, the lexical
meaning does change, but we are not now concerned with that).
On the other hand, if we substitute *curious*, *idly*, or *street* for *stand*,
the structural meaning disappears. This suggests that there must be
different kinds of words, according to the positions they can fill and
the functions they can perform in various structures. Grammarians
long ago recognized this fact and gave the name **parts of speech** to

these various types of words. We shall retain this term, though the methods we shall use to identify the various parts of speech, the number of them we shall find, and the distribution of words among them will all be different from what is found in older grammars. For this reason, the reader is urged to forget all he has ever learned about parts of speech and to follow the ensuing demonstration as if it were in some area of study wholly new to him, like molecular physics or symbolic logic. We shall make heavy demands upon his native speaker's knowledge of English structure, but none at all upon any previous training in grammar he may have had.

In the first place, function words are excluded from this classification of the parts of speech. As we shall see, they often help to mark the parts of speech to which other words belong, but they do not themselves belong to the parts of speech. So different is their operation in the structure of speech that they must be given entirely separate treatment. We shall eventually arrive at a classification of them, but not until the very end of Chapter 7, when we have surveyed all the ways in which they take part in the organization of English utterances. For the present, then, we are concerned with classifying only words like those which are italicized in the sample structures on page 230.

Second, we shall have to note that it is often not possible to classify an English word when we see or hear it in isolation. What this actually means is that a given form may be common to two or more words which are members of different parts of speech. Consider the following substitution patterns, based on simple structures made from our list of lexical words on page 228:

curious people	people come
street	go
window	stand
stand	watch
watch	

We cannot substitute *come* or *go* for *people* in the first column, nor can we substitute *people, street,* or *window* for *come* in the second column. Yet *stand* and *watch* seem to fit equally well into both columns. We must conclude that there are actually two words *stand* and two words *watch*, one of each belonging to the same part of speech as *people* and one to the same part of speech as *come*. They are, in fact, **homophones** (see p. 183). Before we can tell which one we are dealing with, we must see it in a structure with other words, where the environment will indicate clearly what part of speech it belongs to.

Third, we must remember that in the kind of grammatical analysis we are here using, we must make our classification on the basis of form, not of meaning. What this implies is that we must rely on the five signals of structural meaning which we have already identified— word order, prosody, function words, inflections, and derivational contrasts—when we classify words as various parts of speech. Where all of these fail, where there are not enough of them present to indicate clearly what parts of speech the words of an utterance belong to, the utterance is structurally ambiguous. It may not be absolutely ambiguous, because the lexical meanings of the words involved may make one possible structural meaning lexically improbable or ridiculous. Usually, however, we use more of these indicators than are necessary, rather than too few. We can often leave out function words and prosody completely, as in writing headlines or telegrams, and still be understood. But as any newspaper reader knows, headlines are prone to structural ambiguity. The grammarian would attribute this to their habit of cutting out the extra, apparently superfluous, signals of structure.

Setting aside function words, then, and observing the remaining words as they are combined into utterances with clear and unambiguous structural meaning, we find that we must identify four different parts of speech. We can use the traditional names **noun, verb, adjective,** and **adverb** for them, provided we remember that we shall not use traditional definitions or criteria of identification. We can illustrate all four in a relatively simple sentence built from our list of words on page 228:

the curious people are watching the street idly

Here *people* and *street* are nouns, *watching* is a verb, *curious* is an adjective, and *idly* is an adverb. Let us take up each of these parts of speech individually to see how we arrive at the identification.

NOUNS

Nouns are identified by five criteria, some more important than others. In the following, the most important will be taken up first.

1. The most common and most clear-cut noun-marking signal is a group of function words called **noun-determiners.** These precede the nouns they mark, either immediately or with certain types of words between. But since these intervening words can be left out, the determiner is typically a marker immediately preceding the noun. The most important of these—the only ones that have no other function and, thus, invariably signal the presence of a noun—are given in the following list. The seven forms marked by an asterisk /*/, here classed as noun-determiners, are morphologically classed as *pronouns.* (See pp. 244 ff.)

the	my*	our*
a/an	your*	their*

Other function words that often act as noun-determiners but that have other functions as well are chiefly the following:

this/these	two ... ninety-nine	some
that/those	many (a)	no
his*	more	every
her*	several	(a) few
its*	both	other
one	all	enough

Some of these—*these, those, two* ... *ninety-nine, many, several, both,* and (*a*) *few*—always mark nouns in the plural, that is, with the {*-es*} inflection. Others—*this, that, one, many a,* and *every*—always mark nouns in the singular. The rest may appear with either singular or plural.

2. Nouns have two inflections, the plural {*-es*} and the possessive (sometimes called the genitive) {*-'s*}.

a) We have already discussed the plural inflection {*-es*} and its various allomorphs in the last chapter (pp. 174–80). We saw there that it has three regular allomorphs, /-s, -z, and -ɨz/ and quite a group of irregular ones, including /∅/ (zero).

b) The possessive inflection, which we can write morphemically {*-'s*}, has four allomorphs, /-s, -z, -ɨz, ∅/. The first three of these are distributed according to the same rules as the regular allomorphs of {*-es*}; that is, /-s/ appears with nouns ending in voiceless consonants except /s, š, č/, /-z/ appears with nouns ending in vowels and voiced consonants except /z, ž, ǰ/, and /-ɨz/ appears with nouns ending in the sibilants and affricates /s, š, č, z, ž, ǰ/. The /-∅/ allomorph appears with nouns that already end in one of the regular allomorphs of {*-es*}, and a few other nouns, mostly proper names, ending in /s/ or /z/.

The result of the distribution of these allomorphs of the two inflections is to produce three groups of nouns: (a) two-form nouns, (b) three-form nouns, and (c) four-form nouns. This distinction is really a phonemic one, since all nouns have four forms, morphemically considered. Typical two-form nouns are the following:

kæt : kæts	bɔy : bɔyz
dɔhg : dɔhgz	ǰəǰ : ǰə́ǰɨz
biyč : bíyčɨz	diš : díšɨz

Hearing any one of the right-hand forms in isolation, there is no way to tell whether it is the common plural, stem + {*-es*}, the possessive singular, stem + {-'s}, or the possessive plural, stem + {-es} + the /Ø/ allomorph of {-'s}. This distinction is made in writing; thus /bɔyz/ is written as *boys*, *boy's*, or *boys'*. By far the largest number of English nouns belong to the two-form group.

Three-form nouns are those which show a morphophonemic alteration of the base when the plural suffix is added (pp. 182–83). Typical of this group, a relatively small one, are the following four nouns:

wayf : wayfs : wayvz   haws : háwsɨz : háwzɨz
pæθ : pæθs : pæðz   buwθ : buwθs : buwðz

In these nouns, the first form is the common singular, the second is the possessive singular, and the third is both the common and the possessive plural. Again these last two are distinguished in writing as, for example, *wives* and *wives'*.

The four-form nouns include certain irregulars, especially those which form their plural by a morphophonemic change in the base and the /Ø/ allomorph of {-es}:

mæhn : mæhnz : men : menz   guws : gúwsɨz : giys : gíysɨz
fut : futs : fiyt : fiyts   tuwθ : tuwθs : tiyθ : tiyθs
jíynəs : jíynəsɨz : jénərə : jénərəz

Here the forms in order are the common singular, singular possessive, common plural, and plural possessive, or in standard spelling, *man*, *man's*, *men*, *men's*, etc.

3. Many nouns may be identified as such by various noun-marking derivational suffixes, added either to stems or to other words, usually belonging to other parts of speech. The following list contains those that are clear-cut markers of nouns. They are given in morphemic form for simplicity's sake. It is to be understood that they may have more than one allomorph and more than one conventional

spelling. Thus, {-ance} may be phonemically /əns, ənts, ins/, etc., and may be spelled -ance or -ence.[2]

a) added to verbs:
    {-age}: demurrage, breakage.
    {-ance}: conveyance, contrivance.
    {-er}: boiler, sailor, liar, sawyer.
    {-ee}: payee, employee, draftee.
    {-ment}: payment, agreement, argument.
b) added to adjectives:
    {-ce}: abundance, convenience, compliance, independence.
    {-cy}: consistency, relevancy, intricacy.
    {-ity}: facility, hostility.
    {-ness}: happiness, boldness, friendliness, hopelessness.
    {-ster}: youngster, oldster.
c) added to other nouns:
    {-cy}: advocacy, democracy, captaincy.
    {-er}: lifer, liner, outfielder.
    {-ian}: mathematician, librarian.
    {-ism}: Methodism, monarchism, gangsterism.
    {-ist}: physicist, violinist, Jansenist.
    {-ship}: friendship, professorship.
    {-ster}: gangster, roadster, dopester.
d) added to bound stems (pp. 199–200):
    {-er}: carpenter, tailor, porter.
    {-ism, -ist}: monism, monist; polytheism, communism, Fascism, etc.
    {-ity}: depravity, debility, felicity.

There are many other derivational suffixes each of which appears on a few nouns, such as *auctioneer, hostess, anthracite, kingdom,*

---

[2] These have been classified according to the parts of speech to which they are always or commonly attached, even though the other three parts of speech have not yet been identified. Since derivation may proceed in virtually any direction, this circularity cannot be avoided.

booklet, likelihood, bronchitis, duckling, cigarette. There are also a few derivational suffixes which appear commonly on nouns, but which cannot be relied on as noun-markers because they may mark other parts of speech as well. Thus {*-tion*} may indicate either noun or verb, as in *condition*, which may belong to either part of speech. A special problem is posed by the suffix /-iŋ/, which marks not only nouns but also adjectives, and also serves as a verb inflection, as we shall see. When it functions as a noun-suffix, we can distinguish it as {*-ing₂*}. Nouns with this suffix appear in the following sentences; note that they are also marked as nouns by noun-determiners, noun-inflections, or both:

> his *breathing* is more regular now
> she gives *readings* in poetry
> give the *leavings* to the dogs

4. Nouns fill certain characteristic positions in relation to other identified parts of speech in phrases and utterances. The most obvious of these is the position just before a verb, as in /pléyn dipártid/, where /dipártid/ is clearly identified as a verb by its {*-ed*} inflection, as we shall later see. This leads us to identify /pleyn/ as a noun because of its position. But in /pléyn líyvz/, for instance, /liyvz/ is not unambiguously marked as a verb; it could be the plural of the noun *leaf*, in which case /pleyn/ would be either a verb (*plane*) or an adjective (*plain*).

On the whole, position is seldom used to identify nouns, except in the special grammar of headlines or telegrams. If unambiguous noun-determiners or noun-marking derivational suffixes are present, the word will be distinguished as a noun regardless of position. Only if there are none of these present and the word is one that can belong to two or more parts of speech do we depend on position. Even then, unless the neighboring words are clearly identified by formal or lexical qualities as to the parts of speech to which they belong, a noun cannot be unmistakably marked by position alone.

Such is the case, for instance, with Professor Fries's famous example, "Ship sails today."[3]

5. Certain superfixes occasionally distinguish nouns from otherwise identical words that belong to other parts of speech. Thus in pairs like /ímprìnt : imprínt/ and /sɔ́spèkt : səspékt/ we identify the word with the /´ `/ stress pattern as a noun and the other as a verb. We have already discussed this in our treatment of morphemics (pp. 193–96).

Seldom do we find a noun marked by all five of these noun-indicators. In fact, numbers (3) and (5)—derivational affixes and superfixes—seem to be mutually exclusive, since we only become aware of the superfix when it distinguishes words which are otherwise morphemically alike. Hence, we would not look for a noun-marking superfix on a word which was already morphemically identified by a noun-marking derivational affix.[4] We often find all of the first four present, however, as in

my *arguments* are sound

where *arguments* is marked as a noun by (1) the noun-determiner *my*, (2) the plural inflection {-es}, (3) the noun-determining derivational suffix {-ment}, and (4) the characteristic noun position immediately before the verb *are*, which is further reinforced by the phenomenon of **concord** or **agreement** between the plural inflection {-es} and the plural verb form *are*. Here is structural redundancy in plenty.

More often, however, only three, two, or even one of the noun-markers is present and is sufficient to prevent ambiguity. Consider the italicized words in the three structures which follow.

---

[3] C. C. Fries, *The Structure of English* (New York: Harcourt, Brace & Co., Inc., 1952), p. 62.

[4] We are perhaps at fault here in giving such minor significance to prosodic features as word markers. But such is the present state of our knowledge. The grammar of the future will undoubtedly make more of prosody, which has been almost totally neglected by the writing-based grammar of the past.

a) he seized the *opportunity*

b) the *surrender* took place at Appomattox

c) I like *snow*

In (a), *opportunity* is marked as a noun in three ways: by the noun-determiner *the*, by the derivational suffix {*-ity*}, and by its position after the verb, one often occupied, as we shall see, by the noun as direct object.   In (b), there are only two markers: the determiner *the* and the position just before the verb; in isolation *surrender* can be a verb as well as a noun, or actually it is not either.   Finally in (c), only the position of *snow* tells us that we are dealing with a noun rather than a verb.

These various noun-markers, then, singly or in combination, are enough to identify nouns without any help from lexical meaning. This is borne out by the fact that we can unerringly pick out nouns in a highly technical context where we have no idea of what the lexical meaning is, or even in a "nonsense" sentence where there is no lexical meaning at all.   Consider the italicized words in the following sentences:

> connect the selenium *rectifier* to a .1 mfd. *capacitor*
> Sidney left his *greaves* behind
> shun the frumious *bandersnatch*
> what's this little *dingus* (or *gizmo*, *widget*, *dohickey*, etc.)
> the *snark* was a *boojum*, you see

Without knowing what any of the italicized words mean, we can pick them out as nouns.   The reader might find it instructive to identify all the signals which guide us to this conclusion in each case.

The first three of these noun-markers—determiners, inflections, and derivational contrasts—singly or in various combinations, serve to identify as nouns a tremendous number of English words.   There are in addition a limited number of words which occupy most or all of the characteristic noun positions, but which either make no use at all of the other formal markers, make very restricted use of some of them, or use a somewhat different set. Since the list of these words is quite short, all native speakers of English soon come to know them by heart, so that no other markers beside position are needed to reveal that they are performing noun functions. The traditional grammar lumps them all together, along with certain function words, under the name *pronouns*. But since our classification is quite different at this point from that of the traditional grammar, we shall treat them as two subclasses of nouns, called **pronouns** and **function nouns.**

PRONOUNS. This group comprises eight words whose importance far outweighs their number. They are often classified as a separate part of speech because of their morphological difference from nouns. But in a primarily syntactic classification of parts of speech such as the one used here, it is more convenient to treat them as a subgroup of nouns.

The eight pronouns are *I, we, you, he, she, it, they,* and *who.* All of them have inflectional variants, but they do not have the {*-es*} plural and the {*'s*} possessive characteristic of most other nouns. Instead,

Subjective	Objective	First Possessive	Second Possessive
I	me	my	mine
we	us	our	ours
you		your	yours
he	him	his	
she	her		hers
it		its	
they	them	their	theirs
who	who(m)	whose	

they have forms which are commonly called the **objective** (or **ac-cusative**) and the **first** and **second possessive**. Only three of them—*I*, *we*, and *they*—have four distinct forms; of the rest, *you*, *he*, *she*, and *who* have three forms, variously distributed, and *it* has two. But the three with four forms establish a paradigm in which the others are included (see table on p. 244).

From the table it can be seen that *you* and *it* both double as subjective and objective forms, *her* as objective and first possessive, and *his*, *its*, and *whose* as first and second possessive. Many speakers also use *who* as both subjective and objective form. There are further morphological variations in various dialects, such as a full set of second possessives in /-n/: *ourn*, *yourn*, *hisn*, etc., presumably formed by analogy with *mine*. These are usually considered substandard. It is possible to describe the members of the pronoun paradigm in terms of stems + inflectional suffixes, but the description is somewhat too complicated for our needs here.[5] Not used except in special styles with an archaic or ecclesiastical flavor is a ninth pronoun, *thou/thee/thy/thine*.

All these pronouns except *who* are frequently classed as *personal pronouns*, a distinction borrowed from the grammar of other languages that have other groups of different classes of pronouns. They are also often classified by **person**; thus, *I* and *we*, denoting or including the speaker, are called **first person**; *thou* and *you*, denoting or including the person spoken to and excluding the speaker, are called **second person**; *he*, *she*, *it*, *they*, excluding both speaker and person spoken to, are called **third person**. This is sometimes a useful distinction, as is the denoting of *we* and *they* as **plural**, even though the term here has a different sense from *plural* applied to nouns.[6] All these pronouns to some degree, but especially

[5] For such a description, see Trager and Smith, *Outline*, p. 62.

[6] Thus the meaning of the noun plural suffix {-*es*} can be roughly stated as "more than one of whatever is denoted by the stem." /bɔyz/ then means "more than one /bɔy/." But the meaning of *we* is not "more than one *I*"; it may be "I and you," "I and he," "I and you and they," "I and my associates," etc.

the third-person pronouns *he*, *she*, *it*, and *they*, commonly function as **noun-substitutes;** that is, they can substitute for virtually all other nouns in all structures, according to patterns which, as we shall shortly see, provide an important classification of nouns. They resemble function words in having little or no lexical meaning of their own, being dependent for their meaning on the linguistic or nonlinguistic context in which they occur, to a greater degree than do most other words.

FUNCTION NOUNS. This group includes fifteen words which have the following characteristics:

a) They are morphemically identical with or closely related to certain noun-determiners.

b) They are unchanging in form, showing neither of the characteristic noun inflections {-*es*} and {-'*s*}.

c) They have no noun-marking derivational suffixes.

d) They may appear in most of the structural positions usually occupied by nouns.

These fifteen function nouns can be divided into two groups. The first group are morphemically identical with noun-determiners:

all	enough	much
any	his	several
both	more	some

The members of the second group are morphemic variants of noun-determiners, as the following lists reveal:

Noun-Determiner	Function Noun
no	none
my	mine
our	ours
your	yours
her	hers
their	theirs

It will be noted that the last five words in each list are respectively the first and second possessives of the pronouns *I, we, you, she,* and *they.* But in spite of this close relation, their structural functions are quite different, and therefore in a syntactic classification such as this, we put them in these separate groups of noun-determiners and function nouns.

The following pairs of sentences illustrate these words in their two roles. In the first sentence of each pair the italicized word is a noun-determiner, while in the second sentence the italicized word is the corresponding function noun:

> *all* men are free here
> *all* are free here
>
> will you have *more* turkey
> will you have *more*
>
> this money is *his* property
> this money is *his*
>
> *my* house is older than *your* house
> *mine* is older than *yours*
>
> in courage he is second to *no* man
> in courage he is second to *none*

Occupying a sort of intermediate position between full nouns and function nouns is a group of nine words which are like function nouns in being morphemically identical with certain noun-determiners, and like nouns in having one or another of the formal noun-markers. They are the following:

few	either	this/these
many	neither	that/those
most	each	
	another	

Those in the first column may appear with the determiners *the* or *a/an*. Those in the middle column may have the possessive inflection {*-'s*}. The two in the right-hand column, as shown by the alternate forms, have the plural inflection {*-es*}.

Again these may be illustrated in pairs of sentences, the first showing the word as noun-determiner, the second as noun:

> *few* people liked the music; *most* hearers were annoyed by it
> *a few* liked the music; *most* were annoyed by it

> *either* man's house is like home to me
> *either's* house is like home to me

> please hand me *that* book/*those* books
> please hand me *that*/*those*[7]

Certain other words that are morphemically identical with noun-determiners may also appear as nouns. They are *one*, *other*, and the numbers from *two* to *ninety-nine*. All of these may take the plural inflection {*-es*} and appear with any noun-determiner (not just *the* and *a/an*); *one* and *other* can also take the possessive inflection {*-'s*}. There is therefore no reason to consider them anything but nouns, marked as such in the usual ways. The following pairs of sentences show some of them first as noun-determiners and second as nouns. In the second sentence of each pair, observe the various noun-markers, in addition to position, which mark them as nouns:

> *other* people were present so he was silent
> *others* were present so he was silent

> *two* lions and *two* tigers entered the ark
> the animals entered the ark by *twos*

> *one* man's coat was torn and the *other* man was limping
> *one's* coat was torn and the *other* was limping

[7] One interesting group of forms that should be mentioned here are the noun-determiners *a lot of* and *lots of* (phonemically often /əlátə/ and /látsə/ even in careful speech) and their corresponding function-nouns, *a lot/lots*.

bring *three* friends
any *three* you like

Two more groups of words should be mentioned here because they are frequently classed as "pronouns." The first group includes ·the following:

somebody	anybody	everyone
nobody	anyone	everything
something	anything	someone
nothing	everybody	no one

Those in the first column are clearly full nouns, since they can take either the plural or the possessive inflection or both and can follow many (but not all) of the noun-determiners. The remaining eight can take only the possessive inflection and hence may be considered defective nouns. Historically, of course, all twelve are compounds of the noun-determiners *some*, *any*, *every*, and *no* with the nouns *body*, *one*, and *thing*. But they have long since become single words, and all except the last are so written.

The second group includes the compounds of the personal pronouns with *-self*, *-selves*. Two of these, *himself* and *themselves*, are formed on the objective case form. Four—*myself*, *yourself*, *ourselves*, *yourselves*—use the first possessive. One more, *herself*, has a stem that could be either, while *itself* uses the subjective form as stem (or possibly the possessive with synthesis of the two contiguous /s/'s). This inconsistency of the standard language is not always present in some regional and social dialects, where *hisself* and *theirselves* are analogous to *myself* and *ourselves*.

CLASSIFICATION OF NOUNS BY SUBSTITUTE-GROUPS. A quality of nouns which we frequently rely on in English to prevent ambiguity is the fact that they belong to different classes according to the substitutes which can be substituted for them. Thus, the sentence

I called my friend a porter is ambiguous because both *friend* and *porter* can have *he* as their substitute, and therefore we do not know whether they have the same referent or not. But *I called my friend a taxi* is much less likely to be ambiguous, because friend can have *he* or *she* as substitute, while *taxi* can have only *it*, so they probably have different referents.

This quality of nouns is sometimes called **gender.** Grammarians are wary of speaking of gender in modern English, however, for two reasons: (1) unlike many languages that have gender, English has very few clear formal markers that indicate the gender of nouns; (2) the situation in English is much less rigid and clear-cut since many words (*dog*, for instance) may have *he*, *she*, or *it* as substitutes. It thus seems wisest to restrict the term *gender* to those languages that have precise and mutually exclusive noun-classes marked by clear formal markers.

In present-day English, we can recognize eleven **substitute-groups,** with some dialectal variation in the assignment of words to the various groups. In the list that follows, the slant line is used to separate alternative singular forms, and the dash to separate singular and plural. Thus "he/she—they" means "the class of nouns which may have either *he* or *she* (or, of course, their inflectional variants *him*, *her*, and the -*self* compounds) as substitutes in the singular and only *they* in the plural." It should be noted that for classes (8) and (9) *they* can be a singular substitute.

1. he—they
   man, father, uncle, brother, waiter, priest, monk, king, tenor
2. she—they
   woman, mother, aunt, sister, waitress, priestess, nun, queen, soprano
3. it—they
   house, tree, poem, friendship, complication, snow, rock, sand, red
4. he/she—they
   parent, child, artist, teacher, friend, student, cook, doctor, invalid
5. he/it—they
   bull, ram, rooster, buck, steer, tomcat

6. she/it—they
   cow, ewe, hen, doe, heifer, bitch, ship
7. he/she/it—they
   baby, dog, cat, one, other
8. it/they—they
   group, committee, team, gang, class, jury, government, crew
9. he/she/they—they (or no plural)
   somebody, someone, anybody, everybody, person. (In some dialects, most of the words here listed in [4] are in this group.)
10. it (no plural)
    dirt, mathematics, poetry, music, shrubbery, empathy, bravado, nothing
11. they (no singular)
    pants, scissors, pliers, clothes, people

This classification, though formal in operation, is based chiefly on meaning. Each of the groups could, in fact, be more or less accurately described in terms of the common denominator of meaning of the words it includes. Group 1, for instance, contains those nouns that denote human beings in relationships or occupations reserved for males or for which separate words are used for males. It cannot be called "the class of masculine nouns," however, because groups 4, 5, 7, 8, 9 also contain nouns of masculine reference. The simplest nomenclature is to call it the "*he* substitute-group."

Since these classes are largely meaning-based, they are especially sensitive to changes in the social environment that bring about changes in the referents of nouns. Particularly noticeable in the last fifty years or so has been the transfer of large numbers of words from the *he* substitute-group (1) to the *he/she* substitute-group (4) as women have taken up occupations formerly restricted to men. This has been accompanied by the decline in favor of some words in the *she* substitute-group, such as *authoress* and *poetess*, with the corresponding transfer of *author* and *poet* to the *he/she* substitute-group.

SUMMARY. Let us sum up what we have so far established about nouns under five main headings.

1. **Nouns** are a class of lexical words marked by their appearance following certain noun-determining function words, such as *the*, *my*,

some, two; by their use of two inflections, {*-es*} and {*-'s*}; by certain derivational suffixes; by their appearance in certain positions; and occasionally by certain superfixes of stress.

2. A small group of nouns, the **pronouns**, consists of *I, we, thou, you, he, she, it, they, who*, with their inflectional variants.

3. Another small group of nouns, the **function nouns**, includes words like *all* and *none*, which are either identical with or morphemically related to certain of the noun-determiners, but which bear none of the usual distinguishing marks of nouns except ability to occupy the positions characteristic of nouns.

4. English nouns can be classified in eleven **substitute-groups**, on the basis of the substitutes that may replace them or refer to them. These groups are largely meaning-based, though a few morphemic markers like the suffix {*-ess*} help to distinguish some of them.

VERBS

There are five kinds of verb-marking formal criteria: inflections, function words, derivational affixes, positions, and superfixes.

1. There are four verb inflections, which can be morphemically designated as {*-s*}, {*-ed₁*}, {*-ed₂*}, and {*-ing₁*}. This is the most elaborate set of inflections used with any of the English parts of speech, yet it is exceedingly simple compared with the inflectional system of the verbs of languages like Greek and Russian. Let us look briefly at each of these four inflections.

a) The **third-singular** inflection {*-s*} has three allomorphs, /-s, -z, -iz/, which are identical with the three regular allomorphs of the noun-plural inflection {*-es*} and similarly distributed. That is, /-s/ follows stems ending in voiceless consonants except /s, š, č/; /-iz/ follows stems ending in /s, š, č, z, ž, ǰ/; and /-z/ follows all other stems. There are no irregular allomorphs, and there is a single suppletive form, *is*. Because this inflection is morphemically identical with the plural inflection of nouns, it is virtually useless for identifying verbs in isolation. Such forms as *hopes, walks, rides, lies, catches, noses,* and thousands of others can be either nouns or verbs, depending on their environment. Even in the context of complete utterances, there is a constant danger of structural ambiguity resulting from this identity, particularly in the streamlined grammar of headlines and telegrams. Consider the following headline:

LABOR TRAINS FIRE ON RIGHT TO WORK

Here TRAINS can be either noun or verb. Note that intonation keeps this structure from being ambiguous in speech, as is revealed by full phonemic transcriptions:

(a) ²lèybər trêynz ³fáyr²|²àn râyt tu ³wɔ́rk¹#
(b) ²léybər trèynz²||²fâyr àn râyt tu ³wɔ́rk¹#

Note that the different stress and pitch patterns and the contrasting position and type of juncture clearly indicate that /treynz/ is a verb in (a) and a noun in (b).

Since the allomorphs of {-s} are also identical with those of the noun-possessive inflection {-'s}, ambiguity is possible here too. Forms like /mæhnz, píypəlz, liyfs/ can be either nouns in the possessive case or verbs; while others like /dɔhgz, howps, jɔ́jiz/ can be plural nouns, possessive nouns, or verbs. The apostrophe is a device of the written language to resolve some at least of these ambiguities. As we shall see in Chapter 8, the very fact that it does not correspond to anything in the spoken language is the reason that many people never understand the conventions governing its use.

This ambiguity of the three inflections {-es}, {-'s}, and {-s} is the result of certain historical changes in the grammar and pronunciation of English during the last eight or nine centuries. It is a vivid illustration of the fact that linguistic development is not dictated by logic but by very complex unconscious forces that often work contrary to logic. Certainly from the point of view of logic it is unfortunate that three of the eight inflections of present-day English should be almost identical, in spite of the tremendous numbers of phoneme combinations which could have been used to make completely different forms. But from our point of view, which is not that of logic but that of descriptive grammar, this is simply a fact to be noted and taken account of in our formulation of the structural patterns of our language.

b) The inflection we have morphemically described as $\{-ed_1\}$ is often called the **past-tense** or **preterit** inflection. Its regular allomorphs are /-t, -d, -ɨd/, distributed somewhat as the regular allomorphs of $\{-es\}$ are. That is, /-t/ follows bases ending in voiceless consonants except /t/; /-ɨd/[8] follows bases ending in /t, d/; /-d/ follows all others. Examples of these three are: (1) /howpt, wɔhkt, liyst, wišt, riyčt, læhft, bɨrθt/; (2) /béytɨd, síydɨd/; (3) /rabd, wægd, siyzd, ruwžd, jɔjd, seyvd, beyð̃d, dimd, sind, lɔhŋd, kɔhld, sihrd, howd, preyd/.

A large majority of the verbs of English have these regular allomorphs of the past-tense inflection $\{-ed_1\}$. There are, however, a good many verbs, some of quite common occurrence, which show exceptions to this distribution. We have not space here for an exhaustive list of these irregular forms. Instead, we shall merely list some of the more common varieties.[9]

(1) *Forms with* /Ø/. Some verbs whose base forms already end in /t/ or /d/ have a /Ø/ (zero) allomorph of the suffix $\{-ed_1\}$. The result is that their base and past-tense forms are phonemically identical. A few examples are *set, put, hit; shed, spread, rid.*

(2) *Forms with* /Ø/ + *Vowel Change.* The so-called "strong verbs" and a few others make the past-tense form with a change of vowel in the stem and the /Ø/ allomorph of $\{-ed_1\}$. There are about seventy-five of these plus their compounds, but since most of them are verbs

---

[8] This is the form of this allomorph used by the writer. Others may have /-id/ or /-əd/.

[9] A formulaic statement will be found in Trager and Smith, *Outline,* p. 64. See also Gleason, *Introduction to Descriptive Linguistics* (New York: Henry Holt & Co., Inc., 1955), pp. 102–3.

of common occurrence, they are of greater importance than their relatively small number might indicate. Some examples which illustrate the various kinds of morphophonemic change which may appear are /rayd–rowd, friyz–frowz, driŋk–dræŋk, stiyl–stowl, kəm–keym, stæhnd–stud, giv–geyv, siy–sɔh, šeyk–šuk, sley–sluw, howld–held, grow–gruw, bliyd–bled, miyt–met/.

(3) *Forms with* /-t/ + *Change of Base.* Some verbs which add the /-t/ allomorph of {-ed₁} also show morphophonemic change in the base. Examples are /sliyp–slept, tiyč–tɔht, bay–bɔht, siyk–sɔht, θiŋk–θɔht, liyv–left, luwz–lɔhst, gow–went/.

(4) *Forms with* /-d/ + *Change of Base.* Similarly, some verbs which add the /-d/ allomorph of {-ed₁} also show morphophonemic change in the base. Examples: /sel–sowld, fliy–fled, hihr–həhrd, duw–did, hæv–hæd, sey–sed/.

(5) *Forms with* /-t/ *After Voiced Consonant.* Some verbs have /-t/ instead of the regular /-d/ after the voiced consonants /m, n, l/. These divide into two groups: (1) those that add /-t/ to the end of the base, sometimes with a change of the stem vowel: /bəhrn–bəhrnt, spil–spilt, driym–dremt/; most of these also have regular forms in /-d/: /bəhrnd, spild, driymd/; (2) those that drop a final /d/ before adding /-t/: /bend–bent, bild–bilt/; these do not change stem vowel and do not have regular forms in /-id/ except in archaic context.

c) The inflection we have called {-ed₂} is the **past-participle** inflection. It has the same three regular allomorphs as does the past-tense inflection /-t, -d, -id/, distributed in just the same fashion. Hence, the past-participle forms of the regular verbs listed on page 254 are indistinguishable from the past-tense forms. In isolation there is no way to determine whether such forms as *hoped*, *baited*, and *robbed* are past-tense or past-participle forms. The same may be said of most of the irregular forms listed above. Thus in such verbs as *set*, *shed*, *sleep*, *stand*, *teach*, *buy*, *leave*, *lose*, *sell*, *hear*, *have*, and *say* the past-tense and past-participle inflections are alike.

There is, however, a small group of verbs in which the past-participle form is different from the past-tense form. If it were not for these, we would not recognize separate inflections, but would include them all under a single inflection {-ed}, with its various allomorphs. Hence, this group, though small, is grammatically quite important. It may be subdivided into two subgroups. The first of these have the suffixes /-n/ or /-ən/, which are allomorphs of {-ed$_2$} but not of {-ed$_1$}. They may also show some morphophonemic changes in the base. In the following examples, the first form of each set of three is the base, the second is the past-tense form, and the third is the past-participle form: /now–nuw–nown, drɔh–druw–drɔhn, behr–bɔhr–bɔhrn, lay–ley–leyn, duw–did–dən; giv–geyv–gívən, rayd–rowd–rídən, friyz–frowz–frówzən, breyk–browk–brów-kən/. The second group comprises a few verbs which have /∅/ as inflectional ending in both the past-tense and the past-participle forms, but use a different allomorph of the base for each. In some of these the past-participle form is like the base. Examples are /siŋ–sæŋ–səŋ, rən–ræhn–rən, kəm–keym–kəm/.

d) The **present-participle** inflection {-ing$_1$} has only one allomorph, /-iŋ/, which appears regularly with all verbs except a few that lack forms of this sort entirely (*will, can, may*, etc.). There are, of course, dialectal and individual variants of this suffix, such as /-in, -in, -iŋg/, but these have no grammatical significance. This inflection is not an infallible marker of verbs, since it is phonemically identical with the derivational suffixes {-ing$_2$} and {-ing$_3$}, which respectively characterize nouns (see p. 241) and adjectives (as in "this story is very *interesting*.")

In a class by itself as far as inflections are concerned is the verb *be*, which has not only the third singular /iz, z, s/, the past tense /wəz/, the past participle /bin/ and the present participle /bíyiŋ/, but also a form /æm, əm, m/ which appears with the pronoun *I*, a form /ahr, ər, r/ which appears elsewhere in the present, and a past-plural form /wəhr/.

2. The second kind of formal marker that distinguishes verbs is a set of function words called **auxiliaries,** which combine with verbs to make **verb-phrases.** Auxiliaries are true verb-determiners and might be so called, except that the traditional term is both convenient and unambiguous. Just as most of the noun-determiners also appear as function nouns and some even as full nouns, so the auxiliaries may appear by themselves as **function verbs** or full verbs. Formally the auxiliaries may be divided into four groups on the basis of the forms of the main verb with which they appear. As will be seen, there is some overlapping between the groups.

a) Auxiliaries appearing with the *base* form of the verb are:

can/could	must
may/might	dare
shall/should	need
will/would	(had)better/best
do/does/did	

To this list might also be added the function words *please, do, let's,* and the rather archaic *pray,* which may appear in special combinations with the base form of verbs.

b) Auxiliaries appearing with the *present-participle* (base + {-*ing*$_1$}) form of the verb are the following two:

am/is/are/was/were
get/gets/got

c) Auxiliaries appearing with the *past-participle* (base + {-*ed*$_2$}) form of the verb are the following three:

am/is/are/was/were
get/gets/got
have/has/had

d) Auxiliaries appearing with the **infinitive** form of the verb, which consists of the function word *to* + the base form, are the following.

have (/hæf/) /has (/hæs/)/ had
ought
used (/yuwst/)
am/is/are/was/were
get/gets/got

am/is/are/was/were $\left\{\begin{array}{l}\text{about}\\\text{going}\end{array}\right.$

Particularly noteworthy is the fact that *have, has, used,* and often *going* are phonemically distinct from the related (and similarly spelled) forms that appear elsewhere as auxiliaries or full verbs. In fact, such forms as /hǽstə, hǽftə, yúwstə, ɔ́htə, góntə/, prevalent in American speech on all social levels, indicate that the *to* which is customarily considered a part of the infinitive is often a part of the auxiliary instead. A grammatical change seems to be taking place here, which will have to be dealt with in the grammars of the future.

An interesting quality of the auxiliaries is that they may combine with one another to build quite elaborate verb-phrases, which themselves act as auxiliaries of full verbs. There is no point in producing a full inventory of all the possibilities here, but a few examples will recall to the reader the diversity and multiplicity of English auxiliaries.

(a) The auxiliaries of the first group, those that appear with the base form, make no complex forms in the standard dialect. Many speakers, it is true, have forms like *better had, used to could,* and *might could,* but these belong to regional or social dialects not usually accepted as standard educated speech.

(b) The auxiliaries of the second group, those that appear with the present-participle form of verbs—that is, *be* and *get,* with their inflectional variants—may be used in virtually any type of complex form except one that ends in *being* or *keeping.* Some examples are:

was going
might have been going

> used to have to be going
> was getting going

(c) The auxiliaries of the third group, those which appear with the past-participle form of verbs, may build quite elaborate structures, involving virtually all the other auxiliaries. The following are some of the combinations that can be made with the past participle of the full verb *feed*:

might have fed	might have been fed
can get fed	was being fed
will be fed	should have been getting fed
has been fed	used to have to be getting fed

(d) Of the fourth group of auxiliaries, those that appear with the infinitive form of verbs, only *have*, *about*, and *going* can build complex phrases. Some examples are the following:

> might have had to go
> has been going to eat
> would have been about to leave

When complex forms involving *be*, *ought*, or *used* and the infinitive are built, the complexity appears in the infinitive, not in the auxiliary, as in the following examples:

> ought to have gone
> used to be being fed
> was to have been told

Forms such as *had ought*, though common to many speakers and dialects, are usually considered characteristic of uneducated speech.

The large number of these auxiliaries and the multiplicity of ways in which they may be combined permit a very large repertory of verb structures to be built in English. From a historical point of view, it is interesting to note that many of them are of quite recent development. This seems to be an area of English grammar where change has been taking place rapidly. Indeed, change seems to be still going on, and may continue to for some time to come.

3. The third kind of verb-identifying marker is a relatively short list of derivational affixes. Six of these—five suffixes and a prefix— are frequent enough to be noted here.

a) {-ate₁}, phonemically /-eyt/, added chiefly to bound stems but also to a few nouns. It is to be distinguished from {-ate₂}, phonemically /-it, -ɨt, -ət/, which marks adjectives and nouns. Examples of verbs formed from stem + {-ate₁} are *implicate, operate, corroborate, dehydrate*; from noun + {-ate₁}: *calumniate, salivate, orchestrate*. These verbs characteristically have the superfix {ˊ ˇ ˋ}. Virtually every one of them has a noun derivative in {-ation}, as *implication, operation*, etc. A few also have related nouns and adjectives in {-ate₂} with a different superfix: *duplicate, syndicate* (pronounced /dúwplɨkit, síndɨkit/).

b) {-ize}, added to bound stems, nouns, and adjectives, as in *utilize, recognize; idolize, organize; socialize, modernize*. In some cases the stem may be both noun and adjective, as in *standardize, moralize, particularize*. These verbs have related nouns in {-ism} or {-ation}, or both: *organism, organization; socialism, socialization*, etc.

c) {-fy}, phonemically /-fay/, added to stems, nouns, and adjectives, as in *liquefy, indemnify; countrify, dandify; beautify, simplify*. Nouns related to these verbs end in *-faction* or *-fication*, as *liquefaction, simplification*.

d) {-ish}, added to bound stems, as in *finish, furnish, languish*.

e) {-en}, phonemically /-in, -ən/, added to one-syllable adjectives, some nouns, and a few bound stems, as in *blacken, sharpen, widen, tighten; heighten, hasten; glisten*. Verbs of this group are always of two syllables, (except a few like *enlighten, enliven*, which also have the prefix {en-}) and have the superfix {ˊ ˇ}. This suffix is phonemically identical with the /-in, -ən/ allomorphs of {-ed₂} (see p. 256),

as in *given, woven,* and also with the adjective-forming suffix {-en₂},
as in *waxen, oaken.*

f) The prefix {en-}, with allomorphs and dialectal variants /en-,
em-, in-, im-, in-, im-/, added to nouns primarily, but also to other
verbs and to a few adjectives and stems: *enfold, enslave, empower;
enliven, enlighten; embitter; endure.* The characteristic superfix is
{` + ´}.

4. A few positions serve to mark verbs, though seldom without
aid from other formal devices which mark either the verb or other
neighboring words. Two of these positions are important enough to
be noted here.

a) Utterance–initial position may be filled by a verb in the base
form, alone or preceded by one of the function words *please, let's,
do,* or *pray* (this last is quite uncommon in American English). This
produces a type of sentence structure common in requests:

hope for the best	please answer at once
bring your skates	let's go home
love your neighbor	pray come in

Usually the verb is followed by a noun, with or without determiner.
However, if both the noun-determiner and the initial function word
are missing, such structures may become ambiguous, like the following:

time flies (*cp.* time the flies, please time flies, the time flies)
love blossoms in spring

For many speakers, this ambiguity is avoided by intonational differences. Compare

(a) /²lÃ³v² ‖ ²blÃ¢sÉ™mz in ³sprÃÅ‹¹#/
(b) /²lÃ²v ³blÃ¡sÉ™mz² | ²in ³sprÃÅ‹¹#/

Clearly *love* is a noun in (a) and a verb in (b).

b) The position between two nouns, with or without determiners, may be occupied by many sorts of verbs and verb-phrases. Again, if the noun-determiners are missing and the verb is in the base or third-singular form, ambiguity may result, as in the last two of these examples:

dogs chase sticks	/bírdz ləv nests/
people harbor misunderstanding	/həntərz triy behrz/
the stars light our path	

Again the potential ambiguities are often prevented by contrasting intonation patterns. Thus in /²hə̂ntərz tríy²|³béhrz¹#/, *tree* is a noun, while in /³hə́ntərz²|²trîy ³béhrz¹#/, *tree* is a verb. Note that in both cases the single-bar juncture comes just before the verb.

There are other verb positions, but they seldom serve to identify verbs. In fact, so frequent is the occurrence of either an auxiliary or an inflection that it is seldom necessary to rely on either derivative affixes or position to identify verbs. They are usually the most clearly marked of all the parts of speech.[10]

5. Insofar as prosodic patterns reveal the whole structure of an utterance, they may serve to identify verbs, as we have already seen. But seldom is a verb marked as such merely by an unambiguous superfix. There is one group of verbs, however, which are distinguished from related nouns and adjectives by the stress-superfix {˘ ´}, with or without morphophonemic change. In the following list, the words in the right-hand column are nouns or adjectives, those in the left-hand column verbs.

---

[10] In two items, one an article and the other a short story, in the February 1955 issue of *Harper's Magazine*, there were 1014 verbs. Of these, 93 were in the base form alone, 437 had inflections but no function words, 289 had function words (including the infinitive-marker *to*) but no inflections, and 195 had both inflections and function words. Thus, less than 10 per cent were unmarked, while nearly 65 per cent had inflections and nearly 50 per cent were accompanied by auxiliaries. Of the 93 unmarked verbs, only one was truly ambiguous: "An American official watching the British *blunder* in the Iranian oil dispute..." Here *blunder* could be a noun or a verb.

This count does not include 181 occurrences of the inflected forms of *be*.

imprínt	ímprìnt
səspékt	sэ́spèkt
impórt	ímpòrt
kəntrǽkt	kántræ̀kt
pìrfékt	pírfìkt

Even here there are exceptions, however. Thus, both /kántènt/ and /kəntént/ are nouns, though the latter may also be either a verb or an adjective as well.

AUXILIARIES AS FUNCTION VERBS. Any of the auxiliaries that we have discussed above except *get* may appear without the normally expected form of a full verb, provided a full verb has been expressed (or in rare cases implied) in the immediate linguistic context. Auxiliaries so operating are **function verbs.** The illustrations below show various function verbs in various possible responses to the question, "Are you coming?" They are grouped according to our classification of the auxiliaries on pages 257–58, and the omitted full verb forms are indicated in parentheses.

(a) I *will* (come) if I *can* (come)
I guess I *had better* (come)
must I (come)
(b) yes I *am* (coming)
(c) I already *have* (come)
(d) I suppose I *have to* (come)
I guess I *ought* (to come) though I never *used to* (come)
I'm *going to* (come) pretty soon

In connection with group (d), it is interesting to note that the function word *to*, the "sign of the infinitive" or infinitive-marker, is retained with the auxiliaries *have/has* (phonemically /hæf, hæs/), *used* (phonemically /yuwst/), *going*, and *about*. Thus, a response such as "I'm *going* (to come) as I *used* (to come) unless I no longer *have* (to come)" would be unintelligible to any speaker of American

English.[11]   This is further evidence of the trend, mentioned on page 258, to treat the infinitive-marker as part of the auxiliary.

THE VERB-SUBSTITUTE *Do*. The verb *do* and its various inflectional and phrasal forms may appear in place of any full verb that has already appeared in the immediate linguistic context. Thus *do* is a true **verb-substitute,** and the only one that is used in all varieties of English. The following are some examples of its use:

> he works harder than I *do*   (substituted for *work*)
> the music sounds better than it *did* yesterday   (for *sounded*)
> he has accomplished more in a week than I have *done* in a year
> (for *accomplished*)
> A: please mend my shirt at once
> B: I'm already *doing* it   (for *mending*)

In cases like the last two, involving verb-phrases rather than simple base or inflected forms, American English (in contrast to British English) is inclined to use a function verb rather than a phrasal form of *do*. Thus, in America these two would more commonly appear as:

> he has accomplished more in a week than I *have* in a year
> A: please mend my shirt at once B: I already *am*

The versatile little verb *do* may thus appear in four different roles: as auxiliary, as function verb, as verb-substitute, and as full verb. These four uses are illustrated in the following sentences:

> (a) *do* as auxiliary:
> *do* you often go to the movies
> *do* come to see us
> yes he *does* look like his brother
> I *didn't* finish the job
> how *do* you do

[11] British English permits *used* as a function verb without *to*: "I'm *going to* as I *used* unless I no longer *have to*."

(b) *do* as function verb:

    he liked it but I *didn't*

    I go there frequently; *do* you

(c) *do* as verb-substitute:

    I hope you enjoyed it as much as I *did*

    the child used to behave better than he *does* now

(d) *do* as full verb:

    he *does* a great deal for other people

    how do you *do*

    that will *do* for now, but we must *do* better tomorrow

SEPARABLE VERBS. An important group of English verbs have the formal peculiarity of consisting of two parts, which may appear together or be separated by one or more other elements of the structure of which they are a part. The first of the two parts is a form that also appears as an independent verb; the second is a form that also appears as an adverb or as a function word of the class called *prepositions* (see p. 306), and sometimes as a prefix as well. These verbs are not recognized as single grammatical units by all grammarians; some call them "verb-adverb combinations."[12] They have also been called "merged verbs,"[13] "separable compounds,"[14] "compound verbs,"[15] and "poly-word verbs."[16] Our term **separable verbs** is meant to bring out both grammatical qualities of these verbs: (1) that they function as single parts of speech, and (2) that

[12] R. W. Zandvoort, *A Handbook of English Grammar*, 5th ed. (Groningen: J. B. Wolters, 1953), p. 275; Paul Roberts, *Understanding Grammar* (New York: Harper & Bros., 1954), p. 121.

[13] Janet R. Aiken, *A New Plan of English Grammar* (New York: Henry Holt & Co., Inc., 1933), cited in Margaret M. Bryant, *A Functional English Grammar* (Boston: D. C. Heath & Co., 1945), p. 208.

[14] George O. Curme, *Principles and Practice of English Grammar* (New York: Barnes & Noble, Inc., 1947), p. 24.

[15] J. H. G. Grattan and P. Gurrey, *Our Living Language* (London: Thomas Nelson & Sons, Ltd., 1925), p. 80.

[16] E. W. Stevick, "The 'Deferred Preposition'," *American Speech*, XXV (1950), 214.

their two parts may be separated from each other by intervening elements.

These verbs are quite plentiful. Twenty-four of them can be made by combining any of the eight verbs with any of the three separable elements in the following illustration:

$$
\text{he}
\begin{Bmatrix}
\text{takes} \\
\text{puts} \\
\text{gets} \\
\text{throws} \\
\text{holds} \\
\text{gives} \\
\text{makes} \\
\text{plays}
\end{Bmatrix}
\text{it}
\begin{Bmatrix}
\text{over} \\
\text{out} \\
\text{up}
\end{Bmatrix}
$$

From the point of view of word order, these verbs can be identified by the fact that the following noun can come either between the two parts of the verb or after them both, unless it is a pronoun or function noun, in which case it always comes between the two parts. Thus, we can say:

he puts his message over
hè pùts ³óver² | ²hìs ³méssage¹ # (*note stress and juncture*)
he puts it over
but not
*he puts over it

Ambiguity is possible, at least in written English and rapid speech, when the two parts of a separable verb are not separated, as in the following:

he looked over the old fence

But in slower speech this ambiguity is avoided by intonation. Note the different stress and pitch patterns and the different positions of the single-bar juncture in the following:

(a) /²hìy lùkt ³ówvər²|²ðiy ôwld ³féns¹#/
(b) /²hìy lúkt²|²òwvər ðiy ôwld ³féns¹#/

If these two sentences are read aloud, it will become apparent that (a) reports that the subject was inspecting the fence itself, while in (b) he is reported as looking at something on the other side. Therefore, only (a) can be replaced by the separable form:

> he looked the old fence over

If the substitute *it* is put in for *the old fence*, the sentences will be:

> (a) he looked it over
> (b) he looked over it

This same test will settle the problem raised by the often-cited pair:

> (a) he ran up a big bill
> (b) he ran up a big hill

In (a), we have the separable verb *ran up*, with the single-bar juncture, if any, after *up*. In (b) this juncture, if there is one, comes after the simple verb *ran* and is followed by the prepositional phrase *up a big hill*. The contrasting forms that appear when *it* is substituted can be illustrated as answers to questions:

> (a) A: where did this bill come from B: he ran it up
> (b) A: how did he climb that hill B: he ran up it

SUMMARY. What we have so far learned about verbs may be summed up under five headings.

1. Verbs are a class of lexical words marked by their use of four inflections, {-s}, {-ed₁}, {-ed₂}, and {-ing₁}; by their appearance in **verb-phrases** with certain **auxiliaries,** such as *can, must, is, has, please, about* (*to*), *keep* (*on*); by a small group of derivational affixes, such as {*en-*} and {*-ate₁*}; by certain positions relative to clearly marked nouns; and occasionally by the superfix {˘ ΄}.

2. Most auxiliaries may build complex combinations with other

auxiliaries, making possible a very large repertory of **verb-phrases.**

3. Auxiliaries may appear as **function verbs,** standing in place of a full verb-phrase, when the full verb has been expressly stated or strongly implied in the immediate linguistic context or the nonlinguistic context.

4. The verb *do* in its various inflectional and phrasal forms may appear as a substitute for a full verb which has appeared in the immediate linguistic context. It is the only **verb-substitute.**

5. **Separable verbs,** made up of a full verb followed by an adverblike form, may appear with their two parts together or separated by intervening words.

ADJECTIVES

The primary defining or identifying quality of adjectives is their exclusive ability to fit into both the environments left blank in a structure such as:

the . . . man seems very . . .

To avoid lexical incompatibility, the noun and noun-determiner in this pattern may be varied without affecting the structure. Likewise, the verb may be replaced by *is*, *becomes*, *looks*, and certain similar verbs from a limited list. Thus, the framework identifies as adjectives all of the various italicized words in the following sentences:

the *strong* man is very *strong*
this *uncomfortable* position is very *uncomfortable*
the *relaxed* spectator looks very *relaxed*
the *self-centered* girl seems very *self-centered*
any *interesting* story sounds very *interesting*

These two positions may be described as (1) between noun-determiner and noun, and (2) immediately following the function word *very* (or some other **qualifier** from a list to be given shortly), which in turn follows a verb of the **linking** or **copulative** type, which we shall define when we come to consider structures of complementation. In order to qualify as an adjective, a word must be able to fit both these positions.

If we adopt this frame as the defining criterion of adjectives, we must accept the consequences. Two of these may bother the reader accustomed to classifications of the traditional grammar. The first is that some words customarily considered adjectives do not fit the pattern; thus, *chief* and *main* can fill the first position but not the second, while *alive* and *alone* can fill the second position but not the first. Thus, we can say

the *chief* man is very *alive*

(though many would prefer "very much alive"), but we cannot say

*the *alive* man is very *chief*

A bit of study will lead us to the conclusion that these words do not need to be classed as adjectives. Thus, *chief* and *main* are nouns which behave exactly like the noun *head,* or in more colloquial speech, *boss* or *top.* On the other hand, *alive* and *alone* are adverbs, functioning just like *abroad, away, along,* etc. There are a few adjectives, such as *sole* and *unique,* which do not fit the second position because they are lexically incompatible with the qualifier *very.* But if we substitute *quite* for *very,* they fit the second position quite satisfactorily.

The other problem concerns the last three of our examples, which have the suffixes /-t, -d/ and /-iŋ/, already identified as inflectional suffixes of verbs. At first glance, it would seem that there is no formal distinction between these adjectives and the $\{-ed_2\}$ (past-participle) and $\{-ing_1\}$ (present-participle) inflections of verbs. But again closer scrutiny reveals that though true participles may fit the first of our adjective positions, they will not fit the second. They cannot follow the qualifier *very,* or, indeed, any other qualifier.

Thus we can say "the running horse" but not "the horse is very running." Likewise, we can say "the murdered man" but not "the man is very (rather, quite) murdered." On the other hand, these participles can occupy a position almost never occupied by adjectives alone: the position immediately after a noun. Thus, we can say both "a running horse" and "a horse running;" both "the murdered man" and "the man murdered." But we cannot say "a girl charming" or "the man tired." Clearly, then, there is a sharp distinction on the basis of word order between adjectives and the verb-inflections called participles. Therefore we identify the adjective-forming suffixes /-t, -d, -id/ and /-iŋ/ as distinct morphemes, which we can call {-ed₃} and {-ing₃}[17] to distinguish them from homophonous inflectional and derivational suffixes. Later on we shall note some other formal distinctions between adjectives and participles.

When we come to examine the other formal criteria which help to mark adjectives, we find that we must immediately recognize two large subclasses, which between them include all but a very few adjectives. These subclasses may be called **base adjectives** and **derived adjectives.**

BASE ADJECTIVES. This class includes those adjectives which, in addition to fitting both positions in the adjective-identifying frame, also exhibit the following formal qualities:

(1) Base adjectives take the inflectional suffixes {-er} and {-est} to form the **comparative** and **superlative degrees.** These suffixes are seldom sufficient by themselves to identify adjectives, since the principal allomorph of {-er}, /-ər/, is phonemically identical with the noun-forming derivational suffix {-er} (spelled variously -er, -or, -ar, -our), and the principal allomorph of {-est} may, in some dialects at least, be phonemically identical with the noun-forming derivational suffix {-ist}. Thus, in isolation we cannot tell whether *blinder*, *sharper*, and *cooler*, for instance, are nouns or adjectives. They may even be ambiguous in short phrases like "the blinder bats," "the

---

[17] {-ing₂} is a derivational suffix of nouns; see page 241.

sharper cheats," or "the cooler ices." Similarly, /hyúmənist/ may be either the adjective *humanest* or the noun *humanist*, though it is hard to imagine a context in which they might be confused. The following might serve as a facetious example:

of the deist, the theist, and the humanist, the humanist is húmanest

This is hardly a sentence one is likely to encounter very often.

As we might expect, some morphophonemic changes occur when these inflections are added to base adjectives. Most familiar to all speakers of English is the suppletion which occurs in the following paradigmatic sets:

good	better	best
bad	worse	worst

(2) Base adjectives are also distinguished formally by the fact that they serve as stems from which nouns and adverbs are formed by the derivational suffixes {-ness} and {-ly₁}.[18] This gives us a derivational paradigm of great importance in English, as illustrated by the following examples:

adjective	noun	adverb
strange	strangeness	strangely
black	blackness	blackly
false	falseness	falsely
bad	badness	badly
good	goodness	well

Note that in the last case the force of the paradigm leads us to class *well* as a suppletive equivalent of **goodly*.

Some other variations on this paradigm might also be noted here. For instance, some base adjectives use other derivational suffixes beside {-ness} to form nouns. But in virtually all such cases the noun in {-ness} is also used, though sometimes in a specialized meaning

---

[18] Some, but not all, derived adjectives also use both these suffixes.

or as a so-called **nonce-word.**[19] The result is a situation that can be represented as in the table on the following page. An interesting by-product of this table is the obvious complementary distribution of the noun-forming derivational suffixes {*-th*} and {*-ity*}. Historical linguistics supplies a simple explanation of this: the adjectives which form nouns in {*-th*} are of native (Anglo-Saxon) stock, while those that form nouns in {*-ity*} are ultimately from Latin, borrowed into English either directly or by way of French.

There are a few base adjectives beside *good* which do not form adverbs in {*-ly*$_1$}: *small*, *little*, *long*, *fast*, *ill*, *hard* (*hardly* is best considered as a function word). A few more have related adverbs both in {*-ly*$_1$} and without any suffix at all, hence identical with the adjective (the so-called "flat" adverbs): *slow*, *quick*, *soft*, *clean*.

(3) Most base adjectives are of one syllable, and none have more than two syllables except a few that begin with a derivational prefix like {*un-*}: *uncommon*, *inhuman*.

(4) A fair number of base adjectives form verbs by adding the derivational suffix {*-en*$_1$}, the prefix {*en-*}, or both: *brighten*, *cheapen*, *enlarge*, *embitter*, *enlighten*, *enliven* (see pp. 260–61).

DERIVED ADJECTIVES. The other large class of adjectives, the **derived adjectives,** are those which are formed by the addition of adjective-forming suffixes to free or bound stems. There is a relatively large number of these suffixes, and the resulting array of adjectives is much larger than the class of base adjectives. The relative frequency of the two types varies a great deal from one type of discourse to another. Ordinary speech and simple prose tend to have few adjectives of any sort, with a preponderance of base adjectives; formal, technical, or "highbrow" speech and writing use

[19] *Nonce-word* is a term made up by the editors of the Oxford Dictionary to describe words coined *for the nonce*, that is, to fit an immediate situation. In a way, every newly coined word is at first a nonce-word; it only remains such, how-ever, if it is not taken up and given further use by other speakers. The same form may be a nonce-word many times, if each person to whom it occurs to coin the word is unaware of previous nonce-uses by other people.

Base Adjective	Noun in {-ness}	Adverb in {-ly}	Noun in {-th}	Noun in {-ity}	Other Nouns
dead	deadness	deadly	death		
true	trueness	truly	truth		
young	youngness	youngly	youth		
deep	deepness	deeply	depth		deep
sane	saneness	sanely		sanity	
sober	soberness	soberly		sobriety	
rare	rareness	rarely		rarity	
safe	safeness	safely		safety	safe
human	humanness	humanly		humanity	human
clear	clearness	clearly		clarity	clearing, clear
hot	hotness	hotly			heat
cold	coldness	coldly			cold
green	greenness	greenly			green

more adjectives, with the derived type predominating. Thus, in our simple tale of "Grip the Rat," base adjectives outnumber derived adjectives by more than four to one, while in a recent article in *Harper's Magazine* the proportion was more than two to one the other way.

Some of the more important suffixes which form derived adjectives are the following:

(a) {-*y*}, added to one- and two-syllable nouns and bound stems, as in *faulty, leafy, healthy, rickety; holy.*

(b) {-*al*}, added to nouns and bound stems: *fatal, natural, national, traditional; local, physical, racial.*

(c) {-*able*}, added to verbs and bound stems. This very common suffix is a **live** one which can be added to virtually any verb, thus giving rise to many new coinages and nonce-words. Since it is the descendant of an active derivational suffix in Latin, it also appears as part of many words borrowed from Latin or French. Examples formed from verbs: *remarkable, understandable, adaptable, conceivable*; examples formed from bound stems: *viable, portable, capable, terrible, visible.* Many words of both groups have related nouns formed by adding {-*ity*} to a special allomorph of {-*able*}: *adaptability, capability, visibility.*

(d) {-*ful*} and {-*less*}, added to nouns: *hopeful, hopeless; useful, useless; plentiful; penniless.*

(e) {-*ar*}, {-*ary*}, {-*ic*}, {-*ish₂*}, and {-*ous*}, added to nouns and bound stems: *columnar, popular, regular; legendary, literary; climatic, comic; childish, lavish; marvelous, pernicious.*

(f) {-*ent*} and {-*ive*}, added to verbs and bound stems: *abhorrent, significant, convenient; active, native, impulsive.*

(g) {-*en₂*}, added to nouns: *woolen, waxen, wooden, oaken.* This is phonemically /-ən/, identical with the verb-forming suffix {-*en₁*} (see p. 260). But since the latter is most commonly added to base adjectives rather than to nouns, no ambiguity results. Derived adjectives in {-*en₂*} are relatively few, and what there are seem to be on the way out, being replaced where possible by the stem noun itself. Thus, expressions like *wood floors, wool clothes, an oak chest* are at least as common as those with *wooden, woolen,* and *oaken.*

(h) {*-ed₃*}, added to verbs, nouns, and some bound stems. This suffix has three allomorphs, /-t, -d, -id/, distributed on the whole like the regular allomorphs of the verb-inflectional suffixes {*-ed₁*} and {*-ed₂*}. There are some exceptions, however, notably a group which has /-id/ instead of the expected /-d/ after voiced consonants other than /d/: *ragged, beloved, rugged, aged, learned.* Other examples of {*-ed₃*} added to nouns are *garlanded, overcoated, booted, flowered.* Sometimes an adjective modifier of the noun stem is included in the structure, producing elaborate compound derivatives like *old-fashioned, long-tailed, ruddy-countenanced,* and so on. Examples of this suffix added to verbs are *tired, bored, complicated, devoted.* As adjectives these are distinguished from homophonous verb-inflections by the fact that they may follow the various qualifiers but may not come after the nouns they modify (see p. 270).

(i) {*-ing₃*}, added to verbs: *interesting, exciting, revealing, tiring, pleasing.* These are distinguished from homophonous verb-inflections (present participles) by their ability to follow qualifiers and by the fact that a noun denoting the receiver of the action named by the stem verb appears before the derived adjective but after the present participle. A few contrasting examples will make clear this difference between verbs and adjectives in /-iŋ/:

Verbs	Adjectives
a man eating fish	a man-eating tiger
a job killing chickens	a soul-killing job
a speech rousing the rabble	a rabble-rousing speech
he was boring his friends	he was very boring to them

Note the contrast in prosodic pattern between the first example in the left-hand column and the first one on the right.

Verb: /²ə+mǽhn²|²îytiŋ+³fíš¹#/
Adjective: /²ə+mǽhn+ìytiŋ+³táygər¹#/

In deliberate speech a single-bar juncture will be heard after /mæhn/ in the first example, but never in the second. In fact, the superfix /ˆ ˋ/ together with the closer juncture in the second example entitles us to consider /mǽhn+ìytiŋ/ a single compound word. This is recognized in writing by the use of the hyphen, *man-eating*.

(j) {-*ly*₂}, added to nouns and some bound stems. This is distinguished from the adverb-forming suffix {-*ly*₁} by the fact that its stems are nouns and bound stems, while the stems from which adverbs are formed are adjectives. The following examples illustrate the contrast:

Adjectives	*Adverbs*
Noun or Base + {-*ly*₂}	Adjective + {-*ly*₁}
friendly	widely
orderly	crazily
homely	formally
mannerly	remarkably
ugly	exceedingly

Apparent exceptions to this rule are the adjectives *goodly*, *deadly*, and *lively*, and the adverbs *early*, *chiefly*, and *mainly*.

In addition to being marked by derivational suffixes, derived adjectives contrast with base adjectives in the fact that they virtually never have the inflectional suffixes {-*er*} and {-*est*} except for some two-syllable ones like *friendly*.[20] Their comparative and superlative degrees are formed instead by the use of the qualifiers *more* and *most*. They may, however, form nouns in {-*ness*}, and virtually all of them form adverbs in {-*ly*₁}, including even some of those which themselves end in {-*ly*₂}. The table on the opposite page illustrates some of the complicated paradigms of derivation that may result.

---

[20] Derived adjectives are sometimes given the inflected forms for humorous effect, as in the "Curiouser and curiouser" of *Alice in Wonderland*.

Base Noun	Base Verb	Derived Adjective	Adverb in {-ly₁}	Noun in {-ness}	Other Nouns
act	act	active	actively	activeness	action, activity
friend		friendly	friendlily	friendliness	friendship
marvel	marvel	marvelous	marvelously	marvelousness	
impulse		impulsive	impulsively	impulsiveness	impulsion
	impel	impelling	impellingly		
delight	delight	delightful	delightfully	delightfulness	
		delighted	delightedly		
excess		excessive	excessively	excessiveness	
	exceed	exceeding	exceedingly		
life	(live)	{ live	lively	liveness	
		lively }	livelily	liveliness	livelihood
like		likely	(likely)	likeliness	likelihood

Note that the last of these has the adverb identical with the adjective, instead of the expected *likelily.

ADJECTIVE QUALIFIERS. We have already had occasion to allude more than once to the important group of function words which we have called **qualifiers.** These words, usually classed as adverbs in traditional grammar, appear immediately before an adjective (or in two cases immediately after) and have the function of indicating the degree to which the meaning of the adjective is applicable. The principal qualifiers common to most dialects of English are the following:

very	somewhat	more	enough
quite	a bit /əbít/	most	indeed
rather	a little /əlítəl/	less	
pretty	so	least	
mighty	too		

In addition to these, *real* and *awful* are common qualifiers in all but the most formal spoken English, though they appear less frequently in writing. Various regional and social dialects also use *that, some, right, plenty, wonderful, powerful,* as well as *darn(ed), damn(ed),* and other "swear words," shading off into those usually considered unprintable.

Since virtually all these qualifiers can appear with adverbs as well as with adjectives, they cannot serve as adjective-determiners. Some of them exhibit peculiarities of distribution which can only be touched on here, since we have not space for a complete list. Thus, we may mention that *more* and *most* commonly appear only with derived adjectives, since base adjectives use the inflected forms for the comparative and superlative. The qualifier *enough* always follows the adjective with which it appears except when the adjective is a base adjective in the comparative degree: compare the following two sentences:

the music was *loud enough*
the music was *enough louder* so that it could be heard

On the other hand, the qualifier *indeed* may either precede or follow its adjective:

> the music was *loud indeed*
> the music was *indeed loud*

When an adjective is in the comparative degree, whether the inflected comparative with {-er} or the phrasal comparative formed with *more*, the list of qualifiers that may be used with it is different from the list given on page 278, though there is some overlapping:[21]

rather	much	a { good	} deal
somewhat	lots	a { great	} deal
no	a (whole) lot	a little	
still	a (good) bit	even	

As in the case of the other qualifiers, dialects supply further forms, such as *a heap*, *heaps*, *a touch*, *a mite*, *(a) way*, *some*, *that*, as well as "swear word" forms like /əhéləvəlàt/ and many others.

On the basis of function and meaning, it is impossible to draw the line between these qualifiers and adverbs expressing degree, such as *exceedingly*, *enormously*, *infinitely*, *fairly*, *moderately*, *infinitesimally*, and many others. But we can exclude these from the category of qualifiers on the ground that they are marked as adverbs by the adverbial suffix {-ly_1} and can appear in positions regularly occupied by adverbs. This gives us a formal distinction which permits a clear-cut separation of qualifiers from adverbs.[22]

The qualifiers may combine in certain limited ways to form complex qualifying phrases. The rules for these combinations are

[21] Many of these, such as "a good deal," are phrases, rather than words as defined in the last chapter. They are included here because they have the same function and distribution as the single-word qualifiers. This admittedly rather loose procedure will be followed elsewhere in our discussion of grammar.

[22] For a detailed discussion of this problem, see Paul Roberts, "Fries's Group D," *Language*, XXXI (1955), 20–24.

too detailed for our consideration here, but a few examples will illustrate some of the possibilities:

$$\text{this story is} \begin{cases} \text{not so very} \\ \text{pretty darned} \\ \text{rather more} \\ \text{a bit too} \end{cases} \text{sensational}$$

$$\text{his health seems} \begin{cases} \text{a whole lot} \\ \text{quite a good bit} \\ \text{not quite so much} \\ \text{very much} \end{cases} \text{better}$$

his health doesn't seem any better

$$\text{he is} \begin{cases} \text{indeed strong} \\ \text{very strong indeed} \\ \text{quite strong enough} \\ \text{indeed strong enough} \end{cases}$$

SUMMARY. What we have so far established about adjectives can be briefly summarized under five headings.

1. Adjectives are a class of lexical words identified by their ability to fill the position between noun-determiner and noun and the position after a linking verb and a **qualifier** such as *very*, *rather*, and *quite*.

2. Virtually all adjectives fall into one of two groups: **base adjectives** and **derived adjectives.**

3. **Base adjectives** are mostly of one syllable, though some have two or even three. They have no derivational suffixes, and usually form their **comparative** and **superlative degrees** by means of the inflectional suffixes {-*er*} and {-*est*}. They form nouns by adding the derivational suffix {-*ness*}, and adverbs by adding {-*ly₁*}.

4. **Derived adjectives** are formed from bound stems, nouns, and verbs by means of quite a large group of derivational suffixes, such

as {*-ous*}, {*-al*}, {*-able*}, and {*-ing₃*}. They usually form phrasal comparatives and superlatives by means of the qualifiers *more* and *most*.

5. **Qualifiers** are a select list of function words indicating the degree to which the meaning of the adjective they appear with is applicable. The list of those that appear with comparative adjectives is different from the list of those that appear with positive adjectives, though there is some overlapping. Since qualifiers also appear with adverbs, they are not exclusive adjective-determiners. They follow rather complicated patterns of word order, and may be combined into certain complex groups.

ADVERBS

Adverbs make up a rather complicated group of words, varying widely in form and distribution. Their primary identifying characteristic is their ability to fill certain positions in utterances, the chief of which is illustrated in the following sentence:

the man told (us) his story
{
(1) hopefully
(2) eagerly
(3) aloud
(4) actor-wise
(5) backwards
(6) somehow
(7) over
(8) here
}

This position, which may be described as utterance-final following a noun or nouns in the position of what we shall later call a complement, is the primary structural criterion for adverbs. Any word which fits this position is an adverb (though in other positions the "same word"—or its homophone—may be another part of speech). Furthermore, any adverb will fit this position, though we may have to change the specific words in the framework to avoid lexical incompatibility, as in the following:

$$\text{the man walked his dog} \begin{cases} \text{(3) away} \\ \text{(7) past} \\ \text{(8) home} \\ \text{(8) back} \end{cases}$$

$$\text{the man drove his car} \begin{cases} \text{(6) anywhere} \\ \text{(8) fast} \\ \text{(8) right} \end{cases}$$

the man measured the rug (4) lengthwise

There are, of course, other environments where all kinds of adverbs can appear, and still others where only those belonging to certain subgroups will fit. We shall see what some of these are later on, when we come to discuss the various syntactic structures, particularly structures of modification. For the present, however, we are concerned only with the ways in which adverbs may be distinguished from other parts of speech.

If we go back to our first illustration of the basic adverb position on the preceding page and look at the assortment of adverbs there, it is immediately apparent that there are various formal markers which identify certain words as adverbs, even when they appear in isolation rather than in a syntactic context. In fact, we have numbered the eight illustrative adverbs to show that they are examples of the eight subgroups into which the whole class of adverbs may be divided on the basis of their form. Let us now look briefly at each of these.

1. The largest and most clearly marked group of all comprises those adverbs which are formed by the addition of the derivational suffix $\{-ly_1\}$ to derived adjectives, as in our example *hopefully*. Assuming that we know the derivational suffixes that characterize

derived adjectives (see pp. 274–76), we can infallibly identify adverbs of this sort. Furthermore, the adverb-forming suffix $\{-ly_1\}$ can be added to any derived adjective except a few in $\{-ly_2\}$, so that there are just about as many adverbs in this group as there are in the large class of derived adjectives. It is hardly necessary to cite examples, but we may list one derived from each main type of derived adjective (pp. 274–76): *healthily*, *traditionally*, *remarkably*, *visibly*, *hopefully*, *uselessly*, *climatically*,[23] *legendarily*, *marvelously*, *popularly*, *impulsively*, *conveniently*, *woodenly*, *learnedly*, *exhilaratingly*, *friendlily*.

2. Almost as unmistakable are the adverbs formed by the addition of the suffix $\{-ly_1\}$ to base adjectives, such as our example *eagerly*. Others are *slowly*, *strangely*, *falsely*, *blackly*, and so on. Provided we have already identified the base as an adjective (by its ability to form nouns in $\{-ness\}$, for instance), we can almost always be sure that we are right in calling derived forms in /-liy/ adverbs. There are a few which do not run true to form, however, such as *goodly*, *deadly*, and *lively*, which are usually adjectives, though they are formed by the addition of /-liy/ to base adjectives.[24]

[23] It is to be noted that adverbs formed from adjectives in *-ic* end in *-ally* rather than in simple *-ly*. Phonemically this suffix is /-əliy/ or /-liy/. Morphemically we explain /-əliy/ as another allomorph of $\{-ly_1\}$, in most cases appearing in free variation with /-liy/, since a word like *basically* is commonly pronounced either /béysikəliy/ or /béysikliy/. Where there is also an adjective in *-al*, the adverb suffix is simply /-liy/, with synthesis of the two /l/'s (pp. 214–15). Thus there are two different paradigms here:

	Base Noun	Adjective in *-ic*	Adj. in *-ical*	Adverb in *-ically*
A {	beys	béysik		béysik(ə)liy
{	kláymit	klàymǽtik		klàymǽtik(ə)liy
B	ìykánəmiy	ìykənámik	ìykənámikəl	ìykənámik(ə)liy

The adjectives in *-ical* were once much more common than they are in present-day English, where they survive usually only when they have acquired meanings different from those of the related adjectives in *-ic*, as in the pairs *comic*: *comical*; *classic*: *classical*; *economic*: *economical*.

[24] *deadly* and *lively* are also adverbs, but much less frequent as such; *goodly* is never an adverb in standard English.

3. Another well-marked group of adverbs consists of those that are formed by adding the derivational prefix {a-} (phonemically /ə-/) to nouns, verbs, adjectives, and stems, like our example *aloud*. These adverbs are further marked by the fact that they have the superfix {˘ ′}. Of about sixty of them in more or less common use, nearly half are formed from nouns: *ahead*, *away*, *aboard*, etc. The rest are about equally divided among those formed from verbs (*adrift*, *astir*), from adjectives (*anew*, *abroad*), and from bound stems (*akimbo*, *anon*). The traditional grammar classes most of these as both adjectives and adverbs, and they are so listed in most dictionaries. But since they all fit our basic adverb position and since none of them can fit the basic adjective position between determiner and noun (we do not say *the aloud voice* or *the adrift boat*), it is clear that from our structural point of view they are always adverbs.

4. A group of adverbs originally small but at present exhibiting signs of rapid growth includes those formed by adding the derivational suffix {-*wise*} to nouns. A few in this group are well-established words like *lengthwise*; others are recent coinages or nonce-uses like *crabwise* and our example *actor-wise*. In the speech of some Americans, {-*wise*} is a very active "live" suffix, which can be attached to many nouns to create adverbs like *personnel-wise*. The ephemeral nature of such forms is recognized in writing by the use of the hyphen. Whether the popularity of these forms will add a new large class of adverbs to the language or whether it is only a passing linguistic fad, only time can tell. Careful speakers are inclined to view the proliferation of noun + {-*wise*} adverbs as linguistically disreputable. From our descriptive point of view we need only note that this is the principal way in which adverbs are made directly from nouns without an intervening adjective form. It might further be conjectured that the present popularity of this derivational paradigm is related to the popularity of the noun-adjunct, or noun used as noun-modifier.

5. A smaller group of adverbs is formed by the addition of the derivational suffix {-*ward(s)*} to a limited group of nouns: *back-*

ward(s), forward(s), homeward(s). Most adverbs of this group have two forms, one with final *-s* (phonemically /-z/) and one without, variously distributed. The forms without final *-s* are ambiguous, since they may be either adjectives or adverbs. Usually position prevents ambiguity; thus, in *the backward child, backward* is clearly an adjective, since it occupies an adjective position, while in *he walked backward* it is equally clearly an adverb. When one of these is found in a position that can be occupied by both adverb and adjective, structural ambiguity results, as in:

> the child looks backward

This may mean "the child appears to be backward" (*backward* as adjective) or "the child gazes backward" (*backward* as adverb). The forms with final *-s*, however, are always adverbs; there is no ambiguity about *the child looks backwards.*

6. Another quite important though small group of adverbs comprises those which are formed by combining the noun-determiners *some, any, every*, and *no* with a limited list of nouns and function words, as in *someplace, anyway, everywhere, nowhere*, and so on. There are fewer than twenty of these in common educated speech, and a few more dialectal forms like *nohow.*

7. Another relatively small group of adverbs includes those that are formally identical with certain function words of the class called **prepositions**. We shall discuss these later on, when we take up structures of modification. For the present, we can simply note that a large number of them have homophonous adverbs: *in, on, out, up, down, over, under, inside, around*, etc. As adverbs, they frequently appear, as we should expect, in the characteristic adverb position at the end of an utterance, with primary stress, as in

> hè brôught the cât ín
> the drôwning mân wènt únder
> Ì lèft my hât and côat insíde

The part these adverbs play in **separable verbs** has already been discussed (pp. 265–67).

8. The last group of adverbs is the miscellaneous class of those that have no formal markers at all to distinguish them in isolation; we know them as adverbs because we find them in adverb positions in utterances in which the other parts of speech are clearly identifiable. Many in this group are exceedingly frequent in occurrence and are memorized by all speakers of the language, just as function words are; such are *now, then, here, there, often, seldom, perhaps, still, even, always*. Others in this group are words which may also appear as other parts of speech, such as *yesterday, downstairs, home, later, little, fast, slow, early, far, near*.

ADVERB INFLECTIONS. A few adverbs make comparative and superlative forms by means of the inflectional suffixes {*-er*} and {*-est*}, already discussed in connection with adjectives (pp. 270–71). Most of those that do so are the so-called "flat adverbs," that is, those that are morphemically identical with certain base adjectives like *slow, quick, cheap, hard, fast*. Some irregular and suppletive forms are well known:

well	better	best
bad(ly) ⎱ ill ⎰	worse	worst
far { farther	farthest	
{ further	furthest	

ADVERB QUALIFIERS. Like adjectives, most adverbs may appear with function words of the kind we have called **qualifiers** (p. 278). The complete rules governing the distribution of the various qualifiers with various types of adverbs are matter for a full grammar, not for a sketch such as this, but we may note a few of the more important ones here.

a) All adverbs in *-ly* and a few others, such as *often* and *alive*, may appear with any of the list of qualifiers on page 278, as in *very easily*, *more slowly*, *rather often*, *alive enough*.

b) Many adverbs in group 7 (the "preposition-type" adverbs) and some in group 3 (formed with {*a-*}) use *far* or *much* as a qualifier: *far ahead*, *far down*, *much alive*.

c) Adverbs in the comparative degree, whether formed with the inflectional suffix {*-er*} or with the qualifier *more*, may use the same set of qualifiers that comparative adjectives use (listed on p. 279), as in *lots oftener*, *still more easily*, *a little slower*.

d) Some of the adverbs of groups 7 and 8 use *right* as a qualifier, as in *come right in*, *he drove right past*, *I want my dinner right now*.

e) Older English used *well* and *full* as qualifiers. The latter survives in the phrase *know full well*.

ADVERB-SUBSTITUTES. Four adverbs, *then*, *there*, *thus*, and *so*, and the adverb-phrases *this way* and *that way* frequently act as **adverb-substitutes.** That is, they appear in place of an adverb already expressed in the immediate linguistic context. In this respect they operate just as do the noun-substitutes *he*, *she*, *it*, and *they*, and the verb-substitute *do*. Thus, in each of the following examples, the second italicized adverb is the structural and lexical equivalent of the first, and could be replaced by it:

I didn't see him *yesterday* because I wasn't here *then*

I am looking forward to going *abroad*, since I have never been *there*

he writes very *gracefully*; I wish I could write *so* (or *thus*, *that way*)

CLASSIFICATION OF ADVERBS BY SUBSTITUTE-GROUPS. Just as nouns can be grouped according to the substitutes which may replace them (see pp. 249–51), so may adverbs. Specifically we may recognize three groups: a *then*-group, a *there*-group, and a *thus/so*-group. A few examples from each will show that, like the substitute-groups of nouns, these groups of adverbs are based on meaning rather than on form.

then-group	*there*-group	*thus/so*-group
today	outside	easily
daily	ahead	slowly
seldom	backward	regularly
early	somewhere	aloud
still	past	fast
sometimes	indoors	(most -*ly* adverbs)

These classes are rather flexible and subject to change, and some adverbs like *instead*, *perhaps*, *again*, do not fit readily into any of them. But this classification is important because it governs the order in which adverbs appear in certain complex structures of modification.

SUMMARY. What we have so far established concerning adverbs may now be summarized under five headings:

1. **Adverbs** are a class of lexical words identified by their ability to appear in utterance-final position following a noun or nouns functioning as complement.

2. Adverbs may be classified in eight groups or form-classes on the basis of their morphemic structure. The two largest groups are those formed from derived and base adjectives by the addition of $\{-ly_1\}$.

3. A few adverbs, mostly those identical with adjectives ("flat adverbs"), use the inflectional suffixes $\{-er\}$ and $\{-est\}$ to form comparative and superlative degrees.

4. Like adjectives, adverbs appear with function words called **qualifiers.** The qualifiers that may appear with adverbs are the same ones that appear with adjectives, with some exceptions and with variation in distribution.

5. In addition to the phrases *this way* and *that way*, there are four **adverb-substitutes,** *then*, *there*, *thus*, and *so*. These form the basis for a threefold classification of adverbs into a *then*-group, a *there*-group, and a *thus/so*-group. Some adverbs are outside this classification, which is important for its relation to word order.

PARTS OF SPEECH: SUMMARY

It has taken us a good many pages to describe the four parts of speech and to list the criteria by which they are identified. Our next task will be to study the various ways they are combined into larger structures, which is the province of **syntax.** But before we do, a few general observations about parts of speech and how they are actually identified by a listener or reader are in order. The reader who has accompanied us through the last four sections of this chapter may indeed wonder how anyone ever learns to speak or understand at all, so complicated does the process seem upon analysis. We do not want to leave him in the position of the unfortunate centipede, who managed all his many legs quite efficiently until another insect asked him how he knew which one to move first, whereupon he got so tangled up he couldn't walk at all. So, lest the reader find himself tongue-tied amongst a tangled mass of nouns, verbs, adjectives, adverbs, substitutes, determiners, and qualifiers, let us hasten to reassure him.

In the first place, the recognition of the parts of speech is a wholly unconscious process in ordinary listening or reading. We do not mentally tag each word with a label as it goes by in the stream of speech. There is not time to do so; and even if there were, the act of labeling would so monopolize our attention that we would not know what was being said. In fact, most people get along quite well without ever consciously knowing what the labels are or what are the criteria for applying them. The situation is something like driving a car: the experienced driver turns the wheel, shifts the gears, and operates the other controls without consciously thinking about it. But if through some slip he pushes the accelerator instead of the brake, he knows that something is wrong. In the same way, the speaker who inadvertently uses an adverb where an adjective belongs is aware that he has made a "mistake in grammar," and may correct himself before he continues.

Secondly, the recognition of parts of speech is merely part of the process of recognizing larger structures. We take in phrases and utterances as wholes, and seldom bother to analyze them, even unconsciously, into their parts. Just as we recognize a friend by the whole pattern of his appearance, posture, and movement, without analyzing his face into features and his body into individual limbs, so we comprehend a linguistic structure as an organized whole, into which the various parts fit harmoniously. It is only when we wish to describe our friend, or when he shows up with a broken nose or a new kind of haircut, that we become conscious of his individual features. Similarly, it is only when we wish to describe a linguistic structure, or when there is something out of place or novel about it, that we analyze it into its component parts of speech.

In the third place, the formal criteria we have described in the preceding sections are primarily concerned with identifying new or unfamiliar words and assigning them to the various parts of speech. Actually, of course, most of the words in any utterance we may hear are old friends which we learned to know long ago. We don't have to identify words like *hopeful* or *remarkable* as adjectives by their suffixes; we just know that they are adjectives because we have encountered them acting like adjectives many times before and have used them often ourselves. It is only strange words, or ambiguous ones like *round* (which can be any one of the four parts of speech and a function word beside) that we must identify, even unconsciously, by the formal criteria we have been discussing.

COLLATERAL READING, CHAPTER 5

Collateral reading for this chapter and for the next two will be found at the end of Chapter 7 (p. 428).

Chapter 6

Grammar—Part II:
Syntactic Structures

THE FOUR SYNTACTIC STRUCTURES

Early in the last chapter we made the elementary grammatical observation that words are combined with one another to make larger structures that convey more meaning than the mere aggregate of the independent meanings of the words themselves. We found that when this is done, speakers use, along with the full or lexical words, other words that we called function words, as well as inflections, and that the order of arrangement and the prosodic factors of pitch, stress, and juncture are other important indicators of structural patterns. Finally, we found that the lexical words belong to four classes or parts of speech according to the way in which they are combined. This discovery involved us in a rather lengthy investigation into these parts of speech and how they identify themselves both in isolation and as members of larger structures. This excursion being now concluded, we are ready to return to a consideration of the structures themselves. We are, in short, ready for **syntax.**

If we were to collect a group of minimal syntactic structures —combinations of no more than two lexical words, with or without function words—and study them, we would soon discover that they are not all alike either in the parts of speech that make them up or in the structural meanings that they convey. In fact, we could divide them into four principal groups, on the basis of their structural meaning:

1. hungry people
    home town
    easily superior
2. money talks
    soldiers have been killed
    snow kept falling
3. speak truth
    be careful
    love your neighbor
4. pins and needles
    hope and pray
    neither war nor peace

These are the four basic types of syntactic structure. All larger structures are simply combinations of these; no matter how complicated a structure may be, it can always be analyzed in terms of these four. Those in group (1) are **structures of modification;** their two component parts are a **head** (in our examples, *people, town, superior*) and a **modifier** (*hungry, home, easily*). Those in group (2) are **structures of predication;** their two components are a **subject** (*money, soldiers, snow*) and a **predicate** (*talks, have been killed, kept falling*). Those in group (3) are **structures of complementation;** their two components are a **verbal element** (*speak, be, love*) and a **complement** (*truth, careful, your neighbor*). Those in group (4) are **structures of coordination,** consisting of equivalent grammatical units (in our examples either nouns, like *pins, needles, war, peace,* or verbs, *hope, pray*) joined often but not always by a special kind of function word (*and, neither . . . nor*).

In the four sections that follow, we shall take a look at each of these structures in turn, noting what parts of speech go into them, the function words they employ, and the principal patterns of word order and prosody that mark them. Once again we must warn the reader that this treatment of these matters cannot be exhaustive. An exhaustive treatment of English syntax would fill a volume larger than this. What can be done here is to sketch the main outlines and provide the student with a framework of ideas and a basic terminology, so that he may pursue his own studies of grammar with assurance and efficiency.

In the discussion that follows, a simple system of diagramming will be used to represent graphically the various structures which are encountered in English syntax. Most systems of diagramming in common use depend on rearranging the words and word groups of the structure being diagrammed in order to place them in a geometric pattern which reveals their logical relationship. There are two serious objections to this procedure. (1) Since it is based on a logical (meaning-based) understanding of what the structure means, it reveals the *logic*, rather than the *grammar*, of the structure. (2) By rearranging words, it obliterates the part played by word order, one of the basic syntactic devices of English. Systems of diagramming that depend on rearrangement thus conceal grammatical structure instead of revealing it.

In contrast, the system used here will leave the words in the order in which they appear. It is intended to be a graphic representation of structure based on two main principles: (1) English syntax is a many-layered organization of relatively few types of basic units; (2) every structure may be divided into its **immediate constituents** (often abbreviated IC's by linguists), almost always two, each of which may in turn be divided and subdivided until the **ultimate constituents** (in grammar, the words) are reached. This is graphically indicated by enclosing each ultimate constituent in a box and drawing larger and larger boxes around the immediate constituents of each of the increasingly complex structures into which they combine. The result is something like those famous "Chinese boxes" that fit one within another. The difference is that each of our syntactic boxes contains not one but usually two smaller boxes, thus:

Here the outer box incloses a syntactic structure whose immediate constituents are A and B. If this structure joins with another, whose immediate constituents are C and D, into a larger structure, we have

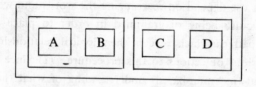

In this fashion, the immediate constituents on every layer of structure are made clearly apparent.

The four different structures are identified by placing simple symbols between the two immediate constituents. **Modification** is indicated by an arrow → pointing from the modifier toward the head:

Predication is indicated by a capital P with its back to the subject and its front facing the predicate. In the relatively few structures of predication where the subject follows the predicate, the P is reversed:

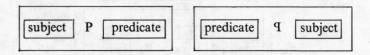

Complementation is similarly indicated by a capital C with its back to the verbal element:

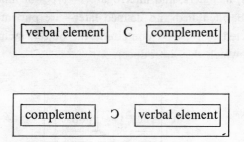

Coordination is indicated by parallel lines connecting the constituents. If a function word (**coordinator**) is present, it is written between these lines:

Split structures are indicated as in the following diagram, where the constituent A has two parts, separated by the constituent B, as in, for instance, *do you swim*:

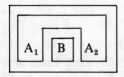

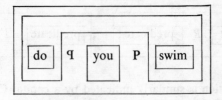

Prepositions, includers, and interrogators—types of function words which will be identified and defined later—are put into a smaller box, connected to the box containing the object, included clause, or question which they introduce:

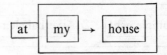

Within the complement, which is one of the two immediate constituents of a structure of complementation, the various kinds of complements are identified by labeling their boxes with initials: DO for direct object, IO for indirect object, SC for subjective complement, and OC for objective complement (these various elements will be discussed later):

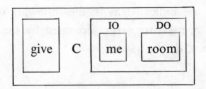

In many of the diagrams that appear later in this chapter, not every structure will be analyzed down to its ultimate constituents. But it should be understood that every "Chinese box" that contains more than one word surrounds a structure which can be further analyzed until the individual words have been reached.

STRUCTURES OF MODIFICATION

As we have seen, the two components of a structure of modification are a **head** and a **modifier,** whose meaning serves to broaden, qualify, select, change, describe, or in some other way affect the meaning of the head.. In the examples cited above—*hungry people, home town, easily superior*—both head and modifier are single words. But this is by no means always the case. Both the head and the modifier which are the immediate constituents of a structure of modification may themselves be structures of more or less complexity. Grammatical organization, as we have already observed, is a complex of many structural layers.

Each of the four parts of speech, and certain function words as well, may serve as the head of a structure of modification. Likewise, each of the four parts of speech, sometimes in special inflected forms, and certain function words may function as modifier. Furthermore, though certain patterns are so frequent as to be considered in some sense "standard" or "regular," in actuality virtually all possible combinations of the four parts of speech are possible in structures of modification. The reader must clear his mind of the notion that it is somehow more "correct" for an adjective to modify a noun, for example, than it is for a noun to modify a noun, or for an adjective to modify a verb. These notions are derived from the grammar of other languages than English, and are not relevant to the grammar of present-day English. Instead of being influenced by them, let us take a look at some of the simpler types of structures of modification which actually appear in present-day English. Since the prime position in such structures is occupied by the head, we shall classify them according to the part of speech to which the head belongs.

NOUN AS HEAD. Nouns appear very frequently as heads of structures of modification. The modifiers in such structures may belong to any of the four parts of speech. Noun-determiners may also be classed as modifiers, so that function words may also perform this task.

The most common noun-modifier is the adjective, which outnumbers all the others except determiners in the proportion of two or three to one.[1] When an adjective is the sole modifier of a noun, its position is almost always directly before the noun—between the noun-determiner, if there is one, and the noun. Structures of this sort are so frequent and well known as hardly to need illustration, but for completeness' sake we may include a few:

barbed wire	intense concentration
the gloomy room	his cheerful smile
a great disparity	both remarkable tales

Occasionally, though very rarely, the adjective may come after the noun. This happens under two kinds of circumstances: (a) in certain fixed phrases, often from technical vocabularies or familiar quotations: *court-martial, grace abounding, darkness visible, fee simple*; (b) when the adjective is not a solitary modifier of the noun, but part of a larger structure that *as a whole* acts as a noun-modifier, as in the following:

> a figure vague and shadowy
> a wish intense beyond belief
> a man taller than I thought

---

[1] In a count of 816 noun-modifiers in two pieces in the February, 1955, issue of *Harper's Magazine*, one an article and the other a short story involving considerable dialogue, adjectives made up about 71 per cent of the total. The other figures were: Nouns, 20 per cent; Verbs, 7½ per cent; Adverbs, 1½ per cent. There were about twice as many noun-determiners (1551) as there were noun-modifiers.

Here the adjectives *vague*, *shadowy*, *intense*, and *taller* are parts of structures which act as unit modifiers of the heads *figure*, *wish*, and *man*.

Nouns make up a considerable number (as many as 25 per cent) of the single-word modifiers of nouns. With the exception of the **appositive,** which will be discussed later on, these nouns come before the noun they modify; they never follow it. Structures of this sort are of two kinds: (a) those in which the modifying noun has the possessive inflection {'s}, and those in which it appears in the base form or with the plural inflection {-es}. The first of these is sometimes called the **possessive** construction and the other the **noun-adjunct** construction. Examples of both, with the same noun as modifier, can be matched with one another:

POSSESSIVE	NOUN-ADJUNCT
child's play	child psychology
a dog's life	the dog days
a day's work	the day shift
my father's house	a father image
that woman's doctor	that woman doctor

The last pair illustrates vividly the difference in meaning there may be between these two structures of modification. The formal difference between them may be described as follows: a construction with *of* may be substituted for the possessive construction, and the determiner (if there is one) will then go with the *modifying* noun; on the other hand, some other kind of construction must be substituted for the noun-adjunct, and the determiner goes with the *head* noun. In the following illustrations the symbol > means "transforms into":

> my father's house > house of my father
>
> *but*   that father image > that image like (a) father
>
> that woman's doctor > doctor of that woman
>
> *but*   that woman doctor > that doctor who is a woman

Because of the phonemic identity of the principal allomorphs of {*'s*} and {*-es*} (p. 238), it is sometimes impossible to distinguish in speech between possessive and noun-adjunct. In such cases a minor structural ambiguity results. /ðòwz bɔ́yz búks/, for instance, may mean "those books for boys" (noun-adjunct) or "books of those boys" (possessive). This ambiguity is sometimes resolved in speech by prosody and in formal writing by the apostrophe. Thus:

/²ðòwz+³bɔ́yz+bûks¹#/ = those boys books (noun-adjunct)
/²ðôwz+bɔ̀yz+³búks¹#/ = those boys' books (possessive)

Other potential ambiguities are avoided by various other peculiarities of morphemic structure or of distribution. Among these we may briefly note the following:

1. The noun-adjunct is almost always singular, hence an ending in /-s, -z, -iz/ usually indicates the possessive: compare *dog days* and *dog's life*.

2. Certain noun-determiners (*this/these* and *that/those*) exhibit the phenomenon of **concord**; that is, they have one form that goes with singular nouns and another that goes with plural nouns. This often helps to indicate whether the determiner goes with the head (in which case the modifier is a noun-adjunct) or with the modifier (in which case the modifier is a possessive). Concord joins with stress and intonation to make such clear distinctions as the following:

/²ðǽt+bɔ̀yz+³búk¹#/ = book of that boy
/²ðǽt+³bɔ́yz+bûk¹#/ = that book for boys
/²ðǽt+bɔ̀yz+³búks¹#/ = books of that boy
/²ðôwz+bɔ̀yz+³búk¹#/ = book of those boys
/²ðôwz+bɔ̀yz+³búks¹#/ = books of those boys
/²ðòwz+³bɔ́yz+bûks¹#/ = those books for boys

3. Most nonpersonal nouns of more than two syllables do not have the {*-'s*} inflection, so that any form ending in /-s, -z, -iz/ must be a plural noun-adjunct. Thus, *communications officer, reparations*

agreement, and *munitions storehouse* are not ambiguous structures.

4. A few nouns have four distinct forms (p. 239), so that the possessive and the plural are always phonemically distinct. For example:

> /wûmən dáktər/ = woman doctor (noun-adjunct)
> /wûmənz dáktər/ = woman's doctor (possessive)
> /wîmɨn dáktərz/ = women doctors (noun-adjunct)
> /wîmɨnz dáktərz/ = women's doctors (possessive)

A special type of noun-modifier is the **appositive.** An appositive is a noun, a noun-headed structure of modification, or a structure of coordination made up of nouns or noun-headed structures, modifying a noun head, which it follows. An appositive is usually marked by single-bar junctures before and after (sometimes a double-bar after) and a /3 2/ or /2 3 2/ pitch contour. The appositive often also has a noun-determiner. Some examples:

> ²his ³brother²|²a ³doctor²|was there also
> Mr. Jones|²the ³art critic²|praised the painting
> the children|²both boys and ³girls²|received presents

Sometimes the terminal junctures before and after the appositive are not present. The resulting pattern, which has been called "close apposition," brings two nouns together in juxtaposition in a potentially ambiguous relationship. The following are examples of the close appositive:

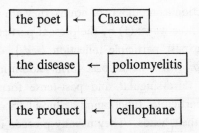

Compare these appositional structures with the following noun-adjunct structures, in which the first noun is the modifier, rather than the second:

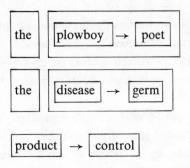

The potential ambiguity here is resolved primarily by prosody, especially stress, though lexical considerations may play some part. The modifier is usually marked by a stronger stress than the head:

> the prôduct céllophàne (appositive)
> próduct contrôl (noun-adjunct)

A special class of close appositives includes those in which the head is a personal or geographical title and the appositive a proper name:

> Professor Jones
> Vice-President Smith
> the River Duddon

When *verbs* function as modifiers of nouns, they are nearly always marked in one of three ways: (1) by the present-participle inflection {-ing_1}; (2) by the past participle inflection {-ed_2}; or (3) by the infinitive-marker *to*. Verbs in the base form seldom modify nouns, and those in the third-singular and past-tense forms never do. Present and past participles functioning as modifiers of nouns may precede or follow their heads. They usually precede if they are by themselves and usually follow if they are parts of larger structures, though there are many exceptions to both these generalizations. Infinitives marked by *to*, however, always follow the noun-head. The following are some examples of various structures of modification with noun as head and verb as modifier:

> running water
> water running in the street
> baked potatoes
> potatoes baked slowly
> money to burn
> the man to see

Since verbs in $\{-ing_1\}$, nouns in $\{-ing_2\}$, and adjectives in $\{-ing_3\}$ can all modify nouns and all appear in the position between noun-determiner and noun, ambiguity is a strong possibility in such cases. It is of interest to observe how delicately the syntax of English discriminates among these three. Consider the three phrases:

> (a) a pleasing table
> (b) a rotting table
> (c) a dining table

Here it is clear that we have three structures of modification with *table* as head. It is also clear from the lexical meaning of the words that (a) means "a table that is pleasing," (b) "a table that is in process of rotting," and (c) "a table for dining." Are there any formal marks of this distinction?

If we allow ourselves to make a few alterations and substitutions, checking the resulting structures against our knowledge of English, or, better yet, that of an impartial native speaker, we will easily find that there are ways of distinguishing these structures on the basis of form. In the first place, we can insert the qualifier *very* before *pleasing*, but not before *rotting* or *dining*. This is enough to mark *pleasing* as an adjective. This identification is corroborated by the fact that we cannot place *pleasing* after *table*. Secondly, we can move *rotting*, but not *pleasing* or *dining*, to the position after *table*: *a table rotting*. This marks *rotting* as a present-participle inflection of a verb. Thirdly, since we can neither place *very* before *dining* nor move *dining* to after *table* without changing the meaning, *dining* can be neither adjective nor verb and must, therefore, be a noun.

Actually a phrase like *a dining table* is structurally ambiguous in the written form. Only avoidance of lexical incongruity guides us to the meaning "a table for dining" and away from the meaning "a table that is in process of dining." When the lexical meaning of the words involved permits either interpretation without incongruity, true ambiguity results, as in *a dancing girl, a trotting horse, a racing yacht, a fighting man*. But this ambiguity is prevented in the spoken language by contrasting prosodic patterns. Thus /²ə+trâtiŋ+³hórs¹#/, with rise in pitch and primary stress both occurring on the head-word *horse*, identifies *trotting* as a verb and signals the meaning "a horse in the process of trotting." But /²ə+³trâtiŋ+hòrs¹#/, with primary stress and rise in pitch both occurring on the modifier *trotting*, identifies *trotting* as a noun and signals the meaning "a horse for trotting."[2] The student should test this point both in his own speech and in that of others; it is a good example of the rôle that prosody plays in syntax.

Adverbs are relatively rare as noun-modifiers, seldom constituting more than 2 per cent of the single-word modifiers of nouns in ordinary prose. When they do appear in this role, adverbs always come immediately after the noun which is the head. The adverbs that function as noun-modifiers are mostly those of the *then*- and *there*-classes (p. 288). Adverbs of the *thus/so*-class, particularly those with the derivational suffix {-ly_1}, modify only one kind of nouns,

---

[2] Combinations like /trátiŋ+hòrs/, with the superfix {´ + `}, can be considered compound words (see pp. 206–7). It would be sound writing practice to indicate this with a hyphen, but this is by no means always done.

those formed from verbs by the derivational suffix {-ing_2}. Examples of structures of modification with noun as head and adverb as modifier are the following:

> the people here
> the temperature outside
> heavens above
> Europe now
> the conversation afterwards
> his speaking rapidly
> our acting together

A rather delicate problem in grammatical analysis is posed by a series of expressions like the following:

> (a) driving slow
> (b) driving slowly
> (c) my driving slow
> (d) my driving slowly $\Big\}$ annoyed him
> (e) my slow driving
> (f) driving a car slow

Clearly *driving* is a noun in (c), (d), and (e), since it is marked by the noun-determiner *my*. Furthermore, *slow* is an adverb in (c), where it follows the noun, and an adjective in (e), where it precedes; *slowly* in (b) and (d) is marked as an adverb not only by position but also by the derivational suffix {-ly_1}. In (f), *driving* is clearly a verb, marked by its complement, *a car*. In (a) and (b) *driving* can be either a noun or a verb; however, since the structural meaning is virtually the same in either case, no ambiguity results. Note also that (b) and (d) are ambiguous in the written language, but not in speech, where a single-bar juncture before *slowly* makes it a modifier of *annoyed*, while one after *slowly* makes it a modifier of *driving*.

Prepositional Phrases. In addition to single-word modifiers of nouns, various other structures can function as noun-modifiers. We must postpone consideration of most of these until we have examined the other kinds of syntactic structure in their simple forms. One that we may treat here, however, is the **prepositional phrase.** In its simple form, this consists of a function word of the class called **prepositions** and a lexical word, usually but not always a noun, customarily (though not too satisfactorily) called its **object.** Together these two form a unit which may function in various ways, one of which is as modifier of a noun.

Prepositions make up a relatively large class of function words, some of very frequent occurrence, others quite rare. On the basis of their morphemic structure they may be divided into three groups: **simple, compound,** and **phrasal prepositions.**

(a) *Simple Prepositions.* These have only one base. There are between fifty and sixty of them in present-day English. About thirty consist of a single morpheme; about twenty more have two morphemes, and a handful have three. The most familiar single-morpheme prepositions are:

after	from	on	through
as	in	out	till
at	like	over	to
but	near	per	under
by	of	round	up
down	off	since	with
for			

Prepositions with two morphemes, one or both of which are bound:

about	around	between	toward
above	before	beyond	underneath
across	behind	despite	unlike
along	below	during	until
amid	beneath	except	unto
among	beside		

Prepositions of three morphemes, all or all but one bound:

> against
> concerning
> considering
> opposite
> regarding

Almost all the simple prepositions may also appear as full parts of speech, usually adverbs. Some may be homonyms of several lexical words; thus, *round* can be noun, verb, adjective, adverb, or preposition, and *like* can be noun, verb, adjective, preposition, or function word of the type we shall later define as *includer*. But whenever these words form with an object a closely integrated structure that functions as a single unit, they are prepositions.

(b) *Compound Prepositions*. These are prepositions that consist of two or more free bases, with or without affixes. They thus belong to the class of compound words (p. 206). Commonly the first element is an adverb (usually but not always one of those that may also be a simple preposition) and the second a simple preposition. Some few of these are of such common occurrence that they are written as single words, but there is no difference from the point of view of morphemics between the ones written as one word and those written as two. Some of the most common compound prepositions are the following:

across from	down from	off of	together with
along with	due to	onto	upon
alongside of	except for	out of	up to
apart from	inside of	outside of	up with
away from	instead of	over to	within
back of	into	throughout	without

(c) *Phrasal Prepositions*. These consist of three words: a simple preposition, a noun, and another simple preposition, usually *to* or *of*.

All of these may be analyzed syntactically into a prepositional phrase followed by a simple preposition. Such, indeed, is their morphemic construction and their historical origin. For this reason, grammarians have not yet provided a clear-cut means of setting limits to this class. Thus, we have classed *instead of* as a compound preposition because *instead* (etymologically a prepositional phrase) is an adverb. Virtually synonymous with it are *in place of* and *in lieu of*, which can certainly be classed as phrasal prepositions. But what of such combinations as *in exchange for*, *in consideration of*, *under circumstances of*, and so on? Formally they are identical with *in place of*, and thus should be entitled to be classed as phrasal prepositions also. It is only when the noun which is the central element of these expressions has a determiner or a modifier that a new formal element enters in. Thus, we can certainly exclude from the class of phrasal prepositions on strictly formal grounds such combinations as *for the sake of*, *in a position of*, *at the back of*, *under the administration of*, *in great danger from*, and so on.

However grammarians may resolve this problem, most of them will agree that the following at least are clear examples of phrasal prepositions:

in regard to	by means of	on top of
on account of	in addition to	in ⎫
in spite of	in front of	on ⎭ behalf of

How many more can be included in this group is at present a matter of individual preference. Fortunately, it makes little difference in grammatical analysis whether we consider expressions like *in time of war* and *in hope of reward* one prepositional phrase or two. In either case they are identified as single modifiers before they are analyzed into their constituents.

As has already been stated, the **object** of the preposition—the lexical word which completes the structure—is usually a noun. It may be an ordinary noun, with or without a determiner, as in:

> above suspicion
> under water
> after dinner
> from the beginning
> like a thunderbolt

Or it may be a pronoun or function noun, as in:

> for us
> because of that
> on behalf of some

It may also be a structure of modification with noun as head, as in:

> for heaven's sake
> in actual practice
> of running water
> for something to do

Note that it is not just the nouns *sake*, *practice*, *water*, and *something* that are objects of the prepositions here, but the complete structures of modification of which these nouns are the heads. Thus, when we analyze a structure like *in actual practice*, we divide it first into two immediate constituents, the preposition *in* and the structure of modification with noun-head, *actual practice*. This latter we may in turn divide into its immediate constituents, the adjective *actual* and the noun *practice*. This may be diagrammatically represented this way:

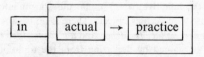

Prepositional phrases that modify nouns may have other parts of speech beside nouns as objects. For instance, the object may be a verb or a verb-headed structure of modification, as in:

> a way of doing
> a day for peacefully resting

Note that *resting* is marked as a verb by the preceding adverb, *peacefully*. In *for peaceful resting*, *resting* is a noun. In *for resting*, *resting* may be either noun or verb; there is an inconsequential ambiguity here.[3] Or the object may be an adverb, as in:

> a mile from here
> the time up to now
> a message from abroad

Finally, the object of a prepositional phrase may itself be a prepositional phrase, as in:

> a book from under the table
> a tale for after dinner
> a trip to beyond the mountains

Note that the combinations *fròm ûnder, fòr âfter,* and *tò beyônd* are not the same as compound prepositions like *ôut òf* and *ûp tò.* This is indicated by the stress-pattern, and may be illustrated by an analysis of two expressions:

(a)
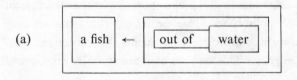

---

[3] The combination *to* + base form of the verb, which we have treated as a special structure, the **infinitive** (p. 257), can quite legitimately be treated as a prepositional phrase with verb as object. There is no basic structural difference between *a place to live, a place for living,* and *a place for life.* On the other hand, nothing seems to be gained by departing from the traditional concept of the infinitive.

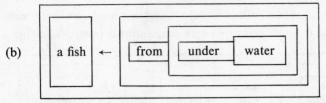

(b)

Observe that in (a) *water* is the object of *out of*, while in (b) *water* is the object of *under*, and the whole phrase *under water* is the object of *from*. The second expression has one more layer of structure than the first, as can be seen by counting the number of "Chinese boxes" we must put within one another to complete the analysis.

Pattern of Noun-Modifiers. When a structure of modification with a noun as head includes several modifiers of different sorts, the result is often quite a complex affair. But it is organized along quite strict and precise lines. The most important fact about it is that unless it contains structures of coordination (which we shall take up later on), it consists not of a series of parallel modifiers like a four-horse team pulling a chariot, but of a series of structures of modification one within the other, in a manner that has already been compared to Chinese boxes. This may best be illustrated by building up such a structure, layer by layer. First comes the noun which is the head:

rate

Next comes a noun-adjunct, if one is present:

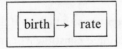

Then, if there are no more noun-adjuncts, come adjectives:

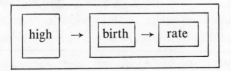

When there are no further adjectives or other modifiers that precede the noun, the next layer may be a prepositional phrase following it:

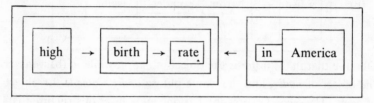

Then an adverb, following the phrase:[4]

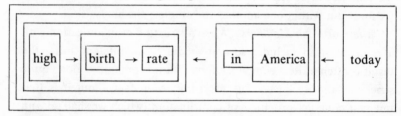

Finally, the noun-determiner introduces the whole business:

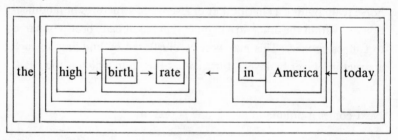

Note that every box except those which contain a single word (or, on this level of analysis, **ultimate constituent**) contains just two smaller boxes. This kind of twofold or **binary structure** is one of the most striking things about the grammatical organization of English. Because of it, virtually any English structure may be divided into two immediate constituents, each of which may in turn be divided into two, until the ultimate grammatical units, the words, are reached.

[4] Prepositional phrases and adverbs may interchange position; we may have *high birth rate today in America* as well.

VERB AS HEAD. At the outset of our discussion of structures of
modification with verb as head, we must make a distinction of
considerable importance, though it is usually overlooked in traditional grammar. We must distinguish, that is, between those structures whose head is a verb alone and those whose head is some other
type of structure containing a verb. As we shall see, the other structures in which verbs are important are structures of predication and
of complementation. Either of these may itself be the head of a
structure of modification. We shall discuss this later on, when we
take up complex structures. But we must make the point here, so
that it will be clear that we are not overlooking many constructions
which the traditional grammar treats as verb-modifiers. A single
illustration will suffice to make the point:

(a) ²Hè ûsually tèlls mè his ³sécrets¹#
(b) ²Hè têlls mè his ³sécrets²|³úsually¹#
(c) ³Úsually²|²hè têlls mè his ³sécrets¹#

In sentence (a), *usually tells* is a structure of modification with the
verb *tells* as head. But in (b), the head is not just the verb but the
whole structure of complementation *tells me his secrets*; while in (c),
the head is the whole structure of predication *he tells me his secrets*.
The differences between the three, signaled by word order and
junctures, may be graphically illustrated by analytic diagrams:

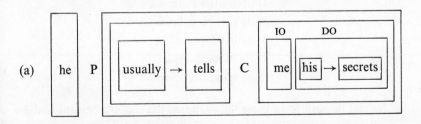

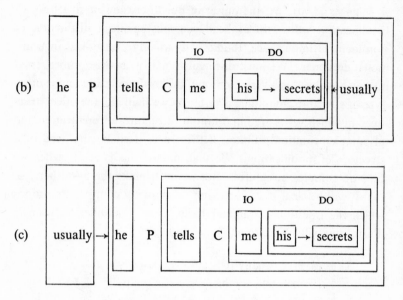

For the present we are concerned with structures like *usually tells* in (a), which have the verb alone as head.

By far the most common single-word modifiers of verbs are adverbs. All of the eight types of adverbs listed on page 281 can function as verb-modifiers:

> (1) he works *successfully*
>
> (2) he drives *rapidly*
>
> (3) he is moving *ahead*
>
> (4) he was looking *sidewise*
>
> (5) he can swim *backward*
>
> (6) he has looked *everywhere*
>
> (7) he stepped *inside*
>
> (8) he speaks *seldom*

As can be seen from these illustrations, the common position of an adverb modifying a verb is immediately after it. All adverbs may take this position. Certain of them may also appear in the other two possible positions: (1) before the verb, (2) between auxiliary and verb or between two auxiliaries. The adverbs that can appear in these positions are those belonging to groups (1) and (2) (those formed with the derivational suffix $\{-ly_1\}$), those of group 8 that belong to the *then*-class (p. 288), a few more from group (8) such as *only* and *even*, and a few from group (6), especially *somehow*, *sometimes*, *somewhere*, and *nowhere*. A few illustrations:

(1) he *successfully* tried
(2) he *slowly* drove
(6) he has *sometimes* seen
(8) he has *seldom* been heard
(8) it may *even* rain

When adverbs other than these appear between the noun subject and the verb, they are modifiers of the preceding noun, rather than of the verb:

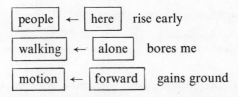

Since most of the adverbs that may precede the verb are those that do not modify nouns (except nouns in $\{-ing_2\}$), the sequence noun-adverb-verb is seldom structurally ambiguous. But when an adverb of the limited group that can both modify nouns and precede the verb appears in this position, structural ambiguity results in the written language, though intonation usually prevents it in speech. For example:

children *nowadays* have many kinds of entertainment
the discussion *thereafter* grew heated
the newspaper *somewhere* said it would rain

In speaking sentences like these, if we wish to show that the adverb modifies the preceding noun, we give it a /3 2/ pitch sequence and introduce a single-bar juncture after it; whereas if we intend the adverb to modify the following verb, we put the juncture before it and apply the /3 2/ pitch sequence to the noun. Thus, a structure like this

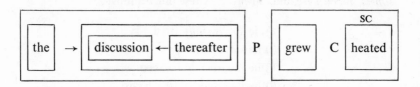

will be spoken: /²ðə dɨskə̂šən ðèhr³ǽftər²|²grûw ³híytɨd¹#/ while a structure like this

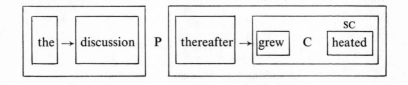

will be spoken: /²ðə dɨs³kə́šən²|²ðèhrǽftər grûw ³híytɨd¹#/

A simple verb + adverb structure of modification may itself be the head of another structure of modification with an adverb as modifier. The result may be patterns like the following:

> he never comes here
> the train moved ahead slowly
> the boy seldom walked along home eagerly

In analyzing such structures, we find that the "outermost layer" of modification is the adverb preceding the verb; next comes the last adverb following the verb; then come the rest, working backward toward the verb. Thus, a complicated structure such as our last example above is constructed this way:

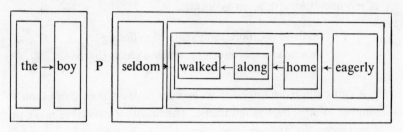

There is not room here to go into the complicated rules governing the position and relative order of verb-modifying adverbs. This is, in fact, one of the most intricate problems of word order in English, and one which grammarians have not yet studied in all its detail. It is to be hoped that they will, since the very intricacy of the conventions of word order here creates difficulty for those learning the language, whether they are children learning their native speech or foreigners learning English as a second language.

Certain *nouns* may function as modifiers of verbs; when they do, they follow the verb and may have noun-determiners. Since a noun following a verb may also be an **object** (as will be discussed later), it becomes necessary to distinguish between these two quite different structures. The test is to replace the noun with one of the substitutes *it* or *them*. If this does not alter the structural meaning, the noun is an object of the verb; if it does alter or destroy the structural meaning, the noun is a modifier of the verb. This contrast appears in the following illustrations:

STRUCTURE OF MODIFICATION (noun modifies verb)	STRUCTURE OF COMPLEMENTATION (noun is object of verb)
he lived a year	he lived his life
he walks this way	he likes his own way
he saw a mile	he measured a mile

In this, as in all other functions which nouns may perform, the simple noun may be replaced by a more or less complicated structure of modification with noun as head:

> he lived six more long years of suffering
> he shaves every morning at six o'clock sharp

A quite limited number of verbs may have an even more limited number of *adjectives* as modifiers. The resulting structures make up a restricted list of stereotyped expressions, of which the following are typical:

> the children ran wild
> the criminal came clean ("confessed")
> the machine ran true
> the dog went crazy
> the show fell flat

It is to be noted that the verbs in structures of this sort are of the type we shall define as **intransitive,** and that nothing can come between verb and adjective except a qualifier or an adverbial modifier of the adjective. We can say "the dog went completely crazy," or "the show fell very flat," but not "the dog went frequently crazy" or "the show fell always flat."

There are also a few types of structure in which a verb may be modified by another *verb*. The modifying verb may be the present-participle form in $\{-ing_1\}$, as in

> the children came running
> I prefer to eat sitting

or the infinitive (*to* + base form), as in

> he lives to eat
> they came to scoff and remained to pray

These verb-modifying verbs may be distinguished from verbs functioning as objects by the same test used above to make a similar distinction regarding nouns—replacing the second verb by *it*. Note that this can be done in the right-hand column below but not in the left-hand one:

INFINITIVE AS MODIFIER	INFINITIVE AS OBJECT
he lives to eat	he loves to eat
he works to succeed	he wants to succeed

If the head-verb is one that may be both intransitive and transitive, ambiguity may result, as in

> he loves to live
> he studies to succeed
> he prays to be saved

There is no way to tell, either in speech or in writing, whether *he loves to live* means "he loves in order that he may live" or "he loves the act of living."

Much more common as verb-modifiers than nouns, adjectives, or other verbs are *prepositional phrases*. Their relative frequency as verb-modifiers in ordinary speech and writing is somewhere near the same as that of adverbs. Their position is after the verb, and they may combine with one another and with adverbs to make quite complicated structures of modification. The following illustrate a few of the possibilities:

> (he) spoke about his work
> (the guests) entered into the game with gusto after dinner
> (the boy) came rapidly down the street on a bicycle
> (he) happily wandered around the town during his vacation

Note that in the last example the adverb *happily* may come after *wandered*, after *town*, or after *vacation*. In each case the layers of modification in the resulting structure are different, and hence the meaning is also different, though the difference is so slight that most native speakers might not recognize it at all. The principle here is the same as was observed in connection with structures of modification with noun as head: such complicated patterns actually consist of several structures of modification, one within the other. On each level there are two immediate constituents, the head and the modifier. Each of these may itself be a structure of some complexity, or it may be a single word. In either case the parts played by the two essential components—head and modifier—are the same, and together they make up a single structure of modification at their level of organization, regardless of how complicated their component parts may be.

ADJECTIVE AS HEAD. Adjectives, which usually function as modifiers themselves, may also serve as heads of structures of modification. The most common adjective-modifiers are the qualifiers, like *very*, *rather*, and *quite*, which have already been discussed (pp. 278–80). But all the parts of speech may occasionally function as modifiers of adjectives.

After the qualifiers, the most frequent modifiers of adjectives are *adverbs*. Adverbs of groups (1) and (2) (those in $\{-ly_1\}$), (6), and (8) may modify adjectives. When they do, they come immediately before the adjective-head, as in the following examples:

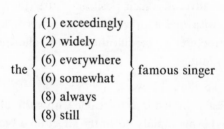

When the adjective is in the predicate position after a linking verb, a following adverb may seem to modify it. But actually the adverb in this position modifies the whole structure of complementation of which the adjective is a part:

(a) it is dark ahead
(b) the house seems clean everywhere
(c) the air feels fresh here

In (a), for instance, the adverb *ahead* modifies the whole structure of complementation *is dark*, not just the adjective *dark*. This is revealed in the diagram:

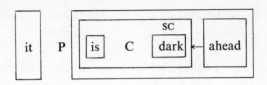

Certain *nouns* modify adjectives in set expressions belonging to a rather restricted list:

> stone cold coffee
> sea green cloth
> house high snowdrifts
> bone dry earth

Many of these combinations take on the superfix $\{' + `\}$ in some dialects or in some contexts; when they do, they can be considered compound words, rather than structures of modification. This is often recognized in writing by hyphenating them or even writing them as single words:

> ice-cold lemonade   lifelong interest
> world-wide fame   praiseworthy conduct

A few *verbs* may function as adjective-modifiers, again in a rather limited list of fairly stereotyped expressions. In such cases the verb is either in the present-participle inflection preceding the adjective head or in the infinitive form following the adjective-head.

freezing cold	hard to get
boiling hot	beautiful to see
hopping mad	easy to know

On rare occasions adjectives may be modified by other *adjectives*. Once again the expressions are likely to be stereotyped, such as the following:

icy cold	dark blue
deathly pale	cold sober
tight shut	crazy drunk

Prepositional phrases are very common adjective-modifiers, being just about as frequent as adverbs in this function. They come immediately after the adjective head, as in the following examples:

easy on the eyes	green as grass
good for nothing	friendly towards everybody
hopeful of success	stronger than ever

It is to be noted that when an adjective is itself modified either by a prepositional phrase or an infinitive, it becomes the head of a structure of modification which in turn follows the noun it modifies:

> a man easy to talk to
> a book interesting to scholars
> a place distant from civilization

A few stereotyped expressions, however, place this kind of structure before the noun-head. Such structures are often hyphenated in writing and bear a special stress pattern in speech which allows us to identify them as compound words, rather than structures of modification with adjective-head:

> a good-for-nothing boy
> a hard-to-get material

ADVERB AS HEAD. When adverbs appear as heads of structures of modification, they may be modified by *qualifiers*, other *adverbs*, *nouns*, or *prepositional phrases*. The first three of these precede the head (except the qualifiers *indeed* and *enough*), and prepositional phrases follow it (as they always do when they function as modifiers). The following illustrate these four types of adverb-modifiers:

Qualifiers: very easily, rather slowly, happily enough
Adverbs: unusually eagerly, far away, sometimes below
Nouns: a foot away, that easily, some way up
Prepositional Phrases: away for a week, behind in his work, outside in the cold, as rapidly as a train

FUNCTION WORD AS HEAD. Since we have not yet observed and named all of the various types of function words, we cannot fully discuss structures of modification in which function words are the head. But we can note at this point that such structures are possible —in fact, fairly frequent—and note a few examples involving the types of function words we have so far identified. Thus, the complex combinations of *qualifiers* we have already remarked on (pp. 279–80) are legitimately considered structures of modification in which the last qualifier in the group is the head:

very much more easily   rather too strong   not quite well

The first of these may be analyzed into its constituents this way:

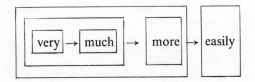

Prepositions may function as heads of structures of modification; when they do, the modifiers are either *qualifiers*, *adverbs*, or certain *nouns*:

very like a whale	slightly off pitch
a bit under the weather	a mile from home
almost beneath notice	a long way off base

When such modifiers follow the prepositional phrase, the head of the structure is not just the preposition but the whole phrase. Thus, we may compare (a) *exactly on the mark* and (b) *on the mark exactly*.

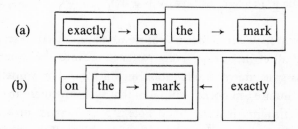

(a)

(b)

This minor difference in structure seldom makes much difference in structural meaning.

Noun-determiners may be modified by *qualifiers*, *adverbs*, or even *prepositional phrases*, as in the following examples:

very many people	almost all people
not a few friends	more than enough money
much more money	

The last of these is actually ambiguous; it may be analyzed in either of the following ways:

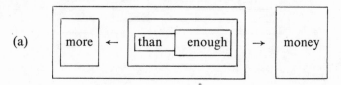

(a)

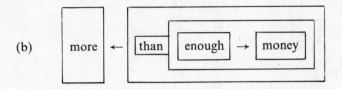

In (a), the phrase *than enough* modifies *more*, and the whole structure *more than enough* serves as a noun-determiner with the noun *money*. In (b), on the other hand, *more* is a function-noun, modified by the phrase *than enough money*, with *enough* serving as noun-determiner with *money*. There is a difference of structural meaning here, which may be quite significant.   Compare:

(a) he left her   more than enough → money   (he left her a fortune)

(b) he left her   more ← than enough money   (in addition to adequate funds, he left her a house, a yacht, and a business)

Meaning (b) would often be indicated in speech by a double-bar (rising) juncture after *more*.

SUMMARY. The simple structures of modification—those that have a single word as head and a single word or prepositional phrase as modifier, may be summarized in the table on pages 326–27. Note that the columns represent the various types of head, printed in capitals in the table, while the rows represent various types of modifiers, printed in italics in the table.

STRUCTURES OF PREDICATION

As we have already noted, the two immediate constituents of a **structure of predication** are a **subject** and a **predicate**, usually, but not always, coming in that order. Each of these may be a single word, a word with accompanying function word(s), a phrase, or one of the three other kinds of syntactic structure—modification,

HEAD Modifier	NOUN	VERB	ADJECTIVE	ADVERB	FUNCTION WORD
Noun	the dog DAYS a dog's LIFE a dining TABLE	LIVED a year SAW a mile	stone COLD bone DRY	a foot AWAY some way UP	a mile OFF base
Verb	running WATER MONEY to burn	CAME running CAME to scoff	boiling HOT HARD to get		
Adjective	the gloomy ROOM barbed WIRE a pleasing TABLE	RAN wild FELL flat	icy COLD cold SOBER		

HEAD → / ↓ Modifier	NOUN	VERB	ADJECTIVE	ADVERB	FUNCTION-WORD
Adverb	PEOPLE *here* / EUROPE *now*	DRIVES *rapidly* / *seldom* SPEAKS	*widely* FAMOUS / *everywhere* DARK	*unusually* EAGERLY / *far* AWAY	*exactly* ON the mark / *soon* AFTER dark
Prepositional Phrase	a MAN *above suspicion* / a PLACE *in the sun*	CAME *down the street* / LIVED *in the country*	GOOD *for nothing* / GREEN *as grass*	OUTSIDE *in the cold* / AWAY *at school*	MORE *than enough* (work) / ENOUGH *for now*
Function-Word	*the* BOOK / MONEY *enough*		*very* STRONG *a lot* STRONGER	*very* EASILY / *much* AHEAD	*very* MUCH / *rather* MORE

complementation, or coordination. In addition, the subject may itself be a structure of predication of the type we shall later define as **included clause.** For the present, we shall confine our discussion to the simpler types of subject and predicate, postponing consideration of more complex structures of predication until we discuss **sentences** in the next chapter.

PREDICATES. Since the best distinguishing mark of a structure of predication is the predicate, let us begin with it. Once a predicate has been identified, its subject usually becomes apparent without difficulty.

Whatever else a predicate may consist of, it always has a verb or verb-phrase in key position. Thus, if a predicate has only one word, that one word is a verb, as in *money talks, the sun set.* If the predicate is a structure of modification, its head is a verb, as in

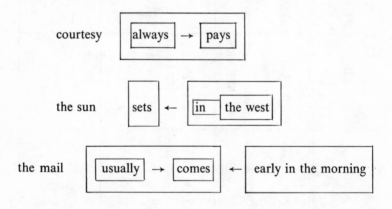

If the predicate is a structure of complementation, one of its immediate constituents is by definition a verbal element, which always has a verb at its core:

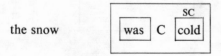

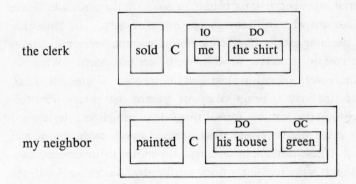

If the predicate is a structure of coordination, its coordinate members are either verbs themselves or structures in which verbs are essential elements:

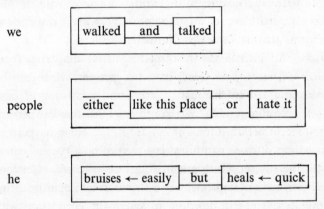

The advice of the traditional grammar to identify a predicate by looking for the verb is thus basically sound. But it should be remembered that the verb by itself is seldom the entire predicate. The predicate is usually a more or less complex structure or structure of structures, with the verb at its core. In analyzing such predicates, we may have to work our way through several structural layers before we can finally isolate the verb. But the verb is the heart of the matter, and certain formal qualities of the verb determine important elements in the structural meaning of the predicate. These qualities are what will engage our attention next. In discussing them, we may use for illustration not only simple verbs but various other types of structure in which verbs are prominent. When we do, the reader should assume that the process of analysis which isolates the verb is being taken for granted, not simply omitted.

English verbs exhibit formal distinctions which can be classed under seven heads: **person, tense, phase, aspect, mode, voice,** and **status.**[5] These distinctions are made by means of inflections, auxiliaries and other function words, word order, and prosody—all the signals of syntactic structure except derivational contrast. In the following discussion we shall concentrate on the first three, since they usually are sufficient to permit identification of the verb-form and are all that are available in the written language. But in one or two cases we shall have to call upon prosody to make distinctions between forms that are otherwise formally identical.

1. *Person.* All English verbs except the modal auxiliaries (*can, may, shall, will, must, dare, need*) have two **persons,** which can be called **common** and **third singular.** Verb forms consisting of base form + {-*s*} inflection (pp. 252–54) are in the third-singular person; all others (except certain forms of *be*) are in the common person. The distribution of these two forms is governed by a type of correlation with the subject which grammarians call **concord.** Concord may be defined as the complementary distribution of linguistic forms having the same syntactic function in systematic correlation with other formally distinct forms with which they are syntactically linked. Since this gives us the two criteria of syntactic similarity and complementary distribution, we have a structural situation similar to that of allophones and allomorphs. Concord is not so prominent in the structure of English as it is in some other languages, but it oc-

---

[5] The terminology used here is that of Trager and Smith (*Outline of English Structure*, pp. 77–80), though the subsequent discussion will depart in a few respects from theirs.

casionally becomes important, as in the matter with which we are now dealing, the person of verbs.

The distribution of the third-singular form of English verbs is quite complicated and exhibits some variation from one dialect to another. It can, however, be described in general terms as follows. The third-singular person is used whenever a simple verb is the head-verb in a predicate whose subject is one of the following:

(1) A noun for which *he, she*, or *it* may be substituted.

(2) One of the pronouns *he, she*, or *it*.

(3) The function-nouns *this* or *that*.

(4) A structure of modification of which one of the above is head.

(5) Any other part of speech beside a noun, or a structure of modification or complementation with such part of speech as head or verbal element.

(6) One of certain special structures of predication: the included clause and the infinitive clause.

(7) A structure of coordination in which the coordinator is *or, nor, (n)either* ... *(n)or*, or *not (only)* ... *but (also)* and in which the last coordinate element belongs to (1)–(6) above; also one of certain other special structures of coordination.

These generalizations are admittedly imprecise. They have been so stated in the interests of brevity and because of dialectal and individual variations.

The seven types of subjects correlating with third-singular verbs may be illustrated as follows:

(1) the man walks; the sun sets; snow falls.

(2) he feels; she speaks; it comes (*but note exception in* watch it come).

(3) this looks good; that goes here.

(4) the tall man in the car drives; that in the dish tastes good.

(5) here seems like a good place; eating candy causes tooth decay.

(6) what I want costs money; how it got there remains a mystery.

(7) either his mistakes or his bad luck keeps him poor; peace and quiet seems (*or* seem) unattainable.

All other kinds of subjects correlate with the common form of the verb. Chief of these are nouns for which *they* can be substituted; the pronouns *I, you, we, they, me, him, her, us, them*; the function nouns *these* and *those*; structures of coordination with coordinators *and, both . . . and*, and the like; a few special included clauses. Some examples:

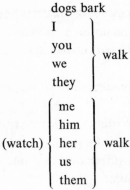

dogs bark

$$\left.\begin{array}{l} \text{I} \\ \text{you} \\ \text{we} \\ \text{they} \end{array}\right\} \text{walk}$$

$$(\text{watch}) \left\{\begin{array}{l} \text{me} \\ \text{him} \\ \text{her} \\ \text{us} \\ \text{them} \end{array}\right\} \text{walk}$$

(both) the knife and the fork shine brightly

either his bad luck or his mistakes keep him poor

whatever jobs are available suit me

One verb, *be*, whether as full verb or as auxiliary, has an additional form, the **first-singular** *am*, which correlates with the subject *I*, and a common person form *are*, which is different from the base, *be*.

2. *Tense.* All English verbs except a few auxiliaries (*ought, must*) have two tenses, the **common tense** (usually called the **present**[6]) and the **past** (or **preterit**) tense. These are formally distinguished by inflections. The past-tense form consists of the base + the inflectional suffix $\{-ed_1\}$; the common-tense forms are the base alone

---

[6] Or by Trager and Smith, the **non-past**.

and the third-singular (base + {*-s*}). As we have already seen (pp. 254–55), the past-tense suffix {*-ed*$_1$} has various allomorphs, sometimes involving morphophonemic changes in the base. But with the single exception of *be*, each verb has a single past-tense form,[7] which correlates with all subjects. The verb *be* has two past-tense forms, *was* and *were* (each with several allomorphs) which show **number concord.** That is, in the standard dialects, *was* correlates with singular subjects (nouns in base form, the substitutes *I*, *he*, *she*, *it*, other parts of speech and special structures), and *were* correlates with plural subjects, including the pronoun *you* regardless of the nature of its referent. In many dialects, however—those usually labeled "substandard"—only the single form *was* is used.

3. *Phase.* All English verbs except a few auxiliaries have two **phases,** the **simple** and the **perfect.** The perfect phase is marked by the use of various forms of the auxiliary *have* with the past-participle form of the verb: *he has spoken, we may have been, I should have worked, he has gone.* In addition, certain verbs, all of the kind we shall later define as **intransitive,** have a **resultative phase,** formed with the auxiliary *be* and the past-participle form of the verb: *he is gone, they are finished ·with the work, I am done with you.* Verbs not formally marked as in the perfect or resultative phase are in the simple phase.

4. *Aspect.* English verbs have three **aspects,** the **simple,** the **durative,** and the **inchoative.** The simple aspect is unmarked. The durative is formed by the auxiliary *be* and the present-participle (base + {*-ing*$_1$}) form of the verb.[8] The inchoative aspect is formed by the auxiliary *get* and the present-participle form of the verb. Examples of these last two are given on the following page.

---

[7] Some verbs, like *wake* and *dive*, have alternative forms in free or dialectal variation.

[8] Forms in the durative aspect are often called "progressive tenses" in the traditional grammar. This is an unfortunate confusion between *tense*, which is semantically related to time, and *aspect*, which is semantically related to the status of an action in regard to its beginning, continuance, repetition, conclusion, etc.

DURATIVE	INCHOATIVE
he is talking	we got talking
she was swimming	let's get going
we ought to be working	we ought to get working

5. *Mode.* English verbs have a variety of **modes,** the number varying somewhat between dialects. The modes can be classified on the basis of form into two groups: (1) those formed by the **modal auxiliaries** with the base form of the verb, and (2) those formed by certain other auxiliaries with the infinitive (*to* + base) form of the verb. The modal auxiliaries are *can, may, shall, will, must, dare, need, do.* All of these except *must* and *need* have past-tense forms; *do* also has a third-singular form, *does.* The auxiliaries which form modes with the infinitive are *have, be, be going, be about, used, ought, get, have got.* The modes formed by these various auxiliaries have no separate names; they can be rather clumsily designated as "the *shall*-mode," "the *ought to*-mode," and so on. The following examples illustrate some of the many possible forms:

MODAL AUXILIARIES	OTHER AUXILIARIES
he can go	they have to go
we might see	we are to see
they should have spoken	he was going to speak
you will come	people were about to leave
everybody must die	she used to sing
nobody dared do it	that man ought to have quit
you need not worry	I never got to see Paris
he does study	he has got to study

A verb-phrase may belong to two modes at the same time. In such a case, only one may be from the modal-auxiliary group, and its auxiliary always comes first in the phrase. Thus, we may have forms such as:

he would have to work
he could be about to work
he may be going to tell us
he used to have to work

but not

*he has to can work
*he is going to must work
*he will can do it

As has already been pointed out (pp. 259–60), the large variety of modal forms is one of the marked features of English, permitting very fine distinctions of meaning in English predicates.

6. *Voice.* English verbs have two **voices,** the normal or **active voice** and the **passive voice.** Passive voice forms consist of some form of the auxiliary *be* with the past-participle form of the verb. Another passive, formed with *get* as auxiliary and the past-participle, seems to be increasing in frequency, though grammarians are at present not agreed as to its status. The three types of voice-forms are illustrated in the following examples:

ACTIVE
he kills
they built a house
we have done the work

be-PASSIVE	*get*-PASSIVE
he is killed	he gets killed
the house was built	the house got built
the work has been done	the work has got done

Two structures which are exactly alike in the written form and sometimes alike in speech are the *be*-passive and the verb *be* with a past participle as **subjective complement.** Consider the following sentences.

(a) the house was built by experts

(b) the house was built of wood

The difference in structure here, sometimes marked in speech by a pause either after or before *built*, can be clearly revealed by diagrams:

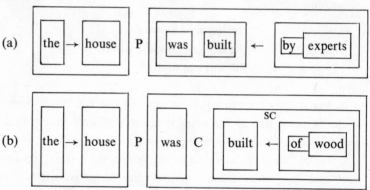

In (a), there is a passive verb, *was built*, as head with the prepositional phrase *by experts* as modifier, the whole structure of modification serving as predicate. In (b), on the other hand, the verb is *was*, with the structure of modification *built of wood* serving as subjective complement. Apart from the juncture which may indicate where the division between the immediate constituents of the predicate falls (either before or after *built*), the only way these structures are formally distinguished is the presence, actual or possible, of a phrase containing the preposition *by*. This always indicates the passive, as in (a). Compare the following examples:

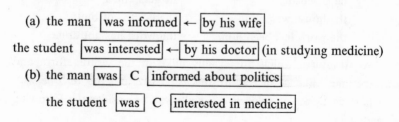

7. *Status.* English verbs have four **statuses,** the **affirmative,** the **interrogative,** the **negative,** and the **negative-interrogative.** The **interrogative status** is marked by a change in word order, involving the inversion of the subject and the auxiliary, or the first auxiliary if more than one are present. Verbs which have no auxiliary in the affirmative status use the auxiliary *do/does/did* to form the interrogative, except *be*, which always simply inverts subject and verb, and *have*, which may invert or may use the forms of *do*.[9] The auxiliaries *get, used* (*to*), and *have* (*to*) also use the forms of *do*. The following examples illustrate interrogative status:

INVERTED FORMS	*do*-FORMS
is he working	does he work
has he worked	did he work
should he have worked	did he get killed
is he going to work	does he have to work
	did he use to work

Note that this inversion produces a structure in which one immediate constituent is split into two parts and the other inserted between:

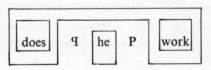

The **negative status** is marked by the insertion of the special function word *not*, which has various allomorphs such as /nat, nt, ənt, ən, n/, immediately after the first auxiliary. Again the forms of *do* are used if no auxiliary is otherwise present, although *do* is not used with *be* and not always with *have*. The forms of *do* are

---

[9] A difference between British and American usage appears here. British prefers the inverted form, such as *has he*, while American prefers the form with *do*, such as *does he have*.

used when the auxiliary is *used* (*to*), *have* (*to*), or a simple form of *get*. The following examples illustrate various cases of negative status:

he is not (/ìz nât, îzənt, z+nât, îzən/) working
he has not worked   he is not here
he should not have worked   he { has not / does not have } any money
he is not going to work
he does not work   he did not use to work[10]

Once again the verb-phrase is split:

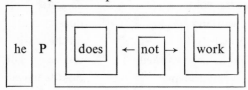

The **negative-interrogative status** combines the two former, as its name indicates. The use of the auxiliary *do* follows the same pattern as in the interrogative forms. This structure brings the subject and the function word *not* together at the same point in the middle of the split verb-phrase. Either of them may come first, but the form with the subject before *not* is somewhat more formal, as the following examples show:

not-FIRST FORM	SUBJECT-FIRST FORM
îsň't hè wórkĭng	îs hè nòt wórkĭng
hasn't he worked	has he not worked
shôuldň't hè hăve wórked	shòuld hě nôt hăve wórked
doesn't he work	does he not work
hasn't he } any money	has he not } any money
doesn't he have	does he not have

---

[10] British usage prefers *used he to work*, *he used not to work*.

Notice that in the left-hand column the allomorph of {*not*} is under weak stress, while in the right-hand column it has at least tertiary and sometimes secondary.

In a negative-interrogative structure, two elements are inserted into the split verb-phrase:

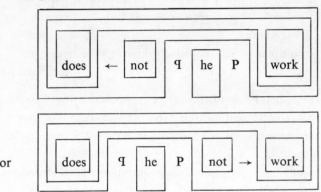

It should be apparent by now that when all seven of these qualities of verbs are considered, a large, varied, and complicated series of verb-phrases is possible. This is one of the most striking aspects of present-day English grammar. Much of this complexity has developed since Old English times (that is, since A.D. 1150), so that the development can be traced in written records. When historical linguists have thoroughly studied this phase of the history of English, it should provide just as spectacular an illustration of the adaptation of the language to new demands as does the tremendous growth of the vocabulary over the same period.

We may summarize this sevenfold classification of verbs by a tabular analysis of four typical verb-phrases:

(a) he is to be told
(b) they should not have been working
(c) ought we to get going
(d) mightn't he have been getting run over

	(a)	(b)	(c)	(d)
Person	third-singular	common	common	common
Tense	common	past	common	past
Phase	simple	perfect	simple	perfect
Aspect	simple	durative	inchoative	durative
Mode	*be to*	*shall*	*ought to*	*may*
Voice	*be*-passive	active	active	*get*-passive
Status	affirmative	negative	interrogative	negative-interrogative

SUBJECTS. In our discussion of person-concord (pp. 330–32) we have already illustrated various types of subjects. We may now somewhat expand what was outlined there and give a few more illustrations.

The commonest subjects are nouns or noun-headed structures of modification:

> *money* talks
> *the weather* has changed
> *the longest day* eventually ends
> *a cold gray day in winter* depresses me.

The other three parts of speech and structures of modification of which they are head may also function as subject:

Adjectives:　*handsome* is as handsome does
　　　　　　　helpful to your friends is a good way to be
Adverbs:　*now* is too soon
　　　　　　never again will be soon enough
Verbs (*Infinitive*):　*to err* is human
　　　　　　　　　　　to work in New York is my ambition
　　(*Present Participle*):　*working there* is pleasant
　　　　　　　　　　　　　living comfortably is expensive

Some other structures that may serve as subject are the following:

(1) Prepositional Phrase:
> *to South America* is a long trip
>
> *in America* is where I choose to live

(2) Structures of Complementation:
> *to make a good living* takes hard work
>
> *sailing a boat* is my favorite hobby
>
> *electing him president* was a mistake

(3) Structures of Coordination:
> *food and drink* can be had here
>
> *to be or not to be* is Hamlet's question

(4) Structures of Predication (Included Clauses)
> *whatever is* is right
>
> *that he did it at all* has not been proved

When the subject is one of the pronouns *I, he, she, we, they,* or *who,* a question of concord arises. These words have the alternative objective-case forms *me, him, her, us, them,* and *whom.* Normally when one of these is a subject, it is the nominative form which appears:

> *he* called me in
>
> *we* were given our instructions
>
> *they* have been sent away
>
> *she and I* met yesterday
>
> *who* will volunteer for the job

But when the verb of a structure of predication is an infinitive, the objective-case form appears as subject:

> I asked *him* to call
>
> I know *them* to have been told

Likewise when a structure of predication not marked as an included clause (to be discussed later) appears as the complement of a verb, the objective-case form appears as subject, as in the following.

> We watched *them* go
> we heard *him* singing

A special type of subject is the function word *there*. This is pronounced /ðər/ or /ðə/ with weak or tertiary stress, which distinguishes it from the adverb *there*, pronounced /ðehr, ðeh/ and often having primary or secondary stress. The function word *there* is sometimes called a **temporary subject,** filling the subject position in place of the true subject, which follows the verb. This interpretation is borne out by the fact that the verb frequently shows concord with a following noun, as in

> there is a tavern in the town
> there were three kings
> there comes a day

There are, however, frequent occasions when the following "true subject" is a structure of coordination, normally calling for a verb in common person, with the verb in the third-singular instead:

> there was a salt-cellar and a pepper-shaker on the table[11]

STRUCTURES OF COMPLEMENTATION

A **structure of complementation** has two immediate constituents: a **verbal element** and a **complement.** The verbal element may be a simple verb, or it may be any structure that has a verb in key position. Thus, it may be a verb-phrase, an infinitive, a structure of modification with verb as head, or a structure of coordination whose components are any of these. The following examples illustrate some of these:

Simple Verb: (he) | gives | lessons

(a man) | hoeing | corn

[11] The prevalence of this construction is documented by R. J. Geist in "'There Is' Again," *College English*, XVI (Dec. 1954), 188–89.

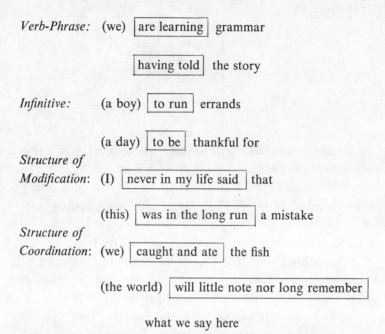

Verb-Phrase: (we)   ⌐are learning⌐   grammar

⌐having told⌐   the story

Infinitive: (a boy)   ⌐to run⌐   errands

(a day)   ⌐to be⌐   thankful for

*Structure of
Modification:*   (I)   ⌐never in my life said⌐   that

(this)   ⌐was in the long run⌐   a mistake

*Structure of
Coordination:*   (we)   ⌐caught and ate⌐   the fish

(the world)   ⌐will little note nor long remember⌐

what we say here

In order to identify and describe different types of complements, we must first note that the verbs which are at the core of the various types of verbal elements may be divided into three main groups: **linking** (or **copulative**) **verbs, intransitive verbs,** and **transitive verbs.** These groups may be identified by the types of structure in which their members are found and by certain other formal indications.

1. *Linking Verbs.* As the name indicates, linking verbs are thought of as a structural link between subject and complement. They therefore never occur without a complement. The most common and typical member of the group is *be* (as a full verb, not an auxiliary). In fact, substitution of *be* can be used as a test for linking verbs. If the appropriate form of *be* can be inserted into a structure of complementation in place of another verb without making a major change in the structural meaning, the original verb is a linking verb. This is illustrated in the following example.

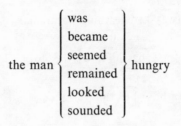

A further formal test is that linking verbs have no passive forms: such verb-phrases as *is remained*, *was seemed*, and *is been* do not occur in standard English. This test is of only limited value, however, for two reasons. In the first place, some linking verbs have homonyms which do have passive forms, as in *the alarm was sounded*.[12] Secondly, as we shall see, intransitive verbs also lack passive forms.

2. *Intransitive Verbs.* Verbs which may appear in the active voice as complete predicates without any complement are **intransitive verbs.** Like linking verbs, they have no passive forms. They may, of course, be modified in various ways. But since they have no complements, they cannot appear as verbal elements of structures of complementation. A few intransitive verbs are the following:

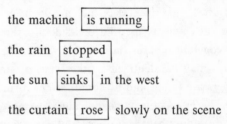

3. *Transitive Verbs.* Verbs which always have a complement when in the active voice, and which have passive forms, are **transitive verbs.** Their most characteristic formal feature is that when a passive form is substituted for an active form, the complement or a part of it must be made the subject if the meaning is to be preserved without a significant change. Thus, in structures like the following two:

---

[12] The form *is become* is not passive voice but resultative phase.

the man ⬚sold⬚ his car

the wind ⬚blew down⬚ the house

the transitive active forms *sold* and *blew down* may be replaced by *was sold* and *was blown down*, requiring that the complements *his car* and *the house* be shifted to subject:

the car ⬚was sold⬚ (by the man)

the house ⬚was blown down⬚ (by the wind)

Many transitive verbs have homonyms which are intransitive or linking. It is therefore necessary to observe a verb in a grammatical context before it can be classified. Thus, verbs such as *turn, blow,* and *sound* can belong to all three classes:

Linking: the weather turned cold
              the wind blew a gale
              the music sounded loud
Intransitive: the earth turns
              the wind is blowing
              the fire alarm sounded
Transitive: the car turned the corner
              the musician blew the trumpet
              the watchman sounds the alarm

The formal distinctions between these three types of verbs may be summarized as follows:

(1) Linking Verb: has complement but no passive;
(2) Intransitive Verb: has neither complement nor passive;
(3) Transitive Verb: has both complement and passive.

Since intransitive verbs have no complements, they do not appear in structures of complementation. Each of the other two types has its own kind of complement. Complements appearing with linking verbs are called **subjective complements;** complements appearing with transitive verbs are called **objects.**

SUBJECTIVE COMPLEMENT. Subjective complements may be single words, with or without related function words, or they may be structures of varying degrees of complexity, from relatively simple structures of modification or coordination to elaborate affairs, containing all sorts of structures within them. We shall illustrate only the less complex types here. The following examples show various kinds of simple subjective complements:

Noun: the woman is ┃ a nurse ┃

Function Noun: ripeness is ┃ all ┃

Adjective: the corn is ┃ ripe ┃

Adverb: the time is ┃ now ┃

Verb (Infinitive): his wish is ┃ to die ┃

(*Present Participle*): his trade is ┃ writing ┃ [13]

(*Past Participle*): this meat is ┃ canned ┃ [14]

Prepositional Phrase: the train is ┃ on time ┃

[13] This structure is identical with the durative aspect of the verb, as in *he is writing.* The resulting structural ambiguity is resolved lexically. It is occasionally a source of verbal humor, as in the hoary joke about the street-cleaner whose business was picking up.

[14] For the formal distinction between this and the passive voice form, see pages 335–36.

Since nouns and adjectives make up a large proportion of the simpler subjective complements, grammarians sometimes use the special terms **predicate noun** (or **predicate nominative**) and **predicate adjective** for them. But since these supply names for only two of the many kinds of subjective complement, it seems wiser to abandon them in favor of the more general term.

When the pronouns *he*, *she*, *we*, and *they* function as subjective complement, they usually appear in the subjective (or nominative) forms in the educated and literary dialects.[15] Usage on *I/me* is divided, both forms being used more or less interchangeably by most standard speakers. But in the spoken and written usage of a large number of people less subject to education and literary practice, the objective forms *me*, *him*, *her*, *us*, and *them* are universal.

There is no need to discuss here the various complex structures which may function as subjective complement. The reader should by this time be able to find and analyze them for himself. A few illustrations will be sufficient to reveal the wide variety of forms that may perform this function:

(a) Structures of Modification

he is | a promising young member of the bar |

his plan is | to retire peacefully to Florida |

this project is | exceedingly simple in its general plan |

(b) Structures of Coordination

the day was | dark, gloomy, and cold |

[15] On this point, see N. C. Stageberg, "Is It Really *We?*" *College English*, XVI (March 1955), 376–378. On the basis of an objective study of spoken usage among educated speakers, Stageberg reaches two "tentatively justified" conclusions: "(1) The choice of case form is a matter of divided usage. (2) The tendency is toward the use of the nominative."

his trouble is | self-induced rather than outwardly caused |

(c) Structures of Complementation

his job is | to supervise the operation of this machine |

his hobby is | collecting stamps |

(d) Structures of Predication (Included Clauses)

the trouble is | that he doesn't want to do it |

the winner is | whoever crosses the line first |

DIRECT OBJECT.   When the complement of a transitive verb consists of a single object, whether it be a single word or a complex structure, this object is called a **direct object.** Pronoun objects are in the objective case.   Some examples of single-word direct objects are the following:

Noun: he found | a friend |

Pronoun: I saw | him |

Function Noun: we sent | several |

Verb (*Infinitive*): they want | to go |

(*Present Participle*): she likes | walking |

Some dialects, notably those of the Midland (Pennsylvania and derivative settlements) use certain adverbs as direct object, especially with the verb *want*, as in *the cat wants out, the passenger wants off.*

As we might expect, various more complex structures also may function as direct objects, as in the following illustrations:

(a) Structures of Modification

    we saw | an excellent new play about Mexico |

    she likes | walking alone in the rain |

(b) Structures of Coordination

    the party needs | a new platform and a new leader |

    the company plans

            | both to find new deposits and to mine them |

(c) Structures of Complementation

    he intends | to make money |

    they dislike | studying grammar |

(d) Structures of Predication

    the teacher had | the students read a book |

    the hot weather caused | us to feel sluggish |

    I know | he is here |

    I wonder | where he is |

INDIRECT OBJECT. When the complement of a structure of complementation whose verbal element is transitive consists of two objects, one of them is always a direct object. The other is either an **indirect object** or an **objective complement.** Structures of this sort are thus potentially ambiguous. They are distinguished by rather subtle formal indications, aided by lexical probability. Let us consider some more clear-cut examples first:

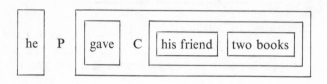

Here, as the "Chinese boxes" indicate, we have a structure of predication with subject *he* and predicate *gave his friend two books.* This predicate is a structure of complementation, with verbal element *gave* and complement *his friend two books.* Assuming (on the basis of the absence of a comma after *friend*) that the intonation of this complement is /²hiz frénd²|²tûw ³búks¹#/, not /²hiz frénd²||²tûw ³búks¹#/, we know that we are not dealing with a structure of coordination or an appositive. Therefore, we recognize that the complement consists of two objects, *his friend* and *two books.*

Scrutiny of these objects reveals that the first is a singular noun of substitute group 4 (*he/she—they*) and the second a plural noun of substitute group 3 (*it—they*). It is thus probable (though not positive) that these nouns have different referents.

Secondly we may observe that if we change the verb to the corresponding passive form, either of the two objects may be made subject, while the other remains as object. Thus, we may say either

          his friend was given two books by him
or   two books were given his friend by him

In the third place, we may further note that instead of the first object, *his friend*, we may use a prepositional phrase, *to his friend*, as modifier either of the verb *gave* or of the whole structure of complementation, *gave two books*. These two alternatives can be diagrammed:

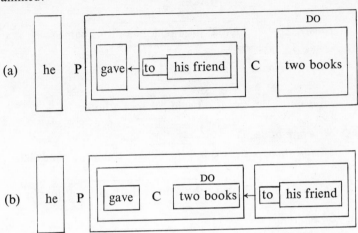

These three circumstances are the formal indications that in this particular complement, *his friend two books*, we are dealing with two objects, the first of which is an indirect object and the second a direct object. We may state the identifying criteria of the indirect object as follows:

(1) With active verbs it occurs only in company with a direct object, as part of a complex complement.
(2) In such complements, it always comes before the direct object.
(3) Its referent is different from that of the direct object.
(4) When verbal elements appearing with such complements are changed to the passive voice, either object may be made subject.
(5) An indirect object may be changed to a prepositional phrase without major change in the total meaning of the structure.

In contrast to direct objects, which may be various parts of speech or more complex structures, indirect objects are always nouns, noun-headed structures of modification, or structures of coordination with noun constituents. The following examples illustrate these various possibilities:

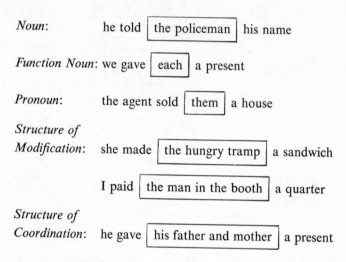

Noun: he told [the policeman] his name

Function Noun: we gave [each] a present

Pronoun: the agent sold [them] a house

Structure of Modification: she made [the hungry tramp] a sandwich

I paid [the man in the booth] a quarter

Structure of Coordination: he gave [his father and mother] a present

OBJECTIVE COMPLEMENT. Certain complements consisting of two objects do not fit the indirect + direct object pattern which we have been discussing. Consider such an utterance as this:

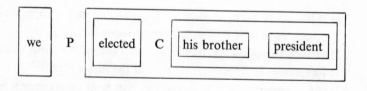

we P | elected C [his brother] [president]

Assuming that the prosodic pattern of the last three words is /²hiz ³brɔ́ðər²|³prézidənt¹#/ (which eliminates the possibility that *brother* is a noun-adjunct modifier of *president*), we can see that the complement consists of two objects, *his brother* and *president*. Looking at these more closely, we observe that though *brother* belongs to substitute-class 1 (*he—they*) and *president* to class 4 (*he/she—they*), they both may have the substitute *he* and, hence, the same referent. Furthermore, if we change the verb to the passive voice, only the first object can be made subject. That is, we can say

> his brother was elected president by us

but not   *president was elected his brother by us

Nor can we substitute a prepositional phrase for the first object; we cannot say

> *we elected to his brother president

nor   *we elected president for his brother

It is clear, then, that we cannot call *his brother* an indirect object. Instead, the two parts of our complex complement are a direct object and an **objective complement,** in that order.

Perhaps the simplest way to define an objective complement is by means of the negative method we have just employed. That is, if a complement consisting of two objects does not meet the requirements for the indirect + direct object structure, its second object is an objective complement. This may be more positively stated as follows:

(1) With active verbs, an objective complement occurs only in company with a direct object as part of a complex complement.

(2) In such complements it always follows the direct object.

(3) Its structural referent is the same as that of the direct object (though it need not belong to the same substitute-class).

(4) When verbal elements appearing with such complements are changed to the passive voice, only the first (direct) object may be made subject.

Objective complements may be nouns (but seldom pronouns or function nouns), adjectives, adverbs, verbs (in past-participle form), prepositional phrases, or structures of modification or coordination, as illustrated by the following examples:

Noun: we made him ┃ a member

Adjective: he painted his house ┃ green

Adverb: we found him ┃ alone

Past Participle: they considered the job ┃ finished

Prepositional Phrase: he left her ┃ in tears

Structure of Modification: we made him ┃ a member of our club

we found it

┃ a trying and difficult task for beginners

Structure of Coordination: He painted his house ┃ red, white, and blue

we consider his conduct

┃ a scandal and a disgrace

OBJECTS WITH PASSIVE VERBS. A verbal element in the passive voice can have a complement, but it always consists of a single object. This may be any of the three kinds we have been discussing —direct object, indirect object, or objective complement. The simplest test for identifying which it is is to change the verb to the active voice. Consider the following:

(a) he was given ┃ a book

(b) a book was given ┃ him

(c) he was elected ┃ president

When the verbs of these structures are changed to the active voice, we have:

(a) gave him | a book |

(b) gave | him | a book

(c) elected him | president |

It is now apparent that *a book* in (a) is a direct object, *him* in (b) an indirect object, and *president* in (c) an objective complement.[16]

STRUCTURES OF COORDINATION

A **structure of coordination** consists of two or more syntactically equivalent units joined in a structure which functions as a single unit. The units so joined may be any of the parts of speech, function words, or more complex structures that we have recognized as taking part in grammatical organization. The joining may be accomplished by word order and prosody alone, or with the additional help of a set of function words and phrases which we can call **coordinators.** These are the following:

and	rather than	not (only) . . . but (also)
but	as well as	either . . . or
nor	together with	neither . . . nor
not	along with	both . . . and
or		

The coordinators in the first column always appear between the elements which they join. Those in the middle column may appear in that position; they may also mark certain split constructions which we shall discuss later. Those in the third column, which are called

[16] The term **retained object** is sometimes used for the objects of passive verbs. But since this fails to distinguish between the three types of objects, it seems more desirable to use the same terms for objects of passive verbs as for those of active verbs.

correlatives, are in two parts, the first part appearing at the beginning of the structure and the second between its last two components.

A structure of coordination which has more than two components is called a **series.** It is the only structure in English which has more than two immediate constituents; clearly, a series has as many immediate constituents as there are items in the series:

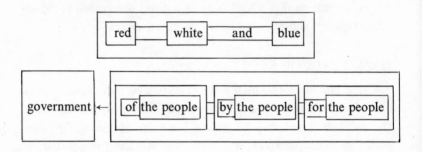

In the second of these examples, the three prepositional phrases make up a series, which in turn functions as a modifier of *government*.

The fact that coordinators are not always used between members of structures of coordination means that such structures may frequently be structurally ambiguous, or at least potentially so. In speech, however, there are prosodic patterns which clearly distinguish the various types of construction. Consider the following sentence:

> he brought his friend a doctor and a gentleman

If we disregard prosody (and punctuation), this has at least three possible meanings:

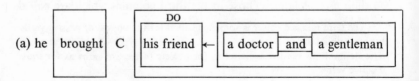

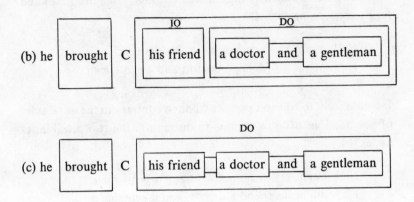

In (a), the structure of coordination *a doctor and a gentleman* is a modifier of *his friend* (of the special sort called **appositive;** see p. 301); therefore *friend, doctor,* and *gentleman* all have the same referent, only one person was brought, and only two are involved in the sentence. In (b), *his friend* is an indirect object and the structure of coordination *a doctor and a gentleman* is the direct object; therefore, the referent of *friend* is different from those of *doctor* and *gentleman,* which may or may not be the same. Thus, either one or two persons were brought, and three or four are involved in the sentence. In (c), the structure of coordination (series) *his friend a doctor and a gentleman* is the direct object; therefore, the three nouns all have different referents, three persons were brought, and four are involved in the sentence. If the reader will pronounce the sentence aloud, concentrating on these three different meanings, he will observe that prosody keeps them distinct. For the author they go like this:

(a) /²hìy brɔ́ht iz ³frénd²‖²ə dâktər ənd ə ³jéntəlmən¹#/

(b) /²hìy brɔ́ht iz frênd ə dâktər ənd ə ³jéntəlmən¹#/
   /²hìy brɔ́ht iz frênd ə ³dáktər²|²ənd ə ³jéntəlmən¹#/

(c) /²hìy brɔ́ht iz ³frénd²|²ə ³dáktər²|²ənd ə ³jéntəlmən¹#/
   /² hiy brɔ́ht iz ²frénd²‖²ə dáktər²‖²ənd ə ³jéntəlmən¹#/

In writing we customarily indicate the terminal junctures in (a) and (c) by commas or dashes:

(a) He brought his friend—a doctor and a gentleman.
(c) He brought his friend, a doctor, and a gentleman.

It would seem to be good practice (though contrary to the usual rules of punctuation) to use a comma to distinguish the two possibilities under (b):

He brought his friend a doctor and a gentleman.
He brought his friend a doctor, and a gentleman.

A special case of this problem concerns structures in which a number of modifiers all ultimately modify the same head. It is of considerable importance to determine whether two or more of the modifiers are coordinate, or whether each successive modifier has as its head the whole previous structure of modification. Consider in this regard the following:

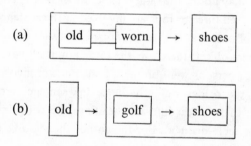

(a) is a single structure of modification, with *shoes* as head and the structure of coordination *old worn* as modifier. The two adjectives are thus coordinate and on the same structural level. Their order may be reversed, or they may be joined by a coordinator: that is, we can say *worn old shoes* or *old and worn shoes*. In (b), on the other hand, there are two structures of modification, one within the other. The head of the inner structure is *shoes*, which is modified by the noun-adjunct *golf*. The whole structure of modification *golf shoes* in turn serves as head of the outer structure, with *old* as its modifier. The order of the modifiers cannot be reversed, nor can they be joined by a coordinator: we cannot say **golf old shoes* or **old and golf shoes*.

This distinction between coordinate and progressive modifiers is signaled in speech by intonation and in writing by punctuation:

(a) /^{3}ówld^2|^{3}wóhrn^2|^{3}šúwz^1#/ = old, worn shoes
(b) /^{2}ôwld ^{3}gálf šûwz^1#/ = old golf shoes (*or* golf-shoes)

In more complex structures of modification, it is sometimes difficult or impossible to be positive about the level on which coordination takes place. Actually, such structures are frequently structurally ambiguous, so that we must rely on lexical probability to resolve them:

(a) he was born and lives in New York
(b) he was born and lived for forty years

Clearly in (a) the phrase *in New York* modifies the structure of coordination *was born and lives*, while in (b) *for forty years* modifies only *lived*, since our common sense tells us that a person cannot be born for forty years. It is the meaning, then, that leads us to analyze these structures differently:

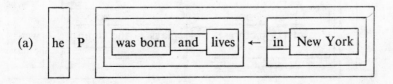

(a) he P was born and lives ← in New York

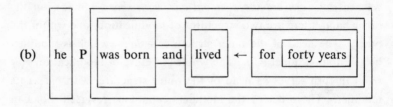

(b)

Sometimes, however, lexical probability is not a reliable guide. In such cases, true ambiguity results, as in:

> a surgeon and a diagnostician of great skill
> (Query: is he a skillful surgeon?)
> he paints pictures and plays the violin well
> (Query: does he paint well?)

When the ambiguity of such utterances might be significant, prosody often makes the difference:

(a) /²hìy pêynts ³píkčərz²|²ənd plêyz ðə vàyəlîn ³wél¹#/

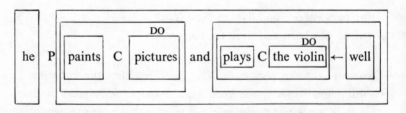

(b) /²hìy pêynts ³píkčərz²|²ənd plêyz ðə vâyə³lín²|³wél¹#/

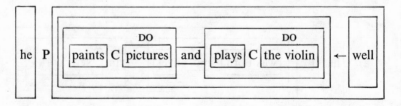

In (b), the adverb *well* modifies the whole structure of coordination, hence applies to both verbs; in (a), *well* modifies only the structure of complementation, *plays the violin*, hence does not apply to *paints* at all. Some writers might make this distinction in writing by a comma after *pictures* in (a):

He paints pictures, and plays the violin well.

ELLIPTICAL STRUCTURES OF COORDINATION. Somewhat of a problem of analysis is presented by structures of coordination such as the following:

(a) I like fresh fish not salted

(b) he told John to come at ten and Bill at noon

(c) the house was painted white and the barn red

In (a), it is clear that *fresh fish* and *salted* are joined by the co-ordinator *not* to make a structure of coordination which functions as the direct object of *like*. But these two components are not syntactically equivalent; to make them so we have to repeat *fish* or use a function noun like *ones* after *salted*. In such a case, analysis is made simpler by assuming an imaginary or omitted repetition of *fish* in this position:

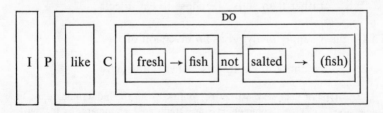

Now we have a true structure of coordination, with syntactically equivalent units (structures of modification) joined by a coordinator, *not*. Such a structure, in which a single component is assumed to be functioning in two different positions in a structure of coordination (or in which it is "understood" to be repeated) can properly be called an **elliptical structure.** Note that we can only "understand" a word or larger unit if it has already appeared in the same structure of coordination, and that we only do so when word order prevents any other analysis. Nothing needs to be repeated or "understood" in *fresh not salted fish*:

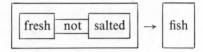

Here *fresh not salted* is a simple structure of coordination modifying the head *fish*. There is nothing elliptical about this structure.

In example (b), *to come* may be understood as repeated between *Bill* and *at*, permitting the analysis on p. 363; while example (c) may best be analyzed by repeating *was painted*. In this case, the two constituents of the structure of coordination are complete structures of predication, the second of which is elliptical.[17]

SPLIT STRUCTURES OF COORDINATION. Normally, the constituents of a structure of coordination appear right next to one another, with the coordinator, if any, between them. But with coordinators of the middle group on page 355, such as *rather than*, split and inverted structures like the following are common:

rather than starve he chose to eat insects

This is most simply analyzed as an inversion of

he chose to eat insects rather than starve

---

[17] This type of analysis must not be confused with the indiscriminate use of "understood" elements common in some traditional grammars, as in "he is stronger than I (am strong)," "(you) come here," "while (he was) at college he fell sick." In the elliptical structure of coordination, no new words are supplied; the only thing that is "understood" is a second occurrence of a word or phrase which has already appeared in an earlier part of the structure.

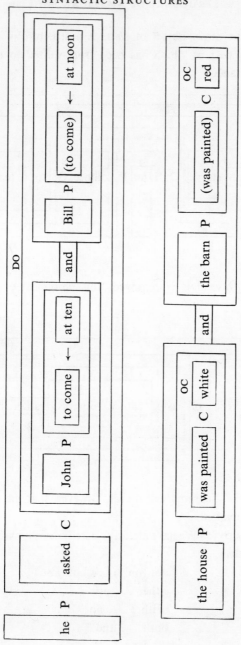

in which the direct object of *chose* is a structure of coordination, the second part of which has been front-shifted to the beginning of the utterance:

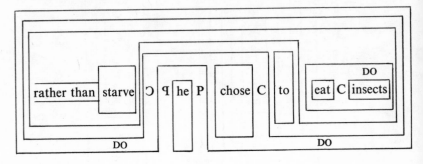

When the inversion is removed, this complicated pattern looks simpler:

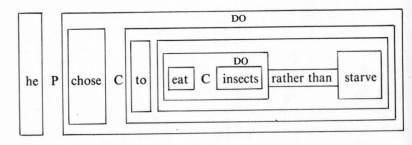

Study of the diagrams will reveal, however, that the two are structurally equivalent.

CORRELATIVES. We have already classed the following coordinators as **correlatives.**

> not (only) ... but (also)
> either ... or
> neither ... nor
> both ... and

In the usual structure of coordination in which one of these appears, the first constituent comes between the two parts of the correlative and the second constituent comes immediately after the second part:

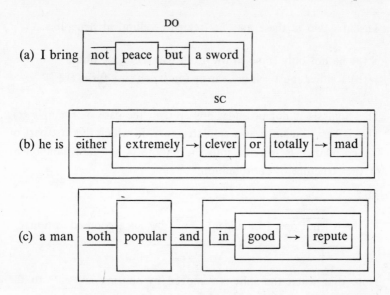

In (a), *not peace but a sword* is a correlative structure of coordination, direct object of *bring*. In (b), *either extremely clever or totally mad* is a correlative structure of coordination whose constituents are themselves structures of modification with adjective as head and adverb as modifier. The whole structure is a subjective complement. In (c), *both popular and in good repute* is a correlative structure of coordination, modifier of the head *man*. In this case, the two components of the structure of coordination are not formally equivalent: *popular* is an adjective and *in good repute* is a prepositional phrase. But they are syntactically equivalent, since both are modifiers of the same head.

A bit of a problem is posed by structures like the following, which are common in both speech and writing, however they may be frowned upon by handbooks of rhetoric.

(a) he not only came to town but to my house
(b) I either must sell my car or my furniture
(c) he is not only intelligent but he has a good education

The first two of these may be treated as elliptical structures:

(a) he not only came to town but (came) to my house
(b) I either must sell my car or (must sell) my furniture

This analysis is not possible, however, in the case of example (c). This is best explained as a split structure, in which the first part of the correlative is inserted into the middle of the first component of the structure of coordination:

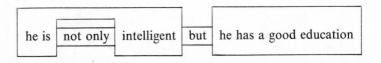

Note that when the split is removed by shifting *not only* to the beginning, the subject and verb of the first structure of predication are inverted:

not only is he intelligent but he has a good education

This actually produces another split construction, in which the subject is inserted into the middle of the predicate.

Occasionally the second part of the correlatives *either . . . or* and *neither . . . nor* may be repeated, producing a correlative structure of coordination with three or more constituents:

neither joy, nor love, nor light, nor certitude,
nor peace, nor help for pain

Such a structure can be called a **correlative series.**

Chapter 7

Grammar–Part III: Sentences

THE SENTENCE DEFINED

The reader accustomed to traditional grammars and handbooks, which usually begin with a discussion of the sentence, may be surprised to see it put off until this far along in a discussion of grammar. But just as we could not discuss the word until we had treated the morphemes of which words are made, so we could not say anything significant about the sentence until we had identified and described the basic syntactic structures of English. For whatever may be our decision as to what can properly be called a sentence, it is clear that it must be composed of one or more of these structures in some sort of combination. Therefore, any objective description of a sentence must take the form of a statement about what linguistic elements— morphemes, words, and syntactic structures—go to make up its parts, and what kind of organization is given to these parts. Any other kind of statement about a sentence—such as that it expresses a "complete thought"—is subjective and unscientific, hence outside the realm of linguistics.

Like the terms *word* and *grammar*, the term *sentence* is part of the common vocabulary, rather than a precise technical term. Its use goes back to a prescientific period of language study, before the need of exactly and objectively defined terms was recognized. In consequence, it is used differently by different people in different contexts. Disagreements over whether a given utterance is or is not a sentence are thus likely to be based not on conflicting observations of the linguistic facts but on conflicting ideas as to what a sentence is. Arguments of that sort cannot be settled by a re-examination of the facts; they can only be resolved by coming to an agreement on definition. An argument as to whether a whale is an animal or a fish ceases as soon as both parties agree that fish are by definition cold-blooded, since the fact that whales are warm-blooded can be verified by observation.

It is thus apparent that if a term in common use like **sentence** is to be used as a technical term in structural grammar, either there must be complete agreement as to the class of things for which it stands (its *referent*, that is), or else each person who uses it must make clear just what he understands its referent to be. This in turn means that there must be one or more objective criteria (like the cold-bloodedness of fish) which can be easily applied and which yield a clear-cut answer. When a group of utterances which comply with these criteria have been gathered together and separated from utterances which do not, they can be studied to see if they have anything else in common beyond the criteria which were used to define them. They may perhaps also be classified in various subgroups upon the basis of further, more refined criteria. But the decision as to whether a given utterance is or is not a sentence and the selection of the subgroup to which it belongs should both be objective; that is, they should be such that all people who are familiar with the criteria will make the same decisions in all cases. This is the way we proceeded in Chapter 5 in our treatment of the parts of speech—noun, verb, adjective, and adverb. As a result, we can use these terms with scientific precision. Can we do the same with *sentence?* If we find that it can be used to cover a class of entities not already named, which is of some significance in grammatical analysis, then the term is worth retaining as a technical term of grammar. If not, we must abandon it to the realm of popular vocabulary, as psychology has abandoned astrologically based terms like *mercurial* and *saturnine*, and physiology has abandoned *complexion* and *animal spirits*.

Although as students of linguistics we are aware of the primary nature of speech, let us begin this quest with the written language, simply because it is easier. I presume that most people, if asked to count the number of sentences on a page of this book, would follow the sensible procedure of counting the periods, question marks, and exclamation points which are immediately followed by a capital letter, except for the special case of abbreviated titles (like *Mr. Jones*). This implies a simple, objective definition: "A sentence is as much as a writer includes between a capital letter and an end mark of punctuation."

If this were all, the business of identifying sentences, at least in the written language, would be quite simple. But a person who would use this method of identifying sentences in a presumably reputable printed book might change his method if given, let us say, a letter written by an uneducated person, in which the whole body of the letter was unbroken by end mark or capital. His comment might well be, "This is really several sentences all run together." Such a statement implies that he is using some other criterion for defining the sentence beside the capital plus end mark one. Suppose, for instance, he were faced with the following:

Two weeks ago I ordered two tires from your catalog so far I have not received them please check on this and let me know.

He would probably say that this is "really" three sentences, the first ending with *catalog* and the second with *them*. If asked why, he might be somewhat at a loss for an answer, but he could at least say that that's how an educated person would write it. From such an explanation, of course, two conclusions are possible: either there is a dialectal difference as to what a sentence is, or our definition must be revised to read "A sentence is as much as an *educated* writer includes between a capital letter and an end mark." But in either case we feel that this definition does not really define; there seems to be some other criterion lurking beneath the surface.

What this is would become apparent if we heard the contents of this letter spoken, either by the original writer of the letter or by the reader who claimed that it is really three sentences. A phonemic transcription of what was said would be approximately as follows (though there might, of course, be considerable dialectal variation, especially in the segmental phonemes):

/²tùw ³wíyks² əgòw²‖²ày ɔ́rdərd tûw ³táyrz²|²frəm yùr ³kǽtəlàg¹#
³sów fâhr²‖²ày hǽvənt ri³síyvd ðəm¹#²plîyz ³čék ɔn ðìs²‖²ən lêt
mìy ³nów¹#/

It can be seen immediately that at the two places where the reader claimed that sentences "really" end, there is a longer pause, preceded by a drop to low pitch, /l/, and a gradual fading away of the voice— i.e., a double-cross juncture. The only other place where this /31#/ intonation pattern appears is at the end of the whole passage, which is, of course, also followed by a long (in fact, permanent) pause. This particular combination, then—drop to lowest pitch followed by double-cross juncture—seems to be a clear-cut indicator of the end of a sentence.

Let us next examine two somewhat similar utterances:

(a) /²hǽd iy kə̀m ³ɔ́rliyər²|²wìy kûdəntəv ³síyn im¹#/
(b) /²hǽd iy kə̀m ɔ́rliyər²‖²wìy ³kúdəntəv²|⁴síyn im²#/

If these are read aloud with careful attention to the stress and intonation patterns, it will be clear that they have quite different meanings. This can perhaps be most simply illustrated by transcribing them in standard spelling and punctuation. Thus (a) would normally be written:

(a) Had he come earlier, we couldn't have seen him.

Contrasting with

(b) Had he come earlier? We couldn't have seen him!

It is also clear that the intonation is what makes the difference, since the segmental phonemes, the internal junctures, and (with one exception) the stresses are alike in both utterances. Specifically, we can observe that the level pitch /2/ followed by the rising double-bar juncture in the middle of (b) is a signal of the end of a sentence, while the one-pitch drop followed by single-bar juncture at the same point in (a) is not. It is by means of signals of this sort that the native speaker recognizes sentence divisions. We may call them **sentence-final intonation contours.** The two we have distinguished—/31#/ and /2||/—are probably the most common in most dialects of American English. There are others, such as the /42#/ which we marked with an exclamation mark at the end of utterance (b). To date the full repertory of them has not yet been listed.

The sentence-final contours thus are used in speech to signal the sentence divisions within an utterance composed of more than one sentence. They are, as it were, the maximal defining criteria for sentences since they establish the outside boundaries of the sentence. Before we can be content, however, that we have defined the sentence, we must establish minimal criteria as well. That is, if the sentence is to be set up as a linguistic entity different from the single word or the various syntactic structures we have so far considered, we must find some objective linguistic phenomenon or group of phenomena whose presence indicates that we are dealing with a sentence and whose absence indicates that we are dealing with a non-sentence.

Various criteria of this sort have been set up by grammarians. The common definition of the sentence as "a group of words containing a subject and a predicate" sets up two of them: it requires that a sentence be of more than one word, and that it be a structure of predication. It is a perfectly acceptable definition in itself; the trouble with it is that most grammarians who use it do not abide strictly by its criteria. They somehow feel that structures like "Come in" and "Help me with this box" must be classed as sentences, although they have no subject, and that structures of predication like "him to come in" (as in "ask him to come in") and "me cutting the grass" (as in "the doctor was opposed to me cutting the grass") are not sentences, though they are groups of words having subject and predicate.

This unwillingness of proponents of the "subject plus predicate" definition of the sentence to abide uncompromisingly by the consequences of the definition is an indication that they are actually—though perhaps unconsciously—applying some other criterion than those named in the definition. This criterion, which is sometimes called "sentence-sense," is to be sought in the actual practice of native speakers, rather than in the grammatical analysis and description of linguistic structures. If we listen to actual conversations for a while, we will be convinced that the only clearly marked unit of speech is the complete utterance of one speaker, bounded on both sides either by silence or by an utterance of another speaker. As we have seen, such an utterance may be divided by sentence-final intonation contours into several sentences. But if it is neither so divided nor interrupted before it reaches its natural conclusion, such an utterance can be considered a single sentence. The minimum criterion for a sentence, then, is that it be an uninterrupted utterance, bounded by silence or change of speaker.

Putting together our criteria, we can arrive at the following objective statement:

Definition: A **sentence** is as much of the uninterrupted utterance of a single speaker as is included either between the beginning of the utterance and the pause which ends a sentence-final contour or between two such pauses.

As corollaries of this definition, we may observe that nothing that cannot stand alone as a complete utterance can be a sentence, and that any complete uninterrupted utterance, no matter what its structural components, is at least one sentence; it is, in fact, as many sentences as it contains sentence-final intonation contours. This further means that many utterances which the "subject plus predicate" definition would class as nonsentences or sentence fragments are recognized as sentences by this definition.

CLASSIFICATION OF SENTENCES.[1] The definition of the sentence we have just given allows us to isolate and identify sentences with certainty. But when we look at the sentences we have so isolated with an eye to finding further elements in common, we find that there are almost none. So great is the variety of linguistic units, from single words to elaborate structures, which meet our definition that we can find no significant common qualities other than those already made part of the definition. But study does reveal that our collection of sentences can be divided into various groups whose members do have further qualities in common. Our next task, then, is to classify sentences.

Let us begin by examining a bit of commonplace conversation, of the kind that most of us take part in many times a day. Let us suppose that two friends encounter one another on the street on a pleasant summer day, and that shortly thereafter a third man, known to them both, joins them. We will report the conversation in standard spelling, but instead of punctuation we shall simply mark the sentence-final contours:

(1) A: Hello ²John² ||
(2) B: Hello ²Joe² || beautiful day ³isn't it¹ #
(3) A: It certainly ³is¹ # perfect for ³fishing² #
(4) B: That's just what I'd like to be ³doing¹ # but I have to ⁴work² #
(At this point the third speaker joins them)

---

[1] The classification of sentences here presented is that of C. C. Fries in *The Structure of English* (New York: Harcourt, Brace & Co., Inc., 1952). The reader is referred to chap. iii of that book, "Kinds of Sentences," for a fuller discussion.

(5) A: Hello ²Bill²||we were just agreeing that this is ³perfect fishing weather¹#

(6) C: Yes if you like ³fishing¹# I'd rather play ³golf¹#

(7) B: Everyone to his ³taste¹# anyhow nobody seems to want to ³work¹||

This conversation consists of seven complete (that is, uninterrupted) utterance units, hence of at least seven sentences. But since each of these utterances except the first has a sentence-final intonation contour within it, there are actually thirteen sentences. If we group these according to their position in the conversation in relation to neighboring sentences, we can make three groups:

1. Those that begin a conversation, representing a linguistic response to a situation. Here belong (1) and the first sentence of (5). For reasons that will be given later, the second sentences of (2) and (5) are also to be included in this group. These can be called **situation-sentences.**

2. Those that continue a conversation, and are thus a linguistic response to a previous utterance of another speaker. Here belong the first sentences of (2), (3), (4), (6), and (7). These are **response-sentences.**

3. Those that continue an utterance of the same speaker. In our sample, these are the second sentences of (3), (4), (6), and (7). They are called **sequence-sentences.**

SITUATION-SENTENCES

Situation-sentences—those that begin conversations—vary considerably in form, chiefly in response to two nonlinguistic factors: the nature of the nonlinguistic situation or context in which they occur, and the nature of the response which they elicit from the other party or parties to the conversation. Thus, one of the simplest is the type illustrated by the first utterance in our sample, *Hello John*, where the nonlinguistic context is the meeting of persons known to each other, and the response, *Hello Joe*, is simply a repetition of the first utterance, with necessary adjustment of names. Situation-sentences of this kind are **greetings**. Every language has a certain rather limited number of these, varying according to the time of day, the season, and the degree of acquaintance and relative status of the speaker and the person addressed. Some of the most common in American English are the following, which may be spoken with various intonation patterns:

> (good) morning (*or* day, afternoon, evening)
> hi
> how are you
> how do you do

We may also class as greetings the stereotyped formulas of leave-taking, since they also arise out of a simple contextual situation and usually elicit as a response a repetition of the same formula or another from the limited repertory:

> good-bye
> good night
> so long
> see you later

These greetings are so stereotyped that they are scarcely linguistic at all; they are vocal equivalents or counterparts of gestures like nodding the head, waving the hand, tipping the hat, offering the hand to shake, saluting, and all the other formalized types of behavior which various societies and social groups expect their members to engage in at meeting and parting. Thus, they are as much a part of the nonlinguistic context as they are communicative utterances. They and the stereotyped responses to them leave the situation virtually unchanged. For this reason, we are justified in classifying the sentences which immediately follow them as situation-sentences, rather than as sequence- or response-sentences. That is why we can consider the second sentences of (2) and (5) on pages 373–74 situation-sentences rather than sequence-sentences.

Similar to greetings in that they are really a part of the non-linguistic context are the attention-claiming situation-sentences, or **calls.** These may be simply names or titles, like *Johnny* or *Mister Chairman*, function words from a very limited list, like *hey* and *oh*, or combinations of the two. Occasionally they may be short structures of modification, such as *you there* or *the boy in the end seat.* Like greetings, these calls are very similar to various gestures which may accompany or substitute for them, such as raising the hand, pointing, ringing a bell, clapping hands, standing up, and so on. We may therefore consider a sentence that follows one of these a situation-sentence also.

A third class of situation-sentences in which the nonlinguistic context is prominent are **exclamations.** These are usually brief—from one to three or four words—and are often spoken with a /(2)42#/ or /(2)41#/ intonation pattern. They represent the response to some unexpected, startling, or untypical condition of the nonlinguistic environment. Thus, one person meeting another in the midst of a violent storm might say /²sə́m ⁴wéðər¹#/, and a person encountering someone he knows at an unexpected place or time might say /⁴yúw¹#/. As with greetings and calls, each language, dialect, and individual speaker has a repertory of stereotyped exclamations, of which the following are typical:

well		what do you know (about that)		
ouch				
what the	heck	for	heavens	sake
	hell		goodness	
	dickens		gosh	
	devil		gods	

As in the case of greetings and calls, exclamations are closely related to various kinds of nonlinguistic gestures, many of them involuntary, such as withdrawing the hand from a hot object, winking the eyes, dodging a blow, and so forth. Any sentence that immediately follows an exclamation may thus also be considered a situation-sentence.

The remaining situation-sentences can be divided into three groups on the basis of the response they customarily stimulate. They differ from the three groups already listed—greetings, calls, and exclamations—in that they arise from less obvious features of the context, are less stereotyped and usually more complex in form, and produce more varied and unpredictable responses in those to whom they are addressed. The three groups of these communicative situation-sentences are the following:

(1) Those that are followed by a linguistic response other than mere attention-signals or the stereotyped responses to greetings and calls. These are **questions.**

(2) Those that are followed by some action response other than the formalized gestures which are used to respond to greetings and calls. These are **requests.** The action response may be positive (like opening a door, sitting down, etc.) or negative (like keeping quiet, remaining seated or standing, etc.). It may be immediate or delayed. It is often preceded or accompanied by a linguistic response of a rather limited kind, such as the following:

> thanks I will
> O.K.
> not now but later

There may, of course, be no action response at all, in which case the response is likely to be an exclamation, a refusal, a question, or a counter-request. But the normal or expected response is action. As Fries puts it, "These utterances are so regularly followed by an 'action' response that they can be said to be directed to eliciting that kind of response."[2]

---

[2] Fries, *op. cit.*, p. 47.

(3) Those that produce as their immediate response a linguistic or nonlinguistic signal of understanding or continued attention. Some of these **attention-signals** are nodding the head, smiling, looking attentively at the speaker, or saying *yes*, *yeah*, [ˀəhə̃], or the like, with a /11|||/ or /22|||/ intonation pattern. Situation-sentences which produce this kind of response are **statements.** Unlike requests and questions, which usually come at the end of an utterance, statements are often followed by sequence-sentences, sometimes in long strings, producing **continuous discourse.** In such a case, the attention-signal responses, whether gestures or vocal, are not so much alternate utterances as a parallel accompaniment to the continuous discourse.

If a listener is to respond in the expected way to situation-sentences of these various types, he must be able to distinguish one from the other easily and rapidly. There must, in other words, be signals in the sentences themselves which indicate without ambiguity whether they are greetings, calls, exclamations, questions, requests, or statements. The description of these signals is an important part of grammar, although some aspects of it are commonly omitted from traditional grammars. In this sketch of the structural grammar of English we cannot be exhaustive on this point. We can, however, indicate the main lines which such a description must follow.[3]

The signals which identify sentence-types are of three kinds: nonlinguistic, lexical, and syntactic (including prosodic). All of these are present in a face-to-face conversational situation. But in a telephone conversation, for example, only the last two are present; the nonlinguistic gestures and facial expressions are not available. In written language, the prosodic signals are also missing, being only imperfectly indicated by punctuation.

Since our concern is with linguistics, we must dismiss the nonlinguistic signals from consideration.

The lexical signals are primarily those that distinguish the stereo-

---

[3] Fries, *op. cit.*, chap. viii, "Structural Patterns of Sentences," for a more complete treatment.

typed sentence-types: greetings, calls, and exclamations. Forms like *how do you do* and *I'll see you later* are structurally question and statement respectively, but native speakers learn them as lexical items serving as greetings, and hence do not respond to them as question and statement, except facetiously. Dialectal differences sometimes cause confusion here. Northerners are sometimes bewildered by the Southern Christmas greeting, "Christmas gift!" and the British may respond to the American /²hâw ³áhr ²yùw¹#/ as if it is a question rather than a greeting eliciting the response /³fáyn¹ ‖ ²hàw ər ³yúw¹#/.

The prosodic and other syntactic signals that identify sentence-types work together in intimate complementary relationship, so they may best be considered together. The nonprosodic signals are of three kinds: (1) the selection of certain structures or combinations of structures from the repertory we discussed in the preceding chapter, (2) the order of arrangement of the constituents of the structures so selected, and (3) the use of certain special function words. The prosodic signals are primarily the rising and falling sentence-final contours. Various combinations of these four elements produce the characteristic patterns of statement, question, and request.

STATEMENTS. Statement situation-sentences commonly consist of one of the following structural patterns, combined with a falling sentence-final intonation contour:

1. A structure of predication whose predicate contains a **finite verb.** A finite verb is one of the following:

    a) A verb in the base form, in concord with a plural subject or one of the pronouns *I, you, we, they.*

    b) A verb in the third-singular form (base + {-s}), in concord with a singular subject or one of the pronouns *he, she, it.*

    c) A verb in the past-tense (base + {-ed₁}) form.

    d) A verb-phrase whose first auxiliary is one of the preceding.

Infinitives, present participles, and past participles are not finite verbs, though they may be part of finite verb-phrases. The following examples illustrate the difference between finite and nonfinite verbs:

FINITE VERBS	NONFINITE VERBS
(they) walk	walking
walks	to walk
walked	been walking
was walking	to have walked
has walked	going to walk
was going to be walking	having had to walk

2. A structure of modification whose head is a structure of the type described in (1) above. Modifiers in such structures are called **sentence-modifiers.** These will be discussed later on.

3. A structure of coordination whose constituents are structures of the type described in (1) or (2) above. These constituents may be joined by coordinators or they may not. In either case, there must not be a sentence-final intonation contour before the end of the structure of coordination. If there is, we are dealing with two sentences, not one. This means that many passages that are written as one "compound" sentence are two or more sentences in speech. In fact, the semicolon and the colon, which are treated as "internal" punctuation marks in writing, very frequently mark the position where sentence-final intonation contours occur when passages are read aloud. The reverse is also sometimes true; that is, a period is sometimes used in writing between two elements which are not separated by a sentence-final intonation contour in speech. This matter, involving as it does the conventions of punctuation, will be taken up in the next chapter. For the present it is sufficient to note that sentences comprising structures of coordination, including series, do exist. The following is an example, which will be seen not to contain a sentence-final intonation contour before the end:

/³mên ²məst ³wə́hrk²|²ənd ³wîmin ²məst ³wíyp¹#/

These are the principal forms of statement situation-sentences, making up a large proportion of the whole. But our statement concerning them is not complete without noting that other structures, or even single words, may function as situation-statements when there are circumstances in the nonlinguistic context, obvious to both speaker and listener (less often, to writer and reader), which in effect become part of the utterance. The most common of these are structures of complementation or structures of modification with verb-head—in effect, subjectless sentences. Sometimes these are called sentences with subject "understood"; but such an analysis, which really amounts to setting up a zero syntactic element, is not necessary, and is sometimes misleading. Certainly we are only justified in maintaining that the subject is understood if we can demonstrate that the speaker and the hearer would both supply the same subject. This is by no means always the case with subjectless statements, though when they are used there is usually something in the nonlinguistic environment which is understood as the referent of a subject that could be supplied by the hearer. Typical of subjectless statements and the environmental situations out of which they might arise are the following:

SITUATION	SENTENCE
Friend at door	thought I'd drop in and see you
One concert-goer to another	sounds even better than I expected
Dark clouds over sky	looks like a storm

Other statement sentences not involving a predication are like these:

SITUATION	SENTENCE
Sound of rain on roof	/³réyn¹#/ or /³réyniŋ¹#/ [4]
Meeting friend in trouble	sorry about your wife (house, child)
Leaving theatre, to one arriving	too crowded
Closing office door	through for the day

[4] Note that with /41#/ intonation these would be exclamations.

REQUESTS. Request situation-sentences usually consist of one of the following structures, often with the same /31#/ or /231#/ intonation pattern that characterizes statements. The intonation may, however, rise to pitch /4/, which is seldom used in statements.

1. A verb in base form or a verb-phrase whose first auxiliary is in base form. The modal auxiliaries do not appear in request sentences, and the perfective and resultative phases are rare, occurring only in rather archaic expressions like *have done* and *be gone*. The verb or verb-phrase may be preceded by the function words *please*, *do*, *let's*, and in some dialects *pray*. *Please* may also follow the verb. The verb may be in the negative status. Some examples are the following:

/³máhrč¹#/

/²gêt ³gówiŋ¹#/ or /³gét gôwiŋ¹#/

/²plîyz bìy ³síytid¹#/

/²lèts ³kîyp ³wóhrkiŋ¹#/

/²dôwnt ⁴gów¹#/ or /³dównt ²gôw²‖/

2. A structure of complementation with verb of the type described in (1). *Please* may come at the end of the structure.

> be careful
> keep your chin up
> give me the book please
> let's not tell him

3. A structure of modification with (1) or (2) as head:

> leave ← at once
> begin work ← without waiting for me
> please wait ← until I can see you
> if you can manage it → don't give in

4. A structure of coordination whose constituents are (1), (2), or occasionally (3) above. As with statements, we must be sure that

there is no sentence-final intonation contour before the end of the structure:

· /²têl ðə ²trúwθ²|²ənd šêym ðə ³dévil¹#/

/²kə̂m ən ³síy mìy¹#/

/³lə́v mìy²|²ər ³líyv mìy¹#/

5. A structure of predication whose predicate is of the type of (1), (2), or (3) above and whose subject is the pronoun *you*, alone or in close apposition (p. 301) with another noun. Occasionally some other noun may be the subject.

> you go home
> you boys stop talking
> volunteers take one step forward

Structurally these are indistinguishable in the written form from statements. Ambiguity is resolved in speech, however, either by the nonlinguistic context or by intonation.

These are the most common types of request situation-sentences. As with statements, however, the nonlinguistic context may be such as to permit other kinds of structures, or even single words, to function as requests. A few examples may be cited; others will readily occur to the reader:

> a) tickets please||
> b) your attention please||
> c) all aboard#
> d) smoking in the outer lobby only#
> e) heads up#
> f) on guard#

In some of these, like (a) and (b), we may find that a verb is "understood," but in others, such as (c) and (d), no two people would be likely to agree on what elements must be understood to fill out a structure belonging to one of the five types described above. It is simpler to recognize these as independent words, prepositional phrases, or structures of modification functioning as request situation-sentences.

QUESTIONS. The fact that a given situation-sentence is a question is signaled by one or more of three devices:

1. the inversion of the principal verb and its subject, producing the split structures which we have called the **interrogative** and **negative-interrogative statuses** of the verb (pp. 337–39);

2. a rising sentence-final intonation contour;

3. presence at the beginning of the sentence (with concomitant adjustments of word order) of one of the following function words, called **interrogators.**

who/whom/whose	who(m)ever
which/whose	whichever
what	whatever
when	whenever
where	wherever
how	however
why	why . . . ever
(whither)	(whence)

Any one of these three devices is enough to signal a question, as in the following:

(1) /²ìz hìy ³híhr¹#/   (inversion)
(2)/²hîy ìz ¹híhr¹|||/   (rising intonation)
(3) /²hwôts ³ðǽt¹#/   (interrogator)

Frequently, however, they appear in combination. Thus, interrogative status and rising intonation may combine:

/³îz hìy ¹híhr¹|||/
/³kǽn yùw ¹dúwit¹|||/

Interrogative status is regular with certain interrogators:

$$/\text{²hwên dìdiy ³kə́m¹}\#/$$
$$/\text{²hwây ər yùw ³lǽhfiŋ¹}\#/$$

Certain environmental circumstances may require the combination of rising intonation and interrogator:

$$/\text{³hwə̂ts ¹ðǽt¹}\|\|/$$

or even the combination of all three:

$$/\text{³hâw ər yùw ¹fíyliŋ¹}\|\|/$$
$$/\text{³hwə̂tsiy ²dúwiŋ²}\|\|/$$

though combinations of this last sort are more common in British than in American English.

The most frequent types of structure that appear as situation-questions are structures of predication with finite verbs or structures of modification or coordination involving such predications.

It is obvious that the interrogative status of verbs can only be present when there is a subject, since this status involves inversion of verb and subject. In speech, however, the initial auxiliary which marks the inverted state of the verb is sometimes omitted, leaving a question which is still a structure of predication, though without a finite verb:

(are) you coming ‖
(does) he like skating ‖
(is) he going to come ‖

These may be considered elliptical structures if it is so desired, since all native speakers would agree in supplying the auxiliaries which have been indicated in parentheses. But it should be observed that questions of this "incomplete" sort are marked as such by the rising intonation, in contrast to questions involving a finite verb or verb-phrase in interrogative status, which may have the falling intonation. Compare:

> (a) do you like ³skating¹#   (question)
> (b)   you like ¹skating³‖   (question)
> (c)   you like ³skating¹#   (statement)

Here (a) is marked as a question by the interrogative verb *do . . . like*, and does not need the rising intonation (though it might have it). But (b) and (c), otherwise identical, are distinguished as question and statement respectively by rising and falling intonation patterns.

As with statements and requests, other structures beside predications, including even some single words, may be situation-questions, deriving a good part of their meaning from the nonlinguistic context. Typical are the following (all with rising intonation):

> yes‖   your name‖
> coming‖   more coffee‖
> lost something‖

Questions making use of interrogators require special examination, since they exhibit some rather unusual features. In the first place, we must note that the interrogators divide into two groups: (1) the **simple interrogators,** whose sole function is to mark a sentence as a certain type of question, and (2) the **interrogative pronouns,** which, in addition to marking a sentence as question, have a further function within the structural pattern of the sentence.

The **simple interrogators** are *when, where, how, why,* their compounds in *ever,* and the archaic *whither* and *whence.* These introduce questions consisting of structures of predication with verbs in the interrogative status. Consequently, if they are removed, the remaining structure is still a question in form, even without the rising intonation:

$$\left.\begin{array}{l} \text{when} \\ \text{where} \\ \text{how} \\ \text{why} \end{array}\right\} \text{was he doing it}$$

The **interrogative pronouns** are *who* (with its inflectional variants *whom* and *whose*), *which*, *what*, and their compounds in *ever*. When one of these comes at the beginning of a sentence, it not only signals that the sentence is a question, but also functions within the sentence as subject, complement, modifier, or object of a preposition:

Subject:	who is there
	whatever made you do that
Direct Object:	who(m) did you see
	what did he tell you to do
Modifier:	what movie did you go to
	whose house is that
Object of Preposition:	who did they give the prize to
	to whom did they give the prize

Two points are to be noted about questions of this type: (1) unless the interrogative pronoun is the subject, the verb is in the interrogative status; (2) since the interrogative pronoun comes first in the question (occasionally preceded by a preposition or one of certain sentence-modifiers), it may be in a position rather far removed from the normal position for a word performing its particular syntactic function. For example, the normal position for the object of a preposition is right after the preposition. But in a question such as *what did he do that for*, the object *what* comes ahead of the preposition *for*, with all the rest of the sentence between. Similarly, in *who did you tell him to see*, *who* is the direct object of the infinitive *to see*, but so far separated from it that most speakers do not use the objective case form, in spite of the efforts of their English teachers to get them to.

This virtually inflexible rule that the interrogative pronoun comes at the beginning of its sentence, regardless of its structural function, produces many rather complicated split constructions. As we have seen in the last two chapters, it is a marked characteristic of English word order to group together the constituents that function together. This characteristic is what has permitted us to reveal the immediate constituents of various structures by the device of enclosing them within "Chinese boxes," nested within one another. In a few cases—interrogative and negative verb-phrases, for example—we have seen that one constituent is inserted within the split parts of another. But on the whole, units which function together are grouped together.

Questions involving interrogative pronouns, however, reveal split and dislocated structures of considerable complexity. Note, for instance, the sentence:

what do you advise me to give my wife for Christmas

Here the interrogative pronoun *what* is direct object of the infinitive *to give*, making up, together with the indirect object *my wife*, a structure of complementation which is modified by the prepositional phrase *for Christmas*, the whole being the predicate of a structure of predication serving as object of *do you advise:*

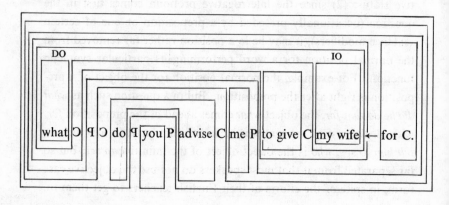

Here the front-shifting of *what* from the normal position of the direct object—immediately after the indirect object, *my wife*—together with the split of the verb-phrase *do advise*, creates a very complicated pattern of constituents. Compare it with the relative simplicity of the statement sentence, in which the members of the various constituents are grouped together, so that there are no split or discontinuous structures:

you advise me to give my wife a ring for Christmas

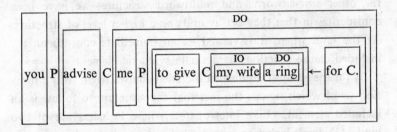

As with the other types of situation-sentences that we have discussed, questions involving interrogators are not always complete predications; they may be various lesser structures. Provided the non-linguistic context supplies a considerable part of the meaning, the linguistic form of the question may be reduced to little more than the interrogator alone. Some examples of this sort are the following:

> what price glory
> where away
> what now
> whose hat   (holding it up)

INCLUDED CLAUSES

Before we go on to discuss the other two classes of sentences—sequence-sentences and responses—we should stop to consider a structural element which we have several times mentioned but not yet fully treated; that is, the **included clause.**[5] Included clauses are structures that have the form of statement sentences as we have described them (p. 379)—basically a structure of predication with a finite verb—but are not set off by sentence-final intonation contours, and have the function of modifier, subject, or complement. It is because of this functional role that we describe them as *included*: instead of serving as complete sentences, they are included in larger structures within the limits of sentences. Although they may be structurally quite complicated within themselves, they are like the other single words and multiword structures we have been considering in that they act as units on a higher level of structure. At the level where it is viewed as an immediate constituent, the included clause functions as a single syntactic element.

By far the greatest number of included clauses begin with a function word which signals the fact that the structure to follow is an included element. Like interrogators, these **includers** are of two kinds: (1) **simple includers,** whose sole function is to mark a structure as a certain type of included clause, and (2) **relative pronouns,** which, in addition to this function, have a further function within the structural pattern of the included clause.

The chief simple includers, both single words and phrases, are the following (those starred are rare in present-day spoken American English).

---

[5] This term is offered as a compromise between Fries's *included sentence* and the terms of traditional grammar, *subordinate clause* and *dependent clause*. The former would be misleading in a treatment of grammar such as this, since it would seem to indicate that any kind of sentence can be "included." The traditional terms, on the other hand, are used in opposition to *main clause* and *independent clause*, which have not been used here. Logically, *clause* alone would be a sufficiently distinct term, since it is not used here for any larger class of forms of which included clauses are a subclass. But it seems worthwhile to retain Fries's distinctive *included*, to prevent confusions arising from the traditional terminology and to emphasize the structural position of clauses of this sort.

after	how(ever)	till
although	in case	unless
as	in order that	until

as{ so} { close / far / long / near / often / soon } as   if   if{ ever / only }   when / whenever / whence*

as if	lest	where
as though	like	wherever
because	now (that)	wheresoever*
before	once	whereas

but{ that / what }   only   provided (that)   what{ if / though }

ere*	since	whether (. . . or)
except (that)	so (that)	while
for	such that	whilst*
	than	whither*
	that	why
	though	

In addition some speakers use certain adverbs, like *directly* and
immediately, as simple includers.

INCLUDED CLAUSES AS MODIFIERS. Clauses introduced by simple
includers function as modifiers of various heads, both single words
and other structures. We have not space here to treat the numerous
types in detail, but the following examples will serve to show the
variety of modification structures in which included clauses may
appear:

Noun as Head:

the fact ← that it is raining is discouraging

we heard the news ← that the war is over

Verb as Head:

he came ← after I left

I will go ← wherever you go

Adjective as Head:

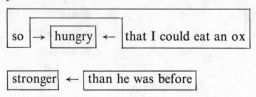

so → hungry ← that I could eat an ox

stronger ← than he was before

Adverb as Head:

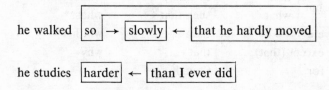

he walked so → slowly ← that he hardly moved

he studies harder ← than I ever did

Verb-Headed Structure of Modification as Head:

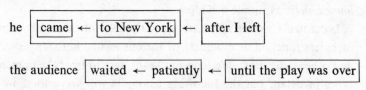

he came ← to New York ← after I left

the audience waited ← patiently ← until the play was over

Structure of Complementation as Head:

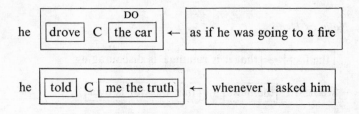

           DO
he drove C the car ← as if he was going to a fire

he told C me the truth ← whenever I asked him

It is noteworthy that the included clause as modifier always follows its head. The single exception to this, the included clause as sentence-modifier, will be discussed later.

RELATIVE CLAUSES. A special type of included clause is the so-called **relative clause,** introduced by one of the following **relative pronouns:**

who/whose/whom	whoever/whosever, whosoever
which	whichever
what	whatever, whatsoever
that	
when	
where	

When modifiers, relative clauses nearly always modify nouns or noun-headed structures of modification, in which case they use only the relative pronouns *who, which,* and *that.* The relative pronouns *who* and *which* are in roughly complementary distribution, in that they show concord with the noun-head according to the substitute-group (pp. 249–51) to which it belongs. Thus, *who* correlates with nouns of substitute-groups (1) (*he—they*), (2) (*she—they*), (4) (*he/she—they*), and (9) (*he/she/they—they*); *which* correlates with nouns of substitute-groups (3) (*it—they*), (5) (*he/it—they*), (6) (*she/it—they*), and (10) (*it*). Nouns of groups (7) (*he/she/it—they*), (8) (*it/they—they*) and (11) (*they*) may be modified by relative clauses introduced by either *who* or *which.* The relative pronoun *that* may introduce clauses modifying any noun.

Relative clauses are formally distinguished from other included clauses by the fact that the relative pronoun not only acts as a function word introducing the clause but also has a structural function within the clause. It may be subject, complement, object of preposition, or modifier. Examples of noun–modifying relative clauses in which the relative pronouns have these various functions follow.

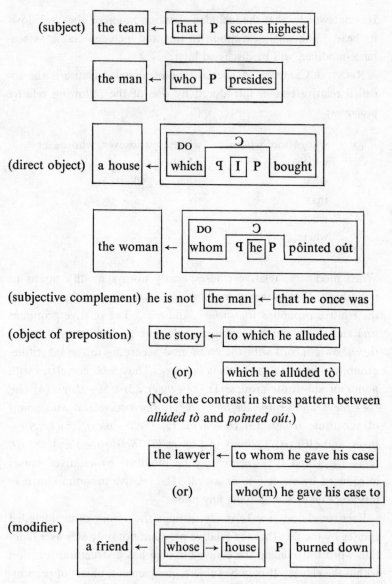

(subject) the team ← that P scores highest

the man ← who P presides

(direct object) a house ← which ꟼ I P bought

the woman ← whom ꟼ he P pôinted oút

(subjective complement) he is not the man ← that he once was

(object of preposition) the story ← to which he alluded

(or) which he allúded tò

(Note the contrast in stress pattern between *allúded tò* and *poînted oút*.)

the lawyer ← to whom he gave his case

(or) who(m) he gave his case to

(modifier) a friend ← whose → house P burned down

(Note that *whose* modifies *house*, while the whole clause modifies *friend*.)

A few details of word order are of interest in these examples. We note that the relative pronoun always comes first in its clause, except that *who* and *which* may follow a preposition. But sometimes with these two and always with *that* the preposition comes in its normal position, so that the prepositional phrase is split in structures like *the man that I gave it to, my wife whom I am always thinking of*, with tertiary stress on the preposition. This front-shifting of the relative pronoun causes other dislocations of the normal statement word order, in all clauses except those in which the relative pronoun is the subject. These dislocations are similar to those we have observed in questions introduced by interrogators (pp. 388–89). In contrast to questions of that sort, however, relative clauses never have a verb in the interrogative status.

Since the relative pronouns *who*, *which*, and *that* do not have distinctive forms for singular and plural, they cannot be said to have number. There can thus be no question of number concord between them and the verb of the included clause when they function as subject. Instead, there is a strong but by no means universal tendency for the verb to be in concord with the noun-head (sometimes called the **antecedent**) which the relative clause modifies. This applies also to the special forms of *be*. Thus:

> I who *am* your friend
> you who *are* my friend
> he who *is* our friend
> they who *are* our friends
> he who *laughs* last beats those who *laugh* first[6]

INCLUDED CLAUSE AS SUBJECT. Included clauses of both types— those introduced by simple includers and relative clauses—may be subjects of structures of predication. It is important to observe that when they are, the whole clause functions as a single unit, even though

[6] For a discussion of a frequent exception to this type of concord, see J. S. Kenyon "'One of Those Who Is'," *American Speech*, XXVI (1951), 161–65.

it may itself be a rather complicated structure of predication. Some examples, the first four with simple includers, the rest with relative pronouns:

> *that he is a scoundrel* is well known
> *however you do it* will be good enough for me
> *where the water is deep* is the best place to dive
> *because you were sick* is no excuse
> *who he is* is a mystery
> *who(m) he married* is unknown to me
> *whoever arrives first* opens the door
> *what you think* does not interest me

INCLUDED CLAUSE AS COMPLEMENT. As we might expect of structures that may be subjects, included clauses may also be various kinds of complements. Both types can be direct object or subjective complement; only the relative type can be indirect object, objective complement, or object of a preposition. The following examples, by no means exhaustive, illustrate some of the possibilities:

Direct Object: tell him *that I am here*
                I don't know *who was there*

Subjective
Complement: this is *where I get off*
                life can be *whatever you choose to make it*
                that was *how we learned the truth*

Indirect
Object: give *whoever comes* this letter
                tell *whomever you can get to listen* my sad story

Objective
Complement: he calls his dog *whatever silly name he likes*
                his wife made him *what he is today*

Object of
Preposition: they agreed to *whatever proposal was made*
                he is friendly with *whoever will flatter him*

In the case of these last two examples, it is important to observe that it is the whole included clause, not just the relative pronoun, that is the object of the preposition. The difference can be clearly seen by comparing the two structures:

(a) a friend of whom he is fond
(b) a friend of whomever he meets

In (a), the clause *of whom he is fond* modifies *friend*. Within the clause, the prepositional phrase *of whom* modifies *fond*. In (b), however, the prepositional phrase *of whomever he meets* modifies *friend*, and the included clause *whomever he meets* is object of the preposition *of*. Diagramming of the constituents of the various structures involved makes clear the differences:

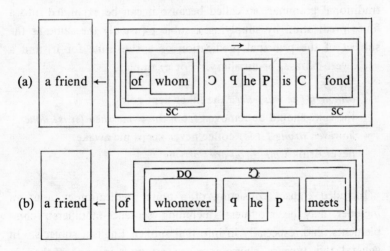

We have established as the normal pattern of included clauses a statement sentence having a finite verb and introduced by an includer. We may also classify as included clauses certain structures lacking one or the other of these characteristics. Thus, we may have a clause introduced by an includer but lacking a finite verb, or a clause comprising a finite predication but without an includer. Without going into all the detailed variations of these patterns, we may examine a few typical examples.

A common type of clause is the **infinitive clause,** which has as its principal constituents a relative pronoun and an infinitive. Clauses of this kind may function as subject, complement, or modifier:

Subject: *what to do next* is my problem
Direct Object: he does not know *where to go*
Subjective Complement: the problem is *who(m) to ask*
Modifier: a quiet place *in which to work*

Another common type, always functioning as a modifier, consists of a simple includer and a modifier. This is the **elliptical clause** of traditional grammar, so called because it can be expanded into a finite predication by supplying a subject (usually the same as the subject of the principal predication or a substitute for it) and a verb, verb-phrase, or auxiliary. For example:

although (he was) tired the hiker kept going
the cake should be removed from the oven *when (it is) done*
however strong (it is) coffee never keeps me awake
never drink *while (you are) driving*

Included clauses consisting of a finite predication without an includer may be modifiers (including sentence-modifiers), complements, and, especially in informal spoken English, subjects. In general this type of clause is more common in spoken than in written English, probably because the potential structural ambiguities may be resolved more easily by intonation than by punctuation. In general, the more formal the context—linguistic or nonlinguistic— the more likely it is that an includer will be present. The reader may test this by supplying more formal variants of the following:

Noun-Modifier:	a place *he goes in summer*
	a story *I heard today*
	the man *he told his story to*
Sentence-Modifier:	that banker *I know* is honest
	($/^1$ây + nów^1 ‖/)
	the door *he told us* will be open
	you were our friend *I thought*[7]
	($/^1$ày + θɔ́ht^1#/)
Direct Object:	he says *he is going away*
Subjective Complement:	the trouble is *he can't swim*
Subject:	*he doesn't try* is why he fails

SENTENCE-MODIFIERS

A function commonly performed by included clauses, as well as by other structures and single words, is that of **sentence-modifier.** As the name indicates, a sentence-modifier is a modifier whose head is all the rest of the sentence of which it is a part. Strictly speaking, then, a sentence containing a sentence-modifier is a single large structure of modification, consisting of the usual two immediate constituents: head and modifier. The most common position for the sentence-modifier is at the beginning of the sentence. In fact, most adverbial or phrasal modifiers occurring in this position are to be considered sentence-modifiers unless some special structural or intonational signal marks them as modifiers of some single word or lesser structure within the sentence.

[7] Note that sentence-modifiers of this type never come at the beginning of the sentence. If one is moved there, it becomes the main predication and the remainder of the sentence becomes its direct object:

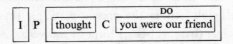

There are six common types of sentence-modifier:

INCLUDED CLAUSES. A very common type of sentence-modifier is the included clause with simple includer, the so-called "adverbial clause" of the traditional grammar. The following are examples of this:

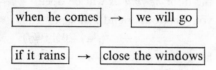

Relative clauses introduced by the relative pronouns in *-ever* may also serve as sentence-modifiers:

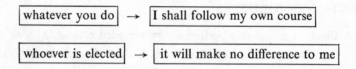

Relative clauses introduced by *who*, *which*, and *what*, as well as other kinds of included clauses, preceded by the function words *no matter* and *never mind* may also be sentence-modifiers:

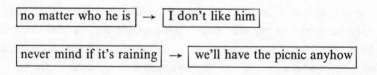

ABSOLUTE CONSTRUCTIONS. An important type of sentence-modifier, but one that is much less frequent than the included clause, is the so-called **absolute construction.** In terms of our analysis in this book, an absolute construction is usually a structure of modification with noun-head and a modifier consisting of or including a participle—either the present-participle (base + $\{-ing_1\}$) or past-participle (base + $\{-ed_2\}$) form of the verb:

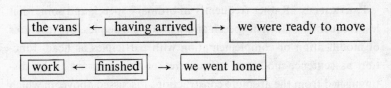

A limited group of other modifiers may appear in this structure in place of the participle. They always follow the noun-head, though their normal position otherwise might be before it:

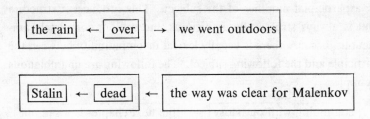

INFINITIVES. Infinitives alone, or structures of modification or complementation with infinitives as head, may serve as sentence-modifiers. Especially common are stereotyped expressions like *to tell the truth*, *to begin with*, *to sum up*, and so on. Some examples are the following:

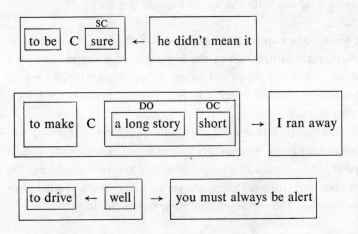

PARTICIPLES. Rather frequently in ordinary speech and somewhat less frequently in formal speech and writing, participles, or structures of modification or complementation with participles as head, function as sentence-modifiers. Structures of this sort are to be distinguished from the absolute constructions discussed above, in which the participle functions as modifier of a noun-head. The structure alluded to here is that commonly called the "dangling participle," since, although it is intended as a sentence-modifier, it occupies the position at the beginning of the sentence which can also be occupied by a participial modifier of the subject. This produces a structure that is always structurally ambiguous, but seldom completely ambiguous, because there is usually lexical incompatibility between the participle and the following subject. The following are unambiguous examples:

| continuing with our story | → | the next chapter is a sad one |

| following a good dinner | → | we heard a brief speech |

Ambiguous examples are often unintentionally comic or ridiculous:

proceeding down the street   a large building came into view
having paid our bill   the waiter brought our hats

It seems to be natural to speakers of English to expect a participle or participial construction at the beginning of a sentence to be a modifier of the subject of the following predication unless lexical incongruity makes this so unlikely as to indicate that it is a sentence-modifier instead.

PREPOSITIONAL PHRASES. An exceedingly common type of sentence-modifier is the introductory prepositional phrase. In fact, most prepositional phrases in this position are sentence-modifiers; the exceptions are front-shifted modifiers of other heads smaller than the sentence. The following are all sentence-modifiers:

according to the paper → it will rain today
after dinner → we chatted for an hour
at the corner → a policeman was directing traffic
in the end → he agreed with me

The following introductory phrases, however, are not sentence-modifiers but front-shifted modifiers of other elements, as the structural analysis reveals:

on the porch sat a large man

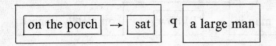

(note inversion of normal order of subject and predicate)

of these books a few are mine

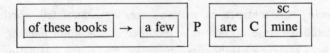

ADVERBS. Various adverbs (or adverb-headed structures of modification) may function as sentence-modifiers:

obviously → he was lying
naturally → I am opposed to war
too late → the truth came out

As we have seen, the beginning of the sentence is the most common position for sentence-modifiers. But they may appear in medial and final positions as well. Since these positions can also be occupied by other kinds of modifiers, not to mention the constituents of other types of structure, sentence-modifiers in medial or final position are often structurally ambiguous, or at least potentially so. As in so many other cases of potential structural ambiguity, intonation frequently provides a clear indication of structural meaning. In general, a sentence-modifier is distinguished from other constructions with which it might be confused by intonation, one of the most common patterns being /|1|||/. Some of the examples to follow will illustrate this.

As we have already seen, one type of sentence-modifier which is never initial, and thus always either medial or final, is the included clause not introduced by an includer:

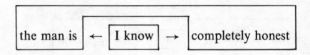

When a clause of this sort follows a noun, it is often potentially ambiguous:

the man I know is completely honest

Seeing this sentence as written here, we cannot tell whether the included clause *I know* is a modifier of the noun *man* or of the whole sentence. Intonation, however, makes the distinction:

/²ðə ³mæhn² |¹ày ¹nów¹ ||²ìz kəm+³plíytliy² |²ánist¹#/

Here the /3 2/ pitch contour on *man* and the /1|||/ intonation pattern on *I know* set it off as a sentence-modifier, to be analyzed as follows:

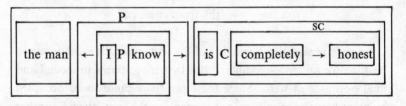

But with the following intonation, *I know* is a modifier of *man*:

/²ðə mæhn ày ³nów² |²ìz kəm+³plîytliy ³ánist¹#/

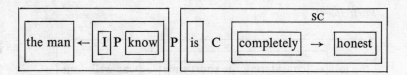

The other types of sentence-modifier that we have listed above may also appear medially and finally, with suitable intonation contours to distinguish them from other structures. There is not space here to illustrate them all in detail, but the following examples show the main types, as well as some of the structures with which they might be confused were it not for the part played by intonation:

Included Clauses: the place *when I finally found it* was suitable
I saw him often *although we were not friends*
it rained heavily *until the ground was soaked*

Absolute Constructions:

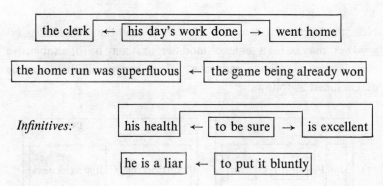

Compare these sentence-modifiers with infinitive-headed structures functioning as modifiers of noun- or verb-heads, which have the intonation /232|/:

his wish ← to be admired is an obsession

he is speaking ← to raise money

Participles:

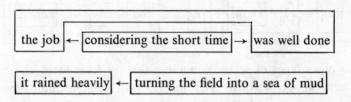

This last example illustrates what is sometimes called the "trailing participle," a sentence-final counterpart of the initial "dangling participle." It is quite common in speech, somewhat less so in formal writing. It is occasionally ambiguous, when there is a noun within the sentence which the participle might modify, or when it might function as a subjective complement. Sometimes even intonation does not resolve this ambiguity. Consider the sentence:

he stood firm considering his weakness

Here the participial structure of complementation *considering his weakness* may be (a) a sentence-modifier, or it may be (b) a subjective complement coordinate with *firm*. These two possibilities may be diagrammed as follows:

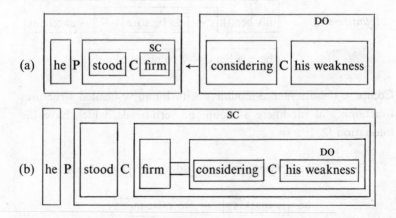

In (a), the speaker is making an allowance for the subject's weakness; in (b), the subject is contemplating his own weakness. In my own dialect, at least, intonation does not distinguish these two; they are truly ambiguous.

Prepositional Phrases:

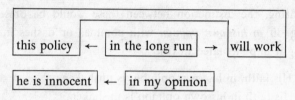

Since prepositional phrases are common modifiers of various types of heads, structural ambiguity is frequently a possibility when they appear medially or finally. However, the characteristic intonation contour of the sentence-modifier—frequently reinforced, it is true, by lexical possibilities—serves to distinguish prepositional phrases functioning as such. Thus, as written here the following sentence is ambiguous:

his faith in his own opinion is unshaken

But with a /3 2/ pitch contour on *faith* and a single-bar juncture before and double-bar after *in his own opinion*, the phrase is clearly marked as a sentence-modifier, and the sentence thus means that it is the opinion of the subject that his faith is unshaken. On the other hand, with level pitch on *faith* and no terminal juncture after it, the phrase becomes a modifier of *faith*, and the sentence thus means that the subject has unshaken faith in his own opinion. Diagrammatically the difference appears as follows:

(a) /²hìz ³féyθ²|²in hìz ôwn əpínyən²||²ìz ə̀n+³šéykən¹#/

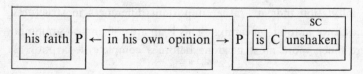

(b) /²hìz fêyθ in hìz òwn ə³pínyən²|²ìz ən+³šéykən¹#/

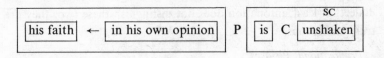

In writing, the distinction between these would be preserved by setting off *in his own opinion* with commas or dashes in (a) and leaving it unpunctuated in (b):

(a) His faith, in his own opinion, is unshaken.
(b) His faith in his own opinion is unshaken.

Adverbs: he thinks *apparently* that he is a genius
he is angry *understandably*

The adverb as sentence-modifier is rare in final position, and when it does occur there, it is usually marked by a rising sentence-final contour.

Once again the potential structural ambiguity implied by a medial or final adverb is clearly resolved by intonation. The reader may analyze the following for himself, observing how a change in intonation can shift the adverbs from sentence-modifiers to modifiers of nearby words or phrases:

the doctor *obviously* knows his business
he is speaking *clearly* of his own experience
he was not *apparently* unwilling to work

The foregoing discussion, brief as it is, should at least indicate the importance of sentence-modifiers in English grammar, and suggest the subtle way in which the structural devices of word order and intonation indicate rather important differences in structural —and hence in total—meaning. This is an area of English grammar where much more must be done before a complete description is available, partly because it has been largely overlooked by traditional grammar, and partly because the binary nature of most English structures has only recently been discovered. The student may pursue the subject further by observing in any page of written prose, as well as in any stretch of continuous speech, how often the first split of a sentence into immediate constituents consists of dividing a sentence-modifier from the rest of the sentence.

SEQUENCE-SENTENCES

As we have seen, only the first sentence of any conversation—or the first one following a greeting, call, or exclamation or the stereotyped response to one of these—can properly be called a situation-sentence. All the rest are either responses or sequence-sentences. They are responses if they begin a new utterance, with change of speaker, and they are sequence-sentences if they continue an utterance, already begun by a situation-sentence or response. We may thus define a **sequence-sentence** as any sentence which immediately follows a situation-sentence (other than greeting, call, or exclamation), a response-sentence, or another sequence-sentence, without change of speaker.

A corollary of this definition is that a sequence-sentence does not stand alone. Both the name we have given it and the definition imply that it is part of a *sequence*, and therefore in some way built into a larger structure. In recognizing the sequence-sentence as a separate kind of structural unit, we have involved ourselves in the grammar of larger units than the sentence, which is usually considered the outside limit of the subject matter of grammar. We cannot go very far into this kind of grammar, primarily because linguists have not yet gone very far with their studies of it. Up to now it has been principally rhetoricians and literary critics who have concerned themselves with the combination of sentences into larger units. What can be called the grammar of continuous discourse remains to be worked out.

We can, however, make a beginning by observing that when two sentences occur together as parts (constituents) of an utterance, their relationship is indicated by at least one and sometimes two or three of the following objectively observable conditions:

(1) The fact that one follows the other in time establishes a presumption as to their relationship in both lexical and structural meaning.

(2) The use of certain linguistic devices in the first sentence sets up an expectation that another (sequence) sentence will follow.

(3) The use of certain linguistic devices in the sequence-sentence recalls certain elements in the sentence which it follows, and thus establishes retrospective links with it, both lexical and structural.

The third of these is the one that primarily concerns us in this discussion of sequence-sentences. But before we come to it, we may take a brief look at the other two.

In the first place, we may note that (1) is always present; it is, in fact, inescapable. No one can speak two sentences at the same time, and even if he could (with the aid of a tape-recorder, for instance), it would be very difficult for a hearer to understand him. One sentence, then, inevitably precedes the other. This in turn implies that while the second sentence is being spoken, the hearer has already heard and, in some degree at least, reacted to the first sentence. This reaction thus becomes part of the context of the second sentence. Therefore, even though the speaker may not make use of this change in context as a justification for formal adaptations in the second sentence, it is none the less there, and changes the total meaning of the second sentence.

Let us illustrate this point by comparing two two-sentence utterances which differ only in the order of their sentences:

(a) now he is my friend#a year ago he was my enemy#

(b) a year ago he was my enemy#now he is my friend#

Clearly, the total meaning of (b) is not the same as the total meaning of (a). Just what the difference is might be hard to describe objectively, but any native speaker will admit to a subjective feeling of difference, which he would probably describe as a matter of "emphasis." Whatever this difference of meaning is, there is no doubt that it exists; furthermore, there is no doubt that it must be due to the relative position of the two sentences, the only objectively ascertainable difference between the two utterances. Therefore, it is clear that part of the total meaning of the second sentence in each pair comes from the fact that it *is* the second sentence, spoken and listened to in a context containing the recollection of the first sentence.

This kind of grammatical relationship based solely upon relative position is sometimes called *parataxis* (Greek "position alongside") in contrast to *syntax* (Greek "position together"). This is an appropriate distinction in the grammar of those languages, like Latin and Greek, which do not employ word order as an important grammatical device. But in those languages, like English and Chinese, where "position alongside" is not more or less accidental or stylistic but an important indicator of grammatical structure, we can hardly say that there is such a thing as parataxis distinct from syntax—not, that is, within the sentence. We have seen throughout these three chapters that the position of words and syntactic structures relative to one another (word order, that is) is an important part of English syntax. As has just been pointed out, relative position seems to have a bearing on the meaning of sentences as well. The grammar of the future may have to take account of "sentence order" as well as word order.

The use of special grammatical devices in a situation-sentence to forecast a sequence-sentence to come is really a special case of an aspect of grammar that has been very little studied: the whole question of the foreshadowing of grammatical structure. Anyone who observes at all closely the process of listening will note that the hearer is often aware of the grammatical structure of part of an utterance before it has been spoken. This can be verified by artificially interrupting a speaker, as by turning off a radio or lifting the needle from a record, in the middle of a sentence and asking a hearer to finish the sentence. Depending on just where the interruption occurs, he may be able to continue for several words, reproducing the correct structure of the sentence, though not, of course, its lexical meaning. He can do this because certain grammatical signals predetermine what is to follow. A noun-determiner like *the*, for instance, must inevitably be followed sooner or later by its noun, and a preposition by its object, unless intonation signals to the contrary. The careful listener, then, like the careful driver, is subconsciously alert to signals that forecast what the situation will be a few seconds later. If it were not for this, we could neither speak nor drive as fast as we do.

When we examine continuous discourse, we find that there are occasional elements in one sentence that look forward to sentences to follow. There are, for instance, sentence-modifiers like *in the first place* and *on the one hand*. Again, the first part of a correlative (p. 364) is a strong forecaster of the second part to come. If, therefore, a sentence-final intonation contour occurs before the second part of the correlative, a strong expectation is set up of another sentence to follow, as in instances like these:

not only is he unable to ³swim¹#but he even hates to get wet#

either I am paid the money at ³once¹#or you know what will happen#

There are many other ways in which one sentence sets up expectations of another or others to follow. It is doubtful, however, whether they belong to the study of grammar. Most of them forecast something about the subject matter, rather than the structure into which it is formed. They are promissory notes, as it were, which the speaker or writer expects to pay in the near future. But there is no presumption that this will be done in the next sentence. In fact, the promise may never be made good. In such case, the hearer or reader may feel cheated, but he does not feel that grammar has been violated. The forecasts in sentences like the following must then be assigned to rhetoric, not grammar:

> let us next consider the second point
> supposing that we are attacked by an aggressor
> what can we say about television

SEQUENCE-SIGNALS. When we turn to the various devices which link sequence-sentences to the sentences that precede them, we are on surer grammatical ground. It is true that rhetorical matters are operating here as well, but we may distinguish certain formal devices that are clearly grammatical. In fact it is these devices that supply the only clear-cut formal difference between sequence-sentences and situation-sentences. We may recognize four main types: (1) substitutes, (2) determiners, function nouns, and function verbs, (3) coordinators, and (4) sentence-modifiers. These may all be grouped together under the general term **sequence-signals,** a term which thus covers all elements that function as grammatical links to a preceding sentence. It is a functional term, like *modifier* or *complement*, not a formal term, like *noun* or *verb*. We have space only for a brief look at each group.

1. *Substitutes as Sequence-Signals.* The noun-substitutes *he, she, it,* and *they,* the verb-substitute *do,* the adjective-substitute *such,* and the adverb-substitutes *then, there, so, thus,* and *that way* are common sequence-signals. In the following examples, the word in the situation-sentence and its substitute in the sequence-sentence are italicized to show the connection.

SITUATION-SENTENCE	SEQUENCE-SENTENCE
I went to see *the doctor*	*he* told me to take a rest
I don't think John *is coming*	if he *does* he will be sorry
the Smiths are very *self-centered*	*such* people bore me
Mr. Smith thinks very *clearly*	he does not speak $\left\{ \begin{array}{l} so \\ that\ way \end{array} \right.$

The substitutes *then*, *there*, *so*, *thus*, and *that way* are common not only as adverb-substitutes but as substitutes for larger structures like prepositional phrases, included clauses, or even whole sentences:

he is free *in the morning*	you can see him *then*
the book is *where it belongs*	I put it *there* myself
I know *that he likes oysters*	he told me *so* himself
I *eat the air, promise-crammed*	you cannot feed capons *so*
I am selling my car now	I'll get more for it *that way*

2. *Determiners, Function Nouns, and Function Verbs as Sequence-Signals.* The noun-determiners *the*, *this*, and *that*, all the words we have classed as **function nouns** (p. 246), as well as certain other nouns, may function as sequence-signals. When they do, they act like substitutes in that they refer back to specific words or structures, usually noun-headed, in a preceding sentence. We cannot illustrate all of them here, but the following are typical of the rest:

he has *a new job*	*this* job is better than the last
I have *two close friends*	*both* live in Boston
give me *halibut or swordfish*	*either* will be fine
one *city I like* is New Orleans	*another* is San Francisco

In addition to these, we may class in this group the nouns *one*, *other*, and the numbers, especially those from *two* to *ninety-nine:*

see those two *girls*	the tall *one* is Alice the *other* Jane
here are six *oranges*	only *three* are good

Function verbs (pp. 263–64) become sequence-signals in a similar manner, by referring back to specific full verbs or verb-headed structures in the preceding sentence:

John *likes sea-food*	at least he always *used to*
I *have* already *resigned*	it was time I *should*
he *isn't speaking today*	at any rate I hope he *isn't*

The negator *not* may function similarly:

he *isn't speaking today*	at any rate I hope *not*

3. *Coordinators as Sequence-Signals.* When the coordinators *and, but, nor, or,* and *yet* function as sequence-signals, they produce what amounts to a structure of coordination whose constituents are separate sentences. In such a case, there must be a sentence-final intonation contour just before the coordinator; otherwise, we have to do not with two sentences but with a single sentence of the kind customarily called **compound.** The only distinction between a pair of sentences linked by a coordinator serving as a sequence-signal, on the one hand, and a compound sentence, on the other, is the presence or absence of a sentence-final intonation contour. In written material, this distinction is marked by a period or sometimes a semicolon in the first case and a comma in the second. The compound sentence is thus a reality in both speech and writing, but it has no formal markings other than intonation in the one case and punctuation in the other. Thus, an utterance such as:

> the spring has come but the weather is still cold

can be spoken (and punctuated) either way:

As two sentences:
  ²the sprîng hàs ³cóme¹#²but the wêather ìs stîll ³cóld¹#
  (The spring has come. But the weather is still cold.)

As one compound sentence:

²the sprîng hàs ³cóme²|²but the wêather ìs stîll ³cóld¹#

(The spring has come, but the weather is still cold.)

An understanding of this simple grammatical point makes clear that the errors classed as "comma fault" and "run-on sentence" in the handbooks of grammar are matters of punctuation, not of grammatical structure.

4. *Sentence-Modifiers as Sequence-Signals.* Three kinds of sentence-modifiers are in common use as sequence-signals: (a) certain adverbs which may at other times also function as modifiers of lesser structures; (b) a group of special sentence-linking function words, called "conjunctive adverbs" in the traditional grammar; and (c) various prepositional phrases, many of them stereotyped.

(a) The sentence-modifying adverbs which serve as sequence-signals are rather numerous. The following list is typical but not exhaustive:

accordingly	hereafter	then
afterward(s)	heretofore	there
also	later (on)	thereafter
before	likewise	thereupon
else	nearby	too
farther (on)	otherwise	thus
	still	

When these function as sequence-signals, they usually come at or near the beginning of the sequence-sentence, and are intonationally set off from the rest of the sentence by a /|2|||/ or /|1|||/ intonation pattern. When medial or final in the sentence, they may be preceded by a single-bar juncture. On the other hand, when they function as modifiers of words within the sentence, they lack these intonational markers.

(b) The most important of the sequence-signals called "conjunctive adverbs" are the following:

consequently   moreover
furthermore   nevertheless
hence   therefore
however

These are properly kept separate from the first group, since their only function is to link sentences.[8] They should, in fact, not be called adverbs at all, but should be treated as a separate class of function words and called by some such name as **sentence-linkers.** In any case, they usually are set off from the rest of the sequence-sentence in which they occur by a /|2||/ (rising) intonation, except at the end of the sentence, when they fit into the final /31#/ pattern.

Two sentences linked in sequence by one of these sentence-linkers are often written as one, with a semicolon at the joint between them. This is, however, wholly a convention of the written language. A sentence so written will virtually always be spoken with a sentence-final contour at the semicolon; hence, in speech it must be considered two sentences. The reader may test this by reading the preceding sentence aloud.

(c) Various prepositional phrases, some of them stereotyped, function just like the sentence-linkers. In fact, the stereotyped ones (like the one which begins this sentence) could just as well be classed with the sentence-linkers. Some typical phrases of this sort are:

at least   in addition
in the next place   as a result
on the other hand   for example
in contrast   after a while

---

[8] There is, of course, an adverb *hence* which may modify single words, as in *he went hence, a mile hence.* But its meaning ("away from here") is so different from that of the conjunctive adverb *hence* ("following logically from the preceding") as to constitute them different though homophonous morphemes. The same point may be made about the two *however*'s.

RESPONSE-SENTENCES

We may define as a **response-sentence** the first sentence of any utterance in a conversation except the opening one.[9]   One point about response-sentences follows immediately from this definition: that is that they occur only in conversation. The response-sentence is not a characteristic component of continuous discourse, whether spoken or written. There we will find situation-sentences at the beginning of major divisions of the discourse and sequence-sentences elsewhere. If we wish to observe response-sentences, we must listen to people talking to one another, or examine written materials like plays, novels, short stories, and stenographic reports of trials, conferences, and discussions. The one exception to this occurs when a speaker or writer employs the rhetorical trick of carrying on a conversation with himself, usually by asking a question and immediately answering it. Apart from this, however, response-sentences are not found in continuous discourse, which is probably why they have been given such short shrift by most traditional grammarians.

Another point about response-sentences that should be made at the outset is that they do not fall into a limited group of structural patterns, as situation- and sequence-sentences do. In fact, virtually any grammatical element, from a single word to an elaborate structure or complex of structures, may function as a response-sentence. Single words, phrases, structures of modification, complementation, or coordination, complete predications, included clauses, statements, questions, requests, greetings, and exclamations—all may function as responses to keep the conversational ball rolling. In the face of this diversity, it is manifestly impossible to arrive at a formal description or set of descriptions which will include all response-sentences. Their variety is as great as that of grammatical forms themselves.

[9] A minor exception to this is the first sentence following a stereotyped exchange of greetings, which is a situation-sentence (p. 375).

A set of meaningful generalizations about the syntactic structure of response-sentences is thus impossible. The alternative is to particularize the types that may appear in response to particular types of sentences that immediately precede them. To do so in any detail would take us far beyond the space we have at hand. Therefore, all we can do here is to give a few examples of the various kinds of response. The reader may expand the lists for himself as he listens to conversations about him.

RESPONSES TO GREETINGS. As we have already seen (pp. 375–76), the responses to greetings are usually as stereotyped as the greetings themselves. They may consist simply of a repetition of the greeting, with necessary adjustment of names, and sometimes with an altered intonation:

^{3}góod ^{2}mòrning^2 || ^{1}Jóhn^1 || ^{2}goòd ^{3}mórning sìr^1#
^{2}goòd ^{3}níght^2# ^{3}góod ^{2}nîght^1#

sometimes the stereotyped response is different:

^{2}how are ^{3}you^1# ^{3}fine^1#^{1}and you^1 ||
^{2}see you ^{3}later^2# ^{3}O.K.^{2}#

Various other responses—questions and statements particularly—may follow greetings, but only as facetious or impatient rejections of the greeting formula:

good morning#   what's good about it#
see you later#   not if I see you first#

RESPONSES TO CALLS. Here again the response is more or less stereotyped, though there is more variety than in the responses to greetings. In general, the responses are likely to have some of the formal elements of questions, either in their intonation or in their other structural patterns as in the following examples.

^{3}waiter^2# ^{1}yés ^{2}sîr^2‖
^{4}Johnny^2# ^{2}what do you ^{3}want^1#

Responses to calls may, however, take other forms, such as statement or request:

A: Mary   B: I'm coming
A: mother   B: be quiet#I'm on the phone#

RESPONSES TO EXCLAMATIONS. In general, exclamations emphasize the expressive function of language more than the communicative. That is, they are themselves responses to the environment, either linguistic or nonlinguistic, and are not primarily concerned with eliciting a response from someone else. Some exclamations, however, do prompt responses, which are usually either exclamations themselves or reaffirmations of statements made prior to the exclamation:

A: ^{3}what a ^{4}day^2#   B: ^{2}it ^{3}sure is^1#
A: ^{3}some ^{4}weather^1#   B: ^{3}I'll say^1#

A:. ^{2}Mrs Smith is getting a di^{3}vorce^1#
B: you ^{4}don't say^1#
A: ^{3}yes^2#^{2}she's already gone to ^{3}Reno^1#

In this last example, A's second utterance is the response to B's exclamation, and consists of a reaffirmation (with further detail) of the situation-statement to which the exclamation was itself a response.

RESPONSES TO STATEMENTS. Since the purpose of a statement is usually to communicate some sort of information, the primary response it elicits is, as we have seen, some sort of **attention-signal** (p. 378), to assure the speaker that his message has been received. If the speaker and hearer can see each other, this may be purely visual or a combination of visual and oral. In any case, the oral attention-signal is little more than a vocal gesture, scarcely linguistic at all. Individual idiosyncrasies enter into the choice of attention-signal, and perhaps dialectal differences as well, though no systematic collection has ever been made by a linguistic geographer. In any case, the attention-signal constitutes the minimum response-sentence. The speaker usually continues straight ahead without pausing, so that the attention-signal overlaps a part of his continuous discourse. But he is still attentive to it, and will falter or even stop after three or four sentences if he does not hear it. The reader may test this by remaining absolutely silent the next time he has a long-winded friend on the telephone.

The attention-signal is the normal response to statements in continuous discourse. Other types of response follow a statement that ends an utterance. The most common type is formally identical with the sequence-sentence—statement, question, or even request. Thus, the second speaker may link his response to the statement that evoked it by the same kind of sequence-signals that a single speaker uses to link his own sentences together. The reader may check this easily by listening to any conversation for a few moments. The following bit of dialogue, in which the sequence-signals are italicized, will illustrate, if illustration be needed:

A: Mary Jones is going to get married
B: *is she* really‖I'm glad of *it* #
A: *yes* # *she*'s been planning *to* for some time‖but *she* couldn't find a man#
B: where did *she* finally find *one*‖at *her* age *it* isn't so easy#*they* don't grow on trees#
A: no *they* don't # but *this one* grew right in *her* office#worked right at the next desk to *hers*#
B: well I hope *they* make a success of *it*#
A: *so do* I#

RESPONSES TO QUESTIONS. By far the largest variety of response-sentences are those that follow questions. Here, however, we should distinguish two general types of questions, on the basis of the kind of response evoked: (1) questions not introduced by an interrogator, but marked as questions by having a verb in the interrogative status, a rising final intonation, or both; and (2) questions introduced by an interrogator.

Questions of group (1) are commonly said "to expect *yes* or *no* as an answer." The range of responses is wider than the two function words *yes* and *no*, but it is still relatively limited. In general, it is either one of a relatively small group of stereotyped responses, or else a sequence-sentence (statement, question, or request) which in some way evades answering the question. The following, all responses to the question *do you like music*, illustrate some of the possibilities:

yes indeed	I'm not very keen about it
not very much	why do you ask
sometimes	none of your business
depends on the music	stop asking questions

But it is responses to questions of the second sort—those introduced by an interrogator—that show the widest variety of all, wider than that of any other kind of sentence. In fact, no formal description can cover the possibilities; all we can say is that anything, from a single word to an elaborately constructed passage of continuous discourse, may function here. The number of possible responses to a simple question like *what are you doing* is very large indeed. The reader may add his own examples to the following brief list:

nothing
just thinking
minding my own business
who wants to know

I am fixing this doorknob so that if a stranger comes and tries to open the door he won't be left with the knob in his hand and a silly smile on his face the way your cousin Harry was when he came to see us last week

Some classification of this great variety of responses is possible. It would have to begin with a classification of interrogator-questions, since the types of responses to *where*-questions, for instance, differ from those to *which*-questions. Such a classification would have its uses, particularly for foreigners learning English. But we cannot attempt it here. Instead, we shall simply conclude our discussion of response-sentences by remarking once more their infinite variety. It is this, more than anything else, that puts conversation into such great contrast with continuous discourse, which is made up almost wholly of situation- and sequence-sentences.

SUMMARY

The last three chapters are little more than an extended summary of the structural grammar of present-day American English. But in the interest of bringing together in shortest possible compass our analysis of English structure, we may present here a sort of tabloid summary of these chapters.

1. There are two kinds of **meaning:**
    a) **Lexical meaning**—the meaning of morphemes and words considered in isolation.
    b) **Structural meaning**—the meaning of the way words are combined in larger structures. This is the business of grammar.
2. There are five **signals of syntactic structure:**
    a) **Word order**—the positions of words relative to each other in time.
    b) **Prosody**—combinations or patterns of pitch, stress, and juncture. Patterns of pitches and terminal junctures are **intonation**

patterns; patterns of stresses and internal junctures are **super-fixes.**

c) **Function words**—words with little or no lexical meaning which are used in combining other words into larger structures.

d) **Inflections**—suffixes, always final, which adapt words to fit varying structural positions without changing their lexical meaning or part of speech.

e) **Derivational contrast**—derivational prefixes and suffixes which change words from one part of speech to another.

3. There are four **parts of speech:**

a) **Nouns** are marked by **noun-determiners** such as *the, his, one*; they have two inflections, the **plural** {-*es*} and the **possessive** {-*'s*}; many of them have derivational suffixes like {-*ance*}, {-*ness*}, and {-*ship*}; a few are distinguished from verbs by the superfix {´ `}. Subclasses of nouns are **pronouns** and **function nouns.** Nouns can be classified in eleven **substitute-groups.**

b) **Verbs** have four inflections, the **third-singular** {-*s*}, the **past tense** {-*ed₁*}, the **past participle** {-*ed₂*}, and the **present participle** {-*ing₁*}; they combine in various ways with **auxiliaries** such as *have, be, get,* and *must* into a large variety of **verb-phrases;** some of them have derivational affixes like {*en-*}, {-*ate*}, and {-*ize*}; they occupy certain characteristic positions; a few of them are distinguished from morphemically related nouns and adjectives by the superfix {˘ ´}. Auxiliaries may operate as **function verbs,** and *do* serves as a **verb-substitute. Separable verbs** consist of two parts, a verb and an element which elsewhere is a preposition or adverb.

c) **Adjectives** are marked by their ability to fill certain positions and to follow **qualifiers; base adjectives** have the inflections {-*er*} and {-*est*} and form nouns and adverbs with the derivational suffixes {-*ness*} and {-*ly₁*}; **derived adjectives** are formed from various bases by derivational suffixes like {-*ous*}, {-*al*}, and {-*able*}.

d) **Adverbs** are marked by their ability to appear in one characteristic position; they are morphemically classifiable into eight groups, the two largest containing those formed from the two kinds of adjectives by the addition of $\{-ly_1\}$; some few have the inflections $\{-er\}$ and $\{-est\}$; most of them can follow qualifiers; they are classifiable into three substitute-groups.

4. There are four types of **syntactic structure:**

a) **Structures of modification** consist of two immediate constituents, a **head** and a **modifier.** The head may be any of the parts of speech, certain function words, or any of the four structures. The modifier may be any of the four parts of speech, a **prepositional phrase,** or various other structures, including the **included clause.** The immediate constituents of complex structures of modification are indicated by patterns of word order and prosody.

b) **Structures of predication** consist of two immediate constituents, a **subject** and a **predicate.** The predicate consists of a verb alone, or some structure in which a verb is prominent, such as a verb-headed structure of modification, a structure of complementation, or a structure of coordination whose constituents are verbs or verb-headed structures. Verbs exhibit formal distinctions by which they can be classed according to **person (common** and **third-singular), tense (common** and **past), phase (simple, perfect,** and **resultative), aspect (simple, durative,** and **inchoative), mode (numerous), voice (active** and **passive),** and **status (affirmative, interrogative, negative,** and **negative-interrogative).** The **subject** is commonly a noun or noun-headed structure, but may be any of the other parts of speech, a prepositional phrase, or other structure, up to included clauses. The function word /ðər/ serves as **temporary subject.**

c) **Structures of complementation** consist of two immediate constituents, a **verbal element** and a **complement.** The verbal element may be a simple verb or one of various kinds of verb-headed structures. Verbal elements are classified as **linking, intransitive,** and **transitive.** Intransitive verbal elements may be predicates, but they do not appear in structures of complementation. Complements appearing with linking verbs are **subjective complements;** they may be any of the four parts of speech, prepositional phrases, or more complex structures, up to included clauses. Complements with transitive verbs are **objects,** which are of three kinds: **direct objects, indirect objects,** and **objective complements,** which are distinguished by various structural signals.

d) **Structures of coordination** have two or more immediate constituents, which are syntactically equivalent units joined in a structure which functions as a single unit. The constituents may be any grammatical units from single words to sentences. The joining may be accomplished by word order and prosody alone, or with the aid of **coordinators.** A structure of coordination with more than two immediate constituents is a **series.** Structures of coordination may be elliptical or split.

5. There are three kinds of **sentences** classified according to position in conversation:

a) A **situation-sentence** is one that begins a conversation. It may also follow a call, greeting, exclamation, or the stereotyped response to one of these.

b) A **sequence-sentence** is one that continues a conversation without change of speaker. A series of sequence-sentences constitutes **continuous discourse.**

c) A **response-sentence** is one that continues a conversation with a change of speaker.

6. There are six kinds of **sentences,** classified according to the context and the responses evoked:

a) A **greeting** is a stereotyped formula used at meeting or parting, eliciting a stereotyped response which often is a repetition of the greeting.

b) A **call** is a brief sentence directed at claiming attention, and eliciting responses of various sorts, commonly brief questions.

c) An **exclamation** is a brief, usually stereotyped, sentence, with characteristic intonation, resulting from some unexpected circumstance in the linguistic or nonlinguistic context. It may evoke no response at all, or a response that is an exclamation or a reaffirmation.

d) A **question** is a sentence that elicits a linguistic response other than the stereotyped responses to greetings, calls, and exclamations. Questions are marked by certain prosodic and word-order patterns, and by function words called **interrogators.**

e) A **request** is a sentence that evokes an action response other than the formalized gestures that follow greetings and calls. The action response may be accompanied by more or less stereotyped linguistic response.

f) A **statement** is a sentence that evokes a linguistic or nonlinguistic response called an **attention-signal.** Statements make up by far the largest part of continuous discourse. An utterance-final statement may evoke various types of linguistic response other than attention-signals.

7. There are eight main groups of **function words** (including some stereotyped phrases) plus some unclassified ones (not all the following lists are complete):

a) **Noun-determiners:** *the, a/an, my, your, her, their, our, this/these, that/those, its, one, two . . . ninety-nine, many* (a), *more, several, both, all, some, no, every,* (a) *few, other.*

b) **Auxiliaries:** *can/could, may/might, will/would, shall/should, must, dare, need, do,* (had) *better, be, get, have, keep* (on), *used, be going.*

c) **Qualifiers:** *very, quite, rather, pretty, mighty, somewhat, too, a bit, a little, so, more, most, less, least, indeed, enough,* (real, awful, that, some, right, plenty), *no, still, much, lots, a* (whole) *lot, a* (good, great) *deal, even.*

d) **Prepositions:**

(1) **Simple:** *after, among, around, before, concerning,* etc.

(2) **Compound:** *back of, due to, together with,* etc.

(3) **Phrasal:** *by means of, in front of, on account of,* etc.

e) **Coordinators:** *and, not, but, nor, rather than, either . . . or,* etc.

f) **Interrogators:**

(1) **Simple:** *when, where, how, why,* (*whence, whither*), *whenever,* etc.

(2) **Interrogative pronouns:** *who, which, what, whoever, whichever, whatever.*

g) **Includers:**

(1) **Simple:** *after, although, how, lest, since,* etc.

(2) **Relative pronouns:** *who, which, that, when, where, whoever,* etc.

h) **Sentence-linkers:**

(1) **Simple:** *consequently, furthermore, hence, however, moreover, nevertheless, therefore.*

(2) **Phrasal;** *at least, in addition, in fact,* etc.

i) **Miscellaneous:**

(1) **Attention-claimers:** *hey, oh,* etc.

(2) **Attention-signals:** *yes, yeah; uh-huh,* etc.

(3) **Responses:** *yes, yeah, no, nope, not at all, maybe, O.K.,* etc.

(4) **Infinitive-marker:** *to*

(5) **Negator:** *not*

(6) **Hesitators:** *well,* etc.

COLLATERAL READING, CHAPTERS 5-7

Books previously listed are cited by author only.

There are very many books on the subject of English grammar. The following readings have been selected because they all approach the subject from the descriptive, structural point of view. The reader will find, however, that they do not agree with one another or with the chapter just concluded in all details of analysis. There is as yet no generally accepted system of English structural grammar.

Bloch and Trager. Chap. v, "Syntax," pp. 71–79.

Fries, Charles C. *The Structure of English*. New York: Harcourt, Brace & Co., Inc., 1952. (The whole book should be read. The chapters listed below, however, are especially valuable.)
Chap. iii, "Kinds of Sentences," pp. 29–53; chap. v, "Parts of Speech," pp. 65–86; chap. x, "Structural Meanings: 'Modifiers'," pp. 202–39; chap. ix, "Structural Meanings: 'Subjects' and 'Objects'," pp. 173–201; chap. xi, "'Sequence' Sentences and 'Included' Sentences," pp. 240–55.

Fries, Charles C. *American English Grammar*. New York: Appleton-Century-Crofts, Inc., 1940. Chap. x, "The Uses of Word Order," pp. 247–82.

Gleason. Chap. viii, "Outline of English Morphology," pp. 92–110; chap. x, "Syntax," pp. 128–42.

Whitehall, Harold. *Structural Essentials of English*. New York: Harcourt, Brace & Co., Inc., 1956. Chap. ii, "Word-groups," pp. 8–28; chap. iii, "Sentences," pp. 29–40.

Trager and Smith. From Part II, "Morphemics," pp. 67–80.

Palmer, H. E., and Blandford, F. G. *A Grammar of Spoken English*, 2d ed. Cambridge, Eng.: W. Heffer & Sons, Ltd., 1939. From Part III, "Parts of the Sentence," pp. 220–36.

Chapter 8

Writing It Down: Graphics

WRITING AND WRITING SYSTEMS

The readers of this book belong to the privileged half of the world's population—those who know how to read and write. What is more, they belong to the much smaller group of those to whom reading and writing are thoroughly conditioned activities, which can be performed rapidly and with very little conscious attention or thought. In this respect they differ not only from the illiterate half of the human race but also from millions of others who are technically literate but to whom reading is a difficult process, involving much brow-knitting and lip-moving, and to whom writing is an infinitely laborious task, requiring the careful tracing out, letter by letter, of complicated patterns that must be consciously recalled and compared. We who read and write so glibly must visit a first-grade classroom if we are to realize what conscious effort these processes involve for the semiliterate.

It is even more difficult for highly literate people to imagine what the world is like to one who is totally illiterate. So conditioned are we to the notion that characters of great variety of shape and size formed into rows must be some form of writing that we find it impossible *not* to read anything even half-legible that comes into our field of vision. As I write this, I sit facing some bookshelves, and every time my eye leaves the paper I see *and read* the titles on the backs of the books. They are in all sorts of type and script, in many colors, against many backgrounds. Some are horizontal and some vertical. Some of the vertical ones read from the bottom up and some from the top down. One is even totally upside-down. A few are in foreign languages. Yet I find it impossible to see these markings merely as markings. All except those in print so fine that my eyes cannot resolve it seem to group themselves automatically into words.

To the illiterate person, on the other hand, these markings are nothing but markings. He may know that they can be read, but they do not form themselves into significant groups in his eye as they do in mine. He is no more able to imagine what they look like to me than I am able to imagine what an orchestral score looks like to a musician, or a complicated formula to a mathematician. To recapture some sense of his view of things, I would have to go to a city in China or Russia or Israel, where every bit of writing was in characters totally meaningless to me. Then I might find that to be illiterate in a literate world is much like being deaf—one important channel of information, relied on heavily by those about me, would be closed.

In the English-speaking parts of the world, as well as in most of western Europe and a few other relatively urbanized population centers scattered around the world, the illiterate person is the exception. But over great areas of the earth's surface and among large masses of its people it is the other way about: the one who has mastered reading and writing is the rarity, and as a result may be a figure of awe, respect, and perhaps even magical power among his fellows. We do not have to go very far back in history to reach a time when this was true everywhere. And if we go back 6000 years, a mere wink of the eye when compared with the length of time man has known how to speak, we reach the virtually simultaneous beginnings of civilization and of writing.

This is not the place to go into the question of which came first, civilization or writing, and whether either can be called the cause of the other. This is a rather futile "hen-and-egg" kind of question, anyhow. The fact remains that our present civilization, and, indeed, any kind of civilization we can imagine, depends on some effective method of making visible and permanent the insubstantial, transient phenomena of speech. By setting the individual man free from the restrictions and limitations of his immediate environment and generation and allowing him to communicate across space and time with those whom he will never meet face to face, writing makes possible the kind of cultural and intellectual accumulation, interchange, and cross-fertilization upon which human civilization depends. Denied the inherited memory which has built and preserved the civilizations of the social insects, man had to invent the written word to serve as his racial memory. It is probably his greatest invention to date, after speech itself, and one which has served him well for sixty centuries. We are now in the midst of an electronic revolution which may ultimately render writing obsolete; it is still too early to tell. Meanwhile it is the business of the linguist to scrutinize the systems and conventions of writing in the same objective, analytic way he looks at speech.

The branch of linguistics concerned with this study is called **graphics.** Specifically, graphics deals with **writing systems.** A writing system has two parts: a set of conventional symbols, used to represent certain aspects of speech, and a set of rules governing the ways in which these symbols are grouped and arranged in order to represent other aspects of speech. Before we undertake an examination of the writing system of present-day English, which is the business of this chapter, a few general observations and definitions are needed to give us our bearings.

In the first place, since it is a branch of linguistics, and since the subject matter of linguistics is language as we defined it in Chapter 1, graphics is concerned only with the visible record of *language.*.

There are many other kinds of visible record which are thus outside its subject-matter. A drawing, a photograph, or a motion picture is a visible record of an event, but it is a nonlinguistic one. A mathematical or chemical formula is the visible record of a relationship or an idea, but it, too, is nonlinguistic, though it might be translated into or explained in linguistic terms. The same is true of other kinds of visible records, such as monetary accounts, radio circuit diagrams, musical scores, statistical graphs, maps and charts of all kinds. We say that these things can be *read*. The reading of them may even have a linguistic accompaniment, but this is a by-product. Two competent radio technicians "reading" the same circuit diagram will have basically the same understanding of its meaning, though their linguistic responses may be quite different. On the other hand, two literate people reading a written record aloud will have basically the same linguistic response, though they may differ widely in their understanding of the meaning of what they are reading.

Graphics, then, is concerned with visible records of linguistic phenomena. From its point of view, we can define **writing** as follows:

Definition: Writing is the systematic visible and permanent representation of the auditory and transient phenomena of speech.

We may have to stretch the meaning of *visible* and *permanent* a bit at times, to include such things as Braille, which is primarily tactile, and airplane smoke-writing, whose permanence extends to only a few minutes. But on the whole this definition will serve to determine our subject matter accurately enough.

Since writing has been in existence for about 6000 years, and since many forms of writing have been and are now used, graphics can be studied from both the historical (or diachronic) and the comparative points of view. Until recently historical and comparative study have completely dominated the field. Great progress has been made, primarily by Egyptologists and Orientalists, in tracing the origins and interrelationships of the various writing systems of the past. Their discoveries make a fascinating chapter in the history of human development, but one which we must, however regrettably, pass over. Instead, our attention is directed to the synchronic description and structural analysis of the writing system now used, with only slight variation, throughout the English-speaking world. This is a much less thoroughly understood and worked-out field. Linguists have only recently turned their attention to it, because their primary task has been to describe and analyze the structure of the spoken language. Now that our understanding of the structure of speech has reached the stage that has been surveyed in Chapters 2–7 of this book, it is possible to look again at our writing system with an eye to two important matters: (1) the structure of the writing system itself, and (2) the relationship of that structure to the structure of speech. Some consideration of these two matters is the purpose of this chapter.

THE STRUCTURE OF OUR WRITING SYSTEM

At the beginning of Chapter 2, and again at the beginning of Chapter 3, the observation was made that in listening to speech we overlook many of its qualities in the interest of concentrating on the **significant features** that carry the message. Some of the things we disregard are absolute pitch (as distinct from relative pitch, which as we have seen is a vital grammatical signal), vocal qualifiers, individual vocal quality, and many nonphonemic phonetic features, such as the aspiration of initial /p, t, k/. We have trained ourselves so well to disregard some of these features that we are sometimes unaware that they are there at all, until we study phonetics or try to learn to pronounce a foreign language accurately. Others, such as absolute pitch and quality of voice, may have a powerful emotional effect on us, but one that we dissociate from the tenor of the message carried by the language.

Much the same process goes on when we read. When we concentrate on getting the message from written material, we disregard such matters as the size and color of the letters, the nature of the material of which they are made (ink, paint, light, smoke, metal, stone, shadow, etc.), the color and material of the background, and the nonsignificant differences in the shapes of the letters. We are influenced by these things, perhaps more than we are willing to admit. Printers, sign-painters, and advertising men know how to use them in ways that will produce desired emotional attitudes toward the message being conveyed. But as readers our primary reaction is to the significant features that carry the message. These features belong almost wholly to two main groups: (1) the basic shapes of the characters, and (2) their relative position in space.

The diversity of modes in which English can be written or printed is, as everyone knows, very great. There are hundreds of type faces available to printers, exhibiting a tremendous variety, ranging from elaborately decorated Old English to the simplicity of plain block. And when it comes to handwriting, our whole system of banking, among other things, is based upon the fact that no two people write exactly alike. These differences may be compared to the dialects of the spoken language. That is, when we read Gothic type or a friend's difficult handwriting, we adjust our reactions in much the way we do when we are listening to an unfamiliar dialect. Our concern here, however, is not with the contrasting details of these various "graphic dialects," but with their common structural features. For this reason we attempt no detailed classification. But from the structural point of view, we should make one broad distinction: that between **print** and **script.** These two major classes are so different that we usually have to learn them separately. The child in school learns to read and make print before he turns to script. The semiliterate, indeed, may never learn to handle script.

Let us now try to look at printed English, as it appears in this book, for instance, as if we had never seen it before. Our first observation is that it is composed of separate, discrete units, differing from one another in shape. These are placed side by side on the page in groups of from one to fifteen or more, with spaces between. These groups are arranged in horizontal rows. Occasionally, two of the units making up a group touch each other, but usually they are separated by just enough space to reveal that they are separate units. The whole patterning suggests a *segmented* kind of structure, with at least two levels of organization, that of the minimum units, which we call **letters** or **characters,** and that of the groups, or **words.**[1]

Further study and analysis, with the help of a "native reader," would allow us to reach some more conclusions. Borrowing some ideas and methods from phonemics and morphemics, for instance, we could conclude that each of the various letters has two or more different shapes, which seem to be in complementary distribution or free variation. This in turn suggests that each different shape can be called an **allograph,** and a family of allographs a **grapheme.** Thus, A, a, *a, A* are four different allographs of the same grapheme, which we write ⟨a⟩, using angle brackets to indicate graphemes, just as we use square brackets for [phones], slant lines for /phonemes/, and wing brackets for {morphemes}. This notation now permits us to use ⟨cat⟩ to stand for any way of writing the accepted spelling of the word /kæt/, including CAT, *cat*, **Cat**, etc.

Taking inventory of the segmental graphemes of standard English writing or printing, we find that there are thirty-seven of them, which can be classified in two groups:

(a) Twenty-six **letters of the alphabet:** ⟨a b c . . . z⟩
(b) Eleven **marks of punctuation:** ⟨, ; : . ? ! ' - — " ()⟩

In addition we must include **space,** a sort of zero grapheme.

We further note that all but the very simplest forms of writing and print make use of two complete sets of letters, the difference

---

[1] It is noteworthy that in print a word is a much more clear-cut entity than it is in speech. The printed word is clearly bounded by space on either side. In fact, for literate people, *word* primarily signifies 'written word.' (See pp. 200–02.)

between which is **suprasegmental.** Thus, the series a b c d ... are called **lower case** and the series A B C D ... **capitals.** We can consider A, for instance, as consisting of the segmental grapheme ⟨a⟩ plus the suprasegmental grapheme of **capitalization,** written ⟨≡⟩. Other common suprasegmental features are **italics,** or ⟨__⟩ as in *a b c d* ..., and **small caps,** or ⟨=⟩ as in ABCD ... . A given letter may exhibit two suprasegmental features at the same time; thus, *A* is ⟨a⟩ + ⟨__⟩ + ⟨≡⟩, or italic capital ⟨a⟩. This is exactly parallel to the situation in phonemics, where /²á/, for instance, represents the segmental phoneme /a/ with pitch /2/ and primary stress.

We could go ahead, if we wished, and make a thoroughgoing descriptive and statistical study of the distribution of the graphemes, which would reveal such things as their relative frequency, the particular combinations which they commonly fall into, and the rarity or absence of other combinations, and so on. We could, in fact, make a great many statements about the structure of English writing, without any appeal at all to what it means. The particular set of statements that could be made about written English would, of course, differ radically from those that could be made about any other written language, even one using the same set of graphemes. There would also be differences depending on the dialect of English being represented, though these would be much less than the differences between the spoken dialects themselves. Such statistical and distributional studies are of considerable concern to cryptographers, addicts of word-games and puzzles, designers of type faces, and many others whose business is with the manipulation of letters. For us, however, the major concern is with the relationship, or fit, of this visible system to the auditory system of the spoken language.

THE RELATIONSHIP OF WRITING TO SPEECH

In the preceding section we noted that the English writing system has a structure of its own, which can be studied independently of what the writing stands for. We made a few sketchy observations about that structure, but did not attempt a thorough description of it. Furthermore, in Chapters 2–7 we made a much more thorough description of the systematic structure of spoken American English. Now since the writing system is a representation of the speech system, we should expect to find a large degree of correspondence between the two. Presumably the goal of a writing system is to make it possible for a speaker to reproduce with complete accuracy an utterance which he has never heard spoken. In order to attain this goal, the writing system must include some means of representing visually all the significant features of speech. In effect, it should provide for representing: (1) the phonemes, both segmental and suprasegmental, (2) the ways in which the phonemes are combined in morphemes, (3) the combination of the morphemes into words, (4) the combination of words into structures, including visual equivalents of all syntactic devices used, and (5) the combination of structures into sentences and of sentences into conversations or continuous discourse. The degree to which a writing system is successful in representing these five things without overburdening the reader with complicated nonsignificant details is a measure of its efficiency.

Before we undertake to examine the way the English writing system represents the structure of English speech, we should make a few general observations about the problems that must be faced in the devising of any writing system. These are all in some way related to the fundamental differences between the sense of hearing and the sense of sight. Everybody knows what these differences are; they are obvious. Nevertheless, some of them are so important that they should be listed here.

1. Hearing is primarily concerned with *time* and sight with *space*. Thus, language is built out of *sounds* having relative existence in *time*, while writing is built out of *shapes* having relative position in *space*. Every culture has its own fundamental notions and conventions about the relationship of time and space. Our Western

culture is deeply committed to a concept of time as progressing steadily in one direction at the same speed. It is therefore easy for us to think of time in spatial analogies like an unwinding spool of ribbon or a flowing river. Accordingly, we find it quite natural to think of speech as something that can unwind like a ribbon or flow like a river, one part after another, always in the same direction. Hence, the printed tape emerging from a teletypewriter or the letters of light flowing in endless succession around the *Times* tower in New York are for us completely natural spatial analogies to the segments of speech succeeding one another in time.

In practice, of course, it is usually easier to hold the writing still and let the eyes do the moving. The effect is the same: the writing moves across the field of vision from right to left. As a matter of convenience of reproducing and handling, the ribbon of writing is customarily cut off into lines of equal length which are placed one beneath another. A "book" consisting of a single line of writing on a reel of ribbon would actually be easier to read than a conventional book like this one, because the eye would not have to swing back and make a new start for each line. But it would be more expensive to produce and more awkward to handle without special equipment.

2. Both speech and writing depend for their effect on various kinds of contrasts. But because of the different media they employ and the different senses they appeal to, they must rely on wholly different kinds of contrast. Thus, speech has available to it such contrasts as the following:

a) between *sound* and *silence*
b) between *noise* and *musical sound*
c) between the numerous tonal *colors* produced by various combinations of harmonics
d) in *pitch*, between high and low, rising and falling
e) in *volume*, between loud and soft

and many others.

Writing, on the other hand, must use an entirely different set of contrasts:

a) between a visible shape and a plain surface
b) in *shape*, with all its possibilities of angular and curved, simple and complex, linear and massive, and so on
c) in *size*, both absolute and relative
d) in *intensity*, between faint and strong
e) in *color*
f) in relative *position*

and so on.

If writing is to correspond efficiently to speech, these visible contrasts must be employed, either separately or in combination, in some systematic correspondence with the audible contrasts of speech.

3. Because of the one-directional flow of time, sounds become unrecapturable as soon as spoken. The attention of the hearer is upon a continuous flow of modulated sound, which his mind segments into phonemes, morphemes, words, and sentences. But actually by the time he is listening to the end of a word, he must supply its beginning from his memory. This is even more obvious in the case of larger structures; even the speaker himself may forget the beginning of a sentence before he reaches its end.

The spatial arrangement of writing, on the other hand, permits two things impossible in speech. (a) First, because of the fineness of discrimination of the eye and the relative breadth of the center of acute vision, it is possible to crowd letters close enough together so that quite a few of them can be seen simultaneously. The skilled reader does not move his eyes from letter to letter or even from word to word; he takes in groups of words or even entire lines of print in one glance. Familiar words and phrases thus come to have recognizable shapes of their own, and are comprehended as units. It is this that makes silent reading potentially much more rapid than listening, though writing (except for specially developed systems of shorthand) is much slower than speaking. (b) Secondly, because the eye may move at will over the printed page, it is possible to go back and look again at material which has been overlooked or incorrectly inter- preted. This cannot be done with speech; if we miss or misunderstand something, we either have to let it go or ask the speaker to repeat.

Disregarding pictographic and ideographic systems, which, as we have seen (pp. 37, 433), are nonlinguistic, a writing system may employ one or more of several methods of arranging its correspon- dences between sounds and shapes. The chief of these are five.

(1) A writing system may have a large number of contrasting shapes (graphemes, that is), each one corresponding to a *word*. This is **logographic writing.** Some simple forms of mathematical notation are logographic, as in $2 \times 4 = 8$, read as *two times four equals eight*. The notation used to record chess games is another example; thus P-KB4 is read *pawn to king's bishop's fourth*, and Q × Q as *queen takes queen*. It is noteworthy that in both these systems the total vocabulary used is very small, so that it is no strain on the memory to learn a separate symbol or **logogram** for each word. It is mani- festly impossible, however, to remember 50,000 or 100,000 distinct arbitrary symbols, though many people have vocabularies of those dimensions. Hence, no fully developed writing systems are logo- graphic, though many of them make use of some logograms. For example, one logogram sometimes used in conjunction with the English writing system is the **ampersand,** ⟨&⟩. Others are ⟨+⟩ for *plus*, ⟨@⟩ for *at*, and ⟨%⟩ for *per cent*.

(2) A writing system may have a separate symbol for each *mor- pheme*, in which case it is **morphemic** or **morphographic writing.** Since the number of morphemes in most languages is in the thou- sands, a morphemic writing system (the Chinese, for example) must have a large number of different graphemes. As we shall see later, there is a considerable mixture of morphographic writing in the basically phonemic English system. Thus ⟨and⟩, though composed

of three separate graphemes, makes a unit that represents not only the phoneme-sequence /ænd/, but all the other allomorphs and dialectal variants of {*and*} in all the dialects of English, ranging from /n/ to /éyənd/. From this point of view it is just as much a morphogram as ⟨&⟩ is.

(3) A writing system may have a separate grapheme for each of the possible *syllables* in the language it represents. Writing of this sort is called **syllabic writing,** and the repertory of graphemes used is called a **syllabary.** Most syllabic systems have separate graphemes for the vowel phonemes alone and for the possible consonant + vowel (CV) combinations in the language represented. Some also have graphemes representing VC and CVC combinations as well. In any case, the number of possible syllables, and hence the number of graphemes needed, is much smaller than the numbers of word- or morpheme-symbols required by logographic or morphemic systems. The most important present-day syllabary is that of Japanese, whose two forms (the *katakana* and *hiragana*) have forty-eight graphemes and several diacritics apiece, though use is also made of morphograms as well. An amusing though limited type of syllabic system, often used playfully by school children, involves using the alphabetic letters as symbols for their syllabic names, as in O I C U (Oh, I see you), I M MT (I am empty), XLNC (excellency), and so on.

(4) A writing system may have a separate grapheme for each of the *phonemes* in the language represented. Ever since Chapter 3 we have made frequent use of such a **phonemic system** for writing English. No standard writing system in present use is truly and completely phonemic, however, though those of Finnish and Turkish approach this ideal. Most systems in use where European, Islamic, or Indian cultures have spread make use of various partially phonemic systems in which the graphemes have a more or less close but imperfect and inconsistent correspondence with the phonemes. Such systems are **alphabetic.**

(5) Finally, a writing system may have graphemes for all the

distinguishable *sound features* of the language represented, whether
they are significant or not. Such a **phonetic system** is much too
cumbersome for ordinary uses, though as we saw in Chapter 2, it is
of great value in the study of phonetics. The International Phonetic
Alphabet, or IPA, is the most successful of many attempts at a
phonetic writing system. Its use is spreading, though chiefly and
properly confined largely to specialists and special purposes. It
would not be desirable to use it for the ordinary purposes of writing,
since it represents too many nonsignificant features, whose inclusion
complicates the reading and writing without adding to the relevant
information communicated.

The foundation of the standard English writing system, both historically and structurally, is phonemic. But during the thirteen
centuries of its use it has departed rather far from a simple and consistent grapheme-to-phoneme correspondence. The principal reason
for this departure is that extensive changes in the language have
occurred which have not always been matched by corresponding
changes in the writing system. Other causes have also been at work,
such as the influence of the writing systems of other languages,
especially French, and the often misguided efforts of scribes with
more learning than common sense. French influence, for instance,
is responsible for the replacement of older ⟨cw⟩ by ⟨qu⟩, and mistaken learning inserted the useless *b* into *debt*, *doubt*, and *subtle*.

In addition to its perceptible but much distorted phonemic foundation, English writing uses several other devices, some of them quite
systematic and others purely arbitrary. Among these, the following
are prominent:

(1) Single graphemes representing various combinations of phonemes, such as diphthongs

(2) Combinations of graphemes representing single phonemes

(3) Arbitrary combinations of graphemes representing combinations of phonemes

(4) Doubling graphemes to indicate which of two possible phonemes or phonemic combinations is represented, and for other reasons

(5) Graphemes used as diacritics, that is as symbols having no phonemic equivalents of their own but serving to indicate the phonemic reference of a nearby grapheme

(6) Alternative representations of the same phonemic combinations used to distinguish homophones from each other

(7) Graphic conventions from other writing systems used to represent words borrowed from other languages

(8) Grapheme-combinations used as **morphograms,** that is as unchanging representations of the same morphemes regardless of morphophonemic variations in the spoken language

In the next two sections of this chapter we shall take up first the phonemic basis of the English writing system and then the eight variations and additional devices listed above.

THE PHONEMIC BASIS OF ENGLISH WRITING

When Anglo-Saxon scribes of the seventh century took over the Latin alphabet and adapted it to the writing of English, they acted on primarily phonemic principles. They were not, of course, consciously familiar with phonemic theory, any more than were the Greeks who adapted a Semitic syllabary into the first nearly phonemic alphabet. In both cases, however, unknown persons with an intelligent and perceptive language sense made skilful use of what was in truth makeshift material. In the case of the Anglo-Saxons, what they did was to use the letters of the Latin alphabet to represent phonemes phonetically similar to those which they represented in written Latin. Where they found gaps, they filled in with letters derived from the old Germanic runic alphabet, such as ⟨þ⟩, and a modification of Roman ⟨d⟩, ⟨ð⟩, both used to represent the phoneme

/ð/, which had allophones [θ] and [ð]. (This duplication, by the way, was one of their mistakes, since only one character was needed.) They also used the rune ⟨ᚹ⟩, called *wen*, for consonantal /w/, leaving the Latin u and v as positional variants (allographs) of a single grapheme, the vocalic ⟨u⟩. What has since become the phoneme /v/ was in Old English simply an allophone of /f/, so the scribes quite properly used the single grapheme ⟨f⟩ for both [f] and [v].

They had somewhat more difficulty with vowels and diphthongs. A short low-back vowel gave them trouble, and they varied in representing it between ⟨a⟩ and ⟨o⟩. But they met other problems with some ingenuity. For instance, they made use of ⟨y⟩, a rare character in Latin, used only in transliterating Greek, to represent a high-front-round vowel, and they employed the **ligature** ⟨æ⟩ for a lower-mid-front-unround, distinct from low-central and low-back. What they produced was not a purely phonemic system—even the segmentals were not wholly phonemic, and no suprasegmentals except length were indicated—but it was an approach and on the whole a consistent one.

Over the centuries that separate us from the first writers of English, many changes have taken place, both in the language and in the writing system. The language has been influenced by contact with many other tongues—Scandinavian and French first, many others later. The writing system has similarly been influenced by scribes familiar with the systems used for these languages. Continuing pressure of Latin and French writing, for instance, led to the dropping of the old runic letters and the substitution of such devices as the **digraph** ⟨th⟩ (originally used in Latin writing to transliterate Greek ⟨θ⟩, which represented phonemic /th/) and the doubled ⟨vv⟩, which came to be treated as a ligature and finally a single character ⟨w⟩, whose name still proclaims its origin. The superfluous Latin ⟨q⟩ was learnedly adopted; also ⟨k⟩ and ⟨z⟩, characters of Greek origin seldom used in Latin. The use made of ⟨z⟩ was intelligent; it primarily appeared as a representation of a new phoneme /z/, which developed out of an allophone of /s/. The substitution was not made completely consistently, however, so that we have *as* beside *us* on the one hand, and *haze* and *raise* on the other. Latin contact with Greek introduced such combinations as ⟨ph⟩ for /f/, which further disrupted the original phonemic basis of the system.

Meanwhile the phonemes of the language were changing—in number, in distribution, in the allophones that constituted them, and in their phonetic constitution. Changes in stress and probably in pitch, morphophonemic alterations such as assimilation, gradation, and synthesis (see pp. 213–18) took place gradually and were often not followed by corresponding changes in the writing system. Finally, the invention of printing introduced a highly conservative force, which has helped preserve our writing system largely unchanged over the last 400 years. The last important adjustment was made during the seventeenth and eighteenth centuries, when i and j, originally allographs of a single grapheme ⟨i⟩, and u and v, originally allographs of one grapheme ⟨u⟩, were given independent graphemic status. Meanwhile, our system of punctuation, which is not phonemic at all but morphemic and syntactic (as we shall see), had been elaborated. The result of all these changes, which have only been suggested here, was to disrupt pretty thoroughly the relatively simple, largely phonemic Old English system and produce the highly complex and frequently inconsistent system we now use.

Since our point of view in this book is structural rather than historical, our concern is not with how our system got the way it is, fascinating though that history is. Instead, we are interested in what it is like now. Specifically, our first task is to look at its phonemic foundation, parts of which are quite firm and reliable, however they may be overlaid and almost obscured by later structures. As a first step, let us take inventory. On the one side are the phonemes of the language; on the other, the graphemes by which they can be represented. Specifically, there are forty-five phonemes, classified as follows:

24 consonants—

    6 stops: /p t k b d g/

    2 affricates: /č ǰ/

    4 fricatives: /f θ v ð/

    4 sibilants: /s š z ž/

    3 nasals: /m n ŋ/

    1 lateral: /l/

    4 semivowels: /r w y h/

9 vowels: /i e æ ɨ ə a u o ɔ/

4 stresses: /ˊ ˆ ˋ ˇ/

4 pitches: /1 2 3 4/

4 junctures: /+ | ‖ #/

On the other side of the ledger, we may list forty-one graphemes (though many others are used in some forms of print). They may be classified as follows:[2]

21 consonantals: ⟨b c d f g h j k l m n p q r s t v w x y z⟩

    4 of these may be called **semi-vocalics:** ⟨h r w y⟩

5 vocalics: ⟨a e i o u⟩

11 marks: ⟨, . ; : ? ! " ' - — ( )⟩

4 suprasegmental features: lower case, italics ⟨—⟩, small

    caps ⟨⹀⟩, capitals ⟨≡⟩.

In addition we should list *space* as a graphemic feature.

Perhaps the most obvious thing we note when we come to study the correspondence between these two systems is that there are no

[2] The terms **consonantal** and **vocalic** will be used here and throughout this chapter to refer to graphemes used primarily to represent consonants and vowels respectively. The terms **consonant** and **vowel** will thus be confined to the discussion of speech. Many confused and fallacious notions can thus be avoided, such as the idea that "English has five vowels, a, e, i, o, u," which is still taught in schools. As we saw in Chapter 3, the number of vowels in English varies with dialect, but a minimum of nine is necessary to provide a scheme that will accommodate most dialects. But it is true that the English *writing system* has five *vocalics*, ⟨a e i o u⟩.

units in the graphic system corresponding to the twelve suprasegmental phonemes of stress, pitch, and juncture. Secondly, there is
nothing in the phonemic system that corresponds to the eleven
punctuation marks and four suprasegmental features of the graphic
system. With these two groups eliminated, we are left with thirty-
three segmental phonemes—twenty consonants, four semivowels,
and nine vowels—on the one hand, and twenty-six letters—seventeen
consonantals, four semivocalics, and five vocalics—on the other.
It is immediately obvious from the numbers that a one-to-one
correspondence is impossible; there would be seven phonemes left
over.

When we look at specific correspondences, we find the possibilities
even more reduced. Let us begin with a table in which the thirty-
three segmental phonemes are set against their most frequent graphic
equivalents. To avoid overcomplicating the table, many unusual
equivalents, such as ⟨ai⟩ for /e/ in *said*, are omitted.

Phoneme	Graphemes	Phoneme	Graphemes	Phoneme	Graphemes
p	p, pp	ð	th	y	y, i
t	t, tt, ed	s	s, ss, c	h	h
k	c, k, ck	š	sh, various	i	i, y
b	b, bb	z	z, zz, s	e	e, ea
d	d, dd, ed	ž	z, s, ge	æ	a
g	g, gg	m	m, mm	ɨ	various
č	ch, tch	n	n, nn	ə	various
ǰ	j, g, dg	ŋ	ng, n	a	o, a
f	f, ff, ph	l	l, ll	u	u, oo
θ	th	r	r, rr	o	o, oa
v	v, ve	w	w, u	ɔ	o, au

It is apparent from the table that all the phonemes except four,
/č θ ð š/, are represented by single graphemes fairly commonly and
in some positions, at least. This is not enough, however, since a true

phonemic system must work in both directions. Approaching the table from the other side, we find that several of the single graphemes are ambiguous. Thus ⟨s⟩ may represent /s z š ž/ (as in *sit, rise, sure, measure*), and ⟨g⟩ may represent /g ǰ ž/ (as in *get, gin, rouge*). Such ambiguities remove /k g s z ž ŋ h w/ and all the vowels from the list. This leaves us with twelve phonemes having a fairly common one-to-one correspondence with single graphemes:

/p/ : ⟨p⟩	/ǰ/ : ⟨j⟩	/n/ : ⟨n⟩
/t/ : ⟨t⟩	/f/ : ⟨f⟩	/l/ : ⟨l⟩
/b/ : ⟨b⟩	/v/ : ⟨v⟩	/r/ : ⟨r⟩
/d/ : ⟨d⟩	/m/ : ⟨m⟩	/y/ : ⟨y⟩

As soon as we study distribution, however, we find that this list is only partially accurate, and exceptions of one sort or another require us to remove one after another from the list. Thus although the phoneme /ǰ/ is relatively common in word-final position, the grapheme ⟨j⟩ never appears there except in a few freak borrowed words like *raj*. Final /ǰ/ is represented instead by ⟨ge⟩ or ⟨dge⟩. The same is true of final /v/, which is represented by ⟨ve⟩, or, in the single word *of*, by ⟨f⟩. When we look at the middles of words, we find all kinds of doublings and combinings of graphemes to represent simple phonemes, and vice versa. We are left with the conclusion that there is not even one single example of a one-to-one correspondence between phoneme and grapheme in the whole system. The nearest to it is /v/ : ⟨v⟩, since /v/ is almost never represented by anything except ⟨v⟩ and ⟨ve⟩, and ⟨v⟩ never stands for anything but /v/ (except in a few proper names and loan-words from German and Slavonic, where it may stand for /f/).

Thus, we are brought to the conclusion that though there is a phonemic foundation for the writing system of English, which is particularly apparent in little words like *pit, man, bed*, it is severely compromised and limited in the following four principal ways.

(1) Some phonemes, e.g., /θ/, are never represented by a single grapheme.

(2) Some graphemes, e.g., ⟨q, x⟩, never represent a single phoneme.

(3) Phoneme-grapheme correspondences that prevail consistently in some positions and environments break down in others.

(4) The suprasegmental phonemes have no graphic representation whatever.

NONPHONEMIC DEVICES IN ENGLISH WRITING

On pages 443–44 we listed eight major devices which the English writing system uses in addition to or in place of the one-to-one correspondence of grapheme to phoneme that constitutes its imperfect phonemic foundation. In this section we shall have a look at each of these in turn, with some examples to illustrate how they work. They are not mutually exclusive, but show some overlapping. Thus, the ⟨kn⟩ representation of the initial /n/ of *knight* can be considered either a combination of graphemes to represent a single phoneme or an alternative representation of the same phonemic combination to distinguish the homophones *knight* and *night*.

Once again we must remind the reader that our treatment can be at best general and suggestive. A detailed and exhaustive study of the relationship of the English writing system to the English language would itself occupy a fair-sized book. No complete study of this sort has yet been made. When it is, it may lead us to far-reaching revisions of our ways of teaching reading and writing, and perhaps to rational and thoroughly considered reforms in the system itself. As it is, suggested reforms in spelling and other aspects of the writing system are usually based on impressionistic or superficial knowledge, and their advocates have often been nonlinguists like the librarian Melvil Dewey and the dramatist George Bernard Shaw.

REPRESENTATION OF PHONEME COMBINATIONS BY SINGLE GRAPHEMES. All five of the vocalic graphemes are used in various environments to represent phoneme combinations of various sorts, principally diphthongs. The following table shows the five vocalics and the principal phoneme combinations they may represent:[3]

⟨a⟩ = /ey/ in *ague, agent, nature.*
⟨e⟩ = /iy/ in *equal, demon, employe.*
⟨i⟩ = /ay/ in *idle, biology, loci.*
   = /iy/ in *machine, unique.*
⟨o⟩ = /ow/ in *over, post, go.*
   = /uw/ in *move, tomb.*
   = /wə/ in *one, once.*
⟨u⟩ = /uw/, /yuw/, or /ɨw/ in *tune, due.*
   = /yuw/ in *unit, futile, emu.*

Consonantals representing more than one phoneme are much less common. One clear case is ⟨x⟩, which almost always represents either /ks/, as in *lexical, six,* or /gz/, as in *exist.* Only in word-initial position does it represent a single phoneme, the /z/ of *xylophone.* The nasal ⟨m⟩ sometimes represents the combination /əm/, as in *prism,* and the semivocalic ⟨y⟩ frequently represents the diphthong /ay/, as in *sky.*

REPRESENTATION OF SINGLE PHONEMES BY GRAPHEME COMBINATIONS. The converse of the preceding is the representation of single phonemes by combinations of two and sometimes three graphemes. Setting aside for later consideration the occasions when one grapheme acts as a diacritic, we may observe three different kinds of grapheme combinations here:

(1) The first group includes those in which a phoneme is represented by its "normal" grapheme (see list on p. 449) accompanied by a so-called "silent letter," as in the following table. Note that the silent letter may precede the normal grapheme, as in ⟨ck, kn⟩, or follow it, as in ⟨mb, rh⟩.

---

[3] In the tables and examples in this section, = is to be read "represents" or "corresponds to."

Graph-eme	Pho-neme	Illustrations	Distribution
⟨ck⟩	= /k/	*racket, sack*	medial and final only
⟨mb⟩	= /m/	*lamb, comb, dumb*	morpheme-final only
⟨mn⟩	= /m/	*damn, column, solemn*	morpheme-final only
⟨mn⟩	= /n/	*mnemonic*	word-initial
⟨kn⟩	= /n/	*know, unknown*	morpheme-initial
⟨ln⟩	= /l/	*kiln*	in this word only
⟨rh⟩	= /r/	*rhetoric*	words of Greek origin
⟨st⟩	= /s/	*glisten, hasten*	word-medial
⟨bt⟩	= /t/	*debt, subtle*	medial and final

(2) The second group includes grapheme combinations used to represent phonemes which are never or only in quite limited environments represented by single graphemes. There are five such phonemes in English: /θ ð č š ŋ/. Since the abandonment of the runic characters þ and ð, the first two of these have been almost universally represented by ⟨th⟩, as in *thin, ether, wrath* and *then, either, smooth*. Of occasional appearance are ⟨tth⟩ for /θ/ as in *Matthew*, and ⟨the⟩ for /ð/, as in *smoothe, breathe*. The phoneme /č/ is commonly represented by ⟨ch⟩ or (except in morpheme-initial position) by ⟨tch⟩, with a few unusual spellings like the ⟨te⟩ of *righteous* and the ⟨ti⟩ of *question*. The phoneme /ŋ/, which is never initial, is most commonly represented by the combination ⟨ng⟩, though it also appears as ⟨n⟩ before ⟨k, g⟩, as in *think, anger*.

The graphic representation of /š/ is considerably more complicated than any of these. This phoneme was not in English at the time the alphabet was adopted, so that no single grapheme was allocated to it. It now appears frequently, sometimes in borrowed words, but usually as the product of the synthesis of contiguous phonemes (pp. 214–15). Since the words in which this synthesis has occurred are of various origin, and since the synthesis took place, usually, subsequent to the standardization of the English spelling system, the words tend to preserve the spellings they had before the synthesis took place. The result is a large number of different ways of representing /š/, some of which are quite common, others rare. They divide into two groups, with some overlapping: those borrowed from the writing system of other languages, such as French ⟨ch⟩ and German ⟨sch⟩, and those resulting from synthesis. In addition there is the combination ⟨sh⟩, a later substitute for the ⟨sc⟩ which represented the Old English combination from which the English /š/ phoneme first developed. This is felt to be the normal representation of /š/, since it occurs in a large number of words and in all positions. It thus has the widest distribution. The borrowed spellings, on the other hand, follow the distribution rules for the writing systems from which they are borrowed. Thus, since ⟨ch⟩ never appears in final position in French, being replaced by ⟨che⟩, it never appears there in English as a spelling for /š/. When ⟨ch⟩ does appear in word-final position in English, it usually represents /č/, as in *each*, though in words borrowed from other languages than French it may represent /k/ or even the velar spirant phoneme /x/, which some educated speakers of English use in words like *loch* and *Bach*.

The spellings for /š/ resulting from synthesis, on the other hand, usually appear at the boundaries between morphemes, where the processes of derivation and compounding bring together phonemes which take part in synthesis. Thus, these spellings are rare in word-initial and word-final position.

The result of all these and other factors in the history of English /š/ is a fantastic variety of ways of representing this common phoneme in English writing. The situation is a delight to etymologists, who can tell at a glance (if they did not know already) that *ship* is of native Anglo-Saxon origin, while *chemise* is French and *schnapps* German. But in the ordinary speaker trying to learn to write his native tongue, the problem of representing /š/ may arouse despair rather than delight, since he is unlikely to be familiar with Latin, French, and German spelling conventions.

The following list gives fourteen different ways of representing /š/.

Graphemes	Illustrations	Distribution
sh	ship, fish, fishing, worship	morpheme initial and final.
ch	chemise, machine	initial and medial, words of recent French origin.
che	cache	final, words of recent French origin.
sch	schnapps, Fischer, Flesch	morpheme-initial, words of German origin; medial and final in proper names.
s	sure, sugar, unsure	morpheme-initial before ⟨u⟩.
ci	vicious	
ti	notion	word-medial at morpheme
sci	luscious	boundary, words of French
si	tension	and Latin origin.
ssi	mission	
ss	issue, fissure	word-medial between a vocalic and ⟨u⟩.
ce	ocean, cretaceous	in *ocean* and its derivatives; medial before -*ous*.
se	nausea, nauseated	only in *nausea* and its derivatives
chsi	fuchsia	only in this word.

3. The third group of grapheme combinations used to represent single phonemes includes those which are less common ways of representing phonemes that are most commonly represented by an entirely different single grapheme. Many of these appear in words borrowed, with their spellings, from other languages, or in native words which have had a special history of some sort. A few illustrations are the following:

⟨ai, ay⟩ = /e/, in *said, says.*

⟨gh⟩ = /f/, in *tough, laughter, enough.*

⟨ph⟩ = /f/, in *phase, gopher, graph.*

⟨que⟩ = /k/, in *unique.*

REPRESENTATION OF PHONEME COMBINATIONS BY ARBITRARY GRAPHEME COMBINATIONS. It is, of course, natural in a phonemic writing system for combinations of graphemes to represent combinations of phonemes. Thus, ⟨pet⟩ is a direct representation of the segmental phonemes of /pet/, though it says nothing about the suprasegmentals, and thus does not distinguish between /²pèt/ and /³pét¹/, for instance. English, however, makes use of some combinations of graphemes which are purely arbitrary; that is, the individual graphemes cannot be assigned to the single phonemes that make up the combination. Thus, in ⟨beau⟩ = /bow/, we must simply say that the whole combination ⟨eau⟩ represents the whole combination /ow/. Some other examples are given here.

⟨ai⟩ = /eh/ in *fair.*

⟨igh⟩ = /ay/ in *sigh, night.*

⟨au⟩ = /ey/ in *gauge.*

⟨ao⟩ = /ey/ in *gaol* (British usage only).

⟨eau⟩ = /yuw/ in *beauty.*

⟨oe⟩ = /uw/ in *shoe, canoe.*

DOUBLING OF GRAPHEMES. The English writing system makes extensive use of the practice of doubling graphemes. The significance of the doubling varies; it may represent nothing at all different from the single grapheme (compare *atom* and *attic*, for instance); it may distinguish one of two phonemic equivalents for the single grapheme (compare *his* and *hiss*); it may distinguish between two phonemic equivalents of a nearby grapheme (compare *diner* and *dinner*); it may occasionally even represent an actual double phoneme (as in *unnamed* compared with *unaimed*). Sometimes the doubling performs more than one of these functions, as in *mussed* compared with *mused*. Here the ⟨ss⟩ indicates that the central consonant is /s/ rather than /z/, but it also indicates that the syllabic is /ə/ rather than /yuw/ and that the final consonant is /t/ rather than /d/. Comparison of the phonemic spellings of these words—/mə́st-myúwzd/—shows what a burden of representation the doubling of the ⟨s⟩ carries. It represents a change in every phoneme except the initial /m/.

The conventions governing the doubling of graphemes are too complicated for us to do more than sketch them here. We may, however, first note that the doubling of vocalics is different in function from the doubling of consonantals. The doubled vocalic was a device originally used in Middle English to indicate a long vowel, and this is still one of its functions in some writing systems. But since the long vowels of Middle English have had a subsequent development different from that of the short vowels, the double spellings have come to represent differences in the segmental phonemes represented, rather than in the suprasegmental feature of length. Actually the doubling of ⟨a i u⟩ has been abandoned, except in some proper names of foreign origin, such as Haag, Riis, and Ruud. As we have seen, the combination ⟨uu⟩ has had another development into the single grapheme ⟨w⟩. Therefore, ⟨ee⟩ and ⟨oo⟩ are the only common double vocalics. In both cases they serve as alternative representations of phonemes or phoneme combinations which may also be represented by the single graphemes ⟨e⟩ and ⟨o⟩ or by other graphemes or grapheme combinations. In general, their range is less extensive than that of the single graphemes.

A few illustrations will make these points clear. Thus, ⟨e⟩ when representing a syllabic commonly stands either for /e/, as in *met*, or /iy/, as in *equal*. But ⟨ee⟩ virtually always represents /iy/, as in *meet*. The situation here is further complicated by the fact that

/iy/ may also be represented by many other graphemes and combinations, as in *meat, field, seize, machine, key, city*, and *people*. Single ⟨o⟩ represents a rather wide variety of phonemes and phoneme combinations, differing from dialect to dialect. The following are the most common in the "General American" dialects:

/ɔ/ or /a/	in *hot, bond*.
/o/	in *comb, only*.
/ə/	in *son, love*.
/u/	in *woman*.
/ow/	in *open*.
/uw/	in *lose, prove, tomb*.
/oh/ or /ɔh/	in *born, gone*.

Of these, only three are also represented by ⟨oo⟩:

/ə/	in *blood, flood*.
/u/	in *wool, good*.
/uw/	in *pool, food*.

The doubling of ⟨o⟩ thus sometimes serves to distinguish pairs like *god*: *good* and *hot*: *hoot*, though not extensively or consistently. There remain unfortunate ambiguities such as *lose*: *loose*, where the syllabic phonemes are the same, though differently represented, and *lose*: *close*, where the syllabic phonemes are different, though similarly represented. To add to the confusion, in *loose* the doubled ⟨o⟩ indicates that the ⟨s⟩ represents /s/ rather than /z/, while in *choose* the reverse is true. It is no wonder that these words present problems for spellers.

Doubling of consonantals in English writing serves several purposes. One of the rarest is the most logical: to indicate an actual double consonant phoneme. These occur only at morpheme boundaries, where derivation, inflection, or compounding brings two instances of the same phoneme together.[4] The example of *unnamed*: *unaimed* has already been cited. But the number of pairs of this sort that can be found is small. There is a much larger number of cases in which the doubled grapheme signifies nothing different from the single: thus for most speakers *holy* and *wholly* both represent /hówliy/. On the other hand, /sówl+liy/, which does have the double phoneme, is spelled *solely*, with an ⟨e⟩ between the two ⟨l⟩'s.

The most common function of the doubled consonantal is to indicate something about the preceding vocalic: usually to signify that it represents a different phoneme or phoneme combination from the one it represents when followed by a single consonantal. Once again this is most common at morpheme boundaries, especially at the point of junction of derivational and inflectional suffixes beginning with a vocalic. In effect, the doubled grapheme here serves as a diacritic on the preceding vocalic. Common examples will occur to anyone. Thus, the doubled grapheme may make distinctions of the sort indicated in the following table:

Vocalic	Phonemic reference when followed by		Illustrative words
	single consonantal	double	
⟨a⟩	/ey/	/æ/	bated : batted
⟨i⟩	/ay/	/i/	diner : dinner
⟨o⟩	/ow/	/a/ or /ɔ/	robing : robbing
⟨u⟩	/uw/ or /yuw/	/ə/	super : supper
			cuter : cutter

When the vocalic is ⟨a i o⟩ this principle does not always apply, as can be seen in the pairs *habit*: *rabbit*, *finis*: *pinnace*, *robin*: *bobbin*.

A third function of the double consonantal is to distinguish one

---

[4] Phonetically, these are usually *long* consonants, rather than double ones. Phonemically, they always are separated by /+/.

of two or more possible phonemic values of the consonantal in certain environments. This especially affects the two graphemes ⟨g⟩ and ⟨s⟩, when they come between vocalics, especially at morpheme boundaries. This function is frequently combined with the preceding, so that the double consonantal indicates not only the nature of the central consonant but that of the preceding vowel as well. The following table illustrates some of the possibilities:

| Grapheme | Phonemic reference when | | Illustrative words |
	single	double	
⟨g⟩	/ǰ/	/g/	rigid : rigging; waging : wagging
⟨s⟩	/z/	/s/	fuses : fusses; loses : losses
⟨s⟩	/ž/	/š/	pleasure : pressure

In the case of ⟨g⟩, certain other distributional factors serve to reduce the occurrence of the double form; thus, when ⟨g⟩ is followed by ⟨a o u⟩, it represents /g/ without doubling, as in *frigate*, *rigor*, *ambiguous*. The doubling may occur anyhow, however, as in *baggage* and *maggot*. On the other hand, in *exaggerate* the double ⟨g⟩ represents /ǰ/, and in *suggest* it represents /ǰ/ or /gǰ/.

Because double consonantals so often occur at the junction-points of bound morphemes, they are much less frequent in word-initial and word-final position than they are in the middle of words. In fact, with the exception of proper names like Lloyd and Ffoulkes, double consonantals never occur in word-initial position. Again excepting proper names, the only ones that may be double in word-final position are ⟨b d f g l n r s t z⟩, and these most commonly in one-syllable words like *ebb*, *odd*, *off*, *egg*, *ill*, *inn*, *err*, and *miss*. Final ⟨tt⟩ and ⟨zz⟩ are especially rare, but they do occur in such words as *batt*, *butt*, *fizz*, *jazz*. Finally, we should note that certain consonantals are never doubled (once more excepting proper names); these are ⟨j k q w x⟩, and ⟨v⟩ except in the colloquial *flivver*.

GRAPHEMES AS DIACRITICS. When a grapheme has no phonemic reference of its own but serves instead to indicate or limit the phonemic reference of a nearby grapheme, we may say that it is being used as a diacritic or distinguishing marker. The most versatile of the graphemes of the English system in this regard is, of course, ⟨e⟩. Largely owing to a series of sweeping changes in English pronunciation in late Middle English times (1350–1500), a grapheme that once had fairly consistent phonemic reference now appears in many words in which it is itself "silent" but in which its presence indicates the phonemic value of one or more other graphemes, sometimes at some distance away. As experienced readers of English, we are so familiar with the multifarious roles of ⟨e⟩ in our spelling that we take them for granted. A bit of close examination, however, will remind us of how much our writing system depends on the proper placing of this grapheme.

The most common use of ⟨e⟩ as diacritic is following a single consonantal, which itself follows a single vocalic, in a syllable bearing at least tertiary stress. In this position ⟨e⟩ indicates that the preceding vocalic has its so-called "long" (really diphthongal) reference. There are hundreds of pairs of English words with the basic phonemic pattern CVC, in which the nature of the vowel phoneme is signaled by the presence or absence of final ⟨e⟩. The following pairs are representative:

$$\langle \text{hat : hate} \rangle \;=\; /\text{hæt : heyt}/$$
$$\langle \text{met : mete} \rangle \;=\; /\text{met : miyt}/$$
$$\langle \text{bit : bite} \rangle \;=\; /\text{bit : bayt}/$$
$$\langle \text{rot : rote} \rangle \;=\; /\text{rat : rowt}/$$
$$\langle \text{cut : cute} \rangle \;=\; /\text{kət : kyuwt}/$$

Occasionally some other convention of English spelling takes precedence over this one and creates an exception. Thus, the rule that ⟨v⟩ is never word-final has led to the spelling of final /v/ by

⟨ve⟩ regardless of the nature of the preceding syllabic. This produces ambiguous spellings like ⟨live⟩, which can represent both /liv/ and /layv/, and misleading spellings like ⟨love⟩, representing /ləv/ rather than */lowv/, which the analogy with *rove* and *stove* suggests. Other cases in point are *have, give, shove, above.*

The grapheme ⟨e⟩ also serves as a diacritic with certain ambiguous consonantals and consonantal combinations. Thus, it may indicate the /s/ value of ⟨c⟩, as in *noticeable*, or the /ǰ/ value of ⟨g⟩, as in *outrageous.* Following ⟨th⟩ it indicates the voiced phoneme /ð/, as in *wreathe* compared with *wreath*, and following ⟨ng⟩ it indicates the pronunciation /nǰ/ rather than /ŋ/, as in *singe*: *sing.* It may also combine its two diacritical functions: thus in the following pairs of words the reference of both the syllabic vocalic and the following consonantal is changed by adding ⟨e⟩:

$$
\begin{array}{ll}
⟨\text{lac}: \text{lace}⟩ & = /\text{læk}: \text{leys}/ \\
⟨\text{rag}: \text{rage}⟩ & = /\text{ræg}: \text{reyǰ}/ \\
⟨\text{us}: \text{use}⟩ & = /\text{əs}: \text{yuwz}/ \\
⟨\text{bath}: \text{bathe}⟩ & = /\text{bæθ}: \text{beyð}/ \\
⟨\text{rang}: \text{range}⟩ & = /\text{ræŋ}: \text{reynǰ}/
\end{array}
$$

Other graphemes beside ⟨e⟩ may also serve as diacritics of various sorts. Thus, ⟨i⟩ may function like ⟨e⟩ to distinguish the /ǰ/ reference of ⟨g⟩, as in *vestigial* compared with *obligatory.* We have treated ⟨ch sh th⟩ as grapheme combinations representing single phonemes. But from another point of view the ⟨h⟩ here could be considered a diacritic, indicating the /č š θ ð/ reference of ⟨c s t⟩. In the same way, the ⟨t⟩ of ⟨tch⟩ serves to limit the combination ⟨ch⟩ to the value /č/, eliminating the alternatives /š k x/. It is of no great importance which way these are classified, so long as we keep in mind the fact that the English writing system uses an elaborate complex of cross-influences to compensate for its deficiencies in direct grapheme-phoneme correspondence.

GRAPHIC DISTINCTION OF HOMOPHONES. The various departures from a straight phonemic system which we have discussed above often make it possible to represent identical combinations of phonemes in different ways. This fact, which is the result of changes occurring during the history of the language, has been used to distinguish homophones by means of alternative spellings. The result is that the writing system makes many distinctions that are not apparent in the spoken language. Examples are numerous; the following are a few of the more spectacular ones:

$$/rayt/ = \text{rite, right, write, wright}$$
$$/rowz/ = \text{rose, rows, roes, row's, roe's}$$
$$/nuw/ = \text{new, knew, gnu}$$
$$/sow/ = \text{so, sow, sew}$$
$$/ruwd/ = \text{rude, rued, rood}$$
$$/feyz/ = \text{fays, faze, phase}$$
$$/ayl/ = \text{isle, aisle, I'll}$$

Sometimes several of these can be combined into complete utterances which are ambiguous in speech but not so in writing, such as /²ðə sânz rêyz ³míyt¹#/, which can be either *the sun's rays meet* or *the sons raise meat*.

INFLUENCE OF OTHER WRITING SYSTEMS. Within a few centuries of the adoption of its writing system, the English language began the extensive borrowing from other languages that has so vastly extended its vocabulary. At first from Latin, Danish, and French, and later from Greek, Italian, Spanish, Dutch, and many of the strange tongues spoken in far-flung posts of empire, the words poured into the language. Most of them were almost immediately adapted to the phonemic system of English, since only educated bilinguals attempt to preserve the foreign phonemes of loan-words unchanged. But the tendency has been for the borrowed words to retain their native spellings, especially during the last three centuries, after the spelling systems of English and the other European languages had been standardized. The result has been that many divergent spelling practices have been introduced into the English system. Some of these have been mentioned above as examples of alternate spellings for the same phonemes or phoneme combinations.

The graphic conventions which our writing has borrowed from other systems are of two sorts. The first group are those which have been so thoroughly incorporated into our system as to displace older native uses. We have already mentioned the displacement of the Anglo-Saxon ⟨þ⟩ and ⟨ð⟩ by the Latin-French ⟨th⟩, resulting in a respelling of all Middle English words containing these phonemes. The Latin-French combination ⟨qu⟩ was also adopted in place of older ⟨cw⟩ as a spelling for /kw/. Also from French come ⟨ch⟩ for /č/, ⟨ou⟩ in place of older ⟨ú⟩, and ⟨o⟩ for ⟨u⟩ in many words like *love* and *son*.

The other group of foreign spelling conventions includes those used only in certain words which have been either borrowed directly from foreign languages or coined by combining morphemes so borrowed. The result is the introduction of alternative spelling conventions parallel to those used in native words or earlier borrowings. Most notable in this regard is the large number of words, many of them scientific terms, which have been borrowed from Greek or coined from Greek morphemes. Greek, of course, has its own alphabet, which includes some graphemes having no counterparts in the Latin alphabet from which ours derives. Greek loanwords thus have to be respelled or **transliterated** into our system. Since Greek also has phonemes and phoneme combinations different from those of English, phonemic adaptations are also made when Greek words are borrowed or coined. The result is an elaborate set of conventions for spelling and pronouncing these words, which amounts to a special subsystem of the English writing system. A few illustrations will reveal the special nature of these conventions.

Greek Grapheme	Greek Phoneme	English Grapheme	English Phoneme	Illustrative Words
⟨χ⟩	/kh/	⟨ch⟩	/k/	character, ichthyology
⟨θ⟩	/th/	⟨th⟩	/θ/	thesis, monolith
⟨φ⟩	/ph/	⟨ph⟩	/f/	philosophy
⟨υ⟩	/ü/	⟨y⟩	/ay, i/	phylum, xylo-phone, hymn, myth

In addition to these arbitrary substitutions, principally based on Latin practice in transliterating Greek, there are other conventions resulting from adopting Greek spellings but changing the pronunciation to accord with the English phonemic system. Thus, initial combinations like /pn, ps, pt, mn/ occur in Greek but not in English. When words involving them were borrowed, the first phoneme was simply ignored, but the grapheme representing it was preserved. The result is the occurrence in English words of "silent" graphemes like the ⟨p⟩ of *pneumonia, psychology,* and *pterodactyl,* and the ⟨m⟩ of *mnemonic.*

Other writing systems beside the Greek have contributed to the complexity of the English system, though not so extensively. Thus, ⟨ch⟩ for /š/, ⟨i⟩ for /iy/, ⟨ge⟩ for /ž/, ⟨gn⟩ for /n/, and ⟨ou⟩ for /uw/ are largely confined to words recently borrowed from French, such as *chemise, rouge,* and *champagne.* German ⟨sch⟩ for /š/ appears in borrowed terms like *schnauzer.* But it is in proper names that the greatest diversity of foreign spelling devices appears. We cannot enter into this large subject here, except to note that no amount of experience with the usual conventions of the English system will guide the uninitiated to the accepted pronunciations of American place-names like *Calais, Bryn Mawr, Sault Ste. Marie,* and *La Jolla.*

MORPHOGRAPHIC COMBINATIONS. We saw earlier in this chapter that a true **morphogram** is a single grapheme used to represent a morpheme (pp. 441–42). It may appear in any context where any allomorph of that morpheme may appear. It thus indicates nothing about the phonemic value of the allomorph it represents in any given context since it may represent any combination of phonemes that is an allomorph of the morpheme it stands for. Let us say, for instance, that $\langle \Sigma \rangle$ is a grapheme representing the English noun-plural morpheme, which we have earlier represented as {-es}. If $\langle \Sigma \rangle$ is to be a true morphogram, it must stand for {-es} wherever that morpheme appears. It thus can represent any of the five allomorphs of {-es}, which are /-s, -z, -ɨz, -ən, Ø/, as we saw in Chapter 4. We would thus revise our writing practice as follows:

Singular	Present Plural	New Plural
hat	hats	hatΣ
rug	rugs	rugΣ
house	houses	houseΣ
dish	dishes	dishΣ
match	matches	matchΣ
spy	spies	spyΣ
ox	oxen	oxΣ
sheep	sheep	sheepΣ
man	men	menΣ

The last column looks rather peculiar, and the reader's first reaction might be that it would be difficult to learn to read writing of this sort, since he would have to know the "correct pronunciation" of $\langle \Sigma \rangle$ after each word. But if he will consider the middle column, he will realize that he must have this knowledge with the present system too, at least for all the words in that column except the last three. He hardly stops to think that he pronounces the final $\langle s \rangle$ of *hats* as /s/, the final $\langle s \rangle$ of *rugs* as /z/, and the final $\langle s \rangle$ of *houses* as /ɨz/. In other words, the final $\langle s \rangle$ used in spelling English plural nouns represents an approach to morphemic writing, since it can represent all three of the regular allomorphs of {-*es*}. But it is not a true morphogram, since it cannot represent the irregular allomorphs /-ən, -∅/, and since the writing system sometimes requires the spelling ⟨es⟩ rather than plain ⟨s⟩, as in *matches*, *dishes*, and *spies*.

Let us consider another example. The following are three environments where the phonemic combination /spayz/ might occur:

(a) The dog /spayz/ his master.
(b) There are /spayz/ in the factory.
(c) He found a /spayz/ tracks.

These three are all identical phonemically but different morphemically. The first is the verb {*spy*₁} + the third-singular inflectional suffix {-*s*}. The second is the noun {*spy*₂} + the plural suffix {-*es*}. The third is the noun {*spy*₂} + the possessive suffix {-*'s*}. According to the conventions of the writing system, the first two are written alike, ⟨spies⟩, and the third is written ⟨spy's⟩. We may arrange the three ways of transcribing these words in a table, as follows:

Phonemic Transcription	Morphemic Transcription	Graphic Transcription
(a) /spayz/	{*spy*₁-*s*}	⟨spies⟩
(b) /spayz/	{*spy*₂-*es*}	⟨spies⟩
(c) /spayz/	{*spy*₂-*'s*}	⟨spy's⟩

It is plain from the table that the graphic system represents a sort of compromise between phonemic (or at least quasi-phonemic) writing and partially morphemic writing. That is, it uses the special combination ⟨'s⟩ to represent the possessive suffix, which is phonemically indistinguishable from {-*es*} and {-*s*}, not only in this one instance but in all occurrences of their regular allomorphs. Thus, the mark ⟨'⟩, the **apostrophe,** is here used as a grapheme of primarily morphemic significance; it tells the reader that he has to do with a possessive inflection. It has no phonemic reference whatsoever, and thus cannot be placed "by ear." That is one reason it is so trouble-some for many people to learn to put it in the conventional positions.

The English writing system shows a morphemic quality in another way. In our discussion of morphophonemics in Chapter 4, we noted the phenomenon of **gradation,** or change of vowel phonemes accom-panying change of stress (pp. 217–18). Some examples we cited were these:

Phonemic Spelling	Standard Spelling
məríyn : mǽrinər	marine : mariner
kəndówl : kándələns	condole : condolence
ədvǽntij : ǽdvəntéyjəs	advantage : advantageous

If we compare the two columns, it is apparent that the pairs of words in the right-hand, or standard spelling, column are much more alike than the pairs in the left-hand, or phonemic spelling, column. All that is done in the standard spelling is to indicate the addition of a derivational suffix by appending the graphemes ⟨r⟩, ⟨nce⟩, and ⟨ous⟩ respectively. There is no indication of the change of stress since the writing system has no means of indicating stress at all. Furthermore, there is no indication of the extensive vowel changes that accompany the addition of the suffix and the resulting shift of stress. Listening to the words spoken, or studying the phonemic transcriptions, we can tell that every single syllabic in the base forms is changed in the derived forms. Thus, in *marine* > *mariner*, $/ə/ > /æ/$ and $/iy/ > /i/$; in *condole* > *condolence*, $/ə/ > /a/$ and $/ow/ > /ə/$; and in *advantage* > *advantageous*, $/ə/ > /æ/$, $/æ/ > /ə/$, and $/i/ > /ey/$. These are radical changes. It is only because we are native speakers and native readers of long standing that we are able to take them for granted. To most of us, I am sure, it is the words in the phonemic column, with their accurate representation of altered pronunciations, which look peculiar. We are quite naturally prejudiced in favor of the standard spellings by our long familiarity with them.

When we approach this situation from the point of view of morphemics, some interesting things become apparent. Thus, we can analyze *mariner*, for instance, as consisting of two morphemes, the base {*marine*} and the derivational suffix {*-er*}. We further note that {*marine*} has two allomorphs, a free one, /məríyn/, and a bound one, /mǽrin-/. In the standard spelling system, however, both of these allomorphs are represented by ⟨marine⟩. In other words, this is a **morphographic combination** which stands for either of the allomorphs of {*marine*}, without regard to morphophonemic changes and thus cannot indicate clearly the phonemic makeup of the particular allomorph it stands for in any given context. It is up to the reader, as a native speaker of the language, to supply the appropriate pronunciation.

Studying the other examples, we may further note the following:

(a) /kən/ and /kán/, two allomorphs of the prefix {*con-*}, are both represented by the morphographic combination ⟨con⟩.

(b) /dówl/ and /dəl/, two allomorphs of the stem {*dole*}, are both represented by the morphographic combination ⟨dole⟩—that is unless we take the ⟨e⟩ of *condolence* to be part of the suffix, in which case /dəl/ is represented only by ⟨dol⟩.

(c) /ij/ and /éyj/, two allomorphs of the suffix {*-age*}, are both represented by the morphographic combination ⟨age⟩.

Countless other examples of morphographic combinations like these can be found. They account for a large proportion of the departures of the English writing system from its phonemic base, and render it a hybrid system of great complexity. We may state this in terms of a general principle which, while admitting many exceptions, is what governs and systematizes many of the apparent inconsistencies of our writing system: The English writing system tends to employ a single combination of graphemes to represent a given morpheme, disregarding for the most part all except the grossest phonemic differences between allomorphs.

As a consequence of this general principle, we may note two qualities of our writing system:

(1) The morphemic relationships between words are usually more apparent in the written form of the language than in speech;

(2) The pronunciations of words are not at all clearly represented in writing.

Three practical effects, among many others, of this use of morpho-graphic spelling are (1) that the writing system is virtually standard for all dialects; (2) that morphemically related words come closer together in standard dictionaries than they would in a phonemically transcribed wordlist; (3) that it is necessary in standard dictionaries to indicate the pronunciation or pronunciations of many words by some form of phonemic or quasi-phonemic respelling. Some further consequences, relating to the role of the teacher, will be touched on in Chapter 10, "Linguistics and the Teacher of English."

THE ROLE OF PUNCTUATION

So far our investigation of the writing system of English has dealt with the relationship of the alphabetic characters or letters of the writing system to the phonemes and morphemes of the spoken language. But this is only part of the story—the largest part, to be sure. There are additional elements in each of these systems which have not yet been accounted for. In the graphic system there are the eleven marks of punctuation and the various suprasegmental features of capitalization, italics, etc. (these last varying in number according to the kind of print or script being used). In the spoken system there are pauses of varying length, and the suprasegmental phonemes of pitch, stress, and juncture, which combine on the level of morphemics into superfixes, and on the level of grammar into intonation patterns.

Speaking broadly, we can say that these two are related to each other. That is, the primary role of punctuation is to supply in the written language some at least of the structural indications which are furnished in speech by pause, stress, and pitch. It does this, however, not by representing pause, stress, and pitch directly, but by means of an almost completely independent system for indicating grammatical structure. A person must be familiar with both systems if he is to transfer an utterance or bit of discourse from one to the other. That is, when he reads aloud, he first must grasp the syntax of the written material by means of the clues afforded by the punctuation and then pronounce the phonemes with the grouping, stresses, and pitch contours appropriate to that syntax in his dialect. When he writes, he must reverse this process. In effect, in both reading and writing he must translate from one system to another quite different one.

This process of translating from one system to the other is a rather complex one, which many literate persons never wholly master. Indeed, it takes a skilled actor or speaker to read written material aloud so that it sounds like natural speech. One of the reasons for this lies in the fact that the controlling syntactic elements of stress and pitch are *suprasegmental*—that is, they go on at the same time as the segmental phonemes, in a sort of counterpoint—while on the other hand the important syntactic indicators of punctuation, except for capitalization, are *segmental*—that is, they are given specific places in the linear stream of writing. Furthermore, they often are placed rather far from the point where some feature of stress or pitch which they call for must be introduced. Consider, for instance, the sentence:

he is coming here tomorrow

spoken as (a) a statement and (b) a question:

(a) /²hìyz ³kɔ́miŋ² hîhr²|²tə ³mɔ́row¹#/
(b) /²hìyz kɔ̂miŋ hìhr tə ¹mɔ́row¹‖/

Note that the first difference between the two is in the pitch of the first syllable of *coming*, and that the major distinction is toward the end, in the rising-falling sentence-final contour of the statement as contrasted with the falling-rising contour of the question. The written language indicates both these differences by the contrast between the final marks ⟨.⟩ and ⟨?⟩:

> (a) He is coming here tomorrow.
> (b) He is coming here tomorrow?

In reading (b), the eye of the reader must go ahead to the end of the sentence and translate the ⟨?⟩ found there into level pitch on *coming* and falling-rising pitch on *tomorrow*. We have all had the experience, when reading aloud, of not seeing a ⟨?⟩ in time, perhaps because it is over the page, and having to apologize and repeat the whole sentence from the beginning with revised intonation. At such times we can appreciate the value of the Spanish practice of putting an upside-down allograph of ⟨?⟩ at the beginning of the sentence. This would be a sound innovation in English practice, especially for those questions which are unmarked by interrogators or subject-verb inversion.

The marks of punctuation, and to a lesser extent the suprasegmental features, thus constitute a subsystem of the English writing system, replacing the suprasegmental features of speech. This is not the place to enter into a detailed account of the operation of that subsystem. Many such accounts are readily available, usually in the form of a set of prescriptive "rules of punctuation." In effect, such rules usually constitute generalizations, more or less objective, based on the practice of "native writers"—or, more accurately, editors and printers, since these professionals are accustomed to normalize the punctuation of material that passes through their hands. It is true that none of these sets of rules is based on a thoroughgoing understanding of the structure of the spoken language as we have described it in Chapters 2–7 of this book, and it is tempting to attempt to supply the deficiency. But space permits only some rather general observations about the functions and operation of the various marks.

In the first place, we may divide the eleven basic marks into four groups, on the basis of their distribution. These are:

> (1) two **morphological marks:** ⟨' -⟩
> (2) three **end marks:** ⟨. ? !⟩
> (3) four **internal marks:** ⟨, ; : —⟩
> (4) two **special marks:** ⟨" ()⟩

1. *The Apostrophe and Hyphen.* We have already seen that one function of the **apostrophe** is to mark the occurrence of the morpheme {-'s}, the inflectional suffix marking the possessive case of nouns, and thus to distinguish this morpheme from the usually homophonous {-es} and {-s}. It is thus a visual morphemic signal, with no direct correspondence to any segmental phoneme. In its other major use, however, it often indicates distinctions apparent to the ear. This use, as in forms like *can't*, *isn't*, and *don't*, is often described as "indicating the omission of one or more letters." This is an accurate account of its function in the graphic system, but says nothing about its relationship to the spoken language. From this point of view, its function is to indicate certain morphophonemic circumstances not ordinarily reproduced in the writing system, which tends, as we have seen (p. 468), to disregard the morphophonemic differences among allomorphs. This may be illustrated from the examples cited above. Thus, while ⟨cannot⟩ = /kǽnət, kənát/ (with dialectal variations), ⟨can't⟩ = /kǽnt, kǽhnt, kéhnt, kǽynt, káhnt/, etc. In effect, it indicates the /nt/ allomorph of {*not*}. In ⟨isn't⟩ = /ízənt, ízint/, on the other hand, the apostrophe indicates the /ənt/ or /int/ allomorph of {*not*}. In ⟨don't⟩, it indicates not only the /nt/ allomorph of {*not*}, but also a special allomorph /dow/ of the verb {*do*}, which appears only in this form. Forms like ⟨shan't⟩ and

⟨won't⟩ represent similar morphophonemic variants of {*shall not*} and {*will not*}.

The **hyphen,** ⟨-⟩, also functions on the morphemic level of structure. Its primary use is to indicate compound words; that is, to indicate the presence of a word-forming superfix, or to join together what may be separate words in speech but which the writer wishes to appear as a single word in writing. We have already noted the distinction between ⟨a man eating tiger⟩ and ⟨a man-eating tiger⟩ (p. 276). Here the hyphen indicates meaningful distinctions of stress and juncture.

The other use of the hyphen is a purely mechanical one, resulting from the practice of breaking up the ribbon of print into lines of equal length. Largely for aesthetic reasons, we like our lines of print to be **justified,** that is, to present an even right-hand margin. This is mostly accomplished by varying the size of the spaces, since spaces of any width above the minimum are all graphically equivalent and, hence, are in free variation. But sometimes it is felt desirable to break a word in two over the line-division. In such case, whether the break comes between morphemes or in the middle of a morpheme, it is marked by a hyphen. There are rather elaborate conventions governing this practice, usually called **syllabication.** They may be found in most handbooks of style or proofreader's guides.

2. *The End Marks.* The three end marks, ⟨.⟩ or **period,** ⟨?⟩ or **question mark** (sometimes called **interrogation point**), and ⟨!⟩ or **exclamation mark** (or **point**), serve primarily to mark the ends of sentences, as these units are understood in the written language. As we saw in the last chapter, the written sentence does not always correspond with the spoken one (see pp. 369–70). But on the whole these marks usually indicate a sentence-final intonation contour. They do not, however, say anything about what kind of contour. The following three sentences, for instance, are perfectly intelligible if spoken with exactly the same distribution of pitch and stress.

(a) ²hè gôt here this ³nóon¹#

(b) ²whàt hâppens ³nów¹#

(c) ²whàt a beâutiful ³dáy¹#

Yet in writing, each has a different end mark:

(a) He got here this noon.

(b) What happens now?

(c) What a beautiful day!

It is clear that the choice of end marks is based not on the intonation of the sentences directly, but on their classification on the basis of expected response (pp. 374–78). Thus, statements have ⟨.⟩, questions ⟨?⟩, and exclamations ⟨!⟩. The other three types—greetings, calls, and requests—may have either ⟨.⟩ or ⟨!⟩.

The end marks have certain other minor functions of an arbitrary sort. The period, for instance, is used in such combinations as ⟨Mr.⟩, ⟨Dr.⟩, ⟨Co.⟩, ⟨etc.⟩, usually called **abbreviations.** From the structural point of view these abbreviations could be called **logograms,** since they serve as unit-symbols for words. The period thus acts as a sort of diacritic to indicate that what precedes it is to be read as a logogram, not as a phonemic combination. It warns us to read ⟨pat. off.⟩, for instance, as /pǽtənt âfis/ rather than /pǽt óhf/. In some cases, of course, we often read the abbreviation phonemically or partially so, thus creating new morphemes. ⟨p.m.⟩, for instance, which may be read logographically as *after noon*, is usually read /píy+êm/ or /píyèm/, which thus becomes a word in the spoken language.

3. *The Internal Marks.* The elaborate conventions governing the use of the four internal marks, ⟨,⟩ **comma,** ⟨;⟩ **semicolon,** ⟨:⟩ **colon,** and ⟨—⟩ **dash,** need not concern us here. But speaking generally, we may observe that these marks always appear in the interior of written sentences, and usually fall at points where pauses come in speech, though by no means all pauses are marked in this way. The

actual function of these marks is to give certain indications of the division of written material into immediate constituents. In performing this function, they substitute for the subtle devices of juncture, pitch, and stress which indicate constituent-division in speech. As with the end marks, the reader or writer must be familiar with both systems and be able to translate back and forth from one to the other.

It is important to realize that all four of these marks, especially the semicolon and colon, may mark points where a sentence-final intonation contour is natural in speech (see p. 415). If the punctuation system were keyed directly to the speech system, this would presumably not be so: all sentence-final contours would be marked by appropriate end marks, while lesser pauses, marking the junction-points of various grammatical constituents, would be marked by appropriate internal marks. Since this is not so, the writer cannot rely wholly on his "ear"—that is, his recognition of the suprasegmental features of speech—to guide him in punctuation. If he does, he will very likely violate the conventions of punctuation by writing what the handbooks call "sentence fragments," "run-on sentences," and "comma splices." These errors, often classed as grammatical, usually result from a failure to understand that the punctuation system as it now stands is to a large degree independent of the intonation system, and hence that it is not always safe to punctuate "by ear."

The ear may, however, sometimes be a helpful guide in punctuation. Consider, for instance, the distinction between the so-called **restrictive** and **nonrestrictive** modifying clauses. This is a distinction resulting from two kinds of structural meaning conveyed by the structural device of modification. It may be roughly described by saying that the restrictive modifier *identifies* or *limits* the meaning of the head, whereas the nonrestrictive modifier *supplies more information* about it. The conventions of punctuation require that the nonrestrictive clause be separated from its head and from the rest of the sentence by commas, and that the restrictive clause be left unpunctuated. Thus, in the following two almost identical sentences,

    (a) Politicians, who are crooked, should be put out of office.
    (b) Politicians who are crooked should be put out of office.

(a) states that all politicians are crooked and should be put out of office, while (b) states that only crooked politicians should be put out of office and thus implies that there are other politicians, not crooked, who should be left in office. In speech this distinction is clearly signaled by pitch and juncture:

    (a) ^{2}pòli^{3}tícians^2 | ^{2}whò are ^{3}cróoked^2 | ^{2}should be pût òut of ^{3}óffice^1 #
    (b) ^{2}pòlitîcians whò are ^{3}cróoked^2 | ^{2}should be pût oùt of ^{3}óffice^1 #

It is plain that the /3 2/ pitch contour on -ticians followed by single-bar juncture in (a) is a reliable indicator of the comma at this point. But it should also be noted that while the second single-bar in (a), after *crooked*, also is marked by a comma in writing, the one after *crooked* in (b) is not so marked, although it indicates the division of the sentence into its two immediate constituents, subject and predicate. Those who rely upon the ear as a guide to punctuation would probably put commas at both pauses in (a), which would be correct, and a comma at the pause in (b), which would be incorrect. The ear, then, is at best an unreliable guide to the placing of internal marks.

The Special Marks. The special marks ⟨"⟩ or **quotation mark** and ⟨()⟩ or **parenthesis** have been put into a group by themselves because they usually mark distinctions in writing or print that have no counterpart in speech. Each of them has two allographs, the initial " and (and the final " and), and they always appear in pairs. They are customarily used to surround material which is to be considered as in some way distinct from that in which it is imbedded. Natural speech affords no way of making similar distinctions. It is true that exceedingly skilful speakers, by using special devices of pitch together with special vocal qualifiers (see p. 53), can make hearers realize that certain passages are quoted or parenthetical material. But this goes beyond the linguistic field into the area of individual art and style. Most of us fall back upon the clumsy device of saying "quote" and "end of quote" or "parenthesis" and "end of parenthesis" when we encounter these marks in written material we are reading aloud. The same is true of other graphemes used in special types of material, such as the [, {, and ⟨ which we have used constantly in this book. Where these are concerned, the written language is capable of effects not possible in speech.

THE SUPRASEGMENTAL FEATURES. All forms of English writing and print make use of at least two types of letters, capitals and lower case. In the kind of analysis we have made in this chapter, we consider these as suprasegmental features, added to the basic segmental graphemes. We treat A, for instance, as an allograph of ⟨a⟩, representing the combination of ⟨a⟩ with the suprasegmental grapheme of capitalization, ⟨═⟩. This in turn permits us to treat two expressions like

TODAY IS A HOLIDAY
today is a holiday

as "the same" in their segmental graphemes, and hence in their linguistic reference, though actually only a few of the letters have the same shape in both versions.

From the point of view of communication, the suprasegmental feature of capitalization is much less important than the segmental letters and marks. Material written wholly in lower case is usually quite intelligible, though rather odd looking, as any reader of the poems of e. e. cummings can testify. This is because the functions performed by capitalization are mostly redundant; that is, the capitals simply duplicate a signal already given in some other way.

This is particularly true of the capital which begins a sentence, since the sentence division has already been indicated by an end mark. Likewise, the special groups of nouns and adjectives called **proper** are usually marked in other ways as well, so that they can be readily identified without benefit of capitals, as they are in speech. No one can hear the difference between *East River* and *east river*, but we can almost always tell which is being used in a given utterance. Therefore, the capitals used to identify the proper name in writing are redundant. But in spite of this redundancy, the conventions governing the use of capitals are both complex and rigid, so that a writer must spend considerable time learning them.

The other suprasegmental features in common use are *italics* and SMALL CAPS. Borrowing from the conventions of proofreading, these can be identified by ⟨—⟩ and ⟨＿⟩, or single and double underlining. The uses of these are various, and to some degree optional with the writer. Both of these may be used, together with capitals, as written counterparts of unusually strong or shifted stress, as in

> I want *him* to do it, not you.
> He spoke *louder* and LOUDER and LOUDER.

There are, of course, other suprasegmental features beside these four, such as *boldface*. In this book we have used italics for cited words and phrases and for special emphasis, and boldface to indicate technical terms.

In conclusion it may be affirmed that structural analysis corroborates what we knew already—that the English writing system is highly complex and frequently inconsistent. It could undoubtedly be improved in many ways. But this analysis further indicates that our writing system is a structure of quite remarkable checks and balances, which interact in very complicated ways. This in turn should lead us to the conclusion that mere tinkering with the system may simply upset some of its adjustments without really improving the whole—something like treating tuberculosis with aspirin. To respell *night* as *nite*, for instance, simply substitutes one morphographic combination for another, without improving the phonemic reference of the spelling. Real improvement of the system must await thoroughgoing analysis, along the lines of the discussion in this chapter, but much more thorough. When such an analysis is available, it will be possible to weigh the consequences of proposed detailed changes to the operation of the whole system. Until then, most proposed reforms of the English writing system would do more harm than good.

COLLATERAL READING, CHAPTER 8
Books previously listed are cited by author only.

Gleason. Chap. xxi, "Writing Systems," pp. 301–17; chap. xxii, "Written Languages," pp. 318–32.

Bloomfield. Chap. xvii, "Written Records," pp. 281–96.

Sturtevant. Chap. iii, "The Relation of Writing to Speech," pp. 19–29.

Gelb, I. J. *A Study of Writing*. Chicago: University of Chicago Press, 1952. Chap. i, "Writing as a System of Signs," pp. 1–23; chap. v, "The Alphabet," pp. 166–89.

Robertson, Stuart. *The Development of Modern English*, 2d ed. (rev. by Frederic G. Cassidy). New York: Prentice-Hall, Inc, 1954. From chap. i, "Writing," pp. 9–14; from chap. xi, "Spelling Today," pp. 353–73.

Summey, George, Jr. *American Punctuation*. New York: The Ronald Press Co., 1949. Chap. i, "General Considerations," pp. 3–14.

Chapter *9*

The Dialects of American English*

DIALECT DIFFERENCES AND THEIR CAUSES

To this point we have been dealing with the structure of American English as if there were only one variety, that of the author. This is a form of fictitious assumption familiar to one who has examined any of the sciences: starting with a special case in order to make a simpler, though no less sound, statement of principles upon which the science depends. Thus, in physics, for example, all the basic formulas for acceleration and velocity assume the absence of friction, although the retarding effects of friction are obvious in any real situation. Similarly, to this point we have dealt with the relatively uniform structure of American English, from phonetics through phonemics and morphemics to syntax, and now turn to the details in which the speech of some Americans differs from that of others. It is perhaps appropriate that the writer of this chapter speaks a variety of American English which differs in many respects from that spoken by the author of the rest of the book.

The idea of a dialect has been previously presented, in its essential features, in Chapter 1 (pp. 42–49): a variety of a language, regional or social, set off (more or less sharply) from other varieties by (more or less clear) features of pronunciation, grammar, or vocabulary.

* By Raven I. McDavid, Jr.

It is often a debatable point as to where one should draw the line between dialect differences and language differences. For instance, Bloomfield[1] shows that Dutch-German actually constitutes one language, with many different local varieties, three of which—Standard High German, Standard Dutch, and Standard Flemish—are recognized as literary and political languages. On the other hand, what are popularly known as "Chinese dialects"—Peipingese, Wu or Shanghai, Fukienese, and Cantonese—are really sharply different languages, though the differences are disguised by their common use of a mutually intelligible morphographic writing system. Similarly, the attitude toward locally differentiated dialects—the kind we are most familiar with—differs widely from language to language.[2] In England (though not in Scotland) and in France, the speaker of the standard language is likely to look upon a dialect as a form of the language one had rather be found dead than speaking, and tries to suppress all purely local speech characteristics he may have grown up with, while in Germany and Austria, especially the Tyrol, the educated speaker is proud of his local origins and often goes out of the way to introduce peculiarly local expressions into a formal utterance. Americans are somewhere in between. Thus, a few speakers strive painfully, but rarely with complete success, to suppress their native speech-forms in favor of those in a dialect of real or imaginary superior social status.[3] On the other hand, at least a part of the success of such political leaders as the late Huey Long and Eugene Talmadge was derived from their ability to discard, when they wished, the grammatical forms of the standard English they could use effectively, and to address a rural audience naturally in the common speech of Louisiana or Georgia.

[1] *Language* (New York: Henry Holt & Co., Inc., 1933), pp. 481–83; see also pp. 44–45, 328–31.

[2] See Eugen Dieth, "A New Survey of English Dialects," *Essays and Studies* by Members of the English Association, XXXII (1946), 74.

[3] See R. I. McDavid, Jr., "Dialect Geography and Social Science Problems," *Social Forces*, XXV (1946–47), 168–72.

To those familiar with the situation in European countries, such as France or Italy or even England, dialect differences in American English are relatively small. Most of the time, any native speaker of any variety of American English can understand a native speaker of any other variety. Furthermore, nearly all these dialects can be fitted comfortably into an over-all framework, such as the analysis presented in Chapter 3 of this book.[4] Nevertheless, every speaker of American English knows that other varieties exist, different from the one he speaks; empirically he has learned to distinguish several of these varieties, sometimes with amazing precision and accuracy. An experienced observer, like Henry Lee Smith, Jr., can often place a speaker within a hundred miles of his home.

Those who have observed dialect differences are often curious as to their origin, and have invented many fanciful explanations. The two most common explanations of this kind are the physiological and the climatic. Certain people whose speech we find objectionably different from our own may be credited with a constitutional malformation of the vocal organs that prevents them from pronouncing the language "normally" (i.e., the way we do). Thus, the American Negro is sometimes supposed to be unable to pronounce a constricted postvocalic /-r/ because his lips are too thick, although what the lips have to do with the constriction or nonconstriction of /-r/ is a mystery to even the most elementary student of articulatory phonetics. More popularly, the "Southerner" is supposed to speak with a drawl (the coastal South Carolinian doesn't!) because the

---

[4] This analysis is fundamentally that of Trager and Smith in their *Outline of English Structure* (Norman: Battenburg Press, 1951). For discussion of some of its weak points as an over-all frame for all American English dialects, see the review by James Sledd in *Language*, XXXI (1955), 312–45. Particularly in many Southern and South Midland dialects, the lower low-front [a] and the lower low-central [ɑ] contrast with each other as well as with /æ/ and /ɔ/, thus making a tenth vowel phoneme necessary. For many of these dialects, and for British dialects as well, it is necessary to posit five semivowels, since length and a centering offglide often contrast.

climate is so hot that it makes him lazy, although Bengali, in a far hotter climate, is spoken at an extremely rapid tempo. A professor of pedagogics at the University of Colorado once declared that Minnesotans nasalize their speech because of the damp climate; Eric Partridge has repeatedly attributed the supposed nasalization of Australian speech to the excessively dry climate. When so many claims, often contradictory and often in complete disagreement with observable fact, are made for the influence of the climate, it is easy to see that the investigator must look elsewhere for the origins of dialect differences. He finds these origins in the relationships among people—in the homes from which they originally came and in the social environment in which they now live.

We are here on surer ground, where our hypotheses can be tested against observable facts of human history. Instead of a simple speculation, which may or may not be true and can never be proved one way or the other, we have a hypothesis which may be checked against older records of settlement, migrations, trade, education, and cleavages in the local culture-patterns. After many hypotheses have been tested, we discover that dialect differences may be explained by the following forces. Occasionally the explanation is simple, attributable to a single force; oftener—since there are no "pure dialects" and probably never have been any—it is more complex, to be explained only by a combination of forces.

1. Any large or influential element in the early population of an area can be expected to contribute materially to the speech of that area, whether in pronunciation, grammar, or vocabulary. To those aware that western Pennsylvania was originally settled in large measure from the Scots Presbyterian counties of northern Ireland, it is not surprising that one can find Ulster Scots features in western Pennsylvania speech.

2. Migrations will carry dialects along their routes. Contrasting forms of Pennsylvania and New York speech have spread across the Great Lakes States in two bands, which show far less overlapping than

the mobility of the American population would lead us to expect.

3. Old political and ecclesiastical boundaries, dating from times when population movements were more restricted than now, may have brought about dialect divisions. Such boundaries often underlie speech differences in Germany (pre-Napoleonic principalities) or England (diocesan boundaries, relatively unchanged since the Middle Ages). In North America, where political boundaries are much younger and do little to restrict population movements, what little effect they have on dialect seems chiefly on the currency of political terms. The South Carolina (and normal U.S.) *county seat* is often the *county site* in Georgia. The chief officer of a township, the *supervisor* in New York State, is the *reeve* in Ontario; in Ontario the chief county official is the *warden*, without a counterpart in the United States.[5]

4. Physical geography, though often overrated as an influence, is nevertheless important. A marsh may hinder communication between settlements, as in the coastal South. A desert will restrict the size or permanence of communities. A mountain range is rarely an absolute barrier, but the passes will determine the routes of migration and communication.

5. A cultural center, for whatever reason its culture is important, will exert an influence on less important communities. "Standard English," particularly the variety emulated in the British Isles, is basically the upper-class speech of the London area, which became a model to imitate when London became not only the capital of England and the residence of the court but the center of trade as well. The relationship of Chaucer to the rise of London English is often misstated; he did not give it status as a standard language, but would likely have written in it even if he had not been a native Londoner (as did a Yorkshireman like Wyclif) because the economic prestige of London had already made its speech the standard. A

---

[5] See R. I. McDavid, Jr., "Midland and Canadian Words in Upstate New York," *American Speech*, XXVI (1951), 245–56.

complex of similar forces operated to make the dialects of Paris and Florence, respectively, the basis of standard French and standard Italian. Although we have no single city dominating American economic and social life the way Paris and London dominate France and England, and though speakers outside of the tributary areas often mock the speech of a city like Boston or Charleston, yet one may detect in the speech of adjacent small-town and rural areas greater or less influence of such cities as Boston, New York, Philadelphia, Richmond, and Charleston—and probably also of San Francisco, St. Louis, and New Orleans.

6. The dialect of an area may reflect its social structure. Are its class distinctions relatively rigid, or relatively flexible? Are educational opportunities open to all, or are they restricted to a favored group? And, even if education is a fairly general advantage, do rich and poor, old families and newcomers, all attend the same kinds of schools?

7. Finally, the dialect may reflect the presence of a large body of new immigrants with a different linguistic and cultural background from that of the older inhabitants. Cultural innovations will lead to innovations in the vocabulary, whether by direct borrowing or by **loan translation.** If the foreign group is relatively large and homogeneous, it may carry over its habits of pronunciation and grammar into English; or the way in which it approaches English may affect the linguistic attitudes of the whole community.

THE STUDY OF LINGUISTIC GEOGRAPHY

The branch of linguistics that deals with the differences within a language area is called **linguistic geography,** or, sometimes, **dialectology.** As with any other branch of linguistics, or of any other scientific investigation, it has developed its techniques over a period of years, with each new project exploiting the advances made by its predecessors and profiting by their mistakes. There are several important projects today which involve the investigation of dialect differences in American English, but we shall spend most of our time upon the project of the *Linguistic Atlas of the United States and Canada* (a group, actually, of several regional atlases) because it has dealt with more aspects of American English than any of the others, and at present has covered about two-thirds of the country in greater or less detail.[6]

The principle upon which all linguistic geography is built is the simple one of observing differences in grammar, pronunciation, and vocabulary, determining the regional and social distribution of these differences, and seeking their historical and cultural explanations. It is a fascinating game which amateurs can play without any formal training in linguistics; it is always a good topic of conversation at a party, and in the hands of an expert like Henry Lee Smith, Jr., it has provided popular radio entertainment on a national scale. After all, since one's speech is the most intimate aspect of one's behavior, the most automatic and least susceptible to conscious alteration, even small children will notice a strange pattern of pronunciation. Farmers in upstate New York identify Pennsylvanians by the farewell "Come back" or "Come back again!" where New York Staters would normally say "Come again!"; and high-school students in the Carolina Piedmont have no difficulty in identifying eastern Virginians by their pronunciation of *out* and *night*, or Charlestonians by *boat* and *date*. What the linguistic geographer does is simply to replace these random empirical obser-

---

[6] C. K. Thomas of Cornell University has made a very extensive survey, using principally informants of college age and a restricted list of pronunciation items in a read text. His conclusions generally support those of the Atlas survey so far as the major dialect areas are concerned; Thomas' investigation is particularly useful for the light it sheds on the recent effects of urbanization. See his *An Introduction to the Phonetics of American English* (2d ed.; New York: The Ronald Press Co., 1958), pp. 191–252.

Henry Lee Smith, Jr., with still another set of criteria, has developed his own analysis of dialect areas. Although he has not yet published his findings, his oral reports suggest substantial agreement with the areas delineated by Thomas and by the Atlas project.

vations by systematic ones, using a larger frame of reference and a larger body of detail.

Modern linguistic geography began in 1876, when Georg Wenker inaugurated the *Deutscher Sprachatlas*. Wenker asked the village schoolmasters of Germany to translate a prepared list of forty sentences into their local dialects. He finally received 44,251 responses from 40,376 villages, which still remains the finest network ever drawn for a dialect survey. It had shortcomings, however, chiefly arising from the method of collecting material, since the schoolmasters varied considerably in their skill as observers and recorders. This was corrected in the next great linguistic atlas, Jules Gilliéron's *Atlas linguistique de la France* (1902–1910). Gilliéron used a single trained field-worker, who interviewed representative informants in six hundred French communities, using a questionnaire of two thousand items. Yet another advance was made by the Swiss scholars Jaberg and Jud in their *Sprach- und Sachatlas Italiens und der Südschweiz* (1925–1940), when they included urban as well as rural speech in their survey of Italy and southern Switzerland.

While linguistic geography was being developed in Germany, France, and elsewhere on the Continent, relatively little was being done in England to provide a model and foundation for the investigation of American dialects. The two major studies of British dialects—the fifth volume of A. J. Ellis's *On Early English Pronunciation* (1889), and the *English Dialect Dictionary* (1895–1905) and *English Dialect Grammar* (1905) of Joseph Wright—relied heavily on volunteer helpers, often with little training, and were sporadic in their coverage of particular items. These faults are not surprising, considering the time when Ellis and Wright worked. But in spite of their inaccuracies and early date, the works of Ellis and Wright held the field until after World War II, when surveys of England (under Harold Orton of Leeds and Eugen Dieth of Zurich) and of Scotland (under Angus McIntosh and Kenneth Jackson of Edinburgh) were undertaken. The completion of these two projects will supply an invaluable foundation for future American dialect study.

Early dialect investigations in the United States were more or less eclectic and of varying quality, with casual wordlists appearing alongside such serious studies as O. F. Emerson's *The Ithaca Dialect* (1891). From its inception in 1889, the American Dialect Society has aimed at the compilation of an American dialect dictionary, comparable to Wright's, an aim that is still far from being realized. With the appearance of the German, French, and Italian atlases, however, it became apparent that a linguistic atlas of the United States and Canada was not only more feasible as an immediate objective, but would actually simplify the work of the proposed dialect dictionary by delineating the areas to which lexical investigators should devote the greatest amount of time. Accordingly, the Linguistic Atlas project was established in 1930, under the sponsorship of the American Council of Learned Societies and the general direction of Hans Kurath, first of Brown and later of the University of Michigan. Kurath himself has assumed responsibility for the Atlantic Seaboard, the area of original settlement. Associated with Kurath's project but constituting autonomous projects in their own right are the regional Atlases of the North-Central States, the Upper Midwest, the Rocky Mountain States, and the Pacific Coast, with some preliminary work under way in other areas (see Map 1, page 579).

The principles upon which the American Linguistic Atlas project is being conducted are derivative from the experience of its European predecessors. Furthermore, they take into account such typical American cultural phenomena as geographical and social mobility, the immigration of foreign-language groups, and the lack of any single prestigious form of speech that may be considered a national standard. More than any of the preceding atlases, it attempts to indicate the spreading of innovations from cultural centers as well as the preservation of relics in isolated areas. Its principles, in brief, are as follows.

In each region a network of communities is selected for detailed investigation. The selection is based upon a study of the economic and cultural history of the region. Besides the obvious need to pick communities at relatively even intervals yet reflecting the population density, various other reasons influence the selection. Some communities are chosen because they were early permanent settlements; some because they were important stations on routes of migration and trade; some because they have become, or always have been, important economically or culturally; some because they have sharply declined from their former grandeur, or have always been relatively isolated, so that old-fashioned forms might be easily preserved; some because they have been or still are foreign-language or bilingual communities; some because they were originally highly homogeneous settlements from England, the Continent, or an older American community. In New England, the "community" is usually considered a township; elsewhere in the United States, a county or part of a county. Along the New England coast, the communities were about fifteen miles apart; elsewhere along the Atlantic Seaboard, nearly every coastal county was investigated along with most of the older counties within a hundred miles of the coast. In the Great Lakes area, the communities are somewhat less numerous—about twenty-five per state.

2. A trained investigator, operating in the field, is responsible for the collection of data. His training includes a general background in linguistics, intensive work in phonetics and phonemics (especially with the Atlas system of notation), some understanding of the history and culture of the region in which he is working, and an ability to work patiently with all kinds of people. It is expected that a field-worker will improve as he acquires experience. Rarely are the American field-workers content to be merely skilled transcribers; practically all have done important analytical work of their own, often in other fields of linguistics. And despite the popular appeal of Professor Higgins in Shaw's *Pygmalion*, the qualities of a successful field-worker are less occult—the pedestrian virtues of sound training, constant practice, and hard-headed willingness to trust his

own judgment and hearing rather than record what previous theories have led him to expect to hear.

3. Data is collected by means of a questionnaire, whose items are designed to provide comparable data on questions of pronunciation (*roof*), grammar (*climbed, clim, clum,* etc., as preterit of *climb*), or vocabulary (names for the *dragonfly* or *earthworm*). In making a choice as to what items to include, the staff of the Atlas followed three principles: (a) items should be familiar to most of the people in the area under investigation; (b) they should be relatively easy to introduce into a conversational situation; (c) they should be known or suspected to have regional or social variants. Even with these precautions, it has not been possible to use a single uniform questionnaire throughout the English-speaking area of North America. For one thing, a number of items of climate, flora, fauna, produce, or culture are regionally restricted—very productive in one part of the continent, yet known in other parts only by hearsay or by commercial names. Some such items are rail fences, stone fences, coasting, chipmunks, peanuts, doughnuts, and crackling bread. For another, an item investigated for pronunciation in one region may turn out to have lexical variants in other regions. Thus, in New England *goal* was used in the context "place to which players run in children's tag games" in order to elicit the pronunciations /gowl, guwl, gul/, but outside the New England area the normal response for this context is *base, bye, home, den,* or *hunk,* so that some other means must be found to elicit the pronunciation of *goal.* As to length, the questionnaires used along the Atlantic Seaboard include about 800–850 items, while the "short worksheets" used in other regions start with a basic 520 items and range up to 700, the total depending on the extent to which items of particular regional interest have been added. With a skilled field-worker and willing informant, these questionnaires can be covered in an interview of four to seven hours.

It is obvious that the questionnaire for such an Atlas does not contain enough material to satisfy either the structural analyst, who may miss some of the items crucial for his minimum phonemic contrasts, or the student of local folk-culture, who does not see enough attention paid to such of his special interests as thieves' cant or hard-rock mining. Theoretically, to be sure, it would be desirable to ask for everything that anybody might conceivably be interested in; practically, investigators are limited not only by the time and funds at their disposal, but also by the time and interest of their informants. The special occupational vocabulary of, say, the shrimp fisherman or the sheepherder is often not known to the average citizen of his community. And some of the minimal pairs on which structural phonemic contrasts may depend, such as /glɔs/ "translation" and /glɔhs/ "sheen" are not only unfamiliar to many speakers but very difficult to get unequivocally in a conversational situation. The staff of the American Linguistic Atlas have repeatedly stated that a linguistic atlas does not and cannot attempt to answer all the questions about dialect differences, but that its principal purpose is to provide a framework of territorial distribution and historical perspective within which further questions may be asked most intelligently. The fact that two branches of a science use different techniques does not render either of them invalid; each may serve to check upon the other. Thus, the structural analysis, the study of geographical and social distribution, and the intense investigation of the vocabulary are all equally legitimate parts of the study of language.

4. The investigator consults representative informants, natives of the community under examination and representative of particular social groups within that community. From the outset it was apparent that the investigation of American dialects could not be adequately conducted if only the oldest and least educated groups were interviewed. Unlike the situation in many European countries, where a "dialect" is clearly differentiated from educated speech, there is no hard and fast line in American English between folk speech and cultured speech. Besides, the cultured speech itself has

regional differences. Furthermore, between folk speech and cultured speech there is a vast body of common speech, sometimes closer to the folk speech, sometimes to the cultured. Little had been written about this common speech, so far as American English was concerned;[7] and in none of the previous linguistic atlases had it been considered. Accordingly, investigators for the American Atlas have normally interviewed at least two informants in every community. Ideally, one of these informants has been of the oldest living native generation, with a minimum of formal schooling, travel, and reading; the other middle-aged, with something like a high-school education and relatively more contact with the outside world. In addition, cultured informants have been interviewed in about a fifth of the communities investigated, and more than one of them in most of the important cultural centers. In some communities, one of the informants (generally the older) represents the "native American" stock, the other (though himself a native speaker of English) a large foreign-language group that has contributed heavily to the early population of the community. Thus, the American Atlas seeks to record data illustrating social differences, the dimension of time, and the process of language and dialect mixture that has been going on everywhere since the New World was settled. The cultured informants interviewed have supplied the largest available body of comparable data on standard English. To be sure, the coverage of no community is exhaustive, but the framework is at hand for more intensive investigations.

5. The basic data for the American Atlas is recorded impressionistically, on the spot, in a finely graded phonetic alphabet. Phonemic contrasts are observed and often deliberately sought during the interview, but the notation is phonetic. Admittedly, it is sometimes difficult to convert from Atlas phonetics to a phonemic notation like that presented in Chapter 3 of this book; nevertheless, for the pur-

---

[7] The nearest approach to such a treatment was the chapter on "The Common Speech" in the various editions of H. L. Mencken's *The American Language*.

poses of linguistic geography, impressionistic phonetics are more practical.

It is obvious, of course, that there will be differences between field-workers in the way they handle such a finely graded phonetic system as the alphabet for the American Atlas.[8] Differences are greater, of course, when the field workers have no training in common; much less if they have worked closely together over a period of time. There is, in fact, a remarkable degree of correlation between the transcriptions of field-workers who have had the same kind of training. Consequently, one may feel considerable confidence in the transcriptions of any experienced field-worker, at least so far as the vowels and consonants are concerned. Since most of the interview is concerned with single words and short phrases, the Atlas does not provide very much evidence about prosodic features of stress, pitch, and juncture. To elicit and preserve these phenomena, the investigator needs a different type of questionnaire and the permanent records now provided by the tape recorder.

Actually, the Linguistic Atlas project was launched and much of the interviewing done before the days of either general rural electrification or portable recording apparatus. It is often felt, with some justification, that tape recordings would facilitate more accurate phonetic recording than is possible with the unaided ear of the field-worker operating on the spot. Yet the best tape recording does not provide as accurate evidence as the unaided ear for consonant quality; and transcription from a raw tape is a very slow and painful process. Moreover, in their desire to get fine phonetic data for their recordings, some field-workers dependent on tapes have neglected to probe adequately for grammar or lexicon, or to allow the informant time for free conversation from which his unguarded use of grammatical forms may be ascertained. As an aid to an experienced field-worker

[8] For some of the problems involved, see Kurath, *et al.*, *Handbook of the Linguistic Geography of New England* (Providence, 1939), chap. iv, "The Phonetic Alphabet and Other Symbols Used on the Maps," pp. 123–46, *passim*.

who makes his preliminary transcription as he goes along, the tape recorder can be extremely useful; but it is no substitute for the field-worker's own impressionistic transcriptions.[9]

6. Finally, the interview is conducted in a conversational situation —or as near to a conversational situation as is possible—so that the informant will be using his normal patterns of stress and intonation and will not be too cautious about avoiding forms he thinks are "incorrect." Free conversation is usually encouraged, especially as a source of the grammatical items.

PROGRESS OF THE AMERICAN LINGUISTIC ATLAS

In the twenty-five years that have elapsed since the *Linguistic Atlas of the United States and Canada* was inaugurated, field investigators have conducted nearly three thousand interviews. Since various parts of the project have proceeded at different rates, it might be well to examine the state of each section in 1956 (see Map 1).

The Linguistic Atlas of New England was the first part of the program to be undertaken, and is the only part to be edited and published so far. Field work was begun in 1931 and completed in 1933, with editing following immediately. The first volume and the *Handbook* were published in 1939, and publication was completed in 1943. The Atlas itself follows the practice of the French and Italian atlases of reproducing the phonetic data, lithoprinted, on

---

[9] In 1933–34, Miles L. Hanley made several hundred phonograph records of continuous discourse, from informants interviewed for the New England Atlas. These records have been indexed and transcribed and are on file at the Atlas office in Ann Arbor.

The *Linguistic Atlas of the Upper Midwest* introduced the practice of systematically recording on tape a sample of connected discourse from every informant, to provide a check on the transcription practices of the field-worker. Investigators for the Rocky Mountain Atlas have followed the same practice, at least in Colorado.

In Indiana, in Washington, and in Wilson's Nova Scotia investigations, the complete field records have been made on tape, with transcription made at a later date.

base-maps. The maps are arranged according to semantic associations, roughly following the plan of the questionnaire, except that maps presenting grammatical data are grouped together in the second part of the third volume. The *Handbook* contains the apparatus needed for interpreting the Atlas—methodology, phonetic alphabet, questionnaire, and sketches of communities and informants—along with a tentative sketch of dialect areas, a survey of settlement history, and bibliographies of linguistic geography and New England history.

The next areas to be investigated were the Middle and South Atlantic States, originally planned as two separate regional atlases on the New England model, but now apparently combined into one project for eventual editing and publication. Field work was begun in 1933 by Guy S. Lowman, Jr., principal field-worker in New England. Upon his death, in 1941, he was succeeded by R. I. McDavid, Jr., who—after the interlude of World War II—finished the field work in 1949. Collections have been assembled at the University of Michigan. Some pre-editing has been done, but final editing and publication have been postponed until funds are available. It is certain, however, that the format will not be the same as that for New England: the costly method of hand-lettered lithoprinting on base-maps. Instead, the data will likely be presented less expensively by photo-offset from typescript, in tabular form, which experience suggests is not only cheaper but also handier for actual charting of individual items.

Pending publication of this Atlas, its significance has been shown not only by frequent articles and reviews, but also by two summary volumes: Kurath's *Word Geography of the Eastern United States* (Ann Arbor, 1949) and E. Bagby Atwood's *Survey of Verb Forms in the Eastern United States* (Ann Arbor, 1953). A third volume, Kurath and McDavid's *The Pronunciation of English in the Eastern United States*, is nearing publication.

The *Linguistic Atlas of the North-Central States*, under the direction of Albert H. Marckwardt of the University of Michigan, began in 1938 as an experimental wide-meshed survey to determine whether it would be worthwhile to conduct an Atlas investigation in the area presumed to be the seat of the allegedly uniform "General American" dialect. Upon the discovery that regional differences did exist in this territory, plans were drawn up for a regional survey, but only Wisconsin was completed before World War II—by Frederic G. Cassidy, one of the participants in the original survey. In 1948, field work was resumed, and with support from various local institutions it was pressed to completion by 1956, chiefly by McDavid, Cassidy, and A. L. Davis. The collections—now including data from Wisconsin, Michigan, southwestern Ontario, Illinois, Indiana, Kentucky, and Ohio—have been assembled at the University of Michigan, where pre-editing has begun. Plans for publication include a preliminary volume analogous to Kurath's *Word Geography*.

In 1947, Harold B. Allen of the University of Minnesota, one of the original field-workers in the North-Central area, began the *Linguistic Atlas of the Upper Midwest*. The last field records were completed în 1957, more than half by Allen himself, in an area including Minnesota, Iowa, the Dakotas, and Nebraska. In addition, Allen has assembled a file of more than a thousand vocabulary check lists. Preliminary editing has been under way for some time. Meanwhile, Mrs. Virginia McDavid has completed a dissertation on *A Survey of Verb Forms in the North-Central States and the Upper Midwest* (Minnesota, 1956), on the model of Atwood's study.

In 1950, work began in the Rocky Mountain area, with Professor Marjorie Kimmerle of the University of Colorado as director and T. M. Pearce of the University of New Mexico as associate director. Because of the greater distances and less certain financial support, work has been even spottier in this area than in most other places. In addition to check-list collections, field work has been completed for Colorado (mostly by Miss Kimmerle) and Utah, more than two-thirds completed for Arizona, an indeterminate amount for New Mexico, and a few scattered interviews for Montana. Presumably the data from each state will be separately published.

Work on the Pacific Coast, though late in beginning, has progressed very rapidly, since several experienced field-workers are available and at least two institutions have provided generous research grants. Codirectors of the project are David Reed of California and Carroll Reed of Washington, with John Moncur of U.C.L.A. and David DeCamp of Washington State as associate directors. About two thirds of the field work and a greater proportion of the check-list collection are complete, in an area embracing Washington, Oregon, California, Idaho, Nevada, and western Montana. One major derivative project has been completed: DeCamp's dissertation on the speech of the San Francisco area.

In Texas and the Gulf States work has been sporadic. A file of vocabulary check lists has been growing at Texas under Atwood's direction. Students of C. M. Wise, at Louisiana State University, have completed more than a hundred field records; though of uneven quality, this collection at least provides clues which more experienced field-workers may utilize in a future survey. More recently, the distribution of check lists has begun in Arkansas and Missouri, with prospects for field investigations awaiting funds and the training of field-workers.

Elsewhere in the United States only fragmentary work has been undertaken. In Canada, except for border communities investigated in connection with the American regional atlases, there are only the incomplete preliminary survey of the Maritime Provinces by Henry Alexander, the study of bilingual relics in Lunenberg County, Nova Scotia, by Rex Wilson, and the projected check-list investigation of eastern Ontario by the Rev. Brother Pius. Cassidy's study of Jamaica speech, now approaching publication, completes the picture of the present state of American linguistic geography.

INTERPRETATION OF THE RESULTS. However romantic field work may be, the task of the linguistic geographer is not complete when he has collected his data, or even when he has published it in the form of maps or tables. Data always requires interpretation—the testing of previous theories and the advancement of new ones—to bring groups of individual facts together into patterns.

Each item investigated in the interview provides a great deal of potential data, which must be sorted and examined piecemeal and then brought together again. For instance, in New England the question dealing with the earthworm was useful primarily for the lexical variants it revealed—the general Northern term *angleworm*, the rare and somewhat bookish *earthworm*, and the definitely localized terms *fishworm*, *mudworm*, *angledog*, and *eaceworm*. However, it also offers data over a wide area on two features of pronunciation: the phonetic quality of the vowel in the first syllable of *angleworm* ([æ, æ·, æ⸲·ᵊ, æ⸲·ɪ] etc.), which may be phonemically significant, and the length and possible constriction of the syllabic nucleus of *worm*. Each of these features may be plotted on a map of the area investigated; some will show patterns of distribution and some will not, but it is not possible to tell until the particular feature has been charted.

When one discovers a regionally distributed feature, it is often possible to draw a line around the outer limits of the area in which it occurs; sometimes one may also be able to draw a line around the inner limits of the area, or around the area in which the feature being examined has no competition. This line is called an **isogloss.** After enough features have been charted, it is then possible to draw a composite map comparing the isoglosses. If several isoglosses approximately coincide for a great part of their length, we have a **bundle of isoglosses,** which may be said to constitute a **dialect boundary** between two **dialect areas.** The formula for evaluating dialect boundaries is rather complicated, since it involves assigning different weights to different kinds of differences; obviously a difference in the phonemic system, such as the absence of a contrast between *cot* and *caught*, *tot* and *taught*, *collar* and *caller*, is of more significance than a difference in the **incidence** in a particular word, such as *creek*, of the syllabic nuclei /iy/, and /i/, which every native speaker of American English has in his inventory. But it usually develops that a dialect boundary involves isoglosses of several types: differences in the phonemic system; differences in the incidence of the phonemes; differences in the pronunciation of the phonemes; differences in the incidence of allomorphs, such as *dived* or *dove*; differences in the morphemic system, as the presence of a second person plural pronoun *you-all* or *youse* or the lack of verbal inflection for preterite or participle; and differences in the incidence of particular vocabulary items, such as *cooter* 'turtle' or *mutton corn* 'sweet corn.'

The number and distribution of the isoglosses determine the kind of dialect area set off. If the isoglosses are bunched rather closely together at a fairly even distance from a major cultural center (a single city like Boston or Philadelphia or a group of interdependent cities like Fredericksburg, Richmond, and Petersburg in Virginia) and forms seem to be spreading outward from the center, we have a **focal area.** If the isoglosses do not group together and the area lacks an important cultural center, so that forms seem to be receding inward, we have a **relic area.** If the area lacks sharply defined characteristics of its own but shares characteristics of two or more adjacent areas, we have a **graded area** or **transition area.** Among the more clearly defined focal areas are the Hudson Valley, the Philadelphia Area, and the Virginia Piedmont; among relic areas, Cape Cod and the offshore islands, the Delmarva Peninsula, and the Albemarle Sound area of eastern North Carolina; among graded areas, northern West Virginia and the Carolina and Georgia Piedmont. Sometimes relatively small pockets turn up with characteristic local speech-forms, such as the New England settlement at Marietta in Southern Ohio, or the Ulster Scots Williamsburg settlement in eastern South Carolina.

FORCES UNDERLYING DIALECT DISTRIBUTION
IN AMERICA

In seeking an explanation of the dialect areas we have found, we must then search for the economic, social, or cultural forces of which these patterns are the result. The most important of these forces, as providing the raw material upon which all the other forces operate, is the history of population, especially the history of the original settlements.

Now it is usually futile to search for the origins of an American dialect in a settlement from any single part of the British Isles. The fact is that dialect mixture was the normal thing in the colonial period, but with the proportions of the mixture varying from one settlement to another. Furthermore, the communications from one settlement to another during the colonial period were generally poor, even when not further handicapped by jealous local administrators or hostile Indians. It is therefore not surprising that the tidewater area, in which the first settlements were made, still has the greatest dialectal diversity to be found in the New World. For a long time —until the middle of the eighteenth century—expansion inland was slow, chiefly by secondary settlement from older colonies, some of which developed into important centers of trade, such as Boston, New York, Philadelphia, the Piedmont Cities of Virginia, and Charleston. But not until the great migration of the Ulster Scots in the eighteenth century did settlers cross the Blue Ridge, the first and lowest of the mountain barriers the westward migrants would have to pass in settling the continent.

Perhaps paradoxically, the crossing was made in one of the more rugged parts of the barrier—in Pennsylvania—rather than along the northern flank in the Mohawk Valley or through the southernmost extensions in Georgia. But in the Mohawk Valley the Six Nations of the Iroquois and in the Carolinas and Georgia their southern relatives the Cherokees (along with the equally formidable Choctaws and Creeks) prevented expansion. In Pennsylvania the favorable relations between the Indians and the proprietary government permitted the Ulster Scots to push westward unmolested until they encountered the French outposts in the Alleghenies. Deflected southwestward, these settlers followed the Great Valley to the Potomac, and then ascended the Shenandoah Valley to the neighborhood of what is now Lexington, Virginia. Here the stream of migration split. Part of it turned westward and followed the Kanawha river system through what is now West Virginia to the Ohio; part of it continued southwestward into the upper reaches of the Tennessee Valley; another part recrossed the Blue Ridge and followed its eastern slopes into the Piedmont of the Carolinas and Georgia. Thus, the painfully slow migration inland from the Southern Coast was overshadowed within a generation by this new migration which populated not only the Shenandoah Valley but the inland areas of the Carolinas and Georgia with a new group, having a different tradition from the merchants and planters of the coastal plain, equaling or even surpassing in numbers the population of the older southern settlements. As the Ulster Scots settled down—as frontier villages gave way to new towns and colonies to states—the cultural prestige of Richmond, Charleston, and Savannah exerted itself upon the elite of the inland communities, so that coastal words and pronunciations often spread inland with other coastal fashions. Nevertheless, even though the inland spread of plantations, and with them the institution of Negro slavery, disturbed what had been an economy of yeoman farmers, the Southern up-countrymen have never fully accepted the ideals of their coastal compatriots. The secession of West Virginia from Virginia during the Confederate War is the most spectacular example, but even today nearly every statewide election from the Potomac to the Okefenokee Swamp brings out the latent hostility between two different ways of life, stemming back, in large measure, to the two original groups of settlers and their different economic and social interests.[10]

[10] See particularly V. O. Key, *Southern Politics in State and Nation* (New York: Alfred A. Knopf, Inc., 1949), especially the section dealing with South Carolina.

THE SPREAD OF SETTLEMENT WESTWARD. With relatively few exceptions, the settlement of the interior of the North American continent can be seen as an extension of the settlement-patterns along the Atlantic Coast. However, not all groups participated in the westward march of settlement in proportion to their position along the Atlantic seaboard. Upon closer examination, one will find that the major contributions were made by the South Midland and the inland North. The South proper, the North Midland, and eastern New England contributed relatively little and, thus, are dialectally less important, except insofar as settlers from those sections may have weighted the balance between competing dialect forms.

The explanation for this situation is to be found partially in the dominant economic patterns of these areas, and partially in the availability of transportation routes to the westward. Eastern New England was for a long time tied to the sea and commerce; its surplus rural population naturally gravitated to Boston and Providence, to New Bedford and Portland. The sea, furthermore, made it easy for factories to find transportation for their raw materials and finished goods, so that, even before the decline of whaling and the China trade, industry furthered the urbanization that shipping had begun. It is true that the wealth and literary interests of the Boston area and the academic reputation of Harvard gave New England speech a prestige for many years unchallenged by any other American dialect—a prestige possibly enhanced by the fact that in many features of pronunciation and grammar Boston speech resembled polite Southern British. Furthermore, in many parts of the Middle West local academies were organized on New England models, and often staffed largely with New England teachers, so that New England speech-features were often encouraged and sometimes imposed. But the numerical contribution of eastern New England to the westward movement was small.

For analogous reasons, the settlements from the South Atlantic coast contributed little to the newer states. Their economy was largely tied to the plantation system, plantation crops such as rice and tobacco and cotton, and chattel slavery as a source of agricultural labor. Much of the new territory was closed to slavery by congressional action, commencing with the Northwest Ordinance of 1787; and even in the territory where slavery was permitted, large areas—the Southern Appalachians, much of the piedmont, the sandhills along the Fall Line, and large swamps like those in southern Louisiana—were not suitable to plantation agriculture.[11] Occasionally, wealthy planters from the South Atlantic Coast (the Hamptons of South Carolina were a notable example) expanded their holdings to the new lands of the Gulf States, or even transferred their operations completely. But many of the new plantation owners in the Gulf States and Lower Mississippi Valley actually came from outside the older plantation areas, exponents of the American dream of free enterprise and personal advancement as surely as was the New Englander who expanded his machine shop into a large industry. Again, to be sure, settlers from the Old South in the Gulf States, the Lower Mississippi Valley, and east Texas carried with them the cultural prestige of Richmond or Charleston and exerted an influence out of proportion to their numbers; moreover, the polyglot mercantile and planter classes of the New Orleans area rather early developed mores and speech-patterns similar to those of the Charleston-Savannah area. Thus, some Southern coastal influence appeared, especially in the speech of the cultured group, in the Kentucky Bluegrass, the Alabama black belt, and along the fertile river bottoms wherever the plantation system was dominant.

[11] Smaller swamps, such as those of the South Carolina and Georgia coastal plains, were sometimes reclaimed by slave labor and converted to ricelands. But the reclamation to rice cultivation of the large swamps of Louisiana, Texas, and Arkansas demanded corporate financing for large-scale irrigation and mechanized farming. The relative inefficiency of slave agricultural techniques is shown by the rapid decline of South Carolina rice culture despite the low wages permitted by post-Civil War peonage, as soon as the Louisiana ricelands were opened up.

Pennsylvania (or North Midland) settlement in the Great Lakes and Mississippi Valley came relatively late because Pennsylvania emigrants were largely dependent on overland transportation, far more hazardous and expensive than the water routes of the Great Lakes to the north or the Ohio River to the south. Not until 1818 did the National Road reach the Ohio at Wheeling; it was abandoned in 1848 with construction completed only to Indianapolis and grading to within seventy-five miles of St. Louis. Thus, clearly defined Pennsylvania settlements in the Great Lakes region are to be found in a narrowing wedge broadest along the Pennsylvania-Ohio line and tapering to a point along the Mississippi near the Illinois-Iowa-Missouri corner. Some Pennsylvanians, to be sure, chose other routes, either descending the Ohio Valley to mingle with the Kentuckians or crossing the Mahoning-Cuyahoga watershed to join the westward migration of the Yankees near Cleveland. Both of these groups illustrate the basic axiom of linguistic geography (an axiom already illustrated when we compare dialect differences along the Atlantic Seaboard with those in the British Isles) that the more recently settled a country, the less clearly defined will be its settlement patterns and consequently the patterns of dialect distribution.

Thus we find that, as far as its American origins are concerned, the major sources of the population of the Great Lakes area and the Mississippi Valley were the Inland North (Western New England and its derivatives in Upstate New York) and the Southern Uplands or South Midland. Both of these regions possessed good natural routes to the West, the Mohawk Valley and the Great Lakes (a route much improved by the opening of the Erie Canal in 1830) and the Ohio Valley. Both regions, furthermore, had high fertility of the population and low fertility of the soil, and relatively few local opportunities for commerce once the game had been killed off and the best timber cut down. The physical labor and small profits of farming in the hills discouraged the indolent and ambitious alike. Even before the War of 1812 removed the Indians as a menace, thousands of Yankees and Kentuckians poured into the Northwest Territory, attracted by the rich soil where stone fences were not necessary to keep the land cleared.[12]

The patterns of settlement in the Middle West reflected the older ways of living along the Atlantic Coast. The South Midlanders generally moved as families, and worked their way up rivers or creeks until they found land that suited them. The Yankees, whether from New England or New York State, moved in slightly larger units and chose somewhat more level ground. The result is, again, a mingling of streams of migration. Where the South Midlander preferred the bottom land and shunned the prairie, since he felt no human beings could live where trees would not grow, the Yankee devised a new plow and brought the prairie under control. Thus, in the central parts of Ohio, Indiana, and Illinois one may find New Englander and Kentuckian both strongly established in the same county, sometimes with Pennsylvanians alongside them. Moreover, New Englanders and South Midlanders sometimes set up compact colonies outside their normal areas of settlement, like the Ohio Yankee enclaves of Worthington (near Columbus) and Marietta on the Ohio River, or the North Carolina Quaker settlement at Richmond, Indiana. But by and large, the earliest settlements in Michigan and Wisconsin and the northernmost strip of Ohio, Indiana, and Illinois was Yankee, with the southern half of these states South Midland and the Pennsylvania wedge in between.

One further group of settlers must be noted, since they play an increasing part in the settlement of the upper Mississippi Valley and the Great Plains—immigrants direct from Europe. Compact settlements of this type had not been unknown, even before the Revolution. In addition to the well-known settlements of German Dissenters in the Susquehannah Valley of Pennsylvania or the Dutch landed gentry

---

[12] Many older informants in the Middle West recall how their parents or grandparents spoke with hatred of the backbreaking work of building stone fences on the farms of Vermont or eastern Kentucky.

in the Hudson Valley, there were Swedes and Finns in Delaware, Palatine Germans in the Mohawk Valley, Moravians in the North Carolina piedmont, Germans and German-Swiss in the South Carolina coastal plain and lower piedmont, Huguenots and Sephardic Jews in the New York City area and the Charleston-Georgetown plantation area in South Carolina, and Salzburgers in the Savannah Valley of Georgia. With the opening of the Middle West to settlement, the trend was accelerated, the normal practice being the movement of the European group in the second or third wave behind the pioneers who had made the first clearings and displaced the Indians. At first, most of these foreign-language settlements were German, the majority of them along the wedge of Pennsylvania settlement; in fact, there was also some migration of the Pennsylvania Germans themselves, into such tightly knit communities as the Amish settlements in Holmes County, Ohio. Later came Scandinavians, still later Slavs and Finns. A few communities were settled by direct migration from England, such as Albion, Illinois, and Robert Owen's experimental Socialist colony at New Harmony, Indiana. For climatic as well as moral reasons, most of these direct settlements from Europe were made in the northern states, where slavery was forbidden; however, there were Germans and Czechs in Texas at an early date, and their colonies, such as New Braunfels, still retain part of their linguistic heritage. In some states—notably Wisconsin, Minnesota, and the Dakotas—these waves of foreign settlement almost overwhelmed the older American stock. For example, in Wisconsin in 1910 more than half the population was of German birth or German parentage. Since many of these immigrants came to avoid military conscription and dynastic wars, it is not surprising that the north-central states and Upper Midwest were strongholds of neutralist and isolationist sentiment during both World Wars.

The spread of migration across the Great Plains and into the Rocky Mountain States generally followed the traditional patterns, with new modifications. Hostile winters and hostile Sioux retarded settlement in the northernmost part of the plains; drought and rugged terrain, as well as the boom-and-bust cycle of mining operations, made settlement sporadic and fitful in the mountains.[13] The streams of Yankee and South Midland migration crossed and recrossed. A strong Yankee element appeared in the permanent population of Denver and of communities even further south; Kentuckians and Missourians, already strongly established in the Tri-State lead area of Iowa, northwestern Illinois, and southwestern Wisconsin— followed the mining strikes into eastern Idaho and western Montana, and the great cattle-drives led to a constant interchange of cowboy population between west Texas and Wyoming. In the Rockies, furthermore, two new elements of population made their appearance. The long Spanish and Mexican domination had produced a South-western Spanish culture, partly Spanish American, partly Hispan-icized Indian, in permanent town and village settlements (some modeled on the older Indian pueblos) before the English-speaking settlers arrived. In the Rockies, too, the Mormons have had their strongholds since their westward march in 1846. A heterogeneous population of various American and European strains before their great trek, then welded together by religious zeal, fierce external persecution, and strong internal discipline, they established them-selves and multiplied so successfully that by 1870 a decided majority of the native American population of Utah were natives of the territory as well. Throughout the Plains and the Rockies, again, we find foreign-language colonies, reflecting the ever-widening sources of immigration.

The settlement of the Pacific Coast, finally, has shown a pattern of normal expansion in Washington and Oregon with steadily spectacular growth in California. Till the Mexican War, with the annexation of California and the peaceful division of the Oregon

[13] See Marjorie M. Kimmerle, Raven I. McDavid, Jr., and Virginia Glenn McDavid, "Problems of Linguistic Geography in the Rocky Mountain Area," *Western Humanities Review*, V (1951), 249–64.

Territory between the United States and Great Britain, English-speaking settlers on the Pacific Coast had been few, and those mainly trappers and traders. Following the opening of the Oregon Trail and the discovery of gold in California, population expanded so rapidly that both California (1850) and Oregon (1858) were admitted as states before the Confederate War, though Washington did not achieve statehood for another generation. Since 1850, the population of California has doubled with every decade, an increase of a thousandfold since annexation. Oregon and Washington have grown less rapidly, though somewhat faster than the nation as a whole. The population of the Pacific Coast States has been derived from many sources, and the excellent communications by sea and rivers have facilitated the mingling of peoples in all parts of the region. Nevertheless, emigrants from the Northern areas—New England, Upstate New York, and their westward derivatives—bulked large in the early settlement of the whole coast. Oregon and Washington, in roughly the same geographical belt as Minnesota and Wisconsin, drew the same kind of immigrants from Germany and Scandinavia, while California has added to the normal processes of the American melting pot such relatively exotic elements as Chinese, Japanese, Filipinos, and Armenians. In recent years, many dispossessed farmers from the South Midland regions—especially from Arkansas, Oklahoma, and Texas—have drifted to California as migratory laborers on large factory farms. In addition, the original inland-Northern set of much of California has been reinforced by an influx of prosperous retired farmers from the plains, especially Iowa, Nebraska, and Kansas, who have migrated to Southern California in their old age.

SOCIAL FORCES. The final forces in American population history have been sociological rather than ethnic or regional: industrialization, urbanization, and education.

The Industrial Revolution had got under way in England shortly before the American colonies gained their independence. The apparently limitless resources of land and raw materials, the many good harbors and navigable rivers, the available water power, the numbers of energetic, ambitious, and often highly skilled settlers[14] —these forces would have brought the United States into the Industrial Revolution even if there had been no protective tariff to encourage manufactures. A growing population provided a market for more goods; growing industries provided job opportunities for more immigrants, so that the expansion of population, industry, and national wealth reinforced each other, with later immigration from southern and eastern Europe seeking industrial jobs rather than farming as a way of livelihood.

Industrialization, of course, led to the growth of cities. Actually, the colonies were far more urban than is commonly realized. In 1775, Philadelphia and Boston were the second and third most important cities in the English-speaking world, with New York and Charleston as important seaports; all four were centers of wealth and the amenities of urban life. The rise of American commerce stimulated the growth of these seaboard towns, and industrialization both accelerated their growth and created new centers, such as Pittsburgh and Cincinnati. The Erie Canal, Great Lakes shipping, and the railroads fostered more cities, to which flocked the German bourgeoisie dispossessed or at least disillusioned by the abortive revolutions of 1848. These immigrants were particularly noticeable in the Great Lakes area, where every city from Buffalo west sported its gymnastic societies, choral groups, and breweries. Because of their political outlook, these immigrants tended to avoid the slave states; but enough settled in St. Louis to hold Missouri in the Union, and there were important German colonies in Louisville, New Orleans, and Charleston. With the other Germans, and hardly to

---

[14] The shrewd Yankee farmer-mechanic was often from an English town, and at the outset little interested in agriculture. But once confronted with farming as a way of life, he designed implements—notably the American ax—far superior to their English counterparts. This was the beginning of the American tradition of industrial planning.

be distinguished from them, came the German Jews. The bourgeois immigration to the cities was ultimately forgotten in the rush of Hungarians, Poles, Ukrainians, and Serbo-Croats to centers of heavy manufacturing, and of Russian and southern European Jews to the garment centers. For a long time two areas remained relatively free of industry: the open expanses of the Great Plains and the Cotton Kingdom in the South. But the discovery of oil and gas brought industries even to the Plains; and the rise of textiles, steel, and chemicals in the South has taken both Negro and poor white from the cotton fields. For some time, now, the majority of the American population has lived in an urban environment.

General education, finally, has always been part of the American cultural tradition. Both New England and Virginia were largely middle class settlements with some tradition of literacy, and in New England the Puritan tradition made education a prerequisite for understanding Scripture, and hence for salvation. Not only were colleges and academies established early, especially in New England, but also the circulation of newspapers and books in the colonies compared favorably with that in England. It is more than possible that higher standards of literacy prevailed in the New World than in the Old. Although illiteracy was by no means unknown among immigrant groups (the Irish of the potato-blight migration of the 1840's as well as the southern and eastern Europeans of the late nineteenth century), the Scandinavians and Germans in particular brought with them an interest in education equally as strong as that of the Puritans, and for much the same reasons. The earliest territorial act, the Northwest Ordinance of 1787, established the policy of setting aside part of the public lands for education. Noah Webster's blueback speller and William Holmes McGuffey's series of readers became all-time best-sellers, and the possession of certificates and diplomas became a passport to success. In the absence of a well-defined elite (except in parts of the South and some of the older cultural centers), it is not surprising that a citizen population that often sought salvation from the literal (though translated) message of the Bible should seek its path to education in the literal message of the school grammars, regardless of the discrepancies between grammatical rules and the actual language practices of the educated. In fact—for grammar as for morals—the greater the proportion of the erring, the greater the reward of the faithful. With the broadening of education and with the emphasis on the letter of the rule, came also the emphasis on careful articulation, upon spelling as the basis for pronunciation, with an increasing tendency to restore /-ow/ in *borrow* and *tomorrow*, /-ey/ in *yesterday* and *Sunday*, and /l/ (lost since the Middle Ages, long before the words ever appeared in English) in *alms*, *palm*, and *psalm*. More broadly, the spread of education, like industrialization and urbanization, has cut the roots of very old-fashioned pronunciations and vocabulary items, and stigmatized if not destroyed nonstandard variants in grammar.

The cumulative effect of industrialization, urbanization, and education is particularly noticeable in the speech of the college generation in metropolitan areas of the Great Lakes Region. This effect may be generalized as a reduction in the number of phonemic contrasts: *hoarse* and *horse* are nearly always homonymous in the speech of this group; *white* and *whip* have /w-/ about half the time; and (especially in the Cleveland area) *caught* is frequently homonymous with *cot*.

THE PRINCIPAL DIALECT AREAS OF THE UNITED STATES

The resulting patterns of distribution, then, show the effects of all the social and cultural forces mentioned in the last section. In general, on all levels, one may still distinguish, for much of the country, the three major belts of dialects, each with its own characteristics: Northern, Midland, and Southern, Midland being in turn divided into North Midland and South Midland. Map 2 (pp. 580–81) shows the dialect areas that have so far been identified. Other recognizable but not clearly set-off areas have been found in the Northern Plains, the San Francisco Bay area, and parts of the Rockies. Clearer subdivisions will be recognized as a result of more extensive field work and more intensive analysis of the available data.

The dialect areas, to be sure, are most sharply defined along the Atlantic Coast, where settlement was earliest and patterns have had longest to become stabilized. In fact, even within such an area as the Carolina-Georgia Low Country, it is often possible to tell a Charlestonian from a Savannian. As the lines of settlement move west, local distinctions become increasingly hard to find, and even the boundaries between major areas are not easy to indicate. Moreover, regional words or grammatical forms (less frequently regional pronunciations) which were in the speech of people of all ages and educational levels along the Atlantic Seaboard may survive in the Middle West or the Rocky Mountains only in the speech of the oldest and least sophisticated. In the Mississippi Valley, furthermore, some Northern forms have pushed south of St. Louis, while some South Midland forms occur as far north as Minneapolis or Duluth.

The analysis of Atlas materials now makes it possible to summarize the characteristics of many of the more distinctive of these speech-areas, especially along the Atlantic Seaboard. Some of the areas, being transition areas, have almost no distinctive characteristics; for others the statement is brief, as that the Delmarva area (14 on Map 2) is most easily characterized by *caps* 'corn husks,' *lodge* 'bed on the floor,' and *mongst-ye* as second person pronoun; for still others the analysis of the materials is not yet complete.

The following tables, then, are essentially a conflation of work on the regional distribution of linguistic forms in the United States and Canada. Some parts have appeared in published volumes, like those of Kurath and Atwood (see Bibliography); other parts are found in unpublished dissertations like those of Avis, Davis, and Frank; still others appear in articles and reviews; some have been presented only orally. Where phonemic data is presented, the transcriptions have been roughly adapted to the system used in other parts of this book. This adaptation, of course, does not mean that the linguistic geographer feels that his data can be adequately represented by such a system. The structural peculiarities of the Charleston vowel-system, for example, make it impossible to represent it accurately in the nine-vowel-plus-three-semivowel analysis; for other individual Southern and South Midland dialects at least ten vowels and perhaps additional semivowels are necessary. Where these difficulties appear most strikingly, phonemicization according to this system has not been attempted, and the data is presented phonetically;[15] in many other places the phonemicization is done with extreme diffidence. It is probable that a different set of terms and perhaps a different graphic device (such as reverse slants) will be necessary to represent structural phonological differences between dialects.

The numbers in parentheses after each area designate the dialect areas indicated on Map 2. Roman numerals after each item indicate, insofar as it has been determined, the social distribution of the form within the particular area where it is observed. The figures correspond essentially to the social classes of Atlas informants:

I. Old-fashioned, rustic, poorly educated speakers.
II. Younger, more modern, better educated speakers.
III. Cultured, well educated speakers.

When these figures are enclosed in brackets, less currency in that group is indicated.

The North (1–6)

Pronunciation

/o/ and /ɔ/ (or /oh/ and /ɔh/) distinguished in *mourning*: *morning;*

[15] Readers are reminded of the fact that *phonemic* transcriptions are recorded between /slants/ and phonetic between [square brackets].

hoarse: *horse*: *fourteen*: *forty*, etc. I, II, III.

/ɨ/ in unstressed syllables of *haunted, careless*, etc. I, II, III. (Also South).

[æ] (perhaps an allophone of /æ/ or if lengthened, of /æh/) sometimes used in *stairs, care*. [I], [II], [III]. (Also South).

centralized first element in the diphthong of *fine;* phonetically [ʌɨ] or [ɐɨ]; phonemically /əy/. I, [II].

centralized first element in the diphthong of *loud;* phonetically [ʌʊ], or [ɐʊ]; phonemically /əw/. I, [II].

/ð/ regularly in *with*. I, II, III. Possibly receding in Inland Northern.

/-s-/ in *grease* (verb) and *greasy*. I, II, III.

/u/ in *roots*.

/ə/ in *won't*. I, II, [III]. But see New York City.

/uw/, /u/ in *gums*. I, [II]. Receding in Inland Northern.

/bɨkɔ́z/ *because*. I, II, III. Also South Carolina-Georgia Low Country.

Vocabulary

pail I, II, III. (Midland and Southern *bucket*).

swill 'garbage' I, II, III. (Midland and Southern *slop*).

clapboards 'finished siding' I, II, III. (Midland and Southern *weatherboards, weatherboarding*).

brook 'small stream' I, II, III. Rare in Inland North.

(*cherry*) *pit* 'seed' I, II, III.

angleworm 'earthworm' I, II, III.

johnnycake 'cornbread' I, II, III.

whiffletree, whippletree I, II, III.

eavestrough 'gutter on roof' I, II, [III].

spider 'frying pan' I, II. Receding in Inland Northern. (Also South).

fills, thills 'buggy shafts' I, II.

quite (spry) I, II, III. (Midland and Southern *right*).

Morphology and Syntax.

dove /dówv/ as preterit of *dive* I, II, III.

sick to the stomach I, II, [III].

all to once [I], [II], receding in Inland Northern.

(he isn't) *to home* I, II, receding in Inland Northern.

hadn't ought 'oughtn't' I, II.

it wa'n't me I, II. (Also South). Receding in Inland Northern.

see as preterit, I, II. (Also South).

clim as preterit of *climb* I, II. (Also South).

be as finite verb (*How be you? Be I going to?*) I. Rare in Inland Northern.

/-θs/ or /-ðz/ in *troughs.* I, [II], [III].

begin as preterit [I], [II]. (Also South).

scairt 'scared' I, II.

Eastern New England (1, 2)

Pronunciation.

[a] (phonemically /a/) inconsistently in *afternoon, glass, bath, France,* etc.; consistently in *barn, yard,* etc. (phonemically /æh/). I, II, III.

/-r/ "lost" except before vowels: *barn, beard, four, Thursday, horse, father,* phonemically /bæhn, bihd, foh/, etc. (Also New York City and South). Linking and intrusive /r/ are common: *idear of it,* /ày + sóhrim/ 'I saw him,' etc. I, II, III.

/ɔ/ (phonetically [ᴅ]) in "short-*o*" words: *crop, lot, on, fog;* often no distinction between these words and words like *fought, law, horse,* etc. Sometimes the latter group has a higher vowel somewhat lengthened: [ɔ·] (phonemically /ɔh/ or /oh/).

/uw/ after /t, d, n/ (rather than /yuw, ɨw, iw/): *Tuesday, due, new.* I, II, III. (Also North Midland).

/o/ (a shortened and centralized allophone) in *stone, coat,* etc. I, [II], [III]. (Also sporadically in Inland Northern).

/ih/ (with a high allophone of /i/) in *beard, ear,* etc. I, II, III.

Vocabulary.

pig-sty 'pigpen' I, II, III.

bonny-clabber, -clapper 'curdled milk' I, II, III.

sour-milk cheese 'cottage cheese' I, [II], [III].

apple dowdy 'deep-dish pie' I, II, III.

buttonwood 'sycamore' I, II, III.

Morphology and Syntax.

waked up I, [II], [III]. (Also South).

verb-forms found in northeastern New England (1): preterits *riz* 'rose,' *driv* 'drove,' *div* 'dove' I (also South); participle *gwine* 'going' I.

(I was sitting) *agin* him, . . . *against* him 'next to' I.

Inland Northern (4)

(This area usually includes all or part of the Northern settlement areas of the Great Lakes Basin and the Upper Mississippi Valley).

Pronunciation.

/-r/ "kept" after vowels in *horse, four, father,* etc. I, II, III. (Also Midland).

[ɑ] (phonemically /a/) in *on, hog, fog, frog* (but not *dog, log*) I, II, III. (Also eastern Virginia and North Carolina).

[ɑˑ] or [a] (fronted allophones of /a/) in "short-*o*" words. I, II, III.

/ɨw, iw/ (phonetically [ɪʉ, ɪʉ]) sometimes in *Tuesday, due, new, music, beautiful.* I, [II], [III]. Receding in Great Lakes and Upper Midwest.

Vocabulary.

stoop 'porch' I, II, III. (Also New York City and Savannah Valley).

lobbered milk, loppered milk 'curdled milk' I, II, III.

Dutch cheese 'cottage cheese' I, II.

sugar bush 'maple grove' I, II, [III].

stone boat 'sled for hauling stones' I, II, III.

Morphology and Syntax.

there are buttons *onto* the coat [I].

we burn coal *into* the stove [I].

New York City and Hudson Valley (5,6)

Pronunciation (mostly confined to the immediate vicinity of New York City)

/-r/ "lost" except before vowels I, II, III. (Also New England and South).

no distinction between *mourning* : *morning*, *hoarse* : *horse*, etc. I, II, III. (Also North Midland).

/əy/ (phonetically [ɜɪ, əɪ]) in both *adjourn* and *adjoin*, *curl* and *coil*, etc. I, II. (Also New Orleans).

[e] (phonemically /eh/) in *Mary*, *dairy* I, II, III. (Also eastern New England. Cf. South).

[ɑ] (phonemically /a/ or /ah/) in *foreign*, *orange*, *borrow;* also in *on*, *hog*, *frog*, *fog*, *log* (not *dog*) I, II, III.

raised allophone of /ih/ in *beard*, *ear*, etc. I, II, III. (Also eastern New England).

raised and lengthened [æ⁺·] (phonemically /eh/) in *pan*, etc. I, II, [III].

raised and lengthened [ɔ⁺·] (phonemically /oh/) in *lawn*, etc. I, II, [III].

/uw/ in *won't* I, II, III. (Also Charleston).

/w/ regularly instead of /hw/ in *wheelbarrow*, etc. I, II, III.

[ʔ] (allophone of /t/) in *bottle*, *mountain*, etc. I, II.

/d/ instead of /ð/ in *this*, etc. I, II (chiefly in foreignized speech).

/ŋg/ instead of /ŋ/ in *Long Island*, etc. I, II, (chiefly in foreignized speech).

Vocabulary (usually includes Hudson Valley)

Dominie 'preacher' I, II, III.

pot cheese 'cottage cheese' I, II, III.

olicook 'doughnut' I.

hunk 'base' (in tag games) [I] (New York City only).

-kill 'small stream' (proper names only) I, II, III.

barrack 'haystack' I, II (rural only).

suppawn 'corn mush' I, II (rural only).

skimmerton, skimmilton 'mock serenade' I, II (rural only).

Morphology and Syntax.

he lives *in* King Street I, II, [III]. (Also Charleston and Canada).

we stood *on* line I, II, III.

Midland (7–13)

Pronunciation.

/-r/ "kept" after vowels I, II, III. (Also Inland North).

/ɔ, ɔh, ɔw/ in *on* (also South); in *wash, wasp;* in *log, hog, frog, fog* I, II, III.

/e/ (phonetically [ɛ]) in *Mary, dairy* I, II, III.

/ə/ in the unstressed syllable of *haunted, careless,* etc. I, II, III.

/ɨ/ in the unstressed syllable of *stomach* I, II.

/θ/ regularly in *with.*

/r/ frequently intrudes in *wash, Washington* I, II.

Vocabulary.

blinds 'window shades' I, II, III. (Also Canada).

skillet 'frying pan' I, II, III. Spreading.

snake feeder 'dragon fly' I, II, [III]. Competes with *snake doctor* in South Midland.

poke '(paper) sack' I, II [III]. Not in Eastern Pennsylvania.

sook! 'call to cows' I, II, III.

green-beans 'string beans' I, II, III. Not in Eastern Pennsylvania.

a little piece 'short distance' I, II, III. (Also South Carolina).

to *hull* beans 'shell' I, II, [III].

Morphology and Syntax.
  clum 'climbed' I, [II].
  seen 'saw' I, II. Spreading in North Central States.
  you-uns (2nd person plural) I, [II]. Not in Eastern Pennsylvania.
  all the further 'as far as' I, II.
  I'll wait *on* you '. . . for you' I, II, [III]. (Also South Carolina)
    Receding in North Central States.
  I want off I, II, [III].
  quarter *till* eleven I, II, III.

North Midland (7, 8, 10, 11)
Pronunciation.
  /uw/ after /t, d, n/, as in *Tuesday, new, due,* etc. I, II, III. (Also
    Eastern New England).
  no distinction between such pairs of words as *mourning: morning,*
    hoarse: horse, etc. I, II, III. (Also Hudson Valley). Such pairs
    seem to have /ɔr/ in the Hudson Valley and Eastern Pennsyl-
    vania and /or/ in Western Pennsylvania.
  /i/ predominant in *creek.* I, II, [III]. (Also common in North, and
    spreading in Inland Northern).

Vocabulary.
  spouting, spouts 'roof gutters' I, II, [III].
  run 'small stream' I, II, III.
  smearcase 'cottage cheese' I, II, [III].

Eastern Pennsylvania (7, 8)[16]
Pronunciation.
  /a/ in *frog, hog, fog* (not *dog*). [I], II, III. (Also North).

[16] Since eastern Pennsylvania and the Hudson Valley share many phonological features—such as the homonymy of *morning* and *mourning,* /w-/ in *whip,* etc., /eh/ in *had* and /oh/ in *law*—it is possible, on phonological grounds alone, to class them together in a Middle Atlantic area, extending from Albany to the Baltimore–Washington area. Certainly, with the growth of population and the heavy industrialization of this area, the more peculiarly local speech charac-teristics are disappearing.

/ɔr/ in *morning, warning;* also *barn, marbles.*

/iy/ in *me, be, see,* etc. (especially under primary or secondary stress).

Vocabulary.

baby coach 'baby carriage' I, II, [III]. Philadelphia area only.

pavement 'sidewalk' I, II, III.

Germanisms (often scattered through the North Midland):

paper *toot* (/tut/) 'sack' I, II.

clook 'setting hen' I.

ponhaws 'scrapple' I, II.

fatcakes 'doughnuts' I, [II].

thick-milk 'curdled milk' I, II.

spook 'ghost' I, II, III. (Also Hudson Valley).

snits 'dried fruit' I, II.

Morphology and Syntax.

sick *on* the stomach I, II.

Germanisms:

(the oranges are) *all* 'all gone' I, II.

got awake 'woke up' I, II.

Western Pennsylvania (10)

Pronunciation.

no contrast between *cot* : *caught, collar* : *caller,* etc. I, II, III.

/u/ in *food* I, II.

/uw/ in *drouth* I, [II].

Vocabulary.

hap 'comforter' I, [II].

cruds, crudded milk 'curdled milk' I, II.

mind 'remember' I, II, [III]. (Also South Carolina).

hay doodle 'haycock' I, II. Expanding in North-Central area.

grinnie 'chipmunk' I, II.

carbon oil 'kerosene' I, II.

baby cab 'baby carriage' I, II.

South Midland (9, 12, 13)

Pronunciation.

[a·], [a·ᵊ] for /ay/ before voiceless and voiced consonants, as in *nice time* I, II.

Vocabulary.

french harp 'harmonica' I, II, [III].

pack 'carry, tote' I, II.

clabber milk 'curdled milk' I, II, III.

redworm 'earthworm' I, II.

sugar tree 'sugar maple' I, II, [III].

fireboard, mantelboard 'mantel' I, II.

milk gap 'cow pen' I, [II].

Morphology and Syntax.

dogbit 'bitten by a dog' I, II. (Also South Carolina).

(the sun) *raised* I, [II].

drinkt (preterite and participle) I.

shrinkt (preterite and participle) I.

swim (preterite) I.

sot down 'sat' I.

/-n/ forms of second possessive: *ourn, yourn,* etc.

I ran *on* him I, [II].

The South (14–18)

Pronunciation.

/r/ 'lost' except before vowels [I], [II], III. (Also eastern New England and New York City). Linking and intrusive /r/ usually do not occur in the South.

/ey/ in *Mary,* etc. I, II, III.

/ɨ/ in unstressed syllables of *haunted, careless,* etc. I, II, III. (Also North).

/-il, -in/ in *towel, funnel; mountain.* I, II, [III]. (Also eastern New
England).

/ey/ in *bleat* I, II, [III].

palatal allophones of /k-, g-/ in *car, garden.* I, II, [III].

/z/ in *Mrs.* [I], II, III.

Vocabulary.

lightwood 'fatty kindling' I, II, [III].

low 'moo' I, II, III.

tote 'carry' I, II.

carry 'take, escort' I, II, [III].

chittlins 'edible intestines' I, II, III.

co-wench! 'call to cows' I, II, III.

hasslet 'liver and lungs' I, II, III. (Also North).

snap beans, snaps 'string beans' I, II, III. Spreading.

harp, mouth harp 'harmonica' I, II, III. Not in Charleston area.

turn of wood 'armload' I, II, [III].

fritters I, II, III.

Confederate War 'Civil War (1861–65)' I, [II], [III].

Morphology and Syntax.

it wan't me I, II, [III]. (Also North).

he belongs to be careful I, II.

heern tell I. (Also northeastern New England).

he *do* 'does' I.

what *make* (him do it?) 'makes' I.

is I . . . ? I.

gwine 'going' I. (Also northeastern New England).

he fell *outn* the bed I.

(I like him) *on account of* (he's so funny). I, [II].

all two, all both 'both' I, [II].

Eastern Virginia (14–15)
Pronunciation.

[əu, ʌu] (phonemically /əw/) before voiceless consonants (*house, out*) against [æʊ] (phonemically /æw/) before voiced (*down*, *loud*). I, II, III. (Also Charleston area and Canada).

/a/ in *pasture* and a few other words; also in *stairs*. I.

[əi, ɐi] (phonemically /əy/) before voiceless consonants (*white, nice*) against [a·ɪ, a·ɛ], etc., before voiced (*time, ride*). I, II, III. (Also Charleston area and Canada).

/u/ in *home* I.

/e/ in *afraid* I, II, III.

Vocabulary.

batter bread 'spoonbread, soft cornbread' I, II, III.

lumber room 'store room' I, II, III.

croker sack, crocus sack 'burlap bag' I, II, [III]. (Also South Carolina).

cuppin 'cow pen' I.

corn house 'corn crib' I, II. (Also South Carolina).

hoppergrass 'grasshopper' I.

goobers 'peanuts' I, II, [III].

Morphology and Syntax.

clome 'climbed' I.

see (preterit) I, II. (Also North).

I ran *up on* him I, II.

he did it *for purpose* I, [II].

South Carolina–Georgia Low-Country (18)

Pronunciation.

[əu, ʌu] (phonemically /əw/) and [əi, ɐi] (/əy/) before voiceless consonants in *house, night*. I, II, III. Tidewater communities only. (Also eastern Virginia and Canada).

[ɝ] occasional in *bird*, etc. [I], [II], [III]. Not homophonous with *Boyd*.

centering diphthongs: [o·ə] in *road, post*, and [e·ə] in *eight, drain*. I, II, III. Syllabics of *beet, boot, bought* less often in-gliding

diphthongs, often monophthongs, very rarely up-gliding diphthongs.

/w/ in *whip, wheelbarrow,* etc. [I], [II], [III]. (Also Hudson Valley
and eastern Pennsylvania).

/ɔ/ in *pot, crop, oxen.* I, II, III. (Also eastern New England).

[u, ʊ] in *won't* [I], [II], [III]. (Also Hudson Valley).

only one front vowel phoneme before /-r/: homophony of *ear: air,
fear: fair,* etc. I, II, III. Rare above tidewater.

/-b/ in *coop* I, II. (Also eastern North Carolina).

/θ/ in *with, without.* I, II, III. (Also Midland).

/æh/ in *pa, ma, palm, calm* I, II, [III].

Vocabulary.

fatwood 'fatty kindling' I, II, [III]. Tidewater in South Carolina,
further inland in Georgia and Florida.

press, clothespress 'movable wardrobe' [I], [II], [III]. Chiefly in
Santee Valley.

stoop 'small porch' [I], [II], [III]. Chiefly in Savannah Valley.
(Also in North).

cripple 'scrapple' [I], [II], [III]. Savannah Valley.

spring frog 'small green frog' I, II, III.

groundnuts 'peanuts' I, II, III.

joggling board 'springing board anchored at both ends' I, II, III.

awendaw [ˈo-ɪnˌdɔ] 'spoon bread, soft cornbread' [I], [II], [III].
Charleston County only.

savannah 'grassland' I, II, III.

mutton corn 'sweet corn' I, II, [III].

corn dodgers 'dumplings' I, II.

Africanisms of various spread:

bloody-noun 'large bullfrog' I, II, III.

cooter 'turtle' (with /u/ on coastal plain, /uw/ further inland).
I, II, III.

pinders 'peanuts' I, II, [III].

yard-ax 'untrained preacher' [I]. (Widely known, but generally labeled a Negroism).

pinto 'coffin' [I]. Chiefly from Negro informants.

buckra 'white man' I, II, III.

Morphology and Syntax (forms current in Negro speech, occasionally in old-fashioned white speech).

he come over *for* tell me. [I].

Uninflected preterites and participles [I]

South and South Midland (9, 12–18)

Pronunciation.

/yuw/ after /t, d, n/ in *Tuesday, due, new*, etc. I, II, III.

[a·ᵉ, a·], etc., in *five, my*, etc. I, II, III.

/o/ and /ɔ/ contrasting before /r/ in *mourning* : *morning, hoarse* : *horse, fourteen* : *forty*, etc. I, II, III. (Also North).

/æw/ predominant in *mountain, loud*, etc. I, II, III. Not common in Charleston area.

/æ/ in *stairs, care, chair.* I. II, III. (Also North).

/o/ in *poor, your*, etc.

/u/ in *coop, cooper.*

/uw/ as a high-central monophthong or diphthong, [ʉ·, ɵʉ]. I, II, III. Not universal in Charleston area.

/u/ as a high-central rounded vowel, [ʉ] [I], [II], [III]. Not in Charleston area.

/ə/ in *put.* I, [II].

/u/ in *bulk, bulge, budget.* I, II, [III]. Not in Carolina–Georgia coastal plain.

/ɨ/ frequent in *sister, dinner, scissors, pretty, milk, mirror*, etc.

Vocabulary.

light bread 'white bread' I, II, III.

clabber 'curdled milk' I, II, III.

corn shucks 'husks' I, II, III.

pallet 'bed on floor' I, II, III.

jackleg preacher 'unskilled preacher' I, II, [III].
snack 'light lunch between meals' I, II, III. (Also New York City).
pulley bone 'wishbone' I, II, III.
snake doctor 'dragon fly' I, II, III. Not on Carolina–Georgia coast.
ha'nts, haunts 'ghosts' I, II, [III].
disremember 'forget' I.
hay shocks 'haycocks' I, II, III.
branch 'small stream' I, II, III.

Morphology and Syntax.
  you-all (second person plural) I, II, III.
  I might could I, II. (Also Pennsylvania German area).
  I'm not for sure. I, II.
  seed 'saw' (preterite of *see*) I.
  a apple I, II. Apparently spreading.
  I *taken* 'took' [I], II.
  tuck (participle of *take*) I, [II].
  holp 'helped' I, [II].
  riz 'rose' I. (Also northeastern New England).
  div 'dived' I. (Also northeastern New England).
  mought 'might' I.
  /-iz, -əz/ in plural ending of *fists, posts, costs* I.
  perfective use of *done*, as I(*'ve*) *done told you that* I, II.
  bought bread I, II.
  use to didn't I, II.

Canada (*chiefly Ontario*)[17]

Pronunciation.
  /əy/, /əw/ before voiceless consonants, as in *nice, house.* I. II, III.
    (Also eastern Virginia and tidewater South Carolina).
  /a/, /ɔ/ in *shone.*
  /u/, /uw/ in *won't.* (Also Hudson Valley and South Carolina).

---

[17] Linguistic Atlas data supplemented by W. S. Avis, "Speech Differences along the Ontario-U.S. Border: I. Vocabulary; II. Grammar and Syntax; III. Pronunciation", *Journal of the Canadian Linguistic Association,* preliminary issue pp. 13-17 (1954); Vol. I, pp. 14-19 (1955); Vol. II, pp. 41-59 (1956).

Vocabulary.

  chesterfield 'sofa.' (Also northern California).

  county town 'county seat' I, II, III.

  reeve 'township officer' I, II, III.

  warden 'county officer' I, II, III.

  dew worm 'large earthworm' I, II, III.

  tap 'faucet' I, II, III.

  serviette 'table napkin' [I], II, III.

  stook 'pile of sheaves' I, II, [III].

Morphology and Syntax.

He lives *in* King Street. (Also New York City and Charleston).

THE INFLUENCE OF FOREIGN-LANGUAGE SETTLEMENTS

Beside the regional distributions, certain types of cultural distribution seem to appear from the data. One of the most obvious of these is the area with a strong tradition of foreign-language settlement. Such an area may still be partially bilingual, or it may have witnessed the overwhelming of the foreign language by English. Nevertheless, the foreign language always leaves its trace—occasionally in a pronunciation or a grammatical form, oftener in the vocabulary, with local articles of food most likely to keep their older names. If the foreign language survives, one often finds it valuable for evidence on the older state of local English. Frequently, the speakers of German or Norwegian or Portuguese have borrowed the prevailing name (and pronunciation) for an American cultural item which they did not have in their homeland. As time goes by, this word—and its pronunciation—become established as standard in the language of the immigrant group, but the English-speaking group drop it and substitute something else. Thus, *horning*, the western New England and Upstate New York term for the burlesque serenade after a wedding, was carried by Yankee settlers to Wisconsin, where immigrants from Norway learned the Yankee word for a Yankee custom and adopted it into American Norwegian. Today, however, where the custom survives at all in English-speaking communities, the Yankee word has been lost and replaced by *shivaree*, from the French Canadian term *charivari*. Wisconsin speakers of Norwegian have in turn learned *shivaree* and occasionally use it as a conscious "Americanism," while the "real Norwegian word" is the older borrowing, *horning*.[18]

Each of the foreign languages brought to the United States by immigrants, and even each of the surviving American Indian languages, has its own peculiar history in this generally one-sided history of conflict between languages. In fact, each local foreign dialect has its own history, for a language may be flourishing in one community and dying in another. A full record of these conflicts would be outside the scope of this chapter, even if adequate data were available. A few examples will show the kinds of situations in which the relics of non-English languages may be observed in the New World.

Probably the most thoroughly studied of non-English languages in America is Pennsylvania German, known commonly as "Pennsylvania Dutch" or simply "Dutch" to its speakers and others in the regions where it is most strongly entrenched. It is certainly the oldest surviving foreign-language colony. The group, principally German nonconformists (Mennonites and Amish) migrated into Pennsylvania from the Rhineland Palatinate about 1700, with the understanding that the proprietary government would respect their conscientious objections to military service. Their traditional eye for good farmlands and their efficiency as farmers brought them such a high degree of prosperity that they have been able to ignore such details of present-day American culture as high schools, tractors, and instalment credit. Their large families have kept the community

---

[18] See A. L. Davis and Raven I. McDavid, Jr., "*Shivaree*: An Example of Cultural Diffusion," *American Speech*, XXIV (1949), 249–55.

replenished even though there have been some inevitable losses to the outside world; in fact, once a Mennonite or Amish community is established it generally seems to expand its holdings. But despite the persistence of the Pennsylvania German way of life, Pennsylvania German itself is a dying language. Few German monolinguals remain. But to American English it has contributed many items of vocabulary, the most widely disseminated being *smearcase, smear cheese* "cottage cheese"—the most widely spread American folk term for this item of diet. Also fairly widespread are *ponhaws* "Philadelphia scrapple," *thick milk* "curdled milk," and *toot* "paper sack." *Rainworm* "earthworm," *vootsie!* "call to pigs," and *saddle horse* "near horse" appear in other German-language settlements. Also of Pennsylvania German origin is the phrase *got awake* "woke up" (intransitive), while the phonemic system of Pennsylvania German may possibly explain why /-s-/ in *greasy* reaches its most southerly point along the Atlantic Seaboard in the Pennsylvania German area. In addition, the English of many residents of the Pennsylvania German area shows characteristic intonation patterns, and some phonemic variations—such as the replacement of initial /w/ by [β], a bilabial allophone of /v/—which are attributable to Pennsylvania German influence.

Other German settlements show a similar pattern of contribution to the English of their area. In the Savannah Valley area of Georgia and South Carolina, scrapple is known as *cripple*, from South German *kriebele* "drippings," brought by the Salzburgers in 1733. Possibly, too, German influence has facilitated the survival in the Midland areas of such verb phrases as *want in, want out, want off.*[19]

A different type of speech situation is found in the dialect of the Gullah Negroes of the South Carolina and Georgia coast. Around 1800, Negro slaves were imported in very large numbers to work the rice and Sea Island cotton plantations in a climate and terrain so

[19] See A. H. Marckwardt, "*Want* with Ellipsis of Verbs of Motion," *American Speech*, XXIII (1948), 3–9.

unhealthy for whites that during the summer malaria season even the overseer left, entrusting the running of the plantation to the Negro "driver." Although mutually unintelligible, most of the languages spoken by these slaves in their African homes did share structural features. Add the fact that it was forbidden by law to teach slaves to read or write, and one perceives a situation that made for the retention of African elements in the variety of English that the Gullah learned to speak—a dialect that in its structural features resembles such contact languages as Taki-Taki and Melanesian Pidgin more than it does any of the better known dialects of English. Of remarkable uniformity in the pronunciation of its phonemes (in a region where white speech exhibits great phonetic diversity), Gullah has a simpler phonemic system than other dialects of English, with no contrast between /v/ and /w/, and the phonetic territory from [æ] to [ɔ] shared among two vowel phonemes, one low front unrounded and the other low back slightly rounded. The Gullah noun and verb are typically uninflected, but the system of verb phrases is complicated. Several thousand proper names of African origin are used among the Gullah as their private names. Many other African vocabulary items survive, and some of them— like *pinder*, *goober* "peanut," *cooter* "turtle," *benné* "sesame"—have passed into local white speech. Whether *tote* "carry" is purely African in origin is debatable, as is the case for African influence in the peculiar intonation patterns and voice-qualifiers that characterize white speech in the neighborhood of Charleston.[20]

Although the French settlements in North America date from the same time as the English, and for a time it was uncertain whether eastern North America would fall under English or French domination, in most of the area French is a dying language, if not

[20] The most scholarly investigation of Gullah is that by Lorenzo Turner, particularly his *Africanisms in the Gullah Dialect* (Chicago: The University of Chicago Press, 1949). See also Raven I. McDavid, Jr., and Virginia Glenn McDavid, "The Relationship of the Speech of American Negroes to the Speech of Whites," *American Speech*, XXVI (1951), 3–17.

actually dead. Aside from isolated relic communities, such as a few Missouri villages along the Mississippi, North American French survives only in Quebec (with offshoots in the Maritime Provinces and northern Maine) and in southwestern Louisiana. Even in Quebec, where it is strongest—thanks to the scrupulousness with which French Canadian culture has been protected by Dominion constitution and statutes, and to the craftiness with which politicians and ecclesiastics have exploited French Canadian particularism—French is suffering slow attrition. The high degree of industrialization which the province of Quebec has seen in the last two generations is producing the mobility of population that is bound to break down the cohesiveness of the linguistic community. Moreover, even the high birth rate of the Quebec French is not enough to match the fairly high birth rate elsewhere in Canada joined to the considerable immigration from the British Isles and from the European continent.

Louisiana French has an even shorter expectation of life. It survives only as a folk dialect in a region of extremely high illiteracy and—until the Huey Long era—relative inaccessability to the outside world. As transportation, education, and industrial employment have come to southwestern Louisiana, the Louisiana French have not become literate in their own language but rather have learned English, although often painfully and imperfectly. Here, as in Quebec, English words are freely taken into French and adapted to the phonology and morphology: thus, *bookkeeper* may go into Louisiana French as [bu:k-ki:pə(r)] or [bu:k-ki:pœr] and from it is derived a verb [bu:k-ki:pe:] "become a bookkeeper, do a bookkeeper's work," as in [il va bu:k-ki:pe:] "he is going to be a bookkeeper." Conversely, North American French loans into American English are relatively few, and are generally confined to cultural items and seldom known over a wide area. *Bureau* "dresser" is known almost everywhere, but may be a book-loan; *batteau* "rowboat" may possibly have been derived from the Huguenot rice planters of the Carolina coast, since it is most widely known in the Carolinas and Georgia and does not seem to occur in Louisiana or in the New York State communities near French Canada. In southwestern Louisiana, chiefly but not exclusively among bilinguals, a concrete highway is the *pave* /peyv/, and the driver in a car pool is said to *make a pass* for his riders (i.e., call for them).

In Louisiana, French has introduced such originally Indian words as *pirogue* "dugout canoe" and *lagniappe* "something extra given a customer making a purchase"; the crappie is called a *sac-à-lait*, by Cajun and English-speaking fishermen alike.

Scandinavian-language colonies have existed in most of the northern tier of states from Michigan west to the Pacific Coast, and also in Illinois, Iowa, and Wisconsin. Most of these colonies have been set up in rural areas, but there have been sizeable colonies in Cleveland, Chicago, and Brooklyn. Haugen's *The Norwegian Language in America*—a model study of bilingualism in action—demonstrates how the pressure of American civilization first gradually forced the American Norse into bilingualism to communicate with their neighbors, and then reduced the cultural importance of those institutions—church, school, and press—that had helped keep Norwegian a functioning language in the United States. The forces of cultural adaptation were as usual manifested linguistically in several kinds of borrowings, which Haugen groups under two main headings, **loan-words** and **loan-shifts**. A **loan-word** imports new morphemes, in part or whole; a **loan-shift** substitutes native morphemes. Pure loan-words may have much or little phonemic substitution or none at all; thus, American Norwegian has borrowed *haṛ`d-wæ̀ᴵr* "hardware," *stå̀ᴵr* "store," and *haṛ`dwæ̀rstå̀ᴵr*.[21] **Loan-blends** show partial morphemic substitution, as in American Norwegian *far`mar* "farmer," *far`mhuᴵs* "farmhouse," and *ju`lekarᴵd* "Christmas

---

[21] The transcriptions here follow Haugen's practice, a modification of standard Norwegian orthography to the complex phonological situations in American Norwegian, with diacritics to indicate stress, stress-tone, and length. For a full discussion of these symbols, see *The Norwegian Language in America* (Philadelphia: University of Pennsylvania Press, 1953), vol. II, pp. 642–44.

card." A loan-shift by creation may import the morpheme arrangement, literally or approximately, as in American Norwegian *heim-
plassen* "home place" and *hyrehelp* "hired help." One might also cite
the German *Halbinsel* "peninsula," a loan-shift from the Latin word
which English took over with phonemic substitution. Finally, by
extension, native words may take on a wide change of meaning,
under the phonetic or semantic influence, or both, of the lending
language. Thus, in standard Norwegian, *brand* means "fire," but in
some American Norwegian dialects it means "bran"; *god tid* "plenty
of time" in Norway is "good time" in American Norse; and in
American Portuguese *frio* "cold" and *correr* "to run" take on the
added signification of a cold in the head and running for office.[22]
While borrowing so generously from American English, American
Scandinavians have contributed to it some food names, the expression *to cook coffee* ("make coffee"), and certain peculiarities of intonation that persist even into the wholly English-speaking generation.

Much has been written about the contributions to English and
loans from English of the various foreign-language groups in
metropolitan areas, especially the Italians and Yiddish-speaking
Jews. *Pizza* and *spumoni*, *schlemiel* and *kibitzer* are part of the
normal metropolitan vocabulary. But one of the most interesting,
though transitory, linguistic phenomena of urban speech is the Slavic
koiné, often called *Slahvish*, which is found in the heavy-industry
towns of Pennsylvania and the Middle West. The migration to
the steel mills and coal mines about the end of the nineteenth century
tended to bring into such communities colonies of Czechs, Slovaks,
Ukrainians, Poles, Slovenes, Croats, Serbs, and occasionally Bul-
garians and Russians. Although the linguistic colonies attended
different churches (since the American Slavs are still split between
the Roman and Orthodox communions, and the Roman Church
has frequently maintained separate parishes for each nationality
group) and lived in different parts of town, nevertheless there was

[22] See ibid., vol. II, chap. xv, "The Process of Borrowing."

bound to be contact in the stores, the schools, the movies, and the mines or factories. Structurally, the Slavic languages resemble each other very closely, and much of the elementary vocabulary of any one language can be recognized by speakers of the others. What developed, then, was a new Slavic dialect in which inflections were highly reduced and most of the structural eccentricities of the individual languages were lost, or replaced by English devices. Beyond this, there is almost no information available, since most of the centers for linguistic study are not located in the areas in which Slahvish has developed, and the few American Slavicists have other interests which have kept them from doing extensive research in this field.

CLASS DIALECTS

In this discussion of the dialect differences within American English, we have alluded several times to the existence of class differences as well as regional differences and those based on foreign-language ancestry. This involves another dimension of analysis, but since the forces involved have already been shown, a short recapitulation should be sufficient.

Briefly, the prestige of a variety of the language is dependent on the prestige of the people who use it—on the extent to which they fulfil the express or tacit ideals of the society in which they live. The sharper the class divisions in a society, the easier it is to determine what the prestigious variety of the language actually is. For this reason, it has been much easier, for the last few hundred years at any rate, to determine who speaks cultivated British English than who speaks cultivated American. Conversely, the more fluid the society, the greater the difficulty in determining whose speech is the model to emulate. A popular sports announcer like Dizzy Dean, whose grammatical practices are completely uninhibited by education, has often drawn the fire of irate schoolmarms who observed that their charges were emulating Dizzy's multiple negatives and nonstandard verb-forms. Yet, if the schoolmarms had only studied historical linguistics, they would realize that it is hopeless to combat example by prescript, but only by another example. Certainly, in American society there are all sorts of conflicting pressures on the kind of speech one might choose to adopt for social reasons. It is "good American" to seek to raise oneself; it is not "good American" to turn one's back on one's old friends—to "forget your raising." It is American to desire education, but equally American to disparage the precepts of mere book-learning. It is equally American to admire the upper-class metropolitan New York speech of Franklin Roosevelt, to whom /áyðə(r)/ was natural, and to ridicule /áyðər/ when adopted as an elegant form by an up-country South Carolinian or a central Ohioan.

Nevertheless, we may follow Fries, Kurath, and others in recognizing three main types of social dialects: cultivated speech, common speech, and uneducated speech. These types correspond in general to the three types (III, II, and I) of Atlas informants.

Cultivated speech is simply the speech of those who have had educational and social advantages—normally four years of college or beyond—and hold a position of esteem, or at least of responsibility, in the community. This group includes most educators, most professional people, most people in the higher ranks of civil service —in short, most of those whose occupational and social obligations require continuous skill in the use of language.

At the other end of the spectrum, *uneducated speech* is simply that used by people who have had few educational or social advantages, and whose work or status is looked down upon or at best tolerated by the community. It is the natural speech of tenant farmers, unskilled laborers, and probably the majority of workers on assembly lines, even though many of the last are financially better off than many educators.

Common speech—what Mencken called the "American Vulgate"— like all intermediate elements in a series, is less sharply defined than the two extreme varieties. It is characteristic of those with high-school diplomas and likely some additional training; it is the speech of most farmers, most semiskilled and skilled workers, technicians, lower-grade civil service employees, and assorted businessmen—in short, of what is socially the middle class, though the economic status of its users may be very high or very low.

Obviously the terms are relative and vary from place to place. A middle-class "common speaker" of a university community like Ann Arbor, Michigan, would probably be far more cultured in an absolute sense than the doctor or school superintendent in a small town near the Okefenokee Swamp or in the middle of the southern Illinois coalfields. Furthermore, the spread between cultured speech and uneducated speech can be relatively little in a prosperous Iowa farming community, and relatively great in a stratified community of the Old South such as Charleston. In short, in evaluating social differences in language, as in evaluating any linguistic phenomena, one must consider observation more important than previous opinion.

Social differences in language are usually most apparent in morphology and syntax. But in some communities, particularly in the South, they manifest themselves in pronunciation as well. In fact, the more sharply drawn the lines of social cleavage, the more likely that such pronunciation differences will have social significance. In North Carolina, for instance, many people, possibly a majority, have constriction of postvocalic /-r/ in such words as *barn* and *beard*, but none of the cultured (type III) informants interviewed for the Linguistic Atlas had such constriction. Here, the cultivated speech of North Carolina is simply patterning itself after the prevailing forms in eastern Virginia, which to North Carolina is a traditional model of elegance. In central Ohio, however, one would hardly find any great differences in pronunciation between the cultured speakers and the rest of the community; one brother may become a blacksmith and another a judge; and both will maintain their phonemic distributions along with their family ties, though their work may produce differences in their grammatical practice and vocabulary.

Normally, the speech of a group with foreign-language ancestry is relatively lacking in the prestige that attaches to the cultured speech of the older American group in the community; the "foreign-ness" that identifies them suggests lack of complete assimilation to American forms of behavior. Yet here there may be exceptions. In certain parts of the Upper Midwest and the Rocky Mountains —to say nothing of California—the "older Americans" are the shifting element in the population, prospectors or lumberjacks at best, unskilled migratory "Okies" at worst. The stability of such communities comes from the second and third generation Norwegian or Italian or Armenian, who lays out the orchards or vineyards or irrigation ditches upon which the agricultural community depends for its existence, or by his insistence on a college education for his daughters sees that the local schools have competent teachers. Since these newer Americans often learn English directly from books, the models of cultivated speech in such communities hardly escape being a little less relaxed, a little more formal and precise, than one would expect in a New England community like Providence, with its longer and surer tradition of what constitutes cultured speech.

Education, by and large, is the surest index to the cultural status of a speaker. Not only does the educational process of itself tend to eliminate nonstandard grammatical items and old-fashioned pronunciations, but it usually brings a person into an environment where his associates are unlikely to use such forms, and where, consequently, he will have less inclination to revert to his former practices. But formal education, even combined with voracious reading, does not assure one of continuing to use cultured English if one's normal associates do not use it. The drive for functioning in one's society is too powerful. It is a familiar, though uncommon, experience of field-workers to encounter an informant who had received university degrees but then returned to the farm or the country store, to look after his parents or for his own health. Such informants often combine prodigious vocabularies with a natural command of the local folk grammar. In this connection may also be mentioned the experience of many educated speakers who served in the armed forces, especially as enlisted men, during World War II, and became aware of the necessity of readjusting their speech upon their return to civil life.

One of the many contributions to language study of Professor John S. Kenyon is the distinction, which he was the first to draw, between social differences (standard and nonstandard) and functional varieties (formal and informal). One must always remember that cultured or uneducated speech may be used in formal or informal situations. On the other hand, it is true that the cultured speaker, because of his wider experience in using the language, will have at his command many more shades of functional variety than the uneducated speaker, just as the tennis champion has a greater repertory of strokes than the club player. And certainly in his most formal speech or writing, the cultured speaker will be able to utilize more complicated syntactic structures.

Lastly, class dialects must be distinguished from the occupational varieties people use because of their work, hobbies, and special interests. It is true that some occupations normally presuppose (or exclude) certain social levels of language: it is almost unthinkable that a near-illiterate should talk understandingly in the professional argot of biochemistry or nuclear physics. But most of the peculiarities of one's "occupational language" are matters of vocabulary, and vocabulary, as we have all learned, is a matter of cultural experience. Given the opportunity to participate in the group where a special vocabulary is used—whether it be liturgical music, safe-cracking, or model railroading—one can acquire it. In fact, most educated Americans have several special vocabularies which they use in special social situations, with special groups they belong to. But rarely does one's *level* of usage change, unless the groups themselves represent disparate social classes. When they do, the individual may be equally in command of cultivated speech and his local variety of uneducated speech, and be able to shift readily from one to the other. Perhaps bi-dialectalism of this sort is most common in the southern states, in keeping with a tradition of *noblesse oblige;* often the cultured Southerner makes this accommodation and doesn't know it until an outsider calls it to his attention.

In concluding our examination of the dialects of American English, we find that the American situation has two significant characteristics—apparently contradictory, yet mutually dependent—which distinguish it from the dialect situation in almost any other major speech area.

1. In a recently settled country, with a high degree of geographical and social mobility characteristic of the whole population, the English of the United States has relatively few dialect differences, and nothing to compare with the sharp distinctions that one may find in a country like Italy, where a Piemontese peasant and a Calabrian will have great difficulty understanding one another. Nor is there anything like the sharp dichotomy between standard language and "dialect" that one commonly finds in Europe.

2. Nevertheless, regional varieties exist, and exist on all levels of usage. There is no single center with the overwhelming prestige of the London area in England, Madrid in Spain, Paris in France, or Florence and Rome in Italy. Despite temporary ascendancies of Boston or New York or St. Louis, the fact remains that many communities can point with pride to the prestige their cultivated speech has had; and as new centers of culture develop, more local varieties will acquire that prestige. In fact, we can already assert with confidence that the cultured speech native to any American community of importance is as good as one can find anywhere in the English-speaking world.

Thus, we conclude with the observation that the two important characteristics of American English, from the point of view of the linguistic geographer, are its relative unity and homogeneity, and the persistence of variety at the standard level.

A NOTE ON DIALECT IN LITERATURE

The discussion of dialect would hardly be complete without some mention of the representation of dialect in literature, a problem which is partly concerned with graphics and partly with the relationships of linguistics and literature.

The literary use of dialect is inextricably tied up with the theory of comedy. On an elemental level, the speaker of a nonstandard variety of the language appears as a foil to the better educated—either as a farcical contrast to polite behavior, or as a representative of primitive crudity which often is manifested in cruelty. On a slightly more sophisticated level, the folk speaker becomes a manifestation of the ideal of the noble savage, the embodiment of the natural virtues of mankind in contrast to the corruption of civilization. In the hands of the literary artist, the folk speaker may become the voice of a philosopher denouncing the ills of the world; he maintains a clear judgment of good and evil which the conventions of civilization have obscured for the better educated.

It should be obvious by now that literary dialect, by its very nature, has certain limitations, and that it can never be authentic as a full and adequate representation, but can at best merely suggest authenticity. There are three basic limitations upon the writer of literary dialect:

(1) Graphic symbolism is inadequate to represent many of the most characteristic features of a dialect, especially in pronunciation. It can never be used to represent with any consistency differences in the pronunciation of phonemes, though such graphic devices as *aaout* or *aout* for *out* may likely convey something like /æwt/. It can only partially indicate differences in the incidence of the phonemes; thus, whether the nucleus of *room* is /u/ or /uw/ cannot be conveyed

by any conventional spelling. Even differences in the phonemic system can be conveyed only with difficulty, often by reverse transcriptions, as with Cockney speech, in which there is no initial /h-/ phoneme, but only nonsignificant aspiration, usually greatest under extra-heavy stress. The usual way of representing Cockney speech in literature is to write *h-* at the beginning of all words (or at least of all stressed syllables) where it would not normally occur in standard English, and omit it (leaving the ' as a graphic cue to the reader) wherever it does normally occur, as in *Handerson's 'ouse.*

(2) The purpose of the writer of literary dialect is not to represent a dialect but to use the suggestion of one to convey certain literary values. In proportion as he succeeds in representing the dialect faithfully, he is likely to fail as a literary artist, because deciphering the dialect will take too much of the reader's attention.

(3) Finally, the literary artist will not normally convey as "dialect" any linguistic feature he shares with his "dialect characters." For example, one of the most accurate writers of literary dialects is William Gilmore Simms, a native of Charleston, where all speakers use [e·ᵊ] and [o·ᵊ] as the nuclei of *date* and *boat* respectively, rather than the up-gliding diphthongs /ey/ and /ow/ or their equivalents. But nowhere in any of Simms's novels is there any suggestion that any of his Charleston characters has a pronunciation like this. It is not merely that graphic representation of these sounds is difficult: actually the up-country Carolinian's representation as *dayut* and *bo-ut* (or *dehut* and *bohut*) is not too bad, and not much harder to figure out than other graphic devices in common use. The explanation seems to be, simply, that Simms did not realize how "exotic" these sounds were, because he used them himself, and hence he did not try to represent them.

A crude but common device often utilized to convey the illusion of substandard pronunciation is **eye-dialect,** a quasi-phonetic respelling of common words. Some of the usual words chosen are *women, was,* and *says,* which appear in eye-dialect as *wimmin, wuz,* and *sez*, representing the standard English pronunciations /wímin, wóz, séz/. Even Uriah Heep's *'umble* is best classed as eye-dialect, for many who like to consider themselves speakers of standard English (including the author of this chapter) wouldn't think of using any other pronunciation than /ómbəl/.

Probably everyone has his favorite examples of literary dialect, from Aristophanes down to the present. But to name a few of the better writers who have represented American dialects, we have:

James Russell Lowell, in the *Biglow Papers*—old-fashioned north-of-Boston Yankee speech.

Mark Twain, here and there—several varieties, especially dialects of the central Mississippi Valley.

Ring Lardner—chiefly the common speech, urban and rural, of the Middle West. His representation of the grammar of the common speech, appropriately praised by Mencken, is vigorous, without either exaggeration or patronizing.

Edward Eggleston—rural Indiana speech of the period just before the Civil War.

Mildred Haun, in *That Hawk's Done Gone*—somewhat sentimental, highly suggestive rather than detailed, indications of Smoky Mountain speech. Most attempts to represent the speech of the Southern mountaineer are both sentimentalized and exaggerated; she avoids the latter.

Jesse Stuart—a rather sure touch in representing the eastern Kentucky hill speech that he grew up with. Vocabulary more interesting than phonology, though the latter is often effectively suggested. His syntax is particularly good.

William Gilmore Simms—seriously interested in the speech of his characters, and generally effective in representing Negroes, poor whites, and mountaineers. A good study of his use of dialect would be a significant contribution to the study of American English and American literature.

Marjorie Kinnan Rawlings—the "cracker" speech of the natives of the Big Scrub expanse of northern Florida.

Joel Chandler Harris—deservedly well known for his portrayal of the old-fashioned piedmont Negro.

Thomas Nelson Page—the Negro of the Virginia plantation. Less realistic and more sentimental than Harris or Simms, but with considerable suggestive value.

Ambrose Gonzales, in the *Black Border* stories, and Samuel Stoney and Gertrude Shelby, in *Black Genesis*, rather effectively present the Gullah of the Carolina coast. Their stories, to be sure, are rather difficult to follow unless one knows something about Gullah; but genuine Gullah is even more difficult to understand. Other successful representations of Gullah have been written by DuBose Heyward, Julia Peterkin, and—particularly—Chalmers Murray in *Here Come Joe Mungin*.

COLLATERAL READING, CHAPTER 9

Books previously listed are cited by author only.

Bloomfield. Chap. xix, "Dialect Geography," pp. 321–45.

Gleason. Chap. xx, "Variation in Speech," pp. 284–300.

Hall, Robert A., Jr. *Leave Your Language Alone!* Ithaca, N.Y.: Linguistica, 1950. Chap. ix, "Language Covers Territory," pp. 130–51.

Kurath, Hans. *A Word Geography of the Eastern United States*. Ann Arbor: University of Michigan Press, 1949. Chap. i, "The English of the Eastern States: A Perspective," pp. 1–10; chap. ii, "The Speech Areas of the Eastern States," pp. 11–49.

Mencken, H. L. *The American Language*: *An Inquiry into the Development of English in the United States*, 4th ed., rev. New York: Alfred A. Knopf, Inc., 1936. Chap. ix, "The Common Speech," especially pp. 416–26, "Outlines of Its Grammar." Also Supplement Two (1948), Chap. IX, especially pp. 332-52

Kurath, Hans, *et al.* *Handbook of the Linguistic Geography of New England*. Washington, D.C.: American Council of Learned Societies, 1939. Chap. ii, "Methodology," pp. 39–54.

Atwood, E. Bagby. *A Survey of Verb Forms in the Eastern United States*. Ann Arbor: University of Michigan, 1953. "Conclusion," pp. 37–44.

Ives, Sumner. "A Theory of Literary Dialect." *Tulane Studies in English*, vol. 2 (New Orleans, 1950), pp. 137–82.

Chapter 10

Linguistics and the Teacher of English

THE POSITION OF THE ENGLISH TEACHER

The first nine chapters of this book have dealt chiefly with facts, analysis, and theory about language in general and present-day American English in particular. This last chapter, on the other hand, will be concerned with opinions, applications, and advice. Though it is more specifically directed to the active or prospective teacher of English, its appeal should be broader, since all of us, as parents and as citizens, should be interested in what is taught about our language. Those who have proceeded with care and understanding through these first nine chapters, whether as private readers or as students in a course, will no doubt already have reached some of the conclusions to be presented here. If they have, so much the better, since our aim throughout has been to provide a solid basis of fact and theory upon which ideas about language and methods of teaching it could be built. The extent to which the reader has anticipated our ideas on these subjects is the measure of his comprehension of their foundation. To the reader who has pondered the implications of what linguistics has to say about our language, as we have presented it in this book, this chapter should be largely redundant. Its value, it is hoped, will be that of a summary, bringing together in one place and in concise form the practical implications of what has gone before.

Let us begin by taking note of two ways in which a person's native language—in this case American English—differs from other subjects he is taught in school.

1. Since a child does not ordinarily go to school until he has learned to talk, he learns many things about his native language from amateur "teachers," who are usually unaware that they are teaching at all. Therefore, the professional teacher of English, even in the first grade, does not start from scratch, as does the teacher of algebra or chemistry, for instance.

2. Since language is the main medium through which other subjects are learned, its use pervades the whole of learning. It cannot be departmentalized. From the most elementary instruction about the world that lies about us in our infancy to the most advanced and recondite philosophy or science, our teachers are teaching us language. The professional English teacher must take account of many accomplices, who may be cooperative, but who may also be indifferent or even competitive. His subject is no monopoly in which he may be an austere authority. In fact, austere authoritarianism is more likely to characterize the uninformed amateur than the teacher learned in the infinite complexities and delicate adjustments of his native language.

The teacher of English thus works under a double handicap. He cannot begin at the beginning, but must build upon a foundation laid more or less ineptly and at random by others. And he is in constant competition with others who often think they know as much about his subject as he does, if not more. On the other hand, he has the satisfaction of knowing that his subject is the most vital of them all, and the one without which no teaching of any sort could go on. His primary responsibility to his students thus consists in making himself an expert in a field where all are more or less competent amateurs. He must justify his position by a more objective, more extensive, and more thorough knowledge of his native tongue than is possible to the nonspecialist. At the same time, he must be aware that he teaches in a field where prejudice and emotion often substitute for knowledge and objectivity. Whether dealing with the "bad grammar" of a substandard speaker, the inaccurate allophones and idioms of the foreign-born, or the thunderings of self-constituted guardians of "good English," he must be aware that most people's attitudes toward language are deeply tinged with emotions, none the less important for being irrational. If he is to win over his pupils and his adversaries in debate, rather than alienate them altogether, he must season his superior knowledge with tact and sensitivity. Only so can sound knowledge and clear thinking about language supplant shame, self-consciousness, narrow-mindedness, and arrogance.

LINGUISTICS AND LEARNING TO TALK

Our first teachers of our native tongue are, in the normal course, our parents, aided at first by older brothers and sisters and other members of the household, and later on by our first playfellows. Whether or not they make conscious attempts at instruction, all these people function as teachers by supplying us with a constant stream of talk, to be attended to, understood, responded to, imitated, and reproduced. They are the most important teachers of English we will ever have, because it is from them that we learn most of the important things about our native speech. From listening to them we make the first tremendous discovery that speech is meaningful. By mimicking them we learn to control our natural babbling and mold it into musical patterns of pitch and stress which are our earliest use of grammar. By long and patient experiment in imitation of their skill we learn to make the adjustments to our articulating organs which produce contrasting sounds at will. By trying out the results of our experimenting upon them, we test the success of our daring attempts to imitate what we hear. By questioning them in one way or another, we build up a stock of words, and by our very first experiments in abstraction, we learn grammatical patterns which allow us to build our words into meaningful structures. Sometimes our first teachers make conscious attempts to instruct us, by repetition, purposeful simplification, and patient correction. But it is not necessary for them to do more than supply us with material to imitate and respond to, by talking to and around us, and occasionally setting us right when we go wrong, whether by the sympathetic correction of a fond parent or the ridicule of a near contemporary. So great is our desire to learn and so indefatigable our devotion to the monumental task, that we master it regardless of bad teaching or none at all. We can be helped a little and hindered more, but we can be prevented from learning to talk only by being cut off entirely from the world of speech.

The language we learn from these first teachers is our **native speech** or **mother tongue.** By the age of five or six we have acquired virtually full command of its phonology, morphology, and syntax, and a vocabulary of several thousand words. In most cases it will remain with us for the rest of our lives, the foundation of all future linguistic development. Its allophones and their distribution in phonemes are so habitual with us that we are unaware of many distinctions that seem large and obvious to speakers of other dialects and languages. Our ear is so well attuned to it that we can immediately detect the speaker of another dialect, though we cannot always say what the differences between his speech and ours are. Because this speech is ours, we feel deeply that it is good, so that we are moved to defend it against encroachment or attack, and we are profoundly shaken if its authenticity or acceptability is questioned or made fun of. In short, it becomes, as no other language or dialect will, a basic part of our personality and an important element in all our thinking. Only recently have linguists, anthropologists, psychologists and philosophers gotten around to studying how profoundly our native speech colors our whole view of the world we live in and our place in it.[1]

Our earliest teachers, then, are amateurs, who cannot be expected to know anything about linguistics. Nor would it help them very much if they did. So overpowering is our motivation in this first stage of our education that we do almost all the work by ourselves, and require chiefly to be left alone to work things out in our own way. Linguists who have observed and worked with their own children have usually learned more than they have taught.[2] Nonetheless there are a few counsels which linguistics can offer to parents and others concerned with the first stages of language-learning. We may here take account of three.

1. The process of acquiring the phonology of one's native speech is a gradual one, extending over several years. After an initial period of babbling, in which all types of sounds are produced in uncontrolled profusion, the child begins his imitative attempts by acquiring two phonemes, a general consonant, which may have allophones as varied as [m, t, d, p, w, β], and a general vowel, whose allophones may wander all over the vowel quadrangle. These are usually put together in CV combinations, repeated and varied in stress and pitch patterns. But since the child can hear further contrasts, he soon begins to expand his phonemic stock by a process of division. His consonant splits into two—perhaps a stop and a continuant. He likewise splits his one vowel phoneme into two, assigning the front allophones to one and the back to another. By this process of increasing refinement, he eventually builds a stock of phonemes which correspond in their allophones and their distribution to those of the speech around him. Some distinctions, such as those between

---

[1] For pioneer work in this field, see *Language, Thought, and Reality: Selected Writings of Benjamin Lee Whorf*, ed. by John B. Carroll (New York: John Wiley & Sons, Inc., 1956), especially, "The Relation of Habitual Thought and Behavior to Language."

[2] See, for example, H. V. Velten, "The Growth of Phonemic and Lexical Patterns in Infant Language," *Language*, XIX (1943), 282–92.

/f/ and /θ/, /v/ and /ð/, and /r/, /l/, /y/, and /w/, may come as late as the fifth or sixth year, or even later. In the course of the phoneme-splitting, some allophones may be wrongly distributed. One of my own children successfully split a generalized voiceless frontal spirant into /f/ and /θ/, but was for a while unsure of their distribution, so that he sometimes said /fəm/ for *thumb* and /θíŋgər/ for *finger*.

Building a phonemic repertory is a long and rather complicated process, in which the principal help the child needs is to hear clear articulation in the speech about him. The worst that people can do to him is consciously to imitate his own phonemic patterns—to "talk baby-talk" to him. This only produces confusion and frustration, and retards the natural process of imitative learning. On the other hand, overcorrecting can be equally fruitless. To insist upon subtle phonemic distinctions before the child is aware of them produces bafflement, not progress. No amount of repeating /mə́ðər/ will help the child who has not yet split his voiced frontal spirant phoneme into /v/ and /ð/; he will just answer, in angry frustration, "I *said* /mə́vər/!"

If, however, some phonemic irregularities persist past the age of six, a parent or teacher with some knowledge of articulatory phonetics can straighten things out calmly and efficiently with a bit of coaching on the placing of the articulatory organs. Except for extreme cases of organic malformation, which are matters for the orthodontist or oral surgeon, anyone can accurately produce all the allophones of any dialect of English. There is no excuse for the perpetuation of a "lisp" or other unconventional allophone into adulthood. But the parent or teacher who attempts such phonemic adjustment must be sure of what he is doing. It is one thing to help the child master his own dialect and quite another to attempt to impose a feature from another dialect upon him. To a teacher from the Midland East or the "General American" area of the Middle and Far West, the interdental [ð̪] of New York City may sound like a "speech defect." Actually, it is as much a dialect feature of New

York speech as is the absence of postvocalic /r/. Many teachers for whom words like *whale* regularly begin with /hw/ spend a good deal of time attempting to teach this pronunciation to those whose native dialects do not contain this initial combination, and for whom *wail* and *whale* are both /wéyl/. This distinction may be aesthetically or socially desirable, though half the speakers of English lack it. But the teacher who insists upon it must be aware that he is imposing a dialect feature, not "correcting an error in speech."

2. This brings us to the second problem about which linguistics can counsel the parent or elementary teacher. This is the problem raised by the fact that the child's various "teachers" of his early speech are often not all speakers of the same dialect. This will be tne case wnen (a) the parents themselves are from different dialect areas or social classes, (b) the family has moved from the parents' native region, so that the dialect of playmates is different from that of parents, and (c) the child's home is in a closely populated urban area, where diverse class dialects may be heard in close proximity. An extreme case is that where one or both parents are not native speakers of any dialect of English, but have acquired English, often imperfectly, as a second language.

Under circumstances of this sort, the best counsel linguistics can give to parents and teachers is to be very cautious about attempting to force a single dialect upon the child under the impression that he must be taught "correct English." Such a procedure may result only in resentment or in cutting the child off from easy and spontaneous communication with his fellows. If left to work out his linguistic problem largely by himself, the child will quite naturally acquire two or more dialects, and will shift naturally from one to another as he shifts his manners and motions in accordance with changes in environment and companions. In this he differs only in degree from the child reared in a foreign-language environment, who becomes easily and naturally bilingual. In time, the dialect of the region and class where his interests, education, and social status place him will predominate. Meanwhile, the wise parent will ignore his occasional use of another regional or class dialect, no matter how distasteful it may seem. In the long run, ability to speak the dialect of another class or region without affectation may prove to be as useful as a knowledge of French or German.

3. The third area where a bit of linguistic knowledge can help the parent and primary teacher is the general field of grammar, especially morphology. Children rather frequently use "incorrect" grammatical forms, which often cause distress to parents and teachers, unless they are quaint enough to be amusing. Time and the child's natural desire to conform to the practices of the world around him will ultimately take care of these, just as they will eventually straighten out most phonemic irregularities. But if the parent or teacher wishes to hasten the process, he should be aware of the nature and origin of nonstandard forms before setting about correcting them.

The child learns to make grammatical forms—that is, to apply inflectional suffixes with concomitant morphophonemic adjustments —in two basic ways, direct imitation and a kind of systematic re-creation which linguists call **analogy.** By direct imitation is meant reproducing, as accurately as his phonemic system will allow, what he hears others say. Thus, if the child has heard parents say *cats* several times, in obvious reference to more than one *cat*, he will begin to use this form himself. Likewise, if he hears *dogs* often enough, he will learn this plural also. In this way he may build a stock of plural forms, such as *blocks*, *trees*, *toys*, *boxes*, *buses*, all learned as individual items. While doing this, he has also been acquiring the raw material for taking another tremendous intellectual step, the use of analogy to create new forms.

Unknown to himself and to most of his amateur "teachers," the child who has learned *blocks*, *dogs*, and *boxes* has learned the three regular allomorphs of the noun-plural inflection {-es}. At first he may use them only with the plural nouns he has learned as separate items. But pretty soon he begins to attach these endings, /-s, -z, -iz/, to other nouns. The problem of deciding which one of the three allomorphs to use with any given noun is solved by analogy; that is, by using an already learned plural as a model. Thus, analogy with /kǽts/ indicates that the plural of /rǽt/ is /rǽts/, and analogy with /tɔ́yz/ supplies the plural /bɔ́yz/. Linguists sometimes indicate the process of analogy by a formula similar to the mathematical proportion, thus:

$$\text{tɔy} : \text{tɔyz} = \text{bɔy} : x$$

The "unknown quantity" x clearly comes out as /bɔyz/.

By means of the constant use, both conscious and unconscious, of analogies of this sort, the child learns the patterns of distribution of the regular allomorphs of {-es}, which are, in effect, the rules for forming regular plurals. He may occasionally make slips, like forgetting that *blocks* is already plural and producing a double plural *blockses* by analogy with *boxes*. But on the whole he learns his lesson well—so well, in fact, that he applies his analogies in situations where usage contradicts their conclusions. So we get "childish" but perfectly logical forms like *sheeps, mans,* and *gooses.* This process is particularly noticeable with verbs, where analogy may produce regular but unconventional past-tense forms like *throwed, seed, goed, comed, bited, hitted,* and *buyed.*

Ideally, it would be a wise and practical course if we parents would learn from our children in this matter at least, and adopt these analogic forms into our own speech. This does happen to some extent in the history of language, though slowly and gradually. The very regularity of the {-es} plural is the result of gradual extension of this form to nouns which formerly used other plural suffixes. Many of the forms we now treat as irregular are fossil survivors of older regular plurals. Similarly, there has been a gradual drift of verbs from the irregular (but once regular) "strong" type to the regular or "weak" type which uses the allomorphs of {-ed} to form the past.[3] That the process is still going on is shown by the existence in present-day English of parallel forms in more or less free variation, like *shined* and *shone*, *thrived* and *throve*. If we were to give the language over to the children for a generation, their rigorous application of analogy would eliminate most irregularities in one clean sweep. But in this as in many other things, our natural conservatism prevails, so that we visit upon each new generation the task of memorizing a large number of irregular forms, whose continued existence is due to the dominance of convention over analogy. It may not be reasonable, but it is very human to do so. However, when we correct a child's *throwed* to *threw*, we should at least have the decency to recognize that he has more right to be amused or shocked than we have!

Many unconventional grammatical forms used by children are thus the result of analogy. Others, however, may be due to contact with speakers of another dialect. Thus, if a child uses /síyd/ as the past of *see*, he is probably applying analogy, while if he uses /síyn/, he is probably echoing a form learned from speakers of a dialect in which this is the standard past-tense as well as past-participle form. After all, a large number of native speakers of English naturally say *I seen him when he come in*. But whether the unconventional form is analogic or dialectal, the cure is the same: refrain from admonishment or direct correction, and simply continue to use the preferred form yourself in talking to the child. Before he grows up, he will naturally relegate /síyd/ to the limbo where go all his frustrated attempts to apply logic to an illogical world, and will learn that /siyn/ as a past tense, though used by many interesting, likable, and admirable people, is a mark of class dialect which many other people are strongly affected by. He will make his own decision as to whether he wishes to preserve it in his informal speech with those to whom it is natural, or ditch it altogether.

[3] For illustrations and statistics concerning this process, see C. C. Fries, *American English Grammar* (New York: Harcourt, Brace & Co., Inc., 1940), pp. 59–63.

In sum, then, the best advice that linguistics has to offer to parents and others concerned with helping children teach themselves their native speech is, first, to be aware of the magnitude of the task and have a wholesome respect for the intelligence and assiduity with which the child goes about it; second, to be sufficiently informed about the nature of language so that an effort to help will be help indeed, and not one more assertion of adult irrationality; and third, to realize that the best help that can be afforded the child is to supply him with a milieu of clear and intelligent talk to imitate. He will do the rest.

LINGUISTICS AND LEARNING TO READ

According to the 1950 census, about 97 per cent of the people in the United States over the age of fourteen know how to read. Their proficiency at this basic skill varies over a tremendous range, from the highly educated business or professional man, who can skim a page for its essential content with great speed and accuracy, to the day-laborer or field hand, who works out passages in his newspaper or Bible slowly and with difficulty. Some few may have learned to read even before they went to school. A few more may not have learned until they were adults, perhaps as part of their military training. But for most people, learning to read is the major pre-occupation and accomplishment of the first two or three years of formal schooling. This in turn means that in a highly literate country like the United States the teaching of reading is an educational enter-prise of vast proportions.

This being so, it is no wonder that there has been in the past and still is considerable controversy about how reading may best be taught. This controversy is not new. It goes back at least to the Renaissance, and has been quite active since the eighteenth century, when the ideal of universal literacy first began to look like a real-izable goal. The intensified study of pedagogy and psychology in the twentieth century has supplied more material both for debate and for solving the problems under debate more efficiently. As with other matters touching the lives of such a large proportion of the population so intimately, the debate about the teaching of reading has not always been carried on in the detached, objective fashion which is most likely to lead to sound solutions. It has not been free from uninformed emotion on the one hand and professional arrogance on the other. Meanwhile, 97 per cent of the people continue, somehow or other, to learn to read.

It is not the business of this book to enter into this controversy. Nor can we claim that linguistics supplies all the answers which render the controversy unnecessary and obsolete. But it is not beyond the range of reason to make two generalizations which seem axiomatic. (1) As the study which has gone farthest in the objective analysis of languages and their writing systems, linguistics has something to contribute to practical training in linguistic skills like reading. (2) Other things being equal, the teacher of reading who has some knowledge of the findings of linguistics about speech, writing, and their interrelationship will be more intelligent and effective than the teacher who knows nothing about these findings.

To begin with, we should note that reading is almost never taught by itself, that is as a simple, self-contained skill, in the way that swimming, for instance, is usually taught. That would be the case only if the prospective reader were an adult, in full command of the literary dialect of his native speech, and desirous of learning only to read, not to write and spell as well. Such a person could learn to read in a few weeks—perhaps even a few days—of intense application. But such persons do not exist in our society, though they are plentiful in predominantly illiterate societies. Instead, the typical beginning reader of our society is a child not far past infancy, frequently undergoing his first experience as a member of a group larger than the family, only recently become proficient in language, and engaged in learning other things, some of them much more interesting to many children than reading. These things add greatly to the problems of teaching reading. Much of the controversy about methods of teaching reading is really concerned not with reading in the simple sense at all, but with some of the other things that are combined with reading instruction in the primary classroom.

Many of these complicating factors are outside our field. But from the point of view of linguistics, the following three are important.

1. While he is learning to read, the child is also continuing the process of learning to speak and understand. This is particularly true in the matter of vocabulary. His knowledge of the structure of English is pretty thorough, but he is only at the beginning of his lifelong task of extending his vocabulary. Therefore, as soon as he gets beyond the simplest primer, he is likely to encounter words he has never heard before. His problem thus becomes more than one of simply translating the unfamiliar written shapes into familiar sounds. He must also learn to deal with new words, which are unfamiliar in speech as well.

2. To a greater or less degree, the child who is learning to read is also encountering a new dialect. The degree to which this is a problem depends upon the nature of his native dialect and of the earliest reading materials he is given. Even in the minimum case, where he has always heard standard English carefully spoken, he will find words, idioms, and constructions in his reading materials that are seldom if ever used in ordinary speech. If his native dialect is widely different from that of his teacher and his primer, his problems will be greater.

3. At the very same time that he begins to learn to read, or soon thereafter, the child also begins to write. This is, of course, both natural and desirable, since he must learn both skills to be literate, and the sooner the better. But it is sometimes forgotten that the two make quite different demands on the learner. To recognize and to reproduce are by no means the same thing, as any untrained person who tries to draw a picture of a familiar object knows very well.

The methods which most efficiently equip the child to read may actually hinder his learning to write and to spell.

Recognition of these three complicating factors leads to three bits of advice which the linguist can offer to the teacher of reading.

1. The very first instruction should be done with materials wholly within the vocabulary of the learner. Very soon, however, he should be taught how to deal with the unfamiliar: how to work out the most likely pronunciation and arrive at an approximation of the meaning in context.

2. Attempts to alter the child's dialect or to familiarize him with standard or literary dialect should be independent of instruction in the mechanics of reading.

3. If an efficient method of training a child in rapid silent reading interferes markedly with his learning to read aloud, to write, and to spell, it should be abandoned in favor of a compromise method that allows him to acquire all three skills equally.

These three factors, and others beside, must be taken account of in any practical consideration of teaching reading to young children. From the theoretical point of view, however, we may set them aside temporarily in order to reach some conclusions concerning the teaching of reading as a simple skill, unrelated to other skills or problems with which teacher and pupil may be engaged. It is clear that such a theoretical approach to the subject must be based on an understanding of two things: (1) the mechanics of the act of reading itself, and (2) the nature of the writing system and its relationship to the already known system of speech.

The actual mechanics of reading is the province of the physiologist and psychologist, not of the linguist. For our purposes, the most important things about it are, first, that the eye cannot clearly discern objects while they are moving across the field of vision, and second, that the central area of acute vision, while narrow in relation to the whole field, is still wide enough to include a sizeable number of distinctly contrasting graphemic symbols. The consequences of these facts are, first, that the material being read does not flow smoothly across our field of vision (as the sounds of speech flow in upon the ear), but appears as a series of distinct pictures, each perceived for a fragment of time before the eye jumps to the next; and second, that each of these separate pictures may include not one but half a dozen or more graphemes, all seen at once as part of a total configuration.

Putting these facts about the mechanics of reading together with the observations about our writing system made in Chapter 8, we reach the following conclusions:

(1) Even if our writing system were wholly phonemic, we would soon come to recognize many combinations of graphemes as *wholes*. If the eye were forced to stop at each individual grapheme, reading would be painfully slow.

(2) Since our writing system departs in various ways from its remote phonemic basis, we tend to read by the word or even by the word-group or phrase. But when we encounter strange configurations that do not immediately suggest familiar linguistic units, we resort to a phonemic or morphemic break-down of the graphemes and grapheme combinations.

These conclusions, in turn, make it apparent that efficient reading is really a combination of two skills, both of which must be taught by any satisfactory method of teaching reading. They are, first, the ability to recognize accurately a large number of words and word groups as wholes, thus minimizing the number of stops the eye must make in scanning a line of print or script, and second, the ability to work out the pronunciation of an unrecognized graphic configuration, in terms of its constituent phonograms and morphograms, until it is recognized as a unit of the spoken vocabulary. Methods of teaching reading based exclusively on developing one or the other of these abilities are often called "sight-word" and "phonic" methods, respectively. It is clear to the linguist, as to the practical teacher, that the best method must equip the child with both skills, so that he may read the familiar with ease and decipher the unfamiliar with accuracy. The linguist would add that efficient and accurate instruction in both must be based upon a sound understanding of English phonemics, morphemics, and graphics. Only with such understanding can the reading teacher be sure he is teaching realities.[4]

LINGUISTICS AND LEARNING TO WRITE

Most societies that train the majority of the population to read also train them to write. So closely allied are these two skills in most contexts that the common term *literacy* is used to mean "ability to read and write." Yet, it does not inevitably follow that they are inseparable. It is conceivable that in a society where communication in writing was a one-way affair—as by the issuing of directions and orders to a large subservient population by a small ruling class—it might be desirable to teach many to read only, since they would have no need to write. Or if someone should invent a typewriter as cheap and as portable as a pencil, the manual skill of tracing out letters on paper would cease to be a necessity and might become a special vocation or hobby, as sign-painting, ornamental calligraphy, sketching, and embroidery are now. Such a machine does not seem to be an immediate possibility, so we must learn to make marks upon paper which bear sufficient resemblance to standard allographs of our writing system to allow a properly trained person to read them without difficulty. Legibility and minimal neatness are all that we ask of ordinary writing. Unlike the Chinese, we relegate the ornamental and aesthetic qualities of writing to engravers, engrossers, sign-painters, stone-cutters, and other specialists.

As has already been noted, writing is customarily taught at the same time as reading, and by the same teacher. This is, of course, sound practice, since the two skills reinforce and supplement each

[4] For specific recommendations of prominent linguists concerning the teaching of reading, see the articles by Bloomfield, Hall, and McQuown in the list of collateral reading at the end of this chapter.

other, just as listening and talking do at an earlier stage. In each case, our incurable human fondness for imitation causes attempts at reproduction to follow close upon recognition. But there is a major difference between learning to talk and learning to write. In the one case, the child creates his own system by a process of consecutive refinements, gradually adjusting it more and more accurately to the system he is imitating. In the other case, the child is systematically introduced to the separate units of a completely formed system, and trained directly in their use. The individual contribution comes later, when, as we say, the child "develops his own handwriting."

Early in Chapter 8 (p. 432), we noted that the significant features of our writing system are of two sorts: the basic shapes of the characters, and their relative arrangement on the paper or other background. This suggests that there are two phases in the process of learning to write: (1) learning to produce recognizable characters, usually called **penmanship,** and (2) learning to arrange them in conventional patterns, which includes the skills of **spelling, capitalization, word division,** and **punctuation.**

Concerning the teaching of penmanship, linguistics has little new to offer. Most children begin by imitating the printed letters which they see in their reading materials, usually called **manuscript** by teachers. At this stage they learn to make both capital and lower case letters, thus unconsciously learning the graphemic principle, according to which A and a, though quite different in shape, can be considered structurally "the same letter." Quite early most children begin to learn the more rapid form of handwriting known as **cursive** or **script** writing. This is somewhat comparable to learning a new dialect in speech, since the script allographs of some of the graphemes may differ quite markedly from their allographs in print. There is hardly enough similarity, for instance, between the four shapes G g *G g* to lead the objective observer to class them as "the same letter." Yet, through much practice and drill, we all learn to produce the script $\mathscr{G}$ and $\mathscr{g}$ almost automatically and to take them for granted as perfect equivalents of the printed forms G and g. It is a rare child indeed who has not mastered the mechanics of producing the letters by the third or fourth grade of school.

Not so with the matter of the proper ordering of the characters into connected written discourse. Spelling and punctuation continue to be formally taught throughout elementary school and on into high school. Yet they are often imperfectly mastered by college students and continue to plague some people throughout life. Nor are the people who never learn to spell conventionally necessarily lacking in intelligence or linguistic skill. William Butler Yeats and John Keats, unparalleled masters of the poetic resources of English, were both notoriously poor spellers.[5] Yet, since the standardization of our spelling in the seventeenth and eighteenth centuries, we have come to consider accurate spelling a mark of education, intelligence, and social acceptability. Hence, the large amount of time devoted to it in our schooling.

As we saw in Chapter 8, our spelling is inconsistent for three main reasons:

(1) The diverse sources of English words, preserving graphic conventions from different writing systems. Compare, for instance, the four morphemes all pronounced /féyn/: Anglo-Saxon *fain*, Latin *fane*, French *feign*, and Greek *phane* (as in *cellophane*).

(2) Changes which have occurred in the pronunciation and distribution of English phonemes without corresponding graphic changes, as illustrated by the falling together in pronunciation of the originally distinct *right*, *write*, and *wright*.

[5] Among many remarkable misspellings in the manuscript of Keats's "Eve of *St. Agnes*" are *shilded* (*shielded*), *tipple* (*triple*), *wereof*, *paradize*. Editors are still arguing over a key word in one of Yeats's most important poems. Yeats apparently wrote *distain* ("Byzantium," line 5), and may have meant it, though *disdain* makes somewhat more obvious sense and is printed in most editions. Since Yeats was a poor speller, all are agreed that even recourse to his manuscript would not solve the question, which must apparently remain forever unsettled.

(3) The semimorphographic nature of our spelling, with its tendency not to represent morphophonemic changes, especially those due to gradation. This produces pairs of words which look more alike than they sound, such as *history*: *historical*, phonemically /hístəriy: histórɨkəl/, and *pacify*: *pacific*, phonemically /pǽsɨfày: pəsífik/.

Linguistics can supply no easy solution to the problems of teaching spelling. It can, however, give some advice that may be of help. Much of it should be obvious to those who have read the earlier chapters of this book, so that it can be rather succinctly stated here, under five headings.

1. The poor speller should not be considered deficient in intelligence or linguistic ability. Some poor spellers are actually more perceptive in linguistic matters than good spellers, since their misspellings often result from attempts to render the English graphic system more phonemic than it actually is. Such misspellers often make better phoneticians than those who always spell correctly.

2. Spelling should be treated as a special phase of the general skill of writing, and one whose importance is more social than linguistic. Misspelling seldom prevents or even hinders communication, but it conditions our estimate of the misspeller.

3. The phonemic basis of the English writing system, slim as it is, should be exploited as fully as possible. It has been estimated that within a 3000-word elementary school vocabulary, four-fifths of the phonemes are spelled by their (more or less) regular graphemic equivalents.[6]

4. The particular problems of each individual misspeller should be individually diagnosed and treated. Thus, the child who has been taught to read exclusively or predominantly by the sight method will often transpose letters and telescope syllables, as in *salior* for *sailor* and *repition* for *repetition*. His cure is a dose of "phonics."

[6] See P. R. Hanna and J. T. Moore, Jr., "Spelling, from Spoken Word to Written Symbol," *Elementary School Journal*, LIII (1952–53), 329–37.

On the other hand, a combination of dialectal divergence and phonemic overaccuracy may produce *artic* for *arctic*, *athelete* for *athlete*, and *signifigant* for *significant*. The teacher with some knowledge of phonemics and intelligent awareness of the dialect of his pupils will know how to straighten out such problems.

5. When the student begins to study foreign languages, especially French and Latin, his new knowledge and interest may be turned to account by revealing to him the historical reasons for many apparently unreasonable spellings. The same may be done by teaching a little elementary historical and comparative linguistics. Such a spelling as *knight*, for instance, becomes more than a mere irrationality to the student who knows its Chaucerian pronunciation [knɪxt] and its German doublet *knecht*.

PUNCTUATION AND CAPITALIZATION. Rules for the conventional use of punctuation marks and capitals occupy a good deal of room in handbooks of English, and the study of these matters often continues even into college courses in composition. The reason for this is the fact already discussed in Chapter 8: the punctuation system is primarily a written substitute for intonation in speech, but it does not represent intonation directly. A writer thus cannot translate the intonational features of juncture, stress, and pitch directly into punctuation marks in the way that a musician can record a tune in musical notation. Instead, the writer must convert from the intonation system to the punctuation system by way of his understanding of the structural meaning. This does not mean that only grammarians can punctuate, because the grammatical knowledge required may be subconscious. But it does mean that learning to punctuate is a fairly complex business, never wholly mastered by some otherwise competent writers.

In spite of the absence of complete correspondence between punctuation and intonation, there are some points where the two systems coincide. It is thus possible to make limited use of intonational clues in teaching punctuation. Some simple training in identifying sentence-final intonation contours, for instance, can help the student to place his end marks properly, and avoid the punctuation errors of sentence-fragment and "run-on" sentence. Recognition of the contrasting intonation patterns of restrictive and nonrestrictive modifiers and of the intonational signals marking structures such as internal sentence-modifiers and coordinate modifiers not joined by a coordinator can help considerably in the placing of commas. The teacher who has made some study of intonation can thus teach students to punctuate "by ear," so far as this is possible. Beyond that, the conventions of punctuation must be taught in relation to grammar.

LINGUISTICS AND RHETORIC

Once the elementary student has mastered the mechanics of reading and writing, his instruction in English usually moves into the broad field of what are often called "the language arts." Even if his formal education ends with high school, he will be in some measure introduced to the art of effective writing, or rhetoric, and to the comprehension and interpretation of literature. If he goes on to college, he will be expected to increase his proficiency in reading, writing, listening, and speaking through courses in composition, communication, and speech, and he may go on to more advanced literary study, including the concepts and techniques of literary criticism. Linguistics has something to contribute to all of these, and the teacher of any of them who has had training in structural and historical linguistics will be more effective—other things being equal—than the teacher who has not. It should hardly be necessary to substantiate this point for those who have pondered the implications of the first nine chapters in this book. Nor have we space here to describe in detail all the ways in which linguistic knowledge can enrich, illuminate, and enliven the study of the language arts. We can, however, point out a few of the important ways in which linguistics can support the teaching of rhetoric and literature, the two main branches of high school and college instruction in English.

The subject of rhetoric is the art of effective writing and speaking. It is important to emphasize the word *art* here, and to contrast its implications with those of the term *linguistic science*. As we have tried to make clear at many points in this book, linguistic science deals only with those aspects of language which are amenable to objective scrutiny, description, and analysis. Whether his approach and preoccupation be historical, comparative, or synchronic, the linguist aims only at description, analysis, generalization, and reconstruction of language considered as a vast and complex system of behavior. His concern is with what has been and is, not with what might or should be. The rhetorician, on the other hand, is concerned with using this instrument as effectively as possible—with language as a medium of communication and influence, even of aesthetic pleasure, though here he begins to encroach upon the territory of the literary critic. His is the more difficult and more important task. But since the medium in which he works is language, he may profit from the knowledge which linguists are steadily accumulating about that medium.

It seems clear, then, that there can be no doubt about the value —indeed the necessity—of some knowledge of linguistics for the teacher of composition, both in high school and in college. Specifically, he must know the phonemic system of English and its relation to the graphic system if he is to teach spelling intelligently. An understanding of morphemics will guide him in helping his students to extend their vocabularies by the study of word groups and derivative classes. A conscious mastery of structural grammar will aid him in teaching sentence structure. A knowledge of the history of English and of the basic principles of semantics—matters outside the scope of this book—will give him a sense of the wealth of the English vocabulary and help him communicate to his students a love of precise and graceful diction. Some knowledge of the dialects of his region and their relation to standard literary English will give him understanding of his students' departures from what he considers "good English," and help him decide to what extent it is wise to attempt to alter their speech and writing habits. But more important than any of these is the fact that his over-all knowledge of the methods, theories, and generalizations of linguistics will free him from provincialism and prejudice, and deepen his wonder and respect for his native tongue. Such knowledge can inspire him to set as a goal for his students, not the attainment of an arbitrary and sterile "correctness," but some degree of mastery over man's most complicated, delicate, and efficient instrument—his language.

Knowledge of linguistics, then, enables the teacher of rhetoric to move confidently and efficiently in many areas where without it he must grope instinctively. There remains the question, much debated nowadays, as to how much knowledge of linguistics should be directly taught as part of the ordinary student's rhetorical training. This is sometimes more bluntly put as the question, "How much grammar should be taught in high school and college composition courses?" But it is really a broader question, which can be stated this way: "How much *theoretical* knowledge of the way language functions is essential to an adequate *operational* knowledge of how to use it?" We have seen that the child has a competent operational knowledge of phonemics, morphemics, and grammar before he even enters school. Must he be given a theoretical knowledge of these subjects as well in order to become a skilful user of language?

The answer is, of course, "No, but it helps." There have been countless skilful speakers and writers of English who have never studied grammar in any form, just as there have been successful painters who never studied draughtsmanship or color harmony. There are many roads to competence in an art. But judicious introduction to some theoretical knowledge about language can be a short cut and an incentive to the improvement of one's operational skill in its use. Specifically, there are four basic theoretical concepts which linguistically trained teachers of composition have found it profitable to introduce to their students.

1. *The Usage Concept.* In this book we have said very little specifically about usage, for the simple reason that our whole study is built upon the premise that language is the actual linguistic behavior of native speakers, which is all that is meant by usage. Nevertheless, the old notion persists—in some quarters as strongly as it ever did in the eighteenth century—that there is some other source and sanction for language, and that the linguistic behavior of the great majority of native speakers is in some way degenerate and corrupt. It is certainly the duty of the English teacher to disabuse his students of this notion, which leads to linguistic uncertainty, self-consciousness, and timid commonplaceness. In its place, the teacher should attempt to establish in his students confidence in their already broad and comprehensive knowledge of their native tongue, and should show them how this knowledge can be used as a firm foundation on which to build a finer, more delicate, and more precise sense of style.

2. *The Dialect Concept.* Even the most superficial study of usage very soon comes upon the problem of divided usage. The usage concept must at this point be supplemented by the dialect concept. The student who has some knowledge of the diversity of regional, class, and occupational dialects is in a much better position to come to decisions on questions of divided usage. If the standards of written English which his teacher is attempting to instruct him in are presented as another dialect—the common dialect of educated persons who write—he will be able to see that it is possible for him to master that dialect and thus become a member of the guild of the educated without eradicating the other dialects in which he conducts the affairs of his everyday life. Above all, he can be trained in standard written English without being made ashamed or self-conscious about his native speech, and thus relegated to some

linguistic limbo because he is unable to speak "correctly" and afraid to speak "incorrectly."

3. *The Structural Concept.* Knowledge about usage and dialect tends to be merely a collection of disorganized details unless there is also some knowledge of structure to give a sense of order to the whole. Language does indeed consist of myriads of details, but these details are part of an elaborately interlocking *system*, as we have been at some pains to make clear throughout this book. The English teacher should thus give his students some sense of the structure of English—phonemic, morphemic, and grammatical—as the framework within which his personal use of language must contain itself. It is an adaptable and flexible framework, but it has its rigidities. Some theoretical knowledge of this structure by student as well as teacher can be of great help in their cooperative effort to increase the student's operational skill—his ability to use the incomparable instrument of language with something like the effectiveness which it permits.

4. *The Semantic Concept.* Finally, the teacher of English is derelict in his duty if he does not give his students at least a basic understanding of the relationship between the world of language and the outside world. This means above all an insight into the relationship between the word and the referent, into the processes of abstraction, metaphor, and analogy, and into the way language controls thought even more powerfully than thought can control language. These matters fall within the areas of semantics and what linguists call metalinguistics, which are outside the range of this book. But there is a good deal being said about them nowadays, and we shall hear more in the future. Meanwhile, the teacher of English must impart enough of their basic concepts to his students to show them how they may free themselves from what Stuart Chase has called the "tyranny of words."

Just how much of the detailed findings of linguistics must be taught in order to transmit these four fundamental concepts, the teacher must decide for himself. In many cases he will have to find and organize his materials himself, since among all the myriads of textbooks in the general field of English rhetoric and grammar, there are very few which are primarily intended for transmitting these important ideas about language. But books of this sort are beginning to appear, and they will be more plentiful as time goes on.

We may summarize the contribution that linguistics can make to the work of the teacher of rhetoric by emphasizing that it can help him set his students free in the world of language. The usage concept frees them from the notion of a transcendental, authoritarian "correctness" in language which is to be approached only by suppressing the instinctive and the natural. The dialect concept sets them free from the idea that all departures from a fixed standard are perforce wrong, and allows them to attain a linguistic versatility which is the counterpart of the social versatility characteristic of the educated man in a democracy. The structural concept shows them the solid substance beneath the glancing surface lights of successful prose and supplies a discipline that sets them free to exercise their creative imagination in stylistic development. Finally, the semantic concept frees them from the shackles that language itself can put upon their thought, and sets them on the way to being the masters, not the slaves, of their own words.

LINGUISTICS AND LITERATURE

During the last two hundred years or so, the branch of linguistics that has contributed most to the study and teaching of literature is the historical. The relationship has been a mutually beneficial one. It was the desire to recover the literature of Old and Middle English times that was largely responsible for the pioneer study of Old English in the seventeenth century. At first it was only a few specialists who had any knowledge in this field, which most scholars considered trivial beside the study of Latin and Greek. Even in the middle of the eighteenth century, Dr. Johnson, who valued learning highly (though he was sometimes too lazy to pursue it), could write an English dictionary complete with etymologies, without having any personal knowledge of Old English. But this was recognized as a deficiency even by contemporaries. During the nineteenth century both the amount of knowledge about the older phases of English and the number of persons possessing that knowledge increased immeasurably. Much of this knowledge has spread outward from the specialists to the general public. Most college sophomores —indeed, many high school seniors—can set right Dryden's errors concerning the pronunciation of Chaucer's English, even though they may not have a tenth of his appreciation for that "perpetual fountain of good sense," writing "in the dawning of our language." Thanks to historical linguistics and its sister-sciences, textual criticism and bibliography, the twentieth-century schoolboy may own an edition of Shakespeare such as the great Shakespearians of the past never dreamed of. The study of the phonology, grammar, and lexicon of the older periods of English has in truth unlocked the treasures of our older literature.

It is clear that some knowledge of the history of the English language and of its structure at various times in the past is essential to any teacher of literature who ventures beyond the elementary and the contemporary. This has long been recognized in regard to more advanced teachers, as is evidenced by the courses in philology or historical linguistics which are required of most graduate students of English. It has not been so generally perceived that knowledge of this sort may illuminate the teaching of literature in high school and grade school as well. There are too many teachers of literature who are inadequately equipped to enhance the reading of a Shakespeare sonnet or a Sheridan play by the insights which a little knowledge of historical linguistics makes possible. Certainly some linguistic history should be combined with the literary history which is standard training for teachers of English literature on all levels.

The contribution which structural linguistics can make to the study and teaching of literature has been much less generally recognized. Though English departments in American colleges are often called departments of "English language and literature," too often the gap between the two branches has been virtually unbridged. Most teachers of literature and literary critics, even at the most advanced levels, have brought to their study little knowledge of the structure of English beyond the smattering of prescientific grammar which they acquired in elementary and high school. Recently, however, there have been signs of a change. On the one hand, the intense scrutiny of literary texts, particularly poems, which is essential to the methods of the so-called "New Critics" has directed the conscious attention of critics and teachers to matters of linguistic structure. On the other hand, some linguists are beginning to venture beyond their characteristic preoccupation with the spoken language of ordinary native speakers and to extend their methods of structural analysis to the language of written literature. There is even a small group of those who, to mix a metaphor, attempt to keep a footing in both camps at the risk of falling between two stools. Speaking as one of that anomalous group, I am pleased to note that as the literary critic and the structural linguist continue to approach one another, the posture of the straddler becomes less precarious and his risk of becoming a pariah, cast out from both camps, less great. Indeed, a major purpose of this book is to help in that desirable *rapprochement*.

Specifically, structural linguistics can aid the study and teaching of literature in two ways. (1) It can supply a solid foundation of linguistic analysis upon which a critical analysis of the artistic structure of a work of literature can be based. (2) It can supply a method of analysis which can be extended into the metalinguistic and artistic realms where the critic works.

The latter of these is at present so new and experimental that we can say nothing significant about it here. But in the former area, two specific ways in which linguistics can aid literary analysis can be pointed out.

1. Knowledge of phonemics and intonation can supply a firm basis for the study of the sounds and rhythms of literature, especially poetry. At present, virtually all discussion of these matters by critics and teachers is impressionistic and inaccurate. Vowel sounds are described as "thin," "rich," "deep," "soft," and so on, and the important distinctions of consonants as stops and continuants, voiced and unvoiced, sibilant, lateral, and nasal, all of which could contribute to a clear discussion of sound-effects in poetry, are ignored. The student of literature who understands basic phonetics and phonemics has both a greater insight into the sound of language and a clear and precise vocabulary for discussing it.

2. Knowledge of grammatical structure and methods of grammatical analysis permits a systematic, objective investigation and description of style. Many of the most characteristic stylistic traits of writers as diverse as Pope, Donne, Joyce, Dylan Thomas, and E. E. Cummings are in the field of grammar. The methods of structural analysis with which the linguist is conversant can supply a descriptive foundation for the aesthetic interpretation and critical comparison of diverse styles. Sometimes a deliberately grammatical attack upon obscurities can supply keys to meaning which no amount of impressionistic reading can furnish. A thorough understanding of the relationship of lexical and structural meaning, and of the ambiguities possible in both, can cast much light on literary irony and word-play. The increasing preoccupation of literary criticism with irony and ambiguity makes this a most promising area where linguistic science can serve the art of literary explication and criticism.

The brief survey in this chapter may be summarized by the conclusion that linguistic science may serve the teacher of English on all levels and in all areas where he works, from the most elementary to the most abstruse. Its objective descriptions, logical generalizations, and inductive methods may cast light on many problems which the

English teacher faces, from the best way to teach reading to the word-play of Joyce and the sprung rhythm of Gerard Manley Hopkins. After all, the common medium of all these things is language, and linguistics is the study most directly concerned with language. It does not profess to know all the answers about language in general or English in particular. In fact, it is the linguist himself who knows how incomplete his knowledge is, and how many gaps there are yet to be filled before we can say we have a complete description and structural analysis of English. But many parts of that description and analysis are ready at hand, and the English teacher who avails himself of them will find them useful aids in many of the difficult tasks which his profession sets for him. If this book has made some of the less abstruse of the findings of linguistics available to the student and teacher of English, it has succeeded in its purpose.

COLLATERAL READING, CHAPTER 10

Books previously listed are cited by author only.

Fries, Charles C. *The Teaching of English.* Ann Arbor: George Wahr, 1949. Chap. vi, "The Problems of the Teacher: Developing Habits," pp. 123–47; chap. vii, "The Problems of the Teacher: Developing Attitudes," pp. 148–59; chap. viii, "The Problems of the Teacher: Acquiring Tools," pp. 161–74.

Carroll. Chap. vi, "Language and Education," pp. 140–68.

Smith, Henry Lee, Jr. *Linguistic Science and the Teaching of English.* Cambridge: Harvard University Press, 1956.

Laird, Charlton. *The Miracle of Language.* Cleveland and New York: The World Publishing Co., 1953. Chap. xvi, "The King's English in a Democratic World," pp. 252–68.

Hall, Robert A., Jr. *Leave Your Language Alone!* Ithaca, N. Y.: Linguistica, 1950. Chap. xi, "Learning Your Own Language," pp. 185–200.

Note: Some of the best material in this field is to be found in articles in various linguistic and educational journals. The following list includes articles by both linguists and practicing teachers of English.

Anderson, Edward L. "Grammar—What and How," *Elementary English*, xxx (1953), 242–46.

ALLEN, HAROLD B., *Readings in Applied English Linguistics.* New York: Appleton-Century-Crofts, 1958.

Bloomfield, Leonard. "Linguistics and Reading," *Elementary English Review*, xix (1942), 125–30, 183–86.

Burnet, MacCurdy. "Structural Syntax on the Blackboard," *College English*, xvi (1954–55), 38–43.

Caffrey, J. "Heresy and the Cultural Lag: English Grammar," *Educational Forum*, xv (1950–51), 353–58.

College Composition and Communication, Vol. v, No. 4 (December, 1954). This issue is largely given over to a series of papers originally presented as a panel discussion on "Modern Linguistics and the Teaching of Freshman English" at the meeting of the Conference on College Composition and Communication at St. Louis in March, 1954. The authors are Karl W. Dykema, J. E. Congleton, James B. McMillan, Sumner Ives, W. Nelson Francis, Donald J. Lloyd, and L. M. Myers.

Francis, W. Nelson. "Revolution in Grammar," *Quarterly Journal of Speech*, XL (1954), 299–312.

Geist, Robert J. "Structural Grammar and the Sixth Grade," *American Speech*, XXXI (1956), 5–12.

Gorrell, Robert M. "Grammar in the Composition Course," *College English*, XVI (1954–55), 233–38.

Hall, Robert A., Jr. "Descriptive Linguistics and the Teaching of English," *Education*, LXXIII (1952–53), 360–67.

Hanna, P. R., and Moore, J. T., Jr. "Spelling, from Spoken Word to Written Symbol," *Elementary School Journal*, LIII (1952–53), 329–37.

Hayakawa, S. I. "Linguistic Science and the Teaching of English," *Baltimore Bulletin of Education*, XXIX (1952), 9–23.

Hill, Archibald A. "Prescriptivism and Linguistics in English Teaching," *College English*, XV (1953–54), 395–99.

Hultzén, Lee S. "Pronunciation," *Elementary English*, XXIX (1952), 402–6+.

Ives, Sumner. "Linguistics in the Classroom," *College English*, XVII (1955–56), 165–72.

Kitchin, Aileen T. "On the Teaching of the English Language," *Teachers College Record*, XLIX (1947–48), 165–78.

Lloyd, Donald J. "The Child Who Goes to School," *Elementary English*, XXX (1953), 411–16.

Lloyd, Donald J. "English and the Liberal Arts Tradition," *College English*, XVII (1955–56), 100–104.

McQuown, Norman A. "Language-Learning from an Anthropological Point of View," *Elementary School Journal*, LIV (1953–54), 402–8.

Moulton, Dorothy E. "Grammar for Future Teachers of English," *Educational Administration and Supervision*, XL (1954), 29–37.

Rich, Elaine S. "How Shall We Think About Grammar in the Basic Course?" *College English*, XVI (1954–55), 307–8.

Sledd, James H. "Teaching Prose Style to College Freshmen," *Journal of General Education*, V (1950), 31–37.

Väänänen, Veikko. "Linguistics in the Classroom," *Modern Language Journal*, XXXIV (1950), 347–50.

Velten, H. V. "The Growth of Phonemic and Lexical Patterns in Infant Language," *Language*, XIX (1943), 282–92.

Appendix

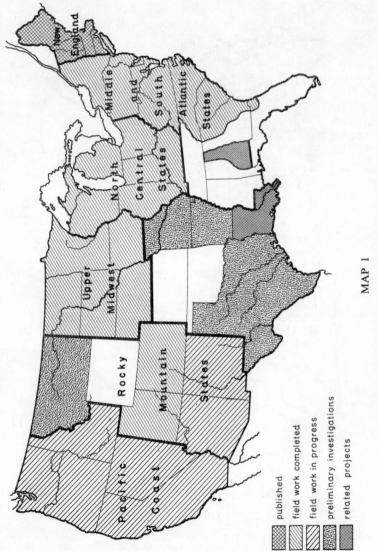

MAP 1

PROGRESS OF THE AMERICAN ATLASES

published

field work completed

field work in progress

preliminary investigations

related projects

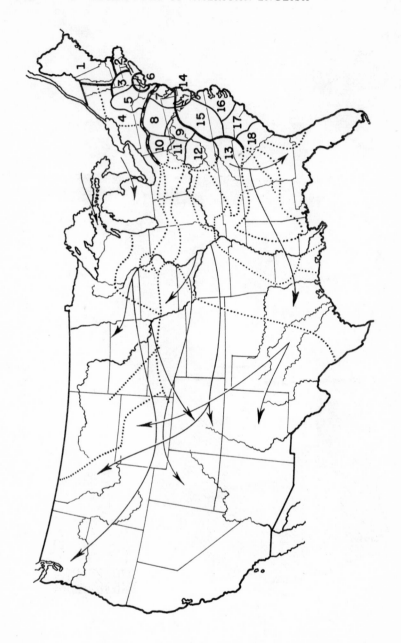

MAP 2

DIALECT AREAS OF THE UNITED STATES

Atlantic Seaboard Areas (after Kurath). Tentative Dialect Boundaries. Arrows indicate direction of migrations.

THE NORTH

1. Northeastern New England
2. Southeastern New England
3. Southwestern New England
4. Inland North (western Vermont, Upstate New York & derivatives)
5. The Hudson Valley
6. Metropolitan New York

THE MIDLAND

North Midland

7. Delaware Valley (Philadelphia)
8. Susquehanna Valley
10. Upper Ohio Valley (Pittsburgh)
11. Northern West Virginia

South Midland

9. Upper Potomac & Shenandoah
12. Southern West Virginia & Eastern Kentucky
13. Western Carolina & Eastern Tennessee

THE SOUTH

14. Delmarva (Eastern Shore)
15. The Virginia Piedmont
16. Northeastern North Carolina (Albemarle Sound & Neuse Valley)
17. Cape Fear & Peedee Valleys
18. The South Carolina Low Country (Charleston)

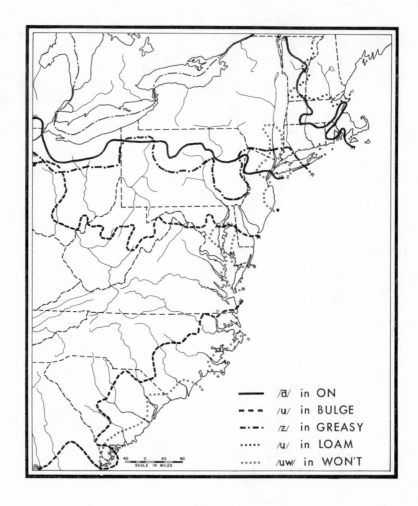

MAP 3

PRONUNCIATION ISOGLOSSES

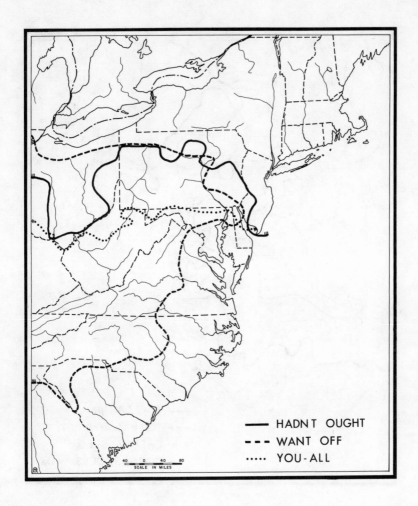

HADN'T OUGHT
--- WANT OFF
····· YOU-ALL

40 0 40 80
SCALE IN MILES

MAP 4

GRAMMATICAL ISOGLOSSES

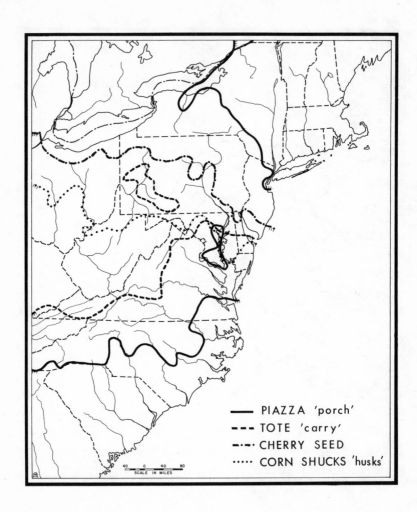

MAP 5

VOCABULARY ISOGLOSSES

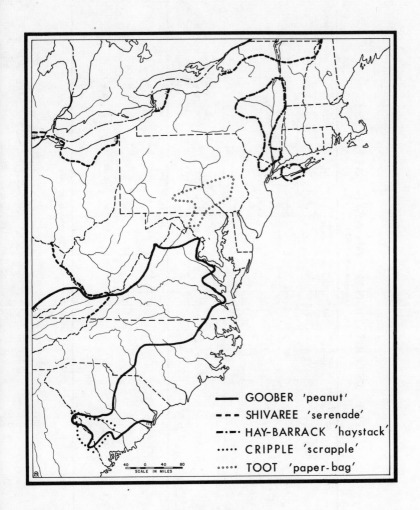

GOOBER 'peanut'
SHIVAREE 'serenade'
HAY-BARRACK 'haystack'
CRIPPLE 'scrapple'
TOOT 'paper-bag'

SCALE IN MILES

MAP 6

LOANWORD ISOGLOSSES

THE INTERNATIONAL PHONETIC ALPHABET.
(Revised to 1951.)

CONSONANTS

	Bi-labial	Labio-dental	Dental and Alveolar	Retroflex	Palato-alveolar	Alveolo-palatal	Palatal	Velar	Uvular	Pharyngal	Glottal
Plosive	p b		t d	ʈ ɖ			c ɟ	k g	q ɢ		ʔ
Nasal	m	ɱ	n	ɳ			ɲ	ŋ	ɴ		
Lateral Fricative			ɬ ɮ								
Lateral Non-fricative			l	ɭ			ʎ				
Rolled			r						ʀ		
Flapped			ɾ	ɽ					ʀ		
Fricative	ɸ β	f v	θ ð s z ɹ	ʂ ʐ	ʃ ʒ	ɕ ʑ	ç ʝ	x ɣ	χ ʁ	ħ ʕ	h ɦ
Frictionless Continuants and Semi-vowels	w ɥ	ʋ	ɹ				j (ɥ)	(w)	ʁ		

VOWELS

		Front	Central	Back
Close	(y ʉ u)	i y	ɨ ʉ	ɯ u
Half-close	(ø o)	e ø		ɤ o
Half-open	(œ ɔ)	ɛ œ	ə	ʌ ɔ
Open	(ɒ)		a	ɑ ɒ

(Secondary articulations are shown by symbols in brackets.)

Other Sounds.—Palatalized consonants : ƫ, ȡ, etc. ; palatalized ʃ, ʒ : ʆ, ʓ. Velarized or pharyngalized consonants : ɫ, ᵭ, ᵶ, etc. Ejective consonants (with simultaneous glottal stop) : p', t', etc. Implosive voiced consonants : ɓ, ɗ, etc. ɼ fricative trill. σ, ϱ (labialized θ, ð, or s, z). ƪ, ƺ (labialized ʃ, ʒ). ʇ, ʗ, ʖ (clicks, Zulu *c*, *q*, *x*). ɺ (a sound between r and l). ɳ Japanese syllabic nasal. ɧ (combination of x and ʃ). ʍ (voiceless w). ɩ, ʏ, ɷ (lowered varieties of i, y, u). ɜ (a variety of ə). ɵ (a vowel between ø and o).

Affricates are normally represented by groups of two consonants (ts, tʃ, dʒ, etc.), but. when necessary, ligatures are used (ʦ, ʧ, ʤ, etc.), or the marks ⁀ or ‿ (t͡s or t͜s, etc.). ⁀ ‿ also denote synchronic articulation (m͡ŋ = simultaneous m and ŋ). c, ɟ may occasionally be used in place of tʃ, dʒ, and ƾ, ƻ for ts, dz. Aspirated plosives : ph, th, etc. r-coloured vowels : eɹ, aɹ, ɔɹ, etc., or eʴ, aʴ, ɔʴ, etc., or ɝ, a˞, ɔ˞, etc. ; r-coloured ə : əɹ or əʴ or ɹ or ɚ or ɚ.

Length, Stress, Pitch.— : (full length). · (half length). ˈ (stress, placed at beginning of the stressed syllable). ˌ (secondary stress). ˉ (high level pitch) ; ˍ (low level) ; ˊ (high rising) ; ˏ (low rising) ; ˋ (high falling) ; ˎ (low falling) ; ˆ (rise-fall) ; ˇ (fall-rise).

Modifiers.— ˜ nasality. ̥ breath (l̥ = breathed l). ̬ voice (s̬ = z). ʻ slight aspiration following p, t, etc. ̫ labialization (n̫ = labialized n). ̪ dental articulation (t̪ = dental t). ˙ palatalization (ż = ʓ). ̣ specially close vowel (ẹ = a very close e). ̨ specially open vowel (ę = a rather open e). ˔ tongue raised (e˔ or e̝ = ẹ). ˕ tongue lowered (e˕ or e̞ = ę). ˖ tongue advanced (u˖ or u̟ = an advanced u, t̟ = t̪). - or ˗ tongue retracted (i- or i̠ = ɨ˖, t̠ = alveolar t). ˒ lips more rounded. ˓ lips more spread. Central vowels : ï (= ɨ), ü (= ʉ), ë (= ə˔), ö (= ɵ), ɛ̈, ɔ̈. ˌ (e.g. n̩) syllabic consonant. ˘ consonantal vowel. ʃˢ variety of ʃ resembling s, etc.

Glossary

This glossary supplies definitions for about one third of the technical terms used in this book which are printed in boldface type at their first appearance. The rest are either defined in the text or used in such a way that the context makes their meaning clear. The reader is referred to the index, where page numbers in boldface indicate these contextual definitions.

ACOUSTIC PHONETICS. The branch of phonetics which studies the nature of the sound-wave or pressure patterns in the air produced by speech-sounds.

ADJECTIVE. A class of lexical words (part of speech) capable of occupying both of the following structural positions: (1) between noun-determiner and noun; (2) sentence-final following a qualifier which follows a linking verb.

ADVERB. A class of lexical words (part of speech) capable of occupying the following structural position: utterance- or sentence-final following a single or double object construction.

ADVERB-SUBSTITUTE. A small class of adverbs and a few brief phrases which appear as substitutes for adverbs which have already been expressed in the immediate linguistic context.

AFFIX. A bound morpheme appearing either before or after the base to which it is bound or another affix bound to the same base.

ALLOGRAPH. One of a group of graphic symbols having the same reference and in free variation or complementary distribution.

ALLOMORPH. A class of morphs having the same phonemic constituency and the same meaning.

ALLOPHONE. A class of identical speech-sounds or phones (i.e., a phone-type) which is one of a group making up a phoneme.

AMBISYLLABIC POSITION. Position occupied by a single consonant phoneme between two syllabic nuclei with close juncture.

ANALOGY. The process of originating linguistic forms by comparing them with a previously learned model, usually a paradigm or paradigmatic set. Thus, the noun-form /*miys/ as plural for /muws/ may be created by analogy with the paradigmatic set /guws : giys/.

ARTICULATION. Alterations in the shape and size of air-passages and resonance-cavities of the human vocal tract to produce the differing sounds of speech.

ARTICULATORY PHONETICS. The branch of phonetics which studies the production of speech-sounds by the human vocal tract.

ASPECT. Variation in the form of verbs and verb-phrases which is semantically related to the status of an action in regard to its beginning, continuance, repetition, completion, etc.

ASSIMILATION. A morphophonemic change resulting in neighboring phonemes becoming more alike in articulation.

AUDITORY PHONETICS. The branch of phonetics which studies the reception of speech-sounds by the human hearing mechanism.

AUXILIARY. One of a group of function words which combine with various forms of verbs to make verb-phrases.

BASE. A morpheme none of whose allomorphs contain open junctures.

BILINGUALISM. The quality of speaking two languages with the facility of a native speaker; the use by a community of two different languages.

BINARY STRUCTURE. A type of structure in which each unit contains just two immediate constituents.

BOUND ALLOMORPH. An allomorph which never appears as an independent unit but is always accompanied by one or more other allomorphs to which it is joined by normal transition or plus juncture.

BOUND BASE. A morpheme which serves as a stem for derivational forms but never appears as a free form.

CALL. A situation-sentence whose purpose is to claim attention.

CITATION FORM. A word or other linguistic form, spoken by itself for the purpose of linguistic illustration.

CLASS DIALECT. A dialect spoken by a speech-community consisting of persons of a certain social class; a **social dialect.**

CLOSE JUNCTURE. The normal rapid transition from one segmental phoneme to another; **normal transition.**

CLOSURE. A form of articulation in which complete stoppage of the stream of air is effected and retained for a brief period.

COLOR. The particular auditory quality of a vowel which allows it to be distinguished from other vowels under diverse conditions of pitch, stress, length, and vocal quality.

COMMON SPEECH. The speech of the great majority of the community, those whose position is neither notably high nor conspicuously low.

COMPARATIVE DEGREE. Adjectives and adverbs having the inflectional suffix {-er} or following the function word *more* are in the comparative degree.

COMPLEMENT. A syntactic element appearing with (and normally following) a verbal element to make a structure of complementation.

COMPLEMENTARY DISTRIBUTION. The members of a set of linguistic entities are in complementary distribution when there is no common environment in which two or more of them appear.

COMPOUND SENTENCE. A structure of coordination whose immediate constituents are structurally separate sentences but without a sentence-final intonation contour at the end of the first; in writing, two sentences separated by a semicolon, comma, or no punctuation rather than by an end mark.

COMPOUND WORD. A word (morphemically a phrase) consisting of two or more free forms and a superfix, with or without affixes.

COMPOUND-COMPLEX WORD. A word whose constituents are a compound word and a derivational suffix.

CONSONANTAL. A grapheme normally used to represent a consonant.

CONTRAST. When two linguistic entities may appear in the same environment with a resulting change of meaning, they are in contrast.

COPULATIVE VERB. A verb which may occupy the same position as the full verb *be* in a structure of complementation; **linking verb.**

DERIVATIONAL PARADIGM. A set of form-classes which contrast systematically in the derivational affixes which determine them.

DERIVATIVE. A word consisting of one or more derivational affixes bound to a stem from which it is said to be derived.

DIALECT. The variety of language spoken by the members of a single homogeneous speech-community.

DIALECT AREA. An area within which a well-defined dialect occurs, distinguished from other dialects by a characteristic group of features of pronunciation, grammar, and vocabulary.

DIALECT BOUNDARY. A bundle of isoglosses constituting the limit of a dialect area.

DIGRAPH. A pair of graphemes, one or both of which have independent use in other environments, used as a single grapheme, as ⟨th⟩, ⟨qu⟩. The term is also used as a name for the low-front vowel phoneme of English, /æ/.

DIRECT OBJECT. The complement of a transitive verb when only one is present; it often indicates the "receiver" of the action and becomes the subject when the verb is altered to passive voice.

DISTINCTIVE FEATURES. The particular qualities of the sounds of speech on which their assignment to phone-types is based.

DISTRIBUTION. The whole set of environments in which a linguistic form appears; **range.**

DISTRIBUTIONAL MEANING. The meaning of a word considered as the sum total of what it contributes to all the utterances in which it appears.

DOUBLE-BAR JUNCTURE. Terminal juncture consisting of relatively gradual cut-off following a rise in pitch.

DOUBLE-CROSS JUNCTURE. Terminal juncture consisting of gradual fading of voice following falling pitch.

EXCLAMATION. A situation-sentence representing the response to some unexpected condition of the nonlinguistic environment, usually brief and marked by special intonation, often including pitch /4/; also a response-sentence having the same formal features but representing a response to something unexpected in the linguistic context.

EYE DIALECT. A literary device used to suggest substandard speech by quasi-phonetic respellings of the standard pronunciations of common words, as *wimmin* for "women" and *wuz* for "was".

FALLING TERMINAL JUNCTURE. The same as DOUBLE-CROSS JUNCTURE.

FEATURES. See DISTINCTIVE FEATURES.

FOCAL AREA. A dialect area, generally with a well-defined center, whose economic or cultural prestige has led to the spread of its characteristic forms into adjacent areas.

FORTIS CONSONANTS. Consonants characterized by tense and energetic articulation.

FREE VARIATION. When two or more linguistic entities may occupy the same position or environment without changing the meaning, they are in free variation in that position or environment.

FUNCTION NOUN. A word which is formally identical with or morphemically related to a noun-determiner but which fills syntactic positions usually occupied by nouns; e.g., *both* and *mine* in *both are mine.*

FUNCTION VERB. An auxiliary appearing without the expected full verb in a context in which a full verb has been previously expressed; e.g., *have* in *He hasn't seen it but I have.*

FUNCTION WORD. A word with little or no lexical meaning which is used in combining other words into syntactic structures.

GRADED AREA. The same as TRANSITION AREA. The term GRADED AREA emphasizes the fact that the isoglosses along its boundary are not compactly grouped into a bundle but spaced irregularly.

GRAMMAR. The branch of linguistics which deals with the organization of morphemic units into meaningful combinations larger than words.

GRAPHEME. A group of graphic symbols (ALLOGRAPHS) in complementary distribution or free variation, having the same phonemic or other reference.

HEAD. One of the two immediate constituents of a structure of modification, the other being a **modifier.** The head is that member of such a structure which can perform by itself the syntactic function performed by the whole structure without radical alteration of the lexical meaning of the whole.

HOMOPHONES. Words which sound alike but have different lexical meanings and/or syntactic classification; e.g., *bore* (noun) in *The gun had a small bore; bore* (verb) in *They bore a hole; bore* (past tense of verb) in *She bore a child;* and (in some dialects, at least) *boar* in *He killed a wild boar.* The first three are **homographs** as well.

HOMORGANIC. Two sounds whose articulation takes place in the same place in the vocal tract but which differ in one or more other features are homorganic; e.g., alveolar [t d n].

IMMEDIATE CONSTITUENTS. The component parts of a structure on its highest level of organization; thus, the parts into which a structure is divided in the first step of analysis. Abbreviated IC's.

INFLECTED FORM. A form consisting of a stem and an inflectional suffix.

INFLECTIONAL SUFFIX. A suffix which adapts a word to a grammatical function without changing its lexical meaning; except for the possessive plural of nouns, inflectional suffixes are always word-final.

INTONATION. Significant variation in pitch from one part of an utterance to another.

INTONATION PATTERN. A sequence of pitch phonemes and a terminal juncture.

ISOGLOSS. An imaginary line delimiting the area in which one may find a particular feature of grammar, pronunciation, or vocabulary.

JUNCTURE. The transition from one segmental phoneme to another; it is either **close** or **open**, and if open, either **internal** or **terminal.**

LENIS CONSONANTS. Consonants pronounced with relatively little tension of the articulating organs.

LEXICAL MEANING. Meaning of a morpheme or word apart from the meaning it acquires by virtue of its position in a larger structure; "dictionary meaning."

LIGATURE. A character formed by combining two characters; e.g., fl, æ.

LINGUISTIC GEOGRAPHY. The study of the regional distribution of linguistic features within a language area.

LOAN-BLEND. A type of linguistic borrowing in which part of a compound or derivative is imported in the phonemic shape of the foreign language while another part is replaced by native morphemes.

LOAN-SHIFT. A type of linguistic borrowing in which the phonemic shape of the foreign word is not imported, so that the loan appears only as a shift of context on the part of a native word.

LOAN-TRANSLATION. A process of linguistic borrowing in which the borrowing language adopts the over-all pattern of the compound or derivative, along with its meaning, but entirely substitutes native morphemes for foreign ones; e.g., English *skyscraper*, German *Wolkenkratzer*, French *gratte-ciel*, Spanish *rascacielos;* or German *Übermensch*, English *superman.*

LOAN-WORD. A type of linguistic borrowing in which the borrowing language imports both the phonemic shape and the meaning of a word.

LOGOGRAM. A grapheme representing a complete word.

MODIFIER. One of the constituents of a structure of modification, the other being the HEAD. The head can be identified as the element which can be substituted for the whole structure.

MORPHOLOGICAL MARKS. The apostrophe and hyphen in the English writing system, which are used to indicate morphological rather than syntactic relationships.

NONLINGUISTIC CONTEXT. The physical and social circumstances in which an utterance is made.

NOUN. One of the **parts of speech**; a lexical word which may follow a noun-determiner such as *the* and is inflectable with the plural and possessive inflections {-*es*} and {'*s*}.

NOUN-DETERMINER. One of a group of function words appearing with and helping to identify nouns.

NOUN-SUBSTITUTE. A word which can be substituted for a noun in a given structure without alteration of the meaning.

NUCLEUS. The most prominent phone in a syllable; **syllabic.**

NUMBER CONCORD. Correlation of syntactically related words on the basis of number, as in *this book*: *these books*, or *he was*: *they were*.

OBJECT OF A PREPOSITION. A word or structure immediately following a preposition and forming with it a syntactic unit.

OBJECTIVE COMPLEMENT. The second object in a complement when the first is a direct object; identified by the fact that it cannot be made subject when the verb is changed to the passive voice.

OPEN JUNCTURE. A transition between segmental phonemes marked by retardation and (sometimes) slight pause; also called PLUS JUNCTURE.

PARTS OF SPEECH. Classes of lexical words distinguished by form and/or syntactic use and distribution.

PHONE. A unique minimal segment of the stream of speech.

PHONE-TYPE. A class of identical phones.

PHONEME. A group of phone-types (**allophones**) which are phonetically similar and either in complementary distribution or free variation.

PHONEMIC TRANSCRIPTION. A transcription of speech in which all phonemes, segmental and suprasegmental, are represented, each by a single grapheme, without regard to allophonic differences.

PHONEMICS. The branch of linguistics whose subject matter is the organization of speech-sounds (phones) into phonemes.

PHONETIC ALPHABET. An alphabet in which a separate character is provided for every discernible kind of speech-sound.

PHONOLOGY. The sound-system (phonetics and phonemics) of a language or dialect.

PHRASE. As much of an utterance as appears between two terminal junctures or between the beginning of an utterance and the first terminal juncture.

PITCH PHONEME. A suprasegmental phoneme whose allophones are slightly different levels of relative pitch.

PLUS JUNCTURE. The same as OPEN JUNCTURE.

POINT OF USAGE. A question concerning the acceptability of a certain linguistic form or structure in a given dialect.

POSSESSIVE CONSTRUCTION. A structure of modification comprising a noun head following a modifier consisting of a noun in the possessive form.

PREDICATE. One of the two immediate constituents of a structure of predication, consisting of a verb alone or some structure in which a verb is prominent.

PREPOSITION. One of a closed class of function words, always followed by a lexical word or syntactic construction, the whole forming a **prepositional phrase.**

PRINT. A graphic style in which the individual graphemes are separated one from another by slight intervening space, except for a few **ligatures,** in contrast to SCRIPT, in which the graphemes comprising a word are linked together.

PROPER NOUNS AND ADJECTIVES. Nouns and adjectives whose referents are specific and unique individuals, as well as some of more general reference derived from these, and a few more included for various reasons, including courtesy, make up a vaguely defined class of PROPER nouns and adjectives, customarily distinguished graphically by capitalization.

PUNCTUATION. The system of distribution of the eleven marks of punctuation; a subsystem of the graphic system, primarily operating as a substitute for the suprasegmental features of speech.

RANGE. The same as DISTRIBUTION.

RELIC AREA. A dialect area, generally lacking a center, whose geographic or cultural isolation has permitted the preservation of old-fashioned forms which have been lost elsewhere.

RISING TERMINAL JUNCTURE. The same as DOUBLE-BAR JUNCTURE.

SCRIPT. A graphic style, adapted to rapid production by hand, in which the graphemes comprising each word are linked together.

SEGMENTAL PHONEMES. Phonemes which follow one another consecutively in the stream of speech; the vowels and consonants.

SEMIVOCALIC. A grapheme principally used to represent a semivowel.

SEMIVOWEL. A vowel-like sound, characterized by rapid transition from one articulatory position to another, and not occupying the nuclear position in a syllable.

SENTENCE-FINAL INTONATION CONTOUR. A suprasegmental morpheme consisting of a series of pitches and a terminal juncture, used to signal the division of an utterance into its largest constituents, or **sentences.**

SHIFT SIGN. A diacritical mark used with a phonetic symbol to indicate that the symbol transcribes a sound whose position is slightly different from that of the sound normally signified by that symbol.

SINGLE-BAR JUNCTURE. Terminal juncture consisting of a sharp cut-off following level pitch.

STEM. That member of a paradigmatic set most conveniently considered as the norm from which the other members of the set are formed.

STRUCTURAL MEANING. The meaning which a linguistic structure has over and above the lexical meanings of the words it contains.

STRUCTURE OF COMPLEMENTATION. A grammatical structure whose immediate constituents are a **verbal element** and a **complement.**

STRUCTURE OF COORDINATION. A grammatical structure consisting of two or more syntactically equivalent units which may be joined by a coordinator.

STRUCTURE OF MODIFICATION. A grammatical structure whose immediate constituents are a **head** and a **modifier.**

STRUCTURE OF PREDICATION. A grammatical structure whose immediate constituents are a **subject** and a **predicate,** usually in that order.

SUBJECTIVE COMPLEMENT. The complement of a linking verb; it characteristically has the same referent as the subject.

SUBSTITUTE-GROUP. A class of words all of which may be replaced by the same substitute.

SUPERFIX. A morpheme whose allomorphs consist of stress phonemes with or without plus junctures.

SUPRASEGMENTAL GRAPHEME. A graphic device, such as capitalizing or italicizing, which alters the shapes of graphemes without altering their reference.

SUPRASEGMENTAL PHONEME. A phoneme (as of pitch, stress, or juncture) which is synchronous with one or more successive segmental phonemes.

SUSTAINED TERMINAL JUNCTURE. The same as SINGLE-BAR JUNCTURE.

SYLLABARY. The repertory of graphemes used in a syllabic writing system, in which each grapheme represents a syllable.

SYLLABIC. The most prominent phone in a syllable; **nucleus.**

SYLLABIC WRITING. A form of writing in which each grapheme represents a syllable.

SYLLABICATION. Division of a written word into syllables for purposes of dividing over the end of a line.

TERMINAL JUNCTURE. Transition from one segmental phoneme to another or to silence, characterized by pause following a distinctive way of cutting off speech.

TRANSITION AREA. A dialect area without conspicuous characteristics of its own but under pressure from two or more adjacent areas; generally bounded by irregularly spaced isoglosses. The same as GRADED AREA.

ULTIMATE CONSTITUENTS. The component parts of a structure on its lowest level of organization.

UNEDUCATED SPEECH. The speech of those with few educational or social advantages and whose work or status is generally looked down upon by the leaders of the community.

VERB. One of the **parts of speech;** a lexical word which has the four inflections $\{-s\}$, $\{-ed_1\}$, $\{-ed_2\}$, and $\{-ing_1\}$, and which combines with auxiliaries to form verb-phrases.

VERB-PHRASE. A phrase consisting of one of the forms of a verb other than the third-singular together with one or more auxiliaries.

VOCAL QUALIFIER. A particular manner of speaking, such as overloudness, staccato utterance, etc., indicating the speaker's attitude toward what he is saying and the person to whom he is saying it, but not altering the basic structure of his utterance.

VOCALIC. A grapheme customarily used to represent vowel phonemes.

WORD. A general term covering any linguistic form considered to be independent in distribution and meaning and capable of being written with space on either side. For a more precise concept, see MORPHEMIC WORD.

WORD DIVISION. Conventional segmentation of written material into groups of graphemes without space between them which corresponds roughly (though not exactly) to the division of spoken language into morphemic words.

ZERO ALLOMORPH. An allomorph with no phonemic content, postulated on the basis of a paradigm.

General Bibliography

This list contains only a small selection of more recent materials relating to the linguistics of English published in book form. Much new and experimental material is published in articles in various journals, which have not been listed here because they would extend this bibliography beyond the bounds of a convenient reading list. Those interested in material in article form are referred to the various annual bibliographies, especially those appearing in *PMLA* and *American Speech*. At least two anthologies of significant articles are currently in preparation.

GENERAL BOOKS ON LANGUAGE AND LINGUISTICS

BLOCH, BERNARD, and TRAGER, GEORGE L. *Outline of Linguistic Analysis.* Baltimore: Linguistic Society of America, 1942.

BLOOMFIELD, LEONARD. *Language.* New York: Henry Holt & Co., Inc., 1933.

BRAM, JOSEPH. *Language and Society* (Doubleday Short Studies in Sociology, No. 8). New York: Doubleday & Co., Inc., 1955.

CARROLL, JOHN B. *The Study of Language: A survey of linguistics and related disciplines in America.* Cambridge: Harvard University Press, 1953.

GLEASON, H. A. *An Introduction to Descriptive Linguistics.* New York: Henry Holt & Co., Inc., 1955.

HALL, ROBERT A., JR. *Leave Your Language Alone!* Ithaca, N. Y.: Linguistica, 1950.

HARRIS, ZELLIG S. *Methods in Structural Linguistics.* Chicago: The University of Chicago Press, 1951.

HAYAKAWA, S. I. *Language in Thought and Action.* New York: Harcourt, Brace & Co., Inc., 1949.

HILL, ARCHIBALD A. *Introduction to Linguistic Structures; from Sound to Sentence in English.* New York: Harcourt, Brace & Co., Inc., 1958.

HOCKETT, CHARLES F. *A Course in Linguistics.* New York: The Macmillan Co., 1958.

598

————. *A Manual of Phonology* (Indiana University Publications in Anthropology and Linguistics, Memoir 11). Baltimore: Waverley Press, 1955.

JOOS, MARTIN, ed. *Readings in Linguistics.* Washington, D. C.: American Council of Learned Societies, 1957.

MARCKWARDT, ALBERT H. *Introduction to the English Language.* New York: Oxford University Press, 1942.

SAPIR, EDWARD. *Language: An introduction to the study of speech.* New York: Harcourt, Brace & Co., Inc., 1921.

SCHLAUCH, MARGARET. *The Gift of Tongues.* New York: Modern Age Books, 1942.

SMITH, HENRY LEE, JR. *Linguistic Science and the Teaching of English.* Cambridge: Harvard University Press, 1956.

STURTEVANT, EDGAR H. *An Introduction to Linguistic Science.* New Haven: Yale University Press, 1947.

TRAGER, GEORGE L. *The Field of Linguistics* (*Studies in Linguistics,* Occasional Papers, No. 1). Norman, Okla.: Battenburg Press, 1949.

TRAGER, GEORGE L., and SMITH, HENRY LEE, JR. *An Outline of English Structure* (*Studies in Linguistics,* Occasional Papers, No. 3). Norman, Okla.: Battenburg Press, 1951.

WELMERS, WILLIAM E. *Spoken English as a Foreign Language, Instructor's Manual.* Washington, D. C.: American Council of Learned Societies, 1953.

WHORF, BENJAMIN LEE. *Language, Thought, and Reality,* ed. by John B. Carroll. New York: John Wiley & Sons, Inc., 1956.

BOOKS OF MORE SPECIALIZED SCOPE

AIKEN, JANET R. *A New Plan of English Grammar.* New York: Henry Holt & Co., Inc., 1933.

ALLEN, HAROLD B., *Readings in Applied English Linguistics.* New York: Appleton-Century-Crofts, 1958.

CURRY, ROBERT O. L. *The Mechanism of the Human Voice.* New York and Toronto: Longmans, Green & Co., Inc., 1940.

FRIES, CHARLES C. *American English Grammar: The grammatical structure of present-day American English with especial reference to social differences or class dialects.* New York: Appleton-Century-Crofts, Inc., 1940.

————. *The Structure of English: An introduction to the construction of English sentences.* New York: Harcourt, Brace & Co., Inc., 1952.

————. *The Teaching of English.* Ann Arbor: George Wahr, 1949.

GELB, IGNACE J. *A Study of Writing.* Chicago: The University of Chicago Press, 1952.

GRAY, WILLIAM S. *On their Own in Reading.* New York: Scott, Foresman & Co., 1948.

HEFFNER, ROE-MERRILL S. *General Phonetics.* Madison: University of Wisconsin Press, 1949.

HERDAN, G. *Language as Choice and Chance.* Groningen: Erven P. Noordhoff, Ltd., 1956.

INTERNATIONAL PHONETIC ASSOCIATION. *Principles of the International Phonetic Alphabet.* London: International Phonetic Association, 1949.

JONES, DANIEL. *The Phoneme, Its Nature and Use.* Cambridge, Eng.: W. Heffer & Sons, Ltd., 1950.

———. *The Pronunciation of English,* 3d. ed. Cambridge, Eng.: W. Heffer & Sons, Ltd., 1950.

JOOS, MARTIN. *Acoustic Phonetics.* Baltimore: Linguistic Society of America, 1948.

KENYON, JOHN S. *American Pronunciation,* 10th ed. Ann Arbor: George Wahr, 1951.

LLOYD, DONALD J., and WARFEL, HARRY R. *American English in its Cultural Setting.* New York: Alfred A. Knopf, 1956.

MYERS, L. M. *American English: A twentieth century grammar.* Englewood Cliffs, N. J.: Prentice-Hall, Inc. 1952.

NIDA, EUGENE A. *Morphology, the Descriptive Analysis of Words,* 2d. ed. Ann Arbor: University of Michigan Press, 1949.

PALMER, HAROLD E., and BLANDFORD, F. G. *A Grammar of Spoken English on a Strictly Phonetic Basis,* 2d. ed. Cambridge, Eng.: W. Heffer & Sons, Ltd., 1939.

PIKE, KENNETH L. *The Intonation of American English.* Ann Arbor: University of Michigan Press, 1946.

———. *Phonemics: A technique for reducing languages to writing.* Ann Arbor: University of Michigan Press, 1947.

———. *Phonetics: A critical analysis of phonetic theory and a technic for the practical description of sounds.* Ann Arbor: University of Michigan Press, 1943.

ROBERTS, PAUL. *Understanding English.* New York: Harper & Bros., 1958.

———. *Patterns of English.* New York: Harcourt, Brace & Co., 1956.

SUMMEY, GEORGE, JR. *American Punctuation.* New York: The Ronald Press Co., 1949.

THOMAS, CHARLES K. *An Introduction to the Phonetics of American English,* 2d. ed. New York: The Ronald Press Co., 1958.

WHITEHALL, HAROLD. *Structural Essentials of English.* New York: Harcourt, Brace & Co., Inc., 1956.

BOOKS ON LINGUISTIC GEOGRAPHY AND AMERICAN DIALECTOLOGY

ATWOOD, E. BAGBY. *A Survey of Verb Forms in the Eastern United States.* Ann Arbor: University of Michigan Press, 1953.

HANSEN, MARCUS L. *The Atlantic Migration, 1607–1860.* Cambridge: Harvard University Press, 1940.

HAUGEN, EINAR. *The Norwegian Language in America: A study in bilingual behavior.* 2 vols. Philadelphia: University of Pennsylvania Press, 1953.

HUBBELL, ALLAN F. *The Pronunciation of English in New York City.* New York: King's Crown Press, 1950.

KURATH, HANS. *Handbook of the Linguistic Geography of New England.* Washington, D. C.: American Council of Learned Societies, 1939.

———, ed. *Linguistic Atlas of New England.* Providence: Brown University Press, 1939–43.

———. *A Word Geography of the Eastern United States.* Ann Arbor: University of Michigan Press, 1949.

REED, CARROLL E., and SEIFERT, LESTER W. *A Linguistic Atlas of Pennsylvania German.* Marburg-an-der-Lahn, 1954.

TURNER, LORENZO D. *Africanisms in the Gullah Dialect.* Chicago: The University of Chicago Press, 1949.

WEINREICH, URIEL. *Languages in Contact.* New York: Linguistic Circle of New York, 1953.

BOOKS ON THE HISTORY OF ENGLISH

BAUGH, ALBERT C. *A History of the English Language,* 2d. ed. New York: Appleton-Century-Crofts, Inc., 1957.

BRYANT, MARGARET M. *Modern English and Its Heritage.* New York: The Macmillan Co., 1948.

ROBERTSON, STUART. *The Development of Modern English,* 2d. ed., rev. by Frederic G. Cassidy. Englewood Cliffs, N. J.: Prentice-Hall, Inc., 1954.

WYLD, HENRY CECIL. *A Short History of English.* London: John Murray, Ltd., 1914.

BOOKS ON VOCABULARY AND SEMANTICS

BERRY, L. V., and VAN DEN BARK, MELVIN. *The American Thesaurus of Slang* (with supplement). New York: The Thomas Crowell Co., 1947.

CRAIGIE, W. A., and HULBERT, J. R. eds. *A Dictionary of American English on Historical Principles.* 4 vols. Chicago: The University of Chicago Press, 1938–44.

ESTRICH, ROBERT M., and SPERBER, HANS. *Three Keys to Language.* New York: Rinehart & Co., Inc., 1952.

GREENOUGH, JAMES B., and KITTREDGE, GEORGE L. *Words and Their Ways in English Speech.* New York: The Macmillan Co., 1901.

LAIRD, CHARLTON. *The Miracle of Language.* Cleveland and New York: The World Publishing Company, 1953.

MATHEWS, MITFORD M. *A Dictionary of Americanisms.* 2 vols. Chicago: The University of Chicago Press, 1951.

———. *Some Sources of Southernisms.* University, Ala.: University of Alabama Press, 1948.

MCKNIGHT, GEORGE H. *English Words and Their Background.* New York: Appleton-Century-Crofts, Inc., 1923.

MENCKEN, HENRY L. *The American Language: An inquiry into the development of English in the United States.* 4th. ed., with Supplements I and II. New York: Alfred A. Knopf, Inc., 1936–48.

PYLES, THOMAS. *Words and Ways of American English.* New York: Random House, Inc., 1952.

SHEARD, J. A. *The Words We Use.* New York: Frederick A. Praeger, Inc., 1954.

ULLMANN, STEPHEN. *The Principles of Semantics.* Glasgow: Jackson, Son & Co., Ltd., 1951.

WEEKLEY, ERNEST. *Words and Names.* London: John Murray, Ltd., 1932.

Index

Definitions in context of technical terms not defined in the Glossary are indicated in boldface type.

C O N S O N A N T

	Bilabial	Labio-dental	Apico-dental
Stops	p b̆		
Fricatives	(ɸ β)	f v	θ ð
Sibilants			
Affricates			
Flaps and trills			
Nasals	m	(ɱ)	
Laterals			
Semivowels	w̥ w		
	(ẙ)		

Syllabic [ˌ]; Voiceless [˳]; Aspirated [ʻ]; Voiced [˴]; Rounded [˻];

V O W E L S

Front   *Central*   *Back*

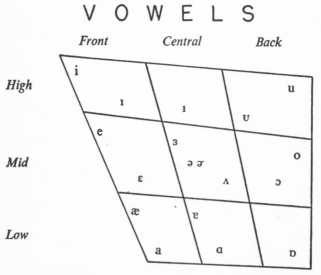

High

Mid

Low

Half-long [ˑ];   Long [:];   Over-long [::];   Short [˘].   Raised [ʻ];
Lowered [ʼ];   Fronted [ʽ];   Retracted [ʻ].   Rounded [˻]; Un-
rounded [˼]; Nasalized [˜]. Voiceless [˳]; Non-syllabic [˯]. Strongest
Stress [ˈˈ]; Strong [ˈ]; Medium [ˌ].